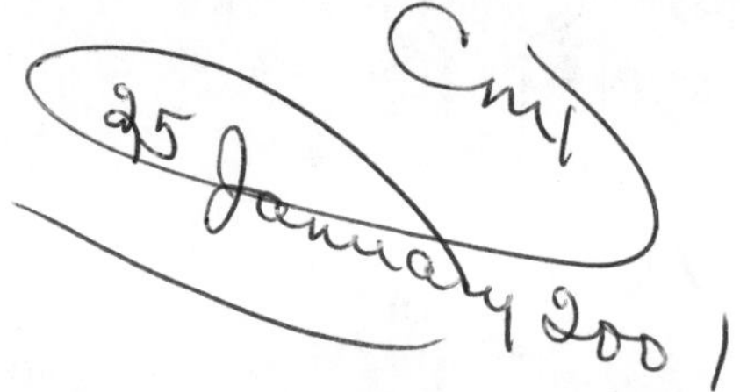

Universal Teaching Strategies

Third Edition

H. Jerome Freiberg
University of Houston

Amy Driscoll
California State University, Monterey Bay

ALLYN AND BACON

Boston London Toronto Sydney Tokyo Singapore

Vice President, Editor in Chief, Education: *Paul A. Smith*
Editorial Assistant: *Bridget Keane*
Marketing Manager: *Brad Parkins*
Editorial-Production Administrator: *Annette Joseph*
Editorial-Production Coordinator: *Holly Crawford*
Editorial-Production Service: *Lynda Griffiths, TKM Productions*
Composition Buyer: *Linda Cox*
Electronic Composition: *Omegatype Typography, Inc.*
Manufacturing Buyer: *Suzanne Lareau*
Cover Administrator: *Linda Knowles*

A Pearson Education Company
160 Gould Street
Needham Heights, MA 02494

Internet: www.abacon.com

Library of Congress Cataloging-in-Publication Data

Freiberg, H. Jerome
Universal teaching strategies / H. Jerome Freiberg, Amy Driscoll.—3rd. ed.
p. cm.
Includes bibliographical references and index.
ISBN 0-205-30285-8
1. Teaching. 2. Classroom management. I. Driscoll, Amy. II. Title.
LB1025.3 .F74 2000
371.102—dc21

99-049035

Printed in the United States of America

10 9 8 7 6 5 4 3 2 04 03 02 01 00

Photo Credits: pp. 1, 55, 118, 176, 240, 270, 396: Will Hart; p. 20: Jim Pickerell; pp. 94, 207, 362: Stephen Marks; p. 143: Suzanne Hunter; p. 304: Brian Smith; p. 334: Mary Ellen Lipionka; p. 433: H. Jerome Freiberg.
Cartoon Credits: pp. 22, 28, 136, 197, 255, 311, 324, 374, 438: © Ford Button and H. Jerome Freiberg; pp. 79, 151, 212: © 1991 Ford Button.

Brief Contents

Contents

CHAPTER ELEVEN
Reflective Teaching and Learning: Students as Shareholders 304

CHAPTER TWELVE
Making Learning Real: Engaging Students in Content 334

CHAPTER THIRTEEN
Using Community Resources, Audiovisuals, Computers, and Multimedia: Varying the Stimuli 362

SECTION III ASSESSING STRATEGIES

CHAPTER FOURTEEN
Assessment of Learning: Let Me Count the Ways 396

Preface

The third edition of *Universal Teaching Strategies* will provide you with an understanding of instruction from a variety of expert perspectives. Your authors will share with you their 54 years of collective teaching and research experience. In addition to the authors' expertise, other expert perspectives are provided throughout the text, through innovative focal points, including **Snapshots, Teacher Talks, Research Vignettes,** and **Samples and Examples.** This edition includes new and updated research in order to bring you the latest innovations and insights concerning instructional practice.

The authors see teachers as a valuable source of information and ideas that should be shared with all current and prospective teaching professionals. The Snapshots, Teacher Talks, and Samples and Examples are derived from classroom experience. Research Vignettes are drawn from the study of teaching that has evolved over the last 30 years to allow the teaching profession to move beyond anecdotes to produce a knowledge base of instruction.

Snapshots give a teacher's detailed perspective on a topic discussed in the text. For example, in Chapter Two (Planning for Instruction: Visualizing What Could Be) a veteran fifth-grade teacher shares her experience of including the students in the planning process. Snapshots appear throughout the text, drawing on the wealth of expertise that is found in our nation's classrooms.

Teacher Talk inserts are brief words of wisdom, strategies, and philosophy from teachers in our elementary, middle, and high schools. For example, in Chapter Fifteen (Self-Improvement through Self-Assessment) a high-school teacher talks about the first time he tape-recorded a class and listened to classroom interactions.

Research Vignettes are summaries of research studies that relate to the chapter topics. For example, Chapter Eight (Questioning and Discussion: Creating a Dialogue) discusses findings of student questions asked during tutoring sessions for seventh-grade algebra students and undergraduate college students studying research methods. Student achievement at both levels was positively correlated with the quality rather than the quantity of questions asked of their tutors. The study design, procedures, research results, and implications for the classroom are included for each Research Vignette. The vignettes have been updated and in some cases rewritten to include new research and perspectives.

Samples and Examples are included at the end of each chapter to provide materials that may be used or adapted to meet your present or future classroom needs. For example, in Chapter Two (Planning for Instruction: Visualizing What Could Be) a "School Year at a Glance" calendar is provided, as well as a script for home calls, a sample syllabus, and a substitute teacher lesson plan. In Chapter Three (Designing Effective Instruction: Creating a Blueprint), three examples of different lesson plans are presented, as well as primary, upper elementary, and secondary lesson starters.

At the beginning of each chapter, *Universal Teaching Strategies* lists **Chapter Outcomes** as well as **Key Terms and Concepts.** The Chapter Outcomes identify what you should expect to learn from each chapter. The Key Terms and Concepts present the most important ideas for your review and study. The summary at the end of each chapter provides a complete review of the chapter.

Universal Teaching Strategies presents teaching from three specific actions: **organizing, instructing,** and **assessing.** The book is divided into three sections that reflect each of these teaching actions. The strategies mirror the universal nature of teaching in that they cut across grade levels, subject areas, and teaching situations.

Decisions about which actions to take in a busy classroom require an understanding of the **context,** the place in which the teaching will occur; the **content,** what will be taught; and, most important, the **learners,** those who will be taught. The thread of the context, content, and learner runs through all the chapters and the three sections of the book. This edition of *Universal Teaching Strategies* adds a feature that discusses the needs of **special learners.** For example, Chapter Six discusses how learners with special needs may require individual behavior plans crafted for them during the admission, review, and dismissal (ARD) process.

The first section, Organizing Strategies, includes Chapters One through Six, beginning with a look at teaching for tomorrow, planning, design, effective use of time, and two approaches to classroom management. Organizing strategies create the conditions necessary for teaching and learning.

The second section, Instructing Strategies, includes Chapters Seven through Thirteen. Each chapter provides a repertoire of teaching strategies that will expand your knowledge about what and how to teach.

The third section, Assessing Strategies, includes Chapters Fourteen and Fifteen. Chapter Fourteen will help you diversify student assessment to accommodate varied content, context, and learners to assess student learning. The last chapter of the text describes strategies for looking at your teaching and determining your effectiveness.

Each chapter has been taught to veteran, mentor, and beginning teachers as well as student teachers and beginning teacher education students. We trust you will find *Universal Teaching Strategies* applicable to both your current and future teaching and learning needs.

This third edition of *Universal Teaching Strategies* is supported by an **Instructor's Manual** with advance organizer transparency masters, teaching and learning activities, and sample test questions. The Instructor's Manual is free of charge and may be acquired from Allyn and Bacon.

ACKNOWLEDGMENTS

We are indebted to many people for their assistance in creating this book, including Susanne Canavan, who convinced us to write the text and to publish it with Allyn and Bacon.

A very special acknowledgment is due to Linda Freiberg for her substantial intellectual and psychological contributions. Thanks go to my wonderful children, Ariel and Oren Freiberg. They have given my work in education greater meaning.

Dear friends have extended much appreciated support and encouragement for this edition—Joan Strouse, Nancy Nagel, and C. S. As always, my family remains an inspiration—thanks to Kerry, Kelly, Katy, Keenan, Keeley, Keesha, and Rikku.

Recognition must be given to the many teachers and colleagues who provided insights, examples, and resources from their classroom and experiences. Thank you Nancy Benson, Josh Weiner, Ken Peterson, Jane Stallings, Robin Lindsley, Carolyn Turkanis, Jeff Cresswell, Maryellen Snyder, Kathleen Gandin-Russell, Myrna Cohen, Gwen Rutledge, Melinda Irwin, Harry Berry, Ann Marsden, Gale Parker, Karen White, Shelly Smith, and Elena Vess for enriching this work. We also extend our gratitude to the reviewers of previous editions of this book: Andrea Bowman, Central Washington University; Douglas Brooks, Miami University; Ronald Doll, Professor Emeritus, The City University of New York; Janis Harmon, Muskingum College; Beth LaForce, George Fox College; Diane Lawler, Arkansas State University; David Payton, New York State Education Department; and Dennie L. Smith, Memphis State University. In addition, we thank the following reviewers of this third edition: Kris Bosworth, The University of Arizona; William A. Harst, Alverna College; Lula Henry, Lamar University; Dee Ann Holmes, Emporia State University; and Kim Truesdell, State University of New York at Buffalo. We also thank Lawrence Kohn, Sunnye Stevens, Heather Clark, and Lyn Liner for their able research, development, and proofing skills, and Saundra McNeese and Holly McMorries for their administrative support.

Finally, this book would not be possible without the expertise, assistance, and support of Stephen Dragin and Bridget Keane at Allyn and Bacon.

CHAPTER

1

TEACHING FOR TOMORROW

Context, Content, and Learners

Chapter Outcomes

At the conclusion of this chapter you will be able to:

1. *Define a universal teaching strategy.*
2. *Describe how you may expand your teaching repertoire.*
3. *Identify and describe organizing, instructing, and assessing teaching strategies.*
4. *Describe the content, context, and learners of tomorrow.*
5. *Describe the role of context, content, and learner in determining the selection of teaching strategies.*

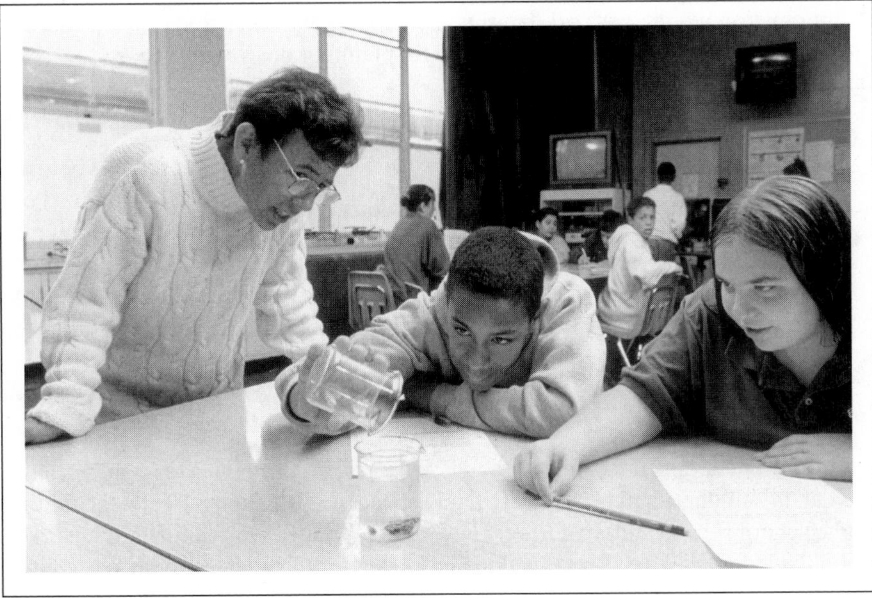

Key Terms and Concepts

Teaching Repertoire
Universal Teaching Strategies
Organizing Strategies
Instructing Strategies
Assessing Strategies
Context of Teaching Tomorrow
Inclusive Education
Content of Teaching
Multicultural Education
Integrated Curriculum
Learners of Today and Tomorrow

The average teacher tells. The good teacher explains.
The superior teacher models. The great teacher inspires.
—Unknown

INTRODUCTION

Listen to the Teachers

Each year one event links all teachers, regardless of location, grade level, or content being taught—it is the first day of school. The first day, like other firsts in a child's education, sets the stage for the future. When we listen to teachers, we hear a common voice: Teaching is exciting, hopeful, and full of challenge.

TEACHER TALK

It's the first day of school. I didn't sleep much last night and it's unusually early for me to be awake. You would think that after 10 years of teaching, the excitement and anticipation would wear off, but this feels like every other first day of school. I'm anxious to meet my students and to begin planning our year together.

Felicia Gomez
Secondary English Literature Teacher

It's a warm sunny day. I'm trying to relax. After all, I've been in schools before. I've spent 16 years going to school, but always as a student, never as the person on the other side of the desk. Memories of my own student experiences flood my mind. I want to be like the best of those teachers I've known. Some made me learn, some made me want to learn, some made me laugh, some made me angry, some made me hope, and some made me despair. I remember feeling smart, and I remember feeling quite dumb. I want to be like those who nurtured me.

Eric Adams
Middle-School Environmental Science Teacher

I'm really energized for this. In fact, I've been waiting for weeks to get started. Last year, my students and I enjoyed so many successes. It's funny—I almost didn't want the school year to end. I've never felt like that before. This summer, the workshops I attended and the reading I've done have caused me to reflect on my teaching and question some of my approaches. My students and I have a lot of decision making to do in the months ahead. The one thing that I am sure of is that I want to empower them—I want them to be much more in control of their own learning.

Pam Rossio
Fourth-Grade Teacher

Meet the Teachers

Felicia Gomez, in her early 50s, is a former training director for a large bank corporation. She made a career change 10 years ago. Her minor in English literature influenced her choice of teaching secondary-school literature courses. She updated her background of novels, short stories, and poetry while pursuing her teaching certificate. Her training background made it possible for her to learn how to teach through a nontraditional teacher education program. The program and career change were right for Felicia and soon she was enthusiastically accepted by students and peers. Her goals for the students in a large urban public school focus on the love for reading that she values so highly.

Eric Adams is a 24-year-old with a degree in environmental science. He just completed a graduate program in teacher education in order to teach middle-school students. He is passionate about his concerns for the environment, is involved in advocacy groups, and spends most of his free time outdoors, hiking and bicycling. He also volunteers with a group of teens in an outdoor recreation program. His goals for the students in his suburban middle school include cooperation and responsible citizenship.

Pam Rossio is a single parent who returned to school once her children were all in elementary classrooms. She completed the college coursework begun 10 years before through a four-year education program, and has been teaching for four years. She is completing a master's degree, one course at a time, in the evening. She puts in long hours preparing for her teaching and is respected and admired by parents, other teachers, and administrators. An extraordinary number of students return to visit her each year. Her goals for her fourth-grade students in a rural elementary school are focused on thinking skills. She wants them to think critically and creatively, and to be able to solve problems and make decisions.

Felicia Gomez, Eric Adams, and Pam Rossio are pseudonyms but they represent the real teachers we observe and listen to in schools. They are the teachers of tomorrow. They chose a teaching career through careful decision making, acutely aware of the problems, criticisms, and challenges so well publicized by the media. After considering other options, and even trying them out, they prepared for the teaching role through varied means: traditional four-year, graduate or fifth-year, and alternative programs. They each joined the teaching profession, having spent at least 16 years in schools, influenced by those student experiences, and thoughtful about their own school memories. They entered their first classrooms with commitments to the kind of teachers they wanted to be, and almost immediately formulated some personal goals for their work. Felicia, Eric, and Pam are teachers who seek knowledge to expand their teaching repertoires.

Teaching Repertoires

A teaching repertoire is an accumulation of skills, concepts, and attitudes based on a person's universe of knowledge and experiences. Each of the three teachers' repertoires is unique, depending on the range of his or her contact with children or adolescents. Although Eric's repertoire is limited by his newness to teaching in public school classrooms, it has already developed through his recent graduate studies in teacher education and his volunteer work with teens.

Pam's repertoire has been expanded by each of her four years of teaching, but is constantly influenced by her own children and the visits of former students. She also subscribes to *The Reading Teacher* and *Educational Leadership.* She just completed a research project for her graduate class on cooperative learning.

Felicia's work with adult learners brought her into teaching with an already developed repertoire from her training work—one that she has adjusted and flexed to the content and learners of her high-school classroom. Felicia has also expanded her repertoire by attending a nationally recognized summer institute on creative writing.

Building a Teaching Repertoire

The process of building a teaching repertoire is never ending. It may be built from a variety of formal and informal sources. Pam is constantly expanding her repertoire through her graduate work, her frequent attendance at workshops, and her journal reading. Felicia's love of reading literature continues to expand her content knowledge, and this often inspires teaching strategies and activities. After a summer of reading, she is bursting with enthusiasm and new ideas. Eric's formal knowledge of both teaching and science content is fresh. His experiences during this first year will build an informal knowledge base, but it will take time for Eric to build a developed teaching repertoire, which will be influenced by the context, content, and students during the next few years. A veteran teacher like Felicia has a well-developed repertoire, and yet it could become less effective as students or curriculum change.

Like Pam, Eric, and Felicia, you have a range of opportunities for building and expanding your teaching repertoire. It expands each time you try out a new idea in your classroom or share an idea with other teachers. Building a repertoire does not require the reinvention of the wheel. Many sources are available beyond your own immediate experiences. You expand your repertoire when you:

1. Observe other teachers.
2. Receive feedback from other professionals about your teaching.
3. Receive feedback from students.
4. Analyze your own teaching.
5. Conduct research in your classroom.
6. Read books, journals, and research studies.
7. Join with other teachers to work on projects.
8. Collaboratively plan with other teachers.
9. Conduct action research to answer questions about your teaching.

Recent research has demonstrated that teacher collaboration can increase achievement (Corbin, 1995). The notion of teachers working together is not only a response to the isolation teachers often feel but it is also an effective approach to the call for new practices in teaching. When teachers work together to understand the foundations or thinking behind teaching strategies and the "how-to" or technical aspects of them, they are able to use these strategies more effectively (Heuwinkel, 1996). Collaboration among teachers has become the most effective approach for reflection and professional growth.

Each of our teachers of tomorrow is involved in some kind of collaboration that will influence this year's teaching. Pam Rossio is serving on a teacher committee to study and make recommendations about assessment. Eric Adams is working with a mentor teacher who has reviewed his plans for the first weeks of school. He has gained feedback on his teaching approaches and management routines, and his mentor has discovered that her teaching repertoire has been enriched by the interaction and sharing of ideas. Felicia Gomez is part of an interdisciplinary team that is developing units of study that will integrate the content areas of literature, world history, art, physics, and personal health.

The three teachers represent their profession well in their efforts to build a teaching repertoire. Felicia, Eric, and Pam know that they will need an expanded repertoire to meet the challenges of teaching for tomorrow. This book's universal teaching strategies respond to that need.

UNIVERSAL TEACHING STRATEGIES

Effective teaching for tomorrow demands teaching strategies that can accommodate the variety of contexts in which teachers will teach, the variety of content that must be taught, and the variety of learners with different backgrounds, needs, and problems. The strategies of this text have been identified as being universal to the act of teaching.

Definition of Terms

The word *universal,* from Latin, means comprehensively broad and versatile. The word *teaching* comes from Greek, meaning to show, point out, direct, or guide. The word *strategy,* from the Greek *strategia,* is defined as the art of devising or employing plans toward a goal. This book, *Universal Teaching Strategies,* can be used to reach a variety of content goals at a variety of grade levels, and is thereby effective with different learners and in different contexts.

Framework of Strategies

This book is designed to add to your teaching repertoire with three kinds of strategies. Figure 1.1 displays a framework of teaching strategies based on our analysis of research and practice (Beck, 1998; Houston, 1990; Wittrock, 1986). The framework provides strategies for organizing your teaching, for instructing, and for assessing teaching and learning. *Organizing strategies* describe much of the work that precedes teaching. They provide a foundation for your instruction—they pave the way for you to teach. *Instructing strategies* are more directly observable. You can see and hear a lecture, a

FIGURE 1.1 *Framework of* Universal Teaching Strategies

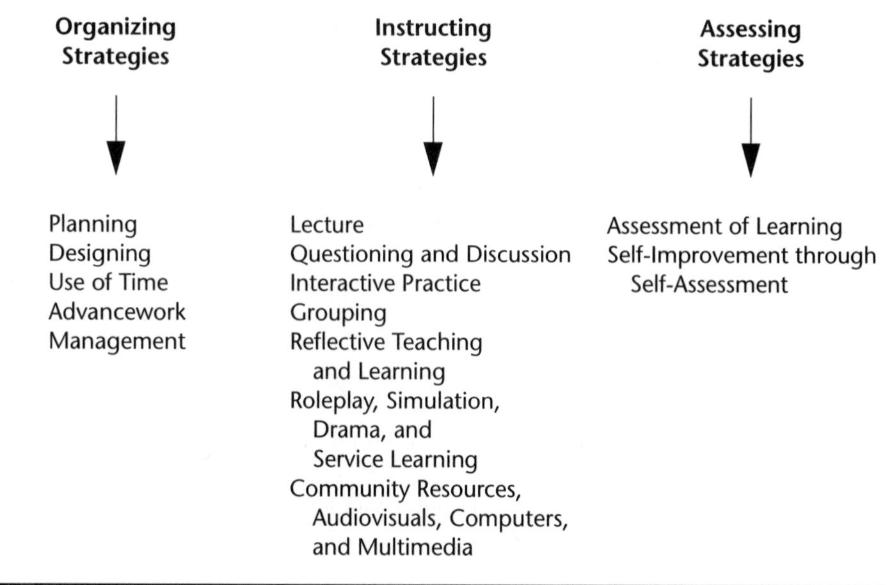

roleplay, or a videotape. They focus on the "how" question to be raised throughout this chapter—how to teach content and learners of tomorrow. *Assessing strategies* are aimed at the measurement of teaching and learning. They provide information about student learning and the effectiveness of your teaching. The chapters of *Universal Teaching Strategies* are arranged as shown in the framework of Figure 1.1. A preview will show you how they will contribute to your teaching repertoire.

Chapter Previews

CHAPTER TWO Planning for Instruction: Visualizing What Could Be

Eric Adams's mentor teacher and Felicia Gomez have many years of teaching experience and engage in the planning we describe in Chapter Two. They visualize and make decisions as they prepare to teach. Their planning gives them an overview of their day, provides order for instruction and management, ensures purposeful learning, indicates an appropriate pace and sequence, connects classroom events with community resources, documents their instruction, helps them order supplies, reduces duplication of effort, and assists them in using a wide repertoire of strategies. Chapter Two begins by encouraging you to listen to the "voices" of planning: your own voice, your colleagues' voices, and the voices of your students. The chapter addresses those functions of planning that Felicia recognizes, and describes the four phases of planning during which teachers think through their alternatives and classroom possibilities.

Eric does and will continue to do a great deal of preplanning, whereas Felicia and Pam make numerous "in-flight" decisions as they teach. You will read many examples of Teacher Talk about planning experiences to guide your own planning process.

CHAPTER THREE Designing Effective Instruction: Creating a Blueprint

We provide a range of design formats that help you prepare for teaching: lesson designs, unit designs, and daily and weekly designs. Eric will benefit from expert design models as he experiments with different ways to prepare for his classes. He is especially interested in problem-solving and inquiry-based models for his teaching. Regardless of the format you use, you will need to attend to goals, objectives, teaching and learning strategies, materials, feedback, and assessment. We describe each and provide examples in Chapter Three. Effective beginnings and endings are emphasized and demonstrations are provided by various teachers. You will see examples of the kinds of designs that teachers like Pam and Felicia use for their planning—designs personalized to meet their needs, reflect their priorities and beliefs, and illustrate efficiency. Finally, we encourage you to plan collaboratively with your students and your professional peers, and describe the efforts of teachers who have done so.

CHAPTER FOUR The Effective Use of Time: Doing More with Less

Felicia, Eric, and Pam are faced with time constraints as they try to incorporate an expanding curriculum in their already full days. Chapter Four will help them and you decide how to use time well for teaching and learning. Many of Felicia's colleagues are engaged in team teaching arrangements and find that they can maximize the benefits of their planning and teaching time. We provide theory and research related to time management, as well as a description of the demands and limits you will be facing. You will read about a teacher whose commitment to her goals for students directs the way she uses her time. You will also find ways to identify and reduce the time losses and wasters that exist in most classrooms.

CHAPTER FIVE Classroom Management: Advancework

Our secondary teacher, Felicia Gomez, has few discipline problems in her teaching. She has created many of her teaching and learning activities to reflect the lives of her students, and she involves them in the selection of literature so that content is meaningful to them. The strategy of advancework has enabled her to do so. Chapter Five discusses advancework—an information-gathering strategy that promotes awareness. Advancework is necessary for making decisions and planning your classroom management. We suggest ways to conduct advancework in the context of your students' neighborhood, classroom, school, and district. Advancework with your curriculum will help you provide the kind of relevant and useful content that Felicia provides for her students. Advancework with students works toward physically and mentally active learning, social learning, confidence about learning, learning in which students are active decision makers, and a safe environment for learning.

CHAPTER SIX Classroom Management: Beyond Discipline

Snapshots of six classroom management models will assist you in developing a cooperative community for your students, much like the one you would find in Pam Rossio's room. We encourage your study of the models in order to develop a system of your own. Much of the climate and routines of your class will be established during the beginning of the year, and we make recommendations for getting started. Your classroom will be affected by transitions, interruptions, crises, and behavior problems, all of which can be addressed effectively. In the final section of Chapter Six, we encourage cooperative work with parents as a way of extending your classroom community.

CHAPTER SEVEN Lecture: From Passive to Active Learning

Felicia decided to make a change from a formal lecture approach, which she had experienced through most of her years in school, to an interactive use of the strategy. She had student groups discuss points in the lecture, provided guided note-taking techniques, and had students prepare outlines on transparencies for the overhead projector. Chapter Seven presents additional ways to make the strategy of lecturing highly interactive and to reduce the level of passivity usually associated with it. A continuum of teacher-centered to student-centered instruction is presented to provide you with a framework for using lecture with other instructional strategies. We also present suggestions that will help you use lecture for informational, motivational, or critical thinking outcomes. You will see how teachers can manage new variations of the old lecture theme.

CHAPTER EIGHT Questioning and Discussion: Creating a Dialogue

Pam, Eric, and Felicia realize how limited they are in using questions or discussion strategies to promote student thinking. They have listened to tapes of their classrooms and are concerned about the low levels of questions and the limited amount of time students are given to answer. Chapter Eight responds to their concerns with strategies for effective questioning and discussion. The chapter describes types of questions as well as questioning for a variety of purposes. Cautions are given about using questions to intimidate or control students and about the length of time you give students to answer questions. The chapter also provides guidelines and strategies for the effective use of discussion. To use discussion, you and your students will need to learn how to listen, reflect, and respond in meaningful ways.

CHAPTER NINE Interactive Practice for Learning: Beyond Drill

Chapter Nine describes outcomes for student learning that match the goal Pam Rossio has set for her fourth-graders—critical thinking. We describe how to incorporate learning strategies with your practice activities in order to help students "learn how to learn." By using the examples in the chapter, you will be able to plan practice activities with different levels of complexity. You will also gain ideas for working with the problems learners often have with practice. Their problems include boredom, indifference, lack of effort or perseverance, and poor time management. We provide descriptions of five practice strategies: review, seatwork, homework, projects, and learning centers. You will learn how to use each strategy in a variety of interesting ways.

CHAPTER TEN Grouping for Instruction: Involvement and Interaction

Chapter Ten examines the context, content, and learner for information that can help you make grouping decisions. We suggest a repertoire of grouping arrangements for accommodating the differences you have in your classroom: different curriculum outcomes, different physical environments, and different student personalities and needs. To support your use of grouping for involvement and interaction, we describe routines and procedures for management and guidelines for using the assistance of volunteers and aides.

CHAPTER ELEVEN Reflective Teaching and Learning: Students as Shareholders

This chapter will also be helpful to Pam in her efforts to teach critical thinking. In it, we guide you in promoting students as sources of curriculum—as "shareholders" in teaching and learning. A climate of trust, necessary for such teaching, is one in which students' thinking and point of view are valued. The strategies of case studies, mapping, and brainstorming are described to expand students' participation and experiences prior to using the actual processes of critical thinking and guided discovery. A survey is presented to help you assess the levels of reflection within your classroom.

CHAPTER TWELVE Making Learning Real: Engaging Students in Content

During his teacher education coursework and practicum, Eric Adams saw the potential for improvisation strategies to provide vicarious experiences for students. With many areas of curriculum, those experiences are necessary for students to be able to learn by doing, thinking, feeling, and responding within the safety of the classroom. Eric also engaged in service learning as a student and has begun to plan for community experiences for his learners. In Chapter Twelve, we help you become aware of and sensitive to your community while using it as a context for service learning and tapping its resources for improvisation. We also attend to the physical and emotional environments for these approaches. The strategies in this chapter are designed for use in all content areas but especially for the problem solving and decision making you will find in tomorrow's curriculum. You will find step-by-step models for roleplay and simulation, guidelines for using drama and service learning as a teaching strategy, and a description of the important roles you play in supporting learning.

CHAPTER THIRTEEN Using Community Resources, Audiovisuals, Computers, and Multimedia: Varying the Stimuli

Drawing on her banking experience, Felicia enjoys the challenges of incorporating technology in her curriculum, but feels limited by the resources and policies of her school. In Chapter Thirteen, we describe the technology available in most schools, from the simplest chalkboards to the most complex computer programs, and recognize the limits Felicia faces. We remind you and her of the purposes that technology can serve, and of the contextual and content considerations that influence use of community resources, audiovisuals, computers, and multimedia. To employ these as stimuli for teaching, we suggest effective and unusual ways to make them part of teaching and learning.

CHAPTER FOURTEEN Assessment of Learning: Let Me Count the Ways

Our three teachers will need another repertoire for their teaching—a repertoire of strategies to assess learning. Chapter Fourteen works to develop that repertoire for the varying content and learners they face. Assessment questions and issues fall into three groupings: diagnostic, formative, and summative. We describe the many purposes of assessment: planning, making decisions, promoting learning, and communicating to students, parents, other teachers, and the general public. You will find over a dozen strategies for assessing student learning, described with guidelines for selection or for development.

CHAPTER FIFTEEN Self-Improvement through Self-Assessment

Knowledge is power, but knowledge about oneself is the greatest power. Felicia, Eric, and Pam continue to develop professionally when they reflect on their teaching. Being able to assess your teaching will help you reflect on your own teaching and will add significantly to your knowledge of teaching. Chapter Fifteen identifies sources of data to improve your teaching. Measures of self-assessment to analyze your teaching are provided, as well as strategies for using student feedback and peer observations for additional information. We describe formal and informal ways of looking at yourself, learning about yourself, and improving yourself in the classroom. The theme of Chapter Fifteen is that learning to be an effective teacher is a lifelong pursuit and requires a variety of information sources.

The chapters of *Universal Teaching Strategies* are arranged in the framework of organizing strategies, instructing strategies, and assessing strategies. Within each chapter you will find opportunities for building and expanding your teaching repertoire. A variety of Research Vignettes, Classroom Snapshots, Teacher Talks, and Samples and Examples will provide you with ideas, activities, examples, observations, and insights. Each chapter has common themes that will make the content more usable for your teaching. For example, each chapter discusses the inclusive classroom and how to organize for, instruct, and assess learners with a wide range of needs, learning styles, and abilities. Considerations of the *context, content,* and *learners* are developed within the descriptions of each teaching strategy; guidelines for their use are given. We look at those themes as we proceed to *teaching for tomorrow.* The challenge of tomorrow's context, tomorrow's content, and tomorrow's learners awaits you.

THE CONTEXT OF TEACHING FOR TOMORROW

Context is another word for setting or environment. The context for teaching may include physical environments such as a country, state, school district, neighborhood, school, or classroom. It may also include less concrete settings such as the political or economic climate. The context for teaching is influenced by the status of the education profession as well as the public's awareness and satisfaction with education. Today's context for teaching emphasizes school reform, school restructuring, and school accountability (Sexton, Kelley, & Aldridge, 1998). Efforts responding to those calls are currently focused around state-mandated standards of student achievement as well as proposed national standards. As our three teachers prepare to teach a new group of students, they are well aware of the many pressures for increased student achievement. They will work with other professionals to decide what they want their students to learn and to be able to do while paying attention to state and national standards. Their decisions about teaching strategies will be significantly influenced by their intent to assess student learning according to those sets of standards. All three teachers will work in the context of reform or change due to concern from within teaching as well as from outside the profession.

Although it is impossible to predict exactly what they will look and feel like, there are definite indications of contextual characteristics to come. Education is being thought of in a much broader sense to include home, neighborhoods, and society. Thus, a better term for the teaching context may be *community.* We suggest that teaching for tomorrow may take place in a "wired" and inclusive community.

A "Wired" Community

In a time when interactive Web TV instruction is being used (Behrmann, 1998) and home/school networking technology brings together a wider audience of parents and teachers (Honey, Carrigg, & Hawkins, 1998), a wired community is clearly a context for your teaching. Yesterday's predictions and prescriptions were for "education that relies on electronic learning" (Mecklenburger, 1990, p. 105), but tomorrow's reality calls for huge restructuring of schools and "inventing new visions of education in the context of a digital world" (Papert, 1998, p. 10).

One example of technology that has captured the imagination of students and teachers alike is the World Wide Web. The Web links text, images, sound, and video resources on computers connected to the Internet. Claims have been made for the Web's capacity to move beyond the physical boundaries of classrooms and schedules, extend lectures and demonstrations to multimedia learning experiences for students, enhance the resources, and even refocus the nation's schools from teaching to learning (Owston, 1997).

It is clear that educational technology is a very high priority for schools. As such, the preparation for using technology in teaching has become a national priority. The 1997 Presidential Advisory Committee on Science and Technology survey found that 20 percent of teachers used advanced telecommunications for teaching and that in more than 50 percent of schools, training for technology was left up to the individual teacher. "The substantial investment in hardware, infrastructure, software, and content will be largely wasted on K–12 teachers that are not provided with the preparation and support they will need to effectively integrate technology into their teaching" (Presidential Advisory Committee on Science and Technology, 1997). You may be able to begin that preparation while you are learning to teach, or you may need to take classes after you begin teaching, as Pam did several years ago.

In addition to preparing themselves to be more computer literate, teachers like Felicia, Eric, and Pam are faced with multiple challenges. They must make decisions about the role of computers in their teaching, appropriate curriculum, quality software, and equal access for students.

Tomorrow's challenge in a complex community of multimedia is for educators to be involved in major decisions about technology and to maintain expertise in an evolving and expanding medium for teaching. The challenge calls for an energetic and active role in policy development and decision making on issues of technology. The challenge also calls for judicious planning on the part of schools if teachers are going to be prepared to use technology to the fullest capacity. Many K–12 educators are currently forming partnerships with businesses, the community, and higher education for collaboration, feedback, and accessibility.

These challenges alone represent major restructuring of the context of teaching. Felicia, with her banking experience, sees many possibilities for meeting the second challenge—expanding the vision of classroom—but feels limited by the resources and policies of her school. Pam, an advocate for educational equality, has already used creative scheduling with her limited computer resources to increase learning opportunities for her students. The challenges of a wired community are many.

A Community of Inclusion

Inclusion is a term used to describe a commitment to educate each child (including children with disabilities) to the maximum extent appropriate, in the school and classroom he or she would otherwise attend (Phi Delta Kappa, 1993). Another way of describing inclusion is that it brings support services to the child rather than bringing the child to the services. The main doctrine of inclusion is that the child will benefit from being in the regular classroom. Communities of inclusion are the context in which many teachers are already working, while others are preparing to do so.

Establishing communities of inclusion requires the acceptance of students with special needs as "full members of the home base schools" and the responsibility of all educators in the school "for all students in that school" (Lombardi, Nuzzo, Kennedy, & Foshay, 1994; McLeskey & Waldon, 1996; Sapon-Shevin, 1996). Both the acceptance and the responsibility have implications for you as a classroom teacher.

Inclusion is based on the understanding that both special education teachers and regular education teachers have expertise about teaching and learning. That is, they have knowledge of human development and the characteristics of learners, assessment, learning styles and other learner differences, curriculum, classroom management, and supportive learning environments. By combining their knowledge and talents, they can develop strategies that focus less on matching a learner's disability with a teaching approach and more on approaches that are effective for *all* learners (Schirmer, Casbon, & Twiss, 1995).

As more and more school districts move to communities of inclusion, new issues emerge for regular education teachers like Eric, Pam, and Felicia. Teaching in an inclusive community may require new time commitments, changes in curriculum and teaching strategies, and physical and emotional accommodations in classrooms. Even the pace of classroom life will need to be adjusted to meet the wide diversity of needs and abilities in a community of inclusion.

Both Felicia and Pam are already experiencing the value and satisfaction of collaborating with teacher colleagues to make changes and improve their teaching. Such team arrangements have proven essential in schools and districts that move to inclusion models. Teachers must have a voice in the decisions and the planning of inclusion. At Souhegan High School in New Hampshire, the faculty was fully involved in the move to full inclusion. Teachers spent considerable time and creative energy during the first year in the collaborative design of learning activities to engage all students' interest and learning styles, while meeting state and local educational requirements (Center for Health Promotion and Research, 1993).

A statement from the Souhegan High School Operating Principles sums up our predictions of the context of teaching communities of tomorrow. It describes the kind of communities in which we hope you will use your repertoire of teaching strategies: "Schools of the future should strive to be communities of learners where intellectual development and adaptability to change become driving forces for everyone—students and staff alike—but where the climate is humane and caring, promoting respect for diversity."

THE CONTENT OF TEACHING FOR TOMORROW

We have been talking about the context demanded for the schools of tomorrow. Now let us discuss the content—the pool of information, skills, and values that our students are expected to learn. *Content* is often called curriculum or subject matter. It can be structured with specifically stated goals and objectives, teaching and learning activities, and materials found in curriculum guides developed by states and school districts. It can also be unstructured and in the control and thinking of individual teachers. Sometimes content refers strictly to what is contained in a textbook. Whatever the source, content changes with the changes in society. Content reflects problems, concerns, values, and priorities of people, as you will see in our projections for the content of tomorrow.

Our three teachers, Felicia, Eric, and Pam, teach different content (English literature, environmental science, and elementary everything), but all three will be affected by the curricular trends of tomorrow. One trend that is influencing all content areas is the move toward integrated curriculum and teaching. *Integrated curriculum* is the blending of several or all content areas around a theme, a problem, or a project. Teachers who teach integrated content often use a unit-planning approach and collaborate with others in planning and implementation stages. Integrated teaching and learning responds to the expanding curricular knowledge base as well as the need for relevant curriculum for an increasingly diverse group of learners (Nagel, 1994). In addition to the move to integrate varied content areas, content associated with social responsibility will be integrated with Eric's science curriculum and with Felicia's literature selections. Among the skills called for in students are critical thinking, problem solving, communication, and the ability to work collaboratively (Uchida, 1996). "Although these skills have always been valued, the renewed call for them represents a demand that schools place increased emphasis on their development" (Owston, 1997).

An additional content prediction involves a drastic change in response to the diversity of learners found in today's schools. Multicultural education has been around for some time, but tomorrow's definition of it calls for empowering all students to become knowledgeable, caring, and active citizens (Banks, 1994).

Thinking Skills Content

Much of the push for thinking skills content has resulted from an awareness that we live in a society that requires us to make complex decisions. It is not likely that tomorrow will be simpler and require less of such thinking and reasoning; in fact, it is likely to require more. The term *thinking skills* refers to "all of the mental processes individuals use to obtain, make sense of, and retain information, as well as how they process and use that information as a basis for solving problems" (Turner, 1999). Some of the thinking skills being addressed by both pedagogy (instruction) and curriculum are logical thinking and creative thinking, problem solving, and inquiry. Such skills will require that students be actively engaged in the learning process.

Teaching thinking skills requires expertise in teaching strategies, the use of curricular materials, and assessment, all of which support students in participatory roles in the education process. We must provide solid preparation for teachers and support their efforts to teach thinking skills. For example, Pam Rossio has been working on curriculum reform and actively implements critical thinking curriculum with her fourth-graders. But she often feels isolated in her efforts and frustrated by lack of resources. Support must be provided for her and other professionals in their efforts by means of workshops, seminars, resources, materials, and recognition. That same level of support is essential for teachers to respond differently to the diversity of learners—that is, to change from "approaches that eliminate differences to thinking of diversity in terms of cultural resources" (Perez, 1994).

Multicultural Education Content

After years of struggling with its definition, educators are becoming clear about what multicultural education is designed to do. The ultimate goal is for all students to acquire the knowledge, skills, and attitudes needed to function effectively in a culturally and ethnically diverse nation and world. Multicultural education is not "an ethnic- or gender-specific movement" (Banks, 1994), and only when it is seen as essential for all students will it become part of our educational institutions.

Grant and Sleeter (1998) considered multicultural education as an approach founded on two ideals: equal opportunity and cultural pluralism. In their words, *equal opportunity* "holds that each student should be given equal opportunity to learn, succeed, and become what he or she would like, with full affirmation of his or her sex, race, social class background, sexual orientation, and disability, if any" (p. 163). *Cultural pluralism* is defined as "a sharing and blending of different ethnic cultures and other forms of culture that constitute the shared mainstream U.S. culture" (p. 163) while supporting distinctive group cultures.

Banks (1994) has reminded us that multicultural education as is multidimensional and cannot be confined to simple curriculum approaches or content. An effective approach begins with a broad and comprehensive view of multiculturalism—a view that promotes the interconnectedness of all peoples (Garcia & Pugh, 1992). This view emphasizes the importance of each individual and each individual's impact on humanity.

This expanded thinking about multicultural education may sound overwhelming, but many teachers are successfully making changes in curriculum, in classroom structures, and in teaching and learning strategies to begin to achieve the goals we have described. A recent approach to further the thinking and goals of multicultural education is antibias and antiracism education. Derman-Sparks and Phillips (1997) described *antiracism education* as "not an end in itself but the beginning of a new approach to thinking, feeling, and acting" (p. 3). The outcomes of such education are the "self-awareness, knowledge, and skills, as well as the confidence, patience, and persistence—to challenge, interrupt, modify, erode, and eliminate all manifestations of racism within one's own spheres of influence" (p. 3). Such a charge requires lifelong learning and begins to communicate the complexity of multicultural education as well as the possibilities for your classroom.

The diversity of learners in the country's classrooms represents the future, and the future will reflect how well educators have included all students in the learning community today. A commitment to multicultural education content in your teaching will be a significant contribution to tomorrow's society.

We have discussed two of the major influences on teaching—context and content. Contextual trends related to technology, cooperation, and inclusion have been predicted, as well as content trends related to critical thinking and multicultural education. Now we look at the third major influence—the learners—and predict what they will look like tomorrow.

THE LEARNERS OF TODAY AND TOMORROW

Today's students are tomorrow's adults. The attitudes, knowledge, skills, and hope provided during growth and development will be the foundations of adulthood. The prophecy is well stated by Freiberg (1990): "Today's children are our leaders for the future and the generation we will depend upon to care for us in our twilight years. We will reap the legacy of both our successes and our mistakes."

The children and adolescents of today are a challenge to teach. They are distracted by their world of video and violence. They have access to over 30 channels of MTV with fast-paced entertainment, rock performances, and occasional pornography. Papert

(1993) stated that most of today's K–12 learners do not know a world without computers. Technology in multiple forms is an integral part of students' lives—they play with, are entertained by, and learn with technology. It is little wonder that today's learners reject teaching approaches such as lectures, films, recitation, reading, worksheets, and independent projects (Grant & Sleeter, 1998).

Tomorrow's learners come from varied family structures and bring to classrooms a myriad of experiences to contribute. In addition, the color of the nation's learners is changing rapidly. It is predicted that nearly half (about 45.5 percent) of school-age children will be young people of color by 2020 (Natriello, Pallas, & McDill, 1989). The most prominent condition influencing the learners to be taught by Pam, Eric, and Felicia is poverty. With poverty comes issues of health, homelessness, violence, abuse, and neglect. The statistics on poverty and its associated issues are bleak and may be enough to discourage you from teaching. We encourage you to study those realities that learners bring to the classrooms to understand as much as possible about these challenges. A look at the following recent statistics on children and their families will focus on the challenges of teaching the learners of tomorrow. A glance at some key facts about American children reveals strong patterns of poverty, violence, poor health, and school failure:

- *1 in 2 preschoolers has a mother in the labor force*
- *1 in 2 children will live in a single-parent family at some point in childhood*
- *1 in 2 children never completes a single year of college*
- *1 in 3 children will be poor at some point in childhood*
- *1 in 3 children is a year or more behind in school*
- *1 in 4 children is born poor*
- *1 in 5 children lives in a family receiving food stamps*
- *1 in 7 children has no health insurance*
- *1 in 8 children never graduates from high school*
- *1 in 11 children lives at less than half the poverty level*
- *1 in 12 children has a disability*
- *1 in 25 children lives with neither parent*
- *1 in 132 children dies before age 1*
- *1 in 680 children is killed by gunfire before age 20 (Children's Defense Fund, 1998, p. xv)*

Children are more likely to be poor than adults, and their disproportionate poverty is getting worse. No racial group is immune: 40.3 percent of Hispanic children, 39.9 percent of Black children, and 16.3 percent of White children are poor (Children's Defense Fund, 1998). Poverty afflicts children in every region of the country—in suburbs, in rural areas, as well as in cities—and in households headed by couples and by single parents alike (p. 4).

To make matters worse, the 1997 Department of Education's *Report on the Condition of Education* found that schools with the highest proportion of poor children have markedly fewer resources than schools serving affluent students. Schools serving large numbers of poor children have fewer books and supplies and employ teachers with less training. Schools in the poorest neighborhoods are also more likely to be in disrepair. Research has shown that environmental factors—such as overcrowded buildings, substandard science facilities, external noise, and other building problems—can lower student performance on academic work.

In sum, the effects of poverty are far reaching and invade many classrooms as obstacles to learning. Lest you finish this chapter completely discouraged about teaching the learners of today and tomorrow, we want to conclude with an assurance that you will have much support from multiple levels. Many states, communities, and districts have committed resources and reform to meet the needs of today's learners.

Important to the effectiveness of those efforts to improve schools is the need for strong expectations that all children can succeed. With those expectations, all teachers must work to be the best they can be and to foster learning in all classrooms for all children.

The statistics only begin to represent the immensely complex learner who arrives at our classrooms. The depth and magnitude of the problems that learners bring to school keep many people from entering the teaching profession, or become the reason given by those leaving the profession. Those who choose to join and stay have learned to address such problems with sophisticated instructional and management strategies. Instructional strategies that promote relevant content and high levels of student involvement will be effective in teaching tomorrow's learners. Management strategies that consider the needs and interests of learners, their families, and their communities will be effective in providing environments that respond to tomorrow's learners.

Felicia has few discipline problems in her teaching. She uses teaching strategies that keep her students involved: interpreting dialogue, creating their own endings to stories, dramatizing scenes, and so on. She also involves her secondary students in the selection of literature so that the content is more meaningful to them.

As Eric contemplates the students in his middle-school classroom, he sees the problems of tomorrow's learners as the core of his work toward the goal of social responsibility. He brings insights from his volunteer work with teens and a repertoire of activities to work toward his goal.

FACING TOMORROW

In addition to the challenges predicted for the context, content, and learners of tomorrow, the teaching profession is faced with increasing demands for changes in instructional approaches, expanded roles for teachers, and a new sense of purpose (Clark & Astuto, 1994). Pam, Eric, and Felicia face these demands for change in their teaching. Their future is full of challenge. It is evident from the demographics of the future that teaching will require greater expertise and a broader repertoire from which to select teaching strategies.

SUMMARY

Teaching is and must be a never-ending quest for new knowledge and ideas to expand our teaching repertoires to meet the needs of a changing world (context, content, and learners). We must begin today if we are to teach for tomorrow and provide tomorrow's adults with the necessary knowledge, skills, attitudes, and dreams for the twenty-first century. This challenge will require us to break from the mold of a limited approach to teaching and expand our options to meet the needs of every learner. This is the challenge of teaching for tomorrow.

REFERENCES

Banks, J. A. (1994). Multicultural education: Development, dimensions, and challenges. *Kappan, 75*(1), 22–28.

Baron, J. B., & Sternberg, R. J. (1987). *Teaching thinking skills: Theory and practice.* New York: W. H. Freeman.

Beck, C. R. (1998). A taxonomy for identifying, classifying, and interrelating teaching strategies. *Journal of General Education, 47*(1), 38–62.

Behrmann, M. M. (1998). Assistive technology for young children in special education. In C. Dede (Ed.), *Year Book 1998: Learning with technology* (pp. 73–93). Alexandria, VA: Association for Supervision and Curriculum Development.

Berman, S. (1990). Educating for social responsibility. *Educational Leadership, 48*(3), 75–80.

Bigelow, B., Christensen, L., Karp, S., Milner, B., & Peterson, B. (1994). *Rethinking our classrooms.* Montgomery, AL: Rethinking Schools Ltd.

Boyer, E. L. (1990). Civic education for responsible citizens. *Educational Leadership, 48*(3), 4–9.

Center for Health Promotion and Research. (1993). *Equity and Excellence, 1*(1).

Charp, S. (1993–1994). *Technological Horizons Education: The multimedia source guide, supplement.* Tustin, CA.

Children's Defense Fund. (1998). *The state of America's children.* Washington, DC: Author.

Clark, D., & Astuto, T. (1994). Redirecting reform. *Educational Leadership, 75*(7), 513–520.

Corbin, G. L. (1995). Collaboration really works. *Teaching Children Mathematics, 2*(3), 190–191.

Department of Education. (1997). *Report on the condition of education.* Washington, DC: Author.

Derman-Sparks, L., & Phillips, C. B. (1997). *Teaching/learning anti-racism.* New York: Teachers College Press.

Freiberg, H. J. (1990). *School and teacher effectiveness for the 21st century child.* Speech given to the West Virginia State Department of Education, Morgantown, WV.

Garcia, J., & Pugh, S. L. (1992). Multicultural education in teacher preparation programs. *Kappan, 74*(3), 214–219.

Grant, C. A., & Sleeter, C. E. (1998). *Turning on learning: Five approaches for multicultural teaching plans for race, gender, class, and disability.* Columbus, OH: Merrill.

Heuwinkel, M. K. (1996). New ways of learning = New ways of teaching. *Childhood Education, 73*(1), 27–31.

Honey, M., Carrigg, F., & Hawkins, J. (1998). Union City online: An architecture for networking and reform. In C. Dede (Ed.), *Year Book 1998: Learning with technology* (pp. 73–93). Alexandria, VA: Association for Supervision and Curriculum Development.

Houston, R. W. (1990). *Handbook of research on teacher education.* New York: Macmillan.

Lombardi, T., Nuzzo, D., Kennedy, K., & Foshay, J. (1994). Perceptions of parents, teachers, and students regarding an integrated education inclusion program. *High School Journal, 77*(4), 315–321.

McLeskey, J., & Waldon, N. (1996). Responses to questions teachers and administrators frequently ask about inclusive school programs. *Phi Delta Kappan, 78*, 150–156.

Mecklenburger, J. A. (1990). Educational technology is not enough. *Kappan, 72*(2), 104–108.

Nagel, N. (1994). *Integrative teaching and learning for elementary students through real world problem solving.* Unpublished manuscript.

Natriello, G., Pallas, A., & McDill, E. (1989). The changing nature of the disadvantaged population: Current dimensions and future trends. *Educational Researcher, 19*(6), 2–15.

Owston, R. D. (1997). The World Wide Web: A technology to enhance teaching and learning? *Educational Researcher, 26*(2), 27–33.

Papert, S. (1993). *The children's machine: Rethinking school in the age of the computer.* New York: Basic Books.

Papert, S. (1998). Let's tie the digital knot. *TECHNOS, 7*(4), 10–12.

Perez, S. A. (1994). Responding differently to diversity. *Childhood Education, 70*(3), 151–153.

Phi Delta Kappa. (1993). *Research Bulletin No. 11.* Bloomington, IN: Author.

Presidential Advisory Committee on Science and Technology. (1997). *Report for support of technology training for teachers.* Washington, DC: Author.

Sapon-Shevin, M. (1996). Full inclusion as disclosing tablet: Revealing the flaws in our present system. *Theory Into Practice, 35,* 35–41.

Schirmer, B., Casbon, J., & Twiss, L. (1995). Diverse learners in the classroom. *The Reading Teacher, 49*(1), 66–68.

Sexton, D., Kelly, M., & Aldridge, J. (1998). Continuing tensions in education. *Childhood Education, 74*(5), 258–261.

Turner, T. N. (1999). *Essentials of elementary social studies.* Boston: Allyn and Bacon.

Uchida, C. (1996). *Preparing students for the 21st century.* Arlington, VA: American Association of School Administration.

Wittrock M. C. (1986). Students' thought processes. In M. C. Wittrock (Ed.), *Handbook of research on teaching* (3rd ed.). New York: Macmillan.

CHAPTER

2

PLANNING FOR INSTRUCTION

Visualizing What Could Be

Chapter Outcomes

At the conclusion of this chapter you will be able to:

1. *Identify the three voices of planning.*
2. *Describe the functions of planning.*
3. *Describe four planning stages.*
4. *Identify considerations of the learner, content, and context in planning.*
5. *Identify the entry characteristics of learners.*
6. *Define how you could initiate or improve your planning.*

Key Terms and Concepts

Definition of Planning
Importance of Planning
Three Voices of Planning
Functions of Planning
Limitations of Planning
Planning Phases
Preplanning
Active Planning
Postplanning
Mental Process
Learner
Content
Context
Special Needs Learners

INTRODUCTION

Planning

Teacher planning is the thread that weaves the curriculum, or the *what* of teaching, with the instruction, or the *how* of teaching. The classroom is a highly interactive and demanding place. Planning provides for some measure of order in an uncertain and changing environment.

Research during the past 40 years on teaching effectiveness supports what most experienced teachers have concluded: Effective teaching is not a haphazard process. Expert teachers plan ahead to create an environment that is conducive for both their teaching style and student learning. Although all effective teachers incorporate some form of planning in their lessons, how a teacher plans seems to be unique to the individual.

Planning Defined

Visualizing

Planning is the ability to visualize into the future—creating, arranging, organizing, and designing events in the mind that may occur in the classroom. Planning allows for purposeful instruction. Consistent planning provides an instructional guide for both teacher and students. It helps with self- and classroom management and allows for easier decision making about the what and how to teach. The goal of planning should always be student learning.

Guiding

Planning for instruction provides a type of road map or guide that assists you in creating a flow of events that has a starting and ending point. Planning is a process that begins with preplanning thoughts and ideas and moves to active planning preparations. Ongoing planning and "in-flight" corrections occur during actual implementation of instruction as events in the classrooms necessitate change. Finally, postanalysis of strengths and weaknesses of instruction and discrepancies between what was planned and what occurred during instruction are noted and become part of the planning process for future lessons.

Managing

Planning is a way of managing time and events. Your plans may be short or long term. A middle-school or junior or senior high-school teacher may plan for five or six 55-minute or four 90-minute time periods throughout the day. An elementary teacher may

plan for 15- to 30-minute segments of instruction. Teachers also develop plans for larger units of time, including daily, weekly, monthly, and yearly plans. The amount of time a teacher plans may be a function of the time allocated by the state or district for the school day, the curriculum or content to be taught, and the knowledge and motivational levels of the students.

Decision Making

Planning for teaching is the ability to make decisions about the how and what of teaching. These decisions are based on three primary considerations: (1) the students' prior (affective and cognitive) learning experiences in the classroom; (2) the content derived from curriculum guides, textbooks, study guides, and teacher-developed materials; and (3) the context or conditions in which the instruction will take place.

Decision making is the ability to select from among several alternatives and implement one or more alternatives within a fixed period of time. During instruction, decision making is almost instantaneous. Planning allows for some decisions to become routine, enabling you to limit the time and energy expended on events that occur frequently. For example, deciding each day how to distribute or collect papers would be an ineffective use of instructional time. Once a routine is established for passing out papers by row and returning the finished papers to a "grading box," the need to make further decisions about assignments is limited to possible future revisions.

THREE VOICES OF PLANNING

In a real sense, the classroom and school provide unlimited possibilities to build a repertoire for planning our lessons, if only we listen to the "voices" of opportunity. The voices are both internal and external and come from three sources: my voice, a colleague's voice, and students' voices. Sometimes we are so busy doing small things that we don't hear these voices of opportunity. When we listen to all three voices, the planning process moves beyond our own limits to engage the larger learning community.

My voice is a starting point for planning. I need to hear myself and determine the best approach to planning a lesson. As a beginning teacher, my voice may be somewhat limited due to a lack of experience. Knowledge of content may be strong but the ability to store and structure knowledge experiences related to teaching in a way that is easily accessible and usable will take time. *Without new instructional experiences and ideas, we tend to teach the way we have been taught.* The ability to transform knowledge about the subject, to include a range of instructional strategies that respond to diverse abilities and backgrounds of the learner, requires more planning at the beginning of one's career than in later years. Also, the ability to translate content in a manner that is understandable to others is a key element of instruction and requires critical thinking and a repertoire of instructional approaches and content-related examples. Planning helps make the transition from novice to expert much smoother and effective. For veteran teachers, spending more time in planning may help in revitalizing instruction and building new ideas. The process of planning alone can become too limited. Much of what is described in this chapter on planning and in the next chapter on designing instruction can be expanded to include other teachers and your students in the planning process.

A colleague's voice will enrich and expand your repertoire of teaching. Two eighth-grade teachers, one in English (Ms. Parker) and the other in American History (Mr. Luther), decided to link their lessons with the same students using a unit on the Civil War as the focal point. While the history class discussed the issues of the Civil War, the English teacher had her students read and discuss *Across Five Aprils,* a historical fiction novel by Irene Hunt. The book, which describes the experiences of living and fighting during the Civil War, gave the students a better understanding of a period in history that shaped the future and their own lives. The students used a timeline of historical events developed in history and overlaid it onto the events discussed in the book. As a closing activity, the students watched a videotape of the film *Shenandoah.* Ms. Parker describes the planning that went into this six-week unit in the following Snapshot.

SNAPSHOT: Cooperative Unit Planning

If you want to stay vital in the classroom, your learning must never end. After 12 years of teaching English at the middle-school level, I had rarely planned an integrated curriculum with another teacher. Attending a graduate-level curriculum course reinforced the importance of integrating across the curriculum what we teach and giving students an understanding that learning is not a series of isolated facts. It was from this perspective that I began a planning process with Lyn Luther, a young energetic teacher who always tried to make history come alive for his students. He was eager to plan a unit that would combine a topic he was teaching about the American Civil War and that would also include the novel *Across Five Aprils* by the Newbery Award–winning author Irene Hunt. This Civil War novel, drawn from the author's family records and from her grandfather's experiences, was reviewed as both historically authentic and beautifully written. Lyn and I met after school to design our six-week unit. From a historical perspective, he wanted the students to understand the personal, economic, and political impact the Civil War had on the nation and its people.

We had decided that the themes of change, conflict, and problem resolution would be a thread that carried through both of our classes. Mr. Luther read the novel and included points made in the novel with a timeline of historical events. This timeline was used in both classes, and events in the lives of the characters were compared along the timeline. The unit culminated in a debate that included issues from perspectives of both the North and South. Students expressed excitement as well as satisfaction that learning can bridge subject areas. (Gale Parker, eighth-grade teacher)

A second example of unit planning with a colleague may be found in Figure 2.1. The authors have developed 12 questions that serve as a guide in planning a unit in the language arts area yet are applicable across the curriculum. The development of unit planning is more complex because of the longer time periods required to accomplish the goals and objectives of the unit and the materials and resources needed to support the learner. The context may also change in that classroom seating arrangements, use of the library, and noise levels may need to be considered. Complex instruction and collaborative units require more detailed planning. The questions may also be helpful in developing student voices in the planning process.

Student voices in planning can change a lesson that is detached from the lives of students to a lesson that is engaged. Student motivation is a challenge to almost every teacher. When students become part of planning a lesson or unit, they have a much greater stake in its success. The following Snapshot shows how this process can begin. Ms. Cohen shared her plans for the following week with her students each Friday. It is an easy transition to seek input from the students once they understand the planning process. Several veteran teachers we have observed ask their students to write down any questions they would like to have answered during the next unit. These questions are then used to assist the teachers in building examples and, in some instances, entire lessons.

SNAPSHOT: A Look Ahead

As I become more experienced, I find myself sharing my plans more with my students. In my fifth-grade class, for instance, each Friday I write on a chalkboard, which is set up as a calendar, the major assignments to come for the following week. It is understood that adjustments may be made, yet the students get a preview of what is to come and it allows them to practice budgeting their homework time. In addition, at the outset of each lesson, I share with the students the planned agenda for the day.

I did not always teach in this fashion. Often, especially when I taught high school, I liked incorporating an element of surprise in my lessons. I felt that the pupils would be more alert if they kept guessing about what was to come next. That worked for me then. But now I feel that sharing my organization with the pupils is more valuable. It gives them a feeling of security. The goals of the lesson become more distinct. Attention spans increase. I find that for students who have slight learning disabilities, this method is extremely beneficial. Once the students are aware of and can follow the schedule, the material becomes familiar because it can be related to as small manageable units. (Myrna Cohen, fifth-grade teacher)

FUNCTIONS OF PLANNING

If you fail to plan, then you will plan to fail. This statement is a truism in life as well as in the classroom. Many travel advisors suggest the local library as a good starting point in planning a trip. Knowledge is an important tool in planning a journey; it is also an important starting point in planning to teach. Planning gives you the advantage of controlling classroom instruction in a positive way. Planning has several benefits, ranging from providing an overview of instruction to establishing a repertoire of instructional strategies that build from daily successes and accumulate from year to year. The following list highlights the functions of planning:

1. *Planning gives an overview of instruction.* A plan presents you with a total picture of the lesson for the day or for the entire year. Knowing where you are going enables you to coordinate the development of materials, resources, and activities that will enrich instruction.

   Many experienced teachers take a calendar at the beginning of the school year and divide the content to be taught for the remainder of the year. (See Samples and Examples, at the end of this chapter, for "School Year at a Glance" planning calendar.) Knowing what should be achieved by specific blocks of time provides guideposts for instruction. Experienced teachers include vacation times, standardized testing periods, site visits from state or regional accrediting agencies, and other important dates that diminish or change actual teaching time. Knowing what will interfere or alter the presentation of a lesson or unit enables you to plan around or incorporate these events.

2. *Planning facilitates good management and instruction.* Planning provides for a sense of order for the teacher and the students. Order is an important part of good management and discipline (Evertson & Harris, 1999). It is evident to the students when the teacher has a clear direction for what is next. Learning flourishes in an environment of order. Students will flounder if you wander from activity to activity without any clear sense of direction or purpose. Valuable instructional time is lost and students become restless when they need to wait for the lesson to begin.

   Experienced classroom teachers recognize the difference in the effectiveness of their lessons when they have not planned. Effective planning reduces the opportunities for student disruptions by providing a smooth flow of instructional events and activities

FIGURE 2.1 *Questions and Considerations for Planning a Thematic Unit in a Ninth-Grade English Classroom*

1. *Start with a "big question" or idea.* What are we trying to find out or answer or explore?

2. *Articulate why this unit is important and what it has to do with our students.* If we don't know why a unit can be important and how it can be connected to student lives and interests, then students certainly won't see the point of what we are doing.

3. *Brainstorm.* Write down any ideas that come to you, any writing connections, questions, material, issues that can be built on. If you find through brainstorming that this "overriding question" has lots and lots of pieces and parts, then it will probably be rich enough to engage the class. If you run into blocks and dead-ends, then rethink your idea for a unit.

4. *Select a centerpiece.* What will you build the unit around? A video, a short story, an audio tape, a piece of nonfiction, a novel, a play, a specific TV show? Use the centerpiece as a focus and as a way to kick off the unit and get the students involved.

5. *Make a list of possible activities that will involve students.* If you see ways to incorporate interviews and small group work and projects and writing assignments, then you can see that this unit is full of possibilities and will likely involve students.

6. *Make a mental inventory of what other materials can be used.* Will children's picture books work? How about fables or fairy tales? Can you think of a movie or a video that would work with the theme and contribute to the unit? How can poetry be worked in? What about nonfiction? Music? Art?

7. *Write down the language art skills that will be emphasized through work on this unit.* Will you focus on having students understand memoir and learn to write descriptively in that genre? Will you ask students to understand the elements in a fable and be able to write one? Will you work with students on improving their ability to use dialogue in their stories?

8. *Figure out the kind of modeling or instruction you need so all the students have the skills necessary to do what you would want them to do.* Do you need to draft a script on the overhead together so students know the necessary conventions? Do you need to construct an activity that includes acting out a scene to help students enter the world of this story?

9. *Consider the classroom organization and the structure of the class.* How much of this unit is teacher-directed and how much is student-centered? Can you see lots of opportunities for students to work in small groups on issues that will concern them? How will you organize class time? What will you expect your students to do each day?

10. *Construct introductory activities and possible end-project assignments.* Have a long-range plan that can be adapted or changed after you see the direction students want to go with the "big question."

11. *Reflect on whether or not the unit is in line with best practice in the field and whether or not the unit is in line with your philosophy on the teaching of language arts.* For instance, does the plan for a unit integrate reading, viewing, writing, speaking, and listening? Are students expected to make meaning and relate this material to themselves or does the teacher control all the outcomes? Are students being given a chance to raise real issues and answer questions for which the teacher does not have a predetermined answer?

12. *Decide how you will access or evaluate student work for this unit.* Will you develop a rubric for projects both oral and written? Will you have students write and reflect on what they have learned? Will you construct essay-like questions on skills you want to emphasize? Will you ask students to evaluate group work using such sentence starters as, "My major contribution to the group was" and "In our group, here's what we accomplished on our task"? How much will you access through observation?

Source: From "Teaching Ideas: Creating Thematic Units" by D. Mitchell, 1997, *English Journal, 5* (86), pp. 80–85. Copyright 1997 by the National Council of Teachers of English. Adapted by permission.

during and between lessons. Order and purpose, however, should not be confused with rigidity and inflexibility. It is easier to change plans to meet student learning needs if you begin with a plan.

3. *Planning makes learning purposeful.* Research on teaching effectiveness strongly supports the belief that purpose must be provided in the instructional process (Freiberg, 1999). The teacher who thinks about the reasons for specific behaviors in the classroom and communicates academic and behavioral expectations to the students will increase student opportunities for learning and reduce anxiety and uncertainty. The Samples and Examples section (at the end of this chapter) contains copies of a weekly calendar and a syllabus, which may also assist you and the students in planning and learning.

4. *Planning provides for sequencing and pacing.* Most textbooks, workbooks, or district curriculum guides present a sequencing of the content. The teacher needs to review these materials at the beginning of the lesson or year to determine if the sequence is reasonable for the students and to decide what enriching activities should be provided along with the text materials. Planning enables you to place one content area in juxtaposition to previous and future instruction. Once information about the content has been reviewed, decisions about the daily, weekly, and monthly sequencing can be determined.

5. *Planning ties classroom instructional events with community resources.* Without planning, those teachable moments where school, home, and community are linked will occur less often. Knowing what will occur, at least in a general sense, two or three months ahead will allow you to coordinate community events with classroom instruction. Exhibits, guest speakers, special television programs, special performances by local art groups all could be missed opportunities if reservations are required several weeks or months in advance and the scope of the content for the year is not evident. Teaching is clearly more than transmitting information from the textbook to the student. The teacher's ability to provide richness to the lessons requires going beyond basic classroom resources.

6. *Planning reduces the impact of intrusions.* There are over 300 teacher/student interactions in a typical 50-minute period at both the elementary and secondary levels. Add to these interactions the intrusions from the public address system or office, visitors at the door, or students arriving late to class, and one can easily see that the classroom is a busy place. Planning reduces the need to wait until the last moment to organize materials. Intrusions into the teaching day are unfortunate, but without planning, the intrusions would take a much greater toll on instructional time. Teachers who have a plan for the day report that they are less affected by the daily intrusions into the classroom.

TEACHER TALK

If I am interrupted during a lesson, I am usually able to pick up where we stopped when I have a well-thought-out lesson plan. However, those days when I haven't spent the time planning can be a problem. It seems the number of things that can go wrong on those days always escalates.

Eleventh-Grade Science Teacher

7. *Planning economizes time.* Time is the greatest natural resource for the classroom teacher. Like any resource, it can be easily wasted. Time is lost when materials are not ready, equipment has not been tested, students are unaware of what comes next, and the teacher lacks a plan for the day. Planning enables you to portion out time for specific activities and lessons throughout the day. Many lesson plans include a space for the time a particular activity will take during a lesson. Beginning teachers may benefit from a timed lesson plan, whereas most experienced teachers usually internalize the timing sequence or make brief notes about the time needed for specific activities.

8. *Planning makes learner success more measurable, which assists in reteaching.* It is easy to lose track of student learning in the dynamics of day-to-day interactions. You need to determine the specific outcomes as well as level of mastery for instruction before moving on to the next lesson or unit. By identifying the outcomes of learning before instruction begins, the teacher has a better gauge of student success and teaching effectiveness. For example, a 95 percent accuracy level for addition is a reasonable expectation for first-graders. Moving on to subtraction before mastering addition will present serious problems for the students and their future teachers.

9. *Planning provides for a variety of instructional activities.* Incorporating new instructional strategies into your current teaching practices requires conscious effort and practice. Many veteran classroom teachers have expressed concerns about attempting

new instructional strategies. Planning plays an important role in making unfamiliar strategies more familiar. New instructional strategies, such as cooperative learning groups or peer tutoring, initially require more planning and preparation time for successful implementation. An absence of planning also reduces the options for incorporating or enriching more complex lessons that require audiovisual equipment, guest speakers, or manipulative materials into the learning experience.

The following Snapshot supports the importance of planning for incorporating new instructional activities into the classroom. The teacher is planning a unit on environmental science, and the lesson described in the Snapshot focuses on the effects of civilization on animal habitats. The teacher has decided to develop a simulation for the students, entitled "Habitat: A Game of Chance," which simulates the problems wild animals face in coping with civilization. Each student selects a card, which describes the type of animal he or she is to be for the game (e.g., deer, rabbit, or raccoon). The object of the game is for the animal and its habitat to survive the challenges faced by interacting with civilization. The Snapshot describes the development of the game and the teacher's thinking about the planning process.

SNAPSHOT

I learned more about the benefits of planning with this lesson. Because I was using a complicated strategy and was designing a complex game from scratch, a lot of preparation went into this lesson. During the process of making the cards for the game, I was able to think through the game. Up to teaching time I was still making minor revisions and additions. The fact that the game went smoothly and was successful made all the planning worthwhile.

I knew that for any chance of success with this game I was going to have to be on top of things. I often take lectures for granted and do not do the planning and preparation that I should. An aspect that I overplanned for in my lesson plan I feared would not be reached—that of an emotional connection—developed as a result of the game. I wanted something more than just a detached acquiring of information.

I did not have the time in the lesson to have an activity focused specifically in the affective domain, but it came out on its own. After being an animal struggling through this game, students had a much better feeling about the fragile life situations of animals. It made the students stop and think. The simulation game took a great deal of planning and preparation, but the students benefited and I realized the importance that planning plays in adding new strategies to my teaching repertoire. (Maryellen Snyder)

Planning for transitions is an important element in planning. Plan to change instructional strategies based on the age of the students—for example, 5-years-olds should have a change in activities about every 5 to 10 minutes, whereas every 20 to 30 minutes is adequate for 17- to 18-year-olds.

10. *Planning creates the opportunity for higher-level questioning.* Most teachers ask lower-order factual questions of their students (e.g., Who was the first president of the United States?) (Dillon, 1984). Incorporating higher-level thinking skills begins with higher-level questions (e.g., How would you feel if you were a deer in the "Habitat: A Game of Chance"?). Additional effort is needed if you are to make higher-level questioning a normal part of the lesson. Writing higher-level questions (on 3" × 5" cards or a sheet of paper) prior to the lesson in the lesson plan book will reduce the chance that key questions will be omitted during instruction.

11. *Planning assists in ordering supplies.* Planning for next year begins now. The lesson that lacked enough manipulatives for the students will need to be noted if the same problem is to be avoided the next time the lesson is taught. Most districts collect supply requisitions during the spring and place orders during the summer. Knowing the requisition system of your district will greatly reduce the disappointment faced by many teachers who forgot to make a list of needed instructional materials and supplies for the following year.

12. *Planning guides substitute teachers.* The hard work of creating order and routine in the classroom may be sidetracked by a substitute teacher who has no plan to follow. If the school district does not have a specific format for substitutes, then a detailed lesson plan should be provided. (See the sample substitute lesson letter in the Samples and Examples section at the end of this chapter.)

13. *Planning provides documentation of instruction.* We live in a highly legalized bureaucratic society. Teachers need to provide documentation for evaluation purposes as well as to reduce the possibility of liability. Most school districts require some form of lesson planning. Principals may require daily plans be turned in at the end of the week. Also, most evaluators require a lesson plan prior to observing in the classroom. According to Richard Henak, who writes for the National Educational Association, teachers may be held liable for not teaching proper safety procedures in laboratory settings: "If the teacher can offer proof that safety procedures are taught in certain classes, it is more difficult to show negligence on the teacher's part. A lesson plan which includes safety content is one way to help establish such proof" (1980, p. 22).

14. *Planning establishes a repertoire of instructional strategies.* Planning enables you to build on the past, examining and changing those elements of teaching that were ineffective and including those elements that were successful. Expertness in teaching is more than years of doing the same lessons. It requires building a repertoire of instructional strategies that are both global and specific in responding to changing teaching situations.

Planning Limitations

The planning process has some limitations. In a study on the effects of planning on teaching, Zahorik (1970) indicated that "planning makes the teacher's thinking rigid and puts him on a track that is nearly derail-proof" (p. 149). Zahorik suggested that greater flexibility on the part of the teacher, as well as sensitivity to the needs of students, would alleviate teacher inflexibility that may occur in planning. Beginning teachers may see planning as a script to follow rather than as a guide through the lesson.

Planning provides a framework for instruction that is constantly being buffeted by the events of the school day. Fire drills, shortened class schedules, assemblies, guest speakers, bomb threats, and severe weather are but a few of the events that impact on the instructional plans for the day.

Planning takes time, and many beginning as well as experienced classroom teachers find time to be in short supply. Most teachers indicate that out-of-school time must be used for planning. Some school districts provide a planning period, however. Parent conferences, grade-level or team meetings, school functions coordination, student tutorials, and other tasks compete for time that may be designated for planning during the school day.

Although there are no absolutes for teaching, and change is an inevitable part of the teaching profession, the limitations of planning are outweighed by the benefits.

PLANNING PHASES

The action of planning is a highly developed process of thinking through various alternatives and possibilities. There are several distinct phases of planning: (1) Preplanning, (2) Active planning, (3) Ongoing planning, and (4) Postplanning. Each phase has a function in the planning process, and key decisions are made at each level, which determines movement to the next phase (see Figure 2.2).

The first two phases, Preplanning and Active planning, occur prior to actual instruction. During the *Preplanning* phase, tentative mental plans are developed and decisions are made regarding the design and implementation of a lesson or larger instructional unit. *Active planning* entails the physical gathering of resources and materials in preparation for teaching. Written lesson plans are usually developed during this phase of the planning process. *Ongoing planning* occurs during instruction and requires the teacher to think quickly to modify a plan that is not working. These corrections are an everyday part of teaching. Rigid adherence to a plan that does not help students learn is clearly counterproductive. *Postplanning* is the self-assessment and the last stage in the planning process. Making notes at the postplanning stage serves as feedback to you for future lessons. It also becomes part of the planning repertoire each teacher acquires through reflective assessments of the lessons and the teaching day.

Preplanning

During the Preplanning stage, information is being gathered about the students' past and present achievements and motivational levels, the content that is to be presented, and the conditions in which the instruction is to be presented. The Preplanning stage represents the mental process of considering various instructional alternatives and deciding on one or several approaches for teaching. It is also during this stage that a mental picture of the sequence of instructional events and the resources needed to implement instruction are considered. Expert teachers report their ability to visualize a lesson from beginning to end by mentally testing their plans against the teaching/learning environment. The ability to visualize what has yet to occur requires either a repertoire of past experiences or a systematic plan to gather enough information to create the image.

FIGURE 2.2 *Planning Phases*

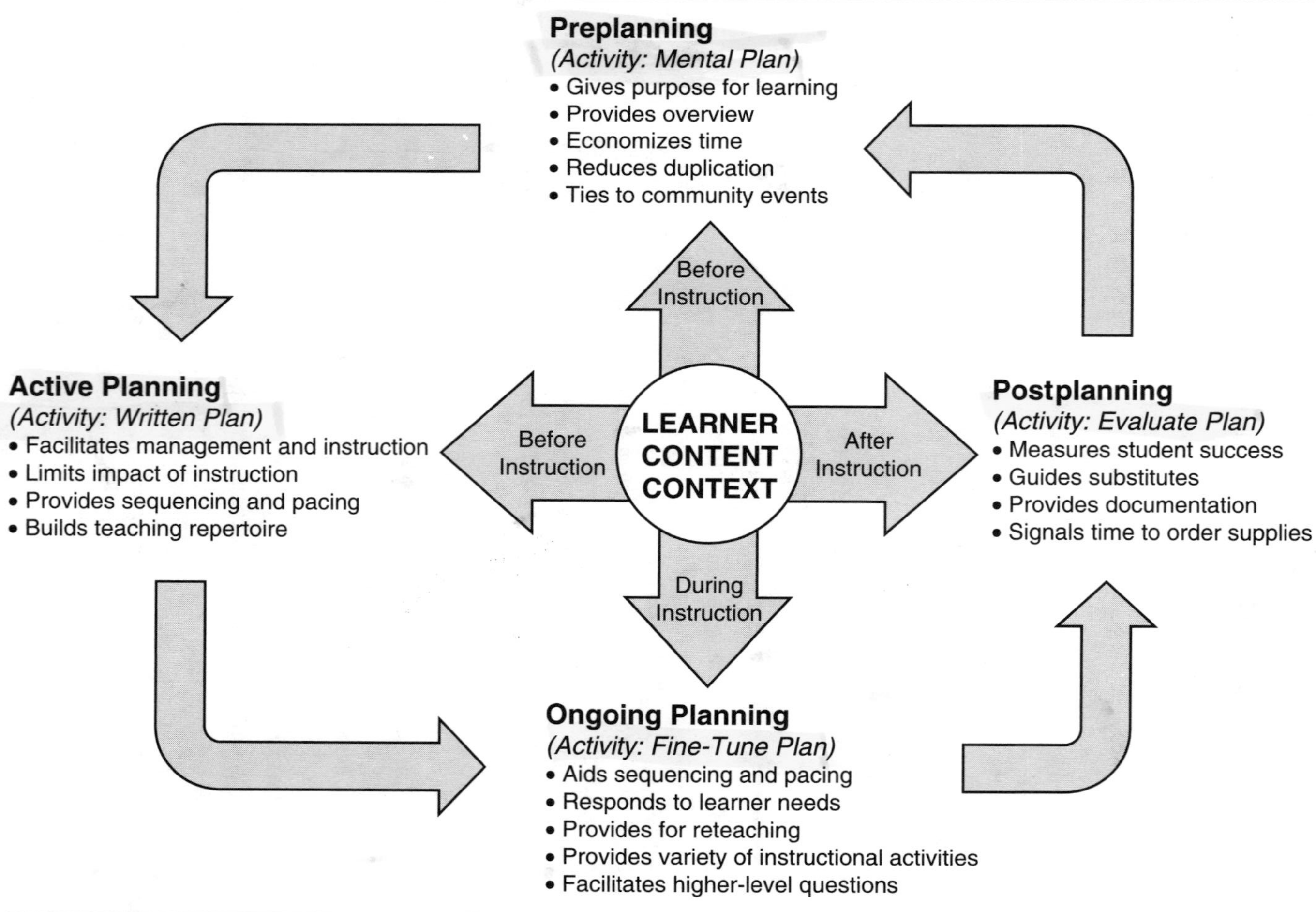
Preplanning
(Activity: Mental Plan)
• Gives purpose for learning
• Provides overview
• Economizes time
• Reduces duplication
• Ties to community events
Active Planning
(Activity: Written Plan)
• Facilitates management and instruction
• Limits impact of instruction
• Provides sequencing and pacing
• Builds teaching repertoire
Before Instruction
Before Instruction
LEARNER
CONTENT
CONTEXT
After Instruction
During Instruction
Postplanning
(Activity: Evaluate Plan)
• Measures student success
• Guides substitutes
• Provides documentation
• Signals time to order supplies
Ongoing Planning
(Activity: Fine-Tune Plan)
• Aids sequencing and pacing
• Responds to learner needs
• Provides for reteaching
• Provides variety of instructional activities
• Facilitates higher-level questions

Mental Processes

Preplanning may occur during the summer months, driving to school, during lunch, after school, and on weekends. Preplanning activities for the first day of school are very different from preplanning activities for the 51st day of school. Planning is a cumulative process that builds on previous experiences. The more familiar a teacher becomes with the course content, students, and school and classroom environment, the easier it is to plan.

Cognitive Monitoring

Manning (1984) described four times when teachers could monitor their own thinking. This process, called *cognitive monitoring,* may occur during (1) planning, (2) instructing and interacting with students, (3) listening to students, and (4) evaluating instruction.

The monitoring points suggested by Manning parallel the four phases of planning described in this chapter. Cognitive monitoring could occur during Preplanning and Active planning (planning); Ongoing planning (instructing and interacting with students, and listening to students); and Postplanning (evaluating instruction). Awareness of what is occurring during planning and instruction will enable you continually to build on past experiences in a systematic manner.

In her research using cognitive monitoring, Neely (1986)* identified 16 questions teachers should ask themselves to improve the quality of the planning process:

1. *How should I plan for the seating arrangement to use during this lesson?*
2. *Which students have special needs that should be attended to during the lesson?*
3. *What discipline and management techniques will I incorporate?*
4. *What role will I take on during this lesson?*
5. *Where will I place the materials I have listed?*
6. *How well do I understand the content of the lesson?*
7. *What changes will I feel most comfortable with during the lesson?*
8. *Why should I teach this lesson?*
9. *Is this going to be too easy/difficult for this group?*
10. *What attention do I need to give the other students while I'm working with this small group?*
11. *How will I handle interruptions to limit interference in this lesson?*
12. *How will I check on student understanding?*
13. *What are my alternative plans if problems arise in this first plan?*
14. *How will I conclude the lesson?*
15. *What will students do as this lesson ends?*
16. *How will I make transitions to the next lesson? (Neely, 1986, p. 31)*

The self-probing that occurs during the preplanning stage of instruction will enable thoughts to effectively influence subsequent actions in the implementation of a lesson. Neely reported that using the 16 questions as a source of self-monitoring improved student teachers' ability to "identify goals and objectives, organize lessons, predict outcomes, establish alternative plans and be sensitive to student needs" (p. 32).

Thoughts to Actions

The mental actions of deciding what to do is a continuous process once a plan is selected. The decision to move from the preplanning to the active planning stage is identifiable in talking to experienced teachers. We asked three teachers—a first-grade

Source: Reprinted with permission from the *Journal of Teacher Education,* Volume 37, Number 3, pp. 29–33.

teacher, a seventh-grade social studies teacher, and an eleventh-grade science teacher—to think aloud about their planning. The first-grade teacher was planning a phonics lesson for the letter *a*.

TEACHER TALK

I am going to teach the *a* sounds on Monday and Tuesday during language arts time. I have 15 to 20 minutes each day in the mornings. I will use the phonics program, which includes hand puppets and a cassette tape with songs that sound out the different combinations for the *a* sound. I need to have the children practice the different *a* sounds in small groups so I can hear them. What I don't finish on Monday I will continue on Tuesday.

AUTHOR'S NOTE: *The first part of this teacher's preplanning includes a global overview of the lesson. She is an experienced classroom teacher, so this segment took her only a few seconds to determine. She then moved on to some specific sequences:*

I will hold up the puppet with a big letter on his front and ask the children to tell me what the letter is. Most of my students will be able to identify the letter. From there, we will move on to identifying other words that begin with the letter *a.* I will then play the cassette to reinforce with songs what we have discussed and to introduce the different *a* sounds. To keep the noise levels manageable, I will pair the students and ask them to whisper the sounds to each other. I will also want each child to talk into a tape recorder (giving the *a* sounds) and to listen to themselves.

First-Grade Teacher

The more specific steps of the lesson begin to take form as the teacher concludes the Preplanning stage and moves to the Active planning stage. It is during the Active planning stage that materials and other resources are physically gathered. Maps, stories, handouts, manipulatives, or materials the teacher will need for the lesson are prepared during this stage. The Active planning stage is the preparation for teaching. The first-grade teacher will need to check the cassette tape recorder and the availability of the song tape and puppets, which are shared by four first-grade teachers.

A seventh-grade social studies teacher described his third-period class: "They come to history very unmotivated and I need to give them a sense of being there before learning will occur." He is going to start a unit on the American Civil War.

TEACHER TALK

I decided that, given their lack of motivation, I would try to create a feeling of the times. I plan on going to the local library to photocopy some newspaper stories and editorials from 1855 to 1860. I will select my stories and editorials from the Northern and Southern newspapers. I want them to see how the political climate changed during the five years prior to the Civil War and read what were the key issues. The newspaper stories will be more on their reading level than the textbook we are currently using.

I plan to divide the class into a Northern and a Southern group and give each group the news articles and editorials from their region. I will ask the students to debate the issues from their articles' perspective. If time allows, I will have the groups switch sides and read the other group's articles and take a new position. I may have the students take the articles home for homework to read if I find the lesson is taking too much time.

This is the first time I have started the unit this way, but I recently read in my professional journal about more motivating approaches to the Civil War. I plan to spend two classes on the lesson. This is a lot for a warm-up, but I am hoping the added interest will pay dividends during the remainder of the Civil War unit.

Seventh-Grade Social Studies Teacher

This teacher is developing a lesson that incorporates a new teaching approach. Additional thought at the Preplanning stage is required due to the newness of the format. The details of the lesson are still to be developed. His decision to use a "you-are-there" approach to the Civil War topic was based on his understanding of the students, the difficulty of the textbook for their reading levels, and the need to motivate them. He had prior experience with teaching the Civil War unit and was familiar with the use of original source materials from reading his professional journals.

The following eleventh-grade chemistry teacher is about to teach a unit on periodic laws, and the starting point for her unit is the periodic table.

TEACHER TALK

I presented a lecture on the development of the periodic table developed by Dmitry Mendeleyev in 1869 to my eleventh-grade chemistry class. I described how Mendeleyev put small slips of paper on the wall with the known elements of his time and their atomic weights and how he arranged the elements according to the magnitude of their atomic weights (for example, H-1 hydrogen would be first on the list and H-2 helium would be second). Based on this chart, Mendeleyev was able to predict the atomic weights of elements still undiscovered. I presented the periodic table as it exists today and discussed the importance of this discovery to modern chemistry.

I felt the presentation was effective, but when I gave my students a quiz the next day, the results were dismal. The students had memorized the specifics about the periodic table, but they failed to understand the relationships of the elements to each other.

I decided to teach it a different way to my seventh-period class, which was a day behind my fifth-period class. This time, I had them go through the same process that Mendeleyev experienced in developing the periodic table. I gave them the elements and atomic weights known in 1869 (without being in any order) and asked the students working in their table teams to develop some logical order for the elements. Once they achieved this, I asked them if they could predict the atomic weights of any future elements. I then showed them the current periodic table and they compared their predictions with the existing table. The results were exciting and the students began to see the relationships between the elements.

This seventh-period lesson took much more planning, preparation, and thinking before I felt comfortable with the approach. I only had one day and was up until 11:30 that night preparing for the lesson. I needed to prepare 3" × 5" cards for each of the six groups in my class. After the lesson started and one group began to place the elements on the blackboard, I discovered that the cards were too small for the class to see. So, in the middle of the lesson, I handed out blank sheets of 8½" × 11" paper for them to write the elements. They needed the 3" × 5" cards to do the sorting and the larger sheets took only one or two minutes to create, with each student in the team having a few elements to complete.

Sometimes you need to make in-flight corrections while teaching. I was too tired to think about the size of the cards the previous evening, but I was able to readjust during the lesson. The results were well worth the extra effort. The students all passed the quiz and I felt a real sense of excitement on their part when they discovered Mendeleyev's periodic table.

Eleventh-Grade Science Teacher

This chemistry teacher provides us with an example of how assessing the impact of learning (postplanning) in one class (fifth period) changed the plans for the same lesson with another class (seventh period). The following day, in this case, the teacher's postplanning led back to the Preplanning and Active planning stages to rethink the lesson. The changes made during the lesson with the larger sheets is a good example of the types of ongoing or in-flight changes made during the lesson.

The mental process of planning is rarely discussed or taught in any formal way, yet it represents an important part of teaching. Veteran teachers have the advantage of using past experiences with similar contexts, contents, and learners. New teachers are at a disadvantage with these three important frames of reference. Becoming more aware of the planning process of other teachers and developing a repertoire of planning strategies will provide new teachers and experienced teachers who are not satisfied with their planning, or face changing conditions, a better foundation for planning.

Active Planning

The Active planning stage indicates a decision and commitment have been made toward one specific plan. Active planning and preplanning include all the actions that occur prior to teaching in the classroom. The self-probes and questions have been answered and the teacher's mental plan is beginning to take form. It is during this stage that the content (what to teach) takes on greater meaning. A plan to teach specific facts, ideas, or concepts revolves around your understanding of the students, district curriculum, teacher guides, textbook materials, and the instructional methods needed to communicate, translate, transfer, and create an environment in which students will learn. The methods of teaching (how to teach) are only as effective as your knowledge level of the subject matter to be taught. The how and what of teaching both take on greater importance as the teacher moves from the Preplanning to the Active planning stage.

Content Focus

Although curriculum guides and textbooks exist for most subject areas, it is evident that what is taught is a condition of the mastery of the content by the teacher. Mastery, or at least a level of comfort, with the content is the starting point for many teachers. Some teachers may be content poor, and this may be the greatest limitation in the planning process and in teaching. Many elementary teachers, for example, avoid science instruction because of their limited exposure to advanced science courses in high school and college. This avoidance is evident when students from the United States are compared with students from other nations in science achievement. A deficiency in content knowledge requires the teacher to take the initiative and seek out additional resources. Excellent sources of information include textbooks, other than the one being used for instruction, district curriculum guides, college texts, and college courses with a focus on content as well as methods.

Teaching Strategies

The Active planning stage brings together the content to be taught with the strategies for teaching. The strategies or methods of instruction include the ways in which the content is transformed into new learning for the students. The content can be transformed directly from the teacher to the student through lecture, demonstration, drill, and questioning. The content may also be transformed more indirectly, where the teacher's role is to facilitate learning situations through grouping, discovery, inquiry, roleplay, and simulations.

Including unfamiliar strategies in your teaching repertoire requires more planning than using strategies that you have experienced or utilized previously. In the previous Snapshot, Maryellen Snyder, the environmental science teacher, used a simulation strategy to teach her students the impact of civilization on animal habitats. Moving away from the lecture format for this lesson, which was her usual strategy, to a simulation required additional planning. She had to consider that students would be working in groups of four, materials had to be distributed, and rules and time frames needed to be established and communicated to the students. The Habitat simulation is now part of her curriculum on environmental science, and she will be able to fine-tune the simulation as she uses it with different groups of students.

Ongoing Planning

The Ongoing planning stage arises during instruction. The realities of the rapidly changing classroom, lack of student mastery of previous lessons, and school scheduling changes frequently require modifications of teaching plans during the lesson. Many teachers describe changes in their plans while teaching as *in-flight corrections.* The term is common for airplane pilots who are required to submit a flight plan with air traffic controllers before departing. The best flight plans may need to be changed once a plane is airborne. In-flight corrections allow the pilot to adapt to changing conditions in the weather, at the landing site, or with the mechanical state of the airplane. In teaching, conditions can change more rapidly than in flying. Being able to adjust to these changes is the mark of an adaptive teacher.

In-flight decision making requires experience and a wide repertoire of instructional strategies. In a two-year study of 9 expert and 10 novice health teachers, Cleary and Groer (1994) found that expert teachers remembered making significantly more in-flight decisions regarding pupils, content, procedures, time, and materials. The authors concluded that novice teachers can become more adept at in-flight decision making if they are taught to predict possible problems with lessons and to consider contingency plans to carry out the lesson.

These corrections center on the transitions that are necessary to move from one part of the lesson to another, student understanding of lesson content, and the pace or timing of the lesson. Teachers who check for student understanding frequently during the lesson may realize some instances when the lesson may need to be retaught during the day (at the elementary level) or the next day (at the secondary level). Intrusions and student disruptions may also require changes in the initial plans. It is during this stage that changes are made in response to changing conditions that were not evident during the Preplanning or Active planning stages.

Fine-Tuning

Ongoing planning is also known as *fine-tuning* the lesson. As the plan for the day meets the reality of early dismissals, shortened classes, an assembly, a high-school pep rally, or a Halloween carnival, you are faced with fine-tuning, changing, or completely scrapping your well-designed plan. Fortunately, these events are more the exception than the rule, but they happen often enough to be an important consideration in the planning process. Strategies for fine-tuning a lesson include lengthening or shortening a lesson, integrating the events for the day into the lesson, or reviewing the material taught over the last several weeks rather than beginning new instruction that will be interrupted.

Planning provides a framework for instruction, but the execution of the plan may require several adjustments along the way. There are few absolutes in teaching. The changing dynamics of the classroom reduce the certainties of the lesson plan. However, there are strategies that will assist you in reducing the need for major changes during instructional time. Consider the following:

1. All the resources should be prepared ahead of time, including handouts, materials, other manipulatives for labs, extra paper, and pencils.
2. Create a checklist of the materials needed for the lesson. Check the clarity of handouts to eliminate going over illegible instructions or questions.
3. Prior to the students entering the class, post or display the objectives and activities of the day on the chalkboard or overhead. This will give the students and yourself a clear picture of the sequence of learning activities.
4. As they walk into the room, involve the students in an activity that reinforces prior learning. This will provide an academic focus for the lesson of the day and will determine the level of understanding of prior instruction.

Teacher Planning Research Vignette

INTRODUCTION

In a study reported by Borko, Bellamy, and Sanders (1992), the differences in planning between student teachers and their more expert cooperating teachers in junior high school science were explored. The study examined planning, presentation, and postlesson reflections. Within these areas, the researchers investigated three major components that are central to learning to teach: "schema and schemata," one's cognitive ability to store and structure knowledge experiences in a way that is easily accessible and usable; "pedagogical reasoning," the ability to transform knowledge about the subject with instructional strategies that respond to diverse abilities and backgrounds of the learners; and "pedagogical content knowledge," the ability to translate content in a manner that is understandable to others.

STUDY DESIGN

The planning, instructional thinking, and actions of four secondary student teachers and their cooperating teachers in junior high school science classes were studied. The study was qualitative in design, using observation, field notes, audiotapes, and interviews. Two of the student teachers were male and two female. Two of the four had majors in life sciences, one in chemistry, and one in physical science. The student teachers were placed with cooperating teachers who had been identified as "experts" from several sources. Each of the eight participants was observed for one period each day for a week. The teachers were interviewed before each lesson to determine their planning, observed during the lesson to see the types of instructional approaches employed, and interviewed after the lesson to ask for reflections about their lessons.

RESULTS

The researchers reported on patterns that emerged from the novice student teachers and their expert cooperating teachers. The patterns the authors found were described in extensive narrative detail. We have summarized their findings into the following framework.

PLANNING

Expert teachers had strategies for keeping track of successful lessons. They used folders to store science activities for future years that were matched to units and lessons; they used notebooks to write out factual information, including formulas and other details that could be forgotten; they kept lesson plan books from previous years and reviewed them; and they made annotations in the margins of their textbooks. They also did yearly and unit planning with another teacher at the beginning of the year and met once a week to review weekly plans. Expert teachers in this study did little written planning except for preparing schedules for monthly or weekly assignments and topics.

Novice teachers had a very different planning process. Without the experience of teaching lessons from previous years, novice teachers in this study spent a great deal of time in detailed written lesson planning. Once the plans were written, then more time was spent in securing the materials needed to present the lesson. This was particularly true in the laboratory portion of the class. One novice teacher, Shari, found planning "to be a 'monumental task,' but the planning had paid off" (p. 64). The lesson she had planned in great detail, which included the dissection of a frog during the lab, incorporated "good procedural explanations with some content woven in" (p. 64). The authors found that novice teachers had difficulties when they didn't have detailed written plans or when they didn't follow their plans.

INSTRUCTING

Expert teachers had several ways to present lessons. They used multiple examples to explain a concept when they observed puzzled looks from students or questions that indicated confusion. During laboratory classes, they kept extra props for demonstrations in case students needed another view for explaining the same concept. One expert teacher, Jim, said, "I'll see their confusion and I'll realize I need another way to say the same thing or make it visible to them, so they can see it happen" (p. 61). Expert teachers had more interactive teaching and felt comfortable changing a lesson in midstream if it meant better understanding by the students. The expert teachers had well-defined pedagogical content beliefs. As part of these beliefs, they used the laboratory experiences to link science theory with students' own experiences. In Jim's class, students did not understand that lifting an object took more work than sliding the same object. According to the observations, he proceeded to bring out a 200-gram mass and indicated that this was his suitcase. Using a spring scale and a meter stick, he was able to show the students the formula of Work = Force × Distance, and that lifting a suitcase took more work than sliding it, even when friction was considered.

Novice teachers did not include the variety of instructional activities that were evident in the expert teachers' lessons. Although content knowledge levels were strong, the novice teachers did not have well-defined pedagogical content beliefs; additionally, pedagogical reasoning was limited.

POSTREFLECTION

The authors found that expert teachers had an extensive repertoire of instructional strategies and knowledge structures. Experts had "powerful explanations, demonstrations, and examples for representing subject matter to students; novices must develop these representations as part of the planning process for each lesson" (p. 67).

CONCLUSIONS AND IMPLICATIONS FOR PRACTICE

This study, although limited to investigating the practices of a few novice and expert teachers, has important implications for preparing yourself for teaching. Building a planning and instructional repertoire that includes multiple instructional strategies is an important goal for beginning teachers and others who want to improve their teaching. The links that expert teachers make between concepts and the students' own lives should be part of the planning process. This study may help explain in part why novice teachers spend so much time planning and writing out their plans and why their cooperating teachers seldom write out plans. This study may also help cooperating teachers understand the need to explain the steps in their own planning so beginning teachers can benefit from their developed pedagogical reasoning and pedagogical content knowledge.

It is our goal that *Universal Teaching Strategies* will expand your schemata of planning and instructional repertoires.

---

5. Using 3" × 5" cards, write notes to yourself about specific points to be made during the lesson or higher-level questions you want to ask the students. Many elementary-level teachers will write notes on the chalkboard as a reminder of important tasks for both the teacher and students.

It is always helpful for the success of future lessons to review the day's activities that were effective or that needed revision. This becomes an important part of Postplanning, which is the final stage of the planning process.

Postplanning

The final level in the planning process may occur as an afterthought of the lesson. The lesson is over and the plan book page is turned to the next day. Many teachers will make notes in the margins of their plan book about changes they need to make in the lesson when they teach it again next year. Our interviews with teachers indicate they keep journals, looseleaf books, or large monthly calendars to write down ideas and make notes for themselves. Postplanning affects planning for the next day as well as planning for future use of the lesson, usually for the following year.

Expert teachers realize that the freshness of ideas and feelings about the lesson will diminish with time. Trying to recall a year later, or even a day later, what went well or what needed to be changed is a frustrating task. In addition to assisting in the design of a lesson the following year, notes made about the lesson could assist in reviewing the content two or three months later. The following is a sample checklist of questions to be considered in the Postplanning stage:

_____ What were the strengths and weaknesses of the lesson?
_____ Were the original objectives met in the lesson?
_____ What percentage of the class mastered the objective/content of the lesson?
_____ Was there too much or too little content for the time?
_____ Were the transitions between activities smooth?
_____ What additional resources or materials would be needed next time to make the lesson more successful?
_____ Did the activities fit the content being taught?
_____ Were the students active or passive learners?
_____ Were the support materials (text or workbooks, printed or visual materials) appropriate and available for the lesson?
_____ What changes in the lesson plan would be required to make the lesson more successful?

This list is designed to provide a framework for revising the lesson for future use, rather than be an exhaustive list. You may need to add other questions.

The four phases represent a framework for teacher planning that is cyclical in nature. The decisions made during the Preplanning phase are influenced by the results of previous lessons and experiences in the Postplanning stage. The Active planning and Ongoing planning phases denote the most intensive part of the planning process. The following list summarizes each of the planning phases with key descriptors:

Preplanning:	Visualizing, sequencing, mental processing, cognitive monitoring and questioning, self-probing, and decision making
Active planning:	Preparation, content focus, teaching strategies, and room and material organization
Ongoing planning:	During instruction, in-flight corrections, transitions, and checking for prior understanding
Postplanning:	Lesson analysis, immediate and future planning, written notes, and planning journals (see Figure 2.2)

CONSIDERATIONS FOR PLANNING

The four phases of planning (Preplanning, Active planning, Ongoing planning, and Postplanning) present a workable structure for thinking through the design and implementation of a lesson. The lesson, however, is a template that must match the learner, content, and context of the teaching situation. Designing a lesson that ignores the needs and previous learnings of the students or that poorly integrates the content with the strategies is doomed to failure. Additionally, a lesson that does not consider the context or environment in which the lesson will be taught will make the learning condition that much more difficult for both the teacher and students. We will examine the roles that the learner, content, and context play in planning for instruction.

SOURCES OF INFORMATION FOR PLANNING

Learner

In third-world countries where schooling is not universal, schools have a significant effect on the learner, when these learners are compared with those individuals who have not attended school. In industrialized countries such as England, Japan, France, and the United States, where schooling is compulsory, the family tends to have a greater impact on the learner (Hampton, Munford, & Bond, 1998; Sanders, 1998). All things being equal and regardless of one's race or ethnic heritage, a family that provides books, discussion, a range of learning experiences, and support for school, including assistance with homework (Paschal, Weinstein, & Walberg, 1983; Sanders, 1998; Hampton, Munford, & Bond, 1998), will give its children an advantage. Children and youth who come to school lacking these experiences and support arrive at a disadvantage. This disadvantage takes the form of prior knowledge.

For example, two first-grade children, Charles and Brian, live in the city and have never seen or touched cows, pigs, or sheep. Both students were asked to identify a picture of a cow. Their choices for answers included a dog, a deer, a cow, and a bear. Charles circled the word *cow* as his answer, but Brian circled *dog* for his answer. Brian had never been exposed to four-legged animals other than the dog, cat, and rodents that he had seen in his neighborhood.

Charles's parents read to him each evening before bed. The stories are about animals, the zoo, letters, numbers, and exciting adventures. Brian only has a few books in his house and they are rarely read to him. When both children entered kindergarten, Charles was ready for the world of words, numbers, and discussion. Through the use of storybooks, Charles was introduced to words, ideas, and concepts he would meet again in school. Both children have equal potential for success in school; however, they will not succeed at the same rate or level. What is familiar to one student may seem like nonsense to another.

Entry Characteristics

Students bring to class what Benjamin Bloom (1976) calls a range of "entry characteristics," which Bloom divides into affective and cognitive behaviors. Affective characteristics incorporate the students' motivation to learn, and cognitive characteristics include the students' prior learnings. According to Bloom, the context of the learning environment and the quality of instruction will determine the learning outcomes. These outcomes embody the level and type of achievement, rate of learning, and affective outcomes (p. 11). See Figure 2.3 for Bloom's theory of school learning.

Learner characteristics are also summarized in Figure 2.3. Affective behaviors include the level of motivation and student self-concept. The motivation to learn and personal self-concept begin in the home prior to formal schooling. The values of the parents for learning and the opportunity to learn prior to school play important roles in the formation of affective characteristics. School- and content-related affect result from a student's prior experiences with schooling and subject matter.

Cognitive characteristics include the prior learnings that a student brings to the classroom. Bloom (1976) indicated that a good predictor of reading success at the first-grade level is the extent of the vocabulary a child brings to school. The same is true for mathematics. A child who knows his or her numbers prior to school will be at an advantage.

The intelligence level of a student is another entry characteristic. General intelligence, as measured by IQ tests, is viewed by some as a means of determining the academic potential of a student. In recent years, however, the use of IQ tests has been

FIGURE 2.3 *Major Variables in the Theory of School Learning*

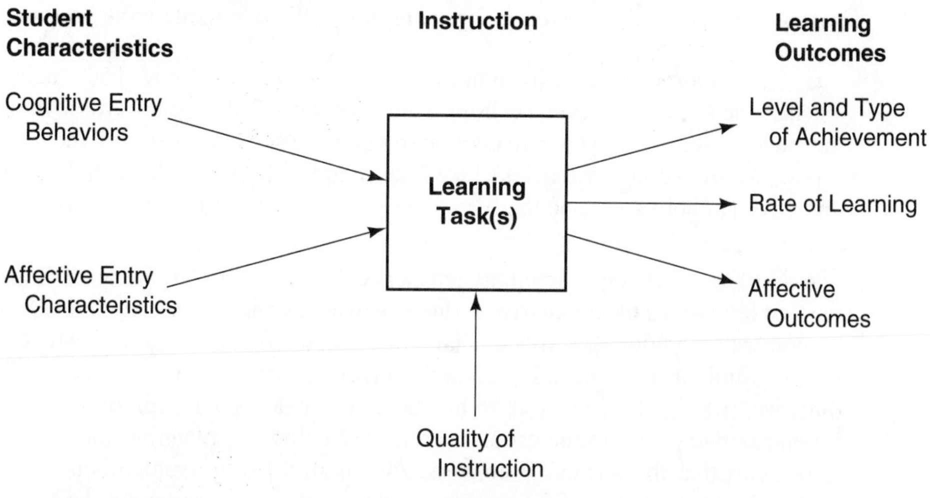

Entry Characteristics

Affective Characteristics
- Motivation
- Personal Self-Concept
- Content-Related Affect
- School-Related Affect

Cognitive Characteristics
- Prior Learnings
- Achievement Level
- Intelligence Level
- Reading Comprehension

Source: From *Human Characteristics and School Learning* by B. Bloom, 1982, New York: McGraw-Hill. Copyright 1982 by McGraw-Hill, Inc. Adapted by permission of The McGraw-Hill Companies.

considered a less valid means of measuring academic potential. Educators have been concerned that IQ scores will be used to establish lower expectations for some students. In addition, the issue of test bias for minority students has raised serious questions about the use of IQ scores as a predictor for academic success.

Achievement levels—as measured by teacher-made tests, report card grades, and standardized tests—form another entry characteristic. In planning for instruction, the entry characteristics identified by Bloom should be used as a starting point rather than as a justification for student academic failure. Knowing the students in the classroom and designing instruction that responds to their needs is an important first step.

Knowing the Student

Creating a positive yet realistic image of the students and the total class may require going outside the usual sources of data (previous standardized test scores, grades, and other teachers' comments). These data sources could be used for some diagnostic purposes, but they may also reflect stereotypes built over the years that are perpetuated from teacher to teacher. A few examples of other sources of data that could be used by the teacher to assist in the planning process are described here. The examples are designed to be illustrative rather than exhaustive.

The research literature is consistent on the importance of knowing students in class as early in the school year as possible (Freiberg, 1999). Planning activities to get to know the students' names and something about their academic and personal interests will provide an excellent avenue for being more effective in planning your instruction.

■ *Class photographs.* It is an arduous process to get to know 150 students if you teach at the secondary level. Although the task is difficult, the rewards will be great if the students sense that you care enough to know them by name during the first week of school. Many secondary teachers take photographs of their students on the first or second day of school and have the film processed at a one-hour photo lab or use a digital camera.

■ *Home calls.* Many elementary teachers call each of the 30 parents of their students the first few weeks of school to introduce themselves and discuss any rules, procedures, homework schedules, or activities that will be occurring in the class. The tone is always positive, and most parents are pleasantly surprised that a teacher is calling when something isn't *wrong*. Teachers report that these calls made at the beginning of the year before academic or discipline problems arise are helpful in planning for the class. They also report that the telephone conversations with a parent or guardian increase their background knowledge of the students and provide an understanding of the home environment. A sample format for home telephone calls is provided in the Samples and Examples section at the end of this chapter.

Some school districts provide secondary teachers with a day off as compensation for calling all the parents in the evenings or on weekends. One high-school mathematics teacher who was required to call parents was initially annoyed at the imposition on her time. However, she later reported that the telephone calls to parents, guardians, and in some cases to older brothers and sisters made a real difference in both the behavior of the students and academic learning. She described it as the best year she had in teaching.

■ *Autobiographies.* Some teachers ask the students on the first day of school to write on a 4" × 6" card or a sheet of paper their name, address, home telephone, and work telephone (for secondary students). On the reverse side of the paper or card, the students are asked the following questions:

What do you feel are your strengths in this subject?
What do you feel are your weaknesses in this subject?
What do you expect to learn this semester from this class?
What could I do to make this class your best learning experience?
What could you do to make this class your best learning experience?

As teachers, we naturally get to know the children who stand out: those who are behavior problems or academically gifted. Those students who sit quietly and rarely interact often become anonymous faces. It is these students whom we must make an extra effort to know.

Content

Content is another name for the curriculum or those learning experiences that are provided to students in school. The curriculum also incorporates the plans that teachers use to guide students through those learning experiences (Glatthorn, 1987). The curriculum is derived from the values of the society. A democratic society like the United States, which values an informed and educated public, includes reading, literacy, and citizenship in the school curriculum. The study of the Constitution, the Bill of Rights, and the steps leading to independence, for example, are weighted heavily in the curriculum. In most states, the part of American history that emphasizes democratic principles is taught several times in both elementary and secondary classrooms.

Written Curriculum

The curriculum is available to teachers in a written form, which becomes the main source of content for teaching. These written sources primarily include published textbooks, state and local curriculum guides, teacher editions of textbooks, and workbooks. The curriculum may also be found in packaged materials, including textbooks, workbooks, videotapes, slide tapes, and film materials.

Many states have specific books they purchase and provide to school districts free of charge on the condition that local districts select their textbooks from a state-approved list. Districts who choose to select their own books face considerable expense in providing texts for all its students. The states are able to control the curriculum and provide continuity from district to district through the use of state-adopted textbook purchases. States also provide state curriculum guides to supplement the textbooks. In Texas, for example, the state has identified "essential elements" that reflect minimal levels of content to be taught in all schools in Texas. These so-called essential elements are later assessed through a state-mandated test given to students each year.

In planning a lesson or mapping out the course of study for an entire year, the teacher must be aware of state, district, and school building requirements and the resources that are provided by each of the levels to support instruction. Current educational reforms of the teaching profession by state legislatures and state education agencies have given greater attention to the standardization of the curriculum between and within school districts. The written curriculum reflects one level of the school curriculum. A second level—the unwritten curriculum—exists in most schools.

Unwritten Curriculum

The unwritten or hidden curriculum (Wenzlaff, 1998) is part of most school environments. The hidden curriculum reflects the values of the community that supports the schools, the administrators and teachers who manage and teach in the schools, and the beliefs and values of the larger society. The hidden curriculum sends a variety of messages to students about their behavior, work habits, and home culture.

Students begin to learn about the hidden curriculum as they observe the reactions of teachers and administrators to specific events that occur each day in school. Students are expected to be in class on time, bring all their materials, respect adults, and attend school regularly. There are rules for functioning in the school that are rarely taught but are usually enforced. The hidden curriculum reflects many of the same virtues required to function later in the world of work. It is only recently that the rules for behavior and academic expectations are being taught in the classroom.

Many students and some teachers are not sensitive to this hidden curriculum. This lack of sensitivity or awareness may be due to their being new to the school or not understanding the norms and values that are part of the hidden curriculum. Teachers who are new to a school may want to find a veteran teacher to be a guide in understanding this phenomenon. Students who enter after the school year has begun may need to be paired with a peer who can help the student understand the new environment.

In many instances, the written curriculum is a given. Printed and/or published materials provided by the state, district, or school present the teacher with a framework or, in some instances, a mandate for what is to be taught. Decisions about specifics for individual lessons, however, require considerable judgment and numerous compromises on the part of the teacher to translate the volumes of written materials to a manageable level for students (Glatthorn, 1987). Teachers who consider only the content when planning a lesson miss the complete picture. The student and the context in which the lesson is to be taught should also be considered in planning instruction.

Textbooks and Other Guides

The content of the lesson is usually considered first in the preplanning stage. A study by McCutcheon (1980) showed that between 85 and 95 percent of the reading and mathematics instruction in 12 elementary classrooms was based on textbooks and other published instructional material. These figures remain true today. From our discussion with secondary teachers and after reviewing their written plans, the same level of textbook use is also evident in middle-school and high-school classrooms.

The teacher's edition of a textbook and the curriculum guide provide a framework for the lesson. There is a tendency for beginning teachers to use these guides as scripts for each lesson. Expert teachers realize that these resource materials are designed to be a starting point for learning rather than an end point. McCutcheon (1980) found in her ethnographic study of 12 experienced elementary teachers that changes in the recommendations of their teachers' guides were based on the following criteria:

1. *Do these children need to learn this or do they already know it?*
2. *Will this activity fit into the amount of time I have?*
3. *Could I ask better questions than the ones in the teacher's guide?*
4. *How can I relate it to what they already know or experience in their daily lives and to other things they are doing?*
5. *Could I do part of this activity as boardwork for the group to do while I work with another group?*
6. *Are the children likely to be able to do it?*
7. *Are there problems with the lesson, errors in the book? (p. 10)*

When we asked secondary teachers to determine their use of teacher's guides, they reported many of these same criteria. Criteria number 5 was not identified, since most secondary teachers use whole-group interactions and rarely teach one group while another is doing seatwork.

A study of 500 randomly selected veteran secondary social studies teachers (Schug, Western, & Enochs, 1997) found that teachers continue to use textbooks because they provide an organized format for teaching and student learning. Teachers will use other sources of information when they enhance learning within the same instructional time period. Technology (computer simulations, the Internet, and CDs) has made some, but limited, inroads into the domination by textbooks. The new decade should see a dramatic change in this area.

It is important for the teacher to move beyond the textbook and enrich the lesson with additional examples from other sources. Building a repertoire of supporting and enriching activities is an important part of teaching and learning. The repertoire of ideas and activities for the lesson requires a building process for cataloguing supporting resources for instruction. Experienced teachers face similar problems of building a new repertoire when new textbook series are adopted by their districts. Considerations of content need to be explored at both the Preplanning and Active planning phases of designing a lesson, and during the Postplanning stage to evaluate needed changes for future lessons. The learner, content, and context are important considerations at all four levels of the planning process. The next consideration in planning is the context or environment in which the lesson will be taught.

Context

The context or environment in which you will teach is an important element in planning. The classroom context includes, for example: (1) the physical arrangement of the classroom (including open space, self-contained environments); (2) desks, chairs, tables, computers, and other furnishings; (3) time of day; (4) class size; (5) other classes or activities that precede or follow the class; (6) class location (e.g., Will the drill team be practicing outside the window?); (7) audiovisual equipment (videodisc, VCR, overhead projector, tape player, slide projector); and (8) duplicators, including copiers and ditto machines. The classroom context—which includes colors in the classroom, noise levels within and around the room, chalkboards, wall space, lighting, toys, comfort levels, storage space, and cleanliness—are additional examples of conditions that affect the planning of a lesson.

Beyond Teacher Control

Many context variables are beyond your individual control but must be considered when planning a lesson. Collectively, through their professional organizations, teachers have tried with some success to affect context variables through collective bargaining of teacher contracts. In general, however, a teacher has little direct effect on most of the following: the number of students in class, socioeconomic status of the students, availability of materials, physical size of the classroom, heating and cooling, physical condition of the school, district requirements for curriculum, standardized testing requirements, teacher evaluation, school administrative policies and procedures, community support, and district tax bases.

Within Teacher Control

The teacher *does* have immediate control over many context variables. Room arrangement, for example, should be determined by the teacher. Placing student desks in a circle, in rows, or in the shape of a horseshoe will change the patterns of interaction in the classroom. There have been several studies of the patterns of interaction with student desks placed in rows. Most of the "action zone" interaction takes place in the front part of the room and down the middle, forming an inverted T. Lack of interaction with the students outside the T significantly reduces the contact the teacher has with these students. Changing the seating arrangement to a circle or a horseshoe, or placing the desks in rows but at angles to each other to form a series of Vs, will improve interaction. However, some teachers feel very comfortable with the students seated in rows, and move around the classroom to reduce the effects of the traditional seating arrangement.

STUDENTS WITH SPECIAL NEEDS

The issue of planning is particularly pertinent with regard to students with special needs. Reaching special needs learners requires a careful plan of action that takes into account each child's particular learning barrier and includes appropriate intervention and/or adaptive strategies. Sugai (1997) suggested the use of flowcharts to plan teaching strategies for all students, but especially for those with specialized learning needs. Flowcharts enable you to see a visual product of your planning and allow you the opportunity to discover any weaknesses before you teach the lesson. Flowcharts are also useful as an evaluative tool, as you participate in the Postplanning stage of the lesson.

SUMMARY

The following 14 functions of planning provide a strong rationale for planning:

_____ Gives an overview of instruction
_____ Facilitates good management and instruction
_____ Makes learning purposeful

_____ Provides for sequencing and pacing
_____ Ties classroom instructional events with community resources
_____ Reduces the impact of intrusions
_____ Provides for economy of time
_____ Makes learner success more measurable, which assists in reteaching
_____ Provides for a variety of instructional activities
_____ Creates the opportunity for higher-level questioning
_____ Assists in ordering supplies
_____ Guides substitute teachers
_____ Provides documentation of instruction
_____ Establishes a repertoire of instructional strategies

You have seen that planning proceeds through four distinct phases: Preplanning, Active planning, Ongoing planning, and Postplanning. Teachers use these four phases to draw on their experiences with the learner, content, and context to develop meaningful instructional plans for both teacher and student. Effective planners are able to visualize future lessons, build from past experiences, and fine-tune lessons while in the midst of instruction. Teachers may improve their planning effectiveness by monitoring their thinking (cognitive monitoring) during and after instruction.

Considerations for planning include the learner, content, and context. Knowing the students in class is an important starting point in planning for instruction. The effective planner will look at both affective and cognitive traits of the learner before making final determinations about how the content should be taught. The teacher who goes beyond the written curriculum and adds something from himself or herself will enrich the learning experience of students. Given the daily press for content coverage, this enrichment must be a planned part of instruction. Planning enables you to challenge the students and broaden your universe of ideas and activities. Although much of the context of the classroom is a given, you have the opportunity to make changes that will benefit everyone.

REFERENCES

Barnette, J. J., et al. (1995). *Wait-time: Effective and trainable.* Paper presented at the Annual Meeting of American Educational Research Association, San Francisco. (ERIC Document Reproduction Service No. 383 706).

Bloom, B. S. (1976). *Human characteristics and school learning.* New York: McGraw-Hill.

Borko, H., Bellamy, M. L., & Sanders, L. (1992). A cognitive analysis in science instruction by expert and novice teachers. In T. Russell and H. Mundby (Eds.), *Teachers and teaching: From classroom to reflection* (pp. 49–70). London: Falmer Press.

Cleary, M. J., & Groer, S. (1994). Inflight decisions of expert and novice health teachers. *Journal of School Health, 64,* 110–114.

DiGisi, L. L., & Willett, J. B. (1995). What high school biology teachers say about their textbook use: A descriptive study. *Journal of Research in Science Teaching, 32,* 132–142.

Dillon, J. T. (1984). Research on questioning and discussion. *Educational Leadership, 42*(3), 50–56.

Evertson, C., & Harris, A. (1999). Beyond behaviorism. In H. J. Freiberg (Ed.), *Beyond behaviorism: Changing the classroom management paradigm.* Boston: Allyn and Bacon.

Freiberg, H. J. (Ed.). (1999). *Beyond behaviorism: Changing the classroom management paradigm.* Boston: Allyn and Bacon.

Glatthorn, A. A. (1987). *Curriculum leadership.* Glenview, IL: Scott, Foresman.

Hampton, F. M., Munford, D. A., & Bond, L. (1998). Parent involvement in inner-city schools: The project FAST extended family approach to success. *Urban Education, 33*(3), 410–422.

Henak, R. M. (1980). *Lesson planning for meaningful variety in teaching.* Washington, DC: National Education Association.

Manning, B. H. (1984). Self-communication structure for learning mathematics. *School Science and Mathematics, 84*(1), 43–51.

McCutcheon, G. (1980). How do elementary school teachers plan? The nature of planning and influences on it. *The Elementary School Journal, 81,* 4–23.

Mitchell, D., & Payne-Young, L. (1997). Teaching ideas: Creating thematic units. *English Journal, 5*(86), 80–85.

Neely, A. (1986). Planning and problem solving in teacher education. *Journal of Teacher Education, 37*(3), 29–33.

Parker, G. (1995). *Planning together across the curriculum.* Unpublished document. Houston: University of Houston.

Paschal, R. A., Weinstein, T., & Walberg, H. H. (1983, April). *The effects of homework on learning. A quantitative synthesis.* Paper presented at the annual meeting of the American Educational Research Association, Montreal, Canada.

Sanders, M. G. (1998). The effects of school, family, and community support on the academic achievement of African American children. *Urban Education, 33*(3), 385–409.

Saur, R. E., Popp, M. J., & Isaacs, M. (1984). Action zone theory and the learning impaired student in the mainstreamed classroom. *Journal of Classroom Interaction, 19*(2), 22.

Schug, M. C., Western, R. D., & Enochs, L. G. (1997). Why do social studies teachers use textbooks? The answer may lie in economic theory. *Social Education, 61*(2), 97–101.

Snyder, M. (1988). *Habitat: A game of chance.* Unpublished lesson plan and teaching analysis.

Sugai, G. (1997). Using flowcharts to plan teaching strategies. *Teaching Exceptional Children, 29*(3), 37–42.

Weade, G. (1992). Locating learning in the times and spaces of teaching. In H. Marshall (Ed.), *Redefining student learning* (pp. 87–118). Norwood, NJ: Ablex.

Wenzlaff, T. L. (1998). Disposition and portfolio development: Is there a connection? *Education, 118*(4), 564–572.

Yinger, R. J. (1980). A study of teaching planning. *The Elementary School Journal, 80,* 107–127.

Zahorik, J. A. (1970). The effect of planning on teaching. *The Elementary School Journal, 71,* 143–151.

SAMPLES AND EXAMPLES

This Samples and Examples section includes the following:

- School Year at a Glance shows how a teacher looks at important dates to have a broad view of the instructional year.
- A Home Calls script will help the teacher make parent contacts.
- A Weekly Calendar and a Syllabus are included as examples of planning for both teacher and students.
- Substitute Teacher Letters are provided for both elementary and secondary teachers.

SCHOOL YEAR AT A GLANCE

Every month: PTO and departmental unit planning
Every 6 weeks (halfway between report cards): Progress reviews

AUGUST	SEPTEMBER	OCTOBER
Mark major events on calendar (end of 6 weeks. Open House, fairs and festivals, holidays, homecoming, tests, papers) Set up room In-service – Find out your extra duties. Find out all you can about students you will have. Fire Drill	Get acquainted with students Establish rules Diagnostic tests	Halloween activities Homecoming activities Six-week exams Open House Teacher observations Progress reports
NOVEMBER	**DECEMBER**	**JANUARY**
Thanksgiving activities Homecoming Community projects Locker clean-up Career Week programs Guest speaker	Holiday program preparation Progress reports	Midterm tests, papers, grade reports In-service Teacher observations Preplanning for spring
FEBRUARY	**MARCH**	**APRIL**
Black History Month activities History Fair	Fairs, festivals Science Fair Spring break	Standardized tests Order materials for next year Teacher observations PTA
MAY	**JUNE**	**JULY**
Cinco de Mayo activities Final tests, papers, grades Recommend kids for summer school, retention, promotion In-service Requisitions & inventories Meet with parents about standardized test results Summer school sign-up	Closing procedures Book returns	Summer workshops

HOME CALLS

Hello. I am Jerome Freiberg, Johnny's teacher. I am calling at the beginning of the school year to introduce myself and to give you an idea of the types of activities we will be including during the first few weeks of school. (Total call time: 5 minutes or less.)

1. Portrait of the day: Describe a typical day in your class.
2. Discuss any specific items (e.g., absence packet).
3. Give a sense of the amount of homework and the days on which it is due.
4. Support the parents in getting their child to school on time: *"I know how difficult it is to get children to school on time, but I would really appreciate your support in having Johnny arrive to school by X o'clock."*
5. If the conversation is positive, you may want to discuss the possibility of the parent becoming a classroom assistant.
6. End the conversation with a note that you hope you can contact the parent at another time, and if he or she has any questions to call the school during your planning time or leave a message and you will call back later that day. It is better *not* to leave your home telephone number.

A WEEKLY CALENDAR

HERE'S WHAT'S HAPPENING

_______________ FOR THE WEEK OF _______________

DAY	PLANS*	WHAT TO BRING
MONDAY		
TUESDAY		
WEDNESDAY		
THURSDAY		
FRIDAY		

*PLANS ARE SUBJECT TO CHANGE

CHILD'S NAME _______________

SYLLABUS

Assignment Sheet

Materials: textbook, notebook, pen, pencil, drawing equipment

	February 27–March 3
Monday	Written assignment from Chapter 9.
Tuesday	SIX-WEEKS EXAM.
Wednesday	Begin discussion of Chapter 9 notes. Answer questions 1–12 in genetics notebook.
Thursday	Go over homework. Learn how to do a monohybrid cross. (Do not miss this lecture.) Answer questions 13–24 in genetics notebook.
Friday	Do monohybrid worksheet in class in small groups.
	March 6–10
Monday	Continue group work on monohybrid problems.
Tuesday	Go over monohybrid problems. Discuss the concept of incomplete dominance. Answer questions 35–40 in genetics notebook.
Wednesday	Learn how to do dihybrid crosses. (Do not even consider missing this lecture.) Do questions 25–34 from genetics notebook.
Thursday	Continue work on dihybrids. Do dihybrid worksheet from notebook.
Friday	LAB: "How Can Inheritance Be Predicted?"
	March 13–17
Monday	Complete work on lab. Turn in at end of the period.
Tuesday	Do review sheet on Chapter 9 from genetics notebook.
Wednesday	EXAM ON CHAPTER 9.
Thursday	Read Chapter 10. Do Chapter 10 worksheet.
Friday	Discuss sex determination, mutations, and nondisjunction.
	March 20–23
Monday	LAB: "Let's Look at Chromosomes."
Tuesday	Discuss sex-linked inheritance from notebook. Do practice problems from genetics notebook.
Wednesday	Check homework from overhead. Do second set of sex-linked problems.
Thursday	Check homework. LAB: "Human Genetics Lab." PROGRESS REPORTS.
Friday	SPRING VACATION STARTS

POP TESTS FOR THESE 4 WEEKS ARE UNANNOUNCED. HINT: YOU WILL USUALLY HAVE ONE THE DAY AFTER A LECTURE OR DISCUSSION.

SUBSTITUTE TEACHER LETTERS

Elementary

Dear Substitute,

Thank you for teaching my students today. I believe that every day my students attend school is important; therefore, your job is very important. Please ask Sarah or Jose to assist you with the roll. They will show you, using the pocket chart on the front wall, how to collect the lunch money or give tickets for students on free and reduced lunch. They will also help you determine which students will be eating a hot lunch or have a lunch sack.

Please leave me a list of students who have been helpful in class. I have talked with them about the importance of assisting a substitute teacher. I have a homework folder in the right top drawer of my desk. Gladys will collect the homework for you.

My lesson plan is beneath the homework folder and should be followed if possible. Please leave a note describing your day and the content you accomplished. Thank you.

Mrs. Eva Johnson

Secondary

Welcome to Earth Science! Each of my classes has students who will assist you in your organization at the beginning and end of each period. A list of all the student assistants for each period is located in the Substitute Teacher Packet, which is kept in my top drawer. In the packet, you will find a picture seating chart for each class, a list of student assistants, and my lesson plan for the day. Please leave me a note about the content you covered in each class. Thank you for being in my shoes while I am out.

Mr. Joseph Evans

design process. Additionally, we suggest that you modify your designs to fit your own needs and those of your students as you gain teaching experience.

Considerations in the Design Process

When you plan for travel, you must consider your destination, time of year, distance, length of time, number of travelers, and your goals for the trip. Then you begin to focus your plans. When you plan for instruction, you must consider the *context* of your teaching, the *content* you intend to teach, and the *learners* who will be taught. You must also consider *yourself.* Then you begin to focus your plans—you design instruction.

Consider the Context of Your Teaching

To help you make some of your planning decisions, ask yourself questions about the context in which you will be teaching:

- Is the setting formal or informal (rows of desks or clusters of tables and chairs)?
- Is it the beginning, middle, or end of the school year? The school day? The class period?
- Is this a group of 8? 12? 20? 30?
- What kind of management routines are established?
- Will you be collaborating with other teachers or team teaching other classes?

Your context concerns must include elements within and outside your classroom. Consider noise levels, potential behavior problems, and movement that affects your teaching and the teaching of those nearby. Note other schedules, such as library period, lunch break, and recess, which may follow or precede your instruction. Remember, too, that there are often administrative pressures imposed on your design process. You may be required to submit teaching plans to administrators, to use a particular format, or to follow a particular schedule.

Consider the Content of Your Teaching

Again, to help you decide on a format for your design, ask yourself questions about the content you will teach:

- Is there a requirement to use a given textbook or other resource material?
- Is the curriculum unstructured and open ended (e.g., curriculum for creative writing)?
- Is there a big idea or concept to be understood (e.g., relationship between societal discontent and politics)?
- Are there skills to be practiced (e.g., map reading)?
- Are there attitudes to be experienced (e.g., appreciation of masterpieces of art)?
- Are there school district objectives to be met?
- Are there connections to be made between several curriculum areas?

What other subject areas can be integrated with this concept? In most subject areas, content should be carefully analyzed to determine the "big ideas" because they are the most effective focus of instructional design. They can be applied more broadly to students' lives, so there is potential for meaningful understanding (Grossen & Lee, 1994). Teachers' individual interests and areas of expertise also influence content decisions. In Chapter Seven, which discusses the lecture strategy, you will see how a teacher's travel experience influences the content of her geography lesson. From content, move to thoughts of your learners.

Consider the Learners to Be Taught

These questions will guide your decision about a format for your instructional design. Ask yourself questions about your learners:

- What kind of learning activities have they experienced? What kind of life experiences? Travel experiences? Activities outside of school?
- Do these learners work well in groups? Do they know how to work in groups?
- What strategies/activities are developmentally appropriate for these learners (e.g., young children need manipulatives for understanding math concepts)?
- Can these learners work independently?
- Have the learners shown interest in the topic? What is their motivation level?
- Is the content relevant to their lives?
- What are the needs of the learners?
- Does this group include learners with special needs?

Economically disadvantaged children unfortunately seem to experience additional disadvantages in schools. Haycock (1998) has reported significant findings concerning the impact of teacher effectiveness on student achievement. In Dallas, Texas, for example, students who were taught by effective teachers in three consecutive years (grades 4–6) moved from the 59th percentile in reading to the 76th percentile. A similar group who were taught by ineffective teachers in three consecutive years (grades 4–6) dropped from the 60th percentile to the 42nd percentile. The same patterns were found in other districts throughout the United States. The importance of effective teaching practices has a direct link with learning and later success. You will need to be sensitive to the social interactions of your learners and to the patterns of class participation that could affect the teaching strategies and learning activities you design. Then you can begin to think about yourself.

Before we provide some models of design, we will look at the basic elements you will find in most formats. Some will be familiar and their descriptions will prepare you to study a range of models.

Elements of Instructional Design

You will find some universal elements in most lesson designs, whether they are written in a detailed format or in mental form. A description of each will assist your understanding of the design models that follow in the next section.

Goals

Educational goals provide overall direction for teaching and learning in broad terms. On a universal level, a goal may be: All students will develop a love of learning. On a district level, a goal may be: Students will become problem solvers. On a class level, a goal may be: Students will become successful in math computation or Students will become literary critics. Notice the broad, general quality of the outcomes and the need for long-range development.

Objectives

Educational objectives specify the learning outcomes in measurable or observable terms. To develop objectives, you must analyze your goals into behaviors that indicate that students are reaching the goal. You may also specify the minimum level of performance necessary for each student that would indicate that the objective and part of the goal are being reached. To be specific, an objective for the goal of math computation (in the preceding paragraph) might be: Students will add 10 sets of 3-digit numbers and get 80 percent of them correct. Objectives for the goal of literary critics (in the preceding paragraph) could be: Students identify the main characters, plot, and setting of five literary selections or Students describe the literary strategies used by authors to build suspense, create a setting, and divert attention.

Teaching and Learning Strategies

Teaching and learning strategies are the vehicle or means we use to transfer facts, ideas, concepts, skills, and attitudes to the thinking and actions of the learner. The transfer of learning may be achieved by teacher-directed strategies of lecture, questioning, and demonstration, or with student-directed strategies of cooperative grouping, discovery, and roleplay. They are the "how" of your instructional design, and the core of this book.

Materials

This is a broad category of tools, equipment, and resources, including anything used by you or your learners in the teaching and learning process. Materials can be simply pencils and pens, paper, and textbooks, or more involved audiovisual stimuli such as films and transparencies. Including materials in your design for teaching contributes to your preparedness.

Feedback

All of us need feedback that recognizes our work, our efforts, our progress, and so on. You may provide feedback to students through individual comments on their papers or through verbal responses to their discussions. Students may provide feedback to each other through peer critiques, checking each other's work, and reading to each other. Students may also provide feedback to themselves by checking an answer sheet, by critiquing work with a set of criteria, or through journal writing.

Assessment

This is the means of determining whether students have met the objectives. You can assess as an ongoing process all through the lesson, as well as at the end of the lesson. You may also use assessment at the beginning of a lesson to see what students already know, before you teach. Short-term assessment includes questions, quizzes, and observations of student work. Long-term assessment includes exams, projects, and research papers. Assessment provides information that will be useful for your next lesson design.

Goals, objectives, teaching and learning strategies, materials, feedback, and assessment are threads that run through the most widely used design models. Other models of instruction elaborate from this universal framework. We present four formal design formats for you to use as you begin teaching or as you expand your teaching experiences. They are appropriate for using in their entirety or in parts, after you consider content, context, learners, and yourself.

MODELS OF INSTRUCTIONAL DESIGN

The Instructional Events Model

Gagne, Briggs, and Wagner (1988) described nine instructional events in their design model. We display them in Figure 3.1, and Ms. Rennie follows the design sequence in the Snapshot below.

SNAPSHOT: Elementary Classroom

On the chalkboard at the side of her second-grade classroom, Ms. Rennie has hung a colorful pizza poster to *gain attention.* "Class, take a look at these pizzas. If you have five people in your family, which pizza would you choose? If you have eight friends over to spend the night, which pizza would you choose? Why?" The students mention the number of slices, or pieces, of pizza as reasons for their choices, and Ms. Rennie continues, "Yes, these pizzas have been cut into different pieces." She writes the word *fractions* on the board, and points to the pizza slices. "These pieces are fractions of the whole pizza. We're going to learn about fractions today, and you'll see why we need them in our lives" (*informs the learner of the objective*).

For several minutes, the class reviews what whole numbers are and talks about some examples to *stimulate recall of prerequisite learning.* Ms. Rennie connects whole numbers to fractions, and together she and the class develop several definitions of fractions. Ms. Rennie writes examples of fractions on the board. "Now class, I've put lots of things on these trays (*presents stimulus materials*) for you to use in your math teams. Look carefully at these things and find as many fractions as you can." (On the trays are newspapers, ads, measuring spoons and cups, pictures of baked goods cut into pieces, and so on.) "Look at the examples on the board to help you remember what fractions are like. You will have 10 minutes to find as many fractions as you can."

While student teams work, Ms. Rennie moves about, commenting to the groups on their efforts and *providing learner guidance.* After 10 minutes, each team reports on the fractions they found (*eliciting performance*). They hear feedback: "You found six sale ads that said prices would be one-half off." Ms. Rennie also summarizes a team's findings with, "You found fractions used in ads, cooking, measuring distances, and shoe sizes (*providing feedback about performance correctness*). Why are fractions useful in our world?"

The students return to their individual places and are asked to draw one example of a fraction. Ms. Rennie moves about the desks and asks individual students, "What is a fraction?" and "Tell me about your fraction." When drawings are completed and turned in to Ms. Rennie (*assessing the performance*), the students are given an assignment to do at home: "Find two examples of fractions at home, and copy or draw or bring them in tomorrow" (*enhancing retention and transfer*). The students write the assignment on a sheet labeled "To Do at Home."

Refer to the instructional events listed in Figure 3.1 and be sure that you can identify each one in Ms. Rennie's lesson. Notice how she *gained attention* with the pizza poster and her questions, then *informed learners of the objectives* (learning about fractions and being able to talk about how we use fractions). She *stimulated* their *recall of*

FIGURE 3.1 *Instructional Events Design Model*

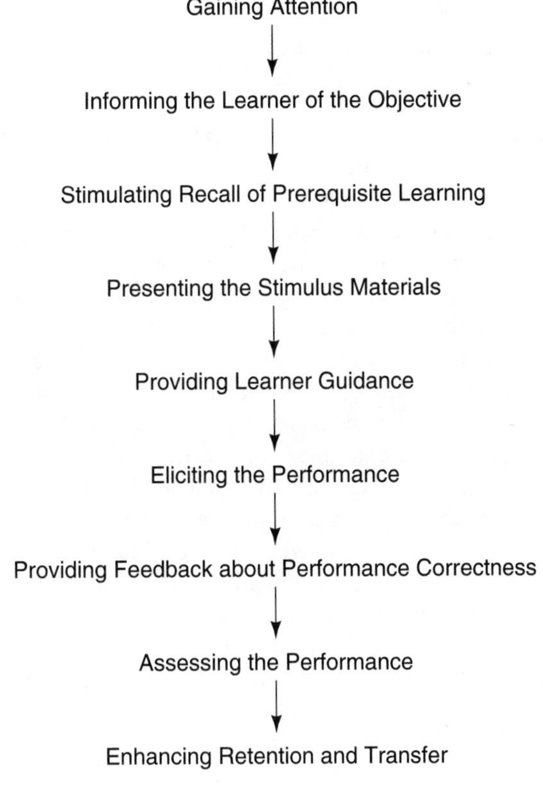

prerequisite learning with a review of whole numbers and examples of fractions. She *presented stimulus materials* with the prepared trays of fraction examples, then moved about the teams at work, finding the examples to *provide learner guidance.*

After the teams had worked for 10 minutes, Ms. Rennie *elicited the performance* when she asked for team reports, and *provided feedback about performance correctness* with her comments about the examples. She collected student drawings and asked questions of individuals to *assess the performance.* Her homework assignment was designed to *enhance retention and transfer.*

As we move to the next model, you will see a similar sequence of teaching and learning. You will also notice as you watch teachers that the sequence can be varied to fit a specific topic or objective or specific learner needs. Although Gagne and other instructional designers propose a particular sequence and format, these can be modified to match the learner, context, and content.

The Lesson Cycle Model

Hunter's (1976) lesson cycle model continues to be widely used in public schools. The model contains nine levels, presented in Figure 3.2. In the Snapshot, Mr. Malter uses the lesson cycle levels in his middle-school math class.

SNAPSHOT: Middle-School Classroom

Mr. Malter begins with newspaper clippings of the recent marathon event in the students' community. On the chalkboard are headlines about the winners and their respective times (*anticipatory set*). "We know that the marathon covered 26 miles, and each of these runners completed the race in the times I have written next to their names. What else would you be interested in knowing about the runners?" The students suggest age of runner, race experience, amount of training, and rate of speed. Mr. Malter writes the suggestions on the board. "Most of these questions would have to be answered by interviewing the runners, but we could answer this one ourselves," Mr. Malter says as he points to rate of speed. "Today we are going to learn how to compute rate of speed, and practice the computation for a number of race examples" (*objective or purpose*).

Mr. Malter discusses with the students the film *Chariots of Fire* and how the runners used the clock tower chimes to determine their speed. "Our formula is a simple way to determine speed," he states. He focuses on the formula: Distance/Time = Rate or Speed (*instructional input*).

Using the marathon distance and each runner's time, Mr. Malter demonstrates the use of the formula for rate (*modeling*). After three examples, he asks, "What information am I using each time I figure a rate of speed for a runner?" (*checking for understanding*). When students suggest distance and time, he writes them on the board. "That's correct. Now what did I do with distance and time?" (*checking for understanding*). With the formula written on the board, he instructs the students to tell him how to compute the next runner's rate. Using the overhead projector, Mr. Malter displays a news clip about an auto race and asks how to figure the rate of speed of the winning drivers. Individual students suggest using the distance and time information with the formula. Two students come up to the board to compute the rate of speed, while others practice on paper at their desks. Those at the board explain what they did to compute the rate of speed (*monitoring and adjusting*).

On the overhead, Mr. Malter displays another problem, this time in pictorial form. Again, students work the problem at the board and at their desks. After discussing the computation process again, students are asked to work three problems at their desks (*guided practice*). Mr. Malter moves about the room, looking at student work, asking questions, and commenting on computation: "How did you get this answer?" "Tell me how you did this computation," "You are using the formula correctly," and "It looks like you know how to use the formula." He checks the final answers for the three problems and comments, "You all used the formula correctly to compute the rate of speed." He assigns 10 problems to be done as *independent practice:* "These examples will give you practice in computing rates of speed so that you can be fast and sure."

At the end of the seatwork practice, Mr. Malter calls for attention and asks, "Class, if you were to tell someone what you learned in math today, what would you say?" (*closure*). After the students describe the process and formula, they are asked, "What information do you need to do this?" Students are told that they can finish their problems at home and are assigned one more task—to "make up a rate of speed problem of your own."

Look at the lesson cycle sequence (Figure 3.2) and identify the levels of the model as Mr. Malter teaches about computing rate of speed. He used the marathon news clips as an *anticipatory set* to direct the students' attention and to prepare them for instruction. He *expressed the objective* directly to the students after creating a need with students' suggestions of other information of interest.

You saw his *instructional input* and *modeling* as he presented a mini-lecture and demonstrated several examples on the board. Students began *guided practice* as they worked the examples displayed on the overhead, and Mr. Malter was able to *check for understanding*. The guided practice continued when students worked on three problems at their desks, and Mr. Malter continued to check for understanding as he moved about, asking for explanations and commenting on work. During this time and during the previous examples, he was *monitoring* (that is, observing to determine student understanding). If he had noticed student difficulty or misunderstanding, he could have *adjusted* (that is, retaught the computation, reworded the process, or asked other students to explain the process again).

The assignment of 10 problems and the homework task comprised *independent practice* (that is, activities without assistance). At the end of the math class, Mr. Malter brought about *closure* by asking students to review what they had learned in class.

You now have two design models with similarities and differences. Continue comparing as we describe a third.

FIGURE 3.2 *Lesson Cycle Design Model*

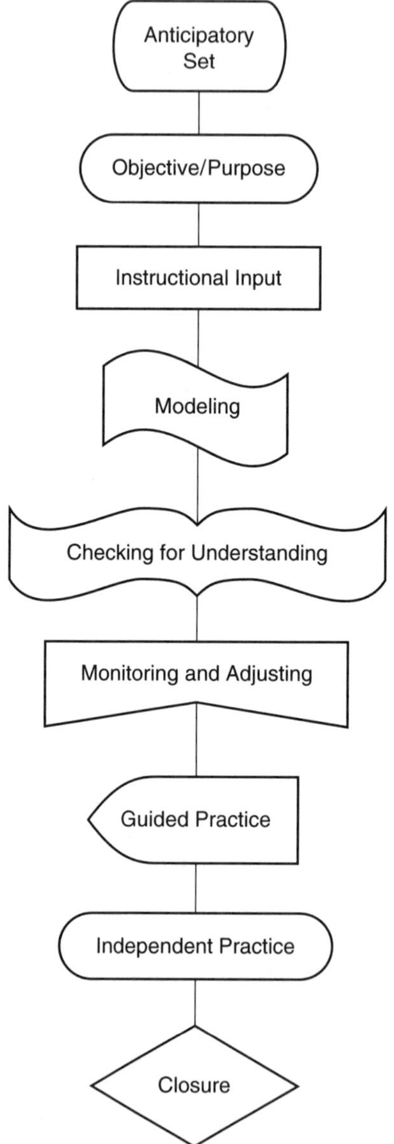

The Instructional Functions Model

When Rosenshine and Stevens (1986) reviewed studies in which teachers increased student achievement, they found a consistent pattern of instructional functions. They noted that these functions are appropriate and effective when used to teach well-structured subjects. Their model is displayed in Figure 3.3 and observed in the next Snapshot of a high-school geometry class. Again, notice that the sequence can be adjusted. Make the sequence meet your needs and those of your students, but include all of the model's elements in your plan to ensure consistency. In an extensive review of research on instruction over a 30-year period, Rosenshine (1995) also found that teaching in small steps (using the frameword described in Figure 3.3) and providing guided practice by giving students examples that are completed together with the teacher prior to independent practice are the two most relevant factors in effective teaching.

SNAPSHOT: Secondary Classroom

Ms. Lasley begins her geometry class with, "OK, class, we have been using *deductive reasoning* and developing *conditionals* and *proofs,*" as she points to the terms on the bulletin board. She asks for definitions of each, and describes how the students are using all three in their lives (*daily review*). "I want to check your assignment from yesterday to be sure you understand the work we have been doing. Then, we will move on to using conditionals and proofs in more complex examples." The assignment is checked and a brief review of writing hypotheses is conducted. Ms. Lasley says, "We have a theorem that states that if a point is not on a line, then the point and the line determine exactly one plane. If you need to write a hypothesis for the theorem, how do you begin?" She reteaches the process when she notices confusion. She provides another theorem example and moves around the room, observing student answers and looking for evidence of confidence. "It looks like you are more clear about writing a hypothesis, so we will move on to today's work."

Ms. Lasley reminds the class that they are going to be working on more complex examples—"writing two-column proofs" (*presents new content*). She turns on the overhead projector and displays an example in which the givens are that angles A and C are supplementary, and angles B and C are supplementary. She reads to the class, "Prove: A ≅ B." She continues, "Notice that we have more givens and when you look at the example, it looks more complex than the proofs we have been doing" (*new skills phased in with old skills*).

Ms. Lasley completes the proof by directing the sequence of steps and using student input. She reviews the entire proof when they finish. "Now, let's try another and work it together," she says, as she reveals a second example on the overhead. When the second example has been completed, she assigns a third example to be worked on, and asks five students (one from each row) to do it at the chalkboard. She observes their work and, as they finish, encourages them to check the work of students in their row. This process is followed three more times at a fast pace (*initial student practice*).

"OK, it looks like you understand how to do these problems quite well (*feedback*). Here are three more to figure out while I check everyone's work. If you feel uncertain, raise your hand and I will come to you."

After 10 minutes, everyone appears finished. "Let's look at these two different conclusions and reasons given for the second problem. Lorianne gave this reason, and Roy gave this one. Lorianne, where did you get your reason? Roy, where did you get yours?" Ms. Lasley makes certain that the class members understand that the figure can provide some conclusions and reasons (*correctives*).

The students are assigned five examples from their textbooks to be worked on during the last few minutes of class and for homework (*independent practice*): "I will continue to check your work and am available if you have questions."

Ms. Lasley followed the instructional functions model for her lesson on two-column proofs, beginning with a *review,* which checked the previous day's work, and a quick reteaching of hypothesis writing. She gave students an overview with her description of using the previous steps of givens and proofs to work with more complex examples. She *presented the new content on the overhead projector and repeated the process of writing two-column proofs three times.* Students *practiced* the proofs throughout most of the lesson and were given *feedback.* When Ms. Lasley discovered a discrepancy between Roy and Lorianne's answers and realized potential problems for students with the particular examples, she clarified for all students. When most class members understood how to write the proofs, she assigned *independent practice.* In the weeks to come, Ms. Lasley will conduct periodic *reviews* and reteach if necessary.

The three design models we have just described and illustrated are classic. They have been adjusted and adapted by teachers for years. In addition to the models, there are

FIGURE 3.3 *Instructional Functions Model*

1. *Daily Review*	Check previous day's work Check homework Reteach when necessary
2. *Teach New Content*	Give an overview Give detailed explanations Present in small parts Maintain a rapid pace Relate new content with previously learned content
3. *Student Practice*	Observable practice tasks Frequent question/answer Frequent feedback Monitor practice Check for understanding
4. *Feedback/Corrections*	Frequent feedback Notice student errors Explain and review Reteach
5. *Independent Practice*	Seatwork Monitoring
6. *Reviews*	Regular schedule (weekly, monthly) Reteach

design formats for some of the curricu
describe one of them, a format for scie
state-of-the-art thinking in each discipline a

The Learning Cycle Model

The learning cycle model is an effective lesson plan
levels. It reflects the development work of the Science C
and consists of three important phases: exploration, conce
application.

Exploration precedes any formal instruction—it is a time ... manipulate, experiment, and "mess about." During this time, learne ... ons and
try out ideas. It will be important for them to record their observatio ... e data col-
lected. Exploration is a time of intense interaction: between teacher and student, between student and student, and between student and materials. As you guide learners, you will hear comments such as the following:

"Look at what happened when I mixed these colors!"
"Let's make a list of which items float and which ones sink."
"Why do these feel so different?"
"Maybe we should count the seeds inside."

Concept introduction is a more teacher-directed phase in which learners begin to organize information, articulate discoveries, and compare ideas and information. Your role will be to help clarify ideas, add information and relevant vocabulary, and encourage further exploration and research. During this phase, you will probably ask many questions, such as:

"What did you notice about the different magnets?"
"When you compare each column of data, what conclusions can you make?"

Concept application is a time when new situations, problems, related materials, or data are brought in so that learners can apply the new concept or information. This is a time of application, reinforcement, and some additional manipulation.

The learning cycle model is appropriate for all grade levels and for most science concepts (Tolman & Hardy, 1999). We encourage you to try it as is and to adapt and use its components. When you consider the span of curriculum and the diversity of learners for whom you are responsible, you will understand our recommendation for using varied lesson formats. We especially recommend adaptations for an inclusive classroom.

DESIGNS FOR VARIED TIME PERIODS

Most of the design formats you have seen thus far have been appropriate for short-term teaching—one or two lessons. Another kind of design has become very important at all levels of teaching. Unit designs are being used for teaching a single subject and for integrated teaching. We will describe both and illustrate an integrated design.

Like lesson designs, unit designs enable you to teach with a sense of direction, knowing what you expect to do, what you will need, and what you expect will happen. They have been described as a way of organizing materials and activities, relating learning activities to each other, and designing experiences around a central theme or purpose. Unit designs consist of general goals or purposes, specific objectives, activities, resources, and assessment. They may also include an outline of content as well as background information or knowledge, and they may be aligned with a textbook. When units are designed to teach a single-subject area (math, writing, etc.), they may be for shorter time periods, but when they are designed to connect several subject areas, they may extend for a longer amount of time.

Listen to the following Teacher Talk about a unit design for the study of weather for two first-grade classes. We have included part of the unit design for you to see the activities and materials that are organized around a central purpose.

TEACHER TALK

We wanted students to know a lot about weather—the different kinds of weather, how it affects our lives, and the changes that occur in the four seasons. We also wanted them to appreciate weather. In addition, it's important to us that students learn some skills related to weather. We don't have a textbook for first grade, so we had to use a lot of library sources. We decided to spend three weeks on this unit and to incorporate science and social studies goals. We'll also integrate language arts activities, some math practice, and art and music projects.

WEATHER UNIT

Goals: Understanding Weather and How It Influences People

Objectives

Students will:

1. Identify and describe different kinds of weather conditions.
2. Predict daily weather and explain reasons for predictions.
3. Describe some of the changes that can occur in weather conditions.
4. Match appropriate clothing and activities with different kinds of weather conditions.
5. List characteristics of each season and describe the associated weather changes.
6. Discuss safety precautions for different weather.
7. Observe, measure, and record weather in graphic and narrative forms.
8. Read a weather thermometer and record daily temperatures.
9. Create a weather report using the unit's concepts and skills.
10. Describe the advantages and disadvantages of seasons and different weather conditions.

Vocabulary

rainy	blizzard	calendar	fall
forecast	meteorologist	snowy	graph
hurricane	temperature	seasons	cloudy

Teaching/Learning Activities

1. Student groups of four will prepare bulletin boards of different weather conditions.
2. Student group construction of "Fog in a Bottle."
3. Teacher demonstration of varied materials for protection in rainy weather (rubber, plastic, wool, cotton, paper).
4. Class discussion of videotaped weather forecast.
5. Class construction of a weather calendar using symbols to indicate conditions.
6. Student independent use of flannel board cutouts of weather symbols and clothing in matching exercises.
7. Students make season collages, write season poems, and pantomime seasons.

Materials

The Snowy Day. Ezra Jack Keats. New York: Scholastic.

What Happens in Autumn. Suzanne Venino. National Geographic Society.

The Day the Sun Danced. Edith Hurd. New York: Harper & Row.

Films: *Farm Families in Autumn*
Thermometers and How We Use Them
Thunderstorms
Spring Comes to the Forest

Cloud Charts from P.O. Box 1122, Glen Allen, VA 23060

People: meteorologist, farmer, construction worker

Picture File: seasons, weather, clothing

Assessment

1. Student portfolios that include weather recordings; poems, drawings, and songs about weather; weather stories; weather calendars; checklists of thermometer use; and weather graphs.
2. Observations of children playing matching games: Weather—Clothing; Weather—Activities; Weather—Careers; Weather—Seasons.
3. Picture/symbol matching test of weather vocabulary.

The two teachers had planned a total of 30 teaching and learning activities, some for students' independent work, some for whole-class instruction, and others for use at learning centers. Some of the activities were brief and simple, and others were complex and demanded large time blocks. They planned more activities than they actually needed for three weeks, just in case they needed to reteach, enrich, or extend student learning.

Some secondary teachers have used a different format for planning; Figure 3.4 displays that format. We have often observed teachers planning together on large sheets of paper with formats such as this one. The same format could be used for brainstorming with your students to give them an opportunity to have input in the planning. In our section on collaborative planning at the end of this chapter, we talk more about planning and designing with others.

FIGURE 3.4 *Unit Plan—Secondary*

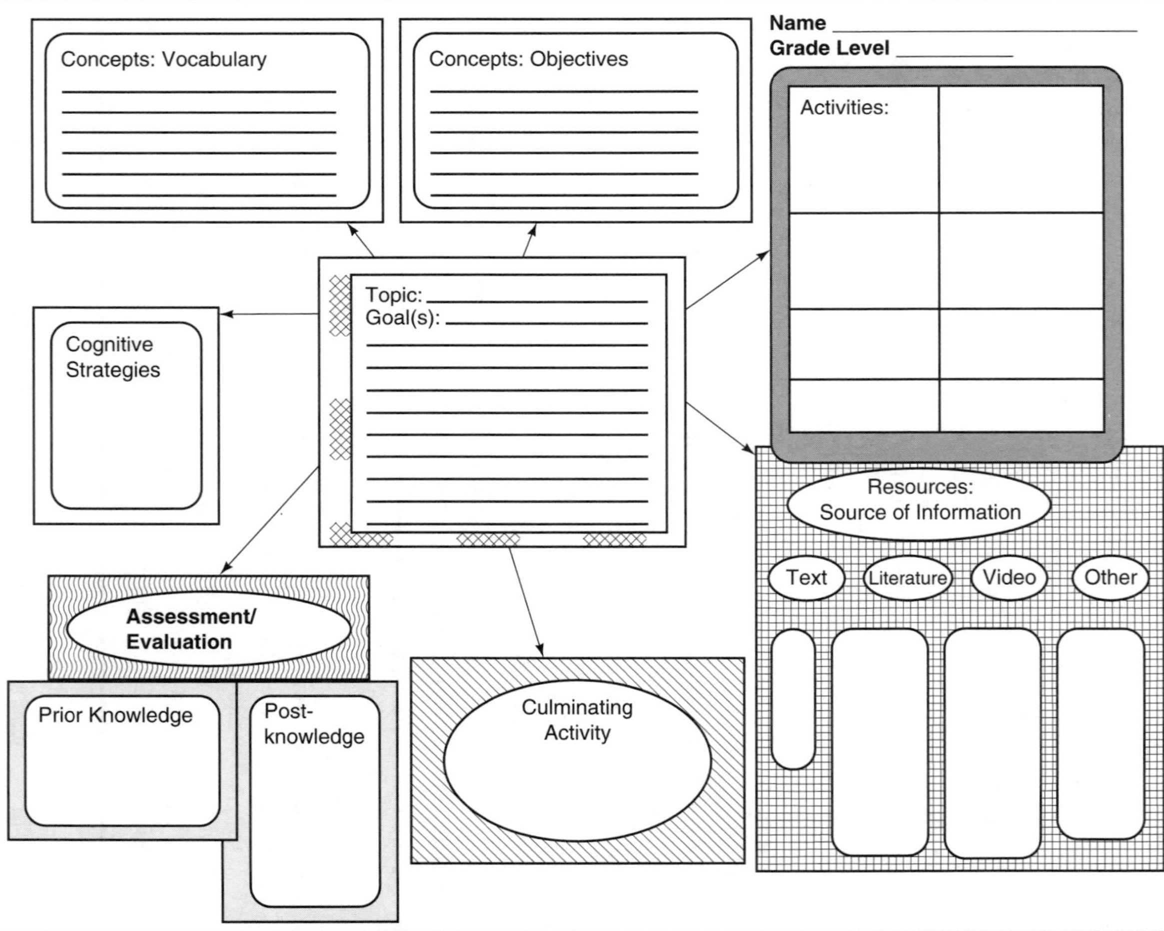

Source: Dannelle Stevens, Whitman College, Walla Walla, Washington. Used by permission.

Integrated Unit Designs

Integrated curriculum and integrative teaching make sense in the complexity of today's society because, as people know from experience, "rarely are we confronted with a problem that requires only one discipline to reach a solution" (Nagel, 1996, p. 1). Integrated unit designs are purposeful in their access of different subject areas and are meaningful approaches to ensure curricular relevance for learners.

The unit example on weather that we just reviewed (in its brief form) demonstrates the ease with which varied topics can be connected to a single theme. Thematic unit design makes sense to many teachers and learners. Other approaches to integrated units are problem-solving models, inquiry-based formats, and the project approach.

In *problem-solving models,* learners "work in meaningful situations as they examine problems, gather data, research information and resources, contact experts, work collaboratively on tasks, and test possible solutions" (Nagel, 1996, p. 12). Generally, the solution and related information are presented or published as a culminating activity. Nagel's (1996) *Learning through Real-World Problem Solving* is an excellent source of examples of problem-based units and stories of their implementation. *Inquiry-based units* (sometimes called *discovery approaches*) are similar to problem-based designs except that they originate with and focus on a question. Such designs begin with the interest and curiosity of the learners and engage them in the gathering and processing of information. Designs for *the project approach* are similar to problem-based and inquiry-based units. They are thematic and they culminate in a significant project (see Chapter Nine for a complete description).

What is exciting and promising about these alternatives for integrative teaching is that they promote the kind of active learning experiences that will be especially effective in an inclusive classroom. They also structure teaching and learning with enough flexibility to meet widely diverse learner needs, strengths, interests, and experiences.

Daily Designs

Teachers use blueprints of a day to set up and arrange their classrooms, to fit the daily schedule to last-minute intrusions, and to prepare students for the day's activities. They often display the daily plan for students and use it as a kind of checklist for getting materials ready and for accomplishing the day's intentions. We have observed teachers reviewing the daily plan with their classes and assigning students to check off the activities on the day's agenda as they are completed. Daily designs are often incorporated into a format of weekly designs, as you can see in Figures 3.5 and 3.6.

Weekly Designs

To structure the week's activities, teachers generally use weekly plans. These blueprints are often adjusted to accommodate interruptions and special needs. Most weekly plan formats are scheduling tools, often with nothing more than the times and names of activities. As you can see in Robin's weekly plan (Figure 3.6), the format is handy for writing all kinds of reminders. Many of the details Robin records would be appreciated by a substitute teacher.

FIGURE 3.5 *Weekly Plan from a Secondary Teacher*

NAME G. Rutledge
SUBJECT English 2B PERIOD(S) 1, 2, 5
Adjectives & Letter Writing
SCHOOL Scarborough H. S.
WEEK OF March 16–20

DAY	ELO	INSTRUCTIONAL OBJECTIVES	RELATED ACTIVITIES	RESOURCE/MATERIALS	T.T. CODES	ASSIGNMENTS
16 MONDAY		The student will compare a request letter using the model on p. 27	1. Letter of request 2. Model — p. 27 3. Complete practice 4— p. 275	English Writing & Skills pp. 274-275	01 02 04 05 07 09	Use evening to work on competition
17 TUESDAY		The student will order a product by mail	1. Letter to order something 2. Model-p. 277 3. Complete practice 5— p. 278 4. Test	English Writing & Skills pp. 276-278	01 02 04 05 07 10	Oral or written UIL next week
18 WEDNESDAY		The student will explain correction in an order by mail	1. Letter of adjustment 2. Model — p. 279 3. Writing practice 6 — p. 280	English Writing & Skills p. 278-280	01 02 04 05 07	Practice for UIL or polish written contest entry
19 THURSDAY		The student will write a letter of appreciation to be mailed	1. Letter of appreciation 2. Model — p. 281 3. Complete practice 7	English Writing & Skills p. 280- 282	01 02 04 05 07	Proof final copy of essay contest for mailing
20 FRIDAY		The student will apply in letter for a position	1. Letter of application 2. Model — p. 283 3. Complete practice 8	English Writing & Skills pp. 282- 283	01 02 04 05 07	

LEARNING ACTIVITIES/TEACHING TECHNIQUES = CODES 01-10

Independent Study–01 Questions & Answers–02 Group Work–03 Discussion–04 Supervised Study–05 Demonstration–06 Illustration–07 Lecture–08 Review–09 Evaluation–10

HOUSTON INDEPENDENT SCHOOL DISTRICT
SECONDARY LESSON PLAN SHEET

Source: Gwen Rutledge, G. C. Scarborough Senior High School, Houston, Texas. Used by permission.

FIGURE 3.6 *Weekly Plan from a Elementary Teacher*

Sept. GRADE OR CLASS First (Robin) WEEK BEGINNING

	Before Sch.	Enter :40-9	Arrival (rug) 9-9:30	Whole Group 9:30-10	Recess 10-10:		Literacy Centers 10:15-11:15	Clean & Inspect 11:15 to 11:25	Lunch 11:30-12	Quiet Reading 12-12:30	Share books 12:20 to 12:30	Math 12:30-1	Learning Centers 1-1:40		Recess 1:50-2	Gathering 2:05-2:20
18 MONDAY	Ann Carstiom here PSU (new jobs) (Zero's 1st B'day)	journals	✓New jobs ✓Calendar ✓Zero's B'day ✓Read: Wet this Bear	Writing (review use of writers' workshop boxes)			finish spelling assess.			Theme tubs Beavers & Squirrels Roombooks otters & racoons		Discovery time Ask kids rules (review) +Q+Q! write down "Math News" (on easel chart?)		↕ clean up & inspection 1:40-1:50		Read: Buzzy Bear or the Garden take home Zero dittos!
19 TUESDAY	Pam here	↓	Calendar shoe patter 8 rules Read: Bledford Bear	↓	Library		Recess 10:30 to 10:45 / Lit. Centers 10:45-11:15 Label room "otter clan" (take pics) Diana 10:50-11:10		↓	Roombooks Beavers & Squirrels / Theme tubs Otters & Racoons		Pattern pages (little brown bears) (first do up real bears again)	Redo Math Assess.			Read: ~~Ernest & Celestine~~ discuss care of records
20 WEDNESDAY		↓	Calendar (Dot chart patterns) (Read: Break-fast time)	↓	P.E.		Literacy Centers 10:30-11:15 (no recess on gym day a.m.) Label room "Squirrel Clan"		↓	Magazines to each clan		Discovery time see Mon.	↓			Read: Ernest & Celestine Take home Bear note!
21 THURSDAY	get math books for Fri.	↓	Calenda (Dot chart patterns) Read:	Make an award for your bear	Music		Recess 10:30 to 10:45 / Lit. Centers 10:45-11:15 Meeting Nate, Meagan, and Matt Rewriting time expectations	Pam here	cindy here	Textbooks to each clan in color tubs (New-sh how to)		Bear Measuring Stations unifix cubes scale string make booklet	↓ early clean up! do math Assess!	ready to go home		Computer 2-2:23 (no recess and leave from comp. lab. room)
22 FRIDAY	✓Math pages!	↓	Calendar (Dot chart patterns) Read: Who will be my friend?	↓ Write about your bear (use blank bear ditto)	Recess 10-10:15		Lit. Centers 10:15-10:50 → Meeting Caritza, Mario, Jesus — ABC cards / Clean time 10:50 / Entertainment time 11-11:25		↓	Library books Otters & Racoons / Theme tubs Beavers & Squirrels		Math books pp. 1-16	↓ Math Assess.	clean & inspect		Outside w/ Bears (Recess & stories)

Source: Robin Lindsley, Boise Elementary School, Portland, Oregon. Used by permission.

In sum, no matter which format you use to design your lesson or plan your day or week, doing so provides a way for you to feel prepared. Many school districts provide a format for you to use, but you can always adapt it to meet your needs. What's important is for you to *consider yourself* as you design instruction, and to be sure that your blueprint enables you to feel confident and, ultimately, to teach well. Many successful teachers say that they emphasize the strategies for beginning and ending a lesson in their designs because of their effect on the lesson effectiveness. Because they are so important, we will describe some specific approaches for you.

LESSON BEGINNINGS AND ENDINGS

As you observed the four models in action, did you notice how important it was to begin the lesson effectively—that is, to gain attention, or to set some anticipation, or to diagnose what students know? Did you also notice how the lessons ended with a sense of closure, or a feeling of completion?

Think about what it is like for you to be in a class that begins in an interesting way, in which the instructor immediately gets you thinking about the subject or arouses your curiosity. Most of us attend well, stay involved, feel positive about the class, and even learn more in those situations. The next time you attend a class, check the ending and see what effect it has on what you remember from the class. Endings generally influence our impression of a class or lesson and our memory. For those reasons, we want to develop strategies for your lesson beginnings and endings. We begin with three beginning strategies: set induction, advanced organizers, and sponges.

Set Induction

A *set* is a mental state of readiness, and an *induction* brings it on, so a *set induction* gets learners thinking and ready for the lesson. Set inductions can provide a reference point between what the student knows and new material, thus creating a link from one lesson or class to the next (Schuck, 1985). How important is set induction? Hudgins and Cone (1992) determined that set induction ranked second only to school climate on a list of effective teaching elements and their practical values in the classroom. Gee (1991) found that most effective lessons contained set inductions using audiovisual aids to create interest and motivation.

Facilitating Sets

Facilitating sets are used to summarize information presented in previous lessons and/or information that will occur. The intent is to bring the students' attention to the current lesson. You may use an outline on the board or on a transparency or verbally present a short summary of key points. Ask your learners to summarize what they have learned from previous lessons.

Motivating Sets

Whereas a facilitating set emphasizes the cognitive aspects of a new lesson by reviewing or summarizing previous learning, a motivating set is intended to catch the students' attention. It arouses curiosity, poses interesting questions, uses dramatic appeal, and creates a need or interest. It induces an affective or emotional response from the learners.

TEACHER TALK

"I want you to watch something on videotape." After enjoying Phil Collins's music video, "One More Night," students were intrigued. "Where did people of those times get their entertainment?" After a discussion of minstrels and balladeers, the teacher picked up her guitar and proceeded to sing "Greensleeves." Upon completion, she said, "This type of song is called a ballad, and today we are going to learn the characteristics of a ballad."

Tenth-Grade English Teacher

With a colorful quilt displayed at the front of the classroom, students were asked to find as many shapes as they could. In time, the teacher said, "Yes, there are polygons, and today we are going to learn to identify various polygons and describe their critical attributes."

Fifth-Grade Math Teacher

Children were directed to a clock with some numbers and one hand missing: "Look at this clock for a minute—does it look funny or odd to you? Now compare it with our clock on the wall. What is missing?" The children talked about the missing numbers and hand. "That's right. Important parts of the clock are missing and today we are going to learn about why we need them to tell time."

First-Grade Math Teacher

As you might have guessed, it is ideal to provide both motivating and facilitating sets in your set induction. The first-grade teacher in the preceding Teacher Talk could have begun her sets with, "What do you remember about clocks?" followed by, "Now, look at this clock—does it look funny or odd to you?" The fifth-grade teacher could have reviewed various triangles and their critical attributes to show a similarity with the information about polygons.

Advanced Organizers

Ausubel (1968), who developed this strategy for beginning a lesson, came up with two types of advanced organizers. One of these he called the *expository organizer,* which provides students with an overview of the subject. He called the second type the *comparative organizer,* as it provides a link between what the students already know and what they will be learning.

Expository Organizers

Expository organizers are appropriate for lessons or classes when the information is new to students. For example, to begin a unit on democracy, you might introduce the issues of freedom and choice by showing photos of Chinese students demonstrating and by discussing protest issues. By using these expository organizers, you will be encouraging your students to think about the "big picture" of democracy as you start the unit.

Advanced organizers help learners begin the lesson or unit with a frame of reference. For a unit of study, it is ideal to have each new advanced organizer build on previous advanced organizers. Students either begin with the broad abstract concept and fill in the details, or begin with the specific, concrete facts and understandings and build the broad overview.

Comparative Organizers

Comparative organizers are appropriate when information is already familiar to students. You build on the known in order to develop the unknown. For example, if your students have studied about water pollution, you use their knowledge of water pollution to begin a study of air pollution. If your students know about squares, you use their understanding of squares to begin studying about rectangles.

Sometimes, advanced organizers take the form of *setting an agenda* for the class or lesson, such as: "Today we will be studying the parts of a microscope. We will begin by discussing its uses, then look at diagrams of the parts of the microscope. We will work in groups to get to know the equipment, to handle it and find the parts. You will have plenty of time to work with the microscope. We will end by going back to our diagrams and see how many parts you can remember and identify by name." The value of this kind of advanced organizer is that learners know what to expect, know the direction and sequence of the lesson, and know what is expected of them during the lesson.

"Sponge" Activities

The *sponge* is a term used by Hunter (1985, p. 93) to describe activities that "sop up" waiting time at the beginning of a lesson or during the lesson. Sponges take the form of a review or extension of previous learnings, a set or mental readiness for the learning that is to come, or an attention-getting technique to eliminate distractions or behavior that would disturb teaching and learning. They help you maintain the smoothness we describe in Chapter Six.

Necessary management routines often occur at the beginning of a lesson: getting books out of desks, moving into groups, or settling into the room. Routines can also occur during a lesson: passing out materials or papers, moving to look at a demonstration, or changing from whole-class teaching to group work. Many of those routines are called *transitions,* and we provide suggestions for handling them smoothly in Chapter Six. Sponge activities are designed to keep students thinking about the lesson or class focus during those routines or transitions. As you begin a lesson on geometric shapes or as you pass out colored paper in the middle of the lesson, you may say to the students, "Look around the room and see if you can find any triangles, or squares, or ...." As students move to their groups during your lesson on using the microscope, you may suggest, "As you move to your table, see if you can come up with the part of the microscope that begins with *l.*" You will find lists of sponge ideas from elementary and secondary teachers in the Samples and Examples section at the end of this chapter.

Summary of Beginnings

Set inductions, advanced organizers, and sponges are an important part of your lesson design. They help focus and direct both the planning and the teaching. Your introductions or beginnings can accomplish multiple tasks: gain attention, focus on the subject, create interest and need, stimulate readiness, eliminate distractions, and develop positive affect for a subject. Lesson beginnings represent a brief sliver of instructional time and a small section of your overall design, but they have a major impact on the entire design and the actual instruction.

Ending a Lesson

The last thing you do in teaching a lesson is often what students remember. Unfortunately, we often end lessons or classes with a bell ringing to indicate change of classes or with, "Time is up. We have to go to lunch. Put your things away and line up at the door." Instead, we suggest using a closure strategy to end a lesson. *Closure* means to close or to pull together. You provide closure for students when you *review, summarize,* and *repeat your overview* from the beginning of your lesson. You, the teacher, can provide closure, in verbal or written form, or you may involve students in the process.

TEACHER TALK

The focus of our lesson today was using the microscope. We looked at the parts and studied the names of each. You handled the microscope, found each of its parts, and then we reviewed the names using our diagram to check what we learned.

Seventh-Grade Science Teacher

We looked at and talked about rectangles today. What do you remember about rectangles?

Second-Grade Teacher

On your 3" × 5" card, write five terms from our class today that were important to you. Now, compare your terms with a partner, then hand in your cards before leaving for your next class. I will post my terms at the door for you to see as you leave.

Seventh-Grade Civics Teacher

Depending on the lesson taught, the time available, the size of the class, and your preferences, you can use a variety of closure strategies to accomplish the functions of review and summary. What is most difficult for many teachers is leaving enough time for closure. One of us uses reminders, written in big letters on lesson plans. Some teachers ask a student to signal them to indicate that there are five minutes left in the period. Some teachers use a timer to cue them to begin closure.

INSTRUCTIONAL OBJECTIVES

In the models presented earlier in the chapter, you may have noticed that objectives directed all other elements of the design. Objectives also affected beginnings and endings. As we defined them earlier, *instructional objectives* are descriptions of the intended outcomes of teaching:

1. Objectives may describe the *information* that you intend *for students to know or use.*
2. Objectives may describe the *skill* that you intend *for students to perform or demonstrate.*
3. Objectives may describe the *value* or *feeling* that you intend *for students to experience.*

Think of instructional objectives as a description of the learner following your instruction.

Criteria of Instructional Objectives

In order to accomplish what you intend by writing them, instructional objectives need to meet three criteria: describe the *outcomes* for the student, describe the *conditions for learning,* and state the degree or *level of mastery* you intend. The three elements of an instructional objective are displayed in Figure 3.7.

Instructional objectives also need to be specific and to be measurable or observable. Look at another example: "Students will list the 50 states of the United States with 80 percent accuracy." Your outcome is for students to be able to list the 50 states, and you can measure or observe whether they can do it. The degree or level of mastery is 80 percent accuracy. This is a specific objective, in contrast to "Students will learn the 50 states" or "Students will know the 50 states."

To guide your development of instructional objectives, we turn your attention to three frameworks of learner outcomes. These taxonomies classify the learning possibilities of your teaching.

Taxonomies of Learning Domains

Taxonomies are classification systems of the learning hierarchy. They progress from simple to complex. The first and most widely used taxonomy was developed for the *cognitive* domain by Bloom, Englehart, Furst, Hill, and Krathwohl (1956). Shortly

FIGURE 3.7 *Instructional Objective Criteria*

Objectives State:	**Examples (Informational Level):**
1. What will the student learn?	The names of the 50 states in the United States
2. Under what conditions?	By listing the 50 states
3. What degree of mastery?	80 percent of the states correctly listed
Completed Instructional Objective:	The student will list the 50 states of the United States with 80 percent accuracy.

"Hi, Dr. Brewster. Finished looking at my lesson plans yet?"

after the development, the *affective* domain was classified into a taxonomy by Krathwohl, Bloom, and Masia (1964). A taxonomy was also developed for the *psychomotor* domain (Harlow, 1972). We describe each domain and provide specific outcome vocabulary for you to use in writing objectives.

Cognitive Domain

The cognitive domain includes thinking outcomes that range from simple to complex:

1. *Knowledge,* the lowest level, asks your learners to remember previously learned material or to make a factual observation. When you want learners to tell when, how many, who, or where, they are using knowledge.
2. *Comprehension* asks your learners to grasp the meaning of information, to interpret ideas, and to predict using knowledge. Learners are asked to translate knowledge into their own words. When asked why, or to explain, or to summarize, they are using comprehension.
3. *Application* asks your learners to use previously learned knowledge in new and concrete situations, to use information, and to do something with knowledge.
4. *Analysis* requires your learners to break something into its constituent parts. They are asked to organize, to clarify, to conclude, or to make inferences. The process of analysis helps learners understand "big ideas" and the relationship of parts.

5. *Synthesis* requires your learners to put elements together. They are asked to create—that is, to form a whole or combination that is unique for the learner. Synthesis involves abstract relationships.
6. *Evaluation* requires a judgment. Your learners must give defensible opinions with criteria for their judgment. This level of functioning requires all the other cognitive levels—knowledge, comprehension, application, analysis, and synthesis—in order to be achieved (Houston, Clift, Freiberg, & Warner, 1988).

Notice in our descriptions of the levels of the cognitive domain and in the vocabulary in Figure 3.8 that levels of appropriate questions emerge along with levels of objectives. You will find them helpful as you plan your teaching and learning strategies and when you develop the assessment strategies described in Chapter Fourteen.

Affective Domain

This domain is also arranged in a hierarchy from a simple level to a complex level:

1. *Receiving* requires your learners simply to attend—to listen, to notice, to observe—in order to receive.
2. *Responding* asks your learners to discuss, argue, or agree/disagree in response to what is heard or observed.
3. *Valuing* requires your learners to consider what was received, to use it to make decisions about its importance, to regard it as priority, and to place a value on it.
4. *Organizing* requires your learners to place values in relationship with other values, to organize judgments and choices, and to be influenced by the value.
5. *Characterizing,* the highest level, requires that your learners' values become organized to the point of being internalized or become a part of the learners' lives.

There is serious controversy about the role of schools in teaching the affective domain, and yet curriculum about drugs and alcohol, sexuality, and value clarification are the responsibility of teachers in most districts. When writing objectives for such curriculum, the levels of the affective domain will guide your planning. You may intend for learners to listen to information (receive) and discuss the importance of avoiding drugs (respond). Or you may intend for learners to act upon the information (valuing) and avoid situations where drugs are present (organization). Or you may intend for learners to work actively against drugs and to influence others (characterization).

Regardless of your stand on current affective curriculum, we hope that you intend for students to achieve Mager's (1984) minimal affective objective—that they should like your subject matter no less than when they came to your class (Houston, Cliff, Freiberg, & Warner, 1988, pp. 162–163). Today's district goals often reflect the outcomes of "lifelong learners," "love for reading," "responsible citizens," and "humanitarian living," all of which require teaching and learning in the affective domain.

Writing objectives for this domain is often difficult because the outcomes are personal, not often observable or measurable. We recommend that you describe indicators, or behaviors, that may indicate that students *appreciate, value, care about, feel,* and so

FIGURE 3.8 *Cognitive Domain Levels and Learner Outcomes*

Knowledge	defines, repeats, lists, names, labels, asks, observes, memorizes, records, recalls, fills in, listens, identifies, matches, recites, selects, draws
Comprehension	restates, describes, explains, tells, identifies, discusses, recognizes, reviews, expresses, locates, reports, estimates, distinguishes, paraphrases, documents, defends, generalizes
Application	changes, computes, demonstrates, shows, operates, uses, solves, sequences, tests, classifies, translates, employs, constructs, dramatizes, illustrates, draws, interprets, manipulates, writes
Analysis	dissects, distinguishes, differentiates, calculates, tests, contrasts, debates, solves, surveys, appraises, experiments, diagrams, inventories, relates, maps, categorizes, subdivides, defends
Synthesis	composes, proposes, formulates, sets up, assembles, constructs, manages, invents, produces, hypothesizes, plans, designs, creates, organizes, prepares, speculates
Evaluation	compares, concludes, contracts, criticizes, justifies, supports, states, appraises, discriminates, summarizes, recommends, rates, decides, selects

on. An objective for appreciation of classical music may take the form of "Students will choose a classical record for listening during free time" or "Students will describe a selection of classical music." You have no certainty that students appreciate the music, but their behaviors indicate the possibility.

Psychomotor Domain

Many physical and movement activities are included in school curricula, but probably not enough from the standpoint of students. Again, you have a hierarchy of simple to complex abilities:

1. *Reflex movements* are actions that occur involuntarily in response to some stimulus, such as stretching, blinking, and posture adjustments.
2. *Basic fundamental movements* are those innate movement patterns formed from a combination of reflex movements, such as running, walking, jumping, pushing, and pulling.
3. *Perceptual abilities* require the translation of stimuli through the senses into appropriate movements, such as following verbal instructions, dodging a moving ball, maintaining balance, and jumping rope.

abilities combine basic movement and perceptual abilities into skilled nents, such as distance running, toe touching, basic ballet exercises, and ght lifting.

lled movements are more complex movements requiring a certain degree of ef-iciency, such as those used in dance, sports, music, and art.

. *Nondiscursive* (nonverbal) communication is the ability to communicate through body movement, such as gestures, choreographed dance, and pantomime.

For each curriculum area, there are psychomotor objectives to be met. In science, you may intend for your learners to "prepare slides of specimens" or "dissect a frog." In language arts, you may intend for your learners to "pantomime the feeling expressed by a main character" or "use calligraphy to display a haiku." In music, you may intend for your learners to "play a simple melody on the tone flute" or "clap six measures of 4/4 rhythm." In geography, you may intend for your learners to "construct a relief map" or "measure rainfall."

The unit design on weather, which we described earlier, was directed to cognitive, affective, and psychomotor objectives. Go back to those objectives and see if you can differentiate between the three domains. It is also possible to achieve such combinations in an individual lesson or class. Think back to the Snapshots of this chapter. When Ms. Rennie taught her class about fractions, her objective was for students "to talk about all the ways fractions are used." She was working on a cognitive objective at the knowledge level. At the same time, she wanted students to appreciate the usefulness of fractions, an affective objective at the responding and/or valuing level. When Mr. Malter taught his math lesson, he had several cognitive objectives. At the knowledge level, students were expected to know a formula and to describe the necessary information. At the application level, students were expected to use the formula and perform computations, and at the synthesis level, to create a problem of their own. Performing the computations required psychomotor skills of perceptual abilities. As you watched the lesson, you sensed that Mr. Malter intended for his students to feel enthusiastic about math and confident in their ability to perform the computations. Those are affective objectives.

Another Look at Objectives

The process of developing and writing objectives is a reflective one. Earlier in this chapter, we mentioned that teachers currently have more autonomy in planning and can better accommodate their own vision of education. Pratt (1994) suggested that we design objectives that "reflect those aspects of human experience that we value" (p. 78). His classification of objectives reflects the importance of "knowing, thinking, acting, feeling, growing, experiencing, and being." Pratt suggested a typology of objectives (p. 79) that includes:

1. Knowledge objectives
2. Skill objectives
3. Somatic objectives
4. Attitude objectives

5. Process objectives
6. Experience objectives

The first two are not unlike what we described for the cognitive and psychomotor domain, and Pratt's attitude objectives are like those of the affective domain. Pratt's unique objectives need explanation. *Somatic* objectives are those that involve a "bodily, physiological, or cellular change," such as developing a positive disposition or decreasing your levels of stress. Next, *process* objectives describe the experiences in which you intend students to be engaged. Many of our current math approaches, whole-language philosophy, and process-oriented science curricula promote this kind of objective. A process objective may sound like "Students will use a variety of media to communicate a single idea" or "Students will observe the characteristics of a leaf using all senses." *Experience* objectives are similar to process objectives, as they also describe an experience, but in Pratt's words, they are "intrinsically valuable, meaningful, significant, memorable experiences" (p. 79). They are the kinds of experiences we all remember from our school days. You probably remember some. At the City and Country School in New York City, students manage and operate the school store, the printing office, and the mail system. The experiences shared by these students are the kinds that Pratt is describing as valuable and meaningful.

You can see that you have alternatives for the form of your objectives. Regardless of form, objectives represent important decisions in your planning and design process. Remember to consider your learners, your content, your context, and yourself as you develop objectives for your teaching.

INSTRUCTIONAL DESIGN AND INCLUSION

An important point must be made as we begin this discussion. In an inclusive classroom, there is no need to change the content of the curriculum for learners with varied special needs (Thornton & Bley, 1994). Instead, it is critical for you to learn as much as possible about each learner and how he or she learns so that you can design the teaching and learning experiences (not content) to match strengths, needs, and limits of each learner (Van de Walle, 1998). Design will be the most critical process for your effectiveness in an inclusive classroom.

Special education teachers can help you in your design work. Following are some guidelines that will actually promote learning for all children and that can become important elements in your lesson designs. Consider these suggestions:

1. Design learning activities that actively involve students.
2. For all learning tasks, consider subtasks within larger projects or assignments.
3. Have students verbalize often—in written, oral, graphic, or other forms—about their work or their learning.
4. Allow plenty of time for practice and application.
5. Build self-monitoring and self-assessment habits and skills (see Chapter Four).
6. Provide directions in varied forms (verbal, written, taped, etc.).

Incorporating these suggestions into your lesson design will enhance your ability to teach students with diverse needs and to create an inclusive setting.

Our final insight for your inclusive instructional design process comes from the experiences of excellent and experienced teachers. Once their teaching plans have been written, those teachers use the plans to record both reminders and observations. Robin's weekly plan (Figure 3.6) has reminders about reading with individual children and is often used to note individual children's needs for more practice or confidence and an observation of skill or expertise. Human frailty, especially that of memory, may keep people from remembering all the individual needs and strengths that exist in the reality of a fast-paced day in the classroom. Your lesson design is a strong support for the kind of supportive teaching you will plan for inclusion.

Elementary Research Vignette

INTRODUCTION

From every direction, teachers are being urged to "work together as colleagues within and across disciplines and grade levels" (National Research Council, 1998). Planning is the area in which most teachers tend to collaborate for idea sharing, for efficiency, and as preparation for team teaching. A group of educators in a Colorado school district questioned whether collaborative planning among teachers had an impact on student learning. Their study was designed to respond to their question and to check the influence of different curriculum models (Corbin, 1995).

STUDY PROCEDURES

Four elementary schools, 10 third-grade teachers, and their 168 students participated in a quasi-experimental study of the impact of teachers' collaborative planning. The teachers and their classes were divided into four groups:

Group 1	Collaborative planning with a traditional basal curriculum
Group 2	Collaborative planning with a problem-solving, investigative curriculum
Group 3	Individual planning with a traditional basal curriculum
Group 4	Individual planning with a problem-solving, investigative curriculum

The students were given standardized math assessments and some open-ended math questions and tasks in pre- and postassessment forms.

STUDY RESULTS

Those students whose teachers planned collaboratively made higher gains on the tests than those students whose teachers planned individually. Student gains were also higher for those teachers who used the problem-solving, investigative curriculum.

DISCUSSION AND IMPLICATIONS FOR PRACTICE

Those teachers who engaged in collaborative planning reported that they spent approximately 30 minutes per week with their peers to develop and discuss lessons. The study demonstrates that the teachers' 30-minute investment significantly improved student achievement. These findings have an important message for school districts in terms of supporting teachers' collaborative planning with time and resources and for individual teachers to seek colleagues for collaborative planning.

EFFICIENCY IN DESIGN

Figure 3.9 displays a lesson planning format that is concise in its organization. The narrative provided by a veteran teacher for each of the seven elements of this lesson planning format, from *Focus* to *Closure,* provides insights into the rationale and purpose for including specific instructional events into your lesson. Figure 3.9 may be used as a guide for planning by inserting your own descriptors into the boxes next to each instructional element.

FIGURE 3.9 *Lesson Planning Format*

Teacher____________________ Grade ____________________

Date ____________________ Subject ____________________

	Mon. Tue. Wed. Thur. Fri.
Focus	This is my "gotcha" part of the lesson. I want the students to begin thinking about social studies as they walk in the door.
Objective	I ask myself what new ideas, concepts, knowledge, or skills will my students learn.
Explanation	I provide information, demonstrate, and give examples. I provide a link between prior knowledge and the objective for today.
Check for Understanding	This is where I use questioning, discussion, mini-chalkboards, yes/no cards, and simulations to check for understanding.
Guided Practice	A problem is placed on the board and we work it together. I check to see if each student knows the solution.
Individual Practice	I give several other problems for the students to work on individually. Some of the problems the students work on in groups.
Closure	I use several types of closure. The students will tell me one idea/skill they learned today. The students or I will summarize the lesson.

Considerations for efficiency in your design are a reality. As you gain experience, you will develop strategies for streamlining the design process. In the weekly design sample from an English teacher (Figure 3.5), you saw a coding system used for teaching and learning activities. Using codes is a way to be efficient about your planning. We suggest that you consider codes for your materials and equipment, assignments, directions, and groups of students. In another chapter, we suggest that you use a color coding scheme to check your plans for variety (easy–challenging work; whole group–individual activities; quiet–noisy).

Including a margin space along the side of your plans as you have seen in some of the formats in this chapter promotes efficiency when you use the space for reminders, "to-do" lists, evaluative comments for future planning, and individualized strategies for specific learners.

Another efficient strategy used by teachers is the development of a card file of teaching/learning activities, often with the activity coded by subject or curriculum area. Then, on the daily or weekly format, a simple code, such as SC-Air-Rev, might appear to indicate a *Science* activity on *Air,* which is appropriate for *Review.* Initially, developing the file takes time, but once you have developed a repertoire of strategies, activities, and resources, you can plan for exciting and varied teaching in an efficient manner. The card file also encourages you to gather ideas from your colleagues in an efficient and organized way.

So, the answer to the question, Which is the best format for designing a teaching plan? is one that changes with your experiences, your philosophy, your needs, and your learning. The important idea here is to be aware of these influences and to make your design format work for you. In the next section on collaborative planning, you will see that working with others may also influence your design or cause you to change your planning process.

COLLABORATIVE PLANNING AND DESIGNS

With the increased autonomy you have in planning, you may decide, as many teachers have, that you prefer to plan with a group of your teacher colleagues. You may also decide that planning with your students fits your beliefs about teaching and learning. Or you may do both.

Collaboration with Teacher Colleagues

Teachers at the Westwood Public Schools in Westwood, Massachusetts, have been collaboratively planning and designing their instruction and have struggled with some difficult issues. The insights learned from their work may help you as you plan with your colleagues.

The Westwood teachers, and many others like them, have discovered that there are some decisions that are really "collective decisions" and some that are "individual decisions" when planning curriculum (Monson & Monson, 1993). They found that decisions about the central purpose and the major learning outcomes of their school district are collective decisions—decisions best made by teacher committees. The same is true for some decisions about assessment and reporting systems. Individual decisions include those of selecting teaching and learning strategies, themes and concepts, materials, levels of difficulty, and appropriate learning contexts.

Collaborative planning involves extensive discussion and reflection. You may hear ideas that conflict with your beliefs, or you may be forced to rethink your teaching approaches. There is the potential to gain a wealth of new ideas from the shared design process. You may also learn that *you* have expertise or unique approaches as others respond to and appreciate your ideas. Collaborative planning and design takes time but it has extensive benefits. For the many teachers who have felt isolated in the teaching profession, collaboration provides much satisfaction and renewal. As you learned in the Research Vignette, collaborative planning also has the potential to enhance student learning outcomes. We will talk about collaboration again in Chapter Four when we describe team teaching.

Collaboration with Students

Lin Frederick, a first-grade teacher, and her colleague, J. Ron Nelson, a professor at Eastern Washington University, asked the question, "Can children design curriculum?" (Nelson & Frederick, 1994). Their exciting experience not only gives a positive response to the question but it also provides guidance for your collaboration with students in the design process. Lin Frederick regularly designed units for two-week periods with her class, with the design process for one unit overlapping the study of the preceding one. The collaborative planning proceeded through three interrelated steps:

> 1. *Selecting the target theme (the focus for developing the curriculum);*
> 2. *Establishing guiding questions to serve as the scope and sequence of the thematic unit;*
> 3. *Designing the classroom instructional activities. (p. 71)*

To achieve step 1, Lin introduces potential themes that promote district objectives and build on previous learning experiences. The themes must, of course, be interesting to first-graders. From there, Lin introduces the themes to her students and provides related materials for them to explore. For about a week, the class engages in daily discussions of the potential themes. Those discussions reveal information to Lin—information about interest levels of both the group and individuals, and background knowledge of both the group and individuals.

In addition, the discussions begin to focus the unit planning and lead to the next step—that of developing the study questions. As children pose questions of interest, they participate in decisions about the disciplinary context of their own questions. To help you understand this process, listen to Lin and her students.

SNAPSHOT: Elementary Classroom

RUSSELL: I want to know how big whales are.

LIN: That's a great question. Do you mean how long they are or how much they weigh?

RUSSELL: Both.

LIN: (Writes the question under the math question.) I'm thinking that because math involves thinking about numbers, this question should go under the math section.

MARY: We should compare the different sizes of the whales. It could go under the math section because it's a number question, too.

BOB: I want to find out how whales breathe in the water.

LIN: Where do you think we should put that question?

BOB: I think it should go under the science section because how animals breathe and stuff is a natural thing. (Nelson & Frederick, 1994, p. 73)

Of course, Lin and her class have had practice with this step, so the children are quite skilled at posing questions and categorizing them. What is impressive is the learning that is occurring during the planning process. As the class engaged in repeated planning and design sessions, they were also able to classify their questions along the lines of Bloom's Taxonomy (page 78). (Remember that these are first-graders!)

The final step, that of designing activities, usually takes two sessions, according to Lin. Students first brainstorm possible sources of information, and in the second session, they brainstorm possible activities. From each list, Lin and her students make decisions about appropriate materials and appropriate activities with class discussions that encourage the students to think about their own learning styles and those of their peers. To promote this kind of reflection, Lin uses statements such as, "I learn ____________ by ____________" (Nelson & Frederick, 1994, p. 74). Again, think of the learning that is occurring during this step.

Nelson and Frederick's (1994) description of first-graders' collaborative planning and design of units assures us that even very young children are able to participate productively in this process. In addition to a very relevant unit design, such collaboration achieves powerful learning outcomes for teachers and students. Teachers learn about individual interests, background knowledge, experiences, and learning preferences of their students. Students learn about their own learning preferences and those of their peers, and about planning, teaching, and learning. When you consider the multiple outcomes of the time spent in this collaborative planning and design process, you may begin to think of this as an efficient approach. As you will see in the next chapter, time is an elusive commodity in the teaching profession, so you will need efficient approaches.

As you continue your journey through this text, many characteristics of effective teaching will be discovered. From a research standpoint, Harris (1998) reviewed the relevant literature and determined some key areas of effective teaching, three of which are effective teaching behavior, effective teaching skills, and effective teaching repertoire. Table 3.1 illustrates the three areas with added examples. Mastery will take time and patience, but the dividends will be great.

TABLE 3.1 *Effective Teaching: Behavior, Skills, and Repertoire*

Effective Teaching Behavior	Effective Teaching Skills	Effective Teaching Repertiore
States clear instructional goals Ex: Verbalizes goals daily and writes them on board	***Organizational: Sorts and uses material effectively*** Ex: Uses color-coded file folders for each class, picture seating chart, in and out boxes, and other management systems	***Focuses on learner, content, and context in making individual decisions*** Ex: Considers individual learner differences, interest and difficulty level of material, and how classroom climate can affect learning
Knows content well and how to teach it Ex: Is well educated in specific field and uses varied instructional methods	***Analytical: Breaks down complex information*** Ex: Giving/Asking examples along the way	***Develops expertise in organizational strategies, instructional strategies, and assessment strategies*** Ex: See Chapter 1, Figure 1.1
Communicates clear expectations Ex: Develops reasonable expectations with students	***Synthesizes: Builds ideas into arguments*** Ex: Models how to build persuasive speaking and writing	***Recognizes the need for instructional repertoire*** Ex: Uses both student- and teacher-centered instructional initiatives
Teaches metacognitive skills and provides opportunities to use them Ex: Teaches reflection techniques and how to use daily journals and other reflective activities	***Presentational: Clarifies complex information without harming its integrity*** Ex: Explains challenging information using various methods, including webs and other visual organizers	***Moves along the instructional continuum from teacher centered to student centered*** Ex: See Chapter 7, Figure 7.1
Addresses higher- and lower-level cognitive thinking skills Ex: Creates activities, questions, and assessments that use all levels of Bloom's Taxonomy	***Assessing: Judges work so appropriate feedback occurs*** Ex: Provides elaborate comments on student work and assesses using multiple formats such as rubrics, observation, portfolios, aside from tests and quizzes	
Monitors student understanding and gives feedback Ex: Uses questioning skills to assess learning in the classroom and provides relevant feedback when asked	***Managerial: Coordinates dynamics of individuals, groups, and classes*** Ex: Provides opportunities to learn cooperatively; creates person-centered learning environments where students are shareholders	
Integrates with other subject areas Ex: Uses examples from English, science, math, social science, and other disciplines	***Evaluate: Improves teaching continually*** Ex: Attends college classes, workshops, and completes self-assessments	
Accepts responsibility for student outcomes Ex: Realizes one method may not lead to success and holds self responsible to help students achieve by meeting student learning needs		

SUMMARY

The process of designing instruction is a comprehensive one. It begins as you consider your content, context, and learner for information that helps you make planning decisions. From there, look to yourself to determine how much detail and what kind of design will help you feel comfortable and confident as you face teaching. You will probably include the basic elements of any instructional design: goals, objectives, teaching/learning activities, materials, feedback, and assessment.

Four design models are available to guide your efforts: the lesson cycle model, the instructional events model, the instructional functions model, and the learning cycle model. Each offers variations of the basic design elements in a format for a single lesson. There are also designs for longer-term teaching: unit designs as well as daily and weekly designs. You will probably use all four to design instruction.

No matter which design you use, it will be important to begin and end your teaching effectively. Lesson beginnings need to capture student interest, promote a mental readiness, and describe the direction that the lesson will take. You have strategies available to do that: set inductions, advanced organizers, and sponges. As for lesson endings, it is important to bring closure—review and summarize—to what has been taught.

No matter which design you use, it is also important to write objectives for your teaching. They direct all the other elements of instructional design. The taxonomies of the three learning domains—cognitive, affective, and psychomotor—provide levels of complexity in each domain to guide your objective writing. You will want to represent the three domains in your teaching so that you attend to the *whole* learner.

Finally, we encourage you to personalize whatever design format you use to meet your needs and priorities, to incorporate your beliefs, and to be efficient and appropriate for your learners. You might begin with a model, and as you gain experience, personalize it. With the increased autonomy that teachers have in their planning and design processes, many have engaged in productive and satisfying collaborative planning with their colleagues. We also encourage you to plan collaboratively with your students. Teachers have found that collaborative planning and design with students leads to more relevant and meaningful units of teaching. Finally, we urge you to be sure that your planning and designs accomplish what teachers have described:

> *"to provide a feeling of confidence and preparedness,"*
> *"to better meet the needs of students,"*
> *"to organize materials, time, and activity flow,"*
> *"for comfort and knowledge of subject matter,"*
> *"to provide a framework for instruction and evaluation" (McCutcheon, 1980)*

REFERENCES

Ausubel, D. P. (1968). *Educational psychology: A cognitive view.* New York: Holt, Rinehart and Winston.

Bloom, B., Englehart, M., Furst, E., Hill, W., & Krathwohl, D. (1956). *Taxonomy of educational objectives: The classification of educational goals Handbook I, Cognitive domain.* New York: McKay.

Corbin, G. L. (1995). Collaboration really works. *Teaching Children Mathematics,* 2(3), 190–191.

Gagne, R. M., Briggs, L. J., & Wagner, W. W. (1988). *Principles of instruction* (3rd ed.). New York: Holt, Rinehart and Winston.

Gee, J. B. (1991). *New perspectives on teaching in the affective domain.* Paper presented at the Annual Meeting of the Mid-South Educational Research Association, Lexington, KY. (ERIC Document Reproduction Service No. 341 659).

Grossen, B., & Lee, C. (1994). Instructional design considerations for science instruction to accommodate diverse learners. *The Oregon Conference Monograph, 6,* 31–44.

Harlow, A. (1972). *Taxonomy of the psychomotor domain.* New York: McKay.

Harris, A. (1998). Effective teaching: A review of the literature. *School Leadership & Management, 2*(18), 169–183.

Haycock, K. (1998). Good teaching matters: How well-qualified teachers can close the gap. *Thinking K–16, 3*(2), 1–14.

Houston, W. R., Clift, R., Freiberg, H. J., & Warner, A. R. (1988). *Touch the future: Teach.* St. Paul: West.

Hudgins, J. M., & Cone, W. H. (1992). Principals should stress effective teaching elements in classroom instruction. *NASSP Bulletin,* 13–18.

Hunter, M. (1976). *Improved instruction.* El Segundo, CA: TIP Publications.

Hunter, M. (1985). *Mastery teaching: Increasing instructional effectiveness in secondary school, college and universities.* El Segundo, CA: TIP Publications.

Krathwohl, D., Bloom, B., & Masia, B. (1964). *Taxonomy of educational objectives: The classification of educational goals, Handbook II, Affective domain.* New York: McKay.

Mager, R. F. (1984). *Preparing instructional objectives* (rev. ed.). Belmont, CA: Fearon.

McCutcheon, G. (1980). How do elementary school teachers plan? The nature of planning and influences on it. *Elementary School Journal, 81,* 4–23.

Monson, M. P., & Monson, R. J. (1993). Who creates curriculum? New roles for teachers. *Educational Leadership, 51*(2), 19–21.

Nagel, N. G. (1996). *Learning through real-world problem solving: The power of integrative teaching.* Thousand Oaks, CA: Corwin Press.

National Research Council. (1998). *A sampler of National Science Education Standards.* Columbus, OH: Merrill.

Nelson, J. R., & Frederick, L. (1994). Can children design curriculum? *Educational Leadership, 51*(5), 71–74.

Pratt, D. (1994). *Curriculum planning.* Fort Worth, TX: Harcourt Brace College Publishers.

Rosenshine, B. (1995). Advances in research on instruction. *Journal of Educational Research, 88*(2), 262+.

Rosenshine, B., & Stevens, R. (1986). Teaching functions. In M. Wittrock (Ed.), *Handbook of research on teaching* (3rd ed.). New York: Macmillan.

Schuck, R. F. (1985). An empirical analysis of the power of set induction and systematic questioning as instructional strategies. *Journal of Teacher Education, 36*(2), 38–43.

Thornton, C., & Bley, N. (1994). *Windows of opportunity: Mathematics for students with special needs.* Reston, VA: National Council of Teachers of Mathematics.

Tolman, M., & Hardy G. (1999). *Discovering elementary science* (2nd ed.). Boston: Allyn and Bacon.

Van de Walle, J. A. (1998). *Elementary and middle school mathematics: Teaching developmentally.* New York: Longman.

SAMPLES AND EXAMPLES

This Samples and Examples section includes the following:

- Examples of Sponges (or beginning activities) that may be used at the primary, elementary, and secondary levels.
- Internet addresses and other sources of lesson design ideas to expand your design repertoire.

EXAMPLES OF SPONGES

Primary-Grade Sponges

1. Tell one playground rule.
2. Tell the names of students in our class that begin with the letter ________.
3. Draw something that is only drawn with circles.
4. Draw something or list things of the color written on the board.
5. List things you can touch or smell, big things, small things, and so on.
6. List the colors of the clothes you are wearing.
7. Write the words listed on the board in alphabetical order.
8. Write a list of words that rhyme with the word on the board.
9. Draw or write names of objects in the room that are in the shape of a triangle, square, circle, or that begin with the letter ________.
10. List or draw different fruits, vegetables, meals, and so on.

Upper-Elementary Sponges

1. Make up names for three rock groups.
2. Choose a number. Write it on a piece of paper. Make a face out of it.
3. List as many kinds of flowers as you can.
4. List as many teachers in this school as you can.
5. List all the things in your living room at home.
6. List as many kinds of ice cream as you can.
7. Write what you would do if you saw an elephant in your backyard.
8. Name as many balls as you can that are used in sports games.
9. Pretend that you have five children. Make up their names.
10. List as many things as you can that are made of cloth.
11. Scramble five spelling words, trade with someone, and unscramble them.
12. Write one kind of food for each letter of the alphabet.

Secondary Sponges

1. How many countries and their capitals can you list?
2. List five parts of the body above the neck that have three letters.
3. List one proper noun for each letter of the alphabet.
4. How many parts of an automobile can you list?
5. Write as many homonyms as you can.
6. List foods that have sugar in them.
7. Which TV series can you list that have high-school-aged characters as regulars?
8. List the different sections of the newspaper.
9. List as many islands as you can.
10. List all the countries that you know with *e* in the name.

Note: Try to select or make up sponges that relate to the content of the lesson that is to follow.

Source: Effective Use of Time Program by J. Stallings, 1986. Houston: University of Houston. Used by permission.

INTERNET ADDRESSES AND OTHER SOURCES OF LESSON DESIGN

Book

Lyons, P. (1992). *Thirty-five lesson formats: A source book of instructional alternatives.* Englewood Cliffs, NJ: Educational Technology Publications.

Internet Addresses

Teams Distance Learning Site <teams.lacoe.edu> From the Los Angeles Office of Education, this is a list of links to sites with lesson plans, ideas, and online projects.

Houghton Mifflin Education Place <www.hmco.com/school> Although it is commercial, this is a great resource for lesson plans organized by theme or curricular area.

ERIC Lesson Plans <gopher://ericir.syr.edu/11/lesson> For K–12 teachers, myriad curriculum areas are covered.

TeachNet <www.teachnet.com> Lesson plans and discussion forums are given; includes ads.

Busy Teachers' Web Site <www.ceismc.gatech.edu/BusyT/TOC.html> Sites for lesson plans, activities, and resources are listed.

Collaborative Lesson Archive <faldo.atmos.uiuc.edu/TUA_Home.html> This is a collection of lesson plans from far and wide.

The Landmark Project <www.landmark-project.com/ca/> This is a monthly bibliography of educational literature from a large selection of journals on more than 200 topics.

Scholastic Network <scholastic.com/network> This paid service provides an array of student projects and teacher resources, all geared to your curriculum.

CHAPTER

4

THE EFFECTIVE USE OF TIME

Doing More with Less

Chapter Outcomes

At the conclusion of this chapter you will be able to:

1. *Decide how to use time effectively for teaching and learning.*
2. *Use time effectively to accommodate district, school, and classroom contexts, content, and the learners.*
3. *Identify and reduce time losses and wasters.*
4. *Describe and use strategies for effective use of time.*

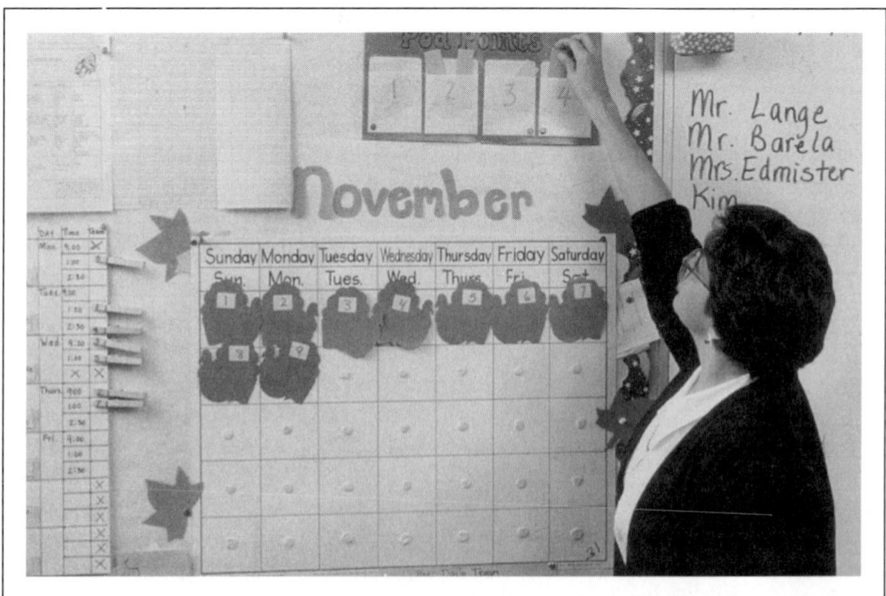

Key Terms and Concepts

Time
Model of School Learning
Context
Content
Learner Differences
Time and Inclusive Classroom
Integrated Curriculum
Teacher-Directed Learning
Student-Directed Learning
Time Savers
Time Losers
Time Wasters
Clarity
Handling Paperwork
Delegating

INTRODUCTION

We recently worked with a group of teachers as they returned to school after summer break. We posed a question: If you could be the best teacher ever, or the teacher you pictured when you decided to teach, what would you need? Of the 28 teachers, 25 said *time.* They described a range of wishes—more time for planning, more time for individual students, more time for teaching. Not a surprising response!

Better use of time in schools has been an ongoing theme of educational reform. As Walberg pointed out some time ago, there's good reason for focusing our efforts on better use of time. "The association of learning with time is among the most consistent that education research reveals" (1988, p. 84). From studies about time (Karweit, 1988), we know that the amount of time spent on teaching and learning is connected to the amount of achievement.

THINKING ABOUT TIME FOR TEACHING AND LEARNING

Today's schools can accurately be described as "restructured or restructuring in terms of reorganization of the school day and substantial changes to better meet student learning needs and improve learning outcomes" (Peterson, McCarthy, & Elmore, 1996, p. 120). With such reform comes the need for even greater amounts of time for teachers to study, plan, implement, and reflect on the changes in their teaching. Adelman and Walking-Eagle (1997) reported from their case studies of schools that time-related effects of educational reform are pervasive: "Time-related innovations in schools reverberate through many aspects of school life, including the professional lives—and sometimes personal lives—of the teachers who work in them" (p. 93).

Unfortunately, we, like so many educators with concerns about time demands on teachers, have no easy answers. We begin this chapter with the realities of time for all that is involved in teaching, not to discourage you, but to urge your awareness. As you prepare to teach, notice how you use your time, check your organizational strategies, and develop clarity about your priorities. In this chapter, we will mentor your development and suggest ways to make better use of the time you will have.

TEACHER TALK

If I don't lock myself in the art office—isolate myself—everyone stops by—students, other teachers—and then I don't get anything done. I want to talk with people, but I don't have enough time to do everything.

Secondary Art Teacher

Model of School Learning

As you think about time for teaching and learning in your classroom, both theory and research offer a framework for your thoughts. Carroll (1985) described a theoretical model for school learning with three factors to consider when you make decisions about time in your classroom.

First, keep in mind *student aptitude*—"the amount of time that a student would need to learn something" (pp. 31–32). Some students catch on in the first few minutes of explanation, and others struggle for days before understanding the same idea. These aptitude differences are important considerations for your teaching schedule.

The second factor is *perseverance*—the amount of time that a student is willing to continue or persist. Some students give up easily or quit after one or two tries, and others will persist for a long time. These perseverance differences are important considerations for your teaching schedule.

The third factor is *opportunity to learn*—the amount of time available to learn. One teacher may provide generous amounts of time for a subject, and another teacher may provide a minimum amount of time for the same subject. Some teachers spend much more time teaching one topic or subject than they spend on another. When teachers record how they spend their day or an individual class or period, they learn about differences in their provision of opportunity to learn. We encourage such recording to make decisions about time for teaching.

When researchers examined the difference between effective and ineffective teachers in the Beginning Teacher Evaluation Study (Fisher et al., 1978), they identified the concept of *Academic Learning Time* (ALT). Three components of ALT will be useful for your thinking about time for teaching and learning.

The first component is *allocated time*—the period of time you allocate or plan for teaching a specific content area. If you schedule a geography lesson from 2:15 to 3:00 P.M., your allocated time is 45 minutes. That time period is affected by your efficiency and preparation. The time you take to find materials, to check on what you are doing, or to pause with, "Now before we begin, are there any questions?" reduces the amount of time you actually have for instruction.

The second component is *student engagement rate*—the amount of time students are engaged in learning. When your students are paying attention, working on tasks, discussing curriculum topics, thinking about ideas, and practicing skills, they are engaged. When they are daydreaming, talking socially, or abusing materials, they are not engaged.

The third component is *student success rate*—the rate at which your students perform tasks correctly, answer questions accurately, and solve problems successfully.

When curriculum and activities are too difficult for students, the rate is low. When curriculum and activities are too easy for students, work becomes boring and repetitive, and the success rate is again low.

When we analyze both theory and research on time, we see the necessity of considering context, content, and learners as we make decisions about how to use our time.

Context

Time for teaching and learning is influenced by society's expanse as well as the confines of a school district. In your classroom context, you may have time wasters and regularly occurring losses (e.g., special programs, announcements, and taking lunch count), as well as productive activity. We will look at each level of context to direct your thinking about time for teaching and learning.

Societal Demands

As society becomes more complex, demands on your teaching expand, but the amount of time available stays the same. You will find yourself making frequent decisions about *what* to teach on the basis of efficiency.

Even if you briefly examine the curriculum standards described in Chapter One, you will see that "there is insufficient time to fully *cover* the curriculum" for all essential disciplines. The time pressures have potential for "hurried curriculum" (Bredekamp & Rosegrant, 1995, p. 167). Many teachers and curriculum developers acknowledge that it is impossible to teach everything without "watering down" content or simplifying ideas to the extent that meaningfulness is lost. Those same teachers have been successful when they find and make connections between curriculum areas—and integrate the curriculum. *Integrated curriculum* (see unit example in Chapter Three) can be defined as the use of an organizing topic or concept within the students' range of experience that promotes engagement in learning activities that draw on several subject-matter disciplines (Bredekamp & Rosegrant, 1995, p. 168). In many ways, integrated curriculum reflects the interconnectedness and complexity of society while responding to the pressures of society's rapidly growing information base and sophisticated demands for new skills and understandings.

The unit sample in Chapter Three provides examples of integration for large-scale planning, but teachers also find ways to integrate on a day-to-day basis. A secondary English teacher designs a writing assignment in which partners critique and provide feedback for each other's work, thus integrating cooperation with writing skills. A third-grade teacher integrates health curriculum with social studies content in a lesson on homeless people. Both teachers increase the scope of learning with their integration and make better use of their time. In addition, their content is more relevant to the society of their learners.

School District Demands

As you make decisions about time, you will feel the effect of school district demands in the form of priorities, expectations, and schedules. There will be variation from district to district, depending on size, philosophy, goals, funding, and administrative structure.

As you will learn from the Research Vignette on page 100, school districts make a number of organizational decisions that support or detract from your efficiency in producing student outcomes.

To become aware of district demands, begin by reading the priorities described in curriculum guides, often in the form of goals and objectives, textbook pages, and suggested schedules. You will also need to read the expectations of your district as you examine the forms of evaluation used to measure student learning. District schedules must also be reviewed for information on holidays, transportation, in-service days, special programs or events, and early dismissals.

What can you do? There aren't simple responses to the widespread demands on your time, but be clear about the priorities of your district so that your efforts are directed accordingly. The good news is that districts also make provisions to help with the demands on your time.

School District Provisions

Districts are aware of and have responded to the time shortages with variations in instructional and scheduling arrangements. *Team teaching,* or *teacher teams,* is an example of an instructional arrangement. With the arrangement, team members divide curricular responsibilities and make use of an individual teacher's interests and expertise. Districts often contribute to this arrangement with time for planning, resources, and reimbursements for related responsibilities. Some team teaching efforts have resulted in achievement gains, more supportive learning environments, and the development of professional communities.

Merenbloom (1996) has reminded educators that the teaming process must be organized as the best means to match curriculum with the needs and abilities of learners. The team arrangements mostly found in middle or high schools include the following:

1. *Interdisciplinary teams* consist of a group of four or five teachers, each responsible for his or her own subject area and group of students, who plan and integrate their curriculum areas.
2. *Disciplinary or single-subject teams* consist of two or more teachers of any subject area who plan and teach together and are able to group students from their combined classes for instruction.

Team teaching requires effective communication and cooperative interactions among team members. The Key Concerns in Team Teaching Rating Scale (found in the Samples and Examples section at the end of this chapter) has been designed to help teachers begin working together in teams that are successful, efficient, and highly supportive of student learning.

Some examples of scheduling arrangements are modular scheduling, block of time scheduling, and variations of the year-round school. *Modular scheduling* offers an alternative to the traditional scheduling format of secondary schools. Modules are short, 20 to 25 minutes each, and teachers have flexibility in using them. For example, on Tuesday, the French teacher meets with students for only one module of lecture presentation, but on Wednesday and Friday, he has three modules in which to conduct conversations, play vocabulary games, continue long-term projects, and read literature.

Another scheduling arrangement is the *block of time schedule.* In it, a group of teachers is assigned to a group of students. They share a common planning period and have flexibility for team teaching.

Year-round school has been tried with variations, such as when students and teachers take a break and how to segment the components (quarters, fifths, etc.). The plan makes year-round use of school facilities and accommodates varied family schedules.

What is noteworthy is that on the national level and on a district level there is awareness and concern about the scarcity of time. Many districts are developing arrangements and making provisions to support your teaching time.

Classroom Demands

Within the classroom are numerous demands on your time. We call some of them time losses and some of them time wasters.

Time losses are situations that are out of your control, such as fire drills, assembly programs, school cancellations (weather), health checks, student illness or accident in class, recesses, lunch, and announcements on the intercom. Our best advice for these losses is to anticipate them and plan accordingly. If you know that an assembly is planned, try to connect your curriculum to the program. Give students specific directions about what to do after the assembly when they return to the classroom. Have a plan of action, well understood by students, for any absences. For example, when a student is absent, an absence packet containing handouts and assignments is placed on his or her desk. Listen to the Teacher Talk that follows for more help with this time loss.

TEACHER TALK

I have a box of carbon paper and students use it for note taking when a "partner" is absent. Each student has a folder for notes, assignments, and handouts. If a "partner" is absent, the folder is used to collect the day's work. I used to hate spending time on the previous day's information.

Eighth-Grade Middle-School Teacher

Time wasters are those situations over which you have some control, such as calling roll, students socializing during a lesson, teaching unprepared lessons, beginning a lesson when students aren't ready, helping students after an absence, looking for lost materials, and dealing with late students and equipment failures. Rather than allowing these to become routine, you can minimize or eliminate them. The teacher in the Snapshot has developed some efficient routines to reduce his time wasters.

SNAPSHOT: Elementary Classroom

When children arrive in Bob Tourtillott's mixed-age classroom (kindergarten, first, and second grades), they stop first at one of the computers and record their own attendance and lunch order. At 9:00 A.M., one of the students goes to the computer and prints up the day's information and takes it to the office.

Later in the morning, when students finish their journal writing, they break into two groups to share their writing. A child is in charge of each group, and Bob and a parent volunteer are present in the groups. The routine is well established. Each child has a turn to read his or her writing, and two children may pose questions about the work. After the questions have been answered, the "reader" selects the next person to read his or her journal. The usual amount of time required for a class of 26 children to read journal entries and respond to questions is reduced by half.

Research Vignette

INTRODUCTION

John Alspaugh (1998) and others have studied the possibilities of achievement loss for students when they make the transition from middle school to high school. With the time concerns of educators escalating, the issue of achievement loss is an important one for investigation. Alspaugh proposed an exploration of the nature of achievement loss with school-to-school transitions.

STUDY PROCEDURES

Alspaugh studied three groups of 16 school districts for a total sample of 48 districts. The first group had a K–8, 9–12 organization. The second group contained districts with one elementary school, one middle school, and one high school, with a linear transition arrangement. The third group had districts with two or three elementary schools, one middle school, and one high school, with a transition from multiple elementary schools into a single middle school. The study used standardized test scores from annual assessments of students' achievement in reading, math, science, and social studies.

STUDY RESULTS

A statistically significant achievement loss was found for students making the transition from elementary school to middle school at sixth grade. The loss was larger when students from multiple elementary schools merged into one middle school. A significant achievement loss was also found for students making the transition from middle schools and K–8 schools to high school at ninth grade, but the loss was larger for those leaving a middle school. Additional data showed that high school dropout rates were higher for districts with grades 6–8 middle schools than for districts with K–8 elementary schools.

The author of this study described the changes encountered by students with the transition from elementary to middle schools. They included different goals, different student/teacher relationships, and different grouping configurations—all of which have potential for declines in student self-perception and self-esteem regardless of age, grade, or ability level.

DISCUSSION AND IMPLICATIONS FOR PRACTICE

The average teacher has little power over schoolwide organization and related decisions, such as whether to have a K–8 school or a K–5/middle school combination. Teachers can, however, learn more about the school to which their students go or the school from which their students come, and use their knowledge to ease the transition process. Alspaugh's data offer strong encouragement for across-district conversations and collaborations among teachers from all levels.

As you prepare to teach, consider learning about elementary schools if you are planning to be a middle or high school teacher. Similarly, if you are planning to teach elementary grades, consider visiting some middle and high schools.

A final suggestion for handling the classroom demands is to maintain *productive activity.* You can hear and feel productive activity when you enter some classrooms—it has a sound or a buzz. There is work being done and there is an attitude of seriousness. You hear, "This is an important study...," "This practice will make a difference in your...," and "This is significant information." To maintain productive activity, you will need to provide the following supports:

- *Pace changers.* After an intense and fast-paced math drill, students stand in place and stretch to music.
- *Student input.* Before beginning a new unit of study, the topic is displayed on a small bulletin board. Students are asked to contribute "what we already know," "what we are curious about," and "how we want to learn."
- *Evaluation and feedback.* Students regularly hear, "You have followed all the steps correctly" or "Your work needs more reference material to support your idea."

So you see that you must balance the demands of your classroom with the demands of your district and society to find as much time as possible for instruction. From there, look to *content* and continue your thinking about time for teaching.

Content

As you make decisions about what to teach, you will be directed by your commitments to content goals and by your attitudes about content. In addition to formal content, you will be teaching time management content informally by the way you use time in your classroom. Rather than rely on it happening casually, you can plan for it, and we give some ideas on how to do so. First, we'll look at how your commitments influence your use of time.

Commitments to Content

Robin, a first-grade teacher who works in an inner-city racially mixed neighborhood, describes independence as a major goal for her students. Her commitment to the goal directs the way she uses her teaching time. Robin is careful to meet district goals, but her decisions about what to teach are influenced by her commitment to independence.

Robin begins by analyzing the components of independence into appropriate skills for first grade: problem solving, decision making, recognition of one's own competence, and communication for help and resources. Notice how specific she is with the components of independence. This is an important first step.

With the skills in mind, Robin plans teaching and management strategies. Time is scarce, so she integrates her goal of independence with other parts of her curriculum:

1. Most of the assignments in her class involve choices, so her students constantly make decisions about materials, tasks, and scheduling their work.
2. When her students write in journals or in group stories, there is an emphasis on expressing "what I can do" or "what I have learned."

3. All the materials and equipment in the room are presented with instruction on how and when to use them during the first month of school. From there, students use the classroom independently.
4. Students are taught and even rehearsed in requesting help or attention from volunteers, parents, and visitors. If you enter the room, you can plan on being asked, "Would you listen to me read?" or "I need you to hold this side of my building while I staple it."

In addition, Robin purposefully assesses student achievement of independence. The measurement is informal and usually includes observations of students, student self-reports, and samples of student work. When parents come in for conferences, she asks, "Can Sam do anything new for himself?" She also screens the student journals to see if they can express confidence or new learning.

Robin gains great satisfaction from seeing independence in her students. That is one of the joys of teaching we don't want you to miss. Commitment means finding time and ways to teach with efficiency. Your attitudes and values have a similar influence.

Attitudes about Content

Most of us would admit that we value or like some curriculum areas more than others, or care more about some topics more than others. If you had a choice, what would you prefer to teach? Why? It's important to be aware of your preferences because they will influence how you plan and how you spend your time. These differences may affect student engaged time, motivation, and your enthusiasm. When you believe certain work is interesting or important, you shape similar beliefs in your students. They hear you say, "We are beginning an exciting unit in economics today" with both verbal and nonverbal messages. You are a source of attitudes and your students model and learn accordingly.

What about the work you do not find interesting and enjoyable due to a lack of interest or knowledge? We asked experienced teachers how to compensate for this attitude and they suggested taking courses and workshops in those curricular areas. Our own experience has shown that if we put extra planning into those subjects, we have better organized lessons, interesting activities, and enthusiasm for teaching. With a few successful experiences, you may discover new preferences.

Time Management as Content

When you consider time as part of your curriculum or content, you may find that student efficiency can be taught through your own management of time. Begin with goal setting, add some time structures, and plan for environmental supports.

As early as possible, students need to learn *goal setting*. You can model by sharing some of your own goals. You may need to define the word *goal* and illustrate it with examples. Students can interview parents for examples. Then students can set goals for themselves. Initially, they can begin with short-term goals like, "Today I will have a neat desk" or "Today I will be helpful." Later, they may learn to set long-term goals. Once students develop some skill in setting goals, you can integrate goal setting with other curricular goals. For example, during a unit on the environment, students may set a goal of "I will start a family recycling program."

At the same time that you are developing goal setting, you can be teaching *time structures* simply by thinking aloud so that students can hear: "We have only 20 minutes left to finish this work" or "Only 15 minutes before the bell rings." Young students learn structures with, "When the second hand is on six, we need to have everything cleaned." They gradually develop a sense of time and how to use it. More mature students need practice in estimating and predicting time structures with, "How much time do you think we need for the lab work today?" or "How many minutes do you think it will take to prepare the room for our group projects?"

Just as you need to identify time losses and wasters, students need the same experience. Class discussions of least favorite times of day, times of boredom, reasons why work doesn't get completed, and reasons for success will prompt awareness. Those losses and wasters that students identify for themselves will be meaningful for them and they will be more likely to take action and become efficient.

To establish *environmental supports,* you will need to instruct students in the use of classroom materials. Teach detailed lessons on using the tape recorder or the stapler. Once taught, provide written instructions for location, use, and storage of many of the classroom materials available during the year. Figure 4.1 provides examples of such instructions for young or nonreading students as well as mature students. Students can make (or decorate) sets of instructions and hang them in appropriate locations. You may want to encourage students to evaluate the directions or to make suggestions for better use. When students know how to use the environment independently, you have environmental supports for your teaching time.

Along with the what and how of teaching, you will need to consider the learner in your thinking about time for teaching.

Learner Differences

Within most classrooms is a range of differences that includes ability, interest, development, and experience. Time becomes an even more precious commodity when you think about accommodating for those differences and meeting individual needs. As you prepare to teach in an inclusive setting, you will need to focus your thinking on how to use your available time on a possibly wider span of student differences.

With respect to differences, teachers often wish for more time to give attention to a low-ability student or wish for extra time to challenge a high-ability student. The same dilemma is true when teachers are faced with students who are very interested in a topic and those who are not, or a student who has had little experience with a concept and one who has had much experience. The ideas in Chapter Three on collaborative planning with students are excellent ways to respond to differences. We also encourage you to consider the use of peer tutors, volunteers, and aides, and to try some of the cooperative learning strategies described in Chapter Ten. You will see that these arrangements are not only efficient but appropriate for student learning.

Another approach to accommodate ability differences is through monitoring, a strategy that checks student understanding of an idea or competence in a skill during the learning process. This strategy will help you determine, before much time passes, who is learning and who is not. Monitoring can be done in a number of ways—questioning,

FIGURE 4.1 *Instructions for Independent Classroom Use*

Using Class References & Materials

Item	Where to use...	How to use...
Encyclopedias	in classroom	Find on back shelf - alphabetical order - return.
Periodicals	in classroom at home	Locate in card file, sign out, return to box.
Filmstrips	in classroom study hall	Locate in card file, sign out, rewind or replace.
Games	at back tables	Locate on side shelf (labeled), return to shelf.

Comments: Fill out a comment slip on needs, lost items, etc.

Using the Tape Recorder

1. Check the classroom — listen
2. Check the plug
3. Put in the tape
4. Push PLAY Play
5. When finished, push REW Rewind

Source: From *Classroom Management Course Materials* by A. Driscoll and K. Peterson, 1988, unpublished materials. Portland State University. Portland, OR. Used by permission.

checking student work, observing facial expressions, and reviewing previous learning. Some examples of teacher monitoring will help you see how it saves time:

EXAMPLE: An eighth-grade algebra teacher instructs students in the use of a new formula, then assigns five problems. She immediately moves about the room, looks at each student's work, and determines who is able to use the formula and who isn't. She asks individual students, "Tell me how you do this problem," and monitors understanding.

EXAMPLE: After giving a lecture on osmosis, Ms. Nagel asks fast-paced questions of the class for about five minutes to determine whether the science content was understood. When one of her questions leads to confused looks and few answers, she knows that some information needs explanation or clarification.

EXAMPLE: While young students practice sequencing pictures of story sets, Mr. Hernandez moves about the room and watches them. He watches for confusion or frustration. He stops and asks often, "Why is this picture last?" or "Why is this picture in the middle?" He can tell from the explanations whether the correct sequence is random or due to student understanding.

Monitoring tells you whether learners understand, whether to slow down or speed up, whether to reteach or go on, and whether to spend some time reviewing. In the end, monitoring will save you time and help you accommodate for ability differences in your learners.

We have been encouraging you to think about time for teaching and directed your attention to the context, content, and learners. Now you are ready to think about how to use time in your classroom.

TIME AND THE INCLUSIVE CLASSROOM

As you are now aware, student differences have the potential to add increased tension to the time issues in your classroom. We suggest that awareness of your teaching, especially those aspects that are directed and controlled by you, is a starting point for making changes that will ultimately use those learner differences as a resource and an asset to your use of time.

Many educators have been encouraging us to look at our traditional teacher-directed classrooms and to examine our roles in those settings. Consider the following behaviors and characteristics:

1. *Teacher sets up class in her way.*
2. *All students get the same assignment.*
3. *All class goals are pre-determined.*
4. *Discipline is punitive.*
5. *Teaching is telling and giving assignments.*
6. *Teaching is controlling and teacher is boss.*

7. *Knowledge is seen as academic achievement.*
8. *No formal attempt to change students' perceptions or attitudes. (Areglado, Bradley, & Lane, 1996, p. 22).*

Have you observed these kind of settings? Have you experienced such teacher roles in your learning history? Research shows that such roles and settings are very demanding of teacher time and energy, and that many students in those classrooms are unmotivated, are engaged in learning without depth or meaning, and eventually drop out.

Making changes in our teaching to replace much of our teacher-directed use of time with student-directed learning will be both efficient and effective in all classrooms and especially in an inclusive classroom. We suggest a few preliminary changes for your thinking and implementation, and encourage you to go beyond these pages to further reading and related workshops. Here are some starting points:

1. Involve students in planning and setting up the classroom environment, routines, and management. Examples include student committees that plan bulletin boards and displays; student discussions that yield management decisions; and the teacher and students who experiment to find the best routines for going to the playground, cleaning up the lab, distributing materials, and so on.
2. Involve learners (and their parents or families) in goal setting. The class, as a whole, may set some group goals, but it is equally important for learners to set individual goals.
3. Instead of being responsible for all of the monitoring described on the previous page, look for ways to involve learners in self-monitoring (e.g., checking own work, describing own learning process, asking peers for help, reflecting on own progress and performance, etc.).
4. Provide opportunities for students to dialog and collaborate in solving problems, explaining concepts, planning learning activities, setting goals, and giving feedback on each other's study skills.

These beginning changes can be combined with the collaborative planning in Chapter Three and some of the classroom management approaches you will learn about in Chapter Five to provide an environment that is characterized by student-directed learning, higher levels of engagement and motivation, and more effective use of available time. The kinds of learning outcomes achieved by student-directed approaches and environments will directly affect academic achievement for the range of learners in an inclusive classroom. Those learners' differences are an important resource in a student-directed learning situation.

TIME SAVERS

Our time savers are generic because they apply to everyday situations, in and out of school, so you can try them out whether you are currently teaching or preparing to teach. We start with *goal setting,* then focus on your *clarity.* From there, we develop some strategies for *handling paperwork efficiently,* and end with *delegating* as a time saver. In spite of time limits on your teaching, there are ways to increase minutes and hours with these time savers.

Goal Setting and Reflection

We suggested earlier that you teach your students to set goals, and we encourage you to do the same with respect to your time management. Begin with specific goals, such as, "Each afternoon, before I go home, I will prepare my materials for the next day" or "I will leave time at the end of each activity for summarizing the ideas." When you achieve these, be sure to notice how good it feels.

Another strategy we recommend is the use of a time journal for reflection. This can be nothing more than a simple record of how you use your time each day. We know some teachers who assign students to keep class time journals. At the end of a week, spend time summarizing your use of time, analyze it for efficiency, and reflect on how it portrays your teaching. The pie charts in Figure 4.2 provide a way of displaying how the day is spent. Analyze the time use of the two teachers whose charts you see. What are their priorities? Problems? If you use this strategy, you may want to discuss the chart with your students and get their responses to some of your questions, such as: Where could we save time? Where could we use 20 more minutes?

FIGURE 4.2 *Pie Chart Recordings of How Time Is Spent in Two Classrooms*

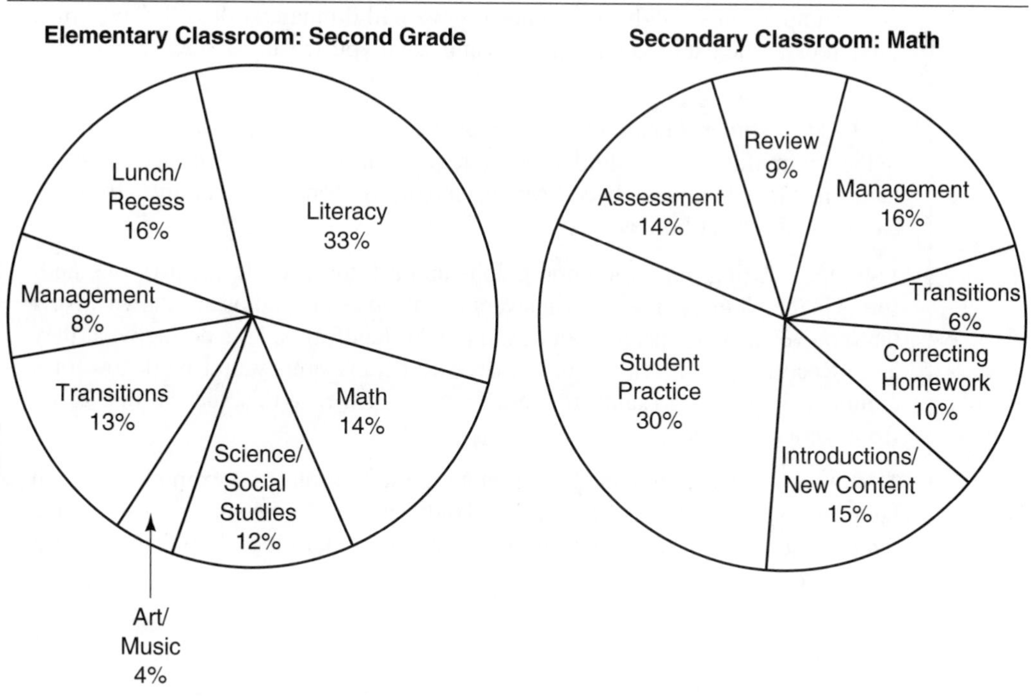

In the next section, we describe how to achieve clarity in your teaching as a time saver. You may want to make it one of your first goals.

Clarity in Teaching

Clarity in your teaching is efficient because students understand better, work more accurately, and are more successful (Gephart, Strother, & Duckett, 1981). When you are not clear, you may have to repeat directions, reteach a concept, undo a misunderstanding, and so on. We have all had occasions in our lives when our lack of clarity had time-consuming and sometimes disastrous results. To keep it from happening in your teaching, we suggest following Ms. Daugherty (in the next Snapshot). She demonstrates five behaviors that provide clarity in her teaching: stating the topic or focus, providing an outline to the students, giving many examples and illustrations, connecting to the students' experiences, and repeating the main points several times in the lesson.

SNAPSHOT: Middle-School Classroom—5th Period

1:38 P.M. Students pick up a study sheet as they arrive. The sheet lists types of landforms, space for examples and definitions, and a reference list.

1:40 P.M. "Take a look at our topic for today. Be ready to begin in one minute."

1:41 P.M. "The topic for today is landforms. We will be working on definitions and examples on your sheets. Tomorrow we will do map work with landforms. First, look at the list of landform types and see if you see any that exist where we live."

1:43 P.M. Students begin raising hands to respond with examples of landforms in the community. "Now, think of your travels and see if you have seen any other landforms listed on your sheet." Again, students respond with examples from vacations and former homes.

1:46 P.M. Bring out large photographs and ask the class to identify the landforms in the pictures. The class answers in unison as the photos are shown. "Now that you've seen and heard about examples of landforms, let's define what they are." Record students' ideas on an overhead transparency and work toward a common definition: "Landforms are features of the earth's surface that result from natural causes."

1:50 P.M. Instruct students to complete the definitions and examples of each landform on their sheets: "Remember, landforms are.... Be sure to describe the feature and the cause." Underline the terms in the definition. Students practice aloud with several examples.

1:55 P.M. "It sounds like you are ready to begin defining. When you finish, check the reference list on your study sheet and see if you can find another new example of landform. You're welcome to come up and write it on the transparency."

Did you notice in the Snapshot that the topic was stated? An outline was provided? Examples and illustrations were used? The topic was connected to students' experiences? The main point was repeated? Ms. Daugherty modeled clarity for you in her instruction. Figure 4.3 is a checklist that will also help you to check your clarity. It can be used by you, as a student or as a teacher, to develop awareness of behaviors that promote *clarity in teaching.*

Handling Paperwork

When we talk with teachers about reasons for being a teacher, they never mention paperwork. Teachers have described an increase in paperwork and consider it a source of stress. Much like other demands on teachers, research on paperwork (Delaware State Department of Public Instruction, 1987) has shown that many paperwork tasks originate with teachers. So, your starting point in handling paperwork is to assess the amount of paperwork you have and determine its necessity. Ask yourself, Does this paperwork contribute to my teaching? To student learning? Could it be accomplished in better or more efficient ways? Paperwork is a reality, so we urge a thoughtful and efficient approach. The Delaware study identified seven major types of paperwork. Although the study was conducted some time ago, the kinds of paperwork haven't changed except for the influence of technology. Many teachers have achieved efficiency in handling all seven types of paperwork by preparing, storing, analyzing, communicating, and organizing with computers. Those teachers also involve students in much of the record keeping (like Mr. Tourtillott in the Elementary Classroom Snapshot earlier in this chapter). To assist you with paperwork responsibilities, we describe each type and suggest time savers for them.

- *Type 1: Classwork paperwork.* Some examples of classwork paperwork include prepared worksheets for seatwork, classroom library information, and collated papers. Several suggestions come to mind for this top time consumer: (1) share materials with other teachers; (2) save successful materials from year to year; (3) get assistance with collating, stapling, and copying; (4) prepare and save classwork materials in a computer file; and (5) search websites and the Internet for class material from other sources. Because this form of paperwork has no easy solution, we encourage you to seek alternatives to doing it yourself—for instance, have students work in groups to prepare their own study guides, use transparencies instead of individual copies of seatwork, use student-made flash cards for drill and practice instead of worksheets, have students develop their own lists of questions to answer, and so on.
- *Type 2: Evaluation and grading paperwork.* Grading tests, writing comments on papers, and recording grades in the grade book are examples of evaluation and grading paperwork. Collins (1987) has shared hints from experienced teachers for grading papers:

_____ "As you walk around the room checking student work, mark those problems which you check with a red pencil. When you later collect the papers to evaluate, you will have part of your work already done."

FIGURE 4.3 *Instructional Clarity Checklist*

Directions: These 32 items describe instructional behaviors that contribute to instructional clarity. To the right of these items is a scale. For each item, put a check mark at the location that best describes how often you, as a teacher, perform the instructional behaviors.

4 All of the time
3 Most of the time
2 Some of the time
1 Never
0 Does not apply

	4	3	2	1	0
1. Explains the work to be done and how to do it	( )	( )	( )	( )	( )
2. Asks students if they know what to do and how to do it	( )	( )	( )	( )	( )
3. Explains something, then stops so students can think about it	( )	( )	( )	( )	( )
4. Takes time when explaining	( )	( )	( )	( )	( )
5. Orients and prepares students for what is to follow	( )	( )	( )	( )	( )
6. Provides students with standards and rules for satisfactory performance	( )	( )	( )	( )	( )
7. Specifies content and shares overall structure for the lectures with students	( )	( )	( )	( )	( )
8. Helps students to organize materials in a meaningful way	( )	( )	( )	( )	( )
9. Repeats questions and explanations if students don't understand	( )	( )	( )	( )	( )
10. Repeats and stresses directions and difficult points	( )	( )	( )	( )	( )
11. Encourages and lets students ask questions	( )	( )	( )	( )	( )
12. Answers students' questions	( )	( )	( )	( )	( )
13. Provides practice time	( )	( )	( )	( )	( )
14. Synthesizes ideas and demonstrates real-world relevancy	( )	( )	( )	( )	( )
15. Adjusts teaching to the learner and the topic	( )	( )	( )	( )	( )
16. Teaches at a pace appropriate to the topic and students	( )	( )	( )	( )	( )
17. Personalizes instruction by using many teaching strategies	( )	( )	( )	( )	( )
18. Continuously monitors student learning and adjusts instructional strategy to the needs of the learner	( )	( )	( )	( )	( )
19. Teaches in a related, step-by-step manner	( )	( )	( )	( )	( )
20. Uses demonstrations	( )	( )	( )	( )	( )
21. Uses a variety of teaching materials	( )	( )	( )	( )	( )
22. Provides illustrations and examples	( )	( )	( )	( )	( )
23. Emphasizes the key terms/ideas to be learned	( )	( )	( )	( )	( )
24. Consistently reviews work as it is completed and provides students with feedback or knowledge of results	( )	( )	( )	( )	( )
25. Insures that students have an environment in which they are encouraged to process what they are learning	( )	( )	( )	( )	( )
26. Makes clear transitions	( )	( )	( )	( )	( )
27. Reduces mazes	( )	( )	( )	( )	( )
28. Avoids vague terms	( )	( )	( )	( )	( )
29. Avoids fillers (uh, ah, um)	( )	( )	( )	( )	( )
30. Reduces nonessential content	( )	( )	( )	( )	( )
31. Communicates so that all students can understand	( )	( )	( )	( )	( )
32. Demonstrates a high degree of verbal fluency	( )	( )	( )	( )	( )

Source: Gephart, W. J., Strother, D. B., & Duckett, W. E. (1981). *Practical applications of research, newsletter.* Phi Delta Kappa Center on Evaluation, Development, and Research, 3(3). Used by permission.

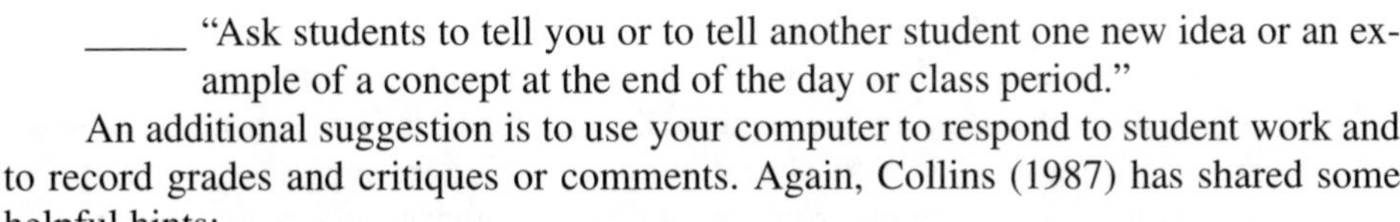

_____ "Ask students to tell you or to tell another student one new idea or an example of a concept at the end of the day or class period."

An additional suggestion is to use your computer to respond to student work and to record grades and critiques or comments. Again, Collins (1987) has shared some helpful hints:

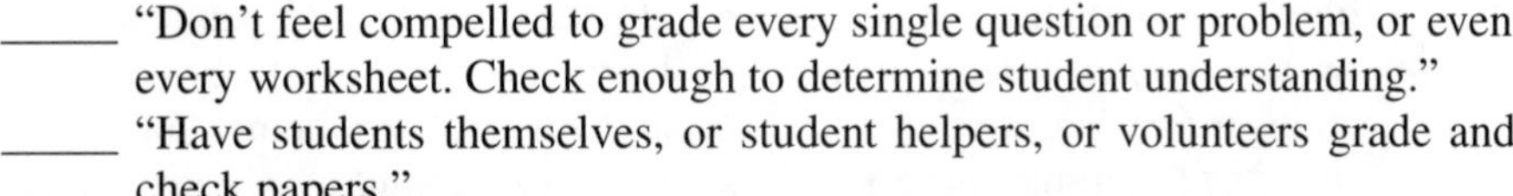

_____ "Don't feel compelled to grade every single question or problem, or even every worksheet. Check enough to determine student understanding."

_____ "Have students themselves, or student helpers, or volunteers grade and check papers."

■ *Type 3: Homework paperwork.* Homework paperwork consists of preparing, grading, and recording homework. Some of the ideas for streamlining classwork and evaluation/grading apply here. In addition, we suggest that you organize specific places and routines for homework distribution and collection (e.g., an IN and OUT box, folders or envelopes for student work, etc.). Consider providing answer keys or samples for students to grade their own work, or involve parents in the review and checking of homework once or twice a week. Many teachers take a few minutes at the beginning of class to allow student partners to check their homework and to record completion and grade.

■ *Type 4: Report card paperwork.* Averaging and recording grades and writing comments on report cards are the typical report card paperwork tasks. There are some generic time savers for any kind of reports due at regular intervals like report cards. First, establish sound procedures for recording and storing data such as test grades, samples of students' work, and commentaries. A good filing system or a computer software program will save you time all year. At report card time, organize your data and materials at a work space that will not be disturbed for the time needed to complete your work. Have plenty of space for spreading out. An important suggestion is that you plan for 50 to 60 minutes of work at a time. If you get too tired, you become inefficient and possibly inaccurate. When you stop, straighten and organize your materials for the next work session.

Because of the nature of this paperwork, this is probably an ideal context in which to use your strategy goal setting: "I have a positive attitude about this task," or "I have completed one-third of my report cards today," or "I have written thoughtful comments on 10 report cards today."

■ *Type 5: Special projects paperwork.* This seems to be a catchall category with familiar-sounding tasks such as, prepare form for promotion committee, lick cafeteria award stickers, and write suggestions for student essay contest. This is probably the best type of paperwork to which you say *no.* Teachers are conditioned not to refuse requests related to professional work. Drawbaugh (1984) suggested that you consider saying no if you have uncertainties about the request, if it will cause you stress, or if it will keep you from or delay your own goals. You should definitely refuse if you are overcommitted or if you just don't want to do it.

Once you have decided, you may have to learn or practice saying no. It is important to be pleasant and tactful, but at the same time be persistent and avoid excuses. Get a friend to help you practice so that you can be successful when the situation occurs. Then you can choose those tasks or requests that you really want to do. You will experience real professional satisfaction and increased efficiency with this strategy.

■ *Type 6: Test-development paperwork.* Even if you have never developed your own tests, you can guess the kinds of tasks teachers do: writing multiple-choice items, typing the test, checking facts and spelling, and so on. The list goes on for every subject area and for every teacher. Three sound strategies are suggested. First, maintain a test question bank with items from previous tests, other teachers, and commercial materials. With computers, an item bank will be easily achieved, and you can add to the bank on an ongoing basis. Consider involving students in test development. An effective study and review strategy is to have students write test items. You can learn from their ideas and you may have some usable items. Second, use answer sheets or other resources for scoring objective tests. Third, pay attention to yourself in this task. Look at your time constraints and teaching conditions. What is your schedule like? How large is your class? Be realistic when you plan your tests.

■ *Type 7: Correspondence within school.* The diversity of paperwork that falls in this category is unbelievable, but a few samples include sending memos to team leaders, completing reports for the principal, and writing congratulatory notes to the student of the month. The strategies for streamlining this type of paperwork apply to all kinds of correspondence, at home and at work. The best advice is to avoid rereading. When you go to the mailroom, take small notes, envelopes, and a pen with you, and jot replies immediately after reading; sometimes, you can reply right on the letter. Throw away those that do not need a reply. Take your calendar with you and you can record scheduling information at the same time. You will no longer have piles of this kind of paperwork on your desk staring at you.

The Delaware study also identified a category called *correspondence out of school,* which consisted of difficult paperwork, but not as time consuming as the types we reported. Many teachers keep a file of sample correspondence for this purpose. In the Samples and Examples at the end of this chapter, you will find a form for corresponding with parents about work missed due to absence. It's a time saver.

There is hope for the reduction of your paperwork burden. It is a professional responsibility you can approach with a few purposeful strategies. We have begun a process for you—that of collecting ideas for saving time. From here, talk to other teachers. They are the best source of time savers.

Delegating

Our final strategy for saving time is delegating. It is a difficult skill to learn, and teachers seem to struggle with it more than most professionals. Most of us feel some guilt when we delegate, as if we are avoiding our responsibilities. Instead, we need to think of delegating as a competent and professional skill. Learning how to delegate is difficult, but we can get you started. From there, you will need to read, discuss, set goals, practice, and check yourself regularly.

Conditions for Delegating

For delegation to work, there must be a high level of trust between you and your students, between you and other teachers, between you and your administration, and between you and your volunteers or aides. Your classroom climate must be positive and communication must be open. Another necessary condition is your recognition of the limitations of delegating. It will not solve all your schedule problems, and it may not even produce more time for you. What it *can* do is allow you to do some of those "extras" that you wish you had time for. Carolyn, the teacher in the following Snapshot, demonstrates some other conditions for delegating.

SNAPSHOT: Middle-School Classroom

Carolyn, a sixth-grade teacher, convinced most of the parents of her students to volunteer, so that each would be scheduled only once every two weeks. She conducted several half-day training sessions on classroom routines, teaching strategies, and management. During one session, parents spent time determining which tasks would be satisfying, and where each would be comfortable working. The parents also had choices about the schedule of days for working in the classroom.

Carolyn also scheduled free time each morning and afternoon, during which she moved about the room supervising both parents and students. She scheduled conference times during lunch so that parents could discuss their classroom experiences, problems, and successes, and get feedback or ideas.

Notice the conditions for Carolyn's successful delegation to parent volunteers. She made sure that they were trained and knew how to do the work, and she provided some choices of work. She also made sure that there were enough people to handle the work. Needless to say, Carolyn didn't have more time. She may have been busier, but she was teaching the way she intended, fitting in all those "extras" that she hadn't had time for previously.

Resources for Delegating

As you observed in the last Snapshot, parents are resources as well as aides and other volunteers. Your most available source of help is students. You will need to observe the same conditions when delegating to students; that is, they will need instruction, alternatives, supervision, and enough of them to divide tasks. Be sure to identify those tasks that are appropriate for student responsibility. As we describe management routines and using audiovisuals in the chapters that follow, we will recommend and describe procedures for using student help.

Be ready to let go and trust that others will do the work as well as you would. Maybe they will do it differently and maybe they will do it better.

SUMMARY

To help you achieve effective use of time and doing more with less, we set out to direct your thinking as you make decisions on use of time for teaching and learning. Consider society's demands and those of your school district. What are the priorities, expectations, constraints, and provisions? Reflect on your own classroom. How do you handle time losses and time wasters? How much productive activity goes on? Look at your content, and be aware of your commitments to goals and attitudes toward curriculum. Look at the "what" and "how" of teaching, and see how you can include time management as content for your teaching.

When you think of your students, consider ways to accommodate a range of differences. Be certain that you are monitoring learning and adjusting the learning time to the differences. In your inclusive classroom, consider the amount of time spent in teacher-directed versus student-directed learning activities.

Finally, reconsider the time-saving strategies of this chapter. We have described goal setting, clarity in teaching, handling paperwork, and delegation. Our advice is to work on only one or two strategies at a time. It would be inefficient to try them all at once. Reflect on your use of time and choose the time saver that will benefit you the most at this time.

As you work on making effective use of time and doing more with less, collect strategies from your own experiences and those of other teachers. Become an expert!

REFERENCES

Adelman, N. E., & Walking-Eagle, K. P. (1997). Teachers, time, and school reform. In A. Hargreaves (Ed.), *Rethinking educational change with heart and mind.* Alexandria, VA: Association for Supervision and Curriculum Development.

Alspaugh, J. (1998). Achievement loss associated with transition to middle school and high school. *The Journal of Educational Research, 92*(1), 20–33.

Areglado, R. J., Bradley, R. C., & Lane, P. S. (1996). *Learning for life: Creating classrooms for self-directed learning.* Thousand Oaks, CA: Corwin Press.

Bredekamp, S., & Rosegrant, T. (1995). Transforming curriculum organization. In S. Bredekamp & T. Rosegrant (Eds.), *Reaching potentials: Transforming early childhood curriculum and assessment.* Washington, DC: National Association for the Education of Young Children.

Carroll, J. B. (1985). The model of school learning: Progress of an idea. In C. Fisher & D. Berliner (Eds.), *Perspectives on instructional time.* New York: Longman.

Collins, C. (1987). *Time management for teachers.* West Nyack, NY: Parker.

Delaware State Department of Public Instruction. (1987). *Teacher paperwork study: Type, time, and difficulty.* Dover: Author.

Drawbaugh, C. C. (1984). *Time and its use.* New York: Teachers College Press.

Fisher, C., Filby, N., Marliave, R., Cahen, L, Dishaw, M., Moore, J., & Berliner, D. (1978). *Teaching behaviors, academic learning time, and student achievement: Final report of Phase III-B, Beginning Teacher Evaluation Study.* San Francisco, CA: Far West Laboratory for Educational Research and Development.

Gephart, W. J., Strother, D. B., & Duckett, W. E. (1981). Practical applications of research, newsletter. *Phi Delta Kappa Center on Evaluation, Development, and Research, 3*(3).

Karweit, N. (1988). Time on task: The second time around. *NASSP Bulletin, 72*(505), 31–39.

McIntosh, M. E., & Johnson, D. L. (1994). An instrument to facilitate communication between prospective team teachers. *The Clearinghouse, 67*(3), 152–154.

Merenbloom, E. Y. (1996). Team teaching: Addressing the learning needs of middle level students. *NASSP Bulletin, 80* (578), 45.

National Research Council. (1998). *A sampler of National Science Education Standards.* Columbus, OH: Merrill.

Peterson, P. L., McCarthy, S. J., & Elmore, R. F. (1996). Learning from school restructuring. *American Educational Research Journal, 33*(1), 119–153.

Walberg, H. (1988). Synthesis of research on time and learning. *Educational Leadership, 45*(2), 143–178.

Walker, D. F., & Soltis, J. F. (1997). *Curriculum and aims.* New York: Teachers College Press.

SAMPLES AND EXAMPLES

This Samples and Examples section includes the following:

- The Absence Packet can take many forms, depending on the age and grade level of the learners, and will assist students who miss class.
- The Key Concerns in Team Teaching Rating Scale is an instrument used to assess and respond to potential concerns about team teaching arrangements.

ABSENCE PACKET

Inside this folder are ______________________ papers for the week. Please take time to review and discuss them with your child. Then date and initial this form and have your child return the completed work as soon as possible. (One day of make-up is allowed for each day missed.)

Thank you,

Mrs. Hawley

Date	*Parent Signature*	*Comments*
____________	______________________	______________________
____________	______________________	______________________
____________	______________________	______________________
____________	______________________	______________________
____________	______________________	______________________
____________	______________________	______________________
____________	______________________	______________________

Source: Hawley, L. (1989). *Instructional materials.* Unpublished materials, Creekwood Middle School, Kingwood, Texas. Used by permission.

KEY CONCERNS IN TEAM TEACHING RATING SCALE

This list of issues might concern teachers who are team teaching for the first time. Teachers separately rate each of the issues as 1 (very important to me); 2 (important but I can be flexible); or 3 (not that important to me). Then for each issue, teachers decide together what they will do about these issues.

1. Classroom Arrangement/Physical Space
   a. Storage
   b. Work spaces for teachers
   c. Teacher desks
   d. Desks or tables for children
   e. Partitions/room dividers
   f. Centers
   g. Bulletin boards
   h. The "look" of the room
   i. Personal neatness preference
   j. Other (explain)
2. Classroom Materials
   a. Supplies for teachers
   b. Supplies for children
   c. Books and other materials for the children (e.g., games)
   d. Children's library books
   e. Whose "stuff" is it? Yours? Mine? Ours?
   f. If the school doesn't provide what we need, how will we get it?
   g. Spending own money in the classroom
   h. Book orders
   i. Other (explain)
3. Behavior Management/Discipline
   a. Classroom routine: lining up, recess, etc.
   b. Rules
   c. Expectations
   d. Consequences
   e. Punishment
   f. Rewards
   g. Other (explain)
4. Planning
   a. Lesson plan book
   b. Yearly plans
   c. Monthly plans
   d. Weekly plans
   e. Daily plans
   f. Sharing ideas
   g. Setting aside time for planning together
   h. Work outside of school
   i. Other (explain)
5. Grading/Communication with Parents
   a. Systems/organizations
   b. When will grading be done?
   c. Who grades what?
   d. Grade books
   e. Grade distribution
   f. Report cards
   g. Communication with parents
   h. Parent conferences
   i. Other (explain)
6. Teaching Style/Philosophy
   a. Spontaneity/teachable moments
   b. Drama
   c. Humor
   d. Interaction with children
   e. Goals for children
   f. Demonstration of affection
   g. Need "own" children in teamed class
   h. Other (explain)
7. Curriculum Issues/Subject Matter
   a. Art
   b. Music
   c. Physical education
   d. Cooking
   e. Health
   f. Science
   g. Social studies
   h. Mathematics
   i. Reading
   j. Writing
   k. Speaking
   l. Listening
   m. Handwriting
   n. Other (explain)
8. Curriculum Issues/Instructional Philosophy
   a. Workbooks
   b. Worksheets
   c. Whole group
   d. Small group
   e. Cooperative learning
   f. Textbooks
   g. Phonics
   h. Literature-based
   i. Whole language
   j. Integrated curriculum
   k. Evaluation/assessment of children
   l. Portfolio assessment
   m. Thematic/integrated teaching
   n. Noise level
   o. Movement within classroom
   p. Inter-classroom: i.e., experiences with other levels or classrooms
   q. Other (explain)
9. When the Substitute Comes
   a. Call team member
   b. Substitutes preference?
   c. Willingness to explain team-teaching situation to sub
   d. Other (explain)
10. Self-Perception
   a. Communication style(s)
   b. Staff development training/graduate course work
   c. Goals
   d. Personality
   e. Constructive criticism
   f. Learning style(s)
   g. Asking for help
   h. Being observed
   i. Work ethic
   j. Teaching
   k. Life outside school
   l. Other (explain)
11. Us as a Team
   a. Decision-making
   b. Division of labor
   c. Social relationship
   d. Commonalities
   e. Differences
   f. Other (explain)

Source: M. E. McIntosh and D. L. Johnson, "An Instrument to Facilitate Communication between Prospective Team Teachers," *The Clearingh-* pp. 152–154, 1994. Reprinted with permission of the Helen Dwight Reid Educational Foundation. Published by Heldref Publications, 1319 Eig- Washington, DC 20036-1802. Copyright © 1994.

CHAPTER

5

CLASSROOM MANAGEMENT

Advancework

Chapter Outcomes

At the conclusion of this chapter you will be able to:

1. *Conduct advancework to gather information on the context, content, and learner.*
2. *Use advancework information about the context, content, and learner to make classroom management decisions.*
3. *Use advancework to help create more positive and active learning environments.*

Key Terms and Concepts

Advancework
Context
Climate: Messages on the Wall
Significant Individuals in Schools
Class Size
Equipment and Materials
Room Arrangement
Use of Space
Location in the School
Content Advancework
Management Messages
Materials' Cues
Content Relevance
Learner Advancework
Physically Active Learning
Mentally Active Learning
Emotionally Safe Environment
Physically Safe Environment

INTRODUCTION

What Is Advancework?

A major computer company prepares to build new facilities in a large urban area, a move involving the transfer of hundreds of employees and equipment. The company sends a group ahead to survey housing costs and availability, schools, shopping, and leisure and recreational facilities with which to develop an information base on the new location. Several company representatives may interview people in some of the neighborhoods to extend the information.

The computer company representative is conducting *advancework.* The example points out the importance of environment, or the context, and uses people as valuable sources of information. In the example, the advancework content is a range of details and facts to be used in making decisions such as where to purchase housing.

Advancework is equally important for you, the teacher, in making classroom management decisions. Advancework in education is about preventing problems before they begin through effective information gathering rather than solving problems once they have occurred because a lack of understanding of the learner, content, and context. Your context is complex—a classroom, a school district, and a community. Your content is curriculum—ideas, knowledge, skills, and attitudes. The important people in your advancework are the learners and those in their lives.

Why Conduct Advancework?

Today's classrooms are complex and dynamic. The expectations of teachers to teach problem solving, to teach critical thinking, and to engage students in quality academic work demand more sophisticated classroom management than ever before (Evertson & Harris, 1999). New methods of organization and management are required (Brophy, 1999), and those methods must not only focus on the content being taught but must also accommodate the expanding diversity of students and settings. In addition, your management must provide those social opportunities we described in previous chapters. The strategy of advancework can help you develop such a responsive classroom management system. It is a first step to meeting the expectations described by Evertson and Harris—expectations that reflect elements of effective teaching in today's society.

In the sections that follow, we will suggest both thinking and action for advancework. Thinking takes the form of questions to ask, information to consider, and awareness to maintain. Action takes the form of examples and models of how advancework is done.

CONTEXT ADVANCEWORK

The context of classroom management has several distinct levels to consider in conducting advancework: the surrounding community, the school and district environment, and the classroom itself. Before teaching, you are an "advance person," surveying each of the levels for information to use in management decision making.

Community Environment

Gathering information about the community context has many advantages for you: an understanding of your students, support for your management decisions, sources of relevant curriculum, and assistance and resources for your classroom. Your best advancework strategy here is to survey the neighborhood and gather information in an organized way for later use.

Surveying the Neighborhood

When you are new to teaching or to a specific school, begin with the neighborhood. A drive or a walk with a teacher who is established at the school might be your starting point. What kind of information could you gather if you traveled through your school's neighborhood at 7 P.M.? At 10:30 A.M.? Many communities have local papers or calendars of events. What kind of information would you find? Look for the local library, park, community center, day-care facility, and shopping center. A visit to the library will tell you about how often it is used, who uses it and when, what resources are available and used, and a little about the neighborhood lifestyle. Experienced teachers have told us that they regularly check community bulletin boards for information such as scheduling of community events, parenting programs, guest speakers, and other teaching resources.

SNAPSHOT: Elementary School

At Washington-Carver Elementary School in Muncie, Indiana, an unusual first-day-of-school meeting took place. Instead of a meeting agenda, teachers were given tickets and directed to a waiting city bus. The chartered bus took the teachers through the streets of their students' neighborhood. Soon, teachers were discussing the community, its businesses, children's routes to school, and other information about the neighborhood. An important discovery of this experience was that for most of the district staff the neighborhood was "new territory," not previously seen. "Our awareness of our neighborhood took on a new meaning. We found out where our students live" (Swetnam & Stokes, 1994).

Gathering Information

When surveying the neighborhood of your school (as the teachers in Muncie did), it is a good idea to record the information you gather. A Community Context Checklist is provided in Figure 5.1 to help you record such information. Notice that it organizes what you see and hear so that you can anticipate problems as well as develop sensitivities.

School Environment

Similar information gathering may be conducted with a simple walk around the inside and outside of your school. Note those features that are going to help your management and those features that have potential for disruption.

School Climate: Messages on the Walls

The walls of *hallways* and *classrooms* reflect the learning environment in a school. Although the fire marshall may play a role in how much is placed on the walls of a school,

FIGURE 5.1 *Community Context Checklist*

Demographics

Population ______________________________

Size in Square Miles ______________________________

Socioeconomic Range ______________________________

Cultural Representations ______________________________

Community Resources	*Description**	*Management Potential†*
Playground(s)		
Community Center		
Newspaper		
Industry(s)		
Civic Organizations		
Medical Facilities		
Mental Health Agencies		
Scout Organizations		
Programs for the Elderly		
Animal Shelter		
Chamber of Commerce		
Public Transportation		
Day-Care Center(s)		
Shopping Center(s)		

*Description can include location, size, use, and condition.

†Management Potential can include influence on or by students and resources for teaching (materials, speakers, field trips).

there is a clear trend of colorful walls in the elementary schools and the barren or institutional walls at middle and high schools. The walls send an important message to the learners and visitors, reflecting the academic focus and climate at the school. In visiting inner-city secondary schools in Houston, Newark, Chicago, and Amsterdam in the Netherlands, two patterns emerged: (1) the halls were devoid of student academic work (there was some artwork and sports trophies) and (2) student work that was displayed in the classroom was selected by the teacher from about 20 percent of the students and hadn't been changed in weeks or months. Also, teacher-selected posters hung in many classroom. The argument made by some teachers and administrators at the secondary level is that students "tag" (graffiti) or tear down materials that are placed in the classroom and particularly in the hallways.

Advancework is about preventing problems before they begin rather than solving problems once they have occurred. A good advancework question might be: What is the root cause of student disregard or destruction for academic work being posted? The root cause may be found in the context and the learner. Rather than having the teacher select a few best works, an effective alternative is asking students to select their own best work for posting. This practice was tested in schools of the four cities mentioned earlier. Teachers asked students to select their best work for placement on the walls, both in the hallways and in the classroom.

A high school mathematics teacher in Chicago in an academically low-performing school took the challenge, assuming that it wouldn't work. All her students handed in their best work but three students gave what amounted to scribble. She posted all the students' work. The next time they had class, the three students asked if they could have their work returned. When the teacher asked why, the students told her they could do much better. The teacher told this story with a smile. Each week, she explained, the quality of work became better, and even though C- and B-level work is posted, students have set the standard for higher quality. Taped interviews indicated that students liked the fairness of this approach to recognition. "We work hard," said a junior at the same high school, "and people needed to know it. I feel good about my work and like that we can select it for the halls." When asked why they think their work in the hallways doesn't get destroyed, they said, "Everyone gets their work displayed; it's cool now" (Freiberg, 2000).

Significant Individuals

Within the school context are individuals with significant influence on your classroom management. You will be wise to make contact with a range of school personnel: custodian, nurse, bus drivers, secretaries, specialists, and cafeteria staff. They can support your management decisions.

For example, most custodians welcome the chance to respond to questions such as, How do you want me to leave my classroom at the end of the day? and What kind of problems do you want me to handle, and for what kind do you want me to check with you? When these questions are posed with sincere intent to listen and cooperate, you will gain support for numerous management situations. When you do not create such cooperation, you may operate in deference to custodial concerns and expectations. You are liable to be left stranded to cope with spilled paint, broken chairs or desks, frayed carpet, or other ordinary management problems. You may not get much support.

Similar contacts with other school personnel will help build supportive relationships. We strongly recommend that you consult with your administrator early in the school year about management expectations, plans, and concerns. It has been our experience that most principals welcome being asked to describe their expectations, being consulted about management decisions, and being informed about management problems. The bottom line is that you will have a difficult time without their support for your classroom management.

Other teachers serve as valuable consultants to your classroom management. Their wealth of experiences, routines, practices, successes, and failures are likely to be your most useful resources for management thinking and decision making. Ignoring other teachers' experiences and preferences has the potential to put you at odds with them in your expectations for student behavior, building use, and routines.

As you can see, school advancework also works to generate information and support for your classroom management. You may want to develop a School Context Checklist similar to the Community Context Checklist (Figure 5.1) for recording and organizing your school advancework information. Make it specific to your school, and don't forget to include noise, traffic, safety hazards, crowded conditions, and resources.

Classroom Environment

Variation in classrooms is almost without limits. You may teach in cramped conditions, noisy locations, and windowless rooms, and have outdated equipment. You may also enjoy bright, carpeted, quiet rooms, well equipped with state-of-the-art materials and furnishings (the eternal optimist in us). To do advancework in your classroom, focus on class size and its effects, equipment and materials, room arrangement, use of space, and your location within the school. You will need to collect information and use it to make management decisions.

Class Size

Many of your management responsibilities are influenced by the number of students placed in your classroom. Simple routines—such as passing out papers, changing activities, leaving the room, grading assignments, and making up missed assignments—are complicated when class size is large. Any routine is smoother and easier with 20 students than with 30 students. Adjustments in routines to accommodate class size are not necessarily difficult, but they require careful thinking and preparation. Some examples of adjustments in large classes are:

1. Dismiss half the class at a time, regularly alternating which half leaves first.
2. Have stacks of papers located in four corners of the room for distribution by student helpers.
3. Stagger transition time for students to change activities—for example, "Rows 1 and 4 move to the reference shelf area"; one minute later, "Rows 2 and 5 move to centers."

The suggestions for grading and recording paperwork in Chapter Four will be especially helpful if you have a large class. Even your room arrangement will be affected by class size. You may need to eliminate all unnecessary furniture, perhaps including your desk, and cluster desks rather than place in rows. Keep class size in mind as you read about equipment and materials.

Equipment and Materials

The kinds of equipment and materials you have to work with will determine a number of your management decisions. Begin by listing what is available and ask yourself if everything on the list is necessary for your teaching. Some teachers have a tendency to store everything available, from fear of not having enough. Ask yourself: Are there potential problems with this equipment? and Where is the best location? Anticipating problems or consequences of use and location is advancework.

Here are some examples in which advancework will help you anticipate problems or limitations. We provide some possible responses for each situation, but there aren't any set answers. Much depends on your classroom environment and your students.

1. You plan to use an overhead projector often. It is on a permanent stand, and three students in the front corner of the room can't see the image.

   Possible Responses:
   - You develop a signal for those three students and a routine for moving their chairs or themselves to other chairs whenever they hear the signal.
   - You describe the problem to the students at the beginning of the year, and ask for their ideas to solve the problem.
   - You rearrange the classroom so that the problem is eliminated.

2. You have five science kits of basic materials that you will use on a weekly basis for your class of 29 students.

   Possible Responses:
   - You organize your students into groups of five and six in your science class, and develop routines for use of the kits.
   - You organize your students into partners (and one group of three for science), then you plan activities that can be done with and without the kits. Each day a different group of 10 partners uses the kits. For example, on Monday, 10 partners use the kits, and the rest of the class is engaged in research projects and small group teaching. On Tuesday, 10 different partners use the kits, and so on.

There are several possibilities, but three guidelines should govern your responses: First, consider *smoothness*. How can you handle the situation with the least disruption? Second, *promote student involvement*. Students have great ideas about solving typical classroom problems. After a few years of school, they have experience with many situations, so involve them in decisions. And third, *be prepared*. Be prepared for anything. With classroom materials, being prepared means having enough, having them organized, and doing it ahead of time.

Room Arrangement and Use of Space

The way you arrange your classroom communicates management messages about your expectations of how to use the room. Emmer, Evertson, Clements, and Worsham

(1994) provided advancework questions for room arrangement from their observations of effective classroom managers:

1. *Are high traffic areas free of congestion?*
2. *Can students be easily seen by teachers?*
3. *Are frequently used materials and supplies readily accessible?*
4. *Can students easily see instructional presentations and displays?*

Adding to the guidelines, we suggest that you separate areas of quiet work from noisy or active work. Then consider some very specific ideas from the Elementary Research Vignette on how to arrange and use the space in your classroom.

Although this research vignette focuses on elementary classrooms, we suggest that Hodgin and Wolliscroft's ideas about arrangement are practical and relevant to secondary settings. Recently, a high school student was raving about his favorite literature class. When asked to talk about why he liked it so much, one of his descriptions included details about the room. "There's plants everywhere and paintings, so it looks like a home, and the desks are arranged in groups so we can talk about books—real comfortable." Students of all ages like the comfort and aesthetics that Hodgin and Wolliscroft describe.

Look at the room arrangements in Figures 5.2 and 5.3 and assess them by using the advancework guidelines from Evertson and colleagues and the research vignette. Try to be sensitive to what it is like to be a student in those rooms. The same awareness is important as you visit real classrooms and as you consider the next topic—location in the school.

Location in the School

Where your room or rooms are located in the school will have advantages as well as disadvantages. The only room at the end of a hallway isolated from general school traffic can be very appealing to some teachers and loathsome to others. Much depends on your personality and teaching style. There are those who shudder when entering the "no wall" arrangements in schools and those who start thinking excitedly about teaching there. Begin with an awareness of personal preference.

Next, assess your location for its advantages and disadvantages. Consider noise, distractions, traffic, and the kinds of activities conducted in nearby areas:

1. What distractions will we experience here?
2. When will this room be most quiet? Noisiest?
3. May I use adjoining hallways, rooms, and closets?
4. Will I disturb others with some of our activities?

Advancework will be important as you plan your teaching so that your location works for you. You will notice how important relationships are with those significant individuals in the school. Your management decisions cannot be made or implemented in isolation.

Conducting advancework on community, school, and your classroom contexts is a comprehensive process, but one with payoffs for an effective classroom management system.

Elementary Research Vignette

INTRODUCTION

June Hodgin, a special education consultant, and Caaren N. Wolliscroft, an elementary school teacher (1997), were interested in basing their classroom instruction on the 21 elements of the Dunn and Dunn Learning Styles Model. In particular, they wished to use the model to create an effective learning styles environment in order to increase achievement and facilitate both student preference and independence.

STUDY PROCEDURES

Hodgin and Wolliscroft implemented a combination of classroom design elements, learning style strategies, and reading strategies in a third-grade elementary class. The class studied had 22 students (10 Hispanic and 12 Anglo); 4 students were identified as learning disabled and qualified for special education, and another 3 had attention deficit disorders. The students' IQs ranged from 74 to 126. The educators concentrated on the following elements of classroom design:

- *Noise.* Areas were created where students could listen to classical music while working. Other students who needed a quiet evironment wore headphones with the cords removed.
- *Light.* Half the fluorescent lights were removed based on student input that called for dimmer lighting. Some students worked under tables to have even dimmer lighting.
- *Temperature.* Students were encouraged to bring sweaters if they preferred a warmer climate. Those who became hot easily were asked to wear layered clothing so they could remove items to become comfortable.
- *Design.* An "informal area" was created in the class as well as several learning centers.
- *Sociological stimuli.* Areas were created where students could work alone, with a partner, or with a small group. Students needing adult presence were sat in the front or near the teacher's desk.
- *Perception centers.* The learning centers and instruction each day contained activities to stimulate auditory, visual, and tactual/kinesthetic modes. Students were also given computers to use and a listening center.
- *Mobility.* Students were given the right to move about the room freely and to utilize special workplaces of their choice.
- *Intake.* Snack times were built into the classroom schedule. Students were encouraged to bring healthy snacks such as fruit, vegetables, cereal, or crackers.

In conjunction with this new environment, the students were introduced to learning styles early in the year and the educators discussed with them how the various elements helped or hindered their learning. They also administered the Marie Carbo Reading Style Inventory. They discussed the results with each child and the learning style indicated by the test. Parents were then brought in and had the results presented along with the classroom design elements. Parents were also educated on learning styles and the Carbo Inventory itself. Finally, students had reading strategies matched to their learning styles.

STUDY RESULTS

The effectiveness of the combined initiatives were demonstrated by the students' scores on the Texas Assessment of Academic Skills (TAAS) during a three-year period from 1993 to 1996. Prior to implementation, only 50 percent of the regular student population passed the test, and none of the special education students passed. In 1994–1995 and 1995–1996, all the regular education students passed; 25 percent of the special education students passed in 1994–1995 and 20 percent passed in 1995–1996. In addition, student mastery of all test objectives rose from 11 percent in 1994 to 67 percent in 1995 to 80 percent in 1996.

Another indicator of success was the improvement of the classroom climate. Students worked together in heterogeneous ability groups unaware of labels or peer ability. All students had increased their self-esteem, motivation, and attitude because they did not feel stress. They found learning to be fun and satisfying, and found success to be much easier.

CONCLUSIONS AND IMPLICATIONS FOR PRACTICE

Hodgin and Wolliscroft advised that creating a learning styles classroom does not happen quickly. In fact, they have suggested that it may take three to five years to develop a successful learning styles environment. In addition, each year brings a new group of students, so plans must be updated annually to meet the unique and individual needs of the new students. The study implies the importance of positive learning climates and how essential they are to student success. All teachers should do advancework and plan accordingly to create positive and quality learning environments for their students.

FIGURE 5.2 *Elementary Room Arrangements*

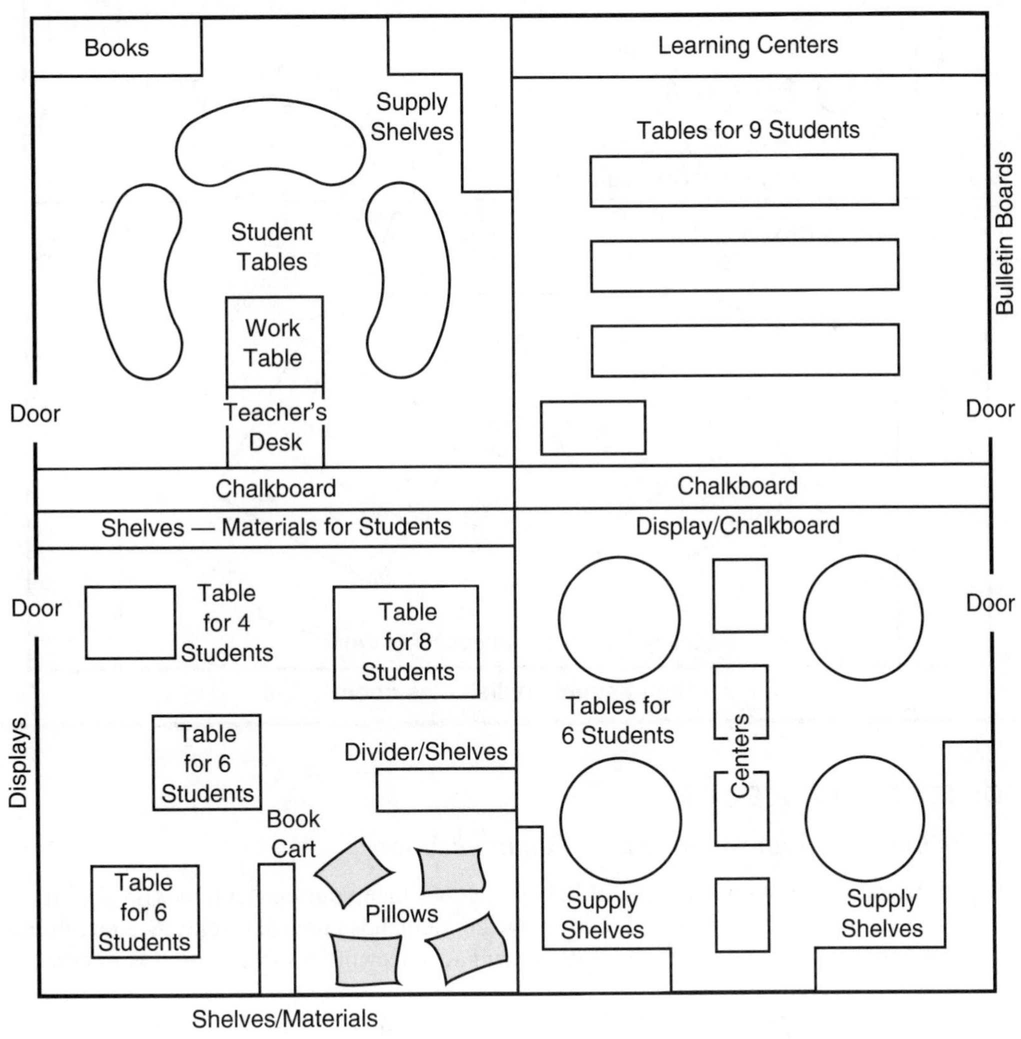

FIGURE 5.3 *Secondary Room Arrangements*

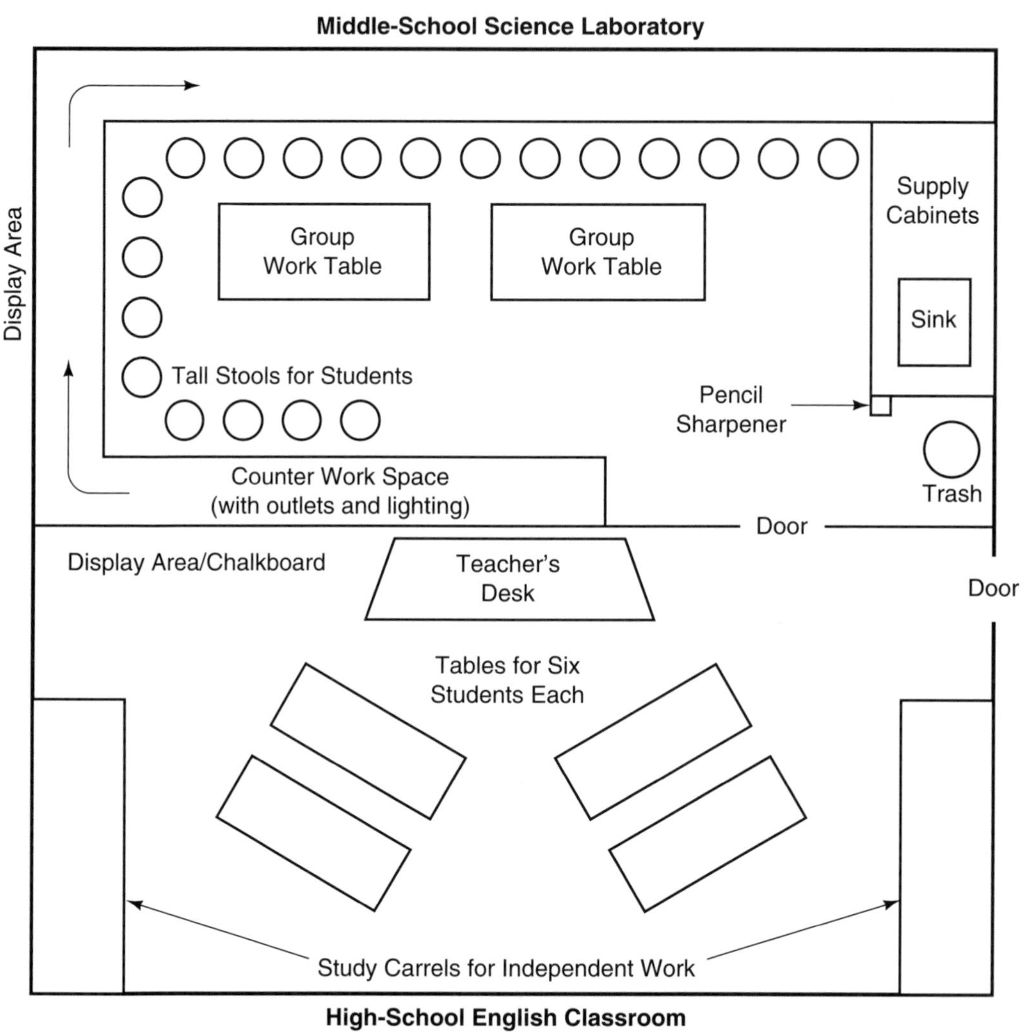

CONTENT ADVANCEWORK

Checking Your Management Communication

Advancework with content will help you coordinate your curriculum with your management. The complexity of today's society demands curricular relevance and utility. We will talk about how to conduct content advancework to determine if your curriculum is relevant and useful.

Begin this advancework with your personal preferences about noise, space, and interactions with students. You might ask yourself: How do I want someone to describe my classroom? Listen to a tape recording of part of your day and examine the messages you are sending to students. When we listen to teachers talk, we hear messages that emphasize orderliness, following directions, and working quietly. Is that how you sound? Is that your intent? With or without your intent, those messages are the informal content of your teaching. From there, you need to consider how students interpret your messages. (See Chapter Fifteen for more information about taped self-assessments.)

Listen to Student Interpretations

Part of the content for students comes from the way they interpret our management messages. We have noticed that students concentrate as much on how to do work and what behaviors to display as they do on actual subject matter. If, in a 20-minute lesson, you spend a great deal of time giving directions, you are probably encouraging students to focus on procedures. You can check on your students' interpretations by asking a few questions before they begin a task: What is the important part of this task? Why are we doing this? What should you be focusing on in your work? In addition to the messages you send and the interpretations students give, your classroom materials are sources of content.

Listen to Your Materials' Cues

Kounin and Gump (1974) noticed that materials act as signals to students. Different materials signal different behaviors, levels of involvement, and the continuity of a lesson. Watch students as they interact with some of the following:

musical instruments	computers
cuisenaire rods	worksheets
magnets	microscopes
photographs	maps

As you plan for students to use materials, stop and think whether the materials will keep the lesson going, bring it to a halt, or interfere with the learning. We recently observed the use of a very exciting set of materials that pulled students completely away from the intended outcome. Instruction was focused on sequencing. Groups of students were given a set of clue cards to solve a mystery, with a process similar to the game of "Clue." The intent was for groups to sequence the clues or information items in order to see the process of building and connecting information. The sequencing process was ignored in the excitement of solving the mystery. Heated discussions of "whodunit" led to the need for management. The noise level and behavior got out of control with the excitement. At first glance, the clue cards looked potentially appropriate and effective, yet they failed miserably. A simple "What will students be likely to do in this activity?" may have predicted the consequences beforehand.

In addition to your informal content with its management messages, student interpretations, and cues from your materials, it will be important to listen to your content for relevance.

Relevance in Content

When subjects or curriculum appear to have little bearing on students' immediate lives, students struggle, they are inattentive, they lack motivation, and they often display distracting or disruptive behavior. When learners do find relevance, their interest and learning increase. Vogel (1994) has urged us to "make learning matter in the lives of our students" by connecting curriculum to the real world and to what's important in students' communities. The way we manage content will enable us to "take seriously the experience of students" (Vogel, 1994, p. 61). You can begin your advancework by listening to content with these questions:

1. Can students connect this knowledge or skill to their daily lives now or in the future?
2. Are there societal trends or examples that parallel this information that I am going to present?
3. Is there an alternative to this learning activity that will be more interesting or engaging?
4. Have any of the students had a similar experience?

Listen to relevance in the Teacher Talk that follows.

TEACHER TALK

Find examples of sentence structures and highlight them in the newspaper articles you have brought for current events.

Middle-School English Teacher

Breaking up a whole number into fractions is like slicing a pizza into pieces.

Third-Grade Teacher

Two people in our class, Tahisha and Sam, have experienced a move like the one we will read about in our story today.

Fifth-Grade Teacher

In some ways, the Boston Tea Party was like the demonstrations you have been reading about in our country today.

Secondary Civics Teacher

Your advancework for content must listen to the content itself as well as how you present it. When students find meaning and use in curriculum, you will see "high levels of student involvement, minimal amounts of interference, and efficient use of instructional time" (Emmer & Evertson, 1981). These are definitely goals of your management.

LEARNER ADVANCEWORK

Much of what we know about how students learn has implications for managing classrooms. As we suggest advancework questions to pose about your learners, we will use that knowledge.

Students Are Active Learners

Active learners move about physically and intellectually to discover, manipulate, experiment, explore, make mistakes, discuss, and problem solve. Physical movement requires you to ask when, where, how, and how much. Intellectual movement requires you to ask about learner differences, needs, and interests. We know that monotony and humdrum tasks result in boredom for learners, so your task will be to provide variety and challenge in activities for intellectually active learning.

Physically Active Learning

Constraint can also contribute to boredom (Wlodkowski & Jaynes, 1990), so you will want to structure learning activities to encourage movement rather than inhibit it. Look at the following examples and determine whether learning can be active:

> "As you work on your individual reports during this time, use your social studies textbooks and materials from home. Work quietly at your desk."
>
> "As you work on your group research reports during this time, consider using reference materials on the back shelves, the magazines in the reading center, or fill out a pass and go to the library."
>
> "You can do your morning seatwork at your desks, at the work table in the back, or on cushions on the floor. When you finish, you may read books, work puzzles, or listen to story tapes."

Can you see the structures that encourage physical movement during learning? To use such structures, students will need to understand how to move about, appropriate times, and limits on movement. Listen again to a structure:

> "If you are ready to critique your geometric construction with a partner, then look around the room for a place where you won't disturb anyone else. Get to that spot quietly, and limit your critiques to five minutes each."

Mentally Active Learning

Those experiences that cause your students to question, process, or apply information are intellectually active. Again, the way you structure the experiences can promote intellectual activity or discourage it. Look at some sets of contrasting examples to see whether such activity will occur:

> "All seatwork is to be placed in the IN box for me to grade."
>
> "When you finish your seatwork, check your answers with the answer key. Record your score in the book, then write a sentence or two describing how you got all your answers correct or how you made mistakes."
>
> "Place punctuation marks in the sentences on page 57."
>
> "Place punctuation marks in the telephone conversation that you recorded last night."

A good advancework question to ask yourself is: What does a student have to do to complete this assignment, or to work on this task, or to answer this question?

Students Are Social Learners

To do your advancework here, think about what it feels like when you have an opportunity to interact with others about something you are learning and when you don't. We suggest this awareness as your first step. The lack of variety that we mentioned earlier minimizes opportunities for social learning. We ask you to check your routines and the way you structure your activities and look for ways to increase social opportunities.

Learning can be exciting when ideas and concepts are discussed and shared. Listen to the following structures providing social opportunities for students:

> "Ask the person next to you to check your sentences while you check his or hers."
>
> "Describe an argument for the new trade law to your partner. When you finish, your partner is to describe an argument against the law."
>
> "Turn to the person behind you and describe one new idea from our class today."

The structures of learning activities such as these support social interactions, communication, and relationships. We also encourage you to use the grouping strategies that we describe in Chapter Ten. We have learned from research that if learners are able to socialize in relation to their academic work, the work is more meaningful and their social needs are met at the same time.

Students Are Confident Learners

Students of all ages learn better if they feel confident and if they experience success while learning. You can use your management routines to communicate to students that they are capable, that you trust them, and that they are responsible. These messages promote confidence. Without awareness, however, you may communicate an opposite message. Here's how that message sounds:

> "When you have a problem with the computer, always check with me before working on it."
>
> "If you can't get work done in your clean-up groups, let me know and I'll help."
>
> "If you can't figure out how to put your folder together, see me."

Those messages say that it would be best if students didn't try, and that you alone are capable of handling the situations. Try changing those messages by turning them into questions. You will express confidence to your students. Listen to the changes:

> "What are some things you could check on the computer before coming to me with problems?"
>
> "If you can't get your work done in your clean-up groups, what can you do about it?"
>
> "When you are putting your folder together, who could you get to help you?"

As students respond, they get involved, make decisions, and usually take care of the work of your classroom. An advancework strategy we suggest here is to survey your management responsibilities. Some possibilities include:

Recording lunch count	Record keeping
Greeting visitors	Collecting work
Distributing materials	Returning work
Storing materials and equipment	Caring for plants
Controlling room temperature	Cleaning
Maintaining safety	Taking roll

Now, ask yourself: Which of these responsibilities could students safely and successfully handle? An example of an appropriate responsibility and how to delegate it to students is seen in the Teacher Talk from a secondary classroom.

TEACHER TALK

I was fed up with interruptions to my teaching, but I was also trying to put students in charge of our room. Students volunteered to be "door greeters" who welcome visitors in a quiet voice and tell them that "Mr. Peterson is busy teaching." Visitors are asked if they would like to sit and observe until class is finished.

Secondary Biology Teacher

Your advancework begins with listing your responsibilities, deciding which ones students can handle successfully, and communicating that expectation to them.

Students Learn by Participating in Classroom Decisions

In many classrooms, students are absolutely powerless with respect to decisions about classroom rules, curriculum, learning activities and materials, and assessment. In many other classrooms, students are able to participate in important classroom decisions about routines, projects, evaluating the class, and planning curriculum. Castle and Rogers (1994) described some compelling outcomes for learners when they have opportunities to make decisions about their classroom lives. Those opportunities can lead to reflection and meaningful connections for learners, a sense of community, and increased cooperation and ownership in the classroom (Heidron & Rabine, 1998). Kohn (1996) also has described more interesting and satisfying work as a benefit for teachers.

To begin the process of student participation in decisions, Kohn (1993) has suggested that you consider the following areas as opportunities for learner involvement:

1. Academic issues to include what, how, how well, and why students are learning
2. Social and behavioral issues to include classroom rules, necessary routines, class problem solving, and limits

Begin your advancework questions with: Who is making these decisions? Might students make the decisions? Who is assessing this? Who is providing feedback for that? and Could students do the assessing or give the feedback?

A few examples will give you an idea of how to provide the kind of opportunities Kohn (1993) suggested:

EXAMPLE: Before beginning a new unit of study, a middle-school geography teacher previews a content outline with her students. Together, they list what information the students already know about the subject, what information makes them curious, and what information is missing.

EXAMPLE: A third-grade teacher regularly checks on class routine and rules from the student perspective with a bulletin board "write in" spot for individual students to comment on "what's working" and "what's not working." Student comments often result in a class discussion to make changes.

EXAMPLE: Senior high-school science students in a nearby school regularly complete their lab assignments with a critique of procedures, an assessment of their own understanding, and a rating of their progress.

Kohn (1993) has encouraged us to engage our learners in conversations and class meetings about what it is like to be controlled and what it is like when learners are really involved in learning (p. 19). By following his suggestions, you will gain important insights about how learners feel about participating in classroom decisions.

Students Need to Feel Safe When Learning

Finally, it is essential to provide for emotional safety if learning is to occur. Your advancework must consider basic human needs and find ways to meet these needs while teaching students.

Providing Emotional Safety

Maslow (1970) represented human needs in a hierarchy with physical needs and safety as essential before others can be met. When children come to school hungry or frightened about a situation on the way to school, they won't be able to learn. If the classroom is an unpredictable, unsafe place where students can be ridiculed, they will be more concerned with protecting themselves than with studying or participating in learning activities.

Many schools and/or individual teachers have adopted the concept of students' rights. You will see an example of those rights in Figure 5.4. They are meant to protect and support the students' right to learn by guaranteeing safety from physical and emotional dangers. Emotionally safe classrooms are those in which students can take risks with creative answers, alternative assignments, or asking a so-called dumb question.

FIGURE 5.4 *Students' Rights (Author Unknown)*

I HAVE A RIGHT TO BE TREATED KINDLY IN THIS ROOM:
THIS MEANS THAT NO ONE WILL LAUGH AT ME OR HURT MY FEELINGS.
I HAVE A RIGHT TO BE MYSELF IN THIS ROOM:
THIS MEANS THAT NO ONE WILL TREAT ME DIFFERENTLY BECAUSE I AM
BLACK OR WHITE,
FAT OR THIN,
TALL OR SHORT,
BOY OR GIRL.
I HAVE A RIGHT TO BE SAFE IN THIS ROOM:
THIS MEANS THAT NO ONE WILL
HIT ME,
KICK ME,
PUSH ME,
OR HURT ME.
I HAVE A RIGHT TO HEAR AND BE HEARD IN THIS ROOM:
THIS MEANS THAT NO ONE WILL
YELL,
SHOUT,
OR MAKE LOUD NOISES.
I HAVE A RIGHT TO LEARN ABOUT MYSELF IN THIS ROOM:
THIS MEANS THAT I WILL BE FREE TO EXPRESS MY FEELINGS AND
OPINIONS WITHOUT BEING INTERRUPTED OR RIDICULED.

Providing a Sense of Belonging

Once safety and survival needs are met, Maslow pointed to the need for a sense of belonging. In your classroom, it is important for students to feel part of a group, to be included in group activities, and to be valued by others. There is evidence that friendships and peer relationships enhance learning activities (Schmuck & Schmuck, 1974). Begin your advancework in this area by asking yourself some questions: Do my routines, comments, and activities encourage competition? Do my routines foster relationships and communication? Can students take risks or try out alternatives?

Listen to the Teacher Talk that follows and decide for yourself if students are going to feel a sense of belonging.

TEACHER TALK

You will be working in teams of four on your projects. First, meet to determine each person's strengths and interests, then plan your display and divide the work.

Secondary Health Teacher

When your partner is absent from school, be sure to take notes, record assignments, and collect an extra copy of everything that is distributed to put in her or his folder. Then welcome her or him back.

Middle-School Homeroom Teacher

We are going to be working on environmental collages at the end of the week. I have begun a collection of materials in these bins. We need more. See if you can come up with more materials by Friday.

Third-Grade Teacher

Providing Physical Safety

The learners' sense of being physically safe will influence their emotional safety. Begin with some questions for students: When and where do you feel safe in our classroom? and When and where do you not feel safe in our classroom? When you work on room arrangement, keep this information in mind.

A second check on students' sense of being physically safe is a look at the transitions that occur in your classroom. A *transition* is a time of change—a change from one place to another, from one activity to another. A common teacher behavior during transitions has been described by Kounin (1970) as *herding.* When a fourth-grade teacher directs students to line up at the door to go to the cafeteria, she is herding students. There is potential for physical danger as well as behavior problems.

Consider an alternative to the herding just described. The fourth-grade teacher asks students in row 3 to line up at the door, then row 5, and on through the rows. A second-grade teacher suggests that everyone who had tortillas for breakfast line up,

then everyone who had pancakes, then everyone who had toast, and so on. Besides worrying about herding, consider how much interest you could bring to a dull routine!

Many upper-elementary and middle-school teachers have students come up with their own categories for transition routines. We've heard fifth-graders suggest birthdays, favorite pizza ingredients, TV shows, and clothing labels. There doesn't seem to be much worry about transitions in high school, yet there are plenty of adolescents who would welcome a less hassled and gentler move to their next class. Our best advice is to discuss transitions with students and ask for suggestions. In the next chapter, we describe other transition strategies for keeping your classroom running smoothly.

In sum, the learner is the most important target for your advancework awareness. That advancework must be maintained for a continual check of the effect of your management on learners.

SUMMARY

Our main objective for this chapter was for you to be able to conduct advancework to gather information to make management decisions. We described your context advancework encompassing the community, the school, and your own classroom. You will need to survey the community and your school, recording the information for those decisions that follow. Remember to make contact with those important people in your school and notice the climate. Check your own room for the influence of class size, equipment and materials, room arrangement and use of space, and location in the school for advancework information.

To conduct content advancework, we encouraged you to listen for the messages of your room, your materials, and your routines. Notice, too, the relevance of your curriculum to students' lives.

Learner advancework considers the qualities that promote learning: active students, social students, confident and successful students, students who participate in classroom decisions, and emotionally and physically safe students. We described structures that promote those qualities and gave you glimpses of structures that could inhibit them. The most important advice we can offer here is to do advancework. Without advancework, management in classrooms is often characterized by repetition, isolation, and lack of joy.

Although some repetition is necessary for learning, our experience tells us that repetition gets boring for you and your students. Without information gathering, many of your management decisions will be made spontaneously. They may not result in clear information for students or the intended outcomes. When this occurs, you will have to rethink the decision, or rephrase it to students, or remind them of it—repetition.

Classroom management without support or contacts may mean that you work in isolation. Without advancework, we have seen teachers facing difficult management problems completely alone. Those problems seem larger or more horrible when faced alone day after day.

When problems can be shared with colleagues, they are often met with, "I remember when I was struggling with a student with temper tantrums and thought I would not survive the year." Knowing that you are not the only one helps you see the situation as less personal, and you can be more effective in your problem solving.

TEACHER TALK

A few years ago, I had a student who "smart mouthed" me when I would call on her or try to get her to pay attention. She was quite loud, used profanity, and I was embarrassed in front of the other students. I tried everything, but I didn't want other teachers hearing it, so I started closing my door. I was close to tears when I finally went to the school counselor for help. I wish I hadn't waited so long.

It took a while but the student and I both made changes. By the end of the year, we were working together.

Middle-School History Teacher

A management system developed without advancework has more potential for behavior problems and, eventually, discipline. A friend of ours says that when discipline is frequent, "teachers get hurt or they get hard." Instead, we wish you the joy of a smooth-running classroom, exciting content, and involved learners. Advancework can help you experience that joy. In the next chapter, we will guide you from advancework to management strategies which extend beyond discipline to effective teaching.

REFERENCES

Brophy, J. E. (1999). Perspectives of classroom management: Yesterday, today, and tomorrow. In Jerome Freiberg (Ed.), *Beyond behaviorism: Changing the classroom management paradigm.* Boston: Allyn and Bacon.

Castle, K., & Rogers, K. (1994). Rule-creating in a constructivist community. *Childhood Education, 70*(2), 77–80.

Cohen, E. (1996). *Designing groupwork: Strategies for the heterogeneous classroom.* New York: Teachers College Press.

Emmer, E. T., & Evertson, C. M. (1981). Synthesis of research on classroom management. *Educational Leadership, 38*(4), 342–347.

Emmer, E. T., Evertson, C. M., Clements, B. S., & Worsham, M. E. (1994). *Classroom management for secondary teachers.* Englewood Cliffs, NJ: Prentice Hall.

Evertson, C. M., Emmer, E. T., Clements B. S., & Worsham, M. E. (1997). *Classroom management for secondary teachers* (4th ed.). Boston: Allyn and Bacon.

Evertson, C., & Harris, A. (1999). Creating a positive learning environment: The classroom organization and management program (COMP). In Jerome Freiberg, (Ed.), *Beyond behaviorism: Changing the classroom management paradigm.* Boston: Allyn and Bacon.

Freiberg, H. J. (2000). *Consistency management & cooperative discipline: Strategies for the classroom.* Houston, TX: Consistency Management Associates.

Heidron, M. E., & Rabine, B. L. (1998). In the zone: Empowering students and teachers to be agents of change. *English Journal, 88*(3), 46–52.

Hodgin, J., & Wolliscroft, C. (1997). Eric learns to read: Learning styles at work. *Educational Leadership, 54*(6), 43–45.

King, L. H. (1983). Pupil classroom perceptions and expectancy effect. *South Pacific Journal of Teacher Education, 11*(1), 54–70.

Kohn, A. (1993). Choices for children: Why and how to let students decide. *Kappan, 75*(1), 8–20.

Kohn, A. (1996). *Beyond discipline: From compliance to community.* Arlington, VA: Association of Supervision and Curriculum Development.

Kounin, J. (1970). *Discipline and group management in classrooms.* New York: Holt, Rinehart and Winston.

Kounin, J., & Gump, P. (1974). Signal systems of lesson settings and the task related behavior of preschool children. *Journal of Educational Psychology, 66,* 554–562.

Maslow, A. H. (1970). *Motivation and personality* (2nd ed.). New York: Harper and Row.

Schmitt, L. (1993). *Classroom design and its relationship to student community.* Unpublished masters' thesis, Portland State University.

Schmuck, R., & Schmuck, P. (1974). *A humanistic psychology of education: Making the school everybody's house.* Palo Alto, CA: National Press Books.

Swetnam, R., & Stokes, P. (1994). Teachers take surprise tour to learn the neighborhood. *Curriculum Review, 33*(6), 7.

Vogel, M. J. (1994). Kids learn when it matters. In Editorial Projects in Education (Eds.), *Thoughtful teachers, thoughtful schools.* Boston: Allyn and Bacon.

Wlodkowski, R. J., & Jaynes, J. H. (1990). *Eager to learn: Helping children become motivated and love learning.* San Francisco: Jossey-Bass.

SAMPLES AND EXAMPLES

This Samples and Examples section includes the following:

- The Student Needs Assessment Questionnaire will give you a sense of student thoughts about the climate of your class.
- The Feedback Form is designed to give you feedback in three areas: difficulty of material, pace of the presentation, and class participation.
- The Advancework Checklist is designed to give you an overview of your advancework implementation.

STUDENT NEEDS ASSESSMENT QUESTIONNAIRE

Check the appropriate box.

Your Thoughts about Our Class	*Always*	*Most of the Time*	*Sometimes*	*Seldom*	*Never*
Physiological Needs					
1. Do you eat a good breakfast each morning?					
2. Can you see the blackboard and screen room from where you are sitting?					
3. Do I talk loud and clear enough for you to hear?					
4. Do you have enough time to complete your assignments?					
5. Is the room a quiet place to work?					
Safety and Security					
6. Does each day in this class seem organized?					
7. Do you follow the school and classroom rules?					
8. Is the discipline used in this classroom fair?					
9. Do you feel free enough to ask me questions?					
10. Can you get help when you need it?					
Love and Belonging					
11. Do you think that the students in this class like you?					
12. Am I friendly and do I smile at you?					
13. Do I take time with you each day?					
14. Do you feel that I listen to you when you have a problem?					
15. Do I praise you when you deserve it?					
16. Do other students respect your property?					
Self-Esteem					
17. Do you feel involved in this class?					
18. What subject area do you feel most successful at? ___________					
19. What subject area could you improve in? ___________					

Source: Adapted from *Comprehensive Classroom Management: Creating Positive Learning Environments for All Students,* 4th ed., by Vernon F. Jones and Louise S. Jones, 1995, Boston: Allyn and Bacon.

FEEDBACK FORM

(No Name) Period ________

Date ________

Rate the material learned today in class:

1	2	3
difficult	just right	too easy
1	2	3
interesting	somewhat	not interesting

Rate today's presentation:

1	2	3
clear	somewhat	not clear
1	2	3
too slow	just right	too fast
1	2	3
energetic	just right	dull

Rate your participation in today's class:

1	2	3
involved	somewhat	not involved
1	2	3
comfortable asking questions	somewhat	uncomfortable asking questions

Do you have any suggestions for this class? ________________________________

____

____

____

____

____

____

____

Source: From *Cooperative Professional Education Program Training Materials* by A. Driscoll, 1988. Portland, OR: Portland State University. Adapted by permission.

ADVANCEWORK CHECKLIST

	Yes	No	In Progress
■ Completed the Community Context Checklist (p. 121)	______	______	______
■ Met at least three significant individuals	______	______	______
■ Matched number of students in class with seating, paper flow, and movement	______	______	______
■ Arranged room and space to minimize congestion and confusion	______	______	______
■ Checked my content advancework	______	______	______
■ Taped a class to check my communication with students, including giving directions, clarifying tasks, and giving material cues	______	______	______
■ Checked my learner advancework	______	______	______
■ Allowed for physically and mentally active learning	______	______	______
■ Encouraged students to be social and confident learners	______	______	______
■ Checked that classroom is an emotionally and physically safe place to learn	______	______	______
■ Received written feedback from students about how we are doing	______	______	______

CHAPTER 6

CLASSROOM MANAGEMENT

Beyond Discipline

Chapter Outcomes

At the conclusion of this chapter you will be able to:

1. *Use management strategies to promote instruction and build student self-discipline.*
2. *Plan management strategies to begin the school year, respond to interruptions and transitions, and communicate with parents and students.*
3. *Use ideas and information from advancework and management models to make decisions.*

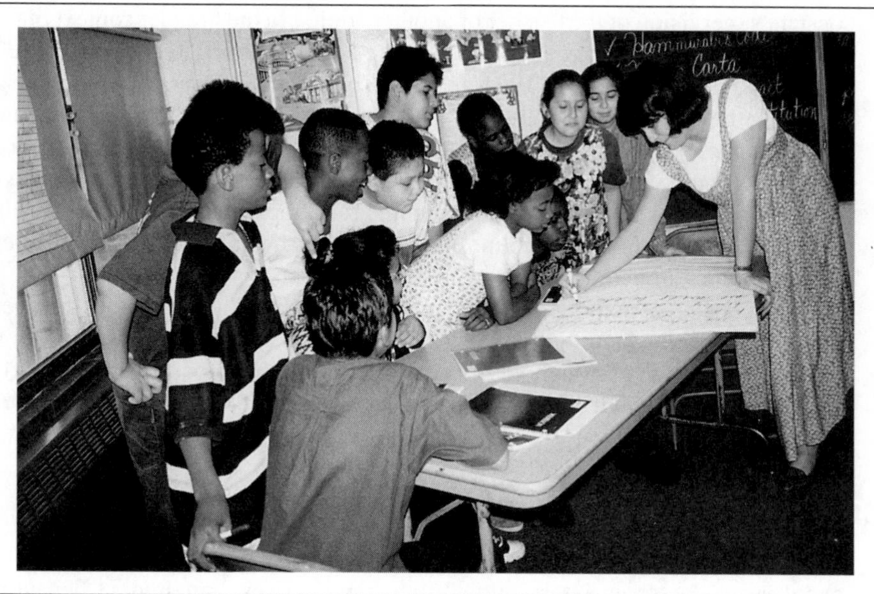

Key Terms and Concepts

Student Self-Discipline
Beginning of the School Year
Interruptions
Transitions
Classroom Crises
Student Behavior Problems
Communicating with Parents
Classroom Management Models
Behavior Modification
Reality Therapy
Judicious Discipline
Assertive Discipline
Adlerian Model (Dreikurs' Approach)
Consistency Management & Cooperative Discipline
Smoothness and Momentum
Special Needs Student

INTRODUCTION

Classroom management can be a pathway or a barrier to better teaching and learning. In most instances, classroom management reflects the ability of the teacher to teach while creating an environment that allows students to learn. When classroom management is working well, it is almost invisible; when it is not working well, disorder and disruptions of learning are obvious. Unwritten and written rules, procedures, routines, tasks, and activities occur in the classroom each and every day. They are intertwined with a learning environment that needs to be caring, supportive, fair, and responsive to needs of students and teachers. Achieving a pathway to positive learning environments is obtained from matching the best elements of different classroom management models to the learner, the context, and the content. This will allow students to become self-disciplined and give teachers the opportunity to facilitate learning.

The leading goal of every teacher we talked with included student self-discipline. Students who are self-disciplined are able to work with each other or alone without constant supervision of the teacher or another adult. "In the broader context of life, self-discipline is knowledge about oneself and the actions needed to grow and develop as a person" (Rogers & Freiberg, 1994, p. 221). There are many models and strategies for managing the classroom and building self-discipline. Six models will be presented later in this chapter. No one model or program will create the same degree of self-discipline in every student. Self-discipline builds over time and requires opportunities to experience responsibility. Too many children come to school lacking in the prerequisite experiences that lead to self-discipline. Classroom management approaches that enhance self-discipline will benefit both you and your students.

The crafting of activities that enhance self-discipline begin prior to the opening of school. The active planning that goes into the first days and weeks of school will set the stage for learning throughout the year. "The planning process should clearly articulate the desired student roles, which then becomes both the goal and rationale for the teacher's management system" (Brophy & Alleman, 1998, p. 58).

CLASSROOM MANAGEMENT STRATEGIES

There are recurring situations that demand your management: the beginning of the school year, classroom interruptions, transitions, crises, and student behavior problems, to cite just a few. Each requires you to use some advancework information—that is, what you know about your students, the context, and your curriculum. From there, use strategies to stay focused on teaching and to manage beyond discipline.

Beginning of the School Year

Studies of effective teachers show that management is well established in the first few weeks of school. Common sense tells you this is important, but the studies actually describe what teachers do. When researchers Evertson, Emmer, Clements, and Worsham (1997) observed effective teachers at the beginning of the school year, they saw the teachers establish rules and procedures, observe students, and begin with energy and enthusiasm. From their observations, Evertson, Emmer, Clements, and Worsham offer advice for beginning the school year.

Establishing Rules and Procedures

To be effective in this process, you will need to follow three steps repeatedly during the first weeks of school: (1) teach the rules and procedures with explanations, modeling, and discussions; (2) practice the rules and procedures with students; and (3) provide feedback to students about whether they are following the rules correctly or incorrectly.

In the following Snapshot, this sequence is used to establish procedures for using reference materials.

SNAPSHOT: Elementary Classroom

Mr. Silva begins the afternoon with, "I want everyone to turn to the back of the room and look at the shelves of materials." He moves to the back and gestures toward the shelves, "Here we have all kinds of materials you can use when you write reports, prepare your presentations, or just look up information. We have old textbooks, paperbacks, and other nonfiction books, magazines, and pamphlets. It's going to be important to use these carefully and return them correctly so that everyone will have the resources they need.

"Let's pick a topic and I'll show you how to use these materials and how to return them. Let's say your topic is dinosaurs and you want to read about them. First, pick the subject area where you think you'll find dinosaurs." Mr. Silva points to a poster list of subject areas and asks for ideas. Tony says, "Science," and Cecilia replies, "History." Mr. Silva responds with, "You may both be correct. Lots of topics could be found in more than one subject area."

Mr. Silva then demonstrates how to look in the science area for textbooks, paperbacks, magazines, and pamphlets. He finds two magazines and a book about dinosaurs. "Now watch this part. First, sign this sheet with your name and the titles of what you have found. Then you may take these to your desk, or work table, or home.

"To return these materials, watch as I put the book in the bin labeled 'Books,' and the magazines in the bin labeled 'Publications.' Then I put a check next to my name here on the list to show that I returned them" (demonstrates on the list). Mr. Silva then asks questions about the procedures.

"Now let's see if Cecilia was correct and look in the history area for information on dinosaurs. Matthew, come up and show us how you would look." As Matthew looks through the book list, Mr. Silva comments, "Yes, that's correct to begin with the book list." Other students are called on to show how to find magazines, how to put away books, and where to use the materials. They also hear, "That's correct, you can use those at the work table" or "No, you need to put those in the bin labeled 'Books.'"

During the next month, students hear, "I noticed you checked your name when you returned the materials," "You followed the procedures correctly when you used the pamphlets," or "You forgot to complete the information on the list."

The students received feedback about whether their procedures were correct or incorrect. Did you also note that Mr. Silva spent enough time describing and practicing the procedures? Reference materials are going to be used all year, so it is important to spend time establishing procedures well. When this does not happen, and you are still reminding students how to check out books or how to put them away in April, how will you feel?

In the Samples and Examples at the back of this chapter, we provide a First-Week Checklist to help you remember important routines and procedures.

Observing Students

During the first month of school, effective teachers plan activities and time schedules that free them to observe students (e.g., an independent practice activity). They are able to see work habits, social interactions, learning preferences, and signs of attitudes toward curriculum and school. You can usually observe students during independent work activities, small group projects, and whole-class discussions. It will help if you observe them in different learning situations. You may want simply to record what is happening during these observations, or you may want to have a checklist of items for which you are looking. (Chapter Fourteen provides several samples appropriate for using to observe students, and the Learner Profile in Chapter Seven offers another form for gathering information on students.)

Some of your observational time may be spent in one-to-one interactions with students, such as interviews, conferences, or just "getting acquainted" conversations. Such interactions begin a relationship and also allow you to observe students.

Being an Enthusiastic Teacher

Years of teaching prompt our advice: Spend the month before school resting, eating well, exercising, and relaxing. Start the school year with lots of energy, both for planning and teaching. Students are impressed and influenced by high-energy teaching.

TEACHER TALK

I put everything I've got into those first few weeks—my best activities, all my energy, and even a few tricks. I want kids to think that I'm the best teacher they've ever seen or heard. Once I get them on my side, then I can ease up a little and we're ready to work together for the year.

Fifth-Grade Teacher

Students generally arrive at school after a summer break with high expectations as well as high energy and enthusiasm. They don't want to be disappointed. If you can communicate that you care about them and about your curriculum, that you are ready to teach with energy and enthusiasm, they will be positive, too.

Interruptions

Interruptions are regular occurrences in classrooms, much to the dismay and frustration of teachers and students. Your advancework with administrators, office staff, and parents can ward off some interruptions. Ideally, a time can be set aside each day for announcements and messages, so that you are interrupted only for emergencies. When school life is less than ideal, begin by prioritizing your interruptions and responding to them in ways that discourage or regulate them.

Prioritizing Interruptions

Start by categorizing your time for interruptions with advancework questions:

- What times of day will interruptions seriously interfere with instruction?
- What times of day will interruptions cause minimal interference with instruction?
- What times of day are you free to respond to messages, questions, and requests?
- Do you need to stop teaching each time a visitor comes to the door, a message arrives, or someone has a question?

From there, identify high-priority or emergency-type interruptions and low-priority or nonemergency-type interruptions that you can anticipate. An example of a high-priority (emergency) interruption occurs when a third-grader announces that his friend is ill or when a tenth-grader informs you that her friend may be in trouble with a dangerous drug reaction. These call for an immediate response. An example of a low-priority (nonemergency) interruption occurs when a parent or another student brings in a forgotten lunch or a note from the library. These do not call for an immediate response.

Responding to Interruptions

Once you identify instructional times that should not be interrupted and categorize anticipated interruptions, you have some options. Depending on school policy, you can request that messages be held for a later time, hang a "Do Not Disturb—Prime-Time Teaching" sign on your door, or assign students to greet and take messages. Such procedures communicate an important message—that teaching and learning are too important to be interrupted.

Much of what happens with interruptions in your class will be determined by the way you respond early in the school year. Evertson, Emmer, Clements, and Worsham

(1997) observed numerous interruptions occurring in the first few days of school. They saw parent requests, administrative questions, visitors, clerical concerns, and late-arriving students. They also noticed that effective teachers did not allow such interruptions to interfere with their work and with the attention being given to students. Effective teachers simply would not be distracted until they had students involved in an activity. These teachers rarely left the room; if necessary, they conversed with parents or faculty inside the room. New students arriving late were assisted by student helpers.

A unique kind of interruption is caused by events that disturb the normal flow or routines of the day. Such events include holidays, special programs, extreme weather conditions, or national events. Kounin (1970) observed teachers trying to proceed with all the normal routines and instruction as if these events didn't exist. He referred to this as "fighting windmills." Teachers are usually unsuccessful and exhausted when they fight windmills.

For example, when school children in southern California witness a snowstorm or when high-school seniors hear that a popular athlete suffered a broken leg, teachers are fighting windmills if they ignore the events and try to proceed as usual. Your alternative is to acknowledge the event, provide time to discuss it, and, if possible, integrate it with your teaching. Stop and experience it with your students, then include it in your teaching. Write poems about the snow or compose a news story about the athlete.

Transitions

Research shows that the smoothness of your classroom can be predicted by the way you handle transitions (Arlin, 1979). Remember the *herding* behavior we described in the last chapter? It usually occurs during transitions from one place to another. Other transitions include changes from one activity to another, from one subject area to another, and even from the beginning of a lesson to the end of a lesson. Transitions occur regularly each day and in each class period.

When Arlin (1979) observed student teachers at the elementary and junior high-school levels, he found that student off-task behaviors and disruptions were twice as frequent during transitions than during other instruction times. Thus, planning for transitions is essential.

Anticipating and Planning for Transitions

Begin by reviewing your daily plan or class schedule and predict times when change or waiting is inevitable. Visualize what your students will need during those times or what could occur. From there, you can plan as these teachers have done:

EXAMPLE: A kindergarten teacher anticipates that the librarian might not be ready for her class at exactly 10:00 and therefore has three quiet fingerplays ready for the wait.

EXAMPLE: A fourth-grade teacher looks at his afternoon schedule and notices that an intense 40-minute math period is followed by a quiet social studies research activity. He plans a 3-minute conversation time for his students to stand near their desks and visit with each other before beginning the research activity.

EXAMPLE: The middle-school history teacher knows that her students have a health class before coming to her room. To make the transition to their history topic, she asks, "Which of today's health problems could have existed during the Civil War?"

Establishing Routines for Transitions

The times when students first arrive, before and after lunch, and at the end of the day are often characterized as ragged, nonproductive, and unpleasant by teachers and students. These transition times occur every day and are appropriate for well-established routines. These routines should be taught with the same practice and feedback we suggested for the beginning of the year. During the year, add some variety to make them interesting, and adjust them to changes. We see classrooms with interesting routines for transitions in these examples:

EXAMPLE: Second-graders know that from 8:00 to 8:10 A.M. (when children are arriving) they are to check the Classroom Chore List for assignments. If they don't have a chore, they can read quietly or work on puzzles.

EXAMPLE: Sixth-grade students check the list of materials written in a box on the chalkboard as soon as they arrive in the classroom after lunch. They know that the materials must be organized on their desks by 12:55, when the afternoon class begins.

EXAMPLE: During the last six minutes of a twelfth-grade composition class, students complete a self-evaluation of the day's work and write a plan for their work the next day.

Ending a class on a positive note or starting the day with a smooth beginning is worth the effort you make with these transitions.

Avoiding Student Waiting

Notice that in the transition examples, students did not have to wait. Students feel frustrated, resentful, distrusting, and disappointed when you have to search for the paint or writing paper, when you have to read through the teacher's guide to see what's next, or when you struggle to decide how to do the history projects.

To avoid student waiting, prepare materials, equipment, and procedures beforehand. Involve students. They are quite competent at setting up and adjusting the overhead projector, counting out and arranging stacks of art paper, distributing materials for math, and even writing the agenda on the board. Your responsibility is a planning one, essential to being ready and involving students. Planning conserves time for teaching and learning, and helps you avoid spending time on discipline.

Classroom Crises

Classroom life is subject to a wide variety of crises at any time. Some are regular occurrences and some are infrequent. What is important, even if a certain crisis never happens, is that you are ready for it.

Anticipating Potential Crises

Again, begin by anticipating what could happen. When groups of elementary and secondary teachers were surveyed for potential and experienced crises, their responses included:

Fire and fire drill
Earthquakes, tornadoes
Bomb scares and alerts
Serious injury
Bees, insects, snakes in classroom
Visits by angry, violent parents
Spilled paint
Power failure
Serious fights
Student "high" (drugs)
Kidnapping of student
Wet pants
Lost student
Broken glass
Gas leak
Student illness

The list could go on. The impact varies, but no classroom is free of crises.

TEACHER TALK

You want to hear about crises? One of our worst is when there are bears on the playgrounds and we can't have recess.

Elementary Classroom Teacher (in Alaska)

Preparing for Crises

Our best advice is to prepare. Most schools have specific procedures for some crises, so your first step is to be informed. From there, predict a list of possibilities like the one we just reviewed, and develop a response plan for each. Other teachers and administrators are ideal consultants when you are planning ahead. You don't have to have a detailed written plan; a simple plan composed in your head will do.

An example of a mental plan for a crisis such as serious student injury would have the following steps:

1. Move students out of the area of the injured student.
2. Make the injured student comfortable and secure.
3. Seek assistance (send another student to the office or call).
4. Get supplies or equipment.
5. Keep everyone calm.

Crises will feel different when they have been anticipated, discussed, and rehearsed. They can also be excellent learning opportunities, so think about how to involve students in your plans. Students gain security from information and practice.

Student Behavior Problems

During the last 30 years, public opinion polls, conducted by Gallup and reported by *Phi Delta Kappan,* show that in 1971, discipline ranked third in leading school concerns. In 1982, a lack of discipline ranked first in public concerns. In 1992, it ranked third, behind school finance and drugs, and in 1994, lack of discipline in schools was joined by fighting/violence/gangs (Rose & Gallup, 1998) as the number-one concern of the public. The trend continues and there seems to be little hope that these concerns will change any time soon as we enter the new millennium. Beyond discipline issues, Wang, Haertel, and Walberg (1993) found that classroom management is the number-one direct influence affecting student learning.

Identifying Student Behavior Problems

Your starting point is one of defining and identifying *problem behavior.* It may mean something different for individual students and for different settings. The important question is: Does the behavior interfere with teaching and learning? The answer is yes when behavior ruins the classroom climate with tension or blocks your teaching with noises or movement.

Remember to use the advancework we urged in Chapter Five to get others' perspectives as well as make you "supportable." Consider the usual causes of behavior problems:

1. *Teacher-student value conflicts*
2. *Physical, mental and social status of students*

"Now about our school's number-one problem: discipline..."

3. *Lack of teacher preparation*
4. *Negative influence of home and community*
5. *Teacher inexperience in coping with problems*
6. *Differences between teachers' expectations and students' responses*
7. *Lack of communication or miscommunication in classroom. (Swick, 1977)*

A profile of teaching in urban schools describes everyday classroom life as characterized by all seven of the major causes (*Education Week,* 1988), so your starting point is to assess your classroom and yourself.

Developing Responses to Student Behavior Problems

Before deciding how you will respond to behavior problems, distinguish between minor and major problems. Just like interruptions, you don't want to respond to all of them in the same way. *Minor* problems are one-time occurrences, irritations, or distractions. *Major* problems are recurring interferences that bring with them tension and other problems. For minor problems, you need responses that do not interfere with your teaching and that are quick and easy to use:

1. *Signals.* Teachers use a hand signal or small body motion (like a third-base baseball coach) to communicate, "Stop what you are doing." Effective teachers can point a finger or nod their heads at a disturbing student without ever stopping their teaching. Students generally know that the message means to stop.
2. *Eye contact.* Teachers simply pause and make eye contact with a student and send the message to pay attention.
3. *Proximity.* Teachers move closer to the student to stop or control the behavior. When students are whispering instead of listening, a teacher walks toward them while continuing a presentation.

For major problems, you will need a more comprehensive approach. Start with the student. Talk in private about the behavior and possible causes. In addition to the student's ideas and feelings, consider the following:

1. Review school records for possible medical or psychological causes.
2. Assess social interactions and peer relationships.
3. Check the classroom for lighting, temperature, room arrangement, furniture condition, comfort, and location of the student.
4. Check your teaching and curriculum for appropriateness to student ability, need, and relevance to the student.

Anticipate what you may find out when you begin this approach. When you ask your student what is happening or why a problem exists, you may hear, "Your class is boring," or "My parents are getting a divorce," or "I work a night shift at McDonald's and I'm tired," or "I'm hungry." Be ready for the possibilities. You may need the assistance of counselors or other personnel. If you have done your advancework, you know what kind of support you will have.

Secondary Research Vignette

INTRODUCTION

Does family income level of adolescents influence the extent and nature of trouble making in school? This is a question that became the focus of a study that examined the influences of student family income on student discipline problems (Brantlinger, 1993).

METHODS

Using qualitative methods (including interviews and observations), 40 low-income and 34 high-income students were part of a study at two junior and two senior high schools in a midwestern city of 60,000 people. Of those in the study, 85 percent of the students were European American and 15 percent were African American. The students were identified through census data and were interviewed for 1½ hours in their homes or apartments. The semistructured (open-ended) interviews examined their lives in school from interactions with teachers to incidence of discipline problems.

STUDY RESULTS

Some 57 percent of misbehavior of low-income students was attributed to hostility and anger, whereas only 8 percent of misbehavior of high-income students could be attributed to these causes. For high-income students, 71 percent felt teacher attitudes toward them were positive, whereas 60 percent of low-income students felt teacher attitudes were negative or ambivalent and their interactions with teachers were adversarial. Students' perceptions of teacher affect carried over to the issue of fairness regarding the consequences of misbehavior. Some 80 percent of low-income students felt their discipline was unfair, "saying that punishment was undeserved, too severe, disproportionate to misdeeds, or that they were picked on or singled out" (Brantlinger, 1993, p. 6). Also, 57 percent of the high-income students felt they were at an advantage when it came to discipline. One student explained, "We are in the popular group—I think teachers kind of respect us. We don't get punished even when we get a little wild"(p. 6). Only 12.5 percent of the students in the low-income group were on grade level and received average or above-average grades.

Many of the low-income students reported feelings of vulnerability, impotence, and humiliation. They saw school as a "humiliating and rejecting" place, whereas high-income students saw school as an "orderly and accepting place." Brantlinger found low-income student behavioral reactions include "sassing back," deliberate nonparticipation (passive-aggressive), and withholding affection. Once a cycle of conflict with teachers and peers begins, it leads to more punishment, increased anger, failure, and being stereotyped as bad or mean, leading to further student alienation from teachers and school.

DISCUSSION AND IMPLICATIONS FOR PRACTICE

School practices and teacher affect that perpetuate differences between students based on social class and income levels can create anger and greater discipline problems with low-income students. Teachers from lower- or middle-income levels may find greater affiliation with the higher-income students. When persistent problems occur, you may want to look beyond the immediate discipline problem to see the root causes of student behavior. Ask yourself if you are being fair to all your students and if lower-income students are receiving harsher consequences than higher-income students for the same infractions. Also, identify friendship patterns in the classroom by using a simple survey that asks students who they would like to work with in the class. If a student is not selected by any peer in class, try giving that student additional attention by highlighting particular strengths and quietly encouraging other students to work with him or her.

School records can help with specific information and a look at homelife to understand what you are seeing in the classroom. Students often reflect what is happening at home, or use school to release feelings and tensions from home.

We know that there is a significant relationship between disruptive behavior and the degree to which a student is accepted socially by peers. The secondary research vignette highlights how economic conditions can influence behavior and friendship patterns among students. You may need to assist some students who are being shunned in class or who are rejected by peers during group work by structuring classroom situations in order to provide opportunities for social acceptance. Chapter Ten discusses strategies for improving the participation of students who are social isolates during cooperative group work.

The third check is based on the influence of physical conditions of an environment. For example, overcrowding is known to have a direct effect on student behavior, causing restlessness, inattention, and aggressiveness. Try putting yourself in the student's place and see how it feels.

The last suggestion asks you to check your own teaching and curriculum. Review the advice of Carroll in Chapter Four and your advancework on students and content in Chapter Five. Listen to your communication and management messages and watch how you interact with students. Be assured that neither you nor the curriculum is the cause of the behavior problem.

You may have a great deal of information when you complete the five steps suggested, but you still have a problem. An important next step in this comprehensive process is to communicate with the student's parents.

Communicating with Parents

Communication with parents can result in information sharing, agreement and support, and consistency between home and school, all of which are especially important when behavior problems exist.

Advancework for Communicating with Parents

Begin with a recognition of the importance and power of parents. Hopefully, they are teaching the student how to express needs and feelings, to cooperate, and to respond to situations. Whether or not you agree with their teaching, recognizing parents' importance is essential to effective communication.

From there, establish informal communication, ideally before a problem exists. This can be done with handwritten notes, brief phone calls, or conversations, after school. The tone is positive and the message is, "I want to work with you," or "I'm glad to have your daughter in my class," or "Your son is involved in our projects." If this advancework is done, a problem-solving session will be part of ongoing communication.

Conferencing with Parents

Think of this step as a two-way process. Each of you has important information for the other. If you have done your advancework, parents will feel secure about asking and answering questions. They can learn about class routines, goals, curriculum, expectations, and their child's behavior. You can learn about the student's experiences, interests, expectations, and behavior at home.

In addition to advancework for conferences, it will be important to keep your talk free from educational jargon. Buskin (1975) found that jargon is a serious barrier to communication with parents. Parents find it meaningless, frustrating, offensive, and insulting. Tape a practice conference and listen carefully to your choice of words. Develop your questions at this time to assure clear wording, nonthreatening quality, and specificity of information you are seeking.

Continue your preparation by establishing an agenda, developing important questions in advance, and gathering and organizing data to share. A conference agenda should be simple and, if possible, the topic to be discussed should be shared in advance. An example of a way to encourage parent input is provided at the end of this chapter in the Samples and Examples section.

When you use actual samples or data in conferences, parents can assess the situation. When they look at a set of unfinished work, or a destroyed desk, they can see the problem for themselves. A Parent Conference Checklist that provides strategies before, during, and after a parent conference is located in the Samples and Examples section of this chapter.

Finally, we suggest a summary at the end of the conference to clarify the discussion, emphasize a decision, or extend the communication. Listen to a middle-school science teacher summarize a conference with Jeff's parents in the following Teacher Talk.

TEACHER TALK

It sounds like we agree that Jeff is enthusiastic and puts effort into his work for this class. We definitely want to encourage his attitude, but his socializing in lab does keep him from the quality of work of which he is capable. We will keep a check on lab work and report writing. Your idea of special social activities with his school friends on Friday nights is great. Let's talk again in three weeks to see how Jeff is doing. I'll call you.

Ninth-Grade Science Teacher

In the Samples and Examples at the end of this chapter, you will also find a form to use for parents to provide input about the success of a conference. It continues the two-way communication after the conference has ended.

Problem Solving with Parents

When student behavior problems are major, a problem-solving approach may be needed in the communication with parents. Rutherford and Edgar (1979, p. 20) recommended a process that is universal for use in other settings. We urge you to follow the steps and develop some skill with the process:

1. Set goals by agreeing on the problem, listing desired outcomes, and deciding how to evaluate the outcomes.
2. Select the solution by discussing alternatives and determining a mutually agreeable solution.

3. Put the plan into action and provide each side with feedback.
4. Evaluate and share results by checking the outcomes and the process.

The first step is best done with some evidence of the problem's existence. Some of Jeff's lab reports, half finished, along with some test scores and a seating chart of the lab were appropriate for the conference with his parents. Identification of the problem was best done with positive language, such as, "Jeff needs to use all of his lab time for experiments and reports" instead of "Jeff needs to stop socializing during lab."

The second problem-solving step requires true collaboration; that is, both parents and Jeff's teacher should suggest solutions and agree on the final decision. When Jeff's teacher wanted to move him from his friends in the lab, his parents suggested a Friday night social as an alternative to socializing in lab. Jeff's parents expressed a wish to have him learn how to control his social behavior in school settings, and his teacher agreed.

Jeff's parents took the lead in implementing the plan, and his teacher followed with a conversation at school. After the first week, his teacher phoned his parents to assure them of his agreement and his already improved work.

It has been our experience that many problem-solving efforts in classroom management stop short of the fourth step—evaluation. Two months after the conference, Jeff's teacher and parents will meet again to look at his lab work, discuss his behavior, hear about the Friday night socials, and generally decide if the solution was effective.

This problem-solving process supports the kind of relationship you seek with parents and students. You will see it used in the Snapshot entitled "Reality Therapy—Elementary Classroom" in the class meeting in Ms. Hathaway's third grade to solve problems on the playground. We encourage you to practice and use problem solving for other aspects of classroom life.

MODELS OF CLASSROOM MANAGEMENT

When you first thought about teaching, you probably said to yourself, "I'd like to be like Mr. Eliot who taught literature in ninth grade" or "I still remember what it was like in third grade with Ms. May." What do you remember about your favorite teachers? Take a few minutes and think about those teachers. Write what you remember, or compare memories with someone to see what you have in common.

Those models in your memories influence your decisions as you prepare to teach or as you manage your classroom. Some of the models help you decide how you want to do things, and some help you decide how you don't want to do things. Both are important to your decision making. Our intent is to add other models to your thinking.

We begin by describing common classroom management models. Some are based on sound theoretical knowledge and others are developed and supported by classroom research. Consider the following:

- Behavior Modification (from the work of B. F. Skinner [1968, 1971], with contemporary modifications)
- Reality Therapy (an extension of William Glasser's [1987] Control Theory for treatment of behavior problems in classrooms)

- Judicious Discipline (a model based on democratic principles that helps build citizenship inside and outside the classroom [McEwan, Gathercoal, & Nimmo, 1999])
- Assertive Discipline (a widely used approach of the 1970s from the work of Lee and Marlene Canter [1979])
- The Adlerian model or Dreikurs' approach (a model emphasizing reasons for behavior [Dreikurs, 1968; Dreikurs, Grunwald, & Pepper, 1971])
- Consistency Management & Cooperative Discipline (a research-based model that builds on shared responsibility between teacher and students (Freiberg, 1983; Freiberg, Prokosch, Treister, & Stein, 1990; Freiberg, 1999)

Figure 6.1 briefly summarizes these six models. For each model, we will take you to classrooms via a Snapshot so that you can see it in action.

Behavior Modification

In the Snapshot that follows, you will see a middle-school physical education teacher using a modified form of the Behavior Modification model. The group of students, male and female, has been difficult to teach, so their teacher is using a number of strategies from the model.

SNAPSHOT: Behavior Modification—Middle-School Classroom

The rules and routines in Mr. Proust's physical education class are clear and well understood by the students. Students are aware that they make the choice to follow or not follow the rules. As the class begins, students check themselves off a sheet to indicate presence, appropriate attire, and equipment readiness. They go immediately into a well-rehearsed exercise routine.

From there, Mr. Proust demonstrates a new skill—a tennis serve. Several students are asked to try the skill in front of the class, with explanations from the teacher. Students then work in pairs and practice the skill with comments from a partner. Mr. Proust moves through the group, commenting on individual performances, "You moved your arm correctly" or "Your follow-through was just right." He will continue this practice until the skill is well learned.

At the end of class, Amanda approaches with a contract regarding her behavior in class. Mr. Proust comments on her participation, effort, and cooperation with her partner, and checks off spaces on her contract. He waits for Dennis to come out of the locker room and talks to him out of earshot of his classmates. Only Dennis hears the recognition of his class participation.

Within the first month of class, Mr. Proust identified those students who followed the rules and those students who didn't. Dennis was generally cooperative and participated in class activities within the rules and routines; Amanda didn't. Mr. Proust reinforces Dennis's behavior and the behavior of classmates like him, to support the behavior, increasing the likelihood that it will continue. He also uses *reinforcement* in his teaching so that students will continue performing skills accurately.

FIGURE 6.1 *Models of Classroom Management*

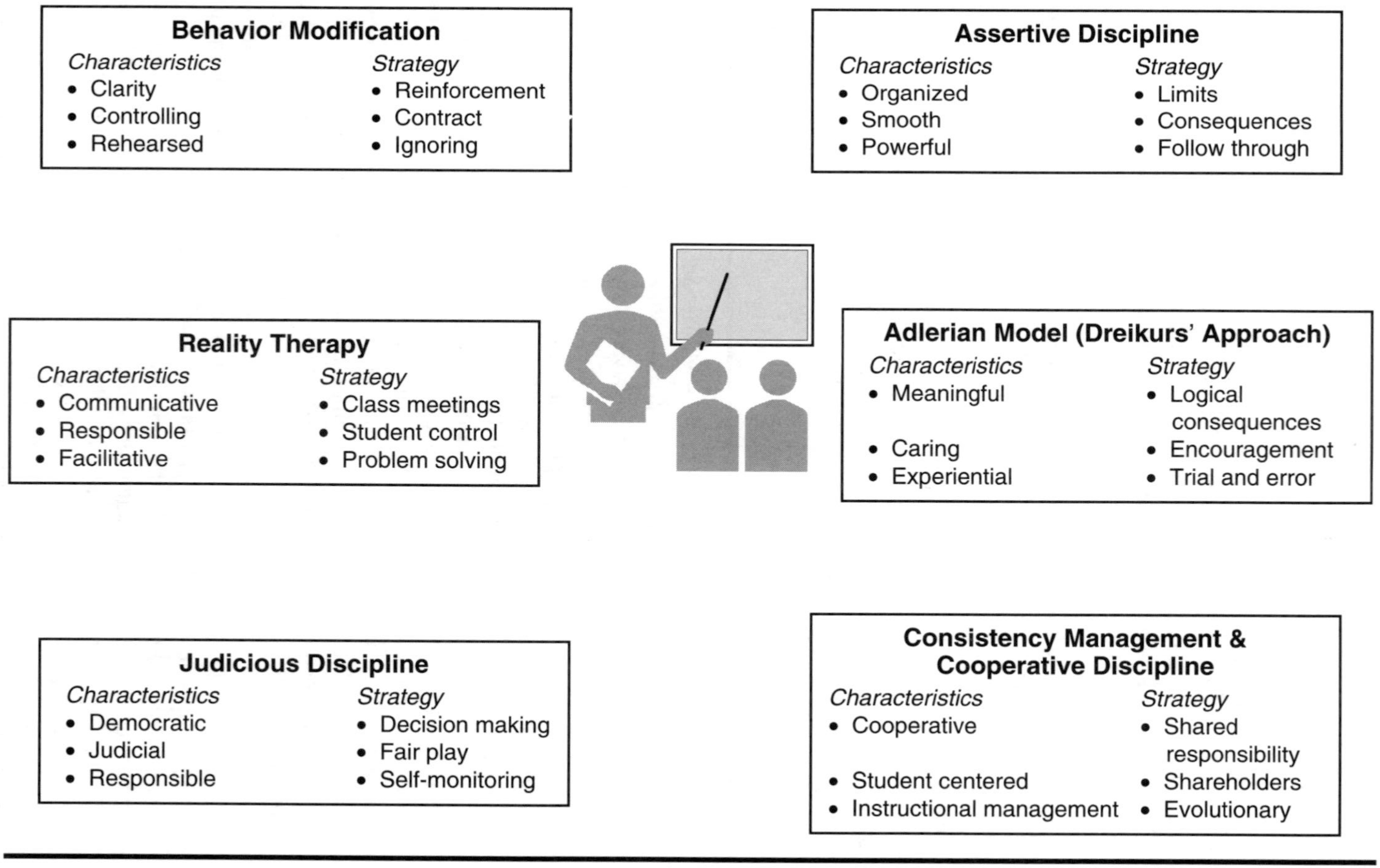

Behavior Modification

Characteristics	*Strategy*
• Clarity	• Reinforcement
• Controlling	• Contract
• Rehearsed	• Ignoring

Assertive Discipline

Characteristics	*Strategy*
• Organized	• Limits
• Smooth	• Consequences
• Powerful	• Follow through

Reality Therapy

Characteristics	*Strategy*
• Communicative	• Class meetings
• Responsible	• Student control
• Facilitative	• Problem solving

Adlerian Model (Dreikurs' Approach)

Characteristics	*Strategy*
• Meaningful	• Logical consequences
• Caring	• Encouragement
• Experiential	• Trial and error

Judicious Discipline

Characteristics	*Strategy*
• Democratic	• Decision making
• Judicial	• Fair play
• Responsible	• Self-monitoring

Consistency Management & Cooperative Discipline

Characteristics	*Strategy*
• Cooperative	• Shared responsibility
• Student centered	• Shareholders
• Instructional management	• Evolutionary

Amanda's behavior in class became more and more of a problem, so Mr. Proust developed a *contract* with her. It specifies expectations, timelines and reinforcers, in this case, free-choice gym activities once a month.

When you use Behavior Modification, you analyze the behaviors you observe in your students and design ways to change or maintain them. Your role in a behavior management system is to control or shape behavior. This is accomplished through reinforcing desired behaviors by using rewards and extinguishing undesirable behavior by ignoring or punishing.

Reality Therapy (Control Theory)

William Glasser's (1987) approach focuses on the here and now of classroom life and helping children understand that what they do in classrooms is their choice. Look at the Snapshot of Ms. Hathaway's fifth-grade class and see what Reality Therapy looks and sounds like.

SNAPSHOT: Reality Therapy—Elementary Classroom

During the first two months of the school year, Ms. Hathaway worked on developing relationships and a kind of classroom community. Opportunity for communication was built into most of the learning activities.

On this particular day, students are working on social studies projects in groups, using maps, art supplies, magazines, bulletin boards, and so on. Ms. Hathaway overhears Jana argue with a classmate about a mess on the storage shelf. When Jana comes to her to complain, she responds with, "What could you do about those feelings?" "What could you say to your classmate?" "Is there a routine we could set up for class that would help with this problem?"

Another student comes to Ms. Hathaway, describing his inability to finish his project because "It won't work" and "Everyone is working on something else." Ms. Hathaway responds with, "It sounds like you regret your choice. You really can't blame it on your group, because you had a chance to look at all the possibilities. I hope that you will carry on with your best work until the project is finished."

Later that day, we see Omar approaching Ms. Hathaway with a problem and saying, "Oh, never mind. I'll bring it up at a class meeting." A week earlier, some of the students came up with the idea of a class store, and the topic became a top priority on the class meeting agenda. As a result of the discussion, four students are currently working on some details of having a store. The same thing happened when special art materials were needed for a project but were unavailable through the usual school supplier.

That afternoon, Sara brought up a problem of fighting and other behavior on the playground. Other students chimed in with comments about boredom: "Not enough balls," "It's too crowded," "They always jump off the platform right in the middle of our game," and so on. Then they brainstormed some solutions: "A schedule for each section of the playground," "Learn some new games," "Some kids can't use the platform," "Assign playground monitors," and others. The meeting ended with a plan for playground time. Students agreed to work in committees for the next week to draw a large playground map, schedule activities for various areas, and read about some new games. Once the committees finished and changes were made, Ms. Hathaway checked back regularly with, "How are things going on the playground?"

Did you notice that *student responsibility* is the emphasis? Student control rather than teacher control goes along with it. Those class meetings are regularly scheduled, and one important rule is that classmates will take turns talking. The teacher's role in this model is that of a facilitator. *Facilitation* is the act of making something (learning, change, and so on) easier. You will facilitate by teaching problem solving and decision making, reviewing choices, asking questions, challenging satisfaction with choices, and accepting no excuses for poor choices.

Judicious Discipline

Judicious Discipline (McEwan, Gathercoal, & Nimmo, 1999) is a classroom management program that uses democratic methods to provide teachers with ways to teach citizenship daily through student/teacher interactions. The main component of the model is facilitating the learning of students concerning the application of "a common language of civility to their daily interactions that occur within and without the school community" (p. 100). Judicious Discipline revolves around the idea that citizenship can be learned via classroom management decisions that show students how the human rights of individuals are balanced against the limitations that guard our needs to be secure and well.

SNAPSHOT: Judicious Discipline—Secondary Classroom

A *classroom constitution* is being created in Mr. Olivas's history classroom. Students are working with their teacher to form classroom rules and norms for the school year. As ideas are suggested, a student scribes them on the board. When all the rules and norms have been written, the class and Mr. Olivas discuss them and vote to accept them. Once finished, the set of rules becomes the constitution for the class; it is then published for posting. Finally, the students and Mr. Olivas sign the constitution that is then displayed on a wall in the classroom. This person-centered approach to creating a classroom constitution is also found in the Consistency Management & Cooperative Discipline (CMCD) model.

Notice in the Snapshot how students work with the teacher in a democratic way to make decisions for their classroom. The self-imposed "teacher rules" are minimized in Mr. Oliva's classroom. This notion is essential to the Judicious Discipline model in that it shows students how to reach consensus in a democratic way on issues that are important to their lives in the classroom and that the process is valuable outside the classroom, as well. The signing of the document further reinforces the idea that democratic-based decisions are important and respected. Finally, as involved members in the decision-making process, students also feel empowered, trusted, and involved in their classroom.

Assertive Discipline

The Assertive Discipline model first appeared during the student rights' movement amidst pro-student court decisions, when teachers were frustrated by disruptive behavior and feeling powerless. Canter and Canter (1979) stated, "Problems or no problems, no child should be allowed to engage in behavior that is self-destructive or violates the rights of his peers or teacher" (p. 56). Watch how that occurs in the next Snapshot.

SNAPSHOT: Assertive Discipline—Elementary Classroom

Mr. Alter's third-grade class has well-established limits about behavior during small group instruction so that distractions and interruptions are kept to a minimum. He uses that instructional time to focus on individual learning needs and paces his teaching accordingly. The behavior limits during this time require quiet work and limited movement around the classroom. On one of the front boards is a sign that says:

NAME ON BOARD	1st misbehavior
CHECK (✔) NEXT TO NAME	2nd misbehavior
TWO CHECKS (✔✔) NEXT TO NAME	3rd misbehavior
THREE CHECKS (✔✔✔) NEXT TO NAME	4th misbehavior

CONSEQUENCES

NAME ON BOARD	Discussion with me
CHECK NEXT TO NAME	Recess cut by 5 minutes
TWO CHECKS	Visit principal's office
THREE CHECKS	Parent conference

During the day, Mr. Alter writes one or two names on the board as he continues his teaching. When Nicola talks continuously during quiet reading, he places a check next to her name.

There is also a list of Our Goals on the front board, listing such items as working together, getting work completed, and listening. Occasionally, Mr. Alter places a check in the box beneath the goal list, commenting, "Everyone really listened to the directions that time. When the number of checks reaches 50, the class will have a popcorn party."

Mr. Alter doesn't have to stop his teaching to respond to Nicola's behavior. Notice that he reinforces the desired behavior for the entire class. It was important that he had established clear limits of behavior beforehand and followed through with the consequences of not minding the limits. Teachers using the Assertive Discipline model make sure that students know and understand the rules and limits. Notice the similarity between this model and the Behavior Modification model with reinforcement strategies.

Adlerian Model (Dreikurs' Approach)

Dreikurs' ideas (Dreikurs & Cassel, 1972), used for parenting and classroom management, are based on two assumptions: Our behavior is goal directed and we learn best through concrete experiences. With those assumptions in mind, look at this Snapshot in which the Adlerian model guides Ms. Conley-Trombley.

SNAPSHOT: Dreikurs' Approach—Middle-School Classroom

There is a climate of conversation in this room—problems are being discussed, questions are posed, effort is urged, and ideas are suggested. The schedule is affected by the time used for conversation; it has large blocks of time for group discussions, individual conferences, and class meetings.

Ms. Conley-Trombley has developed the class rules and limits with her sixth-grade students. Gradually, they have also worked out together the consequences for not following the rules. She guides these discussions to logical consequences with, "What is a logical consequence for leaving a mess in the printing center?" When "staying in the room during recess" is suggested, she asks if it is logical. Gradually, students get the idea, and suggest cleaning up the printing shelves and scrubbing equipment in the area as a logical consequence.

When students have problems, Ms. Conley-Trombley works toward the understanding of behavior and its effects with those students involved. When Bill approaches her with a problem that he had at the drawing table, she asks, "What would the others say happened at the table?" and "How did your behavior affect them?" She encouraged Bill to describe his behavior and the problem from different perspectives.

Ms. Conley-Trombley often holds back and lets experience teach her students. When she observes Kerry using one of the pens incorrectly, she waits. Eventually, Kerry realizes that her sketch isn't going to be acceptable for printing. The logical consequence is that she will start over, this time using the pen correctly. Later she talks with her teacher and classmates about what she learned.

In this middle-school classroom, students hear feedback frequently, generally in the form of encouragement. They hear, "You have carefully followed the steps of the process," "You paid a lot of attention to detail in that sketch," and "Did you notice how clear your print came out?"

Notice how much students are learning from their experiences, from trial and error, and from talking about problems. The intention is that they will become confident and competent problem solvers who are responsible for their own behavior. That is Ms. Conley-Trombley's goal as she follows the Adlerian model.

Consistency Management & Cooperative Discipline (CMCD)

Consistency Management & Cooperative Discipline is a research-based model that builds on shared responsibility between teacher and students (Freiberg, Stein, & Huang, 1995; Freiberg, 1999). The teacher creates a consistent but flexible learning environment and joins with the students in establishing a cooperative plan for the rules and procedures that govern the classroom.

SNAPSHOT: Consistency Management & Cooperative Discipline—High-School Classroom

Mr. Jayson has been teaching algebra for 20 years. For the past few years, he posted his rules at the start of the year. This past year, he decided after much thought and several conversations with Ms. Awad, a world history teacher, that the students needed to be involved in creating a more productive place to learn. He decided to construct a classroom constitution in two classes. If the process was effective, it would be extended to the other four classes.

Mr. Jayson began the first class with a game called "The Unfair Game" to make a point about rules and laws. In the math game, the class was divided into two sides. Questions were given to each side. But the points for a correct answer varied for each response from 1 to 500. The students began to complain that the game was unfair, especially when he declared the team with the fewest points the winner. "Why did they get 500 points for a correct answer, when we only got 5?" asked one student. "How could they win? We had the most points!" declared a student from the other team. Mr. Jayson asked, "Why is this game unfair?" The students began to list the reasons: "We didn't know the rules," "The points aren't in a logical sequence," and finally one student said, "We're not going to play the game anymore unless the rules and procedures are clear to everyone from the start."

Based on the last statement, Mr. Jayson talked about why we have rules in our society, including the classroom and school. He suggested that the class construct a Classroom Constitution for Learning, and this might be a good way to start the school year. The Constitution started out with: "We the people of Room 305, to have a more perfect learning environment, agree to the following." The rules of the class were listed and signed by all members, including the teacher. The Classroom Constitution was posted in front of the room for all to see.

The game and the subsequent Classroom Constitution were designed to involve the students and create rules that reflect the needs of both teacher and students. Building a cooperative learning environment can start with rules and procedures that are cooperatively designed. As part of your continuing advancework, the six models presented in this chapter may be supplemented with others. Models provide alternatives, and you can vary them to accommodate your context, content, and learner. As you will see in the next research vignette, one model may not be the answer.

SMOOTHNESS AND MOMENTUM

As you look at the following Snapshot, watch for the qualities of smoothness and momentum described by Kounin (1970). *Smoothness* refers to the way the classroom happenings appear to be in order, the way changes happen easily, the way routines are established, and the way materials are ready beforehand. *Momentum* refers to the flow of activities and the pace of teaching and learning.

SNAPSHOT: Secondary School Classroom

When the 8:15 A.M. bell rings, Ms. Holloway reminds students, "We will be correcting homework in 30 seconds. Trade your assignment with your partner and have a folder and a clean sheet of paper ready on your desk." As students get ready, their teacher marks an attendance list.

"Ready, class? The following are the answers for the homework problems: Number 1—265 feet, Number 2—39 inches,...(and so on)." After the answers are read, students are seen returning each other's assignments, recording numbers in a folder, and passing assignments to the front. Two students take their papers to a box that has a big red question mark on it (used for assignments with questions or confusion about answers).

"Today we are going to review the formulas for area and we'll practice using them. At your places, draw the shapes for which you can compute the area—just draw them." Ms. Holloway waits 30 seconds as students draw triangles, rectangles, circles, and squares. She flips on the overhead projector with a list of shapes and points to each, saying, "How many of you drew a circle? A square?" and so on.

"Now let's see how many of the formulas you can remember. Next to your circle, write the formula for the area of a circle. Raise your hands when you have it." Within 15 seconds, she calls on Yolanda for the formula and writes it on the transparency, saying, "Check that you have this formula written correctly on your sheet." She proceeds through the shapes with the same process.

"Now we are going to use the formulas. I will assign each of your work groups a shape. You are to find at least three examples of that shape in our classroom and measure them for information to use in your formulas. Then figure out the areas. Group 1, here is a yardstick; your assignment is rectangles. Group 2, here is a ruler; your assignment is triangles. Group 3, here is a tape measure; your assignment is circles."

Groups of four and five students move about the room and measure items. Some students return to their desks and figure the areas. Others remain near objects and measure.

"You have one minute to finish," Ms. Holloway says. "Now we need one person from each group to go to the board and show us one example from the items that you measured. While they are doing so, see if you can compute the area of the parallelogram I have drawn on the overhead."

Notice the following about this Snapshot:

- The lesson began smoothly and the class began with a fast pace.
- Routines for problems had been preestablished so that the pace kept moving.
- The teaching strategies maintained involvement of students and a fast pace.
- There was obvious preparation for this lesson.
- There was change of pace with the group activity.
- Change occurs easily and involvement is maintained.

You didn't hear Ms. Holloway attending to behavior problems. If you were to continue to watch this classroom, you would hear explicit rules and directions; that is, students know exactly what to do and how to do it. They are "ritualized," so well taught that they seem to be automatic. That's why Ms. Holloway doesn't spend much time on rules and organizational activities anymore.

STUDENTS WITH SPECIAL NEEDS

Teachers of students with special needs may need to utilize individual behavior plans. For example, the Admission, Review, and Dismissal (ARD) process for special education students often involves creating a specialized behavior plan for students with special needs. The ARD committee—which consists of an administrator, a regular education teacher, a special education teacher, and the parent(s) of the student—decides if the student can follow the teacher's and the school's discipline policies. If unable, due to the disability, then an individual behavior plan is devised. Included in the plan are reinforcers and motivating initiatives, which are created via committee input. As mentioned earlier in the chapter, transitions are often the problem areas for students, so transitions for students with special needs are extra carefully planned. By utilizing a collaborative effort of teachers and other ARD committee members, students with special needs can have their individual behavioral needs met, which helps them become more successful.

SUMMARY

We conclude by urging you to consider both personal and professional models of classroom management, those teachers you remember, and the models of Behavior

All-Level Vignette

INTRODUCTION

Fashola and Slavin (1998) reviewed a number of schoolwide reform models designed to increase student achievement and create climates in which children can learn effectively. Their focus was to study programs that affected major areas in school functioning: classroom management, curriculum, instruction, assessment, professional development, and governance.

STUDY DESIGN

A program was considered to be effective if evaluations showed significantly better gains in academic performance of program students compared to comparison groups of students on "fair measures of academic performance.... Fair measures were ones that assessed objectives pursued equally by experimental and control groups" (Fashola & Slavin, 1998, p. 371). The programs also had to be widely replicable throughout the United States in sites beyond their initial pilot locations.

STUDY RESULTS

Consistency Management & Cooperative Discipline (CMCD) was the only K–12 program that met Fashola and Slavin's evaluation criteria for student achievement. CMCD has been evaluated in inner-city Houston schools, and is working in schools in Santa Ana, Newark, Norfolk, Chicago, the Netherlands, and Italy. It is a rapidly growing program and "establishing a national dissemination capacity" (Fashola & Slavin, 1998, p. 375). Students in CMCD classes outperformed comparison students by nearly ¾ of a year in national standardized tests (Freiberg, Stein, & Huang, 1995).

In another study of CMCD, Opuni (1998) found that the link between better student discipline and achievement is the time teachers save for teaching that was previously used for discipline and classroom management. He found that teachers in K–12 saved from 14 to 37 minutes of teaching time per day (see the table). He also found that discipline referrals to the office "declined by more than 74%."

CMCD is a schoolwide classroom management reform effort designed to improve discipline in inner-city schools at all levels. CMCD focuses on shared responsibility for classroom discipline and management between teachers and students. Classes are transformed into communi-

Estimate of Additional Time Available for Instruction Resulting from CMCD Practices

Years of CMCD Implementation	Average Time Saved Daily	Total Days Saved per Year
After Year 2: Seven Elem. Schools	14 minutes	7.0 days (1.4 wks.)
After Year 2: Davis High School	14 minutes	7.0 days (1.4 wks.)
After Year 3: Seven Elem. Schools	36 minutes	18.0 days (3.6 wks.)
After Year 1: Marshall Middle School	20 minutes	10.5 days (2 wks.)
After Year 2: Marshall Middle School	30 minutes	15.0 days (3 wks.)
After Year 3: Marshall Middle School	31 minutes	15.5 days (3 wks.)
After Year 1: Twelve Elem. Schools	37 minutes	18.5 days (3.7 wks.)

Source: From *Project GRAD Program Evaluation Report* by K. A. Opuni, 1998 (pp. 4–5). Houston: ISD. Reprinted by permission.

ties in which all shareholders collaboratively arrive at rules and expectations for classroom management. The idea behind this design is that if students are involved with creating and supporting the workings of the classroom, then disrupting learning will no longer be desirable. CMCD has five basic themes: *Prevention, Caring, Cooperation, Organization,* and *Community.* These themes are the core of the program and around which all initiatives are formed and supported.

DISCUSSIONS AND IMPLICATIONS FOR PRACTICE

The analysis of CMCD shows a clear interrelationship between classroom management, discipline, and instructional practices. By utilizing a classroom management program such as Consistency Management & Cooperative Discipline, teachers can begin the school year with a chance to create a positive and productive climate. Teachers need to be aware that discipline should not be the main focus, since other prevention strategies can be overlooked. Equally important to note is that using a flexible discipline program over the "one size fits all" model can have positive effects, since the chances to meet the unique needs of the learner, within the content or context, are possible. (See website www.coe.uh.edu/CMCD/ for further information.)

Modification, Reality Therapy, Judicious Discipline, Assertive Discipline, Dreikurs' approach, and Consistency Management & Cooperative Discipline. We looked at effective teachers for an additional model of managing a classroom with smoothness and momentum.

The theme for handling the recurring situations of beginning the school year—interruptions, transitions, crises, and student behavior problems—was *preparation.* Anticipate and plan your responses to these situations. With student behavior problems, you may need simple responses or a comprehensive approach. Part of your more complex response is communication with parents. Check your attitudes and language for effective communication, and practice problem solving to work successfully with parents on behavior that interferes with your teaching. A foundation for all your management responses is advancework for information and support as you handle situations.

A conclusion of this chapter and of our experiences with classroom management is that effective classroom management requires lifelong learning. Just about the time you think that you have mastered all of the competencies you need to manage a classroom, you have a student or a class that baffles you. Just about the time we think we have all the answers for management problems, a student in one of our classes poses one for which we say, "Hmmmm, I'll have to think about that one."

Be ready to keep learning—read about classroom management, attend workshops, talk about management with other teachers. Most importantly, watch those who are effective. Just as the researchers in this chapter did, you can get the best information from their practices. What you will notice is that their focus is on teaching and learning. Their management goes beyond discipline.

REFERENCES

Arlin, M. (1979). Teacher transitions can disrupt time flow in classrooms. *American Educational Research Journal, 16,* 42–56.

Brantlinger, B. (1993). Adolescents' interpretation of social class influences on schooling. *Journal of Classroom Interaction, 28*(1), 1–12.

Brophy, G., & Alleman, J. (1998). Classroom management in a social studies learning community. *Social Education, 62*(1), 56–58.

Buskin, M. (1975). *Parent power: A candid handbook for dealing with your child's school.* New York: Walker and Company.

Canter, L., & Canter, M. (1979). *Assertive discipline.* Los Angeles: Canter and Associates.

Doyle, W. (1986). Classroom organization and management. In M. C. Wittrock (Ed.), *Handbook of research on teaching* (3rd ed.). New York: Macmillan.

Dreikurs, R. (1968). *Psychology in the classroom.* New York: Harper and Row.

Dreikurs, R., & Cassel, P. (1972). *Discipline without tears.* New York: Hawthorn.

Dreikurs, R., Grunwald, B., & Pepper, F. (1971). *Maintaining sanity in the classroom.* New York: Harper & Row.

Education Week. (1988). A bold step from the ivory tower. *Education Week, 7*(39), 21–31.

Evertson, C. M., Emmer, E. T., Clements, B. S., & Worsham, M. E. (1997). *Classroom management for elementary teachers* (4th ed.). Boston: Allyn and Bacon.

Evertson, C. M., & Harris, A. H. (1995). *Classroom organization and management program. Revalidation submission to the program effectiveness panel, U.S. Department of Education.* (ERIC Document Reproduction Service No. ED 403 247).

Fashola, O. S., & Slavin, R. E. (1998). Schoolwide reform models: What works? *Phi Delta Kappan, 79*(5), 370–379.

Freiberg, H. J. (1999). Consistency Management & Cooperative Discipline: From tourists to citizens in the classrooms. In Jerome Freiberg (Ed.), *Beyond behaviorism: Changing the classroom management paradigm.* Boston: Allyn and Bacon.

Freiberg, H. J., Prokosch, N., Treister, E., & Stein, T. (1990). Turning around five at-risk elementary schools. *Journal of School Effectiveness and Improvement, 1*(1), 5–25.

Freiberg, H. J., Stein, T. A., & Huang, S. (1995). Effects of classroom management intervention on student achievement in inner-city elementary schools. *Educational Research and Evaluation, 1,* 36–66.

Glasser, W. (1969). *Schools without failure.* New York: Harper and Row.

Glasser, W. (1987). *Control theory in the classroom.* New York: Harper and Row.

Kounin, J. (1970). *Discipline and group management in classrooms.* New York: Holt, Rinehart and Winston.

McEwan, B., Gathercoal, F., & Nimmo, V. (1999). Applications of judicial discipline: A common language in the classroom. In Jerome Freiberg (Ed.), *Beyond behaviorism: Changing the classroom management paradigm.* Boston: Allyn and Bacon.

Opuni, K. A. (1998). Executive summary. *Project Grad program evaluation report* (pp. 4–5). Houston: ISD.

Rogers, C., & Freiberg, H. J. (1994). *Freedom to learn* (3rd ed.). Columbus, OH: Merrill.

Rose, L., & Gallup, A. (1998). Phi Delta Kappa 30th Annual Gallop/PDK Poll of the Public's Attitude towards Public Schools. *Phi Delta Kappan, 80*(1): 41–56.

Rutherford, R., Jr., & Edgar, E. (1979). *Teachers and parents: A guide to interaction and cooperation.* Boston: Allyn and Bacon.

Skinner, B. F. (1968). *The technology of teaching.* New York: Appleton-Century-Crofts.

Skinner, B. F. (1971). *Beyond freedom and dignity.* New York: Knopf.

Swick, K. J. (1977). *Maintaining productive student behavior.* Washington, DC: National Education Association.

Wang, M. C., Haertel, G. D., & Walberg, H. J. (1993). Toward a knowledge base for school learning. *Review of Educational Research, 63,* 249–294.

SAMPLES AND EXAMPLES

This Samples and Examples section includes the following:

- The Assessing and Improving Self-Discipline Checklist is designed to help students learn and monitor self-discipline habits.
- The First-Week Checklist is designed for you to review prior to the opening of school.
- The Parent Conference Checklist describes activities that should occur before, during, and after a parent conference.
- The two parent conference forms reflect two sources of data about teacher/parent interactions. The first form is a needs assessment about the topic(s) for the meeting, which would be completed by the parent prior to the meeting. The second form is a feedback form about the meeting. Both forms will facilitate communication between teachers and parents.

ASSESSING AND IMPROVING SELF-DISCIPLINE CHECKLIST

In order to assess their own self-discipline abilities, students may use the following checklist. After completing the checklist, students can work with teachers and other students in order to improve in areas that they identified as needing help.

	Are These Ideas Part of My Own Personalized Discipline Plan?	
Getting Ready for Self-Discipline: Where Am I?	I Need Help	I Understand
1. Good behavior is practiced; it doesn't just come naturally for most people.		
2. How I react to things is a result of how I think inside myself; my reactions are not caused by other people.		
3. I will set some goals of behavior that I know I can master. I will practice these each day.		
4. If I get in charge of myself and control my actions, I will not knowingly break any school rules.		
5. No matter how I feel or if someone "angers" me, if I will just think about what to do, I can think thoughts that will control my behaviors.		
6. I can think about the difference between "good" behavior and "bad" behavior. I have a good self to draw on for good results. I just have to choose to do it.		
7. What I see (perceive) in my mind as my behavior is how I behave in the outside world (outside my mind).		
8. I change whatever behavior I have that feels bad for me.		
9. I have a "good self" because I know I can be good if I choose. From time to time, I need to remind myself I am good and to smile about it.		
10. I have some angry thought patterns of behavior in my brain that are now automatic; I need to look at these behaviors and rethink some of them.		
11. If I have some old automatic behaviors that I wish to get rid of, and substitute a new one, I must practice the new behavior for 21 days before it will be automatic in my life.		

	Are These Ideas Part of My Own Personalized Discipline Plan?	
Getting Ready for Self-Discipline: Where Am I?	I Need Help	I Understand
12. I should take at least one minute a day to review the extent to which my chosen behaviors and goals were carried out successfully yesterday.		
13. The way I treat others should be the way I want to be treated myself.		
14. I must give more love away than hate. I must cause more joy in lives than sorrow. I must take a few more harsh words from others without fighting back. I can do this because others may not have a self-discipline plan in their minds. I can be a good model for them to witness.		
15. When I start to break my self-discipline plan, I must rethink my committment (promise) to myself. I must be honest with myself, and make myself do what my mind tells me to do.		
16. The next time someone irritates me or angers me, I will put off (retrain) any angering behaviors for 5 seconds. I will practice until I can count to 10 seconds, then 60 seconds. Someday I won't have any angering feelings because I have been controlling them.		
17. If I can demonstrate to others that I have control over myself, then I will have fewer people trying to control me.		
18. Controlling myself (my behaviors) at school is just as important a part of my school life as learning the subject matter my teacher teaches.		
19. Every time I'm about to get upset, I must choose more pleasant thoughts.		
20. I must assume the responsibility for every act I do.		

Source: From "Dealing with Angering Behaviors in Students" by R. D. Bradley, 1992, *TESPA Journal* (pp. 24–27). Adapted by permission. Originally printed in the *TESPA Journal,* Texas Elementary Principals & Supervisors Association.

FIRST-WEEK CHECKLIST

Have You:

_______ Learned your students' names?

_______ Greeted students by name on arrival?

_______ Learned information about students' interests, goals, likes, and dislikes?

_______ Made procedures, standards, and limits clear and public knowledge?

_______ Consistently reinforced the procedures and standards you have set up?

_______ Given students overviews prior to an activity to let them know what to expect?

_______ Given students responsibility on a graduated basis?

_______ Used visual aids?

_______ Recorded, distributed, and introduced textbooks?

_______ Set up place and system for keeping records, forms?

_______ Made calendar notes of dates, questions, ideas?

_______ Become familiar with facilities, faculty?

_______ Asked questions of other teachers, principal?

_______ Reviewed and used curriculum guides?

_______ Planned for next week?

_______ Given yourself a pat on the back?

Source: From *Project Entry Teacher Corps Instructional Booklets* by H. J. Freiberg and S. McFaul, 1980, Houston: University of Houston—University Park. Used by permission.

PARENT CONFERENCE CHECKLIST

I. Before

Specific examples of misbehaviors, including dates and time, will be helpful. The data will help the parent conference to be more objective in a potentially emotional meeting.

____ Send a Parent Conference Form (located in this Samples and Examples section).

____ Document and describe student behavior that has interfered with the child's learning, your teaching, or other students' learning. (For example, Jimmy does not have materials or books for class. Sarah is unable to sit for more than 10 minutes without getting out of her seat and distracting others.)

____ Document other contacts with the parents/guardian. (Keep a calendar.)

____ Document what you have tried to minimize the student's disruptions or behavior.

____ Find out the language orientation of the parents (ask for an interpreter when needed).

II. During

The tone of the conference will be important. Parents will be defensive, rather than supportive, if they hear only what's wrong and not how to improve the situation.

____ Start with the positive about the student.

____ Describe and show progress that has been achieved.

____ Describe instructional plans that will produce further achievement.

____ Describe behaviors that are interfering with student learning or your teaching.

____ Describe what the parent and child need to do to improve the situation. Be specific; many parents are at a loss as to what they can do to help. Describe how you will help.

III. After

The follow-up is the key to a successful parent conference.

____ Give a progress report on a daily, then weekly, basis.

____ Give a feedback form for parent feedback.

____ Establish another meeting if the strategies are not working or if parent interest has waned.

PARENT CONFERENCE FORMS

Dear ______________________________,

A parent-teacher conference will soon be scheduled for you. In order for me to plan a useful and informative conference, it is important to ask for your ideas and areas of concern. Please answer the following questions and return one of the copies to me by the end of the week. The other copy is for you to keep and bring to the conference.

1. What are your child's feelings about school? What does he or she say? What does he or she like or dislike about school?

2. Does your child have any "special friends" or talk about other children in class?

3. What kind of changes have you noticed, if any, since your child started school?

4. Are there any problems for you or your child with which I can help?

Please check three topics related to your child's school experiences that you would like to discuss during the conference.

_____ Following directions
_____ Self-confidence
_____ Getting along with others
_____ Working with a group
_____ Listening, attending
_____ Friendships
_____ Self-control
_____ Work habits
_____ Language
_____ Other

Any other thoughts about the conference?

____
Parent signature

PARENT CONFERENCES

Would you please take a moment to evaluate our conference? This will h.. future conferences.

Was there an area which you especially appreciated my sharing or that was helpful?

Was there an area which we neglected to discuss that you feel I should have brought up?

Do you have any other comments to share?

Do you feel the conference time was adequate in length?

Source: Driscoll, A., & Newmann, A. (1989). Materials for communication with parents. Portland, OR: Portland State University and West Linn School District Cooperative Program. Used by permission.

CHAPTER

7

LECTURE

From Passive to Active Learning

Chapter Outcomes

At the conclusion of this chapter you will be able to:

1. *Describe the role of the learner, content, and context in building effective lectures.*
2. *Describe three goals of lecture, including informational, motivational, and reflective, critical thinking presentations.*
3. *Identify guidelines from research that may increase interactive opportunities of lecture.*
4. *Describe the benefits and limitations of lecture.*
5. *Describe six variations of the lecture approach.*

Key Terms and Concepts

Learner
Context
Content
Goals
Informational
Motivational
Reflective/Critical Thinking
Teacher Control
Guidelines from Research
Scope and Pace
Stimulus Variation
Cuing
Pausing
Media
Enthusiasm
Benefits
Limitations
Variations
Lecture with Other Strategies
Student with Special Needs
Teaching Note Taking

lek'-chər, n. *[French* lecture, *from the Latin* lectura, *a reading] a disclosure on some subject read or delivered before an audience; a formal or methodological discourse intended for instruction.*
—Webster, 1972, p. 485

INTRODUCTION

The lecture method is generic across both subjects and grade levels, and ancient in its roots. Lecturing can be found in a seventh-grade English classroom as well as in a college freshman mathematics classroom. It is universal to all content areas and most grade levels, and is the predominant teaching method in secondary and college classrooms. It is ancient in that its roots can be traced back to Greek civilization with the writings and discussions of Socrates, Plato, Aristotle, and Demosthenes. The lecture is well documented as a strategy for communicating ideas to others; it also has been known from Greek times that many a listener has been put to sleep by an uninspired and long-winded lecturer.

The lecture method has survived over 2,000 years because it is both efficient and familiar. In the twentieth century, particularly in the late 60s and early 70s, the lecture approach received a great deal of criticism for misuses and unskilled applications. This criticism is also evident in the commission reports of the 90s. A study conducted by the National Assessment of Educational Progress (NAEP) of achievement for nine million students since 1970 stated, "Across the past 20 years, little seems to have changed in how students are taught. Despite much research suggesting better alternatives, classrooms still appear to be dominated by textbooks, teacher lectures and short-answer activity sheets" (Mullis, Owen, & Phillips, 1990, p. 10).

Research on student learning indicates that motivation is reduced "when students go from lesson to lesson or from class to class, listening to as many as six different teachers telling them what they should know" (Spalding, 1992, p. 33). The research reported on effective teaching (Wittrock, 1986) seems to support a more direct instructional approach at the elementary and secondary levels, often characterized by the use of lecture or presentation strategies. Good and Brophy (1994) indicated that "two key features of good lectures are the *clarity* of the information and the *enthusiasm* of the presentation" (p. 380). Cangelosi (1993) in his analysis of teaching vignettes found "for students to be engaged in lecture-type learning activity, they must attentively listen to what the teacher is saying.... Such engagement requires the students to be cognitively active, while physically inactive" (p. 156).

In a review of 56 research articles on learning retention in 96 studies, Semb and Ellis (1994) in an article entitled "Knowledge Taught in Schools: What Is Remembered?" found that "students retain much of knowledge taught in the classroom" (p. 253). A finding that has implications for this chapter indicates that different instructional strategies produce higher levels of learning but do not produce different levels of forgetting. The exception cited by the authors are those studies that compared strategies that included active learning. For example, active learning might include roleplay rather than lecture for undergraduate accounting students, or hands-on field trips (observing, sketching, and recording events) for middle school students rather than visiting a site without interacting or experiencing the content. The authors concluded: "We hypothesize that these strategies [active learning] produced qualitatively different memories that are more resistant to forgetting" (p. 277).

The implications from the research reviewed by Semb and Ellis, as well as other studies reported in this chapter, are that lecture can and should be a strategy that engages students more in interactions with the content. Lecture is at its best when it actively engages the whole person.

Research (Rosenshine, 1983, 1995) includes excellent guidelines for providing interest, clarity, audience considerations, and organization in response to NAEP criticism. Lecturing, without regard for learner, content, and/or context, however, provides the dull and tedious schooling episodes that most of us would like to forget.

There are perhaps two sources for the problems identified by critics of the lecture method. The first may be a lack of teacher motivation. The second possibility is that teachers are simply unaware of the range of possible options in the lecture method due to a lack of effective role models in high school and college classrooms. Regardless of the reasons, the lecture method is not always seen as a dynamic tool for teaching and learning. In order to understand the potential of the lecture method, this chapter provides an analysis of the benefits and limitations as a teaching tool. Additionally, suggestions for maximizing its effectiveness as a teaching method are presented generically as well as specifically for elementary and secondary settings.

STYLE WITHOUT SUBSTANCE

In contrast to the boredom of many lecture memories are the "entertainers" we have encountered in education. Is the following description a familiar one?

> It is the beginning of September and George Washington High School is about to open its doors for the new school year. The students file into the school and head for their 8:30 A.M. classes. Mr. Johnson, a social studies teacher, is a new member

of the faculty. Many of the students are eager to see the new teacher. They have heard through the grapevine that Mr. Johnson is great. His students are not disappointed by his first lecture. He uses great amounts of humor, enthusiasm, movement, and vocal inflection to embellish his presentation. After a few weeks, the students come to idolize Mr. Johnson, except for Tom, who complains the presentations are entertaining but lack depth or substance. His peers call Tom an egghead and dismiss the objections.

The preceding situation has implications for a series of studies conducted on the effects of lecture on both medical professions and undergraduate college students (Williams & Ware, 1977). The researchers hired a *Hollywood actor* to teach six different types of lectures, varying from high, medium, and low levels of content to high, medium, and low levels of expressiveness. The expressive manner of the "teacher" is reflected in humor, enthusiasm, movement, and vocal inflection (p. 450). The students' ratings of the instructor were not sensitive to the fact that little substance was being presented in a very entertaining manner. The phenomenon has been called the *Dr. Fox Effect* because, in the first study, students thought the lecturer was a professor of medicine.

The point of the story and research is that form without substance is meaningless. Although the expressive manner of the teacher is a very important motivating factor, without knowledge and wisdom the learning experience becomes shallow. Our experiences have demonstrated that mature and committed students are resentful and discouraged by entertainment without relevant content. Many a student has assessed an instructor with, "Sure, it was a fun class but I didn't get what I needed from it. We just listened to stories." We've observed elementary students obviously enjoying an engaging activity or game who are later frustrated with questions or assignments for which they had inadequate preparation.

So we return to the teaching model of our text and examine the lecture strategy with respect to the learner, the content, and the context.

LEARNER, CONTEXT, AND CONTENT

As you learned in the Preface to this book, Chapters One through Six comprise the first section of the book, *Organizing Strategies.*

Considerations for learner, context, and content continue into the second part of the text, *Instructing Strategies,* which consists of Chapters Seven through Thirteen. The chapters in this section include Lecture; Questioning and Discussion; Interactive Practice for Learning; Grouping for Instruction; Reflective Teaching and Learning; Making Learning Real; and Using Community Resources, Audiovisuals, Computers, and Multimedia. Each is designed to expand your teaching repertoire. The strategies work best when the learner, context, and content are considerations during the preplanning, active planning, ongoing planning, and postplanning process.

Lecture, the strategy most widely used in secondary classrooms, tends to be highly teacher directed. Traditionally, as you will see on the instructional continuum in Figure 7.1, this is the view of most learners who have experienced the lecture approach

FIGURE 7.1 *Instructional Continuum*

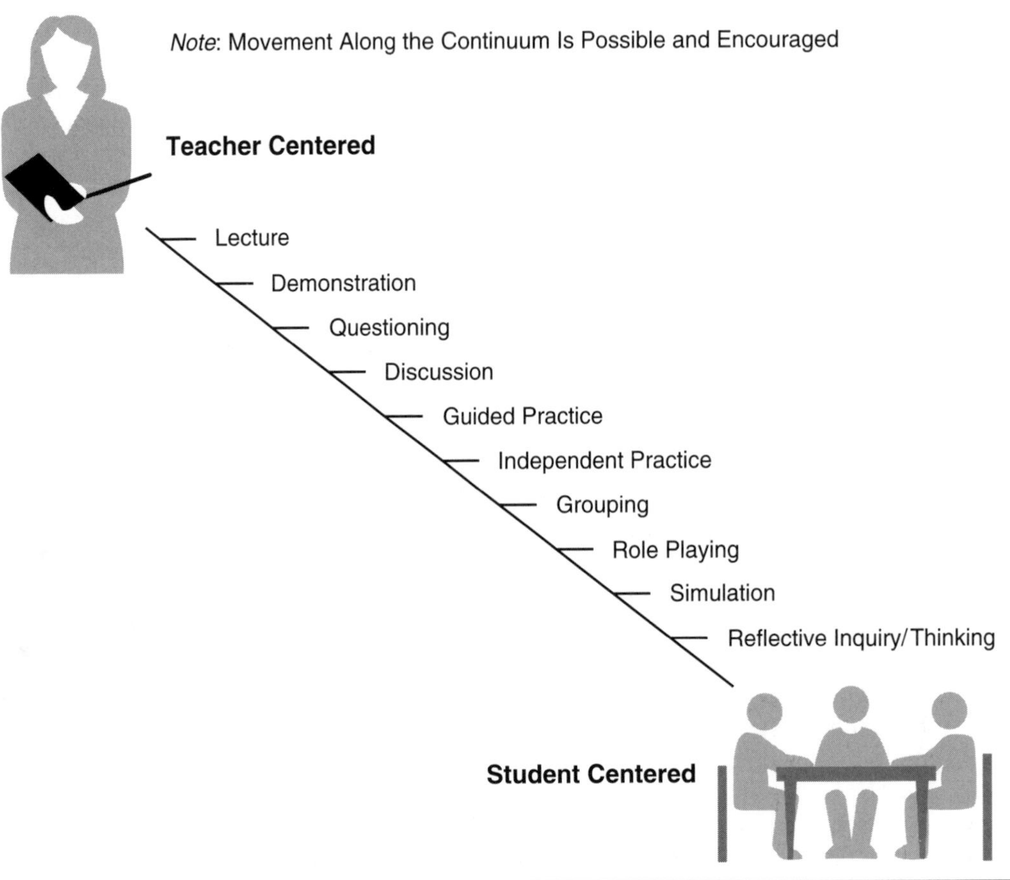

in high school or college. This chapter will provide other more interactive and student-centered ways to view the lecture strategy.

Instructional Continuum

When teachers and other educators were asked to place the instructional strategies in this text on a continuum from teacher focused to student focused, the lecture strategy was placed closest to the teacher-centered end of the continuum (see Figure 7.1). The lecture strategy, although mostly teacher directed, can become much more interactive and student focused. Each instructional strategy presented in the text has benefits and limitations. The instructional continuum is a visual representation of teaching strategies based on what many educators see being used in classrooms today. The lack of student involvement, however, can be minimized if considerations for learner, context, and content become part of the pre- and active planning process. The following Snapshot demonstrates how two teachers in the same school with the same students can get very different results when using the lecture strategy.

SNAPSHOT: Two Secondary Classrooms

Room 107

Ms. Johnson teaches world history in Room 107 to tenth-graders during sixth period, which is from 1:30 to 2:15 each day. The class uses a 400-page world history textbook and the course has a great deal of content to cover. As the students walk into the room and take their seats, Ms. Johnson looks at her attendance list, makes some notations of students who are absent, and begins to present the information for the day's lesson that relates to the fall of the Roman Empire. Fifteen minutes into the lesson, several students begin to fidget with pencils, combs, and other objects. One student drops his pencil and smiles to another student while bending down to pick it up. The teacher reprimands another student for not paying attention. Most students, however, are taking notes. Thirty-five minutes into the lesson, Ms. Johnson explains what will be on Friday's test. A few students ask questions about the test. Five minutes before the bell rings, a homework assignment is given. Students copy the assignment down and are given a few minutes to begin the assignment. The bell rings and the students leave for seventh period.

Room 204

During the last period of the day, from 2:20 until 3:05 P.M., Ms. Bevins teaches biology in Room 204 to the class that Ms. Johnson taught during sixth period. The textbook for the course is 450 pages. As the students walk into the room at 2:16, they turn to a corner of the chalkboard where two questions from yesterday's biology class are listed. The students begin to answer the questions in their notebook, which is collected monthly. Students earn additional credit for work completed before the bell rings. The teacher checks the roll chart and goes to individual students to answer questions. Ms. Bevins begins the lecture on molecular biology at 2:22 P.M. as she places a slide on the overhead and asks if someone could explain what he or she thinks the chemical formula represents.

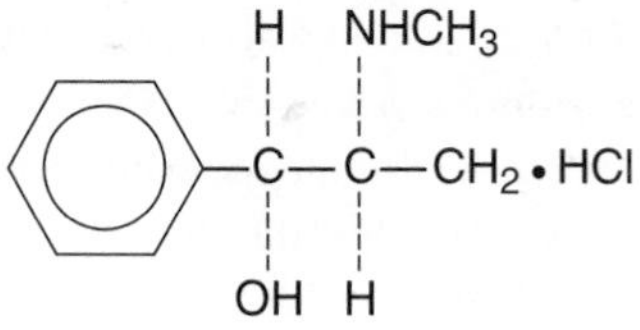

H NHCH3

—C—C—CH2 • HCl

OH H

$$C_{10}H_{16}NO \cdot HCl \qquad MW = 201.70$$

Several students come close to the answer. The formula is for a decongestant used for colds and allergies and found in the information packet with the medicine

(Adams Laboratories, n.d.). The students seem fascinated with the idea that the molecular formula is in some way related to their sniffles from allergies.

Fifteen minutes into the lecture, Ms. Bevins asks the students to turn to a neighbor and summarize for each other the key points in the presentation. The animated discussion lasts for three minutes. Several groups volunteer to present their summaries and questions about the content being discussed. Ms. Bevins continues her lecture and students are given a summary sheet with an outline of the key concepts and terms. The students use this form to complete their notes. Five minutes before the bell rings, students are directed to their homework assignment sheet given each Monday for the week. The remaining time is spent with Ms. Bevins giving an example of a homework problem and the class working together to solve it. The bell rings and the students go to their lockers still discussing what they learned in class.

This Snapshot represents two approaches to lecture. Both teachers lectured, but the classes were different in the way students interacted with the content. Ms. Bevins realized that the context of seventh period (high fatigue and low attention spans) would reduce student motivation and learning. She provided an interactive and stimulating lesson by responding to both learner needs at the end of the day and the requirements of a complex curriculum. On the following day, several students brought additional examples of structural formulas to class and they wanted to talk more about molecular biology.

Returning to the continuum in Figure 7.1, you can see that the lecture strategy in Ms. Johnson's classroom is highly teacher focused. But in Ms. Bevins's classroom, lecture is more interactive, and its position on the continuum would be more student centered, reflecting greater instructional flexibility.

Learner

Knowing about the learner will assist you in making decisions about the type of lecture and the content to be incorporated into the lecture. Although you do not have control over the experiences of the students prior to their entry into your classroom, you should have some knowledge about both the characteristics of the group and the individuals who make up the group. For example, what is the academic background of the students? Have they already mastered some of the information you will present? Do they need a prerequisite set of skills and knowledge level before they can comprehend the information or ideas presented in the lecture? Do the students have an average or less than average attention span (as determined by developmental levels)? Do they have the ability to operate at a formal operational or concrete operational stage of development? Can you rely on symbols or will you need concrete examples?

You want to challenge the students but you do not want to frustrate them. This will interfere with their ability to learn and your ability to be effective. The teacher needs to know if the students are effective in taking notes or if some are having difficulty in synthesizing the information presented during the lecture. The teacher may decide to provide content outlines for the entire class or provide specific training for those students who have poor outlining skills. In either case, the teacher uses data about the students to improve the conditions for learning in the classroom.

Information about the learner can be gained from direct observations of the students, classroom discussions, quizzes or pretests, student interest inventories, standardized test scores, class and homework assignments, and other lecture experiences. Research (Slavin, 1988; Fashola & Slavin, 1998) indicates that effective teachers adapt instructional strategies and materials to the ability level of the students. The process of knowing your students should begin on the first day and continue throughout the year. Knowledge about the students will assist in planning both the content and the format of the lecture.

Knowing your students should not be a justification for lowering expectations or watering down the curriculum. Knowing something about your students will provide you information to create meaningful examples and provide opportunities to build on prior knowledge and experiences. The Learner Profile in the Sample and Examples section provides some important information about the interests, work habits, philosophies, and learning styles of your students in grades 3 through 12. For younger students, the questions are read aloud and the students respond orally. Complete the profile and compare your responses with other members of your class.

Ultimately, effective teachers need to put themselves in the place of the student, to maintain an awareness of the learner, to ask: What would I learn from this lecture? Would I find this material interesting? What am I communicating by my style, my choice of words, my nonverbal language?

One characteristic of teaching that appeals to learners of all ages and that is especially important when using the lecture strategy is enthusiasm. Although enthusiasm is difficult to measure and nearly impossible to teach, we all know it when we see it.

Enthusiasm

Charles Pine, professor of physics at Rutgers University for 36 years, received a national outstanding college teacher award. He is an excellent example of how a teacher can combine form and substance to the benefit of both teacher and student. The summer he received his award for teaching excellence, he shared his teaching methods with (high school) math teachers from over 16 public school districts in New Jersey. A student who nominated Mr. Pine for the award noted:

> *He can transpose his classes into the realm of the subject he is discussing, whether it be climbing into an atom to observe the interaction of atomic forces, standing on a revolving turntable to get the feel for rotating and relative coordinate systems, or venture inside a balloon to observe how the individual air particles contribute to the total pressure.... "You've got to give of yourself," Mr. Pine explains. "In the end, the most important factor, I think, is enthusiasm. Even after all these years, I think it's fun going into a classroom." (Heller, 1984, p. 28)*

You, as a teacher, must ask yourself questions to determine the presence or absence of enthusiasm. Ortiz (1997) found the enthusiasm and positive feedback during lectures were related to higher academic engagement. Check for attitude toward subject matter, students, the school setting, and self; check physical factors (fatigue and enthusiasm don't combine well) and preparation (it's hard to be enthusiastic when you're not sure what comes next). Look at your own learner profile: What characteristics on your profile will contribute to teaching enthusiasm? What characteristics will limit your enthusiasm?

In contrast to the examples of quality lectures found in secondary and higher education, many elementary teachers avoid the lecture strategy. Armed with child-development principles that identify the short attention span of young children, and sold on the advantages of activities and discovery learning, novice elementary teachers plan every possible teaching strategy except lecturing. The common scene in elementary classrooms is a very brief explanation of new material, an abundance of directions, and students doing seatwork for most of the instructional time. In an attempt to be sensitive to young learners and to heed the advice that children learn by doing, elementary teachers have generally ignored lecturing.

As with all of the strategies described in this book, lecturing is appropriate for some curriculum content and for certain learning objectives, just as discovery learning is appropriate for some curriculum content and for certain learning objectives. However, even kindergarten students can and will attend to a brief (5 to 6 minutes) lecture presentation. Although it is important for any lecturer to attend to organization, pacing, focus, clarity, and audience, it is especially critical for elementary teachers to assess these aspects of a lecture. The management and organization of lecture—or as many classify it in the elementary grades, presentation skills—require specific planning and implementation strategies. The following summary of the research provides a framework for the use of lecture with elementary school students.

Research Summary

The following guidelines have been summarized from the work of Rosenshine (1983, 1995) to provide you with ideas from the research on effective instruction and studies of teacher clarity. They give suggestions for effective presentations, specifically in a lecture format. The guidelines reflect a sensitivity to the learner of any age, including middle and high school students, but are especially important for the younger learner.

1. *Content material should be presented in small steps.* Along with guided practice, Rosenshine (1995) found this characteristic to be the most essential to effective teaching. A first-grade teacher is presenting the concepts of maps to his class. Each of the concepts (scale, representation, etc.) is taught in individual lessons and is broken down further into parts for a lecture. *Scale* is first defined, then its purpose is presented, then variations of scale are described, and finally examples of scale are provided. Within the lecture on scale, each of the understandings is developed completely before the teacher continues to the next aspect of the concept.

2. *Presentations should focus on one thought (point, direction) at a time.* When the first-grade teacher is trying to develop the concept of scale, the time would not be appropriate to introduce students to the different kinds of maps, such as aerial maps, topographical maps, and so on.

3. *Digressions should be avoided during presentations.* Young children are notorious for sidetracking presentations, and elementary teachers often yield to the digressions. A

discussion of maps is likely to initiate students' recall of map use on vacations, and discussions can quickly turn to lengthy descriptions of various rides at Disneyland. Elementary teachers need to be especially smooth and skillful in guiding student input to contribute to the subject focus.

4. *When possible or appropriate, modeling should accompany the lecture.* A fifth-grade teacher has been teaching a unit on decision making. When she presents the steps to decision making, she models each step in a scenario from classroom life and demonstrates how to proceed through each step.

5. *Lectures are best accompanied by many varied and specific examples.* During an initial overview lecture on the concept of farms, the kindergarten teacher introduces a wide variety of replicas of farms. These include photographs, dioramas, models, slides, songs, art prints, literature, and so on.

6. *Effective lectures are characterized by detailed and redundant explanations for difficult points.* Many concepts provide difficulty for young children. When teaching the purpose of advertising to first-graders, explanations need to be redundant in order to overcome the students' misconceptions about advertising, then to establish new knowledge about advertising. Such concepts may take several lectures.

7. *Before proceeding to the next point in a lecture, check for student understanding.* As the second-grade teacher presents the process of observation through the sense of vision, he will be coveting the characteristics of an object observed through the eye. Before proceeding to the characteristics that can be observed through the tactile sense, he may begin with, "Before going on, let's list all the things we know about the artichoke by using our eyes."

8. *Student progress should be monitored through the lecture by means of questions.* With the same presentations on observation through the sense of sight, the second-grade teacher may ask, "Can we tell that the artichoke is soft with our eyes? Can we tell that the artichoke is green with our eyes? Can we tell that the artichoke is sour with our eyes?"

9. *Lecturers should stay on the topic, repeating material until students understand.* Again, with the level of difficulty that young students encounter with complex concepts, a lecture on a new and/or abstract concept may extend over a period of several days or a week. The information may be best presented with different examples, continued questioning, and some redundant lecturing over time to accomplish student understanding.

The major obstacles to the success of the lecture strategy at all levels are not student attention span or the inappropriateness of the strategy, but a lack of clarity and organization. Additionally, there may be a lack of sufficient explanations and examples, teachers assuming that everyone knows *without checking for understanding,* and the introduction of more complex material before students master the prior material. These failings reflect a lack of awareness of the learner. Effective lecturing then requires consideration of the learner during the planning phase and during implementation (the actual doing).

Content

The content is the substance of the lesson. The content in the lecture includes facts, skills, ideas, rules, principles, concepts, and generalizations. The teacher must have a mastery level of the content to be able to translate the information effectively to the students. Teaching strategies, motivational techniques, and effective planning cannot substitute for depth in the content area to be taught. Additionally, content knowledge is a prerequisite for the development of goals and objectives of the lesson—a first step in the planning and organization discussed in Chapter Two.

Goals of Lecture: Information, Motivation, and Reflective/Critical Thinking

What are your goals for the lesson? Is your intent *to provide information, to motivate the students,* or *to provide critical thinking, reflective presentations?* All three goals individually, or collectively, could be an instructional outcome of the lesson. Once the goal(s) is(are) determined, then objectives for the lesson need to be developed based on the learner, content, and context. Ask yourself: What do I expect the students to learn from the lesson? The answers to this question lead you to a decision about the strategy or strategies to be used to deliver the lesson. If the lecture method seems to be the most effective strategy for the lesson, then some preliminary organization of the content is necessary.

Informational

For an *informational* presentation, the content information is analyzed into concepts and subconcepts followed by a sequencing process. For example, if you wanted to teach a lesson on selected American inventions (Jefferies & Lewis, 1992), you could develop an outline that is based on *where* the invention is primarily being used rather than *when* the date of the invention occurred. The following outline begins with industry and commerce, then home and electronics, and concludes with communications:

Types of American Inventions

I. Industry and Commerce
  - Machines
    - Cotton Gin
    - Sewing Machine
  - Illuminators
    - Light Bulb
    - Laser

II. Home
  - Labor Savers
    - Washing Machine
    - Vacuum Cleaner
  - Safety
    - Safety Pin
    - Safety Razor

III. Electronics
  - Brains
    - Integrated Circuit
    - Transistor
  - Tools
    - Photocopier
    - Personal Computer

IV. Communications
  - Wire
    - Telegraph (Morse Code)
    - Telephone
  - Wireless
    - Radio (Vacuum Tube)
    - Television

With younger students, an outline based on concepts to be learned is an appropriate starting point. From the following list of concepts, teachers can then anticipate possible questions, examples, and extensions of the basic concepts:

Farms

1. Definition of *farms.*
2. There are different types of farms.
3. Different kinds of farms provide different kinds of products.
4. Different kinds of farms require different kinds of equipment, work, and people.
5. Farms may be different sizes.
6. In our community, there are dairy farms and fruit/vegetable farms.

Here again, awareness of the learner determines the amount of detail we plug into a basic outline. For the primary-grade student, the concept of different kinds of farms might be planned with an outline as follows:

2. There are different types of farms:
   a. Dairy farms
   b. Fruit/vegetable farms
   c. Poultry farms
   d. Grain farms

However, for an upper-elementary student, the outline may extend to regions of the United States or to individual versus corporation farms. An activity to develop sample outlines around given topics (e.g., our community) is provided in the Samples and Examples section at the end of this chapter.

Motivational

If your goal is primarily *motivational,* then the planning process should focus on a lesson of high interest to the students. The teacher should incorporate a high level of stimulus variation and enthusiasm. Providing information would be secondary to creating a high level of interest for the general subject area. For example, a high-school English teacher provides a motivating set induction by entering the classroom dressed like the character in a Shakespearean play. The English teacher then presents a soliloquy on teenage love, using modern-day English for the next five minutes. The students become highly motivated to read about the ancient teenage love story of Romeo and Juliet.

The elementary teacher can promote motivation for learning about farms by having the fifth-grade students prepare a bulletin board of newspaper and magazine headlines and pictures about the woes of the farmer, federal measures influencing farmers, food price fluctuations, or the route food takes from the farm to the table. A kindergarten teacher may set up a display table of products—such as butter, fruits and vegetables, eggs, cereal, beef, rice, and so on—as a stimulation to learn about the different kinds of farms. With younger students, it is important to precede or follow lectures with experiences. Such combinations involve conscientious planning with much advance preparation for such experiences as field trips, visitors, films, and props (costumes, display items, demonstration equipment, etc.).

SNAPSHOT: Elementary Classroom

Mr. Groff instructs the fifth-grade class to get out pencils, a piece of paper, rulers, and math textbooks. "Place all of the items at the corner of your table," he directs the students, "then look at the overhead." On the transparency he had previously written examples of metric and standard measurement. (*Note:* By having the transparency prepared, Mr. Groff saves time and keeps the flow of the lesson moving.)

When the students are ready to attend, he reminds them that they have been studying both metric and standard measurement, quickly reviews the equivalents of each, and begins an explanation of the importance of using the appropriate measurement units. "When we choose the appropriate unit of measure, we can accomplish the task efficiently and easily. If we choose an inappropriate unit, we may make errors, or the task may take us a very long time, or we may be unable to carry out the measurement."

Mr. Groff continues, "Let me give you an example of what I mean by an inappropriate unit of measure. Last week, I observed first-graders studying measurement. Because they don't understand standard units of measure yet, they were using familiar things as units—their fingers, blocks, their feet, and a crayon. One little girl wanted to measure the length of a wall in the classroom with her finger as a unit of measure. The teacher allowed her to begin measuring so that she and her classmates would learn the idea of appropriate measurement units. Now, if I asked you to measure a block in our neighborhood using your rulers and the unit inch, what would happen?"

Students describe the length of time it would take, all the mistakes that would happen, and many potential frustrations. From there, Mr. Groff returns to the list of units on the overhead transparency and asks for appropriate units for measuring the classroom, a building, a book, and so on. He reviews the standard possibilities for measuring his examples, then reviews the metric possibilities for measuring his examples. He follows his review with the question, "Who can tell us why it is important to choose the appropriate unit of measure?" He then proceeds to give directions for practice in making appropriate selections from a handout.

Developing motivational strategies for the beginning of a lecture is an important step in focusing the students' attention.

Reflective/Critical Thinking

If your goal for the lesson is to encourage *reflective and critical thinking,* the lesson should build on the information, ideas, and concepts developed in previous classes. For example, a class that had been studying genetics in biology was presented a lecture on gene manipulation through selective control of the gene pool. The lecturer developed a scenario for the future of a world in which most major genetic diseases were eliminated. At the conclusion of the 20-minute lecture, the students were asked for their reactions to the ideas presented. The lecture led to a very thought-provoking discussion. Garside

(1996) found that active discussion during lecture significantly increased higher-level critical thinking skills.

A reflective/critical thinking lecture could include current research and opinions that were *not* available when the text was written. It could incorporate opposing viewpoints, present critical issues identified by other authors, and identify and present different interpretations and conclusions (McMann, 1979). Nine elements are presented by McMann (1979)* to facilitate higher-level thinking, including:

1. *The lecture should always provide new or supplemental information. Teachers should not abuse the lecture by reciting tedious facts, or chronology, or by restating the obvious material in textbooks.*
2. *Students must be cognizant of the lecture topic and goals, the skills to be learned, and the logical development of the lecture. To achieve this end, a brief outline can be prepared and presented to students.*
3. *Students can be required to analyze the lecture through a developed model similar to the historical model presented [below]. Students' written critiques can also be evaluated by the instructor.*

   Historical Model

   1. *Historical Issue*
   2. *Author and Source*
   3. *Interpretation*
   4. *Supporting Evidence*
   5. *Refuting Evidence*
   6. *Assumptions*
   7. *Logical Consistency*
   8. *Fallacies*
   9. *Questions*

4. *Students should participate by asking questions, clarifying ideas, challenging the evidence, suggesting alternative conclusions and evidence. The lecture is not meant to stifle student response and creativity, and analysis is not meant to be strictly teacher-oriented.*
5. *Questions must be formulated and asked by the instructor during the lecture to emphasize the importance of significant information. Insist that students speculate on questions, clarify values, cite examples, provide arguments, criticize evidence, state assumptions, and cite logical fallacies.*
6. *Facts as facts have an importance secondary to their use as evidence in supporting an interpretation or a point of view. Thus, the students' efforts must be redirected toward the analysis of the facts rather than memorization of the facts.*
7. *Teachers must know their students and the factors which influence their receptivity to a lecture. Such factors might include their academic abilities, physical handicaps, learning disabilities, their interest in social studies (or other subjects) and the specific topic, their understanding of previous material, and the prevalent classroom atmosphere which the students generate.*

**Source:* F. McMann, Jr., "In Defense of Lecture," *Social Studies, 70,* pp. 270–274, 1979. Reprinted with permission of the Helen Dwight Reid Educational Foundation. Published by Heldref Publications, 1319 Eighteenth St., NW, Washington, DC 20036-1802. Copyright © 1979.

8. *Lecture information must not remain in a vacuum. The information must either assist the students in their understanding of the topic or the students must be able to utilize the information in a structured, but creative manner. Conversely, teachers must be creative in extending the lecture information to subsequent classroom activities, particularly in the areas of student research.*
9. *Teachers must exhibit an enthusiastic attitude toward the lecture as an effective method, its content and the skills demanded. A prophetic sense of boredom and impending doom will surely alienate students and diminish their interest and enthusiasm. (p. 273)*

Again, your awareness of the learner will determine the appropriateness of the lecture strategy for reflective/critical thinking. Recognizing the limits of first-graders' higher-level thinking abilities, the teacher can nevertheless plan for lectures that prompt reflection. A mini-lecture of the typical farmer's day with a transparency and slides of the activities could be followed by questions to promote critical thinking. First-graders could be asked: Is the farmer's life a hard or easy life? Why? Would you like to be a farmer? Why or why not? What's different or alike about your parents' work and the farmer's work?

As demonstrated in our examples, the reflective/critical thinking goal may be achieved if you plan for this type of lecture from the beginning. The foundation could be established with an informational lecture and then build to a reflective/critical thinking presentation. The teacher who moves beyond information to analysis, synthesis, comparison, and evaluation can add a unique dimension to the instructional process. This approach would alleviate, but not eliminate, many of the limitations of the lecture method. If you are unfamiliar with the reflective lecture approach, then begin by focusing several weeks ahead in planning a 15- to 20-minute mini-lecture that would challenge the students' higher-level thinking abilities.

Context

The context refers to the total learning environment (discussed in Chapter One), which includes three elements: the classroom, the school, and the community. Each of the elements offers opportunities and limitations for the teacher designing a lesson.

Consider the size of the class or group attending the lecture. The use of slide-tape presentations, overhead projector, chalkboard, or other stimuli will depend on the physical layout of the room. Also consider the sound transmission aspects of the room. Will your voice carry to the last student in the classroom? If the area is an open space environment, then the limitations placed on the lecturer are greater than in a four-wall classroom, especially if other instructors are also lecturing.

Since the effectiveness of the lecture depends on the attention of the students, will there be distractions in the room? Will distractions reduce the effectiveness of the lecture by claiming the attention of the students? (For example, having the classroom overlooking the football practice field would be a real distractor in the fall.) Will the students be seated in such a way that you will have the opportunity to have eye contact with each student? Contextual elements may be incorporated into the lesson if the lecturer considers them in the planning process.

SNAPSHOT: Contextual Elements

Which of the following contextual factors affect the class?

_____ Outside noise levels

_____ Lighting

_____ Types of chairs/desks

_____ Placement of chalkboards

_____ Size of room

_____ Size of class

_____ Time of day

_____ Requirement vs. option

_____ Temperature of the room

_____ Windows

_____ Open arrangement

_____ (Other)

Which of the factors checked in the preceding Snapshot will influence learning?

Many of the suggestions from Rosenshine (1983) demonstrate the importance of contextual considerations, and many of the following management suggestions will provide adjustments to the context.

TEACHER CONTROL

One of the key reasons teachers use lecture as a strategy is the degree of control it provides them over the students. All the attention (or at least most of the attention) is directed toward the teacher. The teacher controls the material, the flow, and the types of questions asked of the students, and monitors the flow of questions from the students. As you will see in the next few pages on the benefits and limitations of the lecture strategy, lecture can be used both to stimulate and stifle learning. If you wish to maximize the effective use of this strategy, then effective planning and preparation are a must. The organization of ideas and examples must flow from the beginning to the end. The first step, then, is to establish a purpose or goal for your lecture and plan an outline accordingly. Once the sequencing or logical organization has been determined, you should:

1. Identify two or three key concepts to be included in the lecture and support these concepts with examples or illustrations within the lecture.

2. Prepare notes that highlight the key concepts, subconcepts, and points to be made during the presentation.
3. Use analogies, stories, and examples to support your ideas and provide a frame of reference for the students.
4. Close your lecture with a summary of the key points in the presentation by writing these points on the board, using an overhead projector, or having the students summarize them.

Guidelines from Research

When

Lecture should be considered primarily to introduce and explain new concepts, to help incorporate smaller units of information into larger logical structures, to add insight and expand on previously presented concepts, and to review and summarize (Bowman, 1979). Although its use is typically limited to providing information, this limitation is imposed by the lecturer, not the strategy. Motivational, reflective, and critical thinking lectures are viable alternatives to lectures that only inform.

Scope and Pace

Many researchers and teacher educators recommend that a lecture be limited to three to five concepts (Stanton, 1978). At the elementary school level, one concept per lecture would be appropriate. The length of the lecture should be limited to 10- to 15-minute segments interspersed by other strategies (e.g., questioning and discussion) and stimulus variations. It is also important to have a pace that most closely matches the absorption rate of the students (Bowman, 1979). If the teacher talks too slowly, the students will become bored too quickly and they will become frustrated. Audiotaping or videotaping a lesson will assist you in determining the proper pace for a lesson. This is discussed further in Chapter Fifteen.

Stimulus Variation

There is a consensus among the researchers that stimulus variation is a key element to an effective lecture (Williams & Ware, 1977; Ebert-May, Brewer, & Allred, 1997). Stimulus variation during the lecture includes the following elements:

1. *Humor.* The use of humor to reinforce examples and illustrate concepts in a lecture is effective in facilitating long-term retention and comprehension. Studies have also shown that humor can be an effective means of reinforcing learning (Desberg, Henschal, & Marshall, 1981). At the school of education at Tel Aviv University, a course is offered for pre-service and in-service teachers in the use of humor in the classroom. Humor, used to reinforce ideas and concepts, can be an effective tool for the lecturer. It should be noted that humor, directed at a student or the class, can interfere with the instructional process by creating a negative climate for learning. Also, sarcasm should never be confused for humor. The students look to the teacher as a role model; sarcasm presents a very negative model for the class.

2. *Cuing.* The lecturer has the advantage of knowing the key ideas and concepts of the presentation. This should be communicated to the students. Key points can be emphasized by:

a. pausing
b. verbally highlighting a word or concept by changing voice tone
c. using gestures (e.g., hand and facial), including physically moving away from the desk to emphasize a point
d. pointing to the chalkboard

The instructor needs to communicate to the learner a level of expectation regarding the material presented. The students should be told if they are to *memorize and recall* (e.g., the periodic table of elements or the battles of the Civil War) or *compare and contrast* (e.g., the causes of the French Revolution with the American Civil War). A study conducted by Kintsch and Bates (1977) found that five days after a lecture, verbatim memory was greatly reduced. However, unique elements (e.g., humor, analogies, and anecdotes) were remembered the best when compared to non-unique elements such as general topics or details of the lecture. Cuing the students to the key points of the lecture will facilitate learning.

3. *Pausing.* A very innovative way of stimulating learning during the lecture is provided by Rowe (1976): "If a lecturer pauses at least two times during a lecture for 2 minutes per pause and has students in adjacent seats share notes and comments, more of the content of the lecture will be learned and retained by more students." The sharing by three students will be an effective overlap for the information presented. The process focuses the students on the lecture material and provides the stimulation of on-task student-student interaction.

4. *Media.* The use of slides (especially those taken by the teacher), overhead projector, chalkboard, films, records, video, posters, maps, and computers (with projector screen) are effective means of providing information. This seems particularly true in the age of visual communication. In many cases, materials developed by the instructor have more impact than packaged programs. For example, before a field trip, take slides of the key points to be viewed by the students during the trip. This is important for trips to museums or institutes where the students may become overwhelmed by the amount of information. For example, the use of visual stimuli and computer simulations of molecules had a dramatic impression on the students studying physics.

The media used during the presentation must be heard and seen clearly by all the students in the classroom. Media can provide the linkage between the familiar (concrete) and the unfamiliar (abstract) elements of the lesson. It should be noted that the first law of any technology is that it may not work. Prepare the lesson with this possibility in mind.

5. *Enthusiasm.* According to Brock (1977, p. 4), a "positive relationship exists between the enthusiasm which students perceived that the lecturer exudes and their learning of the course material." It would be difficult to imagine students becoming excited about a topic if the teacher lacked the interest and enthusiasm for the subject. Enthusiasm is not a skill but an attitude that the teacher brings to the class.

As with any instructional element, the use of stimulus variation should be used in moderation. One study (Henson, 1980, p. 117) found that "movement through the class, gesturing and praising" lowered the effectiveness of lectures to elementary school students. Good judgment in the use of the preceding five elements of stimulus variation will assist you in keeping the interest of the students without distracting them from the focus of the lesson.

Benefits

Every strategy used in the classroom has both benefits and limitations for the teaching/learning process. Three studies—one which covered 50 years of research, reported by Hillocks (1981), another which reviewed 91 studies (Henson, 1980), and the third which encompassed 96 research projects over 40 years (Smith, 1978)—found that the lecture approach is no less effective than other teaching methods. Several studies supported the use of lecture "to introduce a unit or build a frame of reference... [for] demonstrating and clarifying matters... [to] set the atmosphere or focus of students' activities... [and for] introducing and summarizing the major concepts that were presented in a lesson" (Henson, 1980, p. 116).

Some of the benefits of the lecture strategy include the following:

1. The most information may be presented in the shortest period of time.
2. The teacher has a degree of control (pace, content, organization of the material and time) that may not be present with other instructional strategies.
3. It provides an overview of a new concept of unit or learning.
4. It provides the opportunity to sharpen and practice note taking (psychomotor) and listening skills.
5. The same facts and information are presented to all students, which enables the class and instructor to have a common frame of reference.
6. Facts and information have been preorganized to follow a logical sequence. The sequence may flow from a time line of events or build from ideas to form concepts.

Similarly, some research on effective instruction supports the use of the lecture strategy. Studies in grades 4 through 8 (Evertson et al., 1980; Good & Grouws, 1979; Steele, 1993) found that effective mathematics teaching was characterized by twice as much time spent in lecture, demonstration, and discussion than ineffective mathematics teaching. Effective teachers use this additional presentation time to provide redundant explanations, use many examples, provide sufficient instruction so that the students can do the seatwork with minimal difficulty, check for student understanding, and reteach when necessary (Rosenshine, 1983, 1995).

Additionally, data from the Beginning Teacher Evaluation Study (BTES) looking at second and fifth grades, report that students spent about 30 percent of their time in a teacher-directed setting and 70 percent of their time doing seatwork (Fisher, Berliner, Filby, Marliave, Cahen, & Dishaw, 1980). When students were in teacher-led groups, their engagement rate was about 84 percent, whereas during seatwork it was about 70 percent (Rosenshine, 1981). Other studies found that direct instruction or supervision by a teacher is related to higher engagement of students than students working independently. Gump's (1982) third-grade study found that engagement was higher in whole-class presentations, tests, and teacher presentations (approximately 80 percent) than in supervised study and independent seatwork (approximately 75 percent). Garside (1996) found lecture and discussion to be equally effective in facilitating the use of critical thinking skills at the undergraduate level and more effective than reading a chapter without instruction. These kinds of data should cause elementary teachers or those preparing to teach to consider how their teaching time is to be spent. Specifically, their planning may begin to reflect a valuing of the lecture strategy.

Limitations

Research shows that students who are highly motivated and are effective in note taking benefit the most from the lecture approach. A study by Frank (1984) indicates that students who are able to synthesize the information presented in a lecture into an outline are at a distinct advantage over students who write down almost every word the teacher says. This note-taking ability translates into high test scores for some students. However, in a study conducted by Maddox and Hoole (1975) with college students, only 52 percent of the key ideas presented in a lecture were evident in the students' notes. Although lower-achieving students benefit the least from the lecture method, they seem to prefer this method over other strategies that require a more active role in the learning process.

College students who were preparing to become secondary teachers were asked by their instructor (Birkel, 1973) to express their views about the lecture method. The negative views clearly outnumbered the positive. The students felt the following about lecture method: (1) boring and uninteresting; (2) lacked teacher/student or student/student interaction; (3) poorly organized and presented; (4) content was irrelevant, not current, and accessible elsewhere; (5) focused mainly on the lowest level of cognition; and (6) ignored individual differences.

Although the list was developed in 1973, few teachers or students would argue that this is not an accurate reflection of lecture in classrooms of the 2000s. Often, the key of *variability* is missing from the lecture method and this encourages the student to be a passive notetaker, detached from the learning process. Students do not assume a major share of the responsibility for their own learning. Many faculty complain that their students lack "motivation, initiative, responsibility, vision, interest beyond the assigned task, and imagination, but many [faculty] are only dimly aware of the fact that they, with their methods and attitudes, may be creating and perpetuating this condition" (Osterman, 1982).

Some of the limitations of the lecture method cited by educators (Frank, 1984; Gage & Berliner, 1998; Oddi, 1983; Wahlberg, 1997) include the following:

1. The lecture method can be boring if stimulus variations (use of humor, voice modulation, and visuals) are not utilized during the presentation.
2. Student participation is limited to approximately 12 percent of the total interaction in the classroom, thus reducing the opportunity for feedback.

3. The lecture method emphasizes the lower-level cognitive skills of memorization and recall rather than synthesis and evaluation.
4. The lecture approach places students with poor note-taking skills at a disadvantage in the classroom.
5. Students in the lecture class are more passive and take a less active role in their own learning.
6. Due to a lack of interaction, the teacher has difficulty immediately determining the amount of student learning.
7. The lecture method rarely provides the opportunity for the inclusion of the affective learning domain (attitudes, feelings, and values) or the psychomotor domain.
8. Because the lecture approach is directed to large groups of students, individual needs are rarely identified or met.

The limitations of lecture seem to reflect an imbalance between teacher and student interaction. In most lecture situations, the teacher is active and the students are passive. This so-called limitation of lecture is more a function of a narrow teacher repertoire. Lecture as a strategy has greater potential than its current use in most middle- and high-school classrooms. Expanding the operational definition of lecture to include several variations will move lecture along the continuum from being a teacher-dominated strategy to having greater student involvement. The two research vignettes that soon follow provide for additional data on the lecture strategy.

Variations

One way of compensating for some of the lecture limitations is to develop an understanding and ability in implementing variations of the strategy. If you were to observe in classrooms of many different grade levels and instruction of varying curriculum content, you would note the available variations. As you review this list of lecture variations, try to visualize your experiences with each:

1. *Pure lecture.* The teacher talks to a group of students for up to an hour or more. They passively listen without interrupting or asking questions. Many students will be taking notes of the lecture.
2. *Chalk talk lecture.* This approach is more common than the pure lecture. The teacher uses the chalkboard to illustrate points or draw conclusions. By writing on the board, the teacher may limit visual contact with the students.
3. *Guided note-taking lecture.* The teacher may provide detailed notes or outlines for students for the day's presentation. In some cases, the teacher will have the students complete worksheets during different parts of the lecture (Broadwell, 1980, p. 13).
4. *Audiovisual lecture.* The teacher uses a range of media to facilitate the lecture. The overhead projector, slide projector, 16 mm projector, or video cassette recorder are utilized to provide stimulus variation.
5. *Combination lecture.* The teacher uses questioning and discussion, either during the lecture or at its conclusion, to provide feedback and correction if the students do not understand a particular part of the presentation.

6. *Mini-lecture.* The teacher limits the lecture to 15 minutes and focuses on introducing a new unit, summarizing major concepts, or setting the focus for major activities (Henson, 1980). During the remainder of the instructional time, the teacher incorporates other instructional strategies. The mini-lecture is most frequently used at the upper-elementary and middle-school levels.

Lecture with Other Strategies

The blending of lecture with other universal teaching strategies will add to the variability and effectiveness of the presentation. Combining lecture with discussion and questioning, for example, will increase the degree of students' interaction and involvement (Yu & Berliner, 1981; Garside, 1996; Ebert-May et al., 1997). Combining lecture with demonstration reinforces the visual elements of the lesson.

As we move further away from the teacher-centered strategies, the blending process becomes more difficult. Each strategy has its own conditions for effectiveness. The lecture can be conducted with a group of 20 or 200, yet the use of discovery would be limited beyond the range of 30 to 40 students. The learner, context, and content must be considered when planning for one strategy or a combination of strategies. As you master the various strategies presented in this chapter, you will begin to realize the potential of a broad repertoire of instructional options for different teaching situations.

Secondary Research Vignette

INTRODUCTION

Since current literature on school reform often seems to focus on excellence and effective practice, two researchers set out to identify the correlates of effective teaching (Cohen & Seaman, 1997) by going directly to those who are considered the best teachers and observing them at work.

STUDY DESIGN

In order to identify excellent teachers, the researchers relied on administrators, parents, students, and other teachers for such identification. They did this on the premise that colleagues know who are the best and worst in their buildings. Consensus by *all* parties was needed to qualify a teacher as excellent; any disagreement concerning teachers sifted not only the teacher but also the school in which he or she taught. Furthermore, in order to include a broad variety of student views, the researchers selected suburban and city high schools. The questionnaire asked selected teachers to identify their own teaching role models and explain why, and asked them to identify what they considered to be the most important qualities of excellent teachers. It was the belief of the researchers that the combination of observation, identification, and survey methods would result in a "real-search" (Cohen & Seaman, 1997, p. 565) methodology.

RESULTS

Most important in the study were the following correlates of effective teaching identified by the researchers:

Confidence in knowledge of subject matter. Students could sense these teachers had confidence in their subject matter, even if they admitted occasionally to making minor mistakes.

High-quality explanations. The excellent teachers were patient and superior in making explanations to questions, making assignments, and challenging students to think critically and independently.

Attention to individual differences. Effective teachers knew their students well and how they thought and learned. They were also aware of who had physical impediments such as vision and hearing problems and consistently adjusted for those.

Sense of humor. Witty responses, exaggerations, and gentle sarcasm were strategies used by effective teachers to help students learn and feel at ease in the classrooms.

Management through awareness. Despite their individual methods of managing their classes, all exhibited high awareness. These teachers always knew who needed prodding or catching up, and were aware of pacing. The classes were observed to be well managed because the teachers consistently judged student behaviors and based decisions on them.

Active learning. Whether lectures or cooperative activities occurred in these classrooms, students were actively engaged in the lesson's objectives. The excellent teachers consistently bridged the gap between abstractions and students' actual experiences.

CONCLUSIONS AND IMPLICATIONS FOR PRACTICE

The research seems to indicate that excellent teachers do not need to use state-of-the-art restructuring techniques to be excellent teachers, though these might enhance their repertoire or help them find different ways to help students learn. Most would agree that teachers who fit the description of the six correlates would be effective teachers and can serve as a way for new and experienced teachers to look at their own practices in the classrooms.

Students with Special Needs

Students in the classroom who have learning disabilities may need lecture modifications and extra support during lectures. Though admission, review, and dismissal committees may have made modifications for the teacher to follow in the student's Individual Education Plan (IEP), the following are some suggestions to help exceptional learners during classroom lectures:

- Assign a note-taking scribe for the special learners.
- Provide slotted outlines or notes to increase participation in the lecture process.
- Regularly check and discuss the notes with all learners.
- When using mini-lectures or other variations of the lecture, make sure you support the student during independent practice or when in group activities.

TEACHING NOTE TAKING

An aspect of both context and learner is a knowledge of procedures or routines. Research on classroom management (Brophy, 1999; Freiberg, 1999) advocates the teaching of procedures clearly and completely at the beginning of the school year.

An important procedure that is usually ignored is teaching students how to listen to a lecture or how to take notes during a lecture (see Figure 7.2; Hemler, 1990). Molina and collegues (1997) found that "setting a purpose for listening was the most efffective [technique] for improved listening skills" and that "listening lessons enhanced student learning and promoted active participation" (p. 1). A major reason for the lack of success with lectures may be the students' lack of preparation in how to respond to and learn from the lecture strategy. In a classroom management course at the University of Utah, which is characterized by frequent simulations and roleplaying situations, students are taught how to listen to a lecture and practice the strategies. Many university students express the lack of such information in their entire school life, and yet acknowledge the importance of something that sounds so simple.

Teaching is primarily a decision-making process (Shavelson, 1976). Your decisions to use a lecture and to plan and present a lecture involve critical considerations about the learner, the content, and the context. Your decision making is also based on your knowledge about the lecture strategy. You need to be well informed about both the benefits and the limitations of lecturing, variations of the strategy, and research findings on characteristics of its use. What may have seemed to be a simple teaching strategy at the beginning of this chapter should now be appearing as a complex element of teaching, which requires a knowledge base, comprehensive planning, and high levels of awareness. It is a strategy worth the effort, as illustrated in the benefits section of this chapter.

Finally, research has provided numerous additional considerations for teaching with lectures. Guidelines for appropriate times, scope and pace, stimulus variation, and note taking are available for directing your lecture behavior. The research findings and conclusions have been summarized and supplemented with suggestions in this final section of the chapter.

FIGURE 7.2 *Guided Note Taking for Earth Science*

Name ____________________
Date____________________
Class ____________________

The Moon

A. Description
   1. Basic description
   2. Gravity
   3. Structure of the moon
      a.
      b.
      c.
   4. Instruments left on the moon
B. Surface Features of the Moon
   1. Moon after it formed (describe)
   2. Craters—(define)
      a. Rays—
      b. Flat bottoms—
      c. Mare—
C. Origin of the Moon—3 basic theories
   1. Daughter Theory—
   2. Capture Theory—
   3. Sister Theory—

SUMMARY

- Lecture has the longest historical use as a teaching strategy.
- Commission reports of the 80s and 90s are highly critical of teacher-dominated lecture methods.
- Students learn in a variety of ways. Being able to tap several learner strengths through a learner profile or other source will expand the teacher's repertoire.
- Enthusiasm is a starting point for teaching rather than an end point. Depth of content by the teacher is the foundation for teaching. However, enthusiasm draws students into the subject when they see the teacher as a role model of interest.
- The nine steps Rosenshine highlights for effective lecture improve the opportunity for learning by students of any age.
- The three instructional goals of lecture—information, motivation, and reflective/critical thinking—should be blended to enhance the lecture strategy.
- Contextual variables place constraints and opportunities on any teaching strategy. Because of the verbal (and at times) the visual nature of lecture, physical surroundings play an important role in the success of this strategy.
- Humor, cuing, pausing, media, and enthusiasm play important roles in varying the stimuli for lecture.

Postsecondary Research Vignette

INTRODUCTION

With the advent of new technology and its impact on education, research regarding the effectiveness of student note-taking techniques is beginning to provide educators with some clear directions on the issue of note-taking methods and their effectiveness during computer-driven instruction.

STUDY DESIGN

A study performed by Quade (1996) analyzed the effects that note-taking methods (pencil and paper or online computer note pad) and styles (verbatim, paraphrasing, etc.) play in the retention and depth of processing information during computer-delivered instruction. The sample, $N = 112$, consisted of junior and senior undergraduates majoring in computer and information science from a southern Minnesota university. They were asked to view modules from a tutorial and to take notes using either the computer note pad or by pencil and paper. Thirty-two "idea units" (single blocks of information or complete ideas) were chosen from the four modules and used to analyze and evaluate the notes.

RESULTS

After completing the modules, an exit questionnaire and posttest were given to the participants. There was a difference in total posttest scores between the control group that took no notes and the treatment group that took notes online ($p < .05$). This difference, which supported the online note taking, seemed to be caused by the way the control group and the online notetakers responded to the factual-type questions on the posttest.

The study also showed that the type of notes taken did not affect the overall retention of information ($p < .05$) and that the method used to take notes and the type of notes taken did not affect the number of "idea units" recorded by the subjects. Furthermore, the study showed support for verbatim notetakers, as a difference in recall scores was found between the verbatim and both the own style and paraphrase notetakers ($p < .05$). Finally, there was a positive correlation (.69, $p < .01$) between the recall scores and total posttest scores of all subjects (Quade, 1996).

Since there was a significantly better performance by online notetakers versus traditional notetakers based on posttest score analysis, an essential indication came from this study: The research supports the long-held notion that taking and reviewing notes prior to testing increased retention more than not taking notes and only mentally reviewing them. Although this study was conducted at the college level, the implications for secondary educators are important.

CONCLUSIONS AND IMPLICATIONS FOR PRACTICE

Even though teachers continue to encourage students to create quality notes via better retention rates, perhaps the most essential implication of this study was the method used to take notes for review. The online notetakers may have allowed the subjects an improved way to include pertinent ideas in notes, lower fatigue due to traditional pencil and paper note taking, and organize information more effectively (Quade, 1996).

Consequently, these potential advantages may have encouraged the online subjects to take better, more exacting notes, which resulted in their heightened success on the posttests. Secondary teachers often struggle to get students to take effective and meaningful notes. Giving students the option of taking notes via a note pad fashion in class may provide them with the tool that leads to better retention and better organized notes for future use.

You are encouraged to use this technology if it is available to you in your own instructional setting and assess the effectiveness. You can determine which students are benefiting and which may need guidance and alternative methods by comparing their online note pad skills with their pencil and paper notes. The context and learner may cause some variation of the use of note taking, but research provides some clear directions for maximizing its use via computer online note taking.

- Research indicates that lecture is no less effective than other strategies. However, from the teacher and students' perspectives, the strategy has advantages and limitations.
- Variations on the lecture theme can encompass pure lecture, chalk talk lecture, audiovisual lecture, combination lecture, and mini-lectures.
- Lecture is neither good nor bad; it is the way it is used that determines if students will learn from this strategy,

The key to effective teaching is the ability to match the instructional approach with the learner, content, and context. If the lecture method meets these conditions, then the teacher should consider the benefits and limitations in the planning and implementation of this strategy. Chapter 8 presents questioning and discussion strategies that are most frequently combined with lecture.

The lecture strategy can move the learner from being a passive observer to an active participant. Your ability to use an expanded repertoire of approaches within the lecture strategy and combining this strategy with other strategies will improve your teaching options and student opportunities to learn.

REFERENCES

Adams Laboratories Inc. (n.d.). Formula for Deconsal II tablets. Fort Worth, TX.

Birkel, L. F. (1973, July). The lecture method: Villain or victim? *Peabody Journal of Education,* 298–301.

Bowman, J. S. (1979). The lecture-discussion format revisited. *Improving College and University Teaching, 27,* 25–27.

Broadwell, M. M. (1980). *The lecture method of instruction.* Englewood Cliffs, NJ: Educational Technology Publications.

Brock, S. C. (1977). *Aspects of lecturing: A practical guide of IDEA users.* Manhattan, KS: Kansas State University. (ERIC Document Reproduction Service No. ED 171 218).

Brophy, J. E. (1999). Perspective of classroom management: Yesterday, today and tomorrow. In Jerome Freiberg (Ed.), *Beyond behaviorism: Changing the classroom management paradigm.* Boston: Allyn and Bacon.

Cangelosi, J. S. (1993). *Classroom management strategies* (2nd ed.). New York: Longman.

Cohen, F., & Seaman, L. (1997). Research versus "real-search." *Phi Delta Kapan, 78*(7), 564–568.

Desberg, P., Henschal, D., & Marshall, C. (1981). *The effect of humor on retention of lecture material.* Lubbock, TX: Texas Technical University. (ERIC Document Reproduction Service No. ED 223 118).

Ebert-May, D., Brewer, C., & Allred, S. (1997). Innovation in large lecture—Teaching for active learning. *Bioscience, 47*(9), 601–607.

Evertson, C., Emmer, E., & Brophy, J. E. (1980). Predictors of effective teaching in junior high mathematics classrooms. *Journal of Research in Mathematics Education, 11,* 167–178.

Fashola, O. S., & Slavin, R. E. (1998). Schoolwide reform models: What works? *Phi Delta Kappan, 79*(5), 370–379.

Fisher, C., Berliner, D., Filby, N., Marliave, R., Cahen, L., & Dishaw, M. (1980). Teaching behaviors, academic learning time and student achievement: An overview. In C. Denham & A. Lieberman (Eds.), *Time to learn.* Washington, DC: Department of Education, National Institute of Education.

Frank, B. M. (1984). Effect of field independence-dependence and study technique on learning from a lecture. *American Educational Research Journal, 21*(3), 669–678.

Freiberg, H. J. (1999). Consistency Management & Cooperative Discipline: From tourists to citizens in the classrooms. In Jerome Freiberg (Ed.), *Beyond behaviorism: Changing the classroom management paradigm.* Boston: Allyn and Bacon.

Gage, N. L., & Berliner, D. C. (1998). *Educational psychology.* Boston: Houghton Mifflin.

Garside, C. (1996). Look who's talking: A comparison of lecture and group discussion teaching strategies in developing critical thinking skills. *Communication Education, 45*(3), 212+.

Good, T. L. & Brophy, J. E. (1994). *Looking in classrooms.* New York: HarperCollins.

Good, T. L., & Grouws, D. (1979). The Missouri Mathematics Effectiveness Project: An experimental study in fourth-grade classrooms. *Journal of Educational Psychology, 71,* 355–362.

Gump, P. V. (1982). School settings and their keeping. In D. Duke (Ed.), *Helping teachers manage classrooms.* Alexandria, VA: Association for Supervision and Curriculum Development.

Heller, S. (1984). For top professor, teaching is a matter of timing. *Chronicle of Higher Education, 29*(2), 23, 28.

Hemler, D. (1990). *Guided note-taking outline.* Unpublished curriculum materials. Bruceton High School, Bruceton, WV.

Henson, K. T. (1980). What's the use of lecturing? *The High School Journal, 64,* 115–119.

Hillocks, G., Jr. (1981). The response of college freshmen to three modes of instruction. *American Journal of Education, 89,* 373–395.

Jefferies, M., & Lewis, G. (1992). *Inventors and inventions.* Surrey, England: Colour Library Book Ltd.

Kintsch, W., & Bates, E. (1977). Recognition memory for statements from a classroom lecture. *Journal of Experimental Psychology: Human Learning and Memory, 3,* 150–159.

Maddox, H., & Hoole, E. (1975). Performance decrement in the lecture. *Educational Review, 28,* 17–30.

McMann, F., Jr. (1979). In defense of lecture. *Social Studies, 70,* 270–274.

Molina, V., et al. (1997). *Improving student listening skills through the use of teaching strategies.* Unpublished doctoral dissertation, Saint Xavier University, Illinois. (ERIC Document Reproduction Service No. 409 537).

Mullis, I., Owen, E. H., & Phillips, G. (1990). *America's challenge: Accelerating academic achievement, a summary of findings from 20 years of NAEP.* Princeton, NJ: The National Assessment of Educational Progress, Educational Testing Service.

Oddi, L. (1983). Lecture: An update on research. *Adult Education Quarterly, 33,* 222–229.

Ortiz, C. (1997, May). *The relationship between teacher behaviors and student academic engagement.* Paper presented at the Annual Training Conference of the National Head Start Association, Boston. (ERIC Document Reproduction Service No. 411 951).

Osterman, D. N. (1982). Classroom lecture management: Increasing individual involvement and learning in the lecture style. *Journal of College Science Teaching, 12,* 22–23.

Quade, A. M. (1996). An assessment of retention and depth of processing associated with note taking using traditional pencil and paper and an on-line note pad during computer-delivered instruction. *Proceedings of the National Convention of the Association for Educational Communication and Technology, 18,* 560–570.

Rosenshine, B. (1981). How time is spent in elementary classrooms. *Journal of Classroom Interaction, 17*(1), 16–25.

Rosenshine, B. (1983). Teaching functions in instructional programs. *The Elementary School Journal, 83*(4), 335–351.

Rosenshine, B. (1995). Advances in research on instruction. *Journal of Educational Research, 88*(2), 262+.

Rowe, M. B. (1976). The pausing principle—Two invitations to inquiry. *Journal of College Science Teaching, 5,* 258–260.

Semb, G. B., & Ellis, J. A. (1994). Knowledge taught in schools: What is remembered? *Review of Educational Research, 64*(2), 253–286.

Shavelson, R. (1976). Teachers' decision-making. In N. L. Gage (Ed.), *The psychology of teaching methods. Seventy-fifth yearbook of the National Society for the Study of Education. Part I.* Chicago: University of Chicago Press.

Slavin, R. E. (1988). Synthesis of research on grouping in elementary and secondary schools. *Educational Leadership, 46*(1), 67–77.

Smith, I. K. (1978). Teaching with discussion: A review. *Educational Technology, 28*(11), 40–45.

Spalding, C. L. (1992). *Motivation in the classroom.* New York: McGraw-Hill.

Stanton, H. E. (1978). Small group teaching in the lecture situation. *Improving College and University Teaching, 26,* 69–70.

Steele, D. F. (1993). *What mathematics students can teach us about educational engagement: Lessons from the middle school.* Paper presented at the Annual Meeting of the American Educational Research Association, Atlanta. (ERIC Document Reproduction Service No. 370 768).

Thatcher, V. S. (Ed.). (1972). Definition of lecture. *The New Webster Encyclopedia Dictionary of the English Language,* p. 485.

Wahlberg, M. (1997). Lecturing at the "bored." *The American Mathematical Monthly, 104*(6), 551–556.

Williams, R. G., & Ware, J. E., Jr. (1977). An extended visit with Dr. Fox: Validity of student satisfaction with instruction ratings after repeated exposures to a lecturer. *American Educational Research Journal, 14*(4), 449–457.

Wittrock, M. C. (Ed.). (1986). *Handbook of research teaching* (3rd ed.). New York: Macmillan.

Yu, H. K., & Berliner, D. C. (1981). *Encoding and retrieval of information from lecture.* Tucson, AZ: The University of Arizona. (ERIC Document Reproduction Service No. ED 206 738).

SAMPLES AND EXAMPLES

There are four Samples and Examples in this section. The first one includes a Learner Profile that will assist you in matching your instructional approach with your students' interests. The next two ask you to think about different content areas and grade levels and to develop an outline for a lesson. The final activity gives four different situations and asks you to discuss the opportunities and limitations within the framework of a lesson.

- The Learner Profile provides information about your students.
- Activities #1 and #2 develop outlines of different topics and grade levels.
- Activity #3 presents four situations for you to consider in developing your lessons.

LEARNER PROFILE

1. List five things you like to do:
   a. ______
   b. ______
   c. ______
   d. ______
   e. ______
2. What was the title of the last book you read? ______
3. What is your favorite TV show? ______
4. How much time do you spend watching TV each day? ______
5. What is the first thing you do when you come home from school? ______
6. Where do you do your homework? ______
7. What is your favorite school subject? ______
8. What do you think is the purpose of school? ______
9. What do you think is the purpose of homework? ______

The following list contains 10 interest areas. Rank each area from 1 (I like the best) to 10 (I like the least) in the space provided.

_____ Listening to teacher give information
_____ Working in centers
_____ Working in groups
_____ Solving problems in groups
_____ Doing worksheets
_____ Working alone
_____ Seeing films
_____ Doing projects in the classroom
_____ Doing projects outside the classroom
_____ Reading

OUTLINING

The following activities ask you to select one or two topic areas and develop an outline for a specific grade or content area.

Activity #1

Work in a small class group and develop an appropriate outline for content for the following topics and learners:

Topics	Learners
1. Our Community	5-year-olds (kindergarten)
2. Metrics	7-year-olds (second grade)
3. Solar System	10-year-olds (fifth grade)
4. Art Appreciation for the Renaissance Period	12-year-olds (seventh grade)
5. Commodities	14-year-olds (ninth grade)
6. Chinese Cuisine	Adults

Activity #2

Complete the following activity with a class member either during or after class, depending on your professor's instructions.

Return to the content outlines developed in Activity #1, select one outline and brainstorm a list of creative strategies to motivate the intended students to want to focus on the content. Do not limit your ideas—be as creative as possible.

Activity #3

Consider the following scenarios and describe both the opportunity(s) and limitation(s) for your teaching that come from these contexts:

1. You are a middle-school social studies teacher in a small, suburban, blue-collar community. The copper mine located at the edge of the school district has shut down 50 percent of its operations and laid off 180 employees who are parents of your students.
2. The elementary school in which you teach second grade is preparing for a school fair to raise money for computers. The entire school is buzzing with the excitement of the preparations, decorations, and parent involvement.
3. Last night, two students in your high-school senior English class were critically injured in an auto accident after leaving a party where drugs and alcohol were used.
4. You teach fifth grade in an upper-class suburban neighborhood. Most of your students have traveled to other countries; have their own computers; study music, art, and athletics in expensive after-school facilities; and are generally very bright.

Discuss the opportunity(s) and limitation(s) of utilizing the above situations as part of a lesson plan with your peers in class.

CHAPTER

8

QUESTIONING AND DISCUSSION

Creating a Dialogue

Chapter Outcomes

At the conclusion of this chapter you will be able to:

1. *Describe the advantages and disadvantages of questioning.*
2. *Identify and ask a variety of questions.*
3. *Develop several approaches to asking questions and using discussion in the classroom.*
4. *Improve wait time for allowing students to respond.*

Key Terms and Concepts

Why Ask Questions?
Checking for Understanding
Go Around System
Types of Questions
Higher-Level Questions
Bloom's Taxonomy
Convergent and Divergent Questions
Values Clarification
Cautions and Concerns
Questions in Context
Wait Time I & II
Teacher Moves
Why Students Don't Ask Questions
Why Students Should Ask Questions
Advantages and Limitations
Classroom Discussion
Students with Learning Disabilities

Good questions are locks which generate their own keys.
—Maroski, 1987

INTRODUCTION

Did You Know?

- The two most common verbal interactions in the classroom between teachers and students are questioning and discussion.
- Questioning is, by far, the most dominant teaching strategy after lecture in upper-elementary and secondary classrooms (Gall, 1984).
- At the junior, middle, and senior high-school level, the teacher talks 70 to 75 percent of the time, and students talk about 25 to 30 percent of the time.
- Within student talk, recitations or responses to teacher questions form the majority of the interaction in the classroom.
- The types of questions teachers ask can make a significant difference in student achievement. A review of the research on teacher questioning by Redfield and Rousseau (1981) indicates that higher levels of teacher questioning produce greater student gains on standardized tests. For example, if we compared two students on the same standardized achievement test, the student in the class with lower-level (recall type) questioning would score at the 50th percentile, whereas the student in the class where the teacher asked high-level (analysis and synthesis type) questions would score at the 77th percentile (Berliner, 1987).
- In a study of teacher questions in England of 230 lessons by 36 teachers in five high schools, Kerry (1987, p. 33) and his colleagues found the following:
  a. Teachers asked 43.7 questions per hour of observed teaching time.
  b. During the professional lifetime of a teacher, nearly one and one-half million questions will be asked of students.
  c. Only 3.6 percent of all questions were coded as being high order.
  d. Language teachers in the study asked the most questions, with 76.5 questions per hour.

e. Geography, history, and religion instructors asked the least questions, with 21 to 24 each hour.
f. Teachers establish questioning patterns, with the number and types of teacher questions being similar across lessons.

On the surface, all questions may seem alike; however, questioning is a very complex strategy to use effectively. Complete the following common questioning errors self-test (Brown & Wragg, 1993). Mark an X next to those you have committed as a teacher or have experienced as a student. Each common error is followed by a commentary.

___ *Habitually repeating question or students' responses.*
Comment: This causes students to pay less attention because they know the question or response will be repeated (Chuska, 1995). Also, valuable instructional time spent in repeating student statements could be saved if students are asked to speak loud enough for all the students to hear the response.

___ *Asking too many questions at once.*
Comment: This is known as the *bombing rate.* The teacher asks more questions than students can retain. Students are thinking about the first question when the second question is asked. Allowing wait time between questions will give them "think time."

___ *Asking a question and answering it yourself.*
Comment: Known as *rhetorical questions,* these are really not questions but teacher statements placed in the form of a question. They serve little purpose and are usually a function of the teacher being nervous or not allowing students to participate.

___ *Asking questions only of the brightest and most likable students.*
Comment: Perhaps the most important student need is fairness. When teachers show favoritism, the classroom climate and learning for many students suffer. You will see strategies in this chapter to create a fair balance for questioning.

___ *Asking the same types of questions.*
Comment: About 80 percent of all classroom questions would be considered at the lowest levels of the thinking process. Using Bloom's Taxonomy, divergent and convergent questions, and values clarification, you will see that there is a much wider range of questions that may be asked to stimulate student thinking.

___ *Asking questions in a threatening way.*
Comment: Intimidation does not belong in a positive learning environment. Some questions have the effect of inhibiting learning. Although these types of questions may gain the teacher momentary control, a positive climate for learning may be lost in the process.

___ *Not giving students the time to think.*
Comment: Teacher wait time and student think time are important ingredients to teaching and learning. Students with special needs require a few more seconds to think. Waving hands from other students or the hurry-up look from the teacher will cause many students to freeze. Asking more clarifying questions will only

add to the bombing rate. Counting to 5 will help in this circumstance. More ideas will be presented throughout the chapter.

___ *Not correcting wrong answers.*
Comment: The classroom is a very public place. Students look for cues from the teacher about what is accurate. The questioning process gives all students in the class the opportunity to test their own ideas and responses against that of the individual responding to the question and the acknowledgment by the teacher.

___ *Ignoring answers.*
Comment: Perhaps more than being yelled at, being ignored is the cruelest fate. The student with the raised hand who gets no recognition or the student who answers without being acknowledged by the teacher loses a sense of being part of the class.

___ *Failing to see the implications of answers.*
Comment: People often have set answers in mind when they ask a question. This is helpful for recall questions, but frequently preset answers become a barrier to creativity for higher-level questions. Measured against the teacher's answer, the student response may be incorrect but the student may see the question from a different perspective. It is important for the teacher to listen to student responses and to seek out the implications to the answers.

___ *Failing to build on answers.*
Comment: Chapter 15 asks you to use a cassette tape to record your classroom interactions. Often, teachers comment after their self-assessment on the lack of follow-up to important student answers. This process will take some awareness of classroom interactions during questioning and the need to build on student ideas.

Have You Thought About?

The process of teacher questions and students' responses is unique to the classroom. Only in school do those who know the answers—the teachers—ask questions of those who may not know the answers—the students. You can imagine driving up to a gas station and asking the attendant, "I know where 5th and Main Street is, do you?" In everyday life, we ask questions to complete missing information and to increase our understanding of a situation. Young children (especially 2 to 5 years old) ask what seems to be an endless stream of questions. Children ask questions to provide a context or framework for what is occurring. The parents' acceptance or rejection of a child's questions begins to shape both self-concept and early learning. This becomes evident when children are read stories by their parents and they feel free to ask numerous questions about the plot, characters, pictures, or for clarity.

Studies of preschoolers document the spontaneity of children's questions of their parents when being read stories. In one case study, two children asked 810 questions of their parents while being read stories over a total of 75 hours (Yaden, Smolkin, & Conlon, 1988). The spontaneity of children's questions is also evident in daily situations. The first time a child goes with a parent to the gas station, questions and answers may go like this:

CHILD: What is that thing? (pointing to the gas door opening in the car)
PARENT: It is an opening so I can add gas to the car.
CHILD: What is gas?
PARENT: Gas is the food for the car. It gives it the power to go just like food gives you the power to go.
CHILD: Where does gas come from?
PARENT: From oil in the ground. The oil is made into gasoline.
CHILD: Do we drink gas?
PARENT: No. Gas is only for cars. It would make people very sick. It is a poison for people.
CHILD: Why do you give money to the man?
PARENT: Many people work hard to make the gas for the car, and we need to pay them for their time and effort.

The young child is asking questions to provide meaning for what is occurring and to create a frame of reference for future visits to the gas station.

Why Ask Questions?

In the classroom, teachers ask questions for a variety of reasons. The most common include:

1. Checking for student understanding of instruction
2. Evaluating the effectiveness of the lesson
3. Increasing higher-level thinking

In addition to these three primary reasons, teachers may ask questions to control student behavior, manage the pace and direction of the lesson, create a bridge between activities, and increase student participation.

Checking for Student Understanding

A common reason teachers give for asking questions during instruction is to check if students comprehend the information being presented. Questioning allows the teacher to respond immediately to the levels of student comprehension and modify instruction through different examples or instructional strategies. A typical pattern found in many classrooms includes some form of information giving (e.g., lecture, presentation, film, demonstration, etc.) and questioning of the students after the instructional presentation. Questioning may also occur after group activities to determine if the group is on track and using its time effectively. Rosenshine and Stevens (1986) suggested seven steps for checking student understanding. Next to each of the steps is a brief commentary on how each of the steps could be implemented in the classroom.

"No, it's not a horsey or a doggy. It's two squiggles and two dots!"

1. Prepare a large number of oral questions beforehand.
   Commentary: In the upper-elementary, middle, or secondary classroom, writing the questions on 4" × 6" index cards will be useful. This is important in developing a greater variety of questions and in building a bank of higher-order questions.
2. Ask many brief questions on main points, on supplementary points, and on the process being taught.
   Commentary: Using questions that require short answers are appropriate for lessons where basic skills or facts are the objective. For example, knowing that Pearl Harbor was bombed on December 7, 1941, has tripped up many a student, including at least one presidential candidate (George Bush during his presidential campaign).
3. Call on students whose hands aren't raised in addition to those who volunteer.
   Commentary: It is estimated that 80 percent of the questions in the classroom are answered by 20 percent of the students. As a teacher, it is natural to call on students who have their hands raised and will usually provide the correct answer. Questioning provides intellectual stimulation, and all students need this interaction with the teacher. One technique for including all students in question/answer sessions is the *Go Around System,* which is discussed in detail in the Snapshot that follows.
4. Ask the students to summarize the rule or process in their own words.
   Commentary: Students should explain how they arrived at their answers. A

wrong answer may not be as important as the steps the students took to arrive at the answer. Students who have poor learning strategies learn from students who have developed good strategies for solving problems.

5. Have all the students write the answers (on paper or chalkboard) while the teacher circulates.

   Commentary: The use of small hand-held chalkboards will assist many elementary and middle-school students in writing and computation skills. If the teacher asks a question and the students hold up their boards, only the teacher will see their answers, giving students with incorrect answers some privacy. The chalkboards provide a quick check for the teacher, and a mental note can be made for those students who are having difficulty. One-to-one or small group instruction could occur later in the period to provide students further assistance. If a majority of the class is having difficulty, the teacher could stop and reteach the concept or give additional examples.

6. Have all students write the answers and check them with a neighbor (frequently with older students).

   Commentary: If the teacher provides an answer sheet or writes the answers on the board, the students could check each other's work. It is not necessary to have an older student do this. Students working in pairs with mixed abilities will meet the need.

7. At the end of a lecture or discussion (especially with older students), write the main points on the board and have the class meet in groups and summarize the main points to each other (Rosenshine & Stevens, 1986, p. 384).

   Commentary: Groups of two or four could meet at the end of the lesson or class for a few minutes to discuss what they have learned. The teacher should present two or three questions on the board, overhead projector, or a handout for the students to discuss. If there is adequate time, one student from each group could orally give his or her answers to the questions or written responses could be given to the teacher if time is limited.

SNAPSHOT: Go Around System

We have assisted teachers in utilizing a questioning technique called the *Go Around System* (Freiberg, 1987, 1999). The Go Around System has been used in elementary, middle, and high schools in West Virginia, Texas, Italy, New Jersey, The Netherlands, California, and Missouri. It is a strategy for providing question equity through a fairer distribution of questions. The teacher goes around the room in order and says to each student, "Tell me one idea you learned from yesterday or from today's class without repeating another student's answer."

A student who can't give a response when it's his or her turn can *pass.* Students who pass must raise their hands and give a response before the activity is complete. The teacher recognizes a student who has passed after a peer has finished speaking. The teacher will go back to those students who haven't raised their hands to respond by the end of the activity, which takes 3 to 5 minutes.

The students call this the *fair system* because they all need to respond and have the option to pass if another student repeated their response or they forgot. Students in classes where this procedure is used say it takes the pressure of responding off and places the emphasis on learning. Students who finish responding are actively listening to be sure their response is not repeated by another student.

Teachers who have used the Go Around System have shared some humorous stories. One high-school history teacher in West Virginia told of a student in his class who passed when asked a question. The teacher, however, was *not* using the technique in his classroom. The student explained that he was new to the school and his other teacher allowed students to pass if they didn't know the answer and could raise their hands later with a response. After some deliberation, the teacher tried the technique in his class with great success.

A seventh-grade mathematics teacher used the Go Around System with dramatic results. During the first week of use, almost all the students passed. The students were testing the teacher to see if she really meant it. After a week, however, the number of students passing diminished. The teacher was pleased she stayed with the system long enough for it to work.

Questioning techniques like the Go Around System help equalize the opportunity for asking and answering questions. There may be a tendency on our part to ask boys more questions than girls (see Fennema & Peterson, 1987) or ask the right side of the room more questions than the left. Having a system to distribute questions fairly will create a healthier climate for learning.

The Go Around System provides a tool for providing greater variability and equity in questioning. Combine this with other procedures (e.g., volunteers, choral responses, calling on students randomly rather than in order) for questioning students in the classroom.

Evaluating Lesson Effectiveness

Questioning enables the teacher to judge the effectiveness of instruction. Many teachers can see confusion in the eyes of the students, but need a better tool for determining student comprehension than student nonverbal clues. Two studies on teacher understanding of student clues for comprehending the lesson conclude that, even after training, teachers are not good judges of what the students are thinking or understanding during the lesson (Berliner, 1987).

Increasing Higher-Level Thinking

Verbal questioning assists in judging the depth of student comprehension during the lesson. The complexity of your questions determines the ability to measure the level of student understanding. Factual or recall questions will elicit factual responses. The teacher may be willing to limit lesson effectiveness to lower-level factual information, but students will not be able to apply, analyze, synthesize, or evaluate information without the opportunity to practice these skills in the classroom. Asking more complex and demanding questions may not always elicit more complex student responses, but given enough practice, students will begin to respond to teacher questions at increasingly higher levels.

TYPES OF QUESTIONS

There is a range of questions asked in classrooms, including higher level (analytical), lower level (factual), convergent (one answer), divergent (several possible answers), valuing (clarifying student thoughts), and controlling (directing student comments). Each type of question has an important role in stimulating thinking. The literature is very clear, however. In most classrooms, teachers ask higher-level questions only 10 to 20 percent of the time (Dillon, 1988; Wragg, 1993). Few questions are in the higher levels, requiring students to synthesize facts, ideas, and concepts for comparison and analysis. Most classroom questions only require a student to recall simple facts. The mental processing needed to respond to a perplexing question in which a single factual answer is not available requires a student to:

- Analyze the question.
- Search through his or her memory (similar to looking in a file cabinet) to find facts relevant to the question.
- Synthesize the facts and reach a conclusion.
- Respond to the question in less than two seconds.

Allowing students to experience a range of questions will build their cognitive ability to respond to a more complex world in which simple facts can be recalled from computers. However, analysis, synthesis, and evaluation must originate from the individual.

Asking higher-level questions broadens the base of learning and better prepares students for an information society. Asking higher-level questions has numerous stumbling blocks, including the following:

Hurdles to Higher-Level Questions

- The curriculum is driven by textbooks, which until recently emphasized factual information. Teacher editions are just beginning to include higher-level questions.
- Most questioning is spontaneous. It is easier to ask factual questions in the fast-paced dynamics of the classroom.
- Higher-level questions that are clear to the students are more difficult to construct and require greater effort and time on the part of the teacher. Poorly constructed higher-level questions may confuse the students and result in the teacher spending additional time explaining.
- Teachers have rarely experienced higher-level questions in their own learning and have few positive models upon which to draw.
- Higher-level questions require mastery of the content area. In the elementary classroom where the teacher may have 13 different content preparations, achieving mastery in all areas may require years of experience. At the secondary level, it is estimated by the National Educational Association that 20 percent of secondary teachers are teaching in areas in which they were not originally certified. By

the time mastery has been achieved, the pattern of asking lower-level questions may already be ingrained.

- Higher-level questions elicit less predictable responses from the students, requiring more time for student answers and somewhat greater uncertainty for the teacher.
- Lower-level questions do assist students in basic skills learning. It takes time for students accustomed to factual questions to begin to realize the teacher wants more than one-word or short-answer responses.

Although obstacles exist in asking higher-level questions, raising the intellectual climate of the classroom is an important enough goal to seek strategies for implementing a greater range of questions. Building thinking questions is the first step in expanding the range of teacher/student interactions in the classroom.

Using Bloom's Taxonomy of Questions

Bloom's Taxonomy (Bloom, Englehart, Furst, Hill, & Krathwohl, 1956) for designing instruction has also been widely used for distinguishing higher and lower questions (see Chapter Three). Table 8.1 shows questions at each level of Bloom's Taxonomy. The six main headings include Bloom's subheadings and sample questions for each of the subheadings. There are several other ways of developing higher-level questioning strategies in the classroom. The next types of questions—convergent and divergent—also promote higher levels of thinking.

Convergent and Divergent Questions

Another way of looking at lower-level and higher-level questions is from a convergent or divergent perspective. Convergent questions focus on a correct response. The questions can be factual—Who traveled to the land we now call America in 1492?—to more demanding—Why did Columbus name the people he met Indians? The latter question requires more information than relating a name with a date. To answer the second question, students would need to know that Columbus thought he was traveling to India and assumed that he had landed in India, therefore the people he met were Indians.

Divergent questions tend to be more demanding of a student's thought processes. There may be several correct responses to a divergent question, which asks for student opinion or conjecture. However, you may seek student opinion that is "educated" and draws on factual information established through convergent questioning. Divergent questions tend to be at the upper levels of Bloom's Taxonomy (analysis, synthesis, and evaluation), whereas convergent questions tend to be at the lower levels of the taxonomy (knowledge and comprehension). Table 8.2 provides several examples of convergent and divergent questions.

Values Clarification

A third type of questioning was developed by Raths, Harmin, and Simon (1966) to help teachers clarify students' values and focus on the affective elements of learning. Some student comments or questions need to have a more indirect or clarifying response from

TABLE 8.1 *Questioning Strategies in Context with the Cognitive Domain of Learning*

Category	Sample Question
Knowledge	
1-1 Knowledge of specifics	Who discovered the Mississippi River?
1-2 Knowledge of ways and means of dealing with specifics	What word does an adjective modify?
1-3 Knowledge of universals and abstractions in a field	What is the best method for calculating the circumference of a circle?
Comprehension	
2-1 Translation	What do the words *hasta la vista* mean?
2-2 Interpretation	How do the Democrats and Republicans differ in their views of spending?
2-3 Extrapolation	Given the present population birth rate, what will be the world population by the year ____?
Application	How has the Miranda decision affected civil liberties?
	Given a pie-shaped lot 120 ft. × 110 ft. × 100 ft., and village setback conditions of 15 ft. in all directions, what is the largest size one-story home you can build on this lot?
Analysis	
4-1 Analysis of elements	What are the facts and opinions in the article we read?
4-2 Analysis of relationships	How does Picasso organize colors, shapes, and sizes to produce images?
4-3 Analysis of organizational principles	How does John Steinbeck use his characters to discuss the notion of friendship in *Of Mice and Men*?
Synthesis	
5-1 Production of a unique communication	How would you write a simple melodic line?
5-2 Production of a plan	How would you go about determining the chemical weight of an unknown substance?
5-3 Derivation of a set of abstract relations	What are the common causes for cell breakdown in the case of mutations, cancer, and aging?
Evaluation	
6-1 Judgment in terms of internal evidence	What are the fallacies of Hitler's *Mein Kampf*?
6-2 Judgment in terms of external evidence	Who can judge what is wrong with the architect's design of the plumbing and electricity?

Source: From "Questioning: The Essence of Good Teaching" by A. Ornstein, 1988, *NASSP Bulletin, 11*(499), pp. 17–19. Adapted by permission.

TABLE 8.2 *Sample Convergent and Divergent Questions*

Subject and Grade Level	Convergent Questions	Divergent Questions
Social Studies, 5–7	Where did the Boston Tea Party take place?	Why did the Boston Tea Party take place?
Social Studies, 7–9	What are three products of Argentina?	How does wheat production in Argentina affect wheat export prices in our country?
English, 5–7	What is the verb in the sentence, "The girl told the boy what to do"?	How do we rewrite the present and future tense of the verb in the sentence, "The girl told the boy what to do"?
English, 10–11	Who wrote *A Farewell to Arms*?	How does Hemingway's experience as a news reporter affect the story, *A Farewell to Arms*?
Science, 2–5	Which planet is closest to the sun?	How would you compare living conditions on Mercury with Earth?
	Who was the first American astronaut to travel in space?	What planet, other than Earth, would you prefer to visit if you were an astronaut? Why?
Science, 9–11	What are two elements of water?	How is water purified?
Math, 4–5	What is the definition of a triangle?	How have triangles influenced architecture?
Math, 6–8	What is the shortest distance between two points?	What is the best air route to take from New York City to Moscow? Why?

Source: From "Questioning: The Essence of Good Teaching" by A. Ornstein, 1988, *NASSP Bulletin, 11*(499), pp. 17–19. Adapted by permission.

you. By clarifying a response, the student may be better able to understand the implications of the comment.

For example, a student may suggest that homework should *not* be a requirement. If a teacher wanted to *clarify* the student's position on homework, then the questioning strategies would be more indirect. Figure 8.1 provides 20 possible teacher responses to a student's statement on homework. Identify those statements listed in Figure 8.1 that clarify the student's position. Check your answers in the Samples and Examples section at the end of this chapter.

In addition to asking questions to *check for understanding, evaluate lesson effectiveness,* and *develop higher-level thinking,* questions are also used in nonacademic areas. Controlling student behavior and organizational questions are two of the most common uses.

FIGURE 8.1 *Clarifying Responses*

Clarifying responses enable students to identify their own values by using a series of probing or clarifying questions. (*Note:* The answer sheet appears in the Samples and Examples section at the end of this chapter.)

Directions: Circle those questions that you feel clarify the student's position or value.

Value Statement:
JIM: I think students should not do homework.

Teacher Responses:

1. Are you making a rationalization because you usually forget to do your homework?
2. Have you considered any alternatives?
3. Why don't you try doing your homework; it may help you in school.
4. Your parents want you to do homework.
5. You will need homework if you go to college.
6. Is this a personal preference or do you think most people believe that?
7. What are your ulterior motives?
8. How long have you felt this way about homework?
9. Have you expressed this belief to other people?
10. The school requires homework.
11. How can I help you do something about the idea?
12. When did you start to feel this way about homework?
13. Doesn't homework help you in school?
14. What are some of the good things about homework?
15. What do you mean by *homework*? Can you define the word?
16. If I didn't give you homework, the other students would be very upset.
17. What would be the effect of no homework?
18. What are your reasons for not wanting homework?
19. Is this (not having homework) very important to you?
20. I don't think this is a good idea.

CAUTIONS AND CONCERNS

Controlling Questions

Using questions to control student behavior may limit the effectiveness of questioning in academic situations. The following exchange occurred in a fourth-grade classroom. The teacher was giving instructions and two students were poking each other at their desks. The teacher turned to one of the students and asked:

> **T:** John, what's your problem? (tone is negative with the emphasis on "your problem")
> **J:** Nothing.
> **T:** Then there must be a phantom flying around the classroom (teacher walks toward student and class laughs).

J: (John does not respond.)
T: You have to sit next to each other all period. Either you settle it or I'll settle it (some class members make an "ooh-ooh" sound; others laugh nervously).
J: I will knock his teeth out after school.
T: That's going to solve something—"knocking out teeth"? How would you like someone to knock your teeth out?
J: OK.
T: Come here (class laughs very nervously).
J: (John looks down.)
T: Now class, let's turn to page 36.

The questioning sequence is designed to control John's behavior through intimidation. Latter sequences indicate that John continues to be a problem and any relationship the teacher had with John has deteriorated. The teacher is showing a genuine lack of respect for the student in front of his peers. In a secondary classroom, the verbal escalation could have led to a physical confrontation.

The preceding interaction is perhaps more extreme than most situations, but asking students questions when they are not paying attention or purposefully asking questions above the academic level of students to show power begins to destroy the interpersonal fabric of the classroom. Creating more equitable questioning patterns (described in this chapter) could prevent the need for controlling questions or intimidation, which is usually at the expense of student self-esteem. In addition to the actual content of a question, the tone of the teacher also conveys a great deal of meaning.

Questioning Tone

The tone of a question generally speaks much louder than any of its words. The question, How did you arrive at that answer? may seem very neutral. The tone of the question, however, may be perceived by a student to be hostile, intimidating, encouraging, or friendly. The tone combined with nonverbal language (e.g., rolled eyes, standing very close to the student, or smiling) may create feelings in the student that are quite separate from the content of the question. When questioning tones are used as controlling or intimidating factors, students call these *put-downs.* Because the classroom is a very public place, the use of intimidating tones during questioning has a rippling effect beyond a single student. It may intimidate other students listening to the question and create a more negative classroom climate. Students could withdraw from classroom interaction if they experience consistent teacher put-downs during questioning. It is important to be sensitive to tone of voice and nonverbal movements during questioning. The audiotape analysis presented in Chapter Fifteen will assist you in determining the types of questions and the tones in which they are asked.

Clarity in Questions and in Text

There is a time and place for questions. Throughout teacher training and most of a teacher's professional career, we are told to ask questions. But some questions only lead to confusion. Being declarative by making a statement of what is appropriate or expected is, at times, a more appropriate action than asking a question. For example, questions during transitions may not be effective in achieving the objective of moving students from one activity to another.

Unclear directions bring about clarifying or organizational questions from students that may be unnecessary and take time away from instruction. This is the case when teachers ask questions while trying to manage a range of activities. The following provides examples of teacher statements in the classroom. Some are in the form of questions and others are statements of what the student needs to achieve. For example, question number 1 asks, "Will you get back to work?" In some instances, the student could say no. Question number 2 gives the student specific information about what is expected. Review the list and determine how the statements for action differ from the questions.

1. Will you get back to work?
2. You need to keep editing your papers until the bell rings in 10 minutes.
3. Why are you doing that?
4. Anna, take out your reading book and place your story book in your desk.
5. How many times have I asked you to stop that?
6. David, you and Carlos seem to be distracting each other from completing your work. Please focus on your own work. Group time will occur in 15 minutes.
7. Do you want me to keep you after school?
8. Work that is not completed during school time will need to be completed at home or after school.
9. You really want to be excused from the field trip, don't you?
10. You will not have enough information about the exhibit if you don't complete your work, which could make the trip a poor learning experience.

Statements 2, 4, 6, 8, and 10 give the students information about the task at hand. They are direct and clear and provide enough information for the students to follow the directions. The other statements (1, 3, 5, 7, and 9) listed in the form of questions are unclear and rhetorical and give the teacher unusable information. For example, question 3, "Why are you doing that?" usually receives the student response, "I don't know." "What are you doing?" is usually answered, "Nothing."

Questions in Any Content

Many teachers in our interviews about questioning indicated that some content areas don't lend themselves to higher-level questions. Earlier in this chapter, we saw at least seven reasons why teachers don't use higher-level questions. However, with practice and experience, higher-level questions can be used with any type of content. A case in point is the nursery rhyme story of the three little pigs. (In brief, each little pig built a house—one of straw, one of sticks, and one of bricks. The wolf was able to blow down the first two houses but not the third.) We asked elementary, middle-, and high-school teachers to construct questions using higher- and lower-level questions. Given some prior thought and planning, something as basic as a nursery rhyme could lend itself to a range of questions, including higher-level questions. The following is a representative sample of the questions they were able to develop. *L* designates lower-level questions and *H* designates higher-level questions.

1. What material did the first pig use to build his house? (L)
2. Who was the smartest of the three pigs and why? (H)
3. Why is a house important for both pigs and people? (H)
4. Which pig would you rather be? (H)
5. Who was the villain in the story? (L)

The content of a lesson should not be an inhibitor to asking a range of questions. Creating the expectation (for both teacher and student) that higher-level questions will be part of every lesson will eventually make the strategy automatic.

Questions in Context

The type or level of question is context specific. A question that may be considered higher level for a first-grader would be lower level for a fifth-grader. A first-grade class that has studied geometric forms and knows the properties of a right angle would be recalling factual information if the teacher showed a picture of a right triangle and asked the students to identify it. However, the same picture given before any instruction would be at a higher level if the students had to figure or discover what the drawing represented.

Wait Time

The amount of time students have to think during questioning has been an area of concern of educators and researchers for the last 25 years. Rowe (1974) found teachers wait or pause one second or less for students to respond to their questions. She analyzed 900 tapes of teacher wait time and concluded that there are 10 positive effects of teachers waiting 3 to 5 seconds for student responses during questioning:

1. The length of student response increased.
2. Student-initiated and appropriate (related to the topic or subject) responses increased.
3. Student failure to respond to questions reduced.
4. Student confidence in responding (as reflected by confident tone of voice) increased.
5. Student speculative responses increased.
6. Student-to-student interactions increased and teacher-focused instruction decreased.
7. Student evidence to support statements increased.
8. The number of student questions increased.
9. Participation of students who were identified as slower by the teacher increased.
10. The variety of student responses to teacher questions increased.

Allowing students to think during questioning and discussion communicates an expectation that "what you have to say is of importance." Waiting for a student to respond rather than moving on to a classmate also communicates the expectation that everyone's response is important (Barrell, 1991).

Wait Time I

There are different opportunities for teachers to pause or wait during questioning. This pausing or waiting allows students time to think. The *bombing rate,* which results from rapid-fire questions directed toward a student, interferes with student thinking. The advantages to student learning are significant (Tobin, 1986; White & Tisher, 1986). The first opportunity for wait time is after a teacher asks a question to the student (Wait Time I). Research suggests that a teacher wait three to five seconds for students to respond to higher-level questions during this first wait time opportunity. The average interval between teacher question and expected student response is 1 second, but practice and self-assessment will greatly improve your Wait Time I. (See Chapter Fifteen for extending wait-time strategies.)

Wait Time II

A second opportunity for waiting comes after a student has responded to a question. Many teachers immediately respond with an acknowledgment or elaborate on the student's comments and continue to another student. Pausing after students respond to questions has been associated with increases in achievement (White & Tisher, 1986). Student responses tend to be extended in Wait Time II situations. Wait time techniques will work only if students take advantage of the extra time. Students who do not use the extra wait time may need some cues that extra time is available. Encourage students to clarify, expand, or support their initial responses to your questions without your needing to ask them each time.

The next vignette provides additional evidence that wait time plays an important role in teacher questioning and student learning.

Improving Wait Time

The use of wait time needs to be learner, context, and content friendly. Rigidly applying the three- to five-second rule for all questioning opportunities is unlikely to improve the quality of classroom interaction (Carlsen, 1991). The need for extended wait time becomes more critical for higher-level questioning and more complex concepts. A fast-paced verbal drill that requires simple responses would bog down with a three- to five-second wait time. But most other questioning should include a much greater wait time than is presently provided students. The teacher bombing rate (where students have one second to think before the next teacher statement), described in early studies of wait time, creates greater pressure on many students and increases the failure rates in the classroom. The lack of success in answering teacher questions causes some students to withdraw from classroom interaction. Improving wait time requires conscious effort and practice.

Writing down higher-level questions and counting silently to three after asking questions are two strategies for improving wait time. Probing student responses rather than mimicking or providing low-level responses (e.g., "ok," "yes," "uh-huh") will provide greater opportunities for students to respond and think during questioning. An audiotape analysis provided in Chapter Fifteen will also provide a concrete method for checking wait time during actual classroom instruction. After the teacher provides

Middle-School/College Research Vignette

INTRODUCTION

Graesser and Person (1994) investigated the questions asked during tutoring sessions for seventh-grade algebra students who were having difficulties with the class and to undergraduate college students studying research methods. The middle-school algebra students were being tutored by high-school students, and graduate students tutored the undergraduates. The undergraduate tutoring session was part of their course requirements.

STUDY DESIGN

As part of a course in research methods, 27 upper-level undergraduates received tutoring by graduate students over an eight-week period lasting on average 60 minutes. In addition, 13 seventh-grade algebra students received tutoring from high-school students. Sessions were videotaped, coded, and analyzed for the types of questions students and tutors asked of each other. A total of 18 questioning categories, ranging from short to long answer, were given to the coders. Examination scores were used to determine the effects of types of questions on achievement.

STUDY RESULTS

The number of questions asked by students of their tutors did not seem to be of importance as related to achievement. However, student achievement at both levels was positively correlated with the *quality* of student questions asked of their tutors. The questions asked by those being tutored reflected a process of cognitive self-regulation by the students who identified knowledge deficits in the subject areas and asked questions of their tutors to complete their learning.

Students had *241* times greater opportunities to ask questions during tutoring sessions than in the regular classroom. A student in a one-hour regular class asked, on average, less than 1 question (0.17), whereas in a tutoring session, the average was 26.5 questions per hour. Tutors still ask more questions than students (80 percent vs. 20 percent), just as teachers ask many more questions (96 percent vs. 4 percent) than students in the classroom. The 16 percent fewer questions tutors ask translate into greater numbers of student questions. Tutors also ask 1.5 times more questions of their students than classroom teachers.

Only 8 percent of the questions asked by students of their tutors reflected "deep-reasoning questions" that included application, analysis, synthesis, and evaluation on Bloom's Taxonomy. The second half of the course produced a correlation between deep-reasoning questions and achievement, as well as more knowledge-deficit questions asked of tutors by the students. Only 2 percent of the questions asked by tutors or students had a high degree of specification. Within this small range, students' questions were more specific than the tutors' questions.

Tutors asked open-ended questions 35 percent of the time to help them gauge the level of student comprehension. But questions such as Do you understand? elicited a yes response from students when students in fact did not understand. According to the authors, they were being polite, did not want to appear ignorant, or lacked a measure of their understanding.

CONCLUSIONS AND IMPLICATIONS FOR PRACTICE

The traditional classroom with 30 students and one teacher is not a very fertile ground for questions asked by students. This study highlights the power of tutorial settings for giving students greater opportunities to complete gaps in their learning through the formulation of questions answered by their tutors. The use of tutoring pairs in the classroom or upper-grade students tutoring lower-grade students in the same school is a workable option to out-of-class tutoring. Tutors in this study had some specific training in their roles, but the authors suggest more is needed so that tutors and students learn to ask more specific and deep-thinking questions of each other. Students should be asked to give examples to demonstrate their comprehension rather than relying on a verbal yes response to a question. Chapter Ten further develops the use of tutoring in the classroom.

appropriate wait time and the student does not know the answer, then the interaction moves to a different level.

Teacher Moves

When the teacher asks a question and the student answers, several options are presented to the teacher. (See Figure 8.2 for a visual display of teacher options when student responses are correct.) For a correct response, the teacher can (1) acknowledge the answer ("Good, Sally") or praise the student ("Sally, I like the way you brought the facts together to reach a conclusion"); (2) extend the answer to achieve greater clarity by asking the student to elaborate, expand, or give an example; (3) probe student thinking by asking another related more demanding or higher-level question of the student; and/or (4) ask a related question to another student to build on the response of the first student. If the student gives an incorrect response or states, "I don't know," the teacher also has several alternatives. Figure 8.3 shows three teacher options for an incorrect student response.

Why Students Don't Ask Questions

The spontaneity of children's questions becomes drastically reduced as they enter the classroom. Rather than a few children competing for the time of their parents, now 25 or more children are competing for the time of one adult, their teacher. The more socialized to school students become, the fewer questions they ask. The classroom is a very public place; students begin to understand teacher cues about questioning from watching the teacher interact with class members. If one student's question is ignored by the teacher or receives a frown, indicating the student should know the answer, students soon realize that the teacher may not want to hear from them. If the pattern is repeated every day and the teacher provides limited opportunities for student-initiated questions, the message for students regarding their involvement becomes quite clear.

FIGURE 8.2 *Teacher Options after Student Responds Correctly*

Teacher Asks Recall Question: The capital of our nation is named after what president?
Student Responds: George Washington.

Teacher Options:

Same student			***New student***
Acknowledges or Praises Response "Good, Sally."	*or*	*Extends or Probes; Asks Another Question* "Are there any other places named after presidents?" Student responds: "Our school is named after Abraham Lincoln, and the city library is named for Thomas Jefferson."	*Builds on First Student's Response* "Why do you think we name important public places like schools and libraries and cities after our nation's leaders?"

FIGURE 8.3 *Teacher Options after Incorrect Student Response*

Teacher Asks Recall Question (waits 3 seconds): The capital of our nation is named after what president?
Student Responds: I don't know.

Teacher Options:

Same student		***New student***
Gives Clues	*Asks Additional Questions*	*Redirects Question*
"The capital is named after the first president of the United States."	"Who was the first president of the United States?"	It is better to restate the question than to say, "Can someone help Sally?"

Students learn by first grade that answering teacher questions is good but asking too many questions may show ignorance. This lesson is quite universal. Researchers in the former Czechoslovakia found minimal student-initiated questions in the classroom. Mars (1984) (citing Fenclova [1978]) indicates that of 30 lessons in grade schools, vocational schools, and grammar schools, only 60 student-initiated questions were recorded. Nearly half the student questions were related to management or organization concerns. Only 2 of 60 recorded student questions dealt with students attempting to "penetrate more deeply into the subject matter" (Mars, 1984, p. 10). Student passivity, which is reflected in classrooms where teacher talk dominates, creates a classroom climate that discourages student questions. "The pupil is afraid of revealing his ignorance when asking, while the teacher does not encourage the pupils enough to ask questions as he is not sure he could always answer" (Mars, 1984, p. 10).

Why Students Should Ask Questions

Student involvement is a motivator for learning. Encouraging student-initiated questions will create greater involvement and student motivation. However, student-initiated questions require a climate of exploration and reflection. Teaching students to ask questions can also aid them in learning new material on their own. Guided cooperative questioning is a cognitive strategy designed to help students make sense of classroom material. Students use a set of generic thought-provoking questions, such as "What are the strengths and weaknesses of…?" and "What do you think would happen if…?" to create their own specific questions about the material being studied. After generating questions, students work in small cooperative groups or pairs to ask and answer each other's questions. King and Rosenshine (1993) found that when fifth-graders were taught to use guided cooperative questioning, they performed better on comprehension tests than did peers who used unguided strategies. In a review of 26 different studies, Rosenshine, Meister, and Chapman (1996) also found that teaching students to generate questions about material they had read resulted in greater comprehension gains.

Advantages of Teacher Questions

Questioning has a number of important advantages for teachers:

1. *Understanding.* It provides an opportunity for the teacher to check for understanding.
2. *Lesson effectiveness.* It gives an indication of the effectiveness of instruction for the whole class.
3. *Higher-level thinking.* The level of dialogue and thinking is raised when higher-level questions (opinion, synthesis, and evaluation) are used in the classroom.
4. *Student participation.* It increases student involvement in learning.
5. *Communication skills.* Combined with discussion, students can improve on their oral and social communication skills.
6. *Self-checks.* It allows students to hear peer responses to the same question and compare answers with their own.
7. *Review.* It provides students with opportunities for review of recently taught information.
8. *Cues.* It cues students about what the teacher feels is important.

The advantages of questioning begin to show how the teacher can begin to shape a learning community in the classroom through dialogue. However, as with all teaching strategies, questioning also has its limitations.

Limitations of Questions

The use of teacher questions also has its limitations. One researcher (Dillon, 1985) concluded that teacher questions inhibit discussion in the classroom. Teachers can misuse questions to limit dialogue by dominating the interaction, or they can use questions for classroom management rather than academic purposes, addressing students who are not paying attention. The following list provides some insight into the limitations of teacher questions. Suggestions are provided in the notes we developed to assist you in modifying the limitations. See Figure 8.4 for common reasons and responses for nonparticipation.

1. The teacher may ask the same students most of the questions.
   NOTE: For elementary students, drawing popsicle sticks from a can with a student's name on each stick allows the teacher to ask questions in a more random fashion. For upper-elementary and secondary classrooms, the teacher can have the students write their names on two 3" × 5" cards. The teacher collects the cards and uses the two decks of cards to draw the students' names. Two decks are used to increase the chance that a student may be called on more than once.
2. The questions may only be directed at factual recall and ignore higher-level questioning skills.
   NOTE: Writing the higher-level questions on cards in advance will ensure that higher-level questions are asked during the lesson. Classifying questions according to Bloom's Taxonomy helps assure that higher-order questions are included in the discussion.

FIGURE 8.4 *Reasons and Responses for Nonparticipation*

The student is...	*The teacher could...*
afraid to fail	assure students that when they don't know something, it simply means there is room to learn
afraid of ridicule	not allow students to put down other's answers
unsure of the expected response	provide study guides or a list of questions for the week
has little or no confidence because of past failures	give the student time to think and acknowledge effort
apathetic	make connections between the material and students' lives and ask provocative or evocative questions
afraid to speak in front of large groups	allow the students to review the materials in small groups before addressing the questions with the entire class
unwilling to be labeled a "brain" by classmates	create a climate in which knowledge is shared, not exhibited
finds the question too complex or unclear	rephrase the question or encourage students to ask clarifying questions
intimidated by the level of the question	break the question into parts
feeling rushed to answer too quickly	allow a think time of three to five seconds
unable to answer or has difficulty expressing the answer	allow the student to pass, giving him or her an opportunity to respond later

Source: Adapted from *Improving Classroom Questions* by K. R. Chuska, 1995, Bloomington, IN: Phi Delta Kappa Educational Foundation.

3. The students may become bored if the teacher does not try to vary his or her question routine.
   NOTE: Using a combination of volunteers and teacher selection of students to answer questions will reduce boredom. (See Go Around System described in the earlier Snapshot.) Be sure to ask the question first; then call out the student's name.
4. The use of questions can be time consuming if you do not have the questions prepared in advance.
   NOTE: Incorporating questions into the lesson will provide more time to observe and interact with the class than trying to think about the next question during instruction.
5. Adequate wait time needs to be provided for the students to answer the questions.
   NOTE: Rowe (1974) suggested that three to five seconds between the time the teacher asks a question and the next teacher statement will give students adequate time to respond. This is particularly important for higher-level questions (Houston, Clift, Freiberg, & Warner, 1988, p. 201).

6. Questions may be used as a form of feedback for learner comprehension.
   NOTE: Instructional decisions based on a few students' responses may mislead you into thinking all students have the same level of comprehension. Checking for a broader understanding and asking for examples from several students will minimize this issue.

CLASSROOM DISCUSSION

Questioning and discussion are different sides of the same coin. Although both strategies attempt to create a measure of student knowledge, questioning is teacher directed, whereas discussion provides greater student input. Discussion is a universal strategy designed to provide students with active participation in the classroom, either through verbal input or from listening to classroom members speak. It also provides the teacher with insight into students' thinking, which is seldom provided through other strategies.

Discussion Defined

Discussion is the interchange of ideas between students and their teacher or among students. It may take place in whole-class settings, within groups of students, or between two students. Discussion requires a climate of reflective listening, respect for the speaker's ideas, and noninterference from the teacher.

Setting the Stage

Creating a trusting and positive classroom climate is a necessary prerequisite for discussion. A trusting climate is created together with your students. Take the lead in establishing the direction for positive classroom discussions by employing the following guidelines:

1. *Be sure the goals for discussion are clear for both students and yourself.* You and your students may need to determine what you hope to achieve through discussion. For example, the discussion activity could expand on the viewpoints of the text or create alternative strategies for solving a problem. It is useful for a short discussion of the goals to alleviate concerns of students about "What are we supposed to do?"
2. *Actively listen while students are talking.* This includes positive eye contact with the student who is talking and avoidance of interjection with other students or organization activity (e.g., shuffling papers on the desk).
3. *Refrain from commenting after each student statement.* Teachers have a tendency to make comments or elaborate on every student statement. This practice inhibits discussion and limits the available time and the number of students who could participate.
4. *Develop discussions from a series of lessons or a unit that would supply students with enough information, ideas, or concepts to allow for a knowledgeable discussion.*
5. *Encourage student-to-student dialogue without going through the teacher.* Most classroom interactions go through the teacher. For example, during higher-level questioning, a typical pattern looks like the following sequence:

Questioning

T: What are some differences and similarities between ancient Greek forms of democracy and our current American democracy?

SUSAN: Both forms had a group of people called a *Senate* that made decisions for all the people.

T: Yes, that is correct.

T: Victor (hand raised), you have something to add?

VICTOR: Both the U.S. Senate and the Ancient Greek Senate included mostly rich men. (class laughs)

T: Victor has an interesting point. Let's discuss the composition of the two Senates.

The interaction in the classroom stopped at the teacher each time and a pattern of "turn taking" is evident. A discussion on the same topic may look like the following sequence:

Discussion

T: What are some differences and similarities between ancient Greek forms of democracy and our current American democracy?

SUSAN: Both forms had a group of people called a *Senate* that made decisions for all the people.

T: (Remains silent and no one talks for five seconds)

VICTOR: Both the U.S. Senate and the Ancient Greek Senate included mostly rich men. (class laughs)

SALLY: (Looking at Victor) I don't know about the wealth of the Ancient Greek Senate, but the U.S. Senate has members who are not rich.

SUSAN: Yeah, but how many?

MELISSA: We need to look at a reference source for this information.

JANE: Mrs. Thomson, what would be a good source to find out about the wealth and perhaps other information on members of the current U.S. and the ancient Greek Senates?

The role of the teacher is very different in the two sequences. The first interaction is highly patterned, with the teacher taking turns with the students. The teacher, however, would be talking 50 percent or more of the time. In the second sequence, the teacher is more of a moderator or facilitator, with students looking to the teacher as a resource.

Foiling Discussion through Questions

Some researchers indicate that teacher questioning during discussion is the primary inhibitor to implementing this strategy successfully. Because most teachers see their role as being the gatekeeper during questioning, it is difficult to change roles for discussion. The discussion may become too teacher dominated, which, in fact, foils discussion in the classroom (Dillon, 1985). In his study of five high-school classrooms using transcriptions of teacher/student interactions, Dillon began to see patterns of how teacher questioning foiled discussion. One could argue that the teacher was trying to keep the students on track. However, the transcripts indicated the teacher questions moved the class discussion away from the original focus. The difficulty of implementing discussion in the classroom relates to the change of roles the teacher must make during this strategy from giver of information to facilitator of interaction. In addition to the change of roles, most teachers have had little or no opportunities to see effective discussion in their own schooling.

Unfamiliarity with the subject matter can also lead a teacher to inhibit classroom discussion. Carlsen (1992) found that when teaching unfamiliar subject matter, novice teachers tend to close down classroom conversation by postponing instruction at the beginning of the lesson, go off on discursive tangents, resist student efforts to change the topic of instruction, evaluate student responses ambiguously, and follow the textbook too closely.

Student Responsibilities

Some classrooms are dominated by a few students. The Go Around System, notecards for secondary classes, and the use of popsicle sticks or tongue depressors for calling on students (all discussed earlier in this chapter) are designed to equalize the interaction and the opportunity for participation. During discussion the most verbal students will tend to dominate the discussion. The teacher is faced with the decision between free flow of ideas and the need to provide the greatest participation. Following are some rules to which students should agree prior to classroom discussion.

1. *All students should actively listen while classmates are talking.* Talking or other distracting activities will minimize the effectiveness of the discussion.
2. *Students are not permitted to make "killer statements"* (Raths, Harmin, & Simon, 1966). Killer statements inhibit discussion by putting down the student's comments. Examples from the classroom include: "That's a dumb idea" and "You're not very bright today."
3. *Students need to be prepared for the discussion.* If reading or prior meetings in small groups are required, students are expected to have accomplished these tasks before the discussion. Students who are not prepared could listen but not actively participate.

Teacher Approaches

Dillon (1988) suggested two approaches to discussion: (1) pose a single question for discussion and (2) pose a question for which there is no ready answer. Dillon proposed the following action in creating a tone for discussion.

1. *Prepare the question for discussion.*
   a. *Conceive of just the right one.*
   b. *Formulate it in just the right way.*
   c. *Pose just that one in just that way.*
2. *Ask questions that perplex self.*
   (Do not ask questions that do not perplex self.)

3. *Use alternatives to questioning.*
   a. *Statements—State your selected thought in relation to what the student has just said.*
   b. *Student Questions—Provide that a student asks a question related to what the speaker has just said.*
3. *Signals—Signal your reception of what the student is saying without yourself taking or holding the floor.*
4. *Silences—Say nothing at all but maintain a deliberate, appreciative silence for three seconds or so, until the original speaker resumes or another student enters in. (p. 128)*

Students may need to learn how to discuss. Learning a new strategy takes time and requires a progressive building of expertise. Discussion may be a strategy that develops gradually during the school year rather than trying to implement the strategy the first weeks of school. Like the other universal teaching strategies, discussion should be used in combination with other strategies.

The two strategies of questioning and discussion are interrelated. Teachers who ask higher-level questions, wait before and after student responses, respect student ideas, encourage participation by all students, and create a climate of exploration will expand the opportunities for both meaningful questions and discussion. The need to constantly monitor our use of questioning and discussion strategies becomes evident in the following Teacher Talk, in which five teachers reflect on their uses of questioning and discussion.

TEACHER TALK

How should I as a classroom teacher employ the strategy of discussion in teaching literature? I feel strongly that children need to talk about what they have read, and I have used discussion as a teaching tool almost always with literature. After the children have read the Junior Great Books stories, the class is arranged informally in a circle or semi-circle. With the teacher, or sometimes an interested parent, as moderator, the group considers open questions such as "Why do you think that the main character did. . . ?" or "Why do you think that the author has such a character to. . . ?" The students accustomed mostly to questions with definite answers need some time to adjust to this new sort of questioning and for a while will persist in asking, "Well, what *is* the answer?" When they accept the idea of the no-answer question, they begin to feel more free in discussion and enjoy the experience.

Middle-School English Teacher

My classroom setting is first grade. My reading groups are small—nine students—seated at a table. Since the group is small, it is not necessary for the children to raise their hands or for me to call their names. They have already been shown the eye-contact body signal I use for "calling." The first question I ask of the group is designed to arouse curiosity based on the story we are reading (e.g., What could happen if Sally did not go home after school and went with her friends to the haunted house?). The first question is used for a set induction and to set the purpose for reading. Most of these first questions are based on the students' opinions.

First-Grade Teacher

I ask questions all the time; that's the way I learn (as a teacher). Yet in my 18 years of teaching experience, in how many situations have I required students to formulate questions? Two, maybe three. The teachers I know sum up a lesson with "Any questions?" and when there's no response, they say, "Good." Perhaps I'd better add to my teaching repertoire the question "What are you wondering?" because I have a suspicion that, although I haven't missed the boat in asking questions, I may be missing one oar.

High-School Mathematics Teacher

As an observer in the classroom, I noticed that the questions used at the elementary classrooms I am observing are only at the literal (information or factual) levels. The teachers mostly ask the students to comprehend things that are straight out of the book. The students do fine in the reading circle, but when they go back to their desks to do seatwork, they are lost. They seem to forget what seemed so clear to them in the reading circle. Just because the question is worded differently from the text, or goes deeper than the text's meaning, they do not understand what is going on. My observations and work with these students seem to support the findings that students need different levels of questions in order to better comprehend the material and to move their level of reasoning beyond the literal (factual) level.

Graduate Certification Student

Students with Learning Disabilities

Wiig and Wilson (1994) found that the ability of students with learning disabilities (LD) to answer questions at Bloom's *comprehension* and *synthesis* levels was significantly poorer than that of their non-LD peers; therefore, LD students need more opportunities to practice higher forms of reasoning and problem solving. Many LD students need additional time to process questions before they can answer in class. Strategies discussed in this chapter—including allowing students to write their answer, allowing three to five seconds think time, using the Go Around systrem, and implementing the pass option strategy—will allow all learners, including LD students, the extra time they need.

OTHER KEY POINTS

In a book for the National Education Association, William Wilen (1987) summarized the research on questioning and identified nine key points that are presented here.*

1. Plan key questions to provide lesson structure and direction. *Write them into lesson plans, at least one for each objective—especially higher-level questions. Ask some spontaneous questions based on student responses.*
2. Phrase questions clearly and specifically. *Avoid vague or ambiguous questions such as "What about the heroine of the story?" Ask single questions; avoid run-on questions that*

**Questioning Skills for Teachers* (2nd ed.). © 1987. National Education Association. Reprinted with permission.

lead to student frustration and confusion. Ask one question at a time. Clarity increases probability of accurate responses.

3. Adapt questions to student ability level. *This enhances understanding and reduces anxiety. For heterogeneous classes, phrase questions in natural, simple language, adjusting vocabulary and sentence structure to students' language and conceptual levels.*
4. Ask questions logically and sequentially. *Avoid questions lacking clear focus and intent. Consider students' intellectual ability, prior understanding of content, topic, and lesson objective(s). Asking questions in a planned sequence will enhance student thinking and learning.*
5. Ask questions at a variety of levels. *Use knowledge-level questions to determine basic understandings and to serve as a basis for higher-level thinking. Higher-level questions provide students opportunities to practice higher forms of thought.*
6. Follow up student responses. *Develop a response repertoire that encourages students to clarify initial responses, lift thought to higher levels, and support a point of view or opinion. For example, "Can you restate that?" "Could you clarify that further?" "What are some alternatives?" "How can you defend your position?" Encourage students to clarify, expand, or support initial responses to higher-level questions.*
7. Give students time to think when responding. *Increase wait time after asking a question to three to five seconds to increase number and length of student responses and to encourage higher-level thinking. Insisting upon instantaneous responses significantly decreases probability of meaningful interaction with and among students. Allow sufficient wait time before repeating or rephrasing questions to ensure student understanding.*
8. Use questions that encourage wide student participation. *Distribute questions to involve a majority of the students in learning activities. For example, call on nonvolunteers, using discretion for difficulty level of questions. Be alert for reticent students' verbal and nonverbal cues such as perplexed looks or partially raised hands. Encourage student-to-student interaction. Use circular or semicircular seating to create an environment conducive to increased student involvement.*
9. Encourage student questions. *This encourages active participation. Student questions at higher cognitive levels stimulate higher levels of thought, essential for inquiry approach. Give students opportunities to formulate questions and carry out follow-up investigations of interest. Facilitate group and independent inquiry with a supportive social-emotional climate, using praise and encouragement, accepting and applying student ideas, responding to student feelings, and actively promoting student involvement in all phases of learning. (Wilen, 1987, pp. 10–11)*

In addition to the nine points for questioning, the following should be added for classroom discussion.

1. Create a positive climate for discussion.
2. Prepare questions for discussion that have no immediate answer.
3. Limit teacher questions and the role of gatekeeper during discussion.
4. Prepare students for their roles in discussion.
5. Develop the use of discussion gradually.

Intellectual stimulation and improved student participation are two goals of questioning and discussion. Properly used, these strategies can enhance learning and improve the quality of the teachers' and students' lives in the classroom.

SUMMARY

- Questioning and discussion are the most common verbal interactions in the classroom.
- Questioning is the second most dominant instructional strategy after lecture.
- Higher-level questions are missing in most classrooms but can improve student achievement.
- Questions can help the teacher check for student understanding, improve reflective/critical thinking, and evaluate lesson effectiveness.
- Using a system (e.g., Go Around) to distribute questions equally will improve fairness and equality with the strategy.
- Few teacher questions require students to synthesize facts, ideas, and concepts for comparison or analysis. Most questions only require recall of information.
- Bloom's Taxonomy can help provide a range of questions for the learner. Writing down higher-level questions during pre- and active planning will assist the learner during a lesson.
- Convergent questions focus on recall questions at the lower end of Bloom's Taxonomy. Divergent questions focus on analysis, synthesis, and evaluation thought processes located at the upper end of Bloom's Taxonomy.
- Questions can be used inappropriately to intimidate or control students, perhaps solving a short-term problem while creating a longer-term problem of trust between students and the teacher.
- Clear and precise directions help student thinking and create explicit management and organizational expectations in the classroom, reducing the need for student procedural questions that can diminish instructional time.
- Extending teacher wait time for three to five seconds, particularly for higher-level questions, will give students more time to respond and indicate that what a student says is of value.
- The use of tutoring can dramatically increase the quality and quantity of student-generated questions.
- Teacher responses to correct and incorrect student answers require several options, including extensions and appropriate redirecting to new students.
- Some advantages of questioning are: it is a way for checking for understanding; it provides for overall lesson effectiveness; it increases higher-level thinking with higher-level questions; it creates greater student involvement; combined with discussion, it improves student communication skills; it provides for student self-checks; it affords review opportunities for students; and it gives students cues about important content areas.
- There are at least six limitations to questioning: it asks the same students most of the questions; it requires factual recall and ignores higher-level questioning skills; questioning routines become boring without variability; questions become time consuming without effective preplanning; low wait times reduce student responses; and directing questions at a few students may mislead the teacher to think that all students comprehend the lesson.

- Five points should be considered in planning for classroom discussion: (1) clarifying goals for discussion for you and your students; (2) actively listening to your students; (3) refraining from commenting after each student statement; (4) building from a lesson or unit to encouraging a strong knowledge base for discussion; and (5) encouraging student-student dialogue without going through the teacher. Also, some teacher questions can foil discussion.
- Students have several responsibilities during discussion, including the following: actively listening while other students are talking; not making "killer statements" when they disagree with others; and being prepared for the discussion.
- The research on questioning supports nine key elements: (1) plan key questions in advance; (2) phrase questions clearly; (3) adapt questions to student ability levels; (4) ask questions logically and sequentially; (5) ask questions at a variety of levels; (6) follow up student responses; (7) give students time to think and respond; (8) distribute questions widely in the class; and (9) encourage student questions.

REFERENCES

Barell, J. (1991). *Teaching for thoughtfulness.* New York: Longman.

Berliner, D. C. (1987). But do they understand? In V. R. Koehler (Ed.), *Educator's handbook.* New York: Longman.

Bloom, B. S., Englehart, M. D., Furst, E. J., Hill, W. H., & Krathwohl, D. R. (Eds.). (1956). *Taxonomy of educational objectives: The classification of education goals, Handbook I: Cognitive domain.* New York: David McKay.

Brown, G., & Wragg, E. C. (1993). *Questioning.* New York: Routledge.

Carlsen, W. S. (1991). Questioning in classrooms: A sociolinguistic perspective. *Review of Educational Research, 61,* 157–178.

Carlsen, W. S. (1992). Closing down the conversation: Discouraging student talk on unfamiliar science context. *Journal of Classroom Interaction, 27*(2), 15–22.

Chuska, K. R. (1995). *Improving classroom questions.* Bloomington, IN: Phi Delta Kappa Eductional Foundation.

Cuban, L. (1984). *How teachers taught.* White Plains, NY: Longman.

Dillon, J. T. (1985). Using questions to foil discussion. *Teaching and Teacher Education, 1,* 109–121.

Dillon, J. T. (1987). Antique questions. *Questioning Exchange, 1*(1), ii.

Dillon, J. T. (1988). *Questioning and teaching.* New York: Teachers College Press.

Fennema, E., & Peterson, P. (1987). Effective teaching for boys and girls: The same or different? In D. C. Berliner & B. V. Rosenshine (Eds.), *Talks to teachers.* New York: Random House.

Freiberg, H. J. (1987). *Generic teaching strategies: School and teaching effectiveness institute.* Preston County Schools, Kingwood, W.V.

Freiberg, H. J. (1999). Consistency Management & Cooperative Discipline: From tourists to citizens in the classrooms. In Jerome Freiberg (Ed.), *Beyond behaviorism: Changing the classroom management paradigm.* Boston: Allyn and Bacon.

Gall, M. (1984). Synthesis of research on teacher's questioning. *Educational Leadership, 42* , 40–47.

Graesser, C. G., & Person, N. K. (1994). Question asking during tutoring. *American Educational Research Journal, 31,* 104–137.

Houston, W. R., Clift, R. T., Freiberg, H. J., & Warner, A. R. (1988). *Touch the future: Teach!* St. Paul: West Publishing.

Kerry, T. (1987). Classroom questions in England. *Questioning Exchange, 1*(1), 33.

King, A., and Rosenshine, B. (1993). Effects of guided cooperative questioning on children's knowledge construction. *Journal of Experimental Education, 61*(2), 27–148.

Maroski, L. (1987). Question quotes. *Questioning Exchange, 1*(1), i.

Mars, J. (1984). Questioning in Czechoslovakia. *Questioning Exchange, 5,* 8–11.

Ornstein, A. (1988). Questioning: The essence of good teaching. *NASSP Bulletin, 11*(499), 17–19.

Raths, L. E., Harmin, M., & Simon, S. B. (1966). *Values and teaching* (2nd ed.) (pp. 63–65). Columbus, OH: Charles E. Merrill.

Redfield, D. L., & Rousseau, E. W. (1981). A meta-analysis of experimental research on teacher questioning behavior. *Review of Educational Research, 51,* 237–245.

Rosenshine, B., Meister, C., & Chapman, S. (1996). Teaching students to generate questions: A review of the intervention studies. *Review of Educational Research, 66,* 181–221.

Rosenshine, B., & Stevens, R. (1986). Teaching functions. In M. C. Whittrock (Ed.), *Handbook of research on teaching* (3rd ed.). New York: Macmillan.

Rowe, M. B. (1969). Science, soul and sanctions. *Science and Children, 6*(6), 11–13.

Rowe, M. B. (1974). Wait time and rewards as instructional variables, their influence in language, logic, and fate control: Part one—Wait time. *Journal of Research in Science Teaching, 11*(2), 81–94.

Tobin, K. (1980). The effect of an extended teacher wait-time on science achievement. *Journal of Research in Science Teaching, 17,* 469–475.

Tobin, K. (1986). Effects of teacher wait time on discourse characteristics in mathematics and language arts classes. *American Educational Research Journal, 23*(2), 191–201.

Tobin, K., & Capie, W. (1982). Relationships between classroom process variables and middle school science achievement. *Journal of Educational Psychology, 14,* 441–454.

White, R. T., & Tisher, R. P. (1986). Research on natural sciences. In M. C. Whittrock (Ed.), *Handbook of research on teaching* (3rd ed.). New York: Macmillan.

Whittrock, M. C. (Ed.). (1986). *Handbook of research on teaching* (3rd ed.). New York: Macmillan.

Wiig, E. H., & Wilson, C. C. (1994). Is a question a question? Passage understanding by preadolescents with learning disabilities. *Language, Speech, and Hearing Services in Schools, 25,* 241–250.

Wilen, W. W. (1987). *Questioning skills for teachers: What research says to the teacher.* Washington, DC: National Education Association.

Wragg, E. C. (1993). *Primary teaching skills.* London: Routledge.

Yaden, D., Smolkin, L. B., & Conlon, A. (1988). Preschoolers' questions about pictures, print convention, and story text during reading aloud at home. *Reading Research Quarterly, 24*(2), 188–214.

SAMPLES AND EXAMPLES

There are two Samples and Examples in this section.

- The Clarifying Responses answer key for Figure 8.1.
- The Student Survey on Teacher Questioning

TEACHER RESPONSES (ANSWER SHEET)

1. Are you making a rationalization because you usually forget to do your homework?

② Have you considered any alternatives?

3. Why don't you try doing your homework; it may help you in school.

4. Your parents want you to do homework.

5. You will need homework if you go to college.

⑥ Is this a personal preference or do you think most people believe that?

7. What are your ulterior motives?

⑧ How long have you felt this way about homework?

⑨ Have you expressed this belief to other people?

10. The school requires homework.

11. How can I help you do something about the idea?

⑫ When did you start to feel this way about homework?

13. Doesn't homework help you in school?

⑭ What are some of the good things about homework?

⑮ What do you mean by *homework*? Can you define the word?

16. If I didn't give you homework, the other students would be very upset.

⑰ What would be the effect of no homework?

⑱ What are your reasons for not wanting homework?

⑲ Is this (not having homework) very important to you?

20. I don't think this is a good idea.

◯ = Clarifying Response

INTERACTI
FOR LE
Beyo

Review
Seatwork
Guided Practice
Independent Practice
Worksheets
Games
Homework
Projects
Practice and the Inclusive Classroom
Learning Centers

Chapter Outcomes

At the conclusion of this chapter you

1. *Describe a range of content for p*
2. *Provide a context for practice tha tive learning.*
3. *Design interactive practice activ the learners, and are structured*
4. *Design and use review, seatwork, for student practice.*

assroom in Portland, Oregon, children use 14
uire and practice emerging skills in literacy.
oms in Mercer Island, Washington, students
uations by debating their own hypotheses and
, 1994).

ndiana, third-graders learn about and practice
cy in a board game (Gardner, 1991).

ol students gain practice with concepts and
as they prepare video documentaries to pro-
or a redevelopment area in their community

ependent School Districts in rural Texas, stu-
tory together (Shores, 1998).

g various schools and classrooms is a variety
e very often is the use of drill and recitation
he norm in classrooms. In addition to the
s we just described in classrooms, you will
ws, seatwork, and homework. Practice is so
o devote an entire chapter to helping you go
ll *interactive practice.*

and reflect on how you use practice in your
thing? How does it affect your learning? Do
learn something quickly? Notice that some
tlessly and some demands awareness and
e takes different forms, depending on what

you are trying to learn. Our concept of practice for this chapter has the same range of complexity.

Research on learning is showing that complex thinking processes are involved in even the most elementary mental activities (Resnick, 1994). Our teaching and learning activities must be opportunities for critical thinking and problem solving and the acquisition of relevant knowledge and real-world applications. The practice activities we design must provide support for those opportunities. To help you achieve that kind of practice in your classroom, we begin by looking at the content of interactive practice.

CONTENT

Not only do you use practice strategies for students to learn concepts, information, skills, and attitudes, you also intend that your students experience learning itself. We know that successful thinkers of all ages actively monitor their own thinking processes and that they are aware of how they learn (Areglado, Bradley, & Lane, 1996; Resnick, 1994). The content of practice has a wide range of possible outcomes, and we want you to consciously plan for as many of them as possible. We suggest that you start by integrating learning strategies as part of your practice activities because they can expand the possibilities of content for your individual learners.

Practice for Learning Strategies

The learning strategies described by Weinstein and Mayer (1986) in their review of research can help you provide practice with different levels of complexity. Such practice can help students "learn how to learn" as they practice a variety of other content.

Rehearsal Strategies

Rehearsal strategies can be basic or complex. Basic rehearsal is nothing more than repetition of information. You encourage basic rehearsal when you lead your kindergarten students in a singsong repetition of the days of the week. Your middle-school students use basic rehearsal when they recite a conjugation of the verb *to be* in French. You use basic rehearsal when you recite a new phone number over and over to yourself.

There is also complex rehearsal, and you use it when you learn more complicated material or perform a more complex task. Your repetition is combined with more thinking. When fifth-grade students underline adverbs in a sentence, they use complex rehearsal strategies. When you go through your notes from a class and underline the important points, you use complex rehearsal. You think about the information in your notes and decide what is important.

Elaboration Strategies

Elaboration strategies require the learner to develop relationships. Basic elaboration calls for simple relationships, such as pairing items or putting a set of details together into a story or picture. When you have your tenth-grade students match properties with each chemical element, they use basic elaboration. When your sixth-grade students see a list of characteristics (such as angry, defiant, strong, young, and devious) and identify a character in a story, they use basic elaboration.

Complex elaboration is for complicated tasks such as summarizing, paraphrasing, or making comparisons. When your middle-school students relate the information they have learned about drug addiction to other forms of addiction, they use complex elaboration.

Organizational Strategies

Again, there are both basic and complex forms of rehearsal strategies. Organization is an ordering or grouping process that can include sequences, hierarchies, and categories. When your ninth-grade students develop a timeline of events surrounding World War II, they use a basic organizational strategy. When second-graders categorize the foods of a menu into the four food groups, they use basic organizational strategies.

The most common use of a complex organizational strategy is one that many people have used—namely, outlining chapters of textbooks. When you put the teaching strategies of this text into a lesson you plan to teach, you will be using complex organizational strategies.

Comprehension Monitoring Strategies

Comprehension monitoring strategies are quite complex. They involve checking yourself to determine what you understand and what you don't understand, being aware of how you are learning, and identifying what you want to know before reading or studying.

Felicia Gomez (the secondary teacher in Chapter One) helps students use this strategy when she directs them to "think about what you might want to learn about Melville from this film." She models this strategy for students by saying, "I will be interested to see if his early life influenced his writing. So I stop and think to myself, 'What do I know about his writing?' I remember that there is a theme of rebellion against life in his work. Then I ask myself, 'What kind of experiences could have caused him to write with that theme?' I begin thinking that I'll look at his family and his school years." To continue teaching comprehension monitoring, Felicia might turn the film off at intervals to check that students are thinking about the influences: "Have you seen anything in Melville's life that explains his writing theme?" As you can see, Felicia's modeling will be important to teach comprehension monitoring.

Affective Strategies

Affective strategies begin with an awareness of a feeling or an attitude. The strategies are then used to experience motivation, confidence, or positive attitudes, or to change a feeling or attitude. When you are aware and deliberately using strategies to focus attention on a lecture, even though you dislike the subject, you are using an affective strategy.

Research studies show that students can learn to cope with various anxieties by using affective strategies. In the studies, students were taught visualization techniques through teacher modeling and student practice. Students identified fears or negative thinking, and practiced positive "self-talk." The results were changes in feelings and attitudes (Goldfried, Linehan, & Smith, 1978). You probably use these strategies to

study content that you don't value. No
motivate yourself. You are using affec
In sum, the content of practice h
learning strategies along with other c
strategies with other content, it is im
learners (Stevens & Englert, 1993). W
ing strategy while it is being used, you
interactive practice.

CONTEXT

Our goal here is to help you think abou
provide the context for this process in
learning is interactive in your classro
about learning, respond to teaching, a
way you structure practice can reinfor
to determine their own learning.

Providing a Description for Practi

A simple way to begin establishing a
learning strategies as students use the
and why they are doing it. Listen to th

TEACHER TALK

Notice that you are alphabetizing lists
this so you will be able to do it quickl
for looking up words in a dictionary o

That description helped students
doing it. We asked those students, "W
alphabetizing practice several days lat
would make them fast, and they desc
was a note of confidence in their respo
for practice instead of telling them: "
names?" "Why do we want to know th
up with insightful reasons for practice

Providing a Model for Practice

You continue to promote active learn
strategies for them. As you model, y

aching the learning strategies of organization.
to apply the strategies to a chapter in their text-
teaches the students how to go back through
ideas, a complex rehearsal strategy. Again, she
nd why by saying, "Notice that when you un-
you are kind of repeating them. That will help

or a few more days, you would see her continue
the students were successfully taking notes and
nodeling gradually and she listens to students'
er. She is using *reciprocal teaching*. The guided
apter Seven for use with lectures are another way
will now look at one more way to provide a con-
actice.

ce

ns provide a context of verbal assistance. Expla-
you teach students a new process and then give
nay be teaching a writing process or a learning
cit explanations, rather than a quick abbreviated
ueness and ambiguity, leaving nothing implied.
elf is to ask one of the learners to review the ex-
might say, "Tobias, tell us in your words how to
y." If your explanation is elaborate or if there are
lowed, you might say, "Jamal, what is the first
by, "Rhea, what is the next thing?" Modeling the
effective. We also suggest that you tape record
e and describing practice activities. You will be
directions to eliminate interferences to students'

gies—*provide description, model,* and *provide*
or active learning and your students "learn how
ntext, you may find that some learners continue
s look at the learner next to help you with those

problems during practice activities: the student
e activity, the student who doesn't finish most of
who distracts everyone around her, and so on.

Lack of practice may result in lack of understanding or forgetting, so you may have achievement concerns. We suggest that you observe the learner and check yourself when these problems occur.

Observing the Learner

Several possibilities may explain the problems learners have during practice activities: boredom, indifference, lack of effort or perseverance, and poor time management.

Boredom

With respect to boredom, curriculum must be relevant and practice activities must have variety, but students often contribute to their own boredom. Wlodkowski and Jaynes (1990) suggested a series of questions to pose to the bored learner:

> *Are you up to date on your studying and homework?*
> *Do you pay attention?*
> *Are you having success in the class?*
> *Do you participate when you have a chance to participate?*
> *Do you ask questions?*
> *Do you take notes when the teacher lectures?*
> *Do you write personal examples and applications of what you are studying? (pp. 88–89)*

Indifference

Occasionally, a learner's indifference may be due to physical and emotional factors or a home situation. When you can eliminate those possibilities, then you must look at your practice activities for ways to stimulate students. We continue to encourage you to provide variety in all of your teaching and learning activities, especially in practice activities. Some additional ideas for providing more stimulation in practice include:

1. Provide consistent feedback that includes information about progress, effort, and competence, and some encouragement.
2. Assign practice tasks that have natural consequences or finished products so that students can see some direct results of their effort and learning.
3. Provide opportunities for student choice in the practice activities in terms of topic, time period, persons to work with, kind of evaluation, or type of activity.

Lack of Effort or Perseverance

Again, you will need to begin by checking for physical or emotional factors, especially fatigue, when learners display a lack of effort or perseverance. Often, however, these learners have a different kind of problem. Research has identified these learners as "work inhibited." They do not complete assigned work even though they are able to understand and intellectually complete the work (Bruns, 1992). These students seem to need more support and nurturing than other students. Many of the work-inhibited students identified in several studies feel unsuccessful in relationships with parents and lack self-confidence. However, these same students are often quite engaging and participate well in class discussions, and may suffer from perfectionism (Bruns, 1992; Summers, 1993).

The first step in helping work-inhibited learners is the development of new habits of self-control or self-management. Some extrinsic rewards may help get the learner started. In many cases, a team approach (student, parents, teacher, and school counselor) is needed. Consistent routines for both schoolwork and homework are important; the time management suggestions that follow are especially appropriate for these learners.

Poor Time Management

In Chapter Four, we suggested some time management strategies for both you and your students, and they can be a starting point to address this problem. In addition, the ideas that are successful with work-inhibited students apply here.

To assist you with this problem, Davey (1994), in her work with middle-school readers, has come up with suggestions for helping students to use time planning techniques:

1. *Be sure that students understand why and how time planning can help with school assignments.*
2. *Model for students how they might use techniques and provide ample practice with feedback.*
3. *Supply the structure needed for time planning with such items as calendars and daily planning charts. (pp. 61–62)*

Checking Practice Activities and Yourself

When there are learner problems during practice, you may need to check on yourself. Look at the practice activities you have planned. Is the practice connected to the outcomes of the curriculum? Do your students know exactly how to do the practice work and understand why they are doing it? Does the practice activity promote authentic learning—that is, learning that is relevant, interesting, and valuable to the students? Listen to the teachers in the Secondary School Snapshot as they examine their favorite assignments with criteria for authentic learning.

SNAPSHOT: Secondary School

In 1991, three tenth-grade teachers and a former principal in Soquel, California, met to share favorite projects/assignments with the intent of making them more meaningful. Previously, they had developed criteria to guide them in defining authentic learning activities. "Sharing assignments was scary. We believed and had been told that we were excellent teachers, yet every task presented fell short of our own criteria. It took confidence and trust to expose ourselves" (Krovetz, Casterson, McKowen, & Willis, 1993, p. 73).

The criteria for assignments consisted of descriptions of what all students are able to do while working on a task:

1. *Articulate purpose of activity;*
2. *Analyze and practice what they do know;*
3. *Acknowledge what they do not know;*
4. *Formulate questions that lead to further knowledge;*

5. *Synthesize connections between knowledge and life experience now and in the future;*
6. *Evaluate what was learned, how it was learned, and how it could be more effectively learned. (p. 73)*

Such tried-and-true assignments as book reports, research papers, and charts of historical events could not meet the criteria, so new assignments were created to do so.

Student and parent responses to the newly designed assignments have inspired the educators to continue their efforts to create authentic learning activities.

Although the criteria were designed for secondary school assignments, we think that they have relevance for learners of all ages.

As you look at the common forms of practice used in classrooms, you will see the need to vary practice. Variety will be an important quality to observe in your use of practice because learner problems can result from the boredom of using the same approach.

INTERACTIVE PRACTICE STRATEGIES

In our observations of classrooms, we have seen the following practice activities: recitation, review, seatwork, homework, projects, and learning centers. We will describe some guidelines for using these strategies interactively and suggest some variations.

Recitation

Recitation is the simplest form of practice and it is the strategy we described as rehearsal strategies earlier in this chapter. Recitation has the potential for dull teaching and learning, so we urge you to use it with creativity and only for appropriate content.

Review

Literally, review means looking again or relooking at something, going back over material. When you use review this way, it's more recitation. Instead, to use review effectively, you must help students apply and transfer their learning, an interactive process.

Outcomes of Review

In an effective review session, your students will be accurately aware of their own learning, or lack of it, and so will you. This means that review is appropriate for concepts and understandings that have been previously developed and learned.

Effectively Using Review

To conduct a review effectively, we suggest some guidelines:

1. Begin with simple, fast-paced questions to get students thinking about the content.

2. Build from the initial questions and recalled information to other concepts and information.
3. Extend the information or concepts to new situations or problems.

Following the guidelines will take planning. It is difficult to structure questions and a review sequence spontaneously. It takes thinking and organizing beforehand.

Making Review Interesting

After students have checked their homework answers to the social studies questions, Mr. Chang asks, "If you lived in the pioneer days, how would you have answered these questions?"

After each group has conducted a brief review of the problem-solving steps taken by members to work on an assigned problem, Mrs. Piazza asks, "What are some problems in your lives that are similar to the problems that your group solved?"

Students finish a quick review of the previous day's information on the circulation system. They are challenged, "Today we are going to study diseases of the system. See if you can predict them with what you already know about circulation."

Not only are these reviews interesting but they also extend review to application and transfer for individual learners. Whenever the learner feels an involvement of self in the review, it's more interesting.

In sum, review is a form of practice that requires thoughtful planning for effective use, builds from recall to understanding to application, and is interesting when learners see a relationship between self and content.

Seatwork

Seatwork, in its many forms, is the most commonly used practice activity. You could walk into a classroom almost anywhere in the country and find learners engaged in some kind of seatwork activity. Van de Walle (1998) has encouraged the use of seatwork practice for connected and meaningful learning. He also advised that seatwork sessions be brief, provide individualized forms of practice, and provide conceptual help for understanding, and that learners understand why they are practicing (their skills and thinking).

Outcomes for Seatwork

Two functions for seatwork are generally given by teachers: instruction and management. Seatwork offers you a way to engage students in practice activities that do not require your attention for a period of time. The activities are usually quiet and of limited physical activity, so that a large number of students can work independently. The quiet, nondisturbing nature of seatwork allows you to teach individual students or a group simultaneously. This outcome is important when you consider the complexities of your classroom and multiple learner differences.

Fortunately, there are descriptions of successful teachers and classrooms in the research literature from which to provide insights for using practice effectively.

Using Seatwork Effectively

We suggest a sequence of practice that begins with guided practice and moves to independent practice. *Guided practice* is practice in which you lead or direct students in their initial practice and provide guidance. For example, when you give a math seatwork assignment, use the first two or three items or problems for guided practice, saying, "See if you can do the first two problems. Then we'll check them together on the overhead." You can then move about checking for problems or questions.

In guided practice, it is important to check that students understand—to look and listen not only to the answers but to the thinking. This allows you to discover errors before they become habits. It is easier to reteach immediately than after extensive practice.

In addition to checking for understanding during guided practice, it is important to provide feedback to students. *Feedback* is information about understanding or misunderstanding, progress or lack of progress, accuracy or inaccuracy in student work. There is a type of feedback called *process feedback* (sometimes called *academic feedback*) that is helpful to student understanding. Listen as teachers provide process feedback.

TEACHER TALK

"Your steps are done in the correct order."

"You used the criteria of function and characteristics to place each organism in its category."

"Your opening paragraph does two things: It uses a surprise statement to get attention and it tells the reader what topics will be coming."

"I notice that you remember to use quotation marks when someone says or thinks."

Once guided practice is complete (that is, your students are ready to proceed with understanding), they can move to *independent practice.* Much of this practice is done as seatwork. Anderson, Brubaker, Alleman-Brooks, and Duffy (1984) studied how to use seatwork effectively and, together with the teachers observed in the studies, generated a set of guidelines. These guidelines are organized around tasks of using seatwork: selection of seatwork, explanation of seatwork, monitoring seatwork, and evaluating seatwork. They begin with selection, and remind you that it is important to match task and student. They also urge you to consider the quality of your selection, assuring the task will make sense to students.

When Anderson and colleagues describe explanation of seatwork, you are reminded to include information about *how* to do it and *why* you are doing it. Does that sound familiar? Remember to provide the kind of explicit explanations you hear in the Teacher Talk that follows.

TEACHER TALK

Watch as I transfer the data from a table to a bar graph. I look at the entire list of amounts—25 pounds, 40 pounds, 65 pounds, 35 pounds, and 80 pounds—and think to myself, "I will need to break up the scale by 5s. I will have lines at 5-pound intervals." Label your intervals to the left, and label the bottom of your graph with the names of the workers like this. Then you can graph each worker's amount by drawing a bar up to the amount weighed like this.

Middle-School Math Teacher

After explanation, Anderson and colleagues (1984) recommend monitoring seatwork. For this task, the teachers and researchers were specific.

1. *First, do not start another task or instruction immediately after a seatwork assignment is given.*
2. *Second, take a few minutes to circulate among students in between other tasks or group instruction to check on seatwork progress.*
3. *Third, establish systems through which students can get help while you are busy teaching others—a buddy system, a "help card" propped on their desks. (p. 28)*

Finally, evaluate seatwork. You may check the work in the students' presence immediately after completion, or check it later and return it the next day. Be sure to include more process feedback about errors, accuracy, and understanding.

Making Seatwork Interesting

Although there are no limits to the possibilities of content for seatwork, in reality, the majority of it takes the form of worksheets and textbook questions. Our first suggestion is to provide variety in seatwork content. Our second is to use worksheets and textbook questions in interesting ways.

1. *Worksheets.* Start by determining if the worksheet is worth using. Osborn (1981) suggested guidelines for developing worksheets to reading instruction (Figure 9.1) and we find them useful for most worksheet development. Use them to critique commercial worksheets and those that you develop.

Guideline number 6 warrants some discussion. You may be thinking that if you limit your worksheets to a finite number of task forms, or a limited number of types of work, it will get boring. Instead, this limit allows students to focus on the content of the task rather than how to do it. This same advice applies to the "response modes" or ways of answering in guideline number 3. Once students have learned a number of procedures, they can be successful and think about the content.

Another suggestion for making worksheets more interesting will sound familiar. Discuss the purpose with students so that they understand *why.* Scheu, Tanner, and Au (1986) demonstrated that primary-grade students understand worksheet purposes, can explain them, and learn more from practicing with such understanding.

2. *Textbook questions.* Do you remember "Read the chapter and answer the questions"? This assignment often results in boredom and frustration. Those questions and the way that they are assigned have the potential to make this seatwork more interesting if they are used intelligently (Turner, 1989).

Suggestions for intelligent use include giving the assignments in clusters or stages instead of all at once. Students can be overwhelmed because textbooks are generous

FIGURE 9.1 *Guidelines for Developing Worksheets*

1. The layout of the pages should combine attractiveness with utility.
2. Instructions to the students should be clear, unambiguous, and easy to follow. Brevity is a virtue.
3. Most student response modes should be consistent from task to task.
4. Student response modes should be the closest possible to reading and writing.
5. When appropriate, tasks should be accompanied by brief explanations of purpose.
6. There should be a finite number of task forms.
7. Workbook tasks should contain enough content so there is a chance students doing the task will learn something and not simply be exposed to something.
8. The instructional design of individual tasks and of task sequences should be carefully planned.
   a. As students become more competent in using a particular skill, their practice tasks should become increasingly more complex.
   b. Individual tasks should be do-able by students.
   c. Responses should indicate whether or not students understood the task.
   d. Tasks should be designed so that their intent is achieved.
9. The skills being practiced should relate to the main reading.

Source: From "The Purposes, Uses, and Content of Worksheets and Some Guidelines for Teachers and Publishers" by J. Osborn, 1981, *Reading Education Report 27.* Center for the Study of Reading, University of Illinois. Reprinted by permission. Jean Osborn is Associate Director for the Center for the Study of Reading, University of Illinois.

with questions. Consider clustering the assignment around a single topic or theme. Turner also suggested dividing the work among students. In Chapter Ten, we describe cooperative learning strategies in which students work together on a task such as answering textbook questions. Turner also suggested appointing an assignment mentor, someone willing and capable of helping those students who have difficulty.

3. *Games.* We see the value of games in the classrooms of young children but after third grade, most game playing is technology driven. Although some video games can be used for practice, they are also fairly solitary experiences. Casbergue and Kieff (1998) urged us to include traditional games such as cards, dominoes, marbles, checkers, and chess to "consolidate some knowledge and skills, and to develop logical and orderly thinking" (p. 145). Many of the traditional games have more sophisticated versions. *Matador* is a complex dominoes game that provides practice in basic math facts. A more recently popular game, *Mankala,* can be seen in middle elementary classrooms as well as possibilities such as *Boggle, Life,* and *Scrabble.* Games need to be selected with the same care as other forms of seatwork so as to match the practice with the curriculum and the learners.

Most of this advice about seatwork applies to other practice strategies as well, so keep the suggestions in mind as we move to practice through homework.

Homework

One would think that homework means work that one does at home. That was probably the intent; however, homework is often done in a car or bus, at an ice cream parlor or hamburger stand, just outside the school or on a playground. It seems to have taken on the qualities of taste and smell over the years, because dogs and babies frequently chew on it.

Outcomes of Homework

On a serious note, homework is intended to extend teaching and learning outside the classroom. When students are asked, they feel that homework helps them get good grades. Research has demonstrated a positive relationship between homework and achievement. Both educators and parents attribute to homework the development of personal responsibilities, work and study habits, and self-reliance. When students were interviewed about homework, they also felt that homework could help them learn and consolidate what they learned (Warton, 1993).

Using Homework Effectively

To use this strategy effectively, you will make two important decisions. The first is to determine *how much* homework. Begin with sensitivity for family and personal obligations of your students. From there, consider a developmental guide for appropriateness:

Grades K–3:	Short, informal assignments (ten to thirty minutes)
Grades 4–6:	Thirty to sixty minutes a day
Grades 7–9:	One to two hours a day
Grades 10–12:	One to three hours a day

We remind you that no two students or families are alike and no two teachers are alike. Some teachers don't assign homework on weekend or vacation periods. Sometimes students use those times to complete long-range assignments (such as research papers) or to make up work missed.

Your second decision is to determine *what kind* of homework. We could provide a long list of appropriate assignments, but one quality is essential. Unless the homework practice is designed to involve parents, it should be work that can be done independently. Students should have the knowledge and skills to do the assignment and should understand clearly how to do it. Remember your direction giving, checking for understanding, and providing a purpose? Those are important for student homework assignments.

The following categories support appropriate homework assignments:

1. *Rehearsal activities.* Practice through repetition—for example, spelling words or foreign language vocabulary.
2. *Preparation activities.* Practice that gets students ready for new subject matter—for example, reading about a country to be studied and making a list of questions or unfamiliar terms.
3. *Review activities.* Practice that promotes transfer of what was learned to a new situation or application to other situations—for example, using measuring skills used in class to measure items at home.
4. *Integration activities.* Practice that reviews many skills and concepts and requires students to put them together—for example, making a poster about nutrition showing the concepts and skills learned during a two-week unit.

Making Homework Interesting

To help you use this strategy in more interesting and effective ways, we urge you to involve family members (see the following Research Vignette). A number of schools are experimenting with interactive math assignments that involve parents (Epstein & Spann, 1993). In Hayward, California, parents and children coauthor original books as the children learn and practice creative writing (Driscoll, 1995). There is potential for enthusiasm, new perspectives, and increased support for students when families are involved. Begin with basic suggestions for family members who want to help and be involved. You will find ideas in Figure 9.2.

We suggest further that students set up a notebook in which both in-class assignments and homework assignments are listed. Students can be taught to record information about due dates, directions, page numbers, and points to remember about how assignments are to be done. Homework journals are being successfully used in many schools (Wisdom, 1993). The journals allow students to write down their assignments, permit parents to check the assignments, and enable parents, teachers, and students to write notes or comments to each other.

As we have suggested with most of your teaching strategies, the support and assistance of parents and other family members enhance the potential for student achievement. Have you ever seen young children who have just started school? When they first get an assignment, they are thrilled to tell you that they "have homework" and they can't wait to get started. With appropriate assignments, realistic amounts of work, and satisfying involvement of families, we might be able to maintain some of that enthusiasm for homework.

International Research Vignette: Sixth Grade

INTRODUCTION

Studies have shown that homework with feedback, individualized assignments, use of resources not available at school, and parent involvement can make a difference for student learning (Villas-Boas, 1998). Parent support of learners' homework is "probably the most widespread and acceptable form of cooperation between school and home" (Organization of Economic Cooperation and Development, 1997). Many educators have developed interesting and interactive homework assignments for that reason; however, we have only begun to study and innovate in the area of family involvement in homework.

In Lisbon, Portugal, educators planned a research study to examine the effects of parent involvement with homework as a step to improve on the home/school connection and ultimately on student learning.

STUDY METHODOLOGY

Seventy-seven sixth-graders from an urban preparatory school located in Lisbon were studying English and were the subjects of this study (Villas-Boas, 1998). The students were from lower- and middle-class homes. There was wide variation in parents' educational backgrounds.

The students were assigned to three groups as follows:

1. Group A (Treatment) received special homework and the parents received information and instruction on how to be involved in their child's homework.
2. Group B (Treatment) received special homework only.
3. Group C received standard homework assignments.

The "special" homework designed for Groups A and B consisted of activities to enrich and expand on classroom learning. Pre- and posttests were given to all students to determine any achievement differences.

STUDY RESULTS

Significant differences were found in the achievement scores of Groups A and B when compared with Group C. Significant differences were also found in the achievement scores of Group A when compared with the scores of all other students (Groups B and C). "The results indicate that well designed homework combined with parent involvement has a significant effect on student performance" (Villas-Boas, 1998). It was noted that students in Group C scored the highest on the pretest yet scored lower than the other groups on the posttest.

CONCLUSIONS AND IMPLICATIONS FOR PRACTICE

Although this particular study focused on the development of literacy through homework and parent involvement, its findings provide insights for teachers' general use of homework. The homework that was specially designed for the study included interactive activities that were enjoyable for learners and their families. Much of what students take home for practice would never be described as enjoyable, so you will need to be thoughtful in selecting homework activities. It may be useful to design homework as part of your lesson planning process.

It is also useful to know that the teachers in Group A dedicated only one hour to parent preparation. That time investment certainly had dividends in student achievement.

FIGURE 9.2 *Homework Suggestions*

- Provide a quiet, well-lighted place for the student to do homework.
- Help the student budget his or her time so that a regular schedule for study is set.
- Take an active interest in what the student is doing in school. Ask him or her to explain a particular assignment and tell what is being learned by doing it. Compliment good work or when improvement is shown. Make an occasional constructive suggestion, but avoid severe criticism and undue pressure. A positive attitude by parents will encourage students to do their best.
- Encourage the student to seek additional help from the teacher at school if he or she seems to be having any difficulty with the work.
- Insist upon sufficient rest, proper diet, and periodic check ups to maintain good health.
- Encourage, guide, and, at times, help your child with homework, but under no circumstances do it for him/her.
- Consult your child's teacher as soon as problems arise.

Contact the teacher, counselor or principal:

- If your child worries or frets over homework assignments.
- If you or your child do not understand the assigned work.
- If your child does not understand how to proceed with assignments.
- If you think your child is assigned too much or too little homework.
- If other problems regarding homework exist.

Source: Guidelines Regarding Homework, Beaverton School District 48J, Beaverton, Oregon, 1989. Reprinted by permission.

Projects

When high-school students in California developed a videotape on land use, they were participating in the project approach. The use of projects or project work has been part of classrooms since the 1920s when Dewey encouraged the "project method." As you are now aware, there are different ways to describe project work, including one more—project-based learning. Katz and Chard (1992) defined *projects* as "an extended study of a topic usually undertaken by a group of learners, sometimes by a whole class and occasionally by an individual learner. It is a study or an investigation into various aspects of a topic that is of interest to the participating learners and judged worthy of their attention by their teachers" (p. 4). The activities usually included in project work are observation, collecting information, interviews, experiments, collections of artifacts, research, reading and writing, discussion, and reporting.

Projects are the kind of extended curriculum activity that encourages meaningful family participation (Shores, 1998). Projects emerge primarily from children's interests, so there is a natural connection to family interests. Gardner (1991) has encouraged us to see families as "student curriculum brokers" (p. 246)—that is, the source of topics and resources for practice and other learning activities. The project approach is an ideal context for such brokering.

Outcomes of Projects

The project approach supports learner autonomy because the learner actively participates as he or she negotiates questions and experiments. Projects also support integrated curriculum so that learners develop and understand relationships between disciplines. Through project work, students acquire new knowledge and skills, practice and apply skills, are motivated and engaged, and develop feelings of mastery. The most convincing outcome of project work is the potential for such variety in tasks and difficulty levels that "all members of the class are likely to be able to find meaningful work that can enhance feelings of competence, belonging, and contributing to the group effort" (Katz & Chard, 1992, p. 14). Project work responds effectively to the diversity of learners and content in today's classrooms.

Using Projects Effectively

Selecting a topic for project work is the first step. Katz and Chard (1992, pp. 14–16) have encouraged teachers to use questions or titles that indicate the direction of the proposed study. An example is "Who measures what in our town?" From there, Katz and Chard suggested some guidelines for topic selection:

1. The topic is related to the learners' experiences and lives.
2. The topic involves or allows the integration of a range of subjects/disciplines.
3. The topic involves the study of real objects as starting points.
4. The topic has sufficient potential for exploration and investigation so that it can be studied for a period of time.
5. The topic will allow opportunity for problem solving, cooperation, and collaboration.
6. Deeper knowledge of the topic will be useful in later life experiences, and is therefore worthy of further study.

In order to describe the phases of project work in which you and your learners will participate, we will look at a second-grade class at City and Country School in this Snapshot.

SNAPSHOT: Elementary Classroom

In previous years at the school, this group of second-grade students studied their community with intensity. This year, they expressed interest in how their city was connected for water and electricity.

In Phase I (Getting Started), their teacher encouraged discussion related to the utilities. Students shared their personal experiences with water and electricity in their homes. In small groups, the class posed additional questions of interest related to the two utilities. Some of the learners were completely fascinated with the topic of electricity, and wanted to know more about how it works, about how it is transported throughout the community, and how the meters at their homes keep track of usage. The lists of questions were hung around the classroom for all to read. Soon after these discussions, parents were informed of the topic and asked for resources (places to visit, items, access to information, and individuals to interview).

In Phase II (Project in Progress), field trips, interviews, and library research were conducted. Regularly scheduled class meetings were held to discuss findings and clarify ideas. More sheets were hung on the walls as the second-graders listed data they were collecting. The students also had notebooks in which they recorded interviews, field notes, observations, and more questions. Toward the end of this phase, the groups began planning for the wiring of houses and for the construction of water pipes for their city.

In Phase 3 (Concluding a Project), the second-graders were extremely busy with their work on the utilities. Small groups met daily to discuss their progress on various tasks, to solve problems, and to raise and answer questions. As they completed their work, they constructed maps to record the piping and wiring, wrote descriptions of the systems, and labeled many parts of their community to display the utilities. When everything was complete, other classes in the school came to visit and were shown how the utilities worked. Parents and other visitors also viewed the demonstrations. The second-graders played the parts of various managers, supervisors, meter readers, and even the mayor of the city as they gave tours of their community (Driscoll, 1995).

For this particular practice activity, it seemed redundant to include a section called Making Projects Interesting. When learners are able to follow topics of interest, pose their own questions, pursue individual investigations, and report findings in a variety of ways, projects can't help but be interesting. Using Katz and Chard's (1992) criteria will ensure that interest level will be high for both you and your learners. However, as you begin to use the project approach, you may gain unanticipated insights about yourself and your teaching.

Four teachers, who experimented with their middle-school science teaching, studied and implemented the project approach (Marx, Blumenfeld, Krajcik, Blunk, Crawford, Kelly, & Meyer, 1994). Their experiences give us some insights for using projects. Their advice is to start with small-scale projects, implement gradually, and try to enlist a few colleagues to join you. That same advice is appropriate for using the next form of practice—learning centers.

Learning Centers

You may be surprised to find us writing about learning centers in this chapter. We decided to talk about centers here because they help you provide practice in varied forms, interactively, and ranging from simple to complex. Learning centers provide interesting practice in both elementary and secondary classrooms.

Outcomes of Learning Centers

A learning center can be a physical area where a student can work independently or with other students on varied learning activities. It can be a time or a place where students have some choice of activities and can pace themselves. Centers provide an opportunity to practice making decisions, practice following directions, practice new skills, practice using resources and materials, review previously learned information, and enjoy practicing. Centers also provide an opportunity for you to observe students at work, or for you to work undisturbed with a student or small group. You can provide and manage a variety of individualized practice activities with centers.

Using Learning Centers Effectively

The outcomes of learning centers may have overwhelmed you because they make centers sound like a "Super Strategy." It will be important to use them effectively, as you see in Ms. Tannenbaum's classroom.

SNAPSHOT: Elementary Classroom

While teaching about the metric system, Ms. Tannenbaum sets up a learning center for practice in using metric measurement. The activities planned for the center need physical space, so student work tables are shifted to one side of the room. This leaves open floor space along the side of the classroom next to the long counter top where the center will be arranged.

On Monday, Ms. Tannenbaum introduces the learning center to students during math time with, "We will have a week-long set of activities for you to get lots of practice using metrics. I want you to be able to think in metrics when you measure." She walks over to the side of the room and points to a sign, "This is Dr. VonMeter's Laboratory." The students laugh. "In order to use the laboratory, you must be ready to think and work in metrics. At the same time, you will have some fun with measuring."

Ms. Tannenbaum shows students the initial activity, constructing a folder to hold their work records of center activities. Each student has a sheet and she calls attention to it, "Look at the sheet—it's a checklist of the activities at the center. As I show you each activity and explain the directions, check it off on your sheet."

She demonstrates how to do each activity and checks that students understand: "Renee, tell us how to do the Mr. Mouse activity," or "Tomas, what's the first thing to do in the Pacefinder activity?" Each activity has a direction sheet, examples, and an answer key to check when finished.

After directions, Ms. Tannenbaum asks students to look at the checklist again. "Notice that for each activity, I've asked you to indicate how well you did and how well you liked or didn't like the activity. When you finish all of the activities, you earn a metric license." She shows the license and again gets smiles and laughter.

Before students begin trying the activities, Ms. Tannenbaum points to a schedule of group work for the week. Different groups of students will be working with her for 20 minutes each day starting on Tuesday. "On the day that your group works with me, you'll only have 15 minutes in the laboratory."

Ms. Tannenbaum followed some guidelines in her use of learning centers: (1) She placed the centers in areas that will not disturb or be disturbed. (2) She ensured easy movement of students in, out, and within the center. (3) She provided space for materials and supplies, finished and unfinished work (the back of a cabinet door, window sills, bulletin board, and even the floor).

In managing the center, Ms. Tannenbaum also followed some guidelines for us. Did you notice that she gave clear and complete directions for the activities? If we had continued watching her, we would have seen her use the remainder of the first day of the metric center to observe, watching for potential problems or confusion. She provided a record-keeping strategy for students with the folders, and a few of the activities were autotelic (self-correcting). Everything for Dr. VonMeter's Laboratory was organized in advance.

In scheduling the center, it is best begun as part of a class period. An effective use of time is seen in classrooms where student groups follow a rotating schedule with time to work at centers, time to work with their teacher, and time to work independently at desks on assignments. A word of caution: We have often heard, "When you finish your seatwork, you may go to the centers." Our concerns for this scheduling are the student who has difficulty completing seatwork and may never get to use the centers, and for the message it communicates about "just getting done." Did you notice how Ms. Tannenbaum scheduled the centers so that all students had a chance to use them? She also scheduled small groups of students to work with her during that time period. Her schedule gave ample time for all students to try all activities, ample time for her to do some observing, and ample time for her to instruct small groups.

Some other scheduling arrangements include using a sign-up sheet for students to schedule themselves for daily use, and using a buddy system where students use centers in pairs. Our suggestions could go on and on. To capsulate this advice, we offer a checklist for setting up, maintaining, and evaluating your learning centers in Figure 9.3.

Making Learning Centers Interesting

To help you in this task, we suggest student involvement and the assistance of parents, volunteers, or an aide. They can make materials, work with individuals or groups in the center, or observe students as they practice. We encourage student involvement in planning and constructing of centers. Listen to teacher enthusiasm when students are involved.

TEACHER TALK

What more could a teacher ask than to have students ask permission to develop a center on Japanese haiku while the class is studying a unit on poetry?

High-School English Teacher

We were studying Australia and one objective was for students to name and describe the animals native to the country. The students took over a center and painted a mural of the animals and their habitats. They made puppets of the animals and gathered magazines, stories, and poems. They even made a matching game. To tell you the truth, by the time they had the center set up, they had met the objective.

Middle-School Teacher

FIGURE 9.3 *Learning Center Checklist*

______ 1. Have you planned an introductory learning experience to precede the learning center?
______ 2. Does the learning center attract through color, design, and novelty?
______ 3. Does the center challenge, excite, and interest students?
______ 4. Are there easy and difficult tasks?
______ 5. Do activities or tasks provide feedback to students?
______ 6. Are the tasks of activities provided in small, easy to follow sections?
______ 7. Is there a source of information easily available to students?
______ 8. Is the center free from inaccuracies, misspellings, and grammatical errors?
______ 9. Is each activity independent of other activities?
______10. Is there opportunity for independent and cooperative work?
______11. Are directions clear, simple, and complete?
______12. Can the center be used by students independently?
______13. Is the center portable and designed for easy storage?
______14. Are the materials durable?
______15. Do you have a way to determine which students have completed each activity?
______16. Do you have a way of collecting student responses to activities?
______17. Is there a clear procedure for obtaining and storing materials?
______18. Is there a recording system?

Source: From *To Help Children Communicate* by F. B. May (1980), Columbus, OH: Merrill Publishing Company. Copyright 1980 by F. B. May. Reprinted by permission.

> I was hesitant to let my students come up with their own ideas for a center but I decided to try it. They wanted a center for wrapping packages. We gathered wrapping paper, old boxes, lots of tape, cards and envelopes, and ribbon. For three months, they practiced wrapping presents and designed and wrote cards. I watched them practice measuring, writing, predicting, and using materials like tape and scissors.
>
> *Preschool Teacher*

Talk about active learning! Practice can be exciting and relevant to students' lives with learning center activities, especially when students have planning input.

Practice and the Inclusive Classroom

When you use practice strategies in your inclusive classroom or any classroom, you will have an exciting array of variations to accommodate diverse learners. Especially in terms of seatwork, homework, projects, and most review activities, you will be able to adapt a basic practice activity for different learners. Adaptations are small changes that adjust one quality of the learning activity while maintaining the content and learning outcome. The Institute for the Study of Developmental Disabilities (Deschenes, Ebeling, & Sprague, 1994) has provided a set of adaptations for your use. Figure 9.4

FIGURE 9.4 *Adapting Curriculum and Instruction in Inclusive Classrooms: A Teacher's Desk Reference*

Size	***Time***	***Level of Support***
Adapt the number of items that the learner is expected to learn or complete. *For example:* Reduce the number of social studies terms a learner must learn at any one time.	Adapt the time allotted and allowed for learning, task completion, or testing. *For example:* Individualize a timeline for completing a task; pace learning differently (increase or decrease) for some learners.	Increase the amount of personal assistance with a specific learner. *For example:* Assign peer buddies, teaching assistants, peer tutors, or cross-age tutors.
Input	***Difficulty***	***Output***
Adapt the way instruction is delivered to the learner. *For example:* Use different visual aids, plan more concrete examples, provide hands-on activities, place students in cooperative groups.	Adapt the skill level, problem type, or the rules on how the learner may approach the work. *For example:* Allow the use of a calculator to figure math problems, simplify task directions, change rules to accommodate learner needs.	Adapt how the learner can respond to instruction. *For example:* Instead of answering questions in writing, allow a verbal response, use a communication book for some students, allow students to show knowledge with hands-on materials.
Participation	***Alternate Goals***	***Substitute Curriculum***
Adapt the extent to which a learner is actively involved in the task. *For example:* In geography, have a student hold the globe, while others point out locations.	Adapt the goals or outcome expectations while using the same materials. *For example:* In social studies, expect one student to be able to locate just the states while others learn to locate capitals, as well.	Provide different instruction and materials to meet a learner's individual goals. *For example:* During a language test one student is learning computer skills in the computer lab.

Source: Reprinted with permission from Deschenes, C., Ebeling, D. G., & Sprague, J. (1994). *Adapting curriculum and instruction in inclusive classrooms: A teacher's desk reference.* Bloomington, IN: Institute for the Study of Developmental Disabilities.

shows these adaptations and an example of each so that you can see how different adaptations will be appropriate for different learners.

We encourage your practice in using the adaptations in your lesson planning. Start with one or two adaptations and work toward multiple variations. We also urge you to develop learner awareness of each child's own needs and learning approaches. The strategies for helping students "learn how to learn" early in this chapter are excellent starting points for that awareness. From there, learners could begin to take responsibility for their own adaptations, which would be a powerful learning outcome to achieve. That sharing of responsibility promotes the kind of self-directed learning (Areglado et al., 1996) that we have encouraged throughout this book. All students will flourish in an environment that promotes the self-reliance of learners.

SUMMARY

As you use the practice strategies of review, seatwork, homework, projects, and learning centers, remind yourself of the importance of complexity in practice content. Provide an interactive context for practice, and spend time observing learners as they work. Follow the guidelines for using practice effectively. By now, you may have reached a level of automaticity in the use of practice:

- Provide a purpose or reason for the practice activity.
- Give clear directions and spend enough time for students to understand.
- Check for understanding of both the "how to do" and the content of practice.
- Provide feedback and evaluation about the accuracy, understanding, and content of the practice.
- Be sure that the practice is worth doing, connected to learning, and appropriate and interesting to the learner.

Now that you know the guidelines, check yourself on using them. Tape-record your directions for practice activities. Practice writing and giving process feedback. Schedule time to monitor student practice. Ask yourself the purpose of the practice activities before making assignments. Ask students for feedback about the practice activities. Make effective practice a priority in your professional development.

REFERENCES

Anderson, L., Brubaker, N., Alleman-Brooks, J., & Duffy, G. (1984). *Making seatwork work.* Research series #142. East Lansing, MI: Institute for Research on Teaching, Michigan State University.

Areglado, R., Bradley, R., & Lane, P. (1996). *Learning for life.* Thousand Oaks, CA: Corwin Press.

Beach, D. M. (1977). *Reaching teenagers: Learning centers for the secondary classroom.* Santa Monica, CA: Goodyear Publishing.

Bruns, J. H. (1992). *They can but they don't: Helping students overcome work inhibition.* New York: Viking Penguin.

Casbergue, R., & Kieff, J. (1998). Marbles anyone? Traditional games in the classroom. *Childhood Education, 74*(3), 143–147.

Davey, B. (1994). Time planning helps middle-schoolers with reading. *Educational Digest, 59*(9), 61–62.

Deschenes, C., Ebeling, D. G., & Sprague, J. (1994). *Adapting curriculum and instruction in inclusive classrooms: A teacher's desk reference.* Bloomington, IN: Institute for the Study of Developmental Disabilities.

Driscoll, A. (1995). *Cases in early childhood education: Stories of programs and practices.* Boston: Allyn and Bacon.

Epstein, J., & Spann, M. B. (1993). School-home connection. *Instructor, 103*(3), 15–17.

Gardner, H. (1991). *The unschooled mind: How children think and how schools should teach.* New York: Basic Books.

Goldfried, M. R., Linehan, M. M., & Smith, J. L. (1978). Reduction of test anxiety through cognitive restructuring. *Journal of Consulting and Clinical Psychology, 46,* 32–39.

Katz, L., & Chard, S. (1989). *Engaging children's minds: The project approach.* Norwood: Ablex.

Katz, L., & Chard, S. (1992). *The project approach.* Champaign-Urbana, IL: University of Illinois. (ERIC Document Reproduction Service No. ED 149 065).

Krovetz, M., Casterson, D., McKowen, C., & Willis, T. (1993). Beyond show and tell. *Educational Leadership, 50*(7), 73–76.

Marx, R., Blumenfeld, P., Krajcik, J., Blunk, M., Crawford, B., Kelly, B., & Meyer, K. (1994). Enacting project-based science: Experiences of four middle grade teachers. *The Elementary School Journal, 94*(5), 517–538.

May, F. B. (1980). *To help children communicate.* Columbus, OH: Charles E. Merrill.

Organization for Economic Cooperation and Development. (1997). *Parents as partners in schooling.* Paris: OECD Publications.

Osborn, J. (1981). *The purposes, uses, and content of workbooks and some guidelines for teachers and publishers.* Reading Education Report 27. Urbana, IL: Center for the Study of Reading, University of Illinois.

Resnick, L. (1994). The mystery of learning. In Editorial Projects in Education (Eds.), *Thoughtful teachers, thoughtful schools.* Boston: Allyn and Bacon.

Scheu, J., Tanner, D., & Au, K. H. (1986). Designing seatwork to improve students reading comprehension ability. *The Reading Teacher, 40*(1).

Shores, E. (1998). *A call to action: Family involvement as a critical component of teacher education programs.* Greensboro, NC: South Eastern Regional Vision for Education.

Stevens, D. D., & Englert, C. S. (1993). Making writing strategies work. *Teaching Exceptional Children, 26*(1) 34–39.

Summers, S. (1993). *Characteristics of work-inhibited children: A case study.* Unpublished master's thesis, Portland State University, Portland, OR.

Turner, T. (1989). Using textbook questions intelligently. *Social Education, 53*(1), 58–60.

Van de Walle, J. A. (1998). *Elementary and middle school mathematics: Teaching developmentally.* New York: Longman.

Viadero, D. (1994). Thinking about thinking. In Editorial Projects in Education (Eds.), *Thoughtful teachers, thoughtful schools.* Boston: Allyn and Bacon.

Villas-Boas, A. (1998). The effects of parental involvement in homework on student achievement in Portugal and Luxembourg. *Childhood Education, 74*(6), 367–371.

Warton, P. M. (1993). *Responsibility for homework: Children's ideas about self-regulation.* Paper presented at the biennial meeting of the Society for Research in Child Development, New Orleans, LA.

Weinstein, C. E., & Mayer, R. E. (1986). The teaching of learning strategies. In M. C. Wittrock (Ed.), *Third handbook of research on teaching.* New York: Macmillan.

Wisdom, C. (1993). Growing together: Sharing through homework journals. *Teaching PreK–8, 24*(1), 93–95.

Wlodkowski, R. J., & Jaynes, J. H. (1990). *Eager to learn.* San Francisco: Jossey-Bass.

SAMPLES AND EXAMPLES

Four learning center Samples and Examples are provided here to give you ideas for starting your own centers:

- Measure Up
- Metric License and Metric Measuring License
- Spanish Center
- Use Your Senses

MEASURE UP

Your Name ________________________________

Partner's Name ________________________________

Nose to fingertip _____cm

Circumference of head _____cm

Circumference of neck _____cm

Circumference of chest _____cm

Elbow to fingertip _____cm

Arm span (arms outstretched) _____cm

Width of finger span _____cm

Total Height _____cm

Width of thumb _____cm

Width of palm _____cm

Circumference of waist _____cm

Circumference of hips _____cm

Circumference of wrist _____cm

Length of foot _____cm

Width of foot _____cm

Source: C. Holz, Portland State University, 1988. Used with permission.

METRIC LICENSE

Directions: You have already measured all the needed information.

1. Find the information from other activities.
2. Transfer the information correctly onto your license.
3. Make sure to put your name and date on your license.
4. Place your finished sheet in your folder. Congratulations!

Metric Measuring License

This license entitles ____,
upon completion of the form below, to be an OFFICIAL METRIC MEASURER, authorized to measure, at any time, using any OFFICIAL METRIC UNITS (such as cm, dm, m, km, g, or kg), ANYTHING that can be measured either with OFFICIAL MEASURING TOOLS or by ESTIMATION.

For use in estimation:

height ____cm arm spread ____cm nose to fingertip ____cm
plain step (pace) ____cm elbow to fingertip (cubit) ____cm
tip of thumb to tip of little finger with hand widespread (span) ____cm
width of palm (hand) ____cm width of thumb ____cm

For use in buying clothes and accessories:

circumference of head ____cm circumference of neck ____cm
circumference of wrist ____cm foot length ____cm and width ____cm
circumference of chest ____cm circumference of waist ____cm
circumference of hips ____cm Date___________

ALL OF THESE MEASUREMENTS WILL CHANGE—
KEEP YOUR METRIC MEASURING LICENSE UP TO DATE

Source: C. Holz, Portland State University, 1988. Used with permission.

SPANISH CENTER: UN VIAJE POR MÉXICO

Materials Teacher Provides:
The teacher provides the game board with five or more cities in Mexico as the targets in the game. For each city there should be a short narration in Spanish about the city or a filmstrip with written Spanish narration. There should be a deck of question cards for each city with three questions about the city written in Spanish on each card and with the answers on the back of the card. A spinner with moves from 1 to 4 should be included at the game board.

Objective:
Upon completion of the center, the student should be able to demonstrate an understanding of Spanish narration, discuss the cultural aspects of cities in Mexico, and show an increased verbal fluency in Spanish.

Directions:

1. Players should select a token. They are going to take a trip in Mexico, and the object is to visit five cities and collect a token from each one.
2. The player spinning the highest number goes first. Players can start at any of the starting points on the game board.
3. Players spin the spinner to determine the number of spaces they can move. Each time they come to or land on a city, they stop and view a filmstrip on one of the cities, with narration written in Spanish, or they listen to a cassette tape recording with the narration in Spanish. To be able to collect a token from the city visited, the player must answer three questions correctly about the city. The questions are written in Spanish, but the player answers in English. Each city has a set of questions with the answers so that each player gets a different set of questions and answers.
4. The other players should check the answers to the questions. If the player gets them right, he gets a token for that city. If he misses one of the questions, he does not get a token and must come back to the city another time for a token. The first player to get five tokens wins.

SPANISH CENTER

Source: From Don M. Beach, *Reaching Teenagers: Learning Centers for Secondary Classrooms* (Santa Monica, CA: Goodyear Publishing Co., 1977), pp. 160–161. Reprinted by permission.

USE YOUR SENSES

Objective:
The student will write five sentences using ten sense image words selected from a box.

Directions:
1. Draw ten words out of the box.
2. Using the words that you have drawn that appeal to the senses, write five sentences using any combination of two or more words. You must use all ten words at least once in the five sentences.
3. Underline the sense image words you used.

Materials Teacher Provides:
The teacher should provide a box with thirty to forty words that could be used as sense image words. Include
ling," "soft,"
"blazing," "chor
the center activit
worksheet with di

Imagery is a result o
of sight, hearing, t *taste. We respond in various w* *both physically and mentally to the use of sensory-stimulating words, or imagery. Look through your literature books and find two examples each of vague imagery and concrete imagery.*

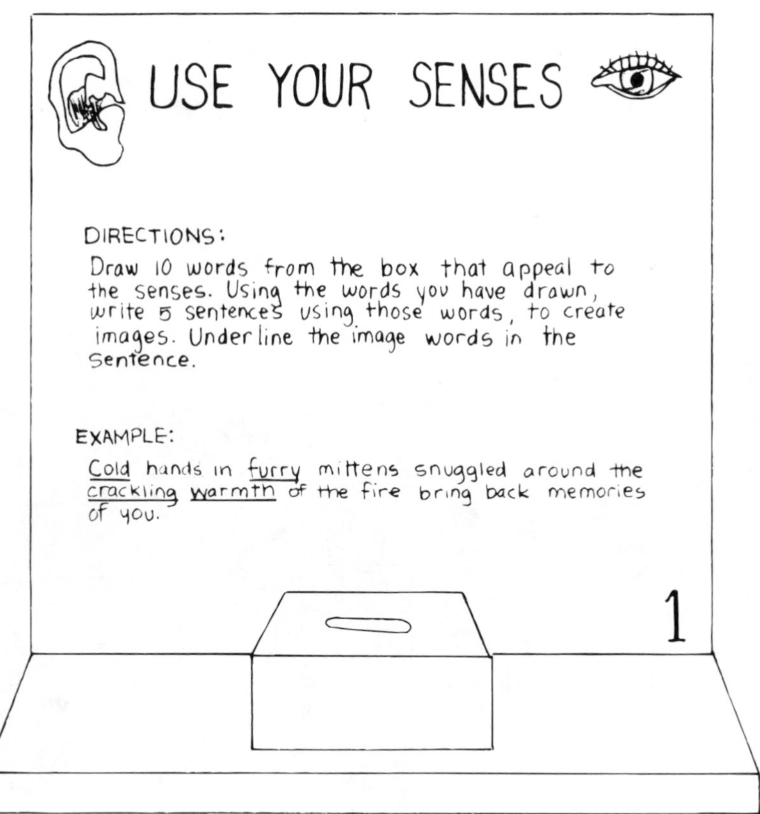

USE YOUR SENSES
DIRECTIONS:
Draw 10 words from the box that appeal to the senses. Using the words you have drawn, write 5 sentences using those words, to create images. Underline the image words in the sentence.
EXAMPLE:
Cold hands in furry mittens snuggled around the crackling warmth of the fire bring back memories of you.
1

Source: From Don M. Beach, *Reaching Teenagers: Learning Centers for Secondary Classrooms* (Santa Monica, CA: Goodyear Publishing Co., 1977), pp. 30–31. Reprinted by permission.

CHAPTER

10

GROUPING FOR INSTRUCTION

Involvement and Interaction

Chapter Outcomes

At the conclusion of this chapter you will be able to:

1. *Examine the context, content, and learner for information to use in making grouping decisions.*
2. *Use different grouping arrangements to accommodate differences in context, content, and learners.*
3. *Develop routines and procedures to manage grouping arrangements and to use volunteers and aides.*
4. *Use grouping practices to support all learners in an inclusive classroom.*

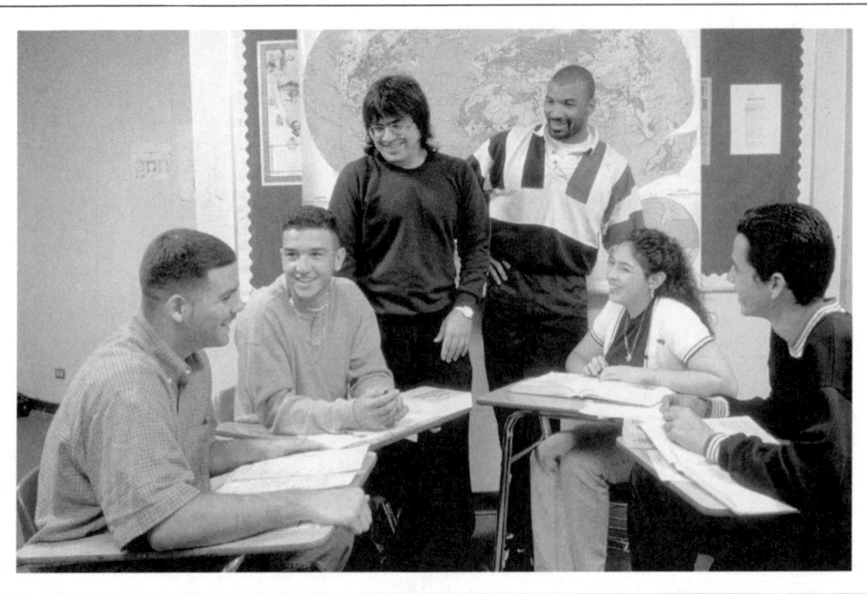

Key Terms and Concepts

Grouping
Cohesive Environment
Group Norms
Interpersonal Skills
Cooperative Work Habits
Varying Student Roles
Varying Student Involvement
Group Size
Assign to Groups
Common Grouping Practices
Within-Class Ability Grouping
Tutoring Groups
Cooperative Learning Arrangements
Cooperative Learning Guidelines
Variations of Cooperative Learning
Cooperative Learning to Support Inclusion
Managing Group Arrangements
Aides and Volunteers

INTRODUCTION

We use *grouping* as a generic term, a way of organizing students for teaching and learning. Many teachers think that grouping helps them individualize or match their teaching to individual learners. Some teachers see grouping as a way of reducing the crowds—that is, allowing them to teach a few students at a time. Many of the first teachers in our country grouped students for the same reasons. We will examine the practice of grouping students as it has progressed in our educational history and see what we have learned.

Grouping—Yesterday and Today

The practice of grouping students for instruction has been with us since the beginning, but it continues to be marked with problems, professional concerns, and legal difficulties. With all of our research and development knowledge, we continue to struggle with effectively teaching all of the different learners in our classrooms, and grouping is our most common response.

Past Practices

In the 1920s, testing came into popular use, and with it came ability grouping. Educators thought that teaching students in homogeneous groups or groups of similar ability would contribute to student achievement. By 1930, studies showed that homogeneous grouping was not effective for achievement and raised questions of effects on student attitudes, self-concept, and educational opportunities (Kelliher, 1931; Mann, 1960; Strauss, 1957).

Ability grouping continued and by the late 1960s, the practice prompted serious equity questions. Some forms of ability grouping were seen as creating racially identifiable classes (McPartland, 1968). Studies of the interactions between teachers and students suggested that ability grouping resulted in low-level expectations expressed by teachers to low-ability students compared to expectations expressed to students of other ability levels (Oakes, 1991).

Today's Practices

Most teachers report using collaborative learning activities in their classrooms—many on a daily basis (Antil, Jenkins, Wayne, & Vadasy, 1997). Grouping strategies are proving to be effective for accommodating the diversity of inclusive classrooms. Studies provide evidence that group work on academic tasks can facilitate student learning (Fuchs, Fuchs, Mathes, & Simmons, 1997). Although current research continues to support the many forms of grouping, we also find cautions about how groups are formed, for what purposes groups are structured, what kind of work groups do, and other decisions related to grouping practices.

We encourage your thoughtful decisions when grouping students for learning. Use the insights from current research and practice. Consider the differences in context, content, and learner. Your decisions will include those related to group size, student assignment, and group configuration. We will describe some common grouping practices, management routines, procedures for using volunteers and aides, and the use of groups in inclusive classrooms.

IMPLICATIONS FOR GROUPING

When you plan to group students for instruction, begin by looking at the context—the physical environment and the socioemotional environment. Look at the content—your intended outcomes and the outcomes possible with the dynamics of group work. Look at the learner—for varying roles and different types of involvement.

Context

To make grouping decisions without considering the physical and socioemotional context of teaching and learning is like packing a suitcase for a trip without knowing anything about the place where you are going. Let's look at your teaching space and assess its arrangement and climate.

Physical Environment

Self-contained classrooms or classrooms designed for one group of students present simple considerations for grouping. Your arrangement of furniture is influenced by number of students, necessary equipment, and your imagination. Since we seldom (or never) hear a teacher say, "I have too much room," your limit is space. To use grouping arrangements with the usual amount of space, try the following:

1. Leave several empty areas (e.g., corners) where students can bring and arrange chairs or pillows to work together.
2. Cluster tables and chairs or desks to accommodate a small work group.
3. Locate groups where students can be easily seen or supervised by you.
4. Arrange the classroom furniture for flexibility, with several movable sets of furniture.
5. Assign "moving committees" of students who go into action when arrangement is needed.
6. Consider adjoining hallways, patios, and storerooms to extend classroom space.

In Chapter Twelve, we describe similar ways to prepare the environment for teaching with roleplay, simulation, and drama, often conducted in small groups of students.

Consult teachers in adjoining rooms and your administrator to prevent misunderstandings and problems of distraction and schedules.

Freedom of space for grouping demands flexibility and creativity, as you will observe in the Elementary Snapshot.

SNAPSHOT: Elementary Classroom

Mrs. Heathman's fifth-grade class at Longwood Elementary in Hayward, California, was a very social, active, and enthusiastic group. Her usual classroom arrangement of clusters of desks wasn't working for the kind of productive climate she wanted in the classroom. Many of her students had difficulty concentrating on their individual work when seated in the clusters. Mrs. Heathman's dilemma was that she used cooperative learning often during the day, and needed an arrangement that supported group work.

When the problems continued, she decided that she needed a more flexible room arrangement. She began by arranging the room into six rows of five desks each. Then she planned a routine for moving into clusters, and rehearsed it with the students until it was smooth.

One day in March, we observed Mrs. Heathman's class as the students prepared to begin a cooperative project in history. Their teacher asked for attention, then announced, "We're going to work in our groups for the next hour, so get ready to move your desks." We watched as the students all stood up and placed themselves beside their desks. "Remember—two hands and two persons to a desk," then "Get ready—move." In less than 30 seconds, the room was ready and groups were sitting together in clusters of five to work on their history project.

Scheduling

Another environmental consideration is time. In your self-contained classrooms, you make decisions about pace and schedule. Grouping is best scheduled in short time periods, with opportunity for movement around the room between activities. Time periods vary with second-grade students (10 to 30 minutes) and high-school juniors (40 to 60 minutes), but there are time limits in terms of attention and comfort for all students. In your open-space classrooms, you are able to have more movement within and between groups, as well as more concurrent group activities, so time is less structured.

Socioemotional Environment

If you were to ask what kind of classroom would best support grouping practices, we would use the word *cohesive.* In a cohesive classroom, students develop socially and emotionally and are able to be group members. Notice the norms of a class to determine its cohesiveness. One way to check for cohesiveness is to look at the group norms. *Group norms* are the "normal" or expected ways of behaving and responding. You initiate norms when you model respect and social relationships. You maintain norms when you prohibit certain behaviors and encourage others. To protect a cohesive environment, prohibit the following:

- Put-downs
- Discrimination in activities (by gender, race, physical differences)
- Negative interactions
- Student rejections

Your use of grouping may not always work well. Silberman (1996) noted that "unequal participation, poor communication and confusion" work against a cohesive classroom and the success of grouping strategies.

To promote a cohesive environment, encourage the following:

- Focus on errors rather than individuals when correcting mistakes.
- Make help available for those who seek it.
- Accept diverse opinions or ideas.
- Structure work for alternative approaches.
- Respect student needs and differences.

If the norms of your class are to work cooperatively and to enjoy individual group members, it will be easier and more effective to use varied grouping strategies. Your students will need to experience peer support and diversity of viewpoints, knowledge, and skills (Silberman, 1996) to be ready for group work. There must also be frequent opportunities for student interaction. Again, research tells us that much of what is learned during group work depends on how students interact (Qin, Johnson, & Johnson, 1995), so you will need to plan activities and assignments carefully for student interactions. We offer ideas for such activities in the Samples and Examples at the end of this chapter.

Content

National Standards in Mathematics (NCTM, 1991) and those of other curriculum organizations as well as many state standards (California Department of Education, 1997) encourage grouping practices for major curriculum areas. As you think about how to use grouping strategies in your teaching, you won't be limited to specific content. Begin by identifying your intended outcomes—these outcomes may be knowledge and understandings, skills, or attitudes. As students learn in groups, they can achieve additional goals related to working in groups.

Knowledge and Understanding Outcomes

Toward these goals, grouping provides opportunity for peer interpretation and sharing of experiences and insights. Haven't you struggled with trying to help someone understand an idea, only to have another person be successful by stating the idea differently? The task of explaining is often made difficult by the difference in student perceptions and experiences. In small groups, students have more opportunity to paraphrase, explain, describe, ask for clarification, and talk about content than whole-class interactions provide.

You are often the only adult in your classroom, and there are limits to the experiences and insights you bring. Each student can contribute additional experiences and insights, and in small groups, they have opportunities to do so. Some examples of how you can provide opportunity for both peer interpretation and student sharing of experiences and insights include:

- When you form groups to study a geographic location or a piece of equipment, mix students who have experience with those who have no experience.
- Have students work together to write definitions of abstract or sophisticated concepts.
- Have students describe their impressions of a field trip or observations of a demonstration in groups.
- Have students describe and compare family customs, holiday celebrations, and home responsibilities.
- Have student groups predict what will happen in a story or a play.
- Have student groups paint a mural to interpret a poem, a feeling, or a stereotype.
- Have students work in groups to develop a response to a crisis, a problem, or an award.

You might look at this list and say that these could all take place in a whole-class setting. Yes, they could. However, hearing 28 to 31 students describe a response is time consuming and does not happen often. When it is done with a whole class, certain students often do the sharing, and others get bored. In small groups, everyone can express and be listened to in a reasonable amount of time.

Skill Outcomes

Toward these goals, grouping assists the practice and feedback that must accompany your teaching. You can effectively model and describe a new skill to 30 students, but it is difficult to provide feedback to each individual. Grouping of students can provide peer coaches as well as peer motivation.

When students work in small groups to practice a skill, they can coach each other's learning. When a sixth-grade student is struggling with long division problems, there is nothing like a friend standing by saying, "OK, now what do you do next? Right. Now, subtract the number. Yes, 23 is correct." The issue of numbers (that is, 30 students and 1 teacher) is not much of an issue if you divide the class into five groups to practice using the microscope. In each group, students can check each other's procedures and provide feedback. You will find more discussion of the coaching role in Chapter Twelve.

There is also the advantage of peer motivation when students work in groups. When students participate in a small group, there is a personal quality to their work because others are aware of their efforts, their successes, and even their struggles. Motivation is higher in these situations, especially when group members work on a group task. Complex tasks requiring well developed skills are much better accomplished through group work than individual work (Johnson & Johnson, 1991).

The following Snapshot gives you a glimpse of how a group of students can practice skills and receive feedback as they work simultaneously on a complex science project and some problem solving.

SNAPSHOT: Secondary Classroom

First-year biology meets in the lab once a week to follow up information from the lecture classes. Today, as students enter the lab, they hear, "We are going to be working on a new process and some important lab skills. As soon as you get to your table, read the chart of tasks for this period."

Soon all students are reading the chart. There are 35 students arranged around six work stations of equipment, sinks, and storage. Ms. Newcomb begins. "Today we are learning the process of making slides, as well as studying slides of bacteria. First, I have a list of procedures for making slides. Your entire group should review the steps carefully and make sure everyone understands. Each of you is to take a turn making a slide. Have others observe you to check your process. When your slide is complete, look under the microscope and compare it with the image on the overhead projector. If your image is different, you have a problem. After everyone in your group checks their images, the group should work on the problems."

Before students begin their small group activity, Ms. Newcomb asks the students at Table 1, "Tell us how you will do your work today." Three students describe the work procedures accurately. The teacher adds, "Here are some group interaction requirements," pointing to the following three requirements (which she has written on the chalkboard):

Group Interaction Requirements

1. Students will be observed by at least two peers and will get feedback on their work.
2. Students will ask at least one peer to check their work.
3. Students will have the assistance of all group members to solve problems.

Ms. Newcomb then says to the students, "I will be observing your work and expect you to follow the requirements. Remember, we are working on being effective group members."

We see students move around to form small groups of three, with one student beginning the steps to make a slide and two others watching. We hear, "Be careful not to touch the slide," and "Wow, that was fast," and "You forgot the solution," and "That's right." When one student struggles, we see at least two others assisting or encouraging, "Try it again, you'll get it."

At Table 4, we hear, "OK, we have two problems here," and "What could be the reasons for the images not matching?" We hear students coming up with several reasons and someone writing them on paper. Then a student asks, "What can we do?" Again, several ideas are expressed and written. Table 4 decides to remake the slides that have problems and to watch the sequence of application carefully. We hear comments of help and encouragement as they begin.

In addition to the illustrations in the Snapshot for grouping students to work on skills, students can help each other edit and rewrite, assess progress, evaluate completed work, set goals, and solve problems. You can move through the groups and listen to the coaching and motivation.

Attitudes and Values Outcomes

The influence of group norms is especially noticed when we work on attitudes with students. Peer pressure is powerful, even for young students. In secondary classrooms, social patterns and group sentiments influence how students respond to an attitude or value that is new or different. To teach content with attitude and value outcomes, it will be necessary to provide opportunity for group discussions so that students can hear different points of view.

To have effective group discussions, everyone must be involved. A group size of 8 to 10 is the absolute maximum. Arrangement is important so that individuals can see everyone in the group. Discussion topics must spark interest. For secondary students, curfews, drug use, ecology, and nuclear power are appropriate topics. Suitable topics for elementary students include allowances, playground rules, and friendships. Students today have quite a bit of savvy and contribute to insightful discussions. With grouping and a small number of students in a group, everyone can be involved.

In situations dominated by you or a few students, few attitudes and values will be developed. One last reason for grouping must be included. We have been told by learners of different ages, "I am more comfortable expressing myself in a small group than in front of the whole class." Grouping is a sensitive approach, an appropriate approach for working on the personal outcomes of attitudes and values.

Outcomes of the Grouping Process

Some of the most frequent outcomes of grouping strategies are active learning, problem solving, student engagement, and personal relationships (McCaslin & Good, 1996). From their extensive studies of learner interactions, McCaslin and Good noted that varied forms of cooperative groups may support student achievement and social relations. They list a number of desirable features of effective small group learning processes:

1. *Subject matter knowledge is increased;*
2. *Students value shared academic work;*
3. *Students can regulate their own resources;*
4. *Students learn to manage other resources;*
5. *Students develop appropriate dispositions toward challenging work on shared tasks;*
6. *School tasks are similar to those outside of school;*
7. *Group members serve as models for one another;*
8. *Students develop an expanded understanding of self and others. (pp. 112–113)*

Many of these features are also outcomes we value for our learners. You will play a critical role in setting up group structures, deciding on appropriate tasks, and promoting that cohesive environment so that a wide array of outcomes is possible.

Interpersonal Skills

Students working in small groups have ample opportunity for practice and talking and listening because everyone can be involved. Even young students learn to wait for a turn, to comment on another's ideas, and to be accepting of different opinions if they regularly experience small group interaction.

In groups, you model those interpersonal skills, so be sure that your listening and speaking are worth noticing by students. You might say, "When Aaron is talking, I sit still and think about only what Aaron is saying." You might paraphrase a student's expression with, "Aaron said that he thinks that raising the bus fares could cause a hardship for students and elderly people. He is worried about their travel if fares increase." Students hear your acceptance and hear Aaron's ideas repeated.

You also have the authority to insist on appropriate respect for each student's expression. Interruptions or judgments are not allowed if you want students to express ideas freely.

Cooperative Work Habits

Working in a small group demands different work habits than working independently within a class. Students have a chance to experience different work styles and a sense of their own and others' strengths and limitations.

In the preceding Snapshot, students learned about the effects of cooperation, everyone working together. In the process of dividing responsibilities, students also learn negotiation strategies. The give and take of life's situations are experienced in cooperative work groups.

The Samples and Examples at the end of the chapter provide you with forms to help your students assess themselves and their group members on their interpersonal skills and cooperative work habits, and to help you with grouping decisions.

Learner

The following Snapshot gives you a glimpse of the diversity of students you will meet. Your learners bring individual differences, especially noticed in their participation and the kind of roles they take in classroom activities.

SNAPSHOT: An Inclusive Elementary Classroom

It is 8:20 A.M. at Raleigh Hills Elementary School and students in a fifth-grade class are already engaged in silent reading. Most of them have a book in front of them and appear to be reading.

In the last row are three girls and three boys. Aletha is the tallest girl in the class, dark skinned with thick hair and glasses. She arrives at school with enthusiasm and can't wait to read. Today she is almost finished with *Johnny Tremaine.* Aletha, to the delight of her teachers, frequently refers to her reading repertoire for information in social studies, science, art, and music. Next to Aletha is Jonathan, who is plump and taller than most of the boys, and is equally enthusiastic about coming to school. His enthusiasm isn't for books, however, it's for his friends. He does not read easily, is constantly moving, and regularly interrupts those around him by making noises or quick comments.

Camille is sitting with her back to Jonathan. She nods at him with a bit of disgust, often in the direction of her girlfriends in the next row. She is reading *Mrs. Wappinger's Secret* but can't remember what it is about. Yesterday she came to school with her hair all braided into plaits with different colored bands. During silent reading she worried about how she looked and kept her mirror on her desk. Today she can't remember what happened in her story.

Jeff stares at Camille a lot. He wants to read but he keeps noticing things that amuse or interest him. Jeff is short, has short brown hair, and wears glasses. His mother decided to get involved with his reading and asks questions about his book each day. Every few minutes Jeff tries to concentrate on his story, *Homer Price.* He actually read it last summer, often in his bed late at night, so he doesn't have to give it much attention. Jeff says very little in class.

Next to Jeff is Martin, a slim active student. He is rapidly reading *The Egypt Game,* a sophisticated mystery. When Martin recommends a book, others in the class try to read it. His choices are usually those of his older brother, a bright and popular middle-school student. Occasionally his choices are beyond his reading ability, but Martin perseveres anyway. He wants his teacher and classmates to notice his reading and the advanced level of his choices, and spends much of his silent reading time looking for such attention.

Yesenia is the last student in the row. She speaks very little English and tries to find books with pictures when she goes to the library. She often reads books written for young children and is pleased with those accomplishments.

In front of this row of fifth-grade students are 23 others. These students are from middle-class homes, a suburban neighborhood with single-family dwellings and a few luxury apartments. About half live with single parents, and all but three have siblings at home. Three of the children have learning disabilities and Tony has Down syndrome. Besides Yesenia, one other child has limited English.

A look at their reading choices suggests that five of these fifth-graders are struggling with books that are aimed at third-grade readers. Eight of the fifth-graders read at levels of secondary students with ease and enjoyment. Some would read for two hours and never notice the time passing. Others last less than a minute and then look for something else to do.

If you were to watch these students all day as they interact in class, work on assignments, and gather at recess, you would see Jeff hesitate to answer when called on and his difficulties with frequent unfinished work. You would see Aletha taking charge of getting a project done for two of her friends, and often looking for something to do. You would see Martin interrupt his teacher to add information, or to disagree, or to volunteer to take care of anything and everything. You would see Yesenia stare out the window when her book is not composed of simple sentences.

If you were hired to teach this fifth-grade class, how would you use this beginning information to group these students? What would you provide for Aletha? For Martin? What would be important to remember as you assign Jeff to a group? Or Camille? We suggest two possibilities that can accommodate the diversity of the fifth-grade class: varying student roles and varying types of involvement.

Varying Student Roles

In a typical class situation, most students perform a listening role (we hope) and a few have a speaking or active role. The level of participation is high for a few and minimal for many.

In traditional group arrangements, students choose or are given leader or follower roles. Some students never experience leadership, some never follow. Cooperative learning strategies offer an alternative with varied roles for different experiences in the same activity. We think that the range of roles can be expanded and can be used in different grouping arrangements. Listen to learner roles:

- *Direction Giver.* Here are the steps we are supposed to follow in our experiment. First, we are to arrange the three beakers in order of size. Then, we are to fill each with 4 ounces of water.... Let's get all the things we need first.
- *Summarizer.* Here is what we have done. We said that our problem is the bullying going on around school, especially outside the back door. We made a list of all the worries kids have. Then we thought of 17 different things to do about the problem, but we decided that only 2 of them were OK. We are going to write a letter to the principal asking for help, and we are going to have a committee to patrol the block around the school.
- *Generator.* Who are some characters who would have lived during this time in history? In a town like Salem, I would expect to find a minister and a shop-keeper. Other ideas?
- *Observer.* I noticed that Ethan and Luanne did most of the talking. Luis took notes all the time and Sharon listened. The only time everyone talked was when we came up with ideas to solve the problem.
- *Record Keeper.* My notes show that we spent 14 minutes trying to agree on the problem. We came up with solutions in 7 minutes but everyone had ideas.
- *Evaluator.* This group did good work today—everyone was quiet and working, the table is clean, and all the equipment is put away.

Add to these roles a Reader, a Time Keeper, an Encourager, a Supply or Resource Person, and a Clarifier, depending on learner maturity and the nature of the learning activity. This variety of roles is appropriate for different grouping arrangements, different content, and definitely different learners. In addition, you can accommodate learner diversity by varying the types of involvement in groups.

In a lesson on the density of matter in his Physical Science class, William Hightower tailored the student roles for a laboratory investigation. His eighth-grade students worked in teams of four and each team member had a role:

Measure master: in charge of group's ruler and ruler measurements.
Mass master: in charge of all weighing.

Engineer: in charge of the group's calculator and calculations.
Graph master: in charge of plotting data on graph paper. (Kellough & Kellough, 1996, p. 293)

You will find that varying student roles and student involvement will be especially important when you want to engage very diverse learners (as described in the preceding Inclusive Elementary Classroom in our Snapshot).

Varying Student Involvement

Within different group structures, learners may be involved independently, cooperatively, and competitively. Even with a group task, some learners go about their work in an isolated way. Some work in coordination with other learners. Others compete and work to be best or fastest. The varying types of involvement that follow allow for differences:

- *Sharing resources or materials.* Here is my set of colored pencils. They are great for maps.
- *Clarifying an idea.* Electricity is not really a conductor; it takes the form of a current.
- *Adding examples.* When I visited a farm, I saw a different kind of fence. It looked like this....
- *Providing controversy.* I disagree. I don't think that our country should put up with another country taking our people as hostages. I think we should be tough and fight.

Remember the fifth-grade we viewed in the earlier Snapshot? Aletha would be challenged and involved if she clarifies an idea. Martin could provide controversy in a noninterruptive way. Jeff could comfortably share resources until another type of involvement was appropriate. Grouping arrangements assist you in accommodating learner differences with varying student roles and varying types of involvement.

GROUPING FOR TEACHING AND LEARNING

As you use grouping strategies, you will be faced with important decisions: How many students to a group? How to assign students to groups? Which grouping practice to use? Before we describe some "how to group" arrangements, we will discuss your decisions.

Grouping Decisions

Begin with your objective. What do you want group members to learn or do? What outcome is intended for the work? What do you want to happen to members? With your objective in mind, move to a decision about the group size.

Group Size

This factor will affect the outcome of group work, so consider some general principles about group size to guide your decision:

1. The larger the group, the broader the range of experiences, expertise, skills, and interests to contribute to the learning activity.
2. The amount of materials or supplies may direct group size.

3. The amount of time available may direct group size. Smaller groups can be more efficient.
4. The size of the task and the number of component responsibilities may determine group size.
5. Larger groups (more than six) require skills of coordination and collaboration for every individual to be involved.
6. Large groups have the potential for members to be or stay uninvolved or to dominate.

In addition to the principles, look at some common group sizes and see what you can expect from this dimension:

- *Two-person group.* This size promotes a relationship and generally ensures participation. This is a good way to begin with inexperienced "groupies" (students who have not been grouped before). In a pair, students gain experience and skill before working in a complex group arrangement.
- *Three-person group.* This arrangement allows for a changing two-person majority. Participation is very likely because no one wants to be the odd person out. Roles in this size group can be those of speaker, listener, and observer, and learners can experience all three roles in a brief period of time. This size group is appropriate for creating descriptions, organizing data, drawing conclusions, and summarizing ideas.
- *Four-person group.* In a four-person group, there will likely be different perspectives. This size is small enough that each member will have a chance to express himself or herself and can be comfortable doing so. Often this size group emerges as two pairs when opinions are expressed. A group of four people requires basic communication and cooperation skills, but offers ideal practice for learning group process.
- *Five-person group.* This size group is considered the smallest size for problem solving, with enough diversity of opinions or perspectives. The odd number of members facilitates decision making. This size group provides continued practice in group process, and even in brief time periods every student has an opportunity to express ideas.
- *Six-person group.* This size group is often used to share data or to develop a report on a topic. In a group this size, leadership or a majority may emerge, and may be needed so that everyone is involved.
- *Seven-person group.* This size group of students works well on a major class assignment or project. In an average class of 30 to 35 students, this means four to five projects or reports to listen to, read, or critique. In this size group, however, subgroups or pairs may develop. There must be enough time for each member to express ideas or to participate. Otherwise, side conversations occur or students become uninvolved.

TEACHER TALK

I don't usually think about how many students to put in each group. I just start assigning them. I do think about those students with behavior problems, because

I can't group certain students in the same group. Once I set up the groups, I usually have to move students around. A group may be too big or too small. Sometimes it goes smoothly, but not often. I keep thinking that I need to plan for it.

Tenth-Grade Teacher

Group size is often determined by curriculum materials. In their study of fifth-grade science groups, researchers (Webb, Baxter, & Thompson, 1997) found that many science kits were designed for groups of four. In most cases, however, you will be making a decision about size. These decisions are not just about numbers of students but about who should be in those particular groups of three, or four, or five.

Assignment of Students to Groups

Again, this decision sounds simple, but it is complex and has significant implications. Your starting point is what you know about your learners. What relationships are possible? What kind of interactions will result? What potential problems?

Consider the outcomes you intend the groups to achieve, and select needed students. If you intend for groups to develop skits, you probably want one or two creative individuals in each group. If you want groups to prepare study outlines, you may want one very organized student in each group. We want to remind you that one objective of grouping is for students to experience diversity of learners, so do consider diversity in group composition. Examine the following strategies for assigning students to groups:

- *Random assignment.* This is a simple process, appropriate when you have decided that student assignment will not influence the outcome and is not necessary for the process. There are a variety of ways to be random:
  a. Have students count off by the number of desired groups. (For example, if you want four groups, have students count off by four. Then have all the "1s" go to one group, all the "2s" to a group, and so on.)
  b. Place group names or numbers in a basket and have students draw for their group assignment.
  c. Use a naturally occurring classroom phenomenon such as rows of desks, table clusters, or room quadrants.
  d. Hand out materials with a group number or symbol on them and have students find other group numbers.
  e. Use creative matching with puzzle pieces, song titles, book characters, or cities in one state. (For example, say, "Find the three other people who have characters in your novel.")

  Random assignments may begin the group process as learners interact to find group members. Some are fun and offer an element of surprise. Some are efficient. Vary your assignment strategies to keep classroom life interesting.
- *Assignment by ability.* You have several options for sources of information with which to group this way: a pretest of new curriculum, current grades, achievement data, and your experience with the learners. You may want to place students of

similar ability levels in one group (a strategy called *ability grouping*) or you may want to structure each group with a representation of high ability, low ability, and middle ability (a strategy called *stratified grouping*). When we talk about grouping arrangements, we will describe when and why you would use these structures.

- *Assignment by social criteria.* Begin by assessing social skills and relationships among your learners, then consider grouping to complement or provide diversity. You may use sociogram information or student lists of desired work partners or team members. Mix your introverts and extroverts, leaders and followers. Have students compose groups with, "Choose two people you know well and two people with whom you have never worked." Try out new ways of assigning, then step back and observe. You will gather new information about your learners for future grouping.
- *Assignment by interest.* For this kind of assignment, survey student interests. (Chapter Seven provides instruments for this purpose.) With groups of students with similar interests, there is usually high motivation and content exploration. When high-school seniors work in groups to study and read favorite authors, those students who enjoy Kurt Vonnegut will work together to study the author with greater depth than in a whole class pursuit. Students enjoy choosing favorite inventions, explorers, countries, kinds of literature, industries, careers, and so on to study in groups. There is nothing more satisfying than observing a group working on a topic in which they are interested, sharing ideas, and working with an exciting momentum.

The next Research Vignette discusses student preferences in grouping structures to consider as you contemplate how to assign students. Before proceeding to a description of common grouping practices or arrangements, we remind you that decisions of group size and assignment of students to groups are not appropriate for "on the spot" thinking.

Common Grouping Practices

You might teach in a school that has structured group arrangements for the entire school. We would like you to be familiar with a few common grouping arrangements:

1. *Between-class ability grouping.* Students are assigned to self-contained classes on the basis of achievement or ability.
2. *Nongraded school.* Students are grouped flexibly according to performance level, not age, and proceed through school at their own rates.
3. *Regrouping for selected subjects.* Students remain in their heterogeneous classes (mixed ability) most of the day and are regrouped for selected subjects, usually reading and math.
4. *The Joplin Plan.* Students are grouped schoolwide for reading without regard for grade level.

Even if you are teaching in a school that has a schoolwide grouping arrangement, you will be able to select and use a number of grouping approaches for your own classroom or course. Most researchers encourage flexible grouping using a variety of grouping formats (Radencich, McKay, & Paratore, 1995), so you will need to develop

Elementary School Research Vignette

INTRODUCTION

As schools move to inclusive educational practices, teachers are asked to teach reading to children with a wide range of reading abilities. That challenge is accentuated by the increasing numbers of students who speak limited English. There is little help for those teachers in terms of research conclusions about group composition, whether group assignments should change, and even the size of ideal reading groups. Researchers (Elbaum, Schuum, & Vaughn, 1997) believed that examining students' perceptions of grouping alternatives would contribute to an understanding of the effects of different group formats.

STUDY DESIGN

Students in grades 3, 4, and 5 in three public elementary schools were studied. The 549 students from an urban setting were distributed ethnically as follows: 43 percent African American, 36 percent Hispanic, 16 percent White non-Hispanic, and 5 percent other. There were 17 students enrolled in English for Speakers of Other Languages and 23 students previously identified as learning disabled. A questionnaire was designed for the study, with sections of questions focused on grouping formats for reading, frequency of grouping formats used by teachers, perceptions of same-ability and mixed-ability groups, and desirability of same-ability grouping. The Student Ideas about Reading Groups (SIRG) questionnaire was administered in students' classrooms.

STUDY RESULTS

With regard to grouping formats, students gave the highest rankings to mixed-ability groups and mixed-ability pairs. Whole-class instruction and same-ability pairs were fairly well liked, and working alone and in same-ability groups were liked least. Both whole-class instruction and working alone were reported to be used more frequently than groups, and groups were used more frequently than pairs. Students thought that they got more help from classmates, worked more cooperatively, and made more progress in reading in mixed-ability groups.

CONCLUSIONS AND IMPLICATIONS FOR PRACTICE

The findings of this study were similar to those of a study of secondary students (Vaughn, Schumm, Klingner, & Samuell, 1995). Both sets of findings suggest that current practice does not always coincide with students' preferences. Current research also suggests that classwide peer tutoring results in achievement gains for all students, and students may be aware of those gains, thus their preferences. Finally, it must be noted that student preferences may influence their motivation and achievement, so it is important to attend to student perceptions of what is effective and what they prefer in terms of grouping structures.

an understanding of skills to use a number of the grouping approaches that follow. We begin with an approach that has a long tradition in classrooms—within-class ability grouping.

Within-Class Ability Grouping

This arrangement takes the form of teachers assigning students to one of a small number of groups for instruction on the basis of ability level. Groups work with different materials, in different activities, and at rates unique to their need and ability. In practice, the best known example is the reading group you see in elementary classrooms. Less common is ability grouping in mathematics. Most teachers limit the number of groups to three in order to provide adequate direct instruction to each.

The abundance of between-class ability grouping and time frame of secondary instruction seems to limit the use of within-class ability grouping. When you find partial ability grouping in high schools, it is usually for skill development, with groups of students with beginning skills, groups with intermediate skills, and so on.

We know from research that ability grouping rarely benefits overall achievement but can contribute to inequality of achievement (Barr, 1995). The number of instructional groups has an effect, and two or three groups have been used for higher achievement effects than four or more groups (Slavin, 1987). Research has also shown that students are keenly aware of other students' ability levels when within-class ability grouping is used, and that teachers demonstrate different levels of enthusiasm, preparation, and expectations with groups of different ability.

The research prompts us to reiterate the complexity of outcomes for ability grouping arrangements. We urge you to use ability grouping with great flexibility. Maintain frequent assessment of students' capabilities and use new information for grouping decisions. Student assignment should be made on the basis of the specific skill or curriculum, not on general achievement.

Be especially aware of your teaching with low-ability groups. Maintain high expectations and put extra effort and your best teaching into this group. For real success with ability grouping, your teaching must be tailored to the needs and ability of the individuals. Adapt your level and pace of instruction for each student in each group.

Tutoring Groups

This practice takes the form of cross-age tutoring (age differences between tutors and those being tutored) and peer tutoring (same age or grade). The intent of this practice is to provide individual help to students.

In practice, peer tutors are usually those students with high ability in a particular subject area or skill, or partners within same ability levels. For cross-age tutoring, older students of any ability level can tutor younger students. Tutoring is also done by volunteers or aides.

Some schools are experimenting with programs in which *all* students participate in giving and receiving tutoring (Gartner & Riessman, 1993). Because the research indicates that gains are often greater for tutors than for those students receiving help, everyone has the opportunity to learn through teaching. This approach also removes the negativity usually associated with receiving help.

What we know from studies of tutoring is that its effectiveness demands a systematic process of planning, training, monitoring, evaluation, and problem solving (Miller, 1993). Other qualities of successful tutoring programs include:

1. A respectful relationship between tutor and tutee
2. Well-organized and long-term arrangements
3. Structured tutoring assignments that prescribe content, sequence, and procedures
4. Matching of same-gender students
5. No evaluation by tutors

Effective tutoring programs depend on your supervision. You will need to provide training or preparation for the tutors, schedule the tutoring, check on progress, and provide liaisons between tutors and tutees.

We see students informally tutoring all the time, so it makes sense to take their lead and organize. Teachers and schools using tutoring approaches describe exciting outcomes for this approach. Both academic gains and improved self-concept are generally reported (Giesecke, 1993). Some tutoring programs have resulted in improvements in academic and social behavior for high-risk transfer students (Weine, 1993).

Cooperative Learning Arrangements

Cooperative learning is defined as "students working together in a group small enough that everyone can participate on a collective task that has been clearly defined, and without direct and immediate supervision of the teacher" (Cohen, 1994, p. 3). There are three common structures for cooperative learning:

1. Assignment of individual students to specific responsibilities within a larger group task or project
2. Assignment of students to work together on a common project or task
3. Assignment of students to groups to study and be responsible for group members' learning (the group goal is the achievement of all group members)

In all three of these structures, for cooperative learning to be effective, there are essential components that must be included in your planning of activities. Johnson and Johnson (1991) described the components as:

1. *Positive interdependence.* This component describes the dual responsibility that learners have in cooperative learning. They are responsible for their own learning as well as the learning of their group members.
2. *Face-to-face promotive interaction.* This component demands that students have maximum opportunity to contribute to each group member's learning by helping, supporting, encouraging, critiquing, motivating, and praising each other's work.
3. *Individual accountability and personal responsibility.* To achieve this component, it will be important to assess the effort and work of individual members and provide feedback to both individuals and groups. The activities will need to be structured to ensure that every member is responsible.
4. *Interpersonal and small-group skills.* This component requires the teaching of communication, problem solving, and conflict resolution, as well as the building of trust, acceptance, and relationships.
5. *Group processing.* This component takes the form of reflection on group work to clarify and improve the group effectiveness, generally soon after a group work session.

You can see some of these components in the earlier Secondary Snapshot (the second Snapshot in this chapter). There is definitely positive interdependence, face-to-face promotive interaction, and individual accountability and personal responsibility. Prior to this lab activity, Ms. Newcomb had taught and promoted interpersonal and small-group skills, or this activity would not have gone smoothly. If we were to continue watching the first-year biology class a little longer, we would see a brief group processing session when the lab work is complete. Within their groups, students are asked to describe helpful and unhelpful actions, make decisions about what to change, give each other feedback on their participation, and celebrate their success. Ms. Newcomb circulates among the group, mostly listening, but occasionally providing feedback to the groups.

Our intention here is not to communicate any simplicity in developing or using cooperative learning. It is a complex and sophisticated approach that must be implemented well to have real effects on student learning. We are providing just a "nutshell" of what it is and how to use it in this chapter. We recommend observing teachers who use it successfully and participating in workshops or classes.

In the meantime, we want to suggest a few more guidelines to get you started. We will also describe your teaching role during this grouping arrangement. Finally, we will inform you of some of the variations in cooperative learning structures that have proved to be highly successful.

Guidelines for Getting Started with Cooperative Learning

Our first guideline is related to the work of *preparing your class* for cooperative learning. Research clearly indicates that time spent on team building, interpersonal and small group skills, and group dynamics techniques ensures the productivity of your group work (Cohen, 1994). There is a wealth of resources with excellent activities for the preparation your class will need for cooperative learning. We list a few in the Samples and Examples at the end of the chapter.

Our next guideline is related to your decisions about *group size and membership.* When teachers who use cooperative learning are studied, their group sizes consisted of pairs and small groups (usually four students) 57 percent of the time (Antil et al., 1998). Until the students are skillful with group work, small groups (usually three students) are appropriate. Heterogeneous groups are generally best, and teacher-made groups are optimal. Johnson and Johnson (1991) have found that there is less on-task behavior in student-selected than in teacher-selected groups. In terms of how long a group should stay together, Johnson and Johnson have encouraged allowing groups to remain stable long enough for them to be successful. We suggest that you vary the terms so that learners get to work with everyone in the class, yet at the same time, be sure that there is opportunity for long-term relationships to develop.

Our third guideline is related to *planning decisions.* When you begin your planning, remember that the teaching and learning task must be appropriate. Ask yourself if the learners will see the goal as important and reachable. Be sure that you are clear and specific when you describe the objectives and the structure of the activity.

Teacher Role in Cooperative Learning

In addition to the three guidelines, research has prescribed some aspects of your teaching role to ensure effectiveness of your cooperative learning arrangements. Managing cooperative learning is quite complex. When classrooms with such complex modes of teaching were studied, the greatest learning gains were seen in those where teachers were successful in delegating authority so that more children could talk and work together (Cohen, 1994, p. 29).

The other teacher behavior that demonstrated positive effects on cooperative learning was giving specific feedback (Cohen, 1994). Giving students specific feedback on their cooperative behaviors and asking them to engage in group processing of their work with respect to specific skills is supported by studies of different contexts and different academic content.

Variations of Cooperative Learning

Once you and your class have mastered cooperative learning, you will be ready to try some of the following variations:

1. *Teams-Games-Tournament (TGT)* is a combination of intragroup cooperation, intergroup competition, and instructional games. In a sixth-grade class, teams of four are studying the classifications of insects and related examples. You see individuals competing with each other in a "What Is It?" game. Both individual and team scores are recorded.
2. *Student Teams-Achievement Divisions,* a modification of TGT, stresses intergroup competition to learn predetermined facts. In the same sixth-grade class, the students are using flash cards to drill each other about insects. When they feel ready, the students take a quiz and their scores contribute to a team score.
3. *Jigsaw* is a combination of cooperative and individualistic learning with resource sharing. Ninth-grade cooperative groups each have an economics unit to learn. The units have been organized into five sections so that each group member is responsible for one section. Each member teaches the group his or her curriculum content, and groups may help each other. When the material has been learned, individuals take a test and are given individual grades.
4. *Group Investigation* is characterized by groups formed with common interests, and group control over what they learn. When a third-grade class began studying their state of Oregon, some individuals were interested in the history while others were interested in the government and industry. Groups were formed based on interests, and within the groups, decisions were made about how to research the topics and how to present the information.

Several other variations of cooperative learning exist and each is well supported by research demonstrating effectiveness. There are *Co-op Co-op, Think-Pair-Share, Cooperative Integrated Reading and Composition,* and *Team-Assisted Individualization.* We encourage you to learn about as many of these arrangements as possible, so that your cooperative learning will truly be varied and learners will be involved and interactive.

Whether you decide to use cooperative learning or tutoring, we urge you to stay flexible. It is also important to manage the grouping arrangements with routines and procedures for student movement, for independent work activities, and for using the assistance of aides and volunteers. You will find flexibility and organization essential in your inclusive classroom.

Using Cooperative Learning Arrangements to Support Inclusion

The challenges of finding effective teaching strategies that address individual differences have been foremost in the minds of educators for some time, and the challenges are increasing (Antil et al., 1998). Cooperative learning has been increasingly popular for its capacity to accommodate individual differences. In fact, it has been described as a teaching and learning strategy that "exploits differences to promote learning" (Johnson & Johnson, 1991; Stevens & Slavin, 1995). Again, we encourage your pursuit of the cooperative learning approach to meet the span of learner needs and to achieve the range of goals in the inclusive classroom.

Cooperative learning is definitely directed to academic goals, but it can work simultaneously toward social and personal development. Few of the other teaching strategies of this book offer opportunities for learning and practicing interpersonal skills. Those skills are essential for effective interactions in any classroom but especially so in the inclusive classroom.

As for the span of learner needs and other differences, cooperative learning approaches are the most recommended for addressing differences in major curricular areas (science, literacy, social studies, and math). Although you might view the span of differences as an obstacle, Borasi (1994) lists some of the benefits of an inclusive setting:

- Regular students serve as learning models for special students.
- Special students can offer unique alternative solutions to challenging problems.
- All students develop awareness of and respect for individual differences.

Those benefits are much more likely to emerge in your classroom if students have the opportunity to be actively involved with each other, have frequent dialogs and discussions, and can form close relationships within the class. Cooperative learning activities provide many more of those opportunities than large groups or whole-class learning.

Management of Grouping Arrangements

Depending on the complexity of your grouping arrangement, you will need a set of routines and procedures. We describe management considerations to use with most arrangements. Adapt them to your context, content, and learners.

Student Movement (In and Out of Groups)

Getting students in and out of groups must be done smoothly because the process affects both the behavior of students and the beginnings and endings of learning activities. The transitions we described in Chapter Six provide ideas for handling these changes. For the transition routines with grouping, you must make some decisions:

- Is there a need for quiet moving in and out of groups?
- Do students need a break in between group work?

- Can two groups move at once?
- Will one part of the classroom be congested?

Teachers often make brief announcements, such as "Group 2, come up to the front now; Group 3, move to the centers," as another group returns to individual desks. Some teachers use a musical signal, a clapping routine, or move quietly from group to group, giving instructions. The latter has the effect of a staggered movement and usually feels less chaotic. For these movement routines to be smooth, they must be taught and practiced. Students can actually rehearse the movement pattern and associated behaviors.

Another effective practice for smooth movement in and out of groups is to provide a description of what is to be done when students get to the location. An example will show what we mean: "When you get to your tables, open your notebooks to the list of equipment necessary for your work and check off each item as you gather equipment," or "When you get to your desk, look up the meaning of *substantive* in your glossary and raise your hand when you find it." These directions influence the pace of movement and efficiency with which students are ready for the next activity.

Effective teachers roam the room between each group activity and check on independent work and student progress. These are pauses of only two or three minutes, but they have positive effects on student achievement and behavior.

Managing Independent Work Activities

If you intend to instruct small groups of students, you will need to be assured that other students are involved in challenging work, have their needs met, and are not disturbing anyone. This is a complex demand and calls for well-developed classroom management. Chapters Five and Six provide many strategies; we will describe additional ways to manage this situation.

A major consideration in the management of independent work activities is the quality of work or activity. Can it be done independently? Do you want it done independently? Take a look at the knowledge and skills needed to do the work and check the difficulty level. Is the work worth doing? Will it interest, challenge, and promote learning? Once you assess the quality of independent work and plans for appropriate worthwhile tasks or activities, there are effective routines that assist the independent workers:

1. Provide generous amounts of direction complete with examples before moving to independent activities.
2. Have work information (directions, schedule, materials) posted in a prominent location.
3. Have alternatives provided for those who complete work with time remaining.
4. Consider the noise level of the independent work.
5. Have clearly defined behaviors for independent work.
6. If the work period is long, provide a physical and social break midway in the period.

A routine that promotes smoothness when you are coordinating group instruction with supervision of independent work is one for getting help when you need it. As we suggested in Chapter Six, have a student or committee assigned to assist others who have trouble with directions or questions. Make tape-recorded sets of directions or a recipe card format posted on the board. What is most important is that students are completely certain of how to get help. The cooperative learning arrangements that we described include this kind of student assistance.

With all of these responsibilities—movement of groups, supervision of independent work, and instruction of small groups—the assistance of another adult can really ease the management. Coordinating the help of another adult is the focus of the next section.

Using Aides and Volunteers to Assist with Grouping

Three areas of concern must be addressed for an effective program of volunteers or classroom aides: training, assignment, and planning time (Rosner, 1997). We describe how they become part of your management.

Training and Preparation of Aides and Volunteers

Depending on the experience of your volunteer or aide, the need for training will vary. Begin by finding out about that experience. You may be comfortable in an informal conversation or you may need a formal set of questions in survey form. Once you have such information, you can plan an outline of essential information for training.

We suggest an orientation session and ongoing training. If you have an experienced assistant, you may want that person to work with the new aide. It will be important for newcomers to observe you and your students, and the time will be profitable if they know what to observe. An example from a group of secondary teachers offers a guide for observing your class.

Classroom Observation Guide

1. Note the time, day, and subject matter.
2. Watch how students follow routines (pencil sharpening, using resources, leaving the room).
3. Listen for the kinds of help students need frequently.
4. Watch what distracts students from work.
5. Watch what kind of behavior is acceptable and unacceptable.

Once an aide or volunteer becomes acquainted with your classroom, other training strategies include:

- Modeling of teaching and management strategies
- Written directions or guidelines for work with groups
- Collaborating with other teachers to hold training
- Student helpers who explain routines and procedures

Be sure to check on state and district policy and procedures regarding other adults working in your classroom.

Assignment of Aides and Volunteers

Your assignment decisions must accommodate both your classroom needs and those appropriate to the other person's experience and preferences. A teacher in Portland, Oregon, offers her volunteers a choice of working directly with students or preparing classroom materials, and writes up job forms for both types of work. Volunteers pick up a job description when they arrive and work efficiently and successfully at their choice. Another teacher who relies on help from other adults writes lesson plans for them. This means extra work for her, but she finds better assistance results from her efforts.

Discuss and put in writing your expectations for assistance, and listen to your aide's expectations. With both aides and volunteers, there is a wide variation in work preferences. Some are comfortable doing clerical work, making materials, or grading quizzes. Some enjoy teaching and interacting with students. Some come with real expertise and need to be able to use their skills. If your assignments reflect those preferences and expectations, you can depend on assistance. Planning will also ensure regular or ongoing help.

Planning with Aides and Volunteers

Once again, the limits of time make planning and coordinating with aides and volunteers a major concern. We don't have any secrets for how to find extra time, but there are ways to be efficient with the time available. Preplanning communication ensures that planning time addresses important topics and concerns. A form for volunteers to complete at the end of the day or class may ask for evaluation, needs, concerns, information, and suggestions. You may want to provide written feedback in similar form. An agenda for planning time will also help.

You have few options for when you can meet and plan: during class time, after school, before students arrive, during a break or lunch, or at a monthly Saturday meeting. Some districts have an early dismissal day, and planning is done after students leave. What will be important is a schedule convenient to you and your aide or volunteer.

When you observe a teacher who has prepared, assigned, and coordinated volunteer assistance, you will see exciting teaching. The time spent getting an aide or volunteer ready has definite payoffs. One advantage reported by teachers is the possibility of working with the same volunteer or aide over a long period of time. The Samples and Examples section at the end of this chapter provides ideas for your work with volunteers and aides.

SUMMARY

Most teachers enter the profession with a genuine liking for people. Is that true for you? In the process of instructing large numbers of students with all the necessary management responsibilities, you may forget or lose sight of that enjoyment. Make it your starting point and think of grouping as a way to appreciate all the unique individuals you have the opportunity to meet and teach.

With that appreciation, begin the process of information gathering. Look at your teaching context. What will support grouping? Where are the obstacles? Check the physical environment for furniture arrangement, space, and movement. Coordinate use of physical space with those around you. Remember to assess your socioemotional environment. What are the group norms? What opportunities exist for student interaction?

Review your content. What are your intended outcomes? With knowledge and understandings, use your grouping to provide peer interaction and broadened experiences. With skills, use your grouping to provide peer coaching and motivation. With attitudes and values, use grouping to provide discussion and individual involvement.

Look at your learners. The diversity is exciting. Plan for your learners to experience different learning roles and different types of involvement within your grouping.

With information about your context, content, and learner, be ready to make decisions. Consider group size and assignment of students to groups. Then proceed to your repertoire of common grouping practices, combinations of grouping practices, and not so common grouping practices.

Once your grouping decisions have been made, check your management for routines and procedures for student movement in and out of groups, for independent work activities. Use aides or volunteers to assist your grouping arrangements. Prepare and train them, assign them carefully, and schedule time to plan together.

Reflect on the kind of groups in which your students will work and live in their adult lives. Provide the same opportunities that await them—that is,working with individuals with the same abilities, interests, needs, and goals, or with different abilities, interests, needs, and goals. Use your grouping arrangements to reflect life.

REFERENCES

Antil, L., Jenkins, J., Wayne, S., & Vadasy, P. (1997). Cooperative learning: Prevalence, conceptualizations, and the relation between research and practice. *American Educational Research Journal, 35*(3), 419–454.

Barr, R. (1995). What research says about grouping in the past and present and what it suggests about the future. In M. Radencich & L. McKay (Eds.), *Flexible grouping for literacy in the elementary grades.* Boston: Allyn and Bacon.

Borasi, R. (1994). *Implementing the* NCTM Standards *in inclusive classrooms.* Presented at the annual meeting of the National Council of Teachers of Mathematics, Indianapolis, IN.

California Department of Education. (1997). *California Standards for the teaching profession.* Sacramento, CA: Author.

Cohen, E. G. (1994). Restructuring the classroom: Conditions for productive small groups. *Review of Educational Research, 64*(1), 1–35.

Elbaum, B., Schumm, J., & Vaughn, S. (1997). Urban middle elementary students' perceptions of grouping formats for reading instruction. *The Elementary School Journal, 97*(5), 475–500.

Fuchs, D., Fuchs, L., Mathes, P., & Simmons, D. (1997). Peer assisted learning strategies: Making classrooms more responsive to diversity. *American Educational Research Journal, 34,* 174–206.

Gartner, A., & Riessman, F. (1993). *Peer-tutoring: Toward a new model.* Washington, DC: Office of Educational Research and Improvement. (ERIC Document Reproduction Service No. ED 362 506).

Giesecke, D. (1993). Low-achieving students as successful cross-age tutors. *Preventing School Failure, 37*(3), 34–43.

Gutierrez, R., & Slavin, R. E. (1992). Achievement effects of the nongraded elementary school: A best evidence synthesis. *Review of Educational Research, 62*(4), 333–376.

Johnson, D. W., & Johnson, R. T. (1991). *Learning together and alone.* Englewood Cliffs, NJ: Prentice Hall.

Kelliher, A. V. (1931). *A critical study of homogeneous grouping.* New York: Bureau of Publications, Teachers' College, Columbia University, Contribution to Education No. 452.

Kellough, R., & Kellough, N. (1996). *Middle school teaching.* Englewood Cliffs, NJ: Merrill.

Mann, M. (1960). What does ability grouping do to the self-concept? *Childhood Education,* 357–361.

McCaslin, M. M., & Good, T. L. (1996). *Listening in classrooms.* New York: HarperCollins College Publishers.

McPartland, J. (1968). *The segregated student in desegregated schools: Sources of influence on Negro secondary students.* Baltimore, MD: Johns Hopkins University, Center for Social Organization of Schools.

Miller, L. (1993). Winning with peer tutoring: A teacher's guide. *Preventing School Failure, 37*(3), 14–18.

Napier, R. W., & Gershenfeld, M. K. (1985). *Groups, theory, and experience.* Boston: Houghton Mifflin.

National Council of Teachers of Mathematics. (1991). *Professional standards for teaching mathematics.* Reston, VA: Author.

Oakes, J. (1991). *Multiplying inequalities: The effects of race, social class, and tracking on opportunities to learn in math and science.* Santa Monica, CA: Rand.

Qin, Z., Johnson, D., & Johnson, R. (1995). Cooperative vs. competitive efforts and problem solving. *Review of Educational Research,* 65, 129–144.

Radencich, M. C., McKay, L. J., & Paratore, J. R. (1995). Keeping flexible groups flexible: Grouping options. In M. Radencich & L. McKay (Eds.), *Flexible grouping for literacy in the elementary grades.* Boston: Allyn and Bacon.

Rosner, R. (1997). *Students teaching students: A handbook for cross-age tutoring.* Atlanta, GA: Center for School Success, Southern Regional Council.

Siberman, M. (1996). *Active learning: 101 strategies to teach any subject.* Boston: Allyn and Bacon.

Slavin, R. E. (1987). Ability grouping and student achievement in elementary schools: A best evidence synthesis. *Review of Educational Research, 57*(3), 293–336.

Stevens, R. J., & Slavin, R. E. (1995). The cooperative elementary school: Effects on students' achievement, attitudes, and social relations. *American Educational Research Journal, 32,* 321–351.

Strauss, S. (1957). Looking backward on future scientists. *The Science Teacher,* 385–388.

Vaughn, S., Schumm, J., Klingner, J., & Samuell, L. (1995). Students' views of instructional practices: Implications for inclusion. *Learning Disabilities Quarterly, 18,* 236–248.

Verduin, J. R., Jr. (1996). *Helping students develop investigative, problem solving, and investigative skills in cooperative settings.* Springfield, IL: Charles C. Thomas.

Webb, N., Baxter, G., & Thompson, L. (1997). Teachers' grouping practices in fifth-grade science classrooms. *The Elementary School Journal, 98*(2), 91–113.

Weine, A. M. (1993). An evaluation of preventive tutoring programs for transfer students. *Child Study Journal, 23*(2), 135–152.

SAMPLES AND EXAMPLES

There are six Samples and Examples that support your grouping arrangements. The first two are forms to help your learners conduct group processing and self-assessment. The third and fourth forms provide help in organizing parent volunteers in the classroom. The fifth and sixth resources are lists of references for more ideas.

- Our Own Observation Sheet is a form developed by a class of fourth/fifth/sixth-graders to process their group work and give feedback to each other.
- The Student Self-Assessment/Group Project form was developed for secondary students to promote both self-assessment and group processing.
- The Volunteer Worksheet is a kind of lesson plan for your volunteers. It enables them to work more independently.
- The Parent Volunteer Survey helps you assess the availability and the resources of the parents of your students.
- The List of References for Use in Developing Cooperative Learning contains resources for more team building, social skill building, and group dynamics activities to use in your classroom in preparation for cooperative learning.
- The Resource List for Tutoring is a helpful set of books and strategies appropriate for learners of varied ages.

OUR OWN OBSERVATION SHEET

We're looking for the positive things each does or can do.

Group name ____________________

Week of ____________ Observer's name ____________________

Name	Cooperating or how are they cooperating?	Being responsible or how are they showing responsibility?	Words of Encouragement? Manners? Praising?	Correct size voice?	Hitchhiking or starting quickly or listening?

STUDENT SELF-ASSESSMENT/GROUP PROJECT

Name: ______________________ Date: ______________

Class: ______________________ Period: ______________

Assignment Description:

____

____

____

____

____

Group Members:

1. ____
2. ____
3. ____
4. ____

Description of How Your Group Approached This Problem:

____

____

____

____

____

Success Record Three things we did really well were:

1. ____
2. ____
3. ____

For Improvement Three things we could have done better:

1. ____

2. ____

3. ____

Overall Satisfaction with the Outcome of This Project:

Very Dissatisfied	Dissatisfied	Neutral	Satisfied	Very Satisfied

| - - - - - - - - - | - - - - - - - - - | - - - - - - - - - | - - - - - - - - - | - - - - - - - - - | - - - - - - - - - | - - - - - - - - - |

The grade my group deserves for this project is ______________________

because ____

The grade I personally deserve for this project is ______________________

because ____

Additional Comments for Teacher Consideration:

____

____

____

Source: Diane Brooks and Ginger S. Redlinger. Reprinted with permission.

VOLUNTEER WORKSHEET

Name ______________________________ Date __________________

I. Task:
Materials Needed—

Instructions—

Children Involved—

Time Frame—

II. Feedback from Volunteer: (Things to consider: Does anyone need additional help? Do you have some suggestions for improving the lesson? Other. . .)

Source: From "Parent Volunteer Materials" by S. Tong, C. Erickson, and J. Weber, 1988, unpublished materials. Portland State University, Portland, OR. Reprinted by permission.

PARENT VOLUNTEER SURVEY

Parents are the key to an enriched and varied school experience for children. No single adult can educate a class of 25 children over a period of 10 months and provide all the information or challenges they need to grow fully. Together we can make this a special year for your child. I invite you to share yourself in any ways that feel comfortable to you. Thanks from all the kids and me!

I can volunteer to help in the classroom (circle the day and time that is best for you):

Days: Mon. Tues. Wed. Thurs. Fri.

Times: Mornings Afternoons Once in a while

_______ I will help out on field trips.

_______ I can make things at home (playdough, math games, etc.). The teacher will provide easy to follow directions and much gratitude!

_______ I have a skill I can share with children.

_______ I have a hobby I can share with children.

_______ I have a collection I can share with children.

_______ I have a talent I can share with children.

_______ I could share information about another country or culture (photos, clothing, objects for example).

_______ I have a job that I could demonstrate/the place where I work is available for a field trip.

_______ I will be a room parent and attend class celebrations.

_______ I will provide treats for class parties.

_______ Call me for special projects. Phone:

Concerns or comments:

Your name: ______________________________

Your phone: ______________________________

Thank you!

Kindergarten teacher

Source: From "Parent Volunteer Materials" by S. Tong, C. Erickson, and J. Weber, 1988, unpublished materials. Portland State University, Portland, OR. Reprinted by permission.

LIST OF REFERENCES FOR USE IN DEVELOPING COOPERATIVE LEARNING

Gibbs, J. (1995). *Tribes.* Santa Rosa, CA: Center Source.

Johnson, D. W., & Johnson, R. T. (1999). *Learning together and alone.* Boston: Allyn and Bacon.

Johnson, R. T., Johnson, D. W., & Holubec, E. J. (1987). *Structuring cooperative learning: Lesson plans for teachers.* Edina, MN: Interaction Book Company.

Kagan, S. (1995). *Cooperative learning: Resources for teachers.* Riverside, CA: University of California.

Slavin, R. E. (1995). *Cooperative learning: Theory, research, and practice.* Boston: Allyn and Bacon.

RESOURCE LIST FOR TUTORING

Cheatham, Judy Blakenship, et al. (1993). *Tutor.* Literacy Volunteers of America, Inc., Syracuse, NY. 198 pages. Collaborative approach to adult literacy instruction. Designed for the professional and nonprofessional reading and writing tutor, it provides a theoretical base and demonstrates the skills and approaches needed for tutoring. Techniques may be applied to one-on-one tutoring or in a small group setting.

Keim, Nancy, & Tolliver, Cindy. (1993). *Tutoring and mentoring: Starting a peer helping program in your elementary school.* Resource Publications, Inc., San Jose, CA. 128 pages. Step-by-step guide to starting a peer helping program in an elementary school. Focuses on two complementary types of peer helping: tutoring and mentoring. Provides information on how to manage the program after its implementation.

MacDonald, Ross B. (1994). *The master tutor: A guidebook for more effective tutoring.* Cambridge Stratford, Limited, Williamsville, NY. 124 pages. Covers aspects of tutoring effectiveness, including how tutors must develop the goals, directions, alternative approaches, and perspectives to build tutee independence rather than dependence. Synthesizes essential, relevant, and proven strategies of tutoring for tutors and trainers. Serves as a reference for tutors after initial reading and training are completed.

Rabow, J., Chin, T., & Fahimian, N. (1999). *Tutoring matters: Everything you always wanted to know about how to tutor.* Philadelphia, PA: Temple University Press. 240 pages. Designed for tutors of all levels of experience. Addresses individual differences. Provides real-life examples and concrete ideas for meeting certain goals for the tutoring experience.

Venezky, Dick, & Linda Sittig (Eds.). (1995). *READ*WRITE*NOW! for reading partners.* United States Department of Education. (*Note:* The information and activities from this workbook may also be printed from the Internet from the following site: <http://www.udel.edu/ETL/RWN.Tutorman.html>.) Designed for adults and older children who serve as reading partners in assisting children through sixth grade to learn to read. Includes activities in sections for infants and preschoolers, children through second grade, and older children. Activities for use in addition to daily reading with students.

CHAPTER 11

REFLECTIVE TEACHING AND LEARNING

Students as Shareholders

Chapter Outcomes

At the conclusion of this chapter you will be able to:

1. *Develop a context for teaching and learning that supports learners as active participants in their own education.*
2. *Provide experiences that promote the learner's ability to take responsibility for learning, think inductively and critically, and solve problems.*
3. *Use the reflective teaching strategies of inquiry and guided discovery.*

Key Terms and Concepts

Reflective Teaching Strategies Defined
How Reflective Is Your Classroom?
Climate of Trust
Constructivism
Valuing Students' Viewpoint and Thinking
Shareholders
Case Study
Active Participation
Brainstorming
Mapping
Inductive Thinking
Critical Thinking
Pyramid of Learning Experiences
Problem Solving
Reflective Teaching Strategies Inquiry
Special Needs Learners
Guided Discovery
Teacher Role

Q. *How do we solve complex problems in the future when the future is unknown?*
A. *You solve complex problems in the future by solving complex problems today.*
—Carl Rogers

INTRODUCTION

Have you ever patted yourself on the back thinking, "I did it," after assembling a new appliance that arrived without a set of directions? Have you ever smiled to yourself knowing, "I could explain that," as you listened to another person struggle to answer a question? Have you ever relaxed your face and neck muscles feeling, "Now I understand," while observing a situation similar to something previously studied? Have you ever resisted taking lessons being certain that, "I can learn it better on my own," because you've done it before and feel more comfortable with your own pace?

Reflective teaching strategies are approaches that support the kind of learning you have experienced if you answered yes to any of the above.

Definition

We are combining the characteristics of several descriptions to create our definition of *reflective teaching and learning strategies:* strategies that stimulate students to use experiences to discover learning for themselves. Their discoveries may lead to knowledge, understandings, skills, and attitudes. They may discover how to solve problems, answer questions, draw conclusions, and take responsibility for their own learning. These strategies reflect a philosophy of education that views the learner as a source of knowledge rather than a blank slate upon which the teacher inscribes information. Because the learner determines the content of learning, it is relevant and important to him or her. These strategies lead learners beyond basic skills to higher levels of thinking and complex reasoning. Brophy (1999) highlighted the term *thoughtfulness* to "summarize the qualities of the discourse observed in classrooms that best exemplify social construction of knowledge within learning communities" (p. 49).

Rationale

In the progressive education envisioned by John Dewey in the 1930s and 1940s, the problems to be studied in schools were created from the everyday needs, interests, and, most importantly, experiences of the students (Dewey, 1938). That kind of curriculum development process can lead to the relevance that students have always demanded and needed. More recently, Harste, Short, and Burke (1988) urged us to make students "curricular informants," that is, the source of ideas, information, and problems to be explored. In *Building COMMUNITY in Schools,* Sergiovanni (1994) referred to the importance of inquiry as a building process of community: "As we learn together and we inquire together, we create the ties that enable us to become a learning community" (p. 167). The reflective teaching strategies of this chapter support the learner role described by Sergiovanni, Brophy, and Harste and colleagues and the process Dewey envisioned.

In order to promote self-learning, your classroom context must be characterized by a climate of trust and the dimensions of constructivism. Learners will need to adjust to the role of shareholder in learning with expanded experiences and participation. The content of self-learning through reflective teaching strategies is not limited to any curricular area, but must include the processes of critical and inductive thinking as well as problem solving. Attention to the context, learner, and content will be important as you use the strategies of inquiry and guided discovery.

CONTEXT

The following survey will help assess the levels of reflection within the context of your classroom. If you are not currently teaching, this survey could be used as a guide for creating a context for a reflective classroom in the future.

How Reflective Is Your Classroom?

On a scale from 1 to 4, mark your classroom according to your response on the following statements and questions: 4 = very often occurs, 3 = often occurs, 2 = sometimes occurs, 1 = rarely occurs. A score of 45 or better would indicate that you are incorporating a reflective learning environment in the classroom.

1. Other sources of knowledge are used in addition to the teacher and the textbook. 1 2 3 4
2. Students are encouraged to think of different ways to solve problems. 1 2 3 4
3. Students' points of view and thinking are valued and encouraged. 1 2 3 4
4. Students have input into what they will learn. 1 2 3 4
5. Students help in constructing questions for tests. 1 2 3 4
6. Students are asked to explain their reasons for an answer. 1 2 3 4
7. Students use brainstorming, mapping, and other strategies to learn new material and solve problems. 1 2 3 4
8. Students are asked questions that require analysis, synthesis, and evaluation thought processes. 1 2 3 4

9.	Lessons present a balance between inductive and deductive teaching and student thinking.	1	2	3	4
10.	Students are encouraged to actively listen to each other.	1	2	3	4
11.	Content examples are drawn from student experiences and other classes.	1	2	3	4
12.	A range of structures for student learning are provided from guided discovery to independent inquiry.	1	2	3	4
13.	Students spend time working with others to learn.	1	2	3	4
14.	When faced with a time limitation, depth of learning is given priority over coverage of material.	1	2	3	4
15.	Assessment measures test the range of learning from information recall to analysis, synthesis, and evaluation thought processes.	1	2	3	4
16.	A climate of trust is established in the classroom.	1	2	3	4

Each of these 16 indicators is explored in this chapter. Of all the indicators, perhaps the last—a "climate of trust"—is the most important.

Climate of Trust

For students to be able to take the risks required of them to be sources of learning, they need classrooms that feel safe. Let's return to the ideas we suggested in Chapters Five and Six for communicating protection and respect for your students' ideas: active listening, class meetings, and encouragement to name a few. When Mrs. Hathaway's students held a class meeting about playground problems, Omar was not afraid to suggest a "playground patrol" as a solution. She knew that everyone's ideas would be accepted as possibilities. When Ms. Conley-Trombley's students heard, "You paid attention to detail in your sketch," they felt respected.

In Chapter Ten, we described the group norms that support a safe context—those of cooperation and respect. We suggested that your role is to promote and maintain the norms by prohibiting put-downs and discrimination, and by encouraging diverse opinions and ideas. Later, in Chapter Twelve, we will describe additional strategies for building a climate in which students can participate in roleplaying, simulations, and drama activities with comfort and trust.

We will now turn to some dimensions of constructivism—those that provide additional ways for you to support students as they develop ideas and solve problems.

Constructivism in Classrooms

Constructivism emerges from the observations of children at an early age as they construct knowledge from their world through various forms of interaction (touching, tasting, seeing, smelling, and hearing). From the constructivist's standpoint, knowledge is built by the child through active participation in real-life situations and interactions with the environments of home, school, community, and the world.

Constructivism in the classroom incorporates three important dimensions: (1) valuing the student's point of view, (2) using higher-level questions to elicit student thoughts (see Chapter Eight), and (3) valuing the process of student thinking rather than student answer or product.

Valuing the Students' Point of View

Students learn at an early age what adults expect to hear when they ask a question. Our favorite story is about a pastor giving a sermon to a group of children. She asked them to think about "something five or six inches high, sometimes brown and sometimes gray, with a big bushy tail, that scampers across the ground, climbs trees, and gathers nuts for the winter." Then she asked the children what it was. There was quiet. Finally, a child raised his hand and tentatively replied, "Well, ordinarily I'd think it was a squirrel, but I suppose you want me to say it was God" (Harste, Woodward, & Burke, 1984, p. xv).

You will need to encourage students to trust their own ideas in order to change established patterns like the one in our story. Your responses to their point of view can quickly communicate approval or disapproval. Listen to the following responses and decide which students feel valued for their thinking:

- "Giacomo, it sounds like you support the tax increase because it's a fair approach to cut the deficit."
- "Andrea, are you sure you want to approach the recycling problem with a voluntary system? Have you looked at all the options?"
- "Matt, you sound sure of your interpretation of this formula. Have you thought about your ideas carefully?"
- "Class, we heard Carol's three reasons for why we should move the gerbil cage to the other shelf. She has been thinking about this problem all week."

Other examples of valuing responses to students are provided in Chapter Eight (see Figure 8.1).

Valuing the Process of Student Thinking

Initially, your students may feel uncomfortable about responding, or unsure of how to provide reasons for their answers. Your patience and support will help them get started, and, in time, they will enjoy the opportunity to share their thinking processes. You will also benefit because teachers who practice this valuing process describe amazing student perspectives. Listen to Julie's ideas when asked about her thinking process:

TEACHER: What are the Nacirema people like?
JULIE: They are poor and not much like us.
TEACHER: What in the story caused you to think they were poor?
JULIE: They seemed to have many superstitions and usually poor people have more superstitions and they were afraid to throw away the charms. They do things differently than I do.
TEACHER: You drew some conclusions I had not thought about. We are going to look at the Nacirema people more closely and think about their superstitions. We will also look for signs of poverty.

You will read a story about the people of Nacirema later in the chapter. When you do, you will see that Julie made a leap from the story to her own information. Without asking her, "What caused you to think they were poor?" you would think that she misread the story. Notice that her teacher's response to her thinking acknowledged and valued the process.

Student explanations offer important information about students. They provide you with the opportunity to see some of their inner-most thoughts. Getting close to their perspectives will help you support their role as "shareholders," while at the same time, expand their experiences and their participation in the learning process.

LEARNER

Teacher-directed strategies such as lecture or recitation require little of your learners. Although Denise may be thinking about the proper nouns you are defining during your lecture, Timothy may be thinking about his baseball game from the previous night. Reflective teaching strategies promote active participation of students. They require students to attend more, to recall previously learned ideas, to draw on existing information, to analyze, to synthesize, to draw conclusions, and to find solutions. In sum, "complex learning requires activity on the part of the learner" (Corno & Snow, 1986, p. 620). In order to achieve the kind of participation we have described, we suggest the role of *shareholder* for students.

Learners as Shareholders

A study by Smith, Johnson, and Rhodes (1993) found that when the students were given a choice and freedom in designing a thematic unit, they actively engaged in content, language activities, social learning, and academic interaction. Adolescents are quite capable of successfully participating in their own learning processes that contribute to increased academic self-concept.

To promote a shareholder role (that is, one in which students share in the planning and decision making), you will need to seek student input at different levels of your teaching. We describe three levels of input for you.

Learner Input in Planning

When you plan instruction, student ideas provide valuable information about previous learning, curiosities, and confusions. Listen to teachers seek student input.

TEACHER TALK

Class, we are going to develop a list of questions that you would like answered when we study about the planets next month. Move into your planning groups and come up with a list.

Fourth-Grade Teacher

This is an outline of the study of nutrition for six weeks. What are some learning activities you would like to have to help you learn and understand more about nutrition?

Middle-School Health Teacher

Learner Input during Instruction

When you are conducting a lesson, it is essential to seek student input to make those in-flight decisions we described in Chapter Two. Learners can inform you about the pace, the difficulty, the interest, and the need for clarification. Listen as teachers check with the shareholders.

TEACHER TALK

Class, we are going to spend about five more minutes practicing this computation. Is that enough time?

We have been working through this process for two days. How does it feel?

Rate this activity with your group members. Record each person's feelings about difficulty, interest, and involvement.

Before we go on, give a thumbs up if you understand the assignment, and a thumbs down if you would like more explanation.

It looks like many of you are confused. Yes, Roseanne? Roseanne says, "I figured it out. Would you like me to explain how I reached a solution?"

Secondary Math Teacher and Student

In classrooms where students begin to take ownership for learning, students like Roseanne are not self-conscious about helping find solutions to problems and sharing their thought processes with others.

Learner Input in Assessment

When you are assessing what has been taught and learned, it is important to seek input from the learner. If you really want students to feel like shareholders in teaching and learning, it is important for them to have a voice in the entire process: in planning, during instruction, and in assessment. You, of course, will benefit with insights for future planning and instruction. And students may develop different attitudes about the assessment process if they feel like shareholders.

To seek learner input in assessment, you may ask them to develop some questions for a test and give their answers. The process of test construction brings students to higher levels of thinking. Teachers from second grade through college who have tried this approach report positive results. You may also interview them for their ideas about the topic studied, and request their critique of the assessment measure (test, project, or paper). Essay-type questions that ask students to "describe three new ideas you learned about nutrition" or "write about how you will use your new computation skills outside of school" provide opportunity for student input.

Seeking their ideas for *planning, instructing,* and *assessing* promotes the shareholder role for learners, and begins the process of expanding experiences and participation.

Expanding Experiences and Participation

Reflective teaching strategies require students to recognize what they know and think about, and to process new information and ideas independently. It will be important to assure that your learners have experiences from which they can process information and ideas. And it will be important to provide some practice in the participation required for their role.

Case Studies

The research vignette on page 314 is a case study of one third-grade teacher's transition from "teller" to facilitator of learning during mathematics instruction. The students became active participants in the learning of mathematics as the teacher changed her role in the way she taught and the way students learned mathematics in her classroom. The case study method of research provides for rich descriptions of single subjects. This method has been used for decades at the Harvard Business School for students to study flourishing companies and individuals. Books on successful practices in education and businesses examine several different types of single subjects to provide the reader with in-depth information on a particular topic.

Carl Rogers, credited with being one of the founders of humanistic psychology, used case studies of the human experience in the 1940s when psychology emphasized experimentation in the laboratory and studies of rat behavior as a predictor of everyday life. His book, *Freedom to Learn,* first written in 1969 and now in the third edition, documents student and teacher learning through case examples (Rogers & Freiberg, 1994). Tracy Kidder, in *Among Schoolchildren*, spent a school year in Ms. Zajac's fifth-grade classroom in Holyoke, Massachusetts. Kidder described the trials, frustrations, joys, and hope of one teacher and her children. Sara Lawrence Lightfoot, in *The Good High School,* described the inner workings of six high schools (four public and two private schools). What is a good learning tool for educators is also an important learning tool for students. Studying cases of history (the original Lincoln-Douglas debates) or mathematics (one or two mathematical problems for an entire period) will give the students needed depth along with breadth. Because a good case analysis involves considering alternatives in decision making, case studies can help to develop free thinking and creativity (Poon Teng Fatt, 1998).

Two more activities for expanding experiences and student participation are *brainstorming* and *mapping.* These two activities have produced independent thinking and the kind of reflection for which the shareholder role is designed. They are reasonably easy to implement in the classroom and are appropriate for learners from kindergarten to university classrooms.

Active Participation

This strategy is used to promote overt (easily seen) participation by students. It involves behavior such as writing, identifying, and responding with gestures. For example,when teaching a lesson about parts of speech, you may ask students to turn to a partner and give an example of a noun. When teaching a lesson in geology, you may ask students to write a term for a description you provide. When teaching a math computation process, you may ask students to hold up the number of fingers that corresponds to their answer.

A study conducted by Pratton and Hales (1986) to determine if active learning improved on-task learning and achievement supported an active learning approach for teaching mathematics to fifth-grade students. Five teachers received in-service in active learning strategies. They taught 30-minute lessons on simple probability to *all* the fifth-grade classes (20 classes, 500 students) in a suburban school district. Each of the five teachers taught four classes, two using active participation and two using traditional methods.

To illustrate the differences in their teaching, one problem from the lesson plan was: "There are 5 checkers in a bag, 3 red and 2 black; what are my chances of getting a red?" (p. 212) In the nonactive lesson, the teacher worked the problem on the board, whereas in the active lesson, the teacher asked the students to work the problem and hold up the number of fingers corresponding to their answer. The teacher then visually checked their responses.

All the students were given a test at the end of the lesson. The class mean for students in the active learning lessons ranged from 78.4 to 87.2 percent, as compared to the nonactive class mean of 71.3 to 77.0 percent correct responses. In all cases, the class means were higher for the active participation group. The researchers noted that active participation allowed teachers to quickly monitor student understanding and promoted student thinking and responding in overt ways.

One word of caution: Simply allowing students to take a more hands-on approach to their learning is not enough. For active learning to be most effective, students should be given the opportunity to reflect on their activity in order to construct meaning from the experience (Wheatley, 1992).

Brainstorming

This activity needs a few ground rules if it is to promote participation and experience for all students. First, all ideas must be accepted. Second, the activity must be fast paced, like a "storm of the brain." Third, the ideas need to be recorded, and fourth, some of the ideas must be used. The following Snapshot provides a look at brainstorming used after an incident in which two students were nearly hit by a car. Notice the ground rules being established and followed.

SNAPSHOT: Elementary Classroom

The third-grade students in Mr. Gindele's class are talking among themselves about the near accident with excitement and anxiety in their voices. "Class, let's talk together about what happened to our friends yesterday. We know that the intersection of Vista and Sherwood is a very busy place, and the only help we have for crossing is a stop sign. Since so many of you use that route to go home, I would like us to work on the problem. We will begin by brainstorming suggestions for making the situation more safe. Remember to let yourself think of everything possible. We want to hear everyone's ideas. Rick, will you record ideas from this side of the room? Mei Ling, will you record ideas from this side of the room? Now spend a quiet minute getting suggestions ready." (pause) "OK, begin."

Every student's idea was recorded, and the process continued until the hum of brainstorming became still. Within three minutes, the lists were full. Some of the suggestions were:

Have students wear a red patch on their jackets so cars can see them.
Hire a crossing guard at the intersection.
Ask students to change their route home.
Ask older students to join a safety patrol for the intersection.
Ask a police officer to present a lesson on traffic safety.
Send a letter to the city council, asking them to add a stop light to the intersection.
Ask students' parents to drive them to and from school.
Have students take the bus.

Many other possibilities were listed. From there, Mr. Gindele asked one group to categorize the suggestions into long term and short term, one group to categorize the suggestions into practical and impractical, and one group to identify the five ideas that sounded safest. Following the group work, decisions were made about the "best" way to begin, and students volunteered spontaneously to carry out various responsibilities.

Elementary Research Vignette

INTRODUCTION

Redefining Student Learning, a book edited by Hermine Marshall (1992), presents research case studies that focus on reform efforts to define classrooms as places where learning for understanding is valued and practiced. This is in contrast to the common view of classrooms where students complete work for external reasons. The book is divided into eleven chapters, each presenting another research perspective on how learning that is meaningful to students can be constructed. This research vignette describes the case study research of Penelope L. Peterson (1992) in "Revising Their Thinking: Keisha Coleman and Her Third-Grade Mathematics Class." Peterson observed Keisha Coleman (pseudonym) and her students for a one-year period, as Coleman began to transform the way she taught and the way students learned mathematics in her classroom.

STUDY DESIGN

Beginning in October and concluding in the spring, the author spent at least one day a week in Keisha Coleman's third-grade classroom observing her teaching and the students learning. Peterson wrote narrative descriptions of what she observed and documented written work on the board and from the students. Teacher and student verbal interactions for each lesson observed were audiotaped and later transcribed. Ms. Coleman was also interviewed by Peterson using an open-ended question format. The interviews focused on how Ms. Coleman constructed her mathematics lessons, her thinking about mathematics, and her thinking about teaching and learning mathematics in the classroom. Students were interviewed three times during the year for one to two hours each in October, January, and June. The interviews were designed to explore student solutions to mathematics problems posed by the interviewer and the students' thinking about these problems. The goal was to explore the depth of understanding of mathematics ideas and concepts throughout the year and to determine student attitudes toward mathematics.

STUDY RESULTS

Ms. Coleman, who had taught 15 years, used materials developed from the Comprehensive School Mathematics Program (CSMP) in her third-grade classroom for a three-year period. The CSMP curriculum focused on problem solving and student verbalization of their mathematical thinking. The program also provided students with tools and manipulatives to understand mathematics (e.g., string pictures, Venn diagrams, and a modern-day abacus). Peterson first observed that Ms. Coleman had a strong dependence on the CSMP teacher's guide. "She held the CSMP teacher's guide in her hand while she was teaching, and she seemed to be reading from the guide much of the time" (p. 157).

During the year, Ms. Coleman began the slow transition from teller to facilitator of learning—mathematical coverage took a back seat to mathematical understanding. As Peterson observed, "Ms. Coleman focused on solving mathematical problems and discussing students' solutions and explanations. Students worked on one or two mathematical problems for the whole period" (p. 170). Ms. Coleman began to realize that she could teach mathematics on any particular day: "and two weeks down the road, the kids didn't even remember one iota of what we dealt with" (p. 169). Students were asked to explain their answers and when an answer was given, the class was asked to respond to the method a student used to arrive at the answer. Interviews with Keisha Coleman indicated that she stopped anticipating what the student should say; "rather, I'm taking what they're giving me and building upon that" (p. 171).

Ms. Coleman gradually began to expand the mathematical knowledge in the classroom to go beyond teacher and textbook as the sole source to include her students. Peterson noted that Coleman discovered the "use of student ideas" as an important source for new knowledge and active engagement by the students. Students began to construct their own meaning for mathematics—one shared with the entire class. Coleman was making the transition from "teaching as telling" to facilitator of learning.

CONCLUSIONS AND IMPLICATIONS FOR PRACTICE

Reflective learning requires an expanded repertoire of teaching strategies and understandings. The shift from teacher telling—from being the primary source of information for students to being one of several sources of information—requires a different way of thinking as well as teaching in the classroom. This study of one teacher gives insight into the pathways teachers can take in building a learning partnership with students. Ms. Coleman had the wisdom to seek knowledge from others, including observing two colleagues in her school who were using a reflective learning approach, attending seminars and workshops on reflective learning, and participating in committees that made decisions about the new mathematics curriculum. Her experience of 15 years was both a blessing and a hindrance. She had the experience and confidence to know that what she was doing needed improvement, but she also had a great deal to unlearn.

For some additional ideas on brainstorming, review the strategies suggested in Chapter Eight. Those ideas will also be helpful for the next topic—mapping.

Mapping

This activity provides a visual image for learners as they think about and build relationships between ideas. In Figure 11.1, a student visualized the term *feudalism* as having three categories: guilds, kings, and church. From those "big ideas" about feudalism, he worked through "small ideas," such as fairs, monks, and manors. Another way of describing the picture in Figure 11.1 is a progression from main headings to subheadings, or from general to specific.

To use mapping with your students, start with simple examples. Have your students suggest words or terms related to feudalism, then write their suggestions in a format of relationships. In the example, crafts are related to guilds, and apprentice and journeymen are related to crafts.

Another example will help you see how relationships can be illustrated with mapping. In the map shown in Figure 11.2, a first-grade teacher began with the word *spring* in preparation for a creative writing project. As you can see, young children come up with relationships quite different from those that you and I might build.

Mapping is an interesting way for students to process a story, a historical event, or a math problem. In the Samples and Examples section at the end of this chapter, we provide a format for mapping about a story or book character that is appropriate for secondary students.

When McTighe and Lyman (1988) reviewed the research on mapping, they found it successful in improving learner retention of information. Their findings also yielded guidelines for your use of the process:

1. *Aid memory by giving tangible cues,* allowing students to focus more quickly on a topic or problem, and providing a visual representation of concepts.
2. *Provide a common frame of reference* by offering common terminology (heading, subheading) and specific cues for action (individual, small, or large group).
3. *Provide an incentive to act* by having students write out their thoughts, allowing teachers to see the results of the thought processes.

FIGURE 11.1 *Mapping Example 1*

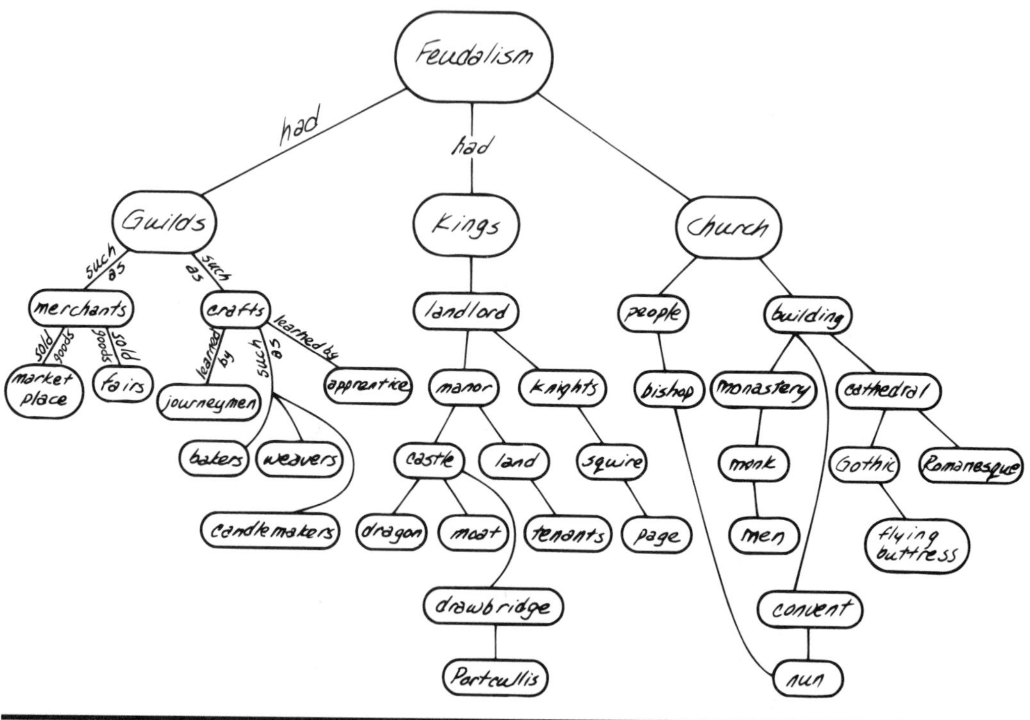

Source: From *Learning How to Learn* by J. Novak and D. Gowan, 1984, London: Cambridge University Press. Copyright 1984 by Cambridge University Press. Reprinted by permission.

4. *Create permanence by imprinting in the mind* a variety of mapping options for transfer to other situations.

When Stahl and Vancil (1986/1987) studied student use of mapping, they concluded that it was important for teachers to discuss the relationship between the words during the mapping process. So, a fifth guideline is:

5. *Promote relationships between ideas and information by questioning and discussion during mapping.*

Seeing, for many students, enhances understanding. In order to help students organize, analyze, and evaluate their representations, Hyerle (1995/1996) developed eight related visual tools he calls *thinking maps*:

Circle map. *Helps define word or things in context and presents points of view*
Bubble map. *Describes emotional, sensory, and logical qualities*

FIGURE 11.2 *Mapping Example 2*

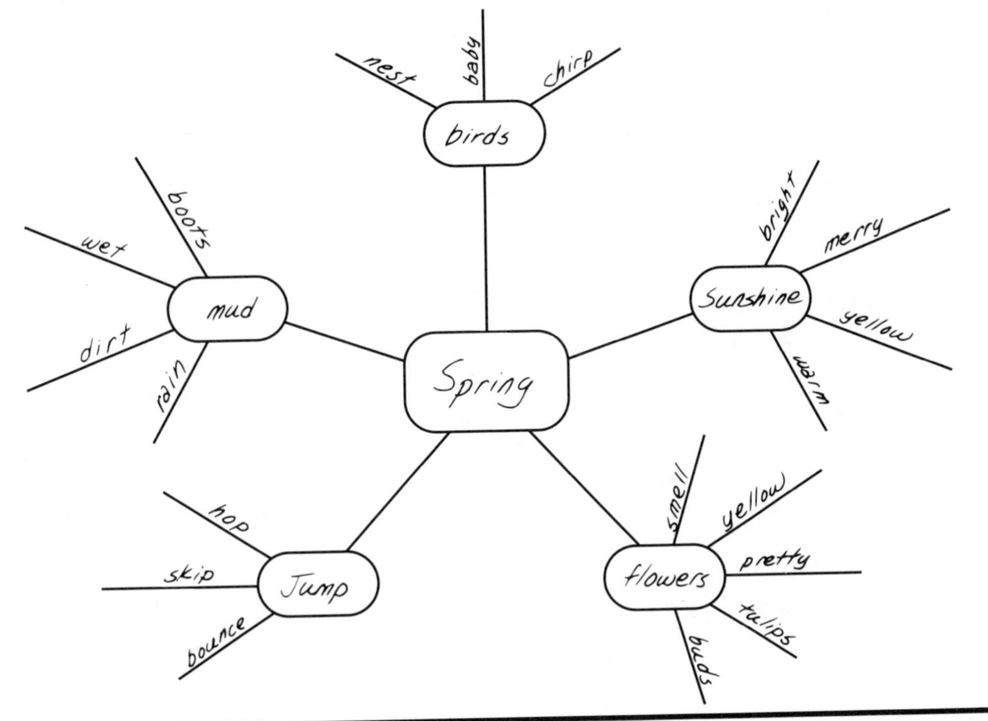

Double bubble map. *Compares and contrasts qualities*
Tree map. *Shows the relationships between main ideas and supporting details*
Flow map. *Shows events as a sequence*
Multi-flow map. *Shows causes and effects and helps predict outcomes*
Brace map. *Shows physical structures and part-whole relationships*
Bridge map. *Helps to transfer or form analogies and metaphors (p. 85)*

Sample templates of these maps are included in the Samples and Examples section of this chapter.

Hyerle (1995/1996) reported that the elementary and junior high schools in North Carolina that used this strategy schoolwide in 1993–94 found significant increases in holistic writing test scores over successive years. Teachers with second-language students also found the mappings very effective for helping students visualize patterns of thinking from one language to another. Students with learning disabilities who are taught to use cognitive mapping demonstrate greater gains in both recall and comprehension of material (Boyle, 1996). In order to maximize the impact of mapping for students with special needs, students should be taught how to generalize mapping techniques to other academic areas and materials.

As learners gain experience and expand their participation through brainstorming and mapping, they take on an authentic shareholder role in teaching and learning. They contribute to their own success in achieving understanding and skill. As we proceed to the content of reflective teaching strategies, you will see how important that success is for learners in today's world.

CONTENT

Whether you are teaching a senior high-school economics course or a second-grade math lesson, the content of reflective teaching strategies is universal across the curriculum. Students will be developing inductive and critical thinking as well as problem-solving abilities.

Inductive Thinking

One approach to learning is through the deductive thinking of the teacher—that is, telling students facts, rules, principles, or generalizations, and then providing practice. Teaching the process of inductive thinking, however, requires you to provide students with a series of related examples or experiences, and supporting them emotionally and intellectually to discover the rules, principles, or generalizations. In this way, your students can create new knowledge from existing ideas and information.

Providing Experiences for Inductive Thinking

The type of experiences you create depends on the development of your learners; you will need to provide a range of experiences from which they produce ideas. The Pyramid of Learning Experiences in Figure 11.3 provides a representation of experiences that move from concrete to abstract, thus encouraging inductive thinking.

Young students need direct contact and experiences (e.g., a visit to the farm) and visual representations (e.g., photos of people from another culture). Older students gain experience from written symbols (e.g., a novel about Asian culture) and verbal symbols (e.g., a lecture on fusion), while continuing to need the more concrete experiences at the base of the cone.

Drawing Inferences from Experiences

A lesson on gravity in an inductive classroom would have students testing the law of physics related to objects of different weights falling at the same speed. They may decide to drop a five-pound rock and a tennis ball from the top of a building at the same time, then develop their own inferences about the nature of gravity and the influence of shape on the rate of acceleration of an object.

Less exciting but appropriate for younger students is an experience with oranges, apples, pears, and grapes. After tasting and examining the seeds, 5-year-olds begin to define fruit as "something sweet, with seeds in the middle, and a skin on the outside." Later, their definition is expanded with categories of fruit as they taste and examine bananas, kiwi, and pineapple.

Critical Thinking

This process begins with questioning by you and by your students. Together, you engage in analysis, synthesis, and evaluation of events, information, and ideas. The kind

FIGURE 11.3 *Pyramid of Learning Experiences*

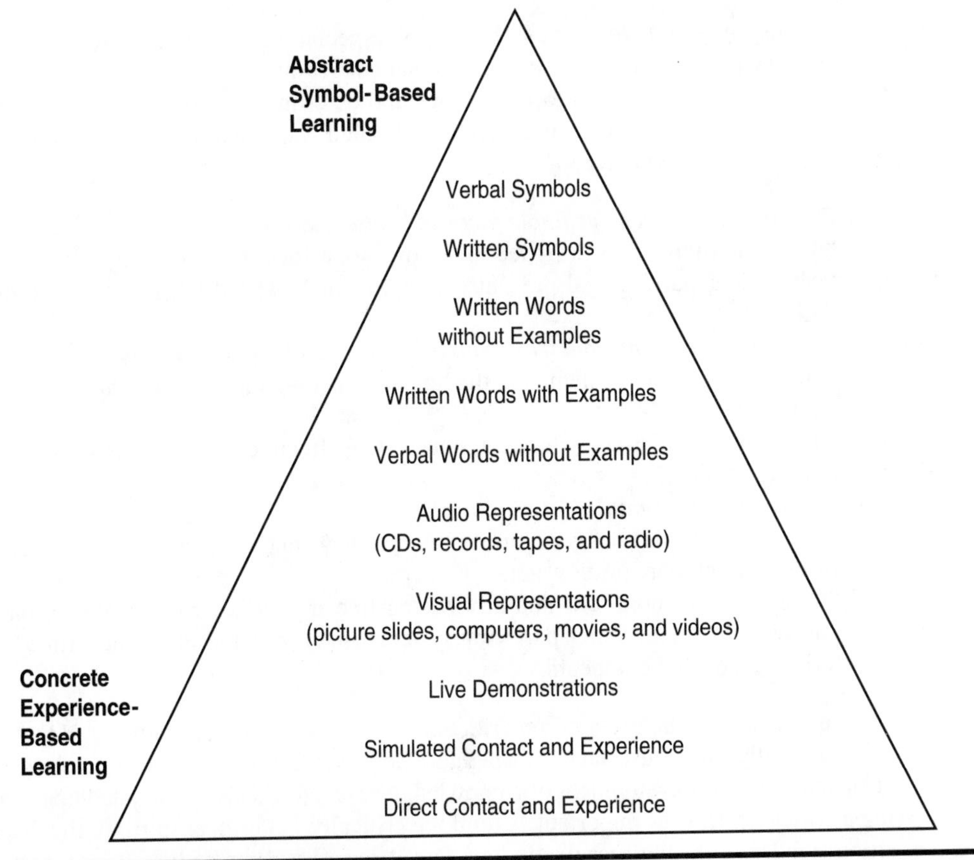

Source: Adapted from *Audio-Visual Methods in Teaching* (rev. ed.) (p. 43) by E. Dale, 1954, New York: Dryden.

of thinking you do before making a major purchase is critical, because you look at options, weigh the advantages and disadvantages, determine the value of your choice, and reach a conclusion.

Critical thinking is a process for determining the value of an idea, a concept, a solution, or information. Beyer (1988) provided a list of eight actions you and your students could use to determine the worth of a statement or idea:

1. *Distinguishing between verifiable facts and value claims.*
2. *Distinguishing relevant from irrelevant information, claims, or reasons.*
3. *Determining the factual accuracy of a statement.*
4. *Determining the credibility of a source.*
5. *Identifying ambiguous claims or arguments.*
6. *Identifying unstated assumptions.*

7. *Detecting bias.*
8. *Determining the strength of an argument or a claim. (p. 27)*

The list of actions for critical thinking is especially relevant to the needs of students faced with today's advertising. Consumer curriculum activities provide even very young children opportunities to detect bias and determine the factual accuracy of a statement. Look at the advertising claims for bottled water and purifying systems and use your critical thinking to:

1. *Distinguish between verifiable facts and value claims.*
   "This water purifier is designed to remove impurities from drinking water."
   "This water purifier will prevent cancer for those who drink from this product daily."
2. *Distinguish relevant from irrelevant information, claims, or reasons.*
   "Our water purifier system is in the homes of people just like you throughout the United States."
   "The water purifier uses charcoal, which is an effective source of removing common impurities."
3. *Determine the credibility of a source.*
   "In interviews with many of our customers, they state the health benefits derived from drinking our spring water."
   "A report from nonprofit and advertising-free magazines for consumers raises concerns that many water-purifying systems attached to the sink concentrate bacteria, which can be unhealthy."

In a review of the research on critical thinking, Norris (1985) concluded that "to think critically, one must have knowledge." So, your first responsibility to students' critical thinking is development of a knowledge base. Norris also concluded that "having a critical spirit is as important as thinking critically." A critical spirit, or the disposition (tendency) to think critically, is relevant for all aspects of life. It may require more sophistication to promote spirit than to provide a knowledge base, especially when students begin examining and questioning your ideas. As you promote this content of your reflective teaching, check your own awareness and ability to be open to critical thinking from your learners. The same sensitivity to thinking different from your own will be important as you teach the content of problem solving.

Problem Solving

Problem solving is one application or product of critical thinking. Once you make a conclusion about the value of information or ideas, you can use the information or ideas to solve a problem. The following list represents the most common steps used in problem solving:

1. Identify and describe the problem.
2. Gather information and/or possible responses.

3. Design a plan or solution.
4. Try out a plan or solution.
5. Check the results of the plan or solution.
6. Determine the effectiveness and select alternative plans if needed.

In an age when standardized test scores are driving many instructional decisions, you may be tempted to choose more conventional methods rather than take the time to construct a problem-based lesson. However, by fostering reflection, problem-based learning can lead to even greater student learning outcomes (Wheatley, 1992). Studies conducted with 93 kindergarten children by Glaubman, Glaubman, and Ofir (1997) found that students at this young age who had specific instruction could develop high-quality questions and self-questioning strategies to produce greater self-directed learning.

When students have not had experience with problem solving, you may have to develop the skills step by step. The "Finding an Apartment" exercise in the Samples and Examples section at the end of this chapter provides practice in steps 2 and 3. In the Snapshot presented earlier in this chapter, Mr. Gindele could have asked, "What is the problem?" before beginning the brainstorm. His students may struggle with, "Our friends nearly got hurt," and "Drivers aren't careful," and "I can't always see the cars coming," before arriving at, "The intersection of Vista and Sherwood is not safe" as the problem. The simplest strategy for achieving step 1 with students is to *ask* rather than tell whenever a problem situation arrives.

Once students have some beginning experiences, they can practice with classroom problems or community situations independently or as a group. Some examples of real-life problems that make sense to students include:

Needing money to finance a class trip
Vandalism on the school playground
Unattractive school hallways
Inefficient school lunch lines
Crowded conditions at the classroom resource shelves
Stray pets near the school grounds
Not enough puzzles for everyone

In Chapter Six, you watched a parent/teacher conference in which problem solving occurred. You also observed the class meeting about playground problems in Ms. Hathaway's room described in the Snapshot. Review the two illustrations to better understand how to use problem solving. Once you have learned the process, it can be modified by you and your students. Again, your acceptance and valuing of student ideas and the suggestions for promoting learners as shareholders will work toward competence in problem solving.

Not all of the content of reflective teaching strategies has relevance for learners and depends on their input. Notice that your teaching focuses on questioning and discussion techniques. You will continue to use those strategies as you teach with the reflective teaching strategies of inquiry and guided discovery.

REFLECTIVE TEACHING STRATEGIES

The two strategies discussed in this section, inquiry and guided discovery, are separated for in-depth description because they require a more subtle role for teachers. Their use requires indirect interaction with students but extensive preparation for the interaction. You are a kind of undercover agent with these strategies; that is, your work is not immediately recognized or easily noticed. Be ready to devote time to these strategies. The use of inquiry and guided discovery in your classroom continues your support of the shareholder role for students, and promotes inductive and critical thinking and problem solving.

Inquiry Approaches

Children are natural inquirers. They find something puzzling and they explore it for information. Teachers of young children need only to support the natural curiosity of students. However, as students get older, you may have to create conditions that stimulate an inquiring nature.

Steps of the Scientific Method of Inquiry

The following are six steps of the process that your students may follow when you teach with inquiry:

1. Forming and refining a question they wish to answer
2. Collecting instances and observing facts likely to be related to a possible answer
3. Putting facts or instances into a class or classes, and making generalizations about them
4. Making intelligent guesses (hypotheses) based on the facts to suggest possible explanations
5. Testing to see which hypothesis, if any, is the correct one
6. Using the new information as a basis for further reasoning

The following example from a 1917 textbook on science teaching (LaRue, pp. 16–18) serves as an excellent illustration of the process we are describing. The question to be answered is: What is the cause of dew? Before answering the question, we must know precisely what we mean by *dew.* Is it the moisture found sometimes on the outside of a pitcher, or on windows, or on waterpipes? We end up with the definition of "the moisture that gathers on any substance exposed in the open air, when there is no rain or other apparent source for the dampness."

Our second step is to *get all possible facts with observations and experiments.* We notice that dew gathers on substances that are dry inside, substances that are damp, and objects that are under cover; it gathers on upper surfaces; and there is no dew on very cloudy nights.

Next, we *generalize* (that is, gather up our facts from all our observations) and notice that dew forms most freely on clear nights. Now, we make guesses, *hypotheses,* as to the probable cause of dew. With each hypothesis, we test it with what we know from our observations. Some examples are:

1. Dew may fall from the sky, as rain does. (No, this can't be because clear nights brought more dew than cloudy nights, and dew formed on our water pitcher, under cover, where anything like rain was out of the question.)
2. Dew may be forced out of the object on which it forms. (No, dew formed on objects that were dry through and through.)
3. Dew may come from the air and settle on objects. (But why does it not form on all objects all the time? We recall the coldness of dewed objects as compared with the temperature of the surrounding air. We know that cold contracts most things. Maybe it contracts the air and squeezes out the moisture, which then settles on whatever is near.)

We now have a hypothesis that the cooling of moist air by a comparatively cold object squeezes out particles of moisture and the particles unite to form drops on the object. We don't expect to find dew on objects that are warmer than the air, nor on any object surrounded by perfectly dry air. We experiment further and find that this third hypothesis holds under every test we can devise. We may use this "new truth" to answer further questions like, "Is there dew on the moon?" or "Could there be dew if there were no air?"

Teaching the Steps of Inquiry

As we suggested with mapping and problem solving, you may need to begin simply or with the individual steps of inquiry. The experience described in this Teacher Talk illustrates the work of a class on steps 1 and 2 (forming and refining questions to answer) and collecting instances and observing facts related to possible answers.

TEACHER TALK

It was December and we were studying the history of religions in our middle-school social studies class. I asked students what holidays were approaching. Many said, "Christmas." I asked if there were others. One student said, "Chanukah" (mispronouncing the word). I restated the word, using the correct pronunciation, and asked if they could tell me something about the holiday. It was quiet. The bell was about to ring. I suggested that they find out about Chanukah for our next class.

The next day, as class began, the students seemed anxious. Before I could ask, several students volunteered that they found out about Chanukah (pronouncing it correctly). They talked about the "holiday of lights," the story of the oil lasting eight days, the fight for freedom that the holiday represented, and the gift-giving customs. Some students had talked with their parents, two had called the local synagogue and asked for information, and others went to the library and looked up the holiday. There was a sense of pride as they described their searches for information.

Their experience with this "new knowledge" was a perfect start for their next assignment. They had two weeks to explore questions about religion, getting ready for a scheduled panel of experts. I had arranged for a Baptist minister, a Catholic priest, and a Jewish rabbi to come to class to discuss and respond to questions.

After much research in the library and discussions among individual students, the students were prepared for dialogue with the panel. The scheduled 45 minutes went on (with principal approval and extension) to an hour and a half. The three clergy indicated that they were totally impressed at the level of student questions. I was thrilled with the pride in students' eyes and the high level of thinking I observed that afternoon and for weeks after.

Sixth-Grade Teacher

The Teachers' Role in Inquiry

In inquiry, your role is quite different from the one you take when lecturing or conducting a demonstration. This role is like an iceberg. Only a small part of the effort is evident above the surface if viewed by the casual observer. Much work has been completed by the teacher before entering the classroom, and more work accompanies the student activity. The efforts are focused on creating the conditions necessary for a successful experience. The sixth-grade teacher in the preceding Teacher Talk guided students as they researched their questions, met with the principal to check policies related to the nature of the discussion and the panel members, scheduled the visits of the clergy, and briefed them on their roles.

Remember the climate of trust and respect we described early in this chapter? The climate in the sixth-grade classroom was one in which the students felt comfortable

seeking answers and raising questions without worry of being considered silly or stupid. Groundwork for the dialogue with the panel members had focused on students' listening to each other, pride in the group, and respect for diversity of opinion.

Did you notice that several weeks went into preparation for the panel? Probably for weeks afterwards, the processing of ideas and information continued. The climate and skills necessary for inquiry require time for development. The same conditions apply when you use guided discovery.

Learners with Special Needs

Students with learning disabilities often misjudge their academic skills (Meltzer, Roditi, Houser, & Perlman, 1998). By adding reflection to your teaching and student learning, the level and complexity of student understanding will develop and students will more accurately perceive their strengths and weaknesses and help channel their efforts to improve. Marlowe and Page (1998) suggested a Think Aloud Program suitable for whole-class instruction that teaches self-talk strategies for solving a range of problems. The program consists of sets of questions students can ask themselves as they set about to learn:

- Identifying problems ("What am I to do? How can I find out?")
- Choosing a plan or strategy ("How can I do it? What are some plans?")
- Self-monitoring ("Am I using my plan?")
- Self-evaluation ("Is my plan working? How did I do? Do I need a new plan?")

The questions may be placed on a bookmark made from card stock by each student. Pictures may be substituted for words for 4- to 6-year-olds to stimulate thinking.

Guided Discovery

This strategy requires that you "examine the cognitive structure of the concepts to be taught and create a series of experiences for students to explore and discover the concepts for themselves" (Simon, 1986, p. 41). For example, when preparing to teach the concept and skill of estimation, you think about the definition of *estimation,* purposes of estimation, a variety of ways of estimating, situations in which estimation is appropriate and inappropriate, and some real-life examples of estimation.

The first experience you might provide would involve the placement of a large jar of jelly beans on display with a sign urging students to estimate how many. From there, a sequence of experiences would gradually guide students to discover that estimation is appropriate for some uses, that estimation is a calculated guess, that there are a number of ways to estimate, and so on.

Steps in Guided Discovery

This strategy draws on prior learning of students and requires active student participation toward a solution or an understanding. The following steps provide a framework for conducting guided discovery:

1. *Present a problem, question, or situation that is interesting or exciting, and will provoke student questions.*

2. *Ask students to define or explain terms, working toward a precise definition of the problem, question, or situation to be studied.*
3. *Aid students in the formulation of specific questions to focus the inquiry and facilitate the collection of data.*
4. *Guide students toward a variety of sources, including yourself and your students, to provide necessary data.*
5. *Assist students in checking the data by clarifying statements or judgments about the problem or situation.*
6. *Support the development of a number of solutions, from which choices can be made.*
7. *Provide opportunity for feedback and revision. Assist in testing the effectiveness of solutions.*
8. *Support the development of a plan of action. (Freiberg, 1973a)*

The context for these steps must be one of openness, and one in which students have consistent opportunities and encouragement to think and develop alternatives. The story of the People of Nacirema provides an ideal step 1 as you see students listen to the story and show interest in the people. Read the story (in Figure 11.4 on page 327) and then watch the fifth-grade students in the next Snapshot as they follow the steps of guided discovery.

SNAPSHOT: Elementary Classroom

After reading the story together, Ms. Stanich worked with her students to underline words that needed explanation. The students were then asked to write two questions they had about the people of Nacirema. They had a library period during which they could search for information and definitions. A collection of resources on other cultures was set up in the classroom.

The next day, students worked in pairs, reading the story again and then drawing what they thought the Naciremans would look like. The students presented their drawings to the class, and the class asked questions. After much discussion of the "weird ways" of the Naciremans and some laughter, Ms. Stanich suggested that students take the word *Nacirema* and rearrange the letters backwards, which then spelled *American.* Once the students saw the connection, the sounds of discovery rippled through the classroom. This was followed by a discussion about their perceptions of other cultures and the biases that accompanied experiences with different ways.

Later, the students brainstormed ways to find better information about different cultures and to avoid stereotypes. They decided that they needed to share their discovery with other classes in the school, so they developed a slide tape about respecting other cultures and understanding your own biases.

Advantages of Guided Discovery

Notice again the time-consuming quality of the guided discovery strategy and the need to simultaneously use a number of strategies. On the surface, this kind of teaching looks easy, but, as in inquiry, you are a skillful "undercover agent," making sure that

FIGURE 11.4 *The People of Nacirema*

Anthropologists are so familiar with the many ways in which different groups of people behave, even the most exotic customs don't surprise them. Let's look at the Nacireman people, a group whose beliefs and practices show just how far human behavior can go.

The Nacireman culture has a highly developed economy. Although many people spend most of their time carrying on the business which makes up the economy, a large part of each day is spent in ritual activities. Their many rituals have to do with the human body. The people are very much concerned about their health and appearance. They believe that the body is ugly and is likely to become weak and diseased. This belief, itself, is not strange. However, the customs that surround this belief are what make it so unusual.

The Naciremans believe that because man is imprisoned in such a weak sickly body, man's only hope of life is through the powerful influences of his rituals and ceremonies. Every household has one or more shrines for this purpose. The more powerful people may have several shrines. In fact, many people feel the more shrines a family has, the richer it is.

The main item in the shrine is a box or chest that is built into the wall. In these chests are magical potions. No Nacireman believes he could live without these charms and potions. These things are gathered from many special people. The most powerful of these people are the medicine men. Help from a medicine man must be repaid with expensive gifts. The medicine men do not actually give the potions to their clients. What they do is decide what the client needs, and then write that down in a secret language. This writing is only understood by the medicine men and the herbalists, who for another gift will give the client the charm he needs.

The charm is not thrown away after its use. Instead it is placed in the charm box in the household shrine. Because there are different charms for different problems, the charm box is usually full to overflowing. There are often so many charms in the charm box, that the Naciremans are afraid to use them again, but we get the idea they believe that just keeping the charm in the house will protect the worshipers.

Beneath the charm box is a small font; each day, one-at-a-time, each member of the family enters the shrine room, bows his head before the charm box, mixes holy water in the font, and does a short rite for cleansing. The holy water comes from the water temple of the community, where priests conduct ceremonies to make the water pure.

Just below the medicine men in importance are specialists known as the "holy mouth men." The Naciremans are almost mad when it comes to the mouth. They believe that the condition of the mouth has a supernatural effect on their relationships with people.

If it weren't for the holy mouth rituals, they believe that their teeth would fall out, their gums would bleed, their friends would desert them. In order to prevent all this from happening, they have one rite that is quite unusual. Each day they put what looks like a small bundle of hog hairs in their mouths along with some magic powder and move this all around. Doing this, they believe, is what saves them.

Besides that mouth rite they see a holy mouth man at least twice a year. These men have a frightening set of tools. These tools are used in an unbelievable ritual that at times is very painful. The holy mouth man uses these tools on decayed teeth. He makes holes in the teeth a little larger and puts in a magic substance. If there are not holes, the holy mouth man makes one. The Naciremans believe that this will help them win friends. In spite of how painful this rite is, it is so important that the Naciremans return to the holy mouth man year-after-year.

There is another ritual which is performed only by men. In this one, the men scrape and cut their faces each day. A rite by women includes having them bake their heads in a small oven for about an hour.

The Naciremans actually seem to enjoy pain. Looking at them from the safety of our civilization, we feel sorry for them, but we must understand that before we could be who we are today we were much like the Naciremans.

Source: From "Body Ritual Among the Nacirema" by H. Miner. Reproduced by permission of the American Anthropological Association from *American Anthropologist, 58*:3, June 1956. Not for sale or further reproduction.

students are guided to their discoveries. With those challenges in mind, we point out the advantages of guided discovery:

1. Most students become more motivated due to greater participation in the learning process.
2. Students have the opportunity to think at more complex levels.
3. Students learn how to seek out information from a variety of sources to solve problems or develop ideas.
4. Students learn to be proactive learners producing new ideas and knowledge.

Your Role in Guided Discovery

You may have realized by now that the iceberg analogy is appropriate again. The role looks simple and easy, but below the surface, you have planned experiences, provided materials, and maintained a clear picture of the sequence and direction for which you have prepared (Houston, Clift, Freiberg, & Warner, 1988). When students discover irrelevant information, you may allow them to go off in an unintended direction, and later support their own redirection. You patiently allow the process of discovery to occur, maintaining the indirect role of guide.

SUMMARY

Reflective teaching strategies can elevate the level of intellectual processing and interaction in your classroom, and make learning more relevant to your students' lives (Oser, Dick, & Patry, 1992). To achieve these goals, we remind you of the following:

1. Develop a *context* for teaching and learning that supports learners as active participants in their own education. The development must attend to a *climate of trust* and the dimensions of *constructivism.*
2. Provide experiences that promote the *learners'* abilities to take responsibility for learning. Support them in a *shareholder* role by providing opportunities for input in planning, during instruction, and in assessment. *Expand their experiences and participation* through the strategies of active participation, brainstorming, and mapping.
3. Provide experiences that teach the *content* of inductive and critical thinking, and problem solving.
4. Use the reflective teaching strategies of *inquiry* and *guided discovery.*

We remind you that the activities and strategies of this chapter will take a greater amount of preparation and time than other more direct teaching strategies. You may feel insecure in your role in these strategies, because you must let go of your direct control of the teaching process. Often, it will not feel comfortable to step back as learners direct their own learning, produce their own knowledge, and develop a high level of competence. Have courage and take risks—because you may get to experience the kind of teaching and learning that drew you to the profession. You read about a sixth-grade teacher in this chapter describe the "thrill" when observing student pride and their high level of thinking. Our hope is for you to feel that same excitement as you use the reflective teaching strategies.

REFERENCES

Beyer, B. (1988). Developing a scope and sequence for thinking skills instruction. *Educational Leadership, 45*(7), 27.

Boyle, J. R. (1996). The effects of a cognitive mapping strategy on the literal and inferential comprehension of students with mild disabilities. *Learning Disability Quarterly, 19*(2), 86–98.

Brophy, J. E. (1999). Perspective of classroom management: Yesterday, today and tomorrow. In Jerome Freiberg (Ed.), *Beyond behaviorism: Changing the classroom management paradigm.* Boston: Allyn and Bacon.

Corno, L., & Snow, R. E. (1986). Adapting teaching to individual differences in learners. In M. Wittrock (Ed.), *Handbook for research on teaching* (3rd ed.). New York: Macmillan.

Dewey, J. (1938). *Experience and education.* New York: Collier.

Freiberg, H. J. (1973a). Inquiry approach. In W. R. Houston & S. C. White (Eds.), *Professional development modules.* Houston: Professional Development Center, College of Education, University of Houston.

Freiberg, H. J. (1973b). Recipe of classroom ideas. In W. R. Houston & S. C. White (Eds.), *Professional development modules.* Houston: Professional Development Center, College of Education, University of Houston.

Freiberg, H. J. (1988). *Generic teaching strategies.* Unpublished curriculum materials. Houston: University of Houston.

Freiberg, H. J. (1991). Consistency management: What to do the first days and weeks of school. *Consistency Management Training Booklet.* Houston: Consistency Management Associates.

Glaubman, R., Glaubman, H., & Ofir, L. (1997). Effects of self-directed, story comprehension, and self-questioning in kindergarten. *The Journal of Educational Research, 90*(6), 361–377.

Gowen, D. B., & Novak, J. D. (1984). *Learning to learn.* New York: Cambridge University Press.

Harste, J. C., Short, K. G., & Burke, C. (1988). *Creating classrooms for authors.* Portsmouth, NH: Heinemann.

Harste, J., Woodward, V. A., & Burke, C. (1984). *Language, stories and literacy lessons.* Portsmouth, NJ: Heinmann.

Houston, W. R., Clift, R. T., Freiberg, H. J., & Warner, A. R. (1988). *Touch the future—Teach!* St. Paul: West Publishing.

Hyerle, D. (1995/1996). Thinking maps: Seeing is understanding. *Educational Leadership, 53*(4), 85–89.

LaRue, D. W. (1917). *The science and art of teaching.* New York: American Book Company.

Marlowe, B. A., & Page, M. L. (1998). *Creating and sustaining the constructivist classroom.* Thousand Oaks, CA: Corwin Press.

Marshall, H. H. (Ed.). (1992). *Redefining student learning.* Norwood, NJ: Ablex.

McTighe, J., & Lyman, F. T. (1988). Cueing thinking in the classroom: The promise of theory embedded tools. *Educational Leadership, 45*(7), 18–24.

Meltzer, L., Roditi, B., Houser, R. F., Jr., and Perlman, M. (1998). Perceptions of academic strategies and competence in students with learning disabilities. *Journal of Learning Disabilities, 31,* 437–451.

Norris, S. P. (1985). Synthesis of research on critical thinking. *Educational Leadership,* 40–45.

Oser, F. K., Dick, A., & Patry, J. (1992). *Effective and responsible teaching: A new synthesis.* San Francisco: Jossey-Bass.

Peterson, P. L. (1992). Revising their thinking: Keisha Coleman and her third-grade mathematics class. In H. H. Marshall (Ed.), *Redefining student learning.* Norwood, NJ: Ablex.

Poon Teng Fatt, J. (1998). Innovative teaching: Teaching at its best. *Education, 118,* 616–625.

Pratton, J., & Hales, L. W. (1986). The effects of active participation on student learning. *Journal of Educational Research, 79*(4), 210–215.

Rogers, C. R. & Freiberg H. J. (1994). *Freedom to learn* (3rd ed.). Columbus, OH: Merrill.

Sergiovanni, T. J. (1994). *Building COMMUNITY in schools.* San Francisco: Jossey-Bass.

Simon, H. (1986). The teacher's role in increasing student understanding of mathematics. *Educational Leadership, 43,* 40–43.

Smith, J. L., Johnson, H. A., & Rhodes, J. W. (1993). *Negotiation: Student-teacher collaborative decision making in an integrative curriculum.* Paper presented at the annual meeting of the American Educational Research Association. (ERIC Document Reproduction Services No. ED 362-488).

Stahl, S. A., & Vancil, S. J. (1986/1987). Discussion of what makes semantic maps work in vocabulary instruction. *The Reading Teacher, 40,* 62–67.

Wheatley, G. H. (1992). The role of reflection in mathematics learning. *Educational Studies in Mathematics, 23,* 529–541.

SAMPLES AND EXAMPLES

There are four Samples and Examples in this section.

- Finding an Apartment is provided as an example of how several different subject areas could be integrated into one activity.
- The Ready Reading Reference Bookmark is designed to be a reminder for students during reading activities.
- The Flowchart is an activity where students could map out the traits of a character related to the events in the story.
- Eight formats for mapping ideas are presented based on the "thinking maps" described on page 316 in this chapter.

FINDING AN APARTMENT

Please review the apartment ads and, using the questions as a guide, select the best answer(s).

1. You have $900 a month to rent an apartment. Which of the nine apartments listed could you afford? Write in the space provided the location or two-word descriptor of the apartments (e.g., Montrose and Central/Air Heat) here. __________
 Yellowstone/Highway 288, Heights, and Galleria Richmond first apartment.
2. How much more would you need to rent the Condo at 2121 Hepburn Street #308 near the medical center? $350.00 + $550 deposit = $900.00
3. Which apartments have two bedrooms? Rockwood Heights, Galleria-Richmond (both apartments) and the Condo at Near Medical Center.
4. How much does it cost for the year to rent the Medical Center Condo and the Galleria-Richmond apartments? $15,000 a year and $10,800 a year. What is the difference in total cost between the two places? $4,200
5. Which apartment gives you the most information about the place and why?__________
 St. Thomas/Rice area. The owners need to fill the apartment which may be the reason for the free rent and all the information.

NEAR MEDICAL CENTER. 2–2 condo, 2121 Hepburn #308. $1,250/month, $550 deposit. 2nd floor flat, stove, refrigerator, washer/dryer, fireplace, 24 hour guard. 528-5311. CLARK MCDOWELL.

YELLOWSTONE/HWY 288: 1 bedroom, $750 monthly or $200 weekly. Individual. 748-8296.

HEIGHTS: NICE one bedroom apartment. Trees, yard, quiet. See what $860/month will rent in the Heights. 869-4516.

MONTROSE GARAGE APARTMENT. Large, clean, a/c. Near River Oaks Center. On bus line. $650 month. 665-3114.

MONTROSE/RICHMOND area. 417 W. Main. Ceiling fans, covered parking. 1 bedroom apartment. $775. Clean, hardwood floors, quiet complex, pets ok. 523-3121. MANAGER.

ROCKWOOD HEIGHTS: 3607 Murworth. 2 bedroom, new carpet, mini-blinds, carport, downstairs. $1,200 a month. 984-9769.

CENTRAL AIR/HEAT. One bedroom in clean, quiet complex. Covered parking, laundry. New grey carpet, mini's. $675. 522-1565.

GALLERIA-RICHMOND two bedroom, $900. Covered parking. On-site manager at 4822 Merwin. Manager speaks Spanish. 439-1784. HYLTON MANAGEMENT.

ST. THOMAS/Rice area. Newly renovated 1 bedroom. All adult living, electronic gates, covered parking, mature landscaping, 24 hour emergency maintenance, mini-blinds, carpet, large walk-in closet, ceiling fan. Quiet neighborhood. Close to universities and downtown. $750. One month free! 528-5151. SOHO.

Source: From "Generic Teaching Strategies" by H. J. Freiberg, 1999, unpublished curriculum materials. University of Houston, Houston, TX.

THE READY READING REFERENCE BOOKMARK

While you read—
Tell
yourself what the author says.
Ask
yourself if what you are reading makes sense.
Picture
what the author describes.
Identify
the main ideas.
Predict
what will come next.

If you don't understand—
Identify
the problem.
Remind
yourself of what you want to find out.
Look Back.
Look Ahead.
Slow Down.
Ask
for help.

After you read—
Retell
what you read in your own words.
Summarize
the most important ideas.
Ask
yourself questions and answer them.
Picture
in your mind what the author described.
Decide
what was especially interesting or enjoyable.

Source: Maryland State Department of Education. Reprinted by permission.

FLOWCHART

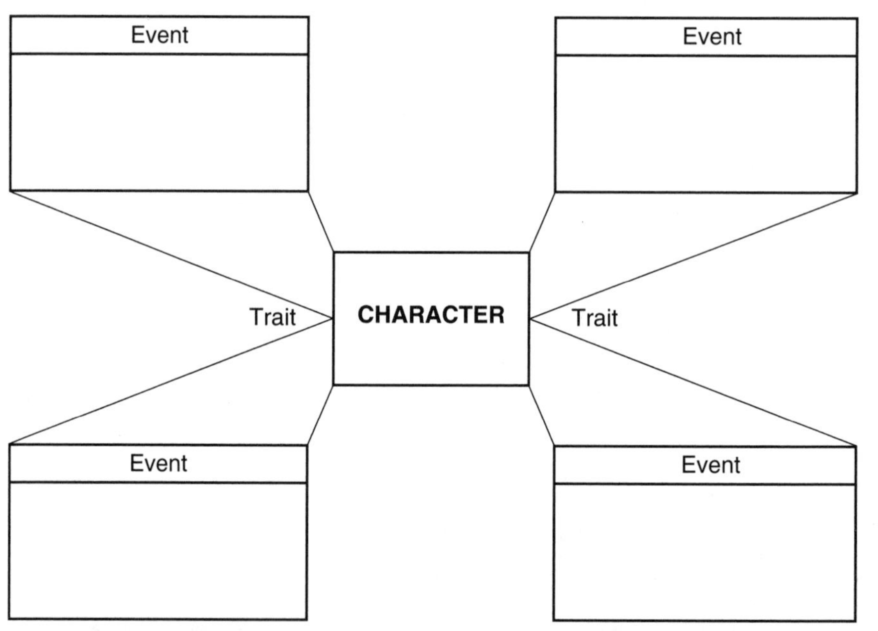

Source: From "Cueing Thinking in the Classroom: The Promise of Theory Embedded Tools" by J. McTighe and F. T. Lyman, 1988, *Educational Leadership 45*(7), pages 21–24. Reprinted with permission of the Association for Supervision and Curriculum Development. Copyright © 1985 by ASCD. All rights reserved.

MULTIPLE FLOWCHARTS

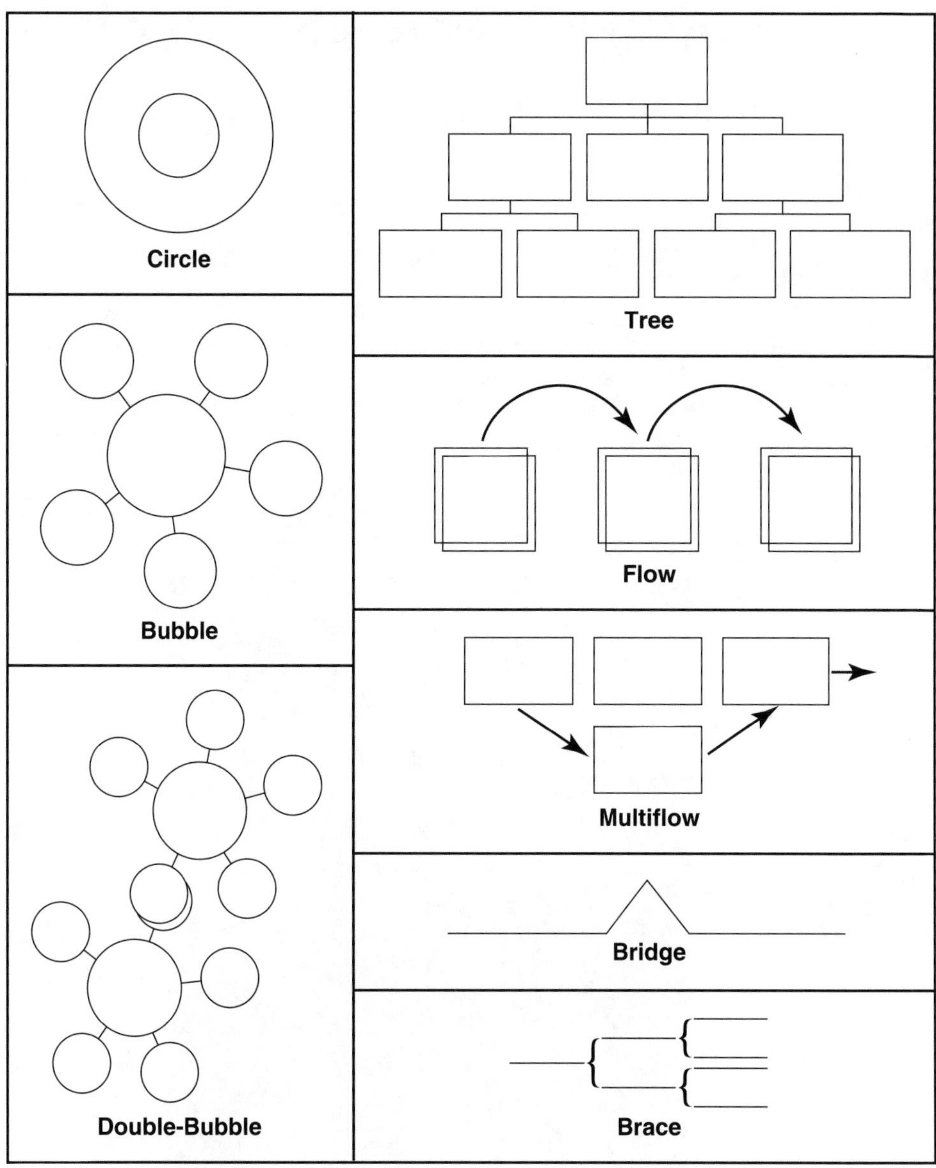

CHAPTER

12

MAKING LEARNING REAL

Engaging Students in Content

Chapter Outcomes

At the conclusion of this chapter you will be able to:

1. *Consider the context, content, and learner in planning for roleplay, simulation, drama, and service learning.*
2. *Plan for and use roleplay, simulation, and drama with appropriate prerequisites, management, and other teaching strategies.*
3. *Design service learning experiences.*

Key Terms and Concepts

Improvisation
Advantage of Improvisation and Service Learning
Context
Content
Learner
Teaching with improvisation and Service Learning
Simulation Model
Drama
Service Learning
Experiential Learning
Teaching Roles

INTRODUCTION

We offer four Snapshots as an introduction to the strategies in this chapter—all forms of experiential learning. In the first, a middle-school class participates in a roleplay activity. In the second, a kindergarten snapshot, you will see a simulation strategy. A high-school teacher uses the third strategy, drama. You will also observe service learning in a middle-school setting.

SNAPSHOT: Middle-School Classroom (Roleplay)

Eric Adams's environmental science class is studying ways to dispose of refuse. To develop understanding of the issues regarding use of landfills, he assigns roles to students and schedules a community forum. One group of students becomes property owners who live in the neighborhood of the proposed landfill site. A second group of students becomes the planning commission proposing the site. A third group is a hearing committee that will review the proposal and take testimony at the forum to make a decision. The last group of students are "interested observers": news reporters, chamber of commerce representatives, and business people.

During three days of research and preparation for the forum, Eric meets with each group to discuss what information they need, what sentiments are felt, and issues that have come up. At the Friday forum, each group speaks on the issues, raises questions, and pleads a case. Some roles are played with intensity for and against the landfill.

After the forum, the class meets for discussion. Students respond to such questions as: What would you say to a community group that approached you for advice on this situation? Students write about what learning occurred during the roleplay, and how they learned.

SNAPSHOT: Elementary Classroom (Simulation)

As the kindergarten students arrive one morning, they are greeted by Mrs. Dunham, who points out the lines and arrows on the floor of their classroom. She instructs children to walk around the room only in the direction of the arrows.

When everyone has arrived, Mrs. Dunham reviews the walking instructions during "circle time," a time when students sit on the floor in a circle to talk. She refers to the walking arrangements as a new rule for the classroom. Within the first 10 minutes of activity time, students find the walking arrangements inconvenient and hard to follow. Mrs. Dunham waits another 10 minutes. She calls the class together for another "circle time" to discuss the new rule. She begins by saying that rules are made to help us work and play together well. She asks, "Is the new rule helping?" Most children say, "No," and she responds, "Rules can be changed."

When Mrs. Dunham asks for ideas for changing the rule, many students suggest turning the arrows the opposite way. She agrees, and students return to their activities.

Within a shorter time, students complain, and their teacher calls another discussion. Again she asks, "Is the new rule helping us work and play together?"

The kindergarten class continues to negotiate and try out new walking rules. By the end of the morning, the students are talking about rules with a beginning understanding of the concept and the rule-making process.

SNAPSHOT: Secondary Classroom (Drama)

Sophomore students are studying the topic of drugs and the pressures for drug use. After filmstrips, readings, a speaker, and instruction, they form groups to develop play scripts about the pressures.

Groups may select a scenario for a play or create one of their own. For example, group #1 writes a script for a situation in which a popular older student approaches a younger student and offers drugs. After two days of script development, they rehearse for a day and then present to the other classes.

After the plays, the students discuss what they learned about drugs in their lives. Importantly, they talk about what it felt like to be offered drugs, to refuse drugs, the pressures to try drugs, and how different individuals influenced the feelings.

SNAPSHOT: Middle-School Classroom (Service Learning)

In the classes of a middle-school team of teachers, students are engaged in three projects to assist a local shelter for homeless families in a fund-raising effort. The teachers have combined their curriculum areas of English composition, technology, graphic design, and marketing, and have engaged their students in the production of posters, television ads, and other promotional material to support the fund-raising campaign.

Their students began by studying homelessness in their community, collecting information about the shelter's program and identifying community issues related to homelessness. From their information, the students developed scripts, content for posters, and other marketing productions. They practiced the skills of teamwork, communication, project planning, and research. "The best thing about our service learning activities was the level of involvement we saw in our students ...they were so committed to producing great results for the community" reported Kellen Akiyama, one of their teachers.

In this chapter you will learn how to use the four strategies observed in the snapshots in different contexts, with different content, and by different learners.

Definition of Terms

All the strategies in this chapter offer experiences to learners that promote their learning. The strategies provide opportunities to experience values, situations, emotions, dilemmas, perspectives, and decisions that probably would not occur in the everyday lives of your learners. These opportunities are a rich source of learning and are generically described as *experiential learning.*

Roleplay, simulation, and drama can be considered together as improvisation strategies. The following characteristics make them exciting approaches to teaching and learning (Farris & Parke, 1993; Johnson, 1998):

1. Active—*Students are involved in their own learning, constructing their own knowledge.*
2. Collaborative—*Students must cooperate in the learning process.*
3. Interactive—*Students share meanings, feelings, thinking, and actions with the group.*
4. Composite—*The concepts and skills of varied curriculum areas are linked. (p. 231)*

Our fourth strategy, service learning, is the newest teaching approach and it has the same characteristics as the improvisation strategies. The difference between service learning and the other three strategies is that students experience reality rather than a representation of it.

As we define the individual strategies, you will see the individual uniqueness.

Roleplay

Roleplay enables participants to think, feel, and act as other persons. It is an enactment or rehearsal of behavior with some reality and with a safe environment for trying out new ideas and making mistakes. Eric Adams's students prepared for their roles to give them some reality, but at the same time, were able to play their roles spontaneously.

Simulation

Simulation enables students to experience the consequence of their own and other's behaviors. Simulations are meant to represent reality as closely as possible. An important quality of simulations is the self-feedback provided by the person experiencing the behaviors or consequences. Mrs. Dunham's students gave their own feedback about the rules and kept making changes based on the feedback.

Drama

A common definition of drama is a composition intended to portray life or a character or to tell a story, often with conflict, emotions, and action and dialogue. The story is often intended for performance. The middle-school students composed their own stories to portray real-life pressures associated with drugs.

One form of drama, *dramatic play,* is an unrehearsed activity with props and accessories in which students play in real or unreal situations of their choice. A common example is found in early childhood settings, with children enacting roles of adults with props of a home.

Another form of drama is *theater games.* These are exercises or games that train participants in communication and theater techniques and skills. They are designed to stimulate action, spontaneity, and creativity. As games, they have a set of rules that keep the playing active.

Service Learning

Service learning is an approach that links community service with learning, or academic programs with community. "The community becomes an extended classroom where students apply their knowledge and practice skills" (Fertman, White, & White, 1996, p. 2). Another way of describing service learning is the involvement of learners in real-life settings and situations in which they use their learning and experiences to solve real problems and address real needs in the community as a regular part of their school curriculum.

Advantages of Improvisation and Service Learning

If you consider using improvisation in your classroom or engaging your students in service learning, and you ask a colleague for an opinion, you may encounter the kind of comments that you hear in this Teacher Talk.

TEACHER TALK

I don't have enough time to do those activities.

Elementary Teacher

I'm uncomfortable, or my students are uncomfortable, with roleplaying.

Middle-School Teacher

I just don't get around to planning for drama. You know, having props ready, thinking through the routines,...there's so many other things to do.

Secondary Teacher

The community is unpredictable; you never know what students will encounter outside the classroom.

Middle-School Teacher

The Time Issue

Improvisational strategies require more time than some other instructional strategies. In the middle-school Snapshot, the actual forum for roleplaying the landfill issues was scheduled for 55 minutes, and preparation took three days of class periods. The discussion that followed lasted another 55 minutes. So, the time issue is real.

A way to look at the time issue is to look at the additional learning benefits—that is, the composite characteristic of improvisation. During the 55-minute forum, students practiced public speaking, questioning, and use of data. They conducted research, used group processes, and planning.

A response to the time consumed as middle-school students wrote scripts, rehearsed, and presented their plays is that the time spent instructing on drug pressures could be lost if students do not get experience or practice responding to the pressures.

Service learning also requires extensive time for preparation, logistics, the actual service activity, and processing of the learning. Teachers frequently mention time as a major barrier to implementing service learning in their classrooms (Wade, 1997). Like improvisation, the outcomes have real depth of learning through application as well as the multiple learning benefits you observed in the Snapshot at the beginning of this chapter.

The Discomfort Issue

We advocate sensitivity to this issue. Some individuals flourish when participating in improvisational strategies; others are shy and uncomfortable. Later in this chapter, we will describe how to provide different levels of participation in improvisation.

The improvisation strategies offer advantages that you will not find with other teaching and learning strategies. Listen to some teachers who do use improvisation.

TEACHER TALK

I watched students as they took on the personas of the characters they chose. The faces and voices were familiar, yet the concentration, the imagination, the group support, I had not seen before (Everson, 1993).

Secondary English Teacher

This was an exciting and stimulating experience where I felt that not only did the students develop a caring, learning, thinking attitude, but they also developed a sense of professionalism in design through their role work. As teachers working together with this learning strategy we felt that, we, too, had learned and grown in new ways (Melnichuk, 1993).

Teachers of Elementary Grades 2/3 and 5/6

The discomfort issue with service learning has to do with the harsh realities of some of society's problems. Both teachers and students studying homelessness in our middle-school Snapshot experienced discomfort with the issues and realities of families without places to live. Sensitivity is essential with this teaching approach as students need preparation and guidance for the experiences they may have in the community.

CONTEXT

Your community context provides planning information and resources, and your classroom context provides physical arrangements, an emotional climate, and a schedule to be considered. Begin by reviewing your advancework information about the community and your classroom.

Community Context

Community awareness is important, whether you use improvisation or service learning. You don't teach in isolation, so the "hows and whats" of your instruction must be sensitive to the attitudes and values of the community. You will need community resources for improvisation and community placements for service learning.

Community Attitudes and Values

The teaching strategies of this chapter have unpredictable outcomes. If students role-play presidential candidates and reporters in a press conference, who knows what issues may be raised? If students participate in a simulation of world trade, moral and ethical decisions may arise. When young children engage in dramatic play of "mother and father," anything is possible.

Our advice is to anticipate some possible directions in which your activities may take students. What could happen? What might be said? What conclusions are possible? If you anticipate topics, feelings, or opinions that may offend students, parents, or community, you can decide whether the outcomes are worth the risk. If they do come up, you can be ready to talk about them with students. Discuss why they happened and how they conflict with community values or attitudes. Use caution not to sanction or judge them.

Our message in this section is not to stay on "safe ground," avoiding all controversial topics, but to be thoughtful and sensitive as you approach such topics. Being aware of community attitudes and values is your first step. That same unpredictability characterizes service learning. When elementary school students go to a home for senior citizens, we cannot be certain of what kind of experiences they may have. You might not want to avoid the difficult and uncomfortable issues of community, but you do want to be clear about the appropriateness of your service placements for the development of your students and the understandings of their families.

Community Resources

Go back to the Community Context Checklist in Chapter Five and look for themes, props, and support persons for improvisation as well as placements, issues, and problems for your service learning approaches. Themes for your use of improvisation come from community issues, events, problems, and other situations. The landfill scenario came from a real-life situation occurring in Eric Adams's students' community. In service learning, there is no need for props, but community partners are critical to the success of both the service and the learning.

Your community is a source of props: libraries, historical societies, chamber of commerce offices, hospitals, universities, realtors, restaurants, grocery stores, newspaper companies, and museums. Your school district may have a resource center. It is a matter of becoming familiar with what is available and being organized enough to schedule use of what you find.

One kind of prop for improvisation is *realia,* objects used to relate classroom teaching to the real life of people or situations studied. Some common examples of realia are costumes, tools, journals, maps, and household furnishings. The advantage of collecting and using realia is that items such as toys from colonial days can motivate authentic drama or roleplay. Students visualize life of the colonists when interacting with toy props.

Once you develop a list of needed items (props and realia), ask for help from parents and neighbors. Our experience has been that this is an easy kind of support for people to give. There is a request letter in the Samples and Examples section at the end of Chapter Ten. If you have time, garage sales are gold mines for props.

The community is also a source of individuals or groups who can support your improvisational strategies and service learning activities. Community partners may need to help with transportation or logistics, or orient you and your students prior to engagement with the community. Consider using them for information, guidance, or as substitutes. The historical society guide can provide information with which to begin a roleplay of early settlers in your state. A construction company manager can provide real-life examples for your math simulations. The local drama group may have an individual who would enjoy coming to your class and conducting a drama activity.

For those of you who feel that discomfort we described earlier, many of these support persons can substitute for you while you gain experience and confidence. They can prepare you and your students for society's realities and help track the skills of community engagement. Chapter Thirteen offers you additional examples and sources of community resources.

Classroom Context

Room arrangements and the emotional climate of your class will influence the effectiveness of your improvisation strategies. Your classroom schedule will be a consideration for your service learning methods.

Room Arrangement

Depending on the number of students in your class, the strategies in this chapter may require some extra classroom space. Students need to be seated or standing close to other students who are participating in the improvisation. If the entire class is not participating, the room may be arranged for separation of activities. Some improvisation requires additional space for physical movement.

Probably our best advice for your room arrangement is to have flexibility. Have an area or corner of the room that can be quickly cleared or set up for improvisation activities. Ideally, a student committee for "set-ups" can be organized in anticipation of the need for space. Decisions about location and student assistance can be made with students in a class discussion.

In addition to using actual classroom space, you will find alternative spaces outside the classroom. Your advancework will pay off as you locate hallways, play yards, and storage areas for rehearsal, planning discussions, and actual improvisation. Sometimes, the alternative spaces provide more supportive contexts than the classroom. When Mr. Hardt, a fifth-grade teacher, looked for a space similar to the living space on the *Mayflower,* he found a covered outdoor pavilion with a mast or support pole for his improvisation activity.

Emotional Climate

In all of the advice on using improvisation, there is a consistent theme of the importance of trust. If you are going to teach with improvisation, you must believe that individuals can and will succeed. You must also be clear that the enacted behavior is neither good nor bad. Along with your beliefs, you must provide the following in your classroom emotional climate:

1. Safety for exploration of feelings and behaviors
2. Permission to express all feelings
3. Respect for ideas and feelings of all

Shaftel and Shaftel (1982) have recommended some procedures to help you provide such an environment. We describe them with some classroom examples:

1. *Demonstrate your acceptance of feelings or experiences.* Ms. Janes demonstrates to her third-grade class when she says, "Sometimes we feel afraid when we don't know anyone or enter a strange place. When I moved to Seattle two years ago, I was afraid. I didn't know anyone. I didn't know where the grocery store was located. I didn't even have the name of a doctor."
2. *Read and discuss stories of emotions, human traumas, relationships, and conflicts.* After sixth-grade students read a story of a moral dilemma, their discussion comments could safely reflect the dilemma of the story's characters. It is secure to talk about, "Justin felt tempted to take the 50 dollars because he could be sure that no one would ever look for the money."
3. *Use active listening.* This kind of listening is described in the Teacher Effectiveness Training model in Chapter Five. As students begin to express feelings, ideas, or actions, you reflect back those same feelings, ideas, or actions, without any judgment. Mr. Rodriguez observed his first-graders roleplaying a library scene and reflected, "You feel angry when books aren't in the right place on the shelf."
4. *Provide guidance and be willing to explore topics in any direction.* When students in Ms. Schumanoff's history class became interested in societal attitudes about working women before and after World War II, she encouraged their research and drama for the rest of the class.

Classroom Schedules

Both improvisation and service learning bring time pressures. The best suggestion for addressing issues of time is integration of curriculum—for example, the earlier Snapshot on homelessness addressed at least four curricular areas in one activity. Another way to think about the fact that students spent four hours per week out in the neighborhood in their study of homelessness as they interviewed people at the shelter, observed and recorded numbers of homeless individuals, and gathered statistics from library resources is that students did the equivalent work of four class sessions. These kinds of arrangements will almost always require collaboration with other teachers to achieve the flexibility of scheduling necessary for service learning.

The awareness of room arrangement, emotional climate, and classroom schedules will help your improvisation and service learning be effective. The same awareness is necessary as you review the content of what you are planning for service learning.

In sum, you and your students interact with the community's attitudes and values in improvisation, so awareness is important. Your classroom can support the strategy with its room arrangement, emotional climate, and use of time, but, again, you begin with awareness. That same awareness is important as you review your content to plan improvisation and service learning.

CONTENT

Some educators confine the use of roleplay, simulation, drama, and service learning to the social sciences—history, citizenship, economics, and so on. A creative teacher will find no curricular limits in using those strategies. Some of our most memorable observations of teaching include:

- The preschool teacher whose 4-year-old students roleplayed the artist Jackson Pollack and created "works of art"
- The first-grade teacher whose students simulated pairs for adding by twos
- The sixth-grade class in which students dressed in costume and addressed the class in the role of the main character of their book reports
- The chemistry teacher who had students wear name tags of various elements, and simulate compounds and equations
- The education professor who had students roleplay parents and teachers meeting in conference about student problems or progress
- The engineer trainer who simulated a steam pipe with body movement and sounds and brought both delight and understanding to his peers with his teaching
- The fourth-grade students who tutored first-grade students in writing, giving them feedback and critique for revising their stories
- The history class in which students paired with senior citizens to record their individual histories

So you see, art, math, science, language arts, education, history, and engineering can be taught with these strategies. We find no curricular limits. In addition, improvisation and service learning respond to a concern for relevant curriculum as students explore "both factual knowledge and content concepts while 'trying on' real-life situations and experiences" (Smith & Herring, 1993; Wade, 1997). Experiential learning is process oriented and is essential to student achievement of the real-life goals of problem solving and decision making.

Learning Problem Solving

Using improvisation to teach problem solving allows students to study serious problems, explore solutions, and make mistakes in the security of the classroom. Students can be guided through a sequence of problems that becomes increasingly more difficult or complex over a period of months. They will gain insights when they try out previously successful solutions or responses on a new problem and are forced to rethink and create different ideas. Problem solving in the community further enhances learner skills and confidence. Service learning experiences offer the chance to follow through the problem-solving process and to obtain feedback from community members about solutions.

Learning Decision Making

The younger the student, the fewer opportunities there are available to practice decision making. Again, the safety of the classroom offers the opportunity for students of all ages to practice repeatedly and to make mistakes. Mistakes in improvisation are not accompanied by failures, judgment, or rejection, as they may be in the real world.

What is important in the decision making that occurs in improvisation is student awareness of process. As students talk about decisions with the reasons behind them, they develop awareness. Your input assists the awareness with, "When you were deciding to run for mayor, you paid attention to all the problems of holding office" or "Review the steps you took when you decided to talk with your parents." The same awareness is important in service learning and equally critical is the development and maintenance of communication with community members during the decision-making process.

LEARNER

The strategies of improvisation and service learning require your sensitivity as you work with individual learners. You can adjust or vary the strategies for individual personalities and experiences.

Learner Personalities

With improvisation, there is often concern for the student who controls or dominates the drama, or for the student who is uncomfortable in the spotlight. We suggest that you accommodate individual personalities with improvisation by assigning roles some of the time, by having students select roles some of the time, and by rotating or reversing the roles, some of the time. Some of the learner personality differences may influence student participation in service learning. Shy students may be hesitant in community situations, others may be too aggressive in particular settings. We have learned that students need extensive preparation for service learning experiences.

Learner Experiences

One of the best things about using improvisation is that your students bring such a range of different experiences. You will have students lacking in experience related to the theme of your improvisation, and students with vivid memories related to the theme of service learning. We encourage you to use some or all of the following approaches to assess learner experiences:

- Student interviews
- Student life timelines
- Student collages of life
- Student self-portraits (verbal and nonverbal)
- Student bulletin boards of life stories
- Student photo albums or scrapbooks

Chapter Seven contained a Learner Profile that you can use to assess learner experiences. In the Samples and Examples of this chapter, there is a Parent Survey to help you determine learner experience. In Chapter Fourteen, you will find information about interviews, surveys, and questionnaires, all of which can be used to assess learner experiences for improvisation activities for planning experiential learning. We have described considerations for your planning and sensitivities for your use of experiential learning. Now we will describe some models for teaching with improvisation and service learning.

TEACHING WITH IMPROVISATION AND SERVICE LEARNING

For the strategies of roleplay and simulation, there are models with specific phases and activities for teaching. We will describe those models and show you their use in classrooms. Drama does not have a specific model, but we will provide a set of recommendations. Service learning has many interpretations, but we will describe some basic components of the strategy. We conclude this section with descriptions of teaching roles to support improvisation activities: facilitator, supporter, and manager.

The Roleplay Model

For roleplay to be effective, two criteria must be met. First, students must act out the roles of the story or situation with believability. As we stated earlier, not all students have a dramatic flair or are comfortable with dramatic roles. However, the roles must be portrayed with quality in the enactment. Students themselves and their peers must be able to believe the role being played. Otherwise, little discussion of the role, feelings, and effects can take place. The second criteria is similar; that is, the role or situation must have a real-life quality. A connection to real life promotes interest and involvement of students. With the two criteria in mind, we turn to the model.

Joyce, Weil, and Showers (1992, p. 59) described nine phases for conducting a roleplay activity. Each of the phases is an important lead-in to the next phase, ultimately ensuring that discussions, evaluations, and generalizations are productive. We would like to take you through the phases of their roleplay model with a middle-school teacher. Her class has been studying the legal system in social studies/government and the use of alcohol in health, so she has integrated these curriculum topics into the roleplay.

Phase One: Warm Up

To warm up the group, Mrs. Fong describes a town in the Northwest that prides itself on being beautiful and free from crime. The townspeople are involved in civic projects, sponsor many cultural events, and participate in educational activities. Mrs. Fong asks students to talk about what it would be like to live in such a place. Then she describes the mayor of the town, the first woman mayor, elected for the second time. The mayor has intense community support and an exemplary record of successes in her office.

"One evening the mayor is returning from a social event to honor an artist and is stopped by the police for reckless driving and possibly for being intoxicated. She describes a very exhausting work day, followed by an event that required her attendance. She did not have time for lunch or supper, but did have several drinks at the social.

"The police officer feels confused about what to do. The mayor asks him to forget the incident and she will take a cab home. She assures him that it won't happen again. He reluctantly agrees. The police officer discusses the incident with his superior officer. The mayor is troubled and discusses it with her major advisor."

Mrs. Fong stops her description and asks, "What are the issues in the situation?" She has students retell the story.

Phase Two: Participant Selection

Students then list the major players in the story and review what they know about each. Together with Mrs. Fong, they decide which students will play each role.

Phase Three: Set the Stage

Mrs. Fong states, "In order to roleplay this situation, what different settings will we need?" Students plan three settings in three corners of their classroom. Chairs are arranged to resemble a car, and a student's bike is brought in for the police officer. In another corner, a chair is pulled next to Mrs. Fong's desk for a setting with the police officer and a superior. In another corner, a conversational arrangement for the mayor and her advisor is set up.

Phase Four: Prepare the Observers

Those students who are not playing other roles are assigned observer roles. Three observers are to describe the feelings of the players, three are to define the goals of each player, and a pair is to critique the enactment for nonverbal expression. Other observers are to describe an alternative to the action when the roleplay is over. Others are charged, "Do you think that this could really happen?"

Phase Five: Enact the Story, Roles, and Situation

The students enact their roles as mayor, police officer, advisor, and superior officer through the plot described by Mrs. Fong. Others listen, observe, and take notes.

Phase Six: Discuss and Evaluate

At first, students talk excitedly about their reactions, some disagreeing with the actions and some commenting on how well the roles were played. Mrs. Fong allows the excitement to ease, then poses questions to help students think about the roles, the feelings and goals, and the interpretations of the behaviors. She asks, "What do you think the mayor intended with her plan?" As discussion slows, she asks, "What other options did these people have?" The class begins planning another enactment of the scenario with alternative actions.

Phase Seven: Enact Again

The situation can be reenacted any number of times, as long as new interpretations of the roles emerge or alternative actions are proposed. Because of time constraints, Mrs. Fong's class enacts the situation three times in small groups: once with the police officer releasing the story to the press, again with the police officer taking a "hard line" and ticketing the mayor for driving while possibly intoxicated, and again with the mayor taking the first step and calling a meeting with the police to plan action.

Phase Eight: Discuss and Evaluate

Students responded intensely to each enactment, some with agreement and righteous defense of the police officer and some with disagreement and empathy for the mayor. They discussed the effects of alcohol, legal issues of driving under the influence of alcohol, and held some heated debates about implications for the mayor.

Phase Nine: Describe Experiences and Generalize

Mrs. Fong asked, "What advice would you give to public officials after your roleplay experiences?" Students offered advice and then were given the assignment: "Think of a situation here at school that would be similar to our roleplay, and think of some individuals here who would experience the same kind of decisions."

The nine-phase model of roleplay from Joyce, Weil, and Showers (1992, p. 59) gives you a sequence of specific activities. It will help you to have a model to follow when you first use roleplay. With experience, you may vary the model.

The Simulation Model

This model is simpler and has just four phases. To teach with simulation, select the activity and carefully direct students through the activities that you see in Mr. Cooley's classroom.

Phase One: Orientation

Mr. Cooley reviews the principles of effective management with students before describing the simulation. Then he proposes, "You are going to face a significant decision as members of the board of trustees of a major international corporation. The most important aspect of your task is to match the qualifications of the candidates with the projections for the corporation."

Mr. Cooley reviews the process of simulation and reminds students of a trade simulation experienced the month before. He then turns on an overhead of the organizational chart of the corporation. "The current president has resigned," he says as he points to the role on the chart. "These administrators are also on the board of trustees. These are not. Many have influential relationships with trustees. There are three candidates being considered, and you will have a resume for each."

Phase Two: Participant Training

Mr. Cooley informs the class that they will be moving to the board room down the hall to engage in the simulation. He encourages them to read the resumés quietly in their classroom and then join him in the board room. He proceeds to the board room and distributes copies of financial statements of the company and name cards at each place around the table. He places a second copy of the flowchart on an overhead projector at the back of the room.

Once students arrive and are ready for more direction, Mr. Cooley sets the schedule for the simulation. "We will be working on this decision for the remainder of the week. On Friday, we will vote for our choice. There will be some time that day for presenting a case for a candidate." Students are grouped into three different boards of trustees, and urged to meet and discuss the candidates. Each board receives a set of role cards with descriptions of board members.

Before dismissing the class, Mr. Cooley reviews the task, the roles, and the schedule for the simulation.

Phase Three: Simulation Operations

On Wednesday and Thursday, students meet in small groups or pairs, and with the candidates to discuss information and views. At the end of each class, Mr. Cooley spends 10 minutes checking on progress, needs, and directions. He asks, "What issue was important for your group today?" or "What success did your group have today?"

On Friday, the class meets with three boards, and votes are cast. Each board announces its decision and reasons for candidate selection.

Phase Four: Participant Debriefing

After the decisions are announced, the groups compare their processes. Students are led through a discussion of the difficulties, insights, unexpected ideas, and a comparison of the simulation with real-world happenings. Mr. Cooley asks, "What information from this course helped your work in the simulation?" After a set of questions, students are assigned to write a critique of the simulation, assessing its effectiveness and making recommendations for revision.

As we recommended for the roleplay model, using the sequence of phases for the simulation model (Joyce, Weil, & Showers, 1996, p. 106) will give you security when you begin teaching with this strategy. Depending on the content, context, and learner, you may decide to adapt the strategy once you have gained experience in teaching with simulation.

Drama

Drama provides an opportunity for your students to explore the concepts of fantasy and reality, cause and effect, language, and sequence. Teachers who use drama describe learner benefits that include increased motivation, improved group interaction, and greater understanding and tolerance of differences. Learners also develop critical thinking, analytic skills, decision making, and creativity when they participate in drama in addition to the intended curricular goals. For teachers, the benefits include enhanced integration of curriculum and opportunity for real individualized instruction (Albert, 1994).

Guidelines for Using Drama

As a starting point, remember that a climate of trust is essential in your classroom if you want students to participate in drama. From there, some simple guidelines will assist you in getting started:

1. Use as few props as possible to promote creativity, and be sure that players are familiar with the props.
2. Make characters in a drama convincing and easy for students to identify with.
3. Be sure the story is suitable in theme, length, and language for the age of students.
4. Rehearse students in parts, create emotional involvement with characters by discussing characters' goals and feelings.

It is recommended that students up to the age of 11 or 12 years participate in informal drama exclusively—that is, drama with minimal planning, and spontaneous action and dialogue. Older students can participate in rehearsed drama because they have the ability to think through dialogue and action and perform with a greater degree of naturalness.

Drama Activities

In addition to dramatic play and theater games defined earlier, there are several short and simple drama formats that will help you and your students become comfortable with drama:

- *Storyreading or storytelling.* These are good preparatory steps for drama that provide practice in using voice, inflection, and clarity. Storytelling involves understanding of sequence, relationship, and detail.
- *Tableaux/pantomime.* This simple process has students arranging themselves into a picture to illustrate a scene or concept. Learners practice facial expressions, body language, and use of props.

- *Monologues.* Learners study and portray the thoughts and feelings of a character, either real or imagined. They have the opportunity to explore different viewpoints or alternative interpretations of a role.

Storyreading, storytelling, tableaux/pantomime, and monologue can be used in conjunction with each other. They offer you a way to begin using drama with little preparation.

Approaches to Drama

According to Smith and Herring (1993), teachers see power and value in drama but acknowledge that drama is not well used in classrooms. They described two approaches for integrating drama into everyday curriculum.

- *Linear drama approach.* This is an ideal beginning approach in which you, as the teacher, plan and outline the drama activities before involving students. During your planning, you select a theme or concept to be explored, appropriate materials, and a strategy to get students involved in the theme. Students dramatize the material through varied drama activities (tableaux, monologues, etc.) and further the development of themes or concepts. An evaluation stage and replay stage follow to promote reflective analysis and enriched experiences (Smith & Herring, 1993, pp. 419–421).

An example of a linear drama session is seen in a second-grade classroom. The teacher, Mr. Powers, has planned activities to develop the concept of transportation. He shows slides of varied forms of transportation (ships, helicopters, etc.) and plays a tape of recorded traffic sounds. He has the children move to the traffic sounds followed by a discussion of the vehicles seen and heard. Later, he forms small groups to present tableaux of varied forms of transportation. From there, the class reads from a book about transportation. Again, small groups are formed to portray sections of the book. After the dramatization, the class evaluates the drama and students discuss their ideas about transportation. Later, Mr. Powers takes the class to the library and the small groups each select another book about transportation. During the week, the groups meet, read their books, and plan another dramatization.

- *Holistic drama approach.* In this approach, students are "dropped" into roles and encouraged to invent material. During the drama, teachers take on roles as characters to help focus or challenge the students. This is called "teacher in role" and it is a key element in holistic drama. In this approach, dramatizations are scheduled in a sequence that builds development of a theme or concept (Smith & Herring, 1993, pp. 421–425).

An example of holistic drama can be seen in a middle-school history class after a brief study of the civil rights struggles in the South. Angela Munro, the teacher, leads the class through a guided imagery activity, reading a newspaper description of the tension and fear in the streets of a town whose schools are to be integrated the following day. From there, she assigns the class into groups to spontaneously play out a town meeting, a school board session, a church gathering, and conversations in the local shops. Later, dramatizations include the first day of school and other scenes that could follow the initial school integration. In all of the dramas, Angela Munro plays a role to probe feelings, to challenge the characters, and to extend the drama.

Notice that in both approaches, the learners have the opportunity to make unique and individual contributions to their own learning. Smith and Herring (1993) reported that student attitudes toward learning are greatly improved when they are engaged in drama.

Service Learning

Service learning is a teaching/learning strategy by which students learn and develop through active participation in carefully organized service experiences that

- Meet community needs
- Are coordinated in collaboration with school and community
- Are integrated into each student's academic learning
- Provide structured time to think, talk, and write about the experience
- Provide opportunities for using newly acquired skills and knowledge in real-life situations in community
- Enhance classroom learning by extending it to community
- Foster a sense of caring for others (Alliance for Service Learning in Educational Reform, 1993; Fertman, White, & White, 1996)

For activities to be called *service learning,* there must be a deliberate connection between the service and the learning accompanied by conscious reflection on the experience. *Reflection* is defined as active, persistent, and careful consideration of the service activity, of behavior, practices, effectiveness, and accomplishments (Fertman, 1994). Reflection gets learners to self-assess and contemplate their motivations, understandings, roles, and the impact of service learning. Figure 12.1 displays a model for generating reflection and illustrates the multiple forms reflection can take to accommodate learner differences.

Experiential Learning and the Inclusive Classroom

Research has demonstrated that students from special education classes can perform in improvisation activities as well as students from regular classes (Miller, Rynders, & Schleien, 1993). Given the varied possibilities for different roles, improvisation can be an effective teaching and learning approach for a class of diverse learners.

Much of the success of an inclusive classroom will be related to the climate, the respect and acceptance among learners, and the willingness to work together. Improvisation can be used early in the class development to help learners understand each other and to share perspectives. When several fourth-graders roleplay physical challenges, they better understand their physically challenged peers. Such improvisation must be facilitated with sensitivity, but the potential outcomes can be powerful for building a community of learners.

Service learning has equal potential for effectiveness in an inclusive classroom. As Urgese describes in the Research Vignette on page 353 and as many university programs

FIGURE 12.1 *Generating Reflection*

Speaking
• one-on-one conferences with teacher leader
• whole class discussion
• small group discussion
• oral reports to group
• discussions with community members or experts
• talks on project — for parents, school board, etc.
• teach younger students
• testimony before policy makers
Writing
• essay, research paper
• journal or log — daily, weekly, or at conclusion
• case study, history
• special project report
• narrative for a video or slide show
• guide for future participants
• self-evaluation or evaluation of program
• newspaper or magazine articles
• portfolio
Generating Reflection
How do we help students develop new understanding, skills, and knowledge from service learning?
Activities
• gather information on a project
• workshop presentations
• surveys or field-based research
• simulation or role playing
• plan training session for others
• celebration programs
• plan future projects
• recruit peers to serve
• plan budget
Multimedia
• photo illustrated or slide essay
• video documentary
• painting, drawing, collage, etc.
• dance, music, or theater presentations

Source: From *Generating Reflection-Model* by National Youth Leadership Council (NYLC), 1991, St. Paul, MN: NYLC. 1910 West County Road B, St. Paul, MN 55113, 651-631-3672. Reprinted by permission.

have discovered, service learning can bring meaning to curriculum and opportunities for success to learners who seldom experience it. The outcomes of caring behaviors and attitudes, improved self-esteem, and understanding of diversity will strengthen the dynamics of an inclusive classroom toward the kind of learning environment where all learners can succeed.

Experiential learning can be an exciting and effective approach to the challenge of teaching in an inclusive setting. We urge you to seriously consider these strategies as a foundation for your teaching.

As you follow the models for roleplay and simulation, and the guidelines for drama, you will notice that you need to facilitate and support the learning as well as manage the activities. In the next section, we will describe how to be a facilitator and a manager with improvisation and service learning.

Middle School Research Vignette

INTRODUCTION

This vignette is focused on a case study of a community service program at the Albert G. Prodell Middle School in Long Island, New York. Case studies typically use multiple kinds of data (observations, interviews, documents, etc.) to create a "picture" of a person, program, or event. This case study includes descriptive information, organizational and logistical information, and evaluative information in order to provide a comprehensive picture of the service learning program (Urgese, 1996).

STUDY DESCRIPTION (METHODOLOGY)

The service learning program at the Prodell Middle School began in 1973, when a teacher and parent took a small group of students struggling to stay in school to a day-care center and nursing home to work. The experience was so positive that the school hired a teacher assistant to help expand the activity. Since then, awareness of the benefits of service work has stimulated consistent program growth with support from teachers, administrators, and community members.

In 1996, every student at the middle school was involved in at least one service unit. Most students have two or three experiences during their three years at the school. The program is run by a coordinator and teacher assistants who plan activities and schedules in coordination with classroom teachers. The program involves use of related video and written materials as well as community speakers to orient teachers and students.

Students write weekly journal assignments about their service experiences. "They are encouraged to be open and honest" (Urgese, 1996, p. 135). The adults involved read and respond to the journals, help students plan their service, and guide group discussions.

STUDY FINDINGS

An obvious question for the Prodell Middle School is whether student outcomes justify the resources, time, and other investments made to the service learning program. The first outcome reported consistently by teachers is that students learn to care for others. Even with the wide range of learner personalities found in any middle school, teachers report observations of thoughtfulness and helpfulness throughout the program. The students report learning about and understanding people different from themselves. They learn to plan, organize, and achieve goals.

Teachers note gains in self-esteem, and observe successes for those students who typically struggle in academic and social settings. Academic content is purposefully reinforced by the service activities, which have been planned with the classroom teachers. The program is evaluated by means of observations of students, their discussions, and journal entries. Students are rated on their preparation, service work, and conduct when traveling to community sites.

CONCLUSIONS AND IMPLICATIONS FOR PRACTICE

An important conclusion by the author (Urgese) of the case study is that the school and community must be committed to a service learning program if it is to be effective. Another conclusion to be drawn is that both partners must experience positive outcomes if they are to continue their commitment. Finally, a schoolwide program requires teacher involvement, school resources, and a supportive environment.

Cases of programs like the one at Prodell Middle School are being reported for every level of education, from preschools (Rowley, 1997) to higher education at universities and colleges (Wofford, 1997). There are abundant resources available to assist an individual teacher, a department, a school, or an entire district to begin to offer service learning for students. A resource list can be found in the Samples and Examples at the end of this chapter.

TEACHING ROLES FOR IMPROVISATION AND SERVICE LEARNING

The Facilitator Role

A *facilitator* is one who facilitates or makes something easier. When you facilitate experiential learning, you make it easier for students to understand, to be involved, and to learn from the strategies. To do so, you guide students into the activity, through the activity, and in analysis of the activity. To be an effective facilitator, you need the skills of a tight-rope artist. You must be directing students and yet be nondirective at the same time. To begin this balancing act, start with your purpose. What do you intend for students to experience, feel, learn, and think?

The Manager Role

Did you notice the many details that were managed in Mr. Cooley's simulation activity (page 348)? The board room was scheduled, transparencies were ready, cards with descriptions of roles were prepared for students. Mr. Cooley was an effective manager and his simulation proceeded smoothly. As you manage improvisation, you will need to be organized and ready to referee when situations warrant.

The time demands of improvisation require careful scheduling. These are not strategies that can be hurried, fit in, left unfinished, distracted, or interrupted. Some scheduling suggestions include:

- Schedule these activities for "quiet" times of day and in "quiet" places.
- Inform others of your need for undisturbed time.
- Schedule visually with a sign on your classroom door.
- Schedule time with students for a discussion of the importance of undisturbed time within the classroom.

In addition to scheduling, think about space, materials, and props. Involve students in the planning and organizing of materials and logistics, arranging the room, gathering props, or listing necessary procedures.

Finally, you will need to be sure that your information is organized. Ask yourself, "Do students know enough about slavery to enact this scene?" or "What data do students need to make this decision?" or "Will students be able to portray an architect with what they know about the profession?" Once you organize what students already know and what they need to know, you can decide to review or teach additional content. When we described review in Chapter Nine, we suggested application as part of the learning. Improvisation and review are an effective teaching and learning combination.

The manager role in service learning is also critical. The Research Vignette gave you a realistic picture of the amount of coordination necessary to ensure student learning and community satisfaction. Unless help is available, teachers are urged to begin service learning on a small scale or to begin collaboratively with other teachers and share management.

The same management of curriculum knowledge and skills will be important so that students are prepared to contribute quality service. Your management role will include all of the following and more:

- Travel arrangements
- Orientation to community sites
- Development of partnerships in community
- Permissions from families
- Scheduling

In sum, your manager role in experiential learning calls for complex organizational skills and wise use of resources.

SUMMARY AND A CHARGE

The strategies of this chapter have the potential for powerful and dynamic teaching and learning. They also have the potential for risk taking and unforeseen experiences and feelings. The flexibility and accommodation required by varied contexts, content, and learners give you good reason to use the strategies of this chapter. Those same foundations require your awareness and sensitivity.

Notice context for:

1. Community values and attitudes
2. Community resources
3. Classroom space and emotional climate
4. Classroom scheduling
5. Community sites

Notice content for:

1. A full range of curriculum use
2. Opportunities for learning problem solving
3. Opportunities for learning decision making

Notice learners for:

1. Differences in personalities
2. Differences in experiences

With your awareness of context, content, and learner, you can proceed to the models for roleplay and simulation, the approaches and activities for drama, and planning for service learning. You will expand your instructional role with the roles of facilitator, supporter, and manager.

The complexity of your instructional role with experiential learning strategies may be just what you need to be excited and challenged as a teacher. The unknown qualities of improvisation may intrigue you and your students. You may develop a closeness as you take risks together. Develop competence with roleplay, simulation, and drama by reading, observing other teachers, and participating in workshops. Practice with your students. Connect with teachers who are using service learning and go out into the community to observe student involvement. Begin with a spirit of adventure, and make learning real.

REFERENCES

Albert, E. (1994). Drama in the classroom. *Middle School Journal, 25*(5), 20–24.

Alliance for Service Learning in Education Reform. (1993). *Standards for school-based service learning.* Washington, DC: Author.

Everson, B. J. (1993). Considering the possibilities with improvisation. *English Journal, 82*(7), 64–66.

Farris, P. J., & Parke, J. (1993). To be or not to be: What students think about drama. *Clearinghouse, 66*(4), 231–234.

Fertman, C. I. (1994). *Service learning for all students.* Bloomington, IN: Phi Delta Kappa.

Fertman, C., White, G., & White, L. (1996). *Service learning in the middle school: Building a culture of service.* Columbus, OH: National Middle School Association.

Johnson, A. P. (1998). How to use creative dramatics in the classroom. *Childhood Education, 75*(1), 2–82.

Joyce, B., Weil, M., & Showers, B. (1996). *Models of teaching.* Boston: Allyn and Bacon.

Melnichuk, M. (1993). Role power. *English Quarterly, 25*(4), 21–25.

Miller, H., Rynders, J., & Schleien, S. (1993). Drama: A medium to enhance social interaction between students with and without mental retardation. *Mental Retardation, 31*(4), 228–233.

Rowley, R. (1997). Service learning in the early childhood classroom. *Childhood Education, 52*(7), 26–31.

Shaftel, F. R. & Shaftel, G. (1982). *Role playing in the curriculum.* Englewood Cliffs, NJ: Prentice Hall.

Smith, J. L., & Herring, J. D. (1993). Using drama in the classroom. *Reading Horizons, 33*(5), 418–426.

Urgese, J. (1996). Shoreham Wading River Middle School, Long Island, New York. In C. Fertman, G. White, & L. White (Eds.), *Service learning in the middle school: Building a culture of service.* Columbus, OH: National Middle School Association.

Wade, R. C. (1997). Community service learning and the social studies curriculum: Challenges to effective practice. *The Social Studies, 88*(5), 197–202.

Wofford, H. (1997). Corporation for national service. *Journal of Public Services & Outreach, 2*(1), 3–8.

SAMPLES AND EXAMPLES

The Samples and Examples for this chapter include resource lists for developing your own improvisation for teaching and learning. There is also a parent survey for improvisation resources.

- The Resource List for Improvisation provides suggestions for roleplays, simulations, and drama described by classroom teachers or curriculum specialists, or available commercially. Brief descriptions of each are included.
- The Resource List for Service Learning includes books, curriculum materials, organizations, and grant agencies, with brief descriptions of each.
- The Parent Survey takes inventory of student experiences and resources for improvisation.

RESOURCE LIST FOR IMPROVISATION

Roleplays

Crowell, L. (1993). Busy with birds in the Springtime. *Communication Education, 42*(4), 296–299.
Roleplay activities in which students draw on each other's information, reasoning ability, and kindliness.

Dufeu, B. (1993). Un exercise ouvert: La prison. *Français dans le Monde, 259,* 56–61.
Activities, including dramatizations, for French language classes.

Hershey, D. (1993). Evaluation of irrigation water quality. *American Biology Teacher, 55*(4), 228–232.
Describes laboratory activities and roleplays for introducing students to the importance of water quality.

McKinnon, M. (1993). How to encourage studying Germany and Europe in the classroom. *Social Education, 57*(5), 231–232.
Activities from an "Idea Bank for Teaching Germany and Europe in U.S. Classrooms K–12" with roleplays, student projects, and addresses for free materials.

Melnichuk, M. (1993). Role power. *English Quarterly, 25*(4), 22–25.
Description of roleplay for cross-grade activities with interviews of students in grade 5/6 and 2/3.

Merrill, M. (1992). The living museum. *Social Studies Texan, 8*(2), 33.
Lesson plan for a second-grade class project in which students portray famous people.

Moore, M. (1993). Talk show science. *Science Scope, 15*(5), 23–25.
Skits in which students play the role of science concepts.

Plavin, A. (1993). A simple economics project that students enjoy. *Social Education, 57*(3), 137–138.
A secondary economics lesson with roleplays of occupations; includes directions and questions.

Simulations

Arce, G. (1992). Nuclear-powered debate. *Science Teacher, 59*(3), 44–49.
Describes an exercise to develop interest and understanding about nuclear energy.

Boston, J. A. (1998). Using simulations. *Social Studies Review, 37*(2), 31–32.
Describes steps needed for a successful simulation.

Davison, B. (1993). Kids development corporation. *Gifted Child Today, 16*(2), 2–6.
A simulation of economic life appropriate for adaptation to grades 4 through 11.

Dedrick, M. (1993). A study of immigrant experience. *Social Education, 57*(1), 45–47.
Describes a week-long unit on late nineteenth-century immigration to the United States; appropriate for elementary and secondary.

Gustafson, K. (1993). Government in action: A simulation. *Social Education, 57*(2), 90–92.
Describes a simulation exercise for secondary curriculum about federalism and the system of checks and balances.

Hartman, J., & Vogeler, I. (1993). Where in the world is the U.S. Secretary of State? *Journal of Geography, 92*(1), 2–12.
A geography instructional game with maps and charts.

Maltby, F. (1993). Teaching mathematics through "thinking actively in a social context." *Gifted Education International, 9*(1), 45–47.
A simulation for grades 5, 6, and 7 detailed for development of problem solving.

Simonis, D., & Staudt, C. (1992). Moonbase America. *Science Teacher, 59*(8), 36–41.
Describes a seven-day simulation for a space science course and a communications network.

Trent, L. (1993). Changing student attitudes about disabilities. *Principal, 73*(2), 32–34.
A program, Handicapped Awareness through Simulation, provides interaction opportunities for children without disabilities.

Drama

Breen, K. (1993). Taking Shakespeare from the page to the stage. *English Journal, 82*(4), 46–48.
An approach to studying Shakespeare and ideas for relating plays to contemporary work.

Ernst-Slavit, G., & Wenger, K. J. (1998). Using creative drama in the elementary ESL classroom. *TESOL Journal, 7*(4), 30–33.
Discusses the benefits of drama in an ESL classroom.

Heath, S. B. (1993). Inner city life through drama: Imagining the language classroom. *TESOL Quarterly, 27*(2), 177–192.
Drama for development of standard English and preparation for job entry.

Jenkins, A. (1993). *Hamlet's suicide soliloquy: A case study in suicide ideology.* Teaching Guide. Washington, DC. ED363590.
A secondary teaching activity for integrated English and health education curriculum.

Labov, J., & Sewell, R. (1993). Command performances. *Science and Children, 31*(2), 23–24.
A program to create and perform original science-related plays.

LaRocca, C. (1993). Civil War reenactments—"A real and complete image." *Educational Leadership, 50*(7), 42–44.
Describes the experiences of a high-school Civil War study group, with data on student attitudes and achievement.

Schoon, S. (1998). Using dance experience and drama in the classroom. *Childhood Education, 74*(2), 78–82.
Presents books and activities that can be used for dance and drama.

Sickbert, C. Deer me. *Science Scope, 16*(5), 38–42.
Describes middle-school activity of a mock trial.

Sprague, M. (1993). From newspapers to circuses—The benefits of production-driven learning. *Educational Leadership,* 50(7), 68–70.
Describes experiences in a first grade and in a high-school journalism class.

RESOURCE LIST FOR SERVICE LEARNING

Cairn, R. W., & Kielsmeier, J. (Eds.). (1991). *Growing hope: A sourcebook on integrating service into the school curriculum.* Roseville, MN: National Youth Leadership Council. (1910 West County Rd. B, Roseville MN 55113. Phone: 612-631-3672).

Council of Chief State School Officers. (1994). *The service learning planning and resource guide.* Washington, DC: Author.

Follman, J., Watkins, J., & Wilkes, D. (1994). *Learning by serving: 2,000 ideas for service learning projects.* Greensboro, NC: SouthEastern Regional Vision for Education (SERVE), affiliated with the School of Education, University of North Carolina at Greensboro.

Goldsmith, S. (1995). *Journal reflection: A resource guide for community service leaders and educators engaged in service learning.* Washington, DC: The American Alliance for Rights & Responsibilities.

Kinsley, C., & McPherson, K. (1995). *Enriching the curriculum through service learning.* Alexandria, VA: Association for Supervision and Curriculum Development. (1250 N. Pitt Street, Alexandria, VA 22314-1453. Phone 703-549-9110).

Lewis, B. A. (1995). *The kid's guide to service projects.* Minneapolis, MN: Free Spirit Publishing. (400 First Avenue N., Suite 616, Minneapolis, MN 55401-1724. Phone: 1-800-735-7323).
This book contains more than 500 ideas for service for young people of all ages. The projects range from simple things kids can do on their own to large-scale commitments that involve whole communities.

Lyday, W. J., & Winecoff, H. L. (1998). Service learning standards for teachers: Guidelines for practitioners and pre-service teacher education programs. *Community Education Journal, 25*(1-2), 43–44.

Melchior, A., & Bailis, L. (1997). Evaluating service learning: Practical tips for teachers. *Social Studies Review, 36*(2), 40–42.

National Center for Service Learning in Early Adolescence. (1991). *Reflection: The key to service learning.* New York: Author. (CASE/CUNY, 25 W. 43rd St., Suite 612, New York, NY 10036-8099. Phone: 212-642-2946).

National Service Learning Clearinghouse, University of Minnesota, Dept. of Work, Community, & Family Education (1954 Buford Ave., Room R-460, St. Paul, MN, 55108).
The National Service Learning Clearinghouse provides leadership, knowledge, and technological assistance to support and sustain service learning program areas, and offers a toll-free information number, national database of programs and resources, a library of materials, an electronic bulletin board, referrals to training, peer consultants, and other resources, and operates regional technical assistance centers.

National Youth Leadership Council. (April 1993). *Learning by giving: K–8 Service Learning Curriculum Guide.* Roseville, MN: Author. (1910 West County Rd. B, Roseville, MN 55113).

Stephens, L. S. (1995). *The complete guide to learning through community service grades K–9.* Boston: Simon and Schuster.

PARENT SURVEY

Name ______________________________

Date ______________________________

1. Describe some travel experiences of your family.

2. Describe some special family customs.

3. List some careers represented in your family (include aunts, uncles, etc.).

4. List some hobbies, crafts, or recreational interests of your family (include aunts, uncles, etc.).

5. What are some special events that your family has attended?

6. What are some common problems at your house? What are some common decisions?

CHAPTER

13

USING COMMUNITY RESOURCES, AUDIOVISUALS, COMPUTERS, AND MULTIMEDIA

Varying the Stimuli

Chapter Outcomes

At the conclusion of this chapter you will be able to:

1. *Describe the purposes for using community resources, audiovisuals, computers, and multimedia for teaching and learning.*
2. *Consider the content, context, and learner when using community resources, audiovisuals, computers, and multimedia.*
3. *Describe how to use community resources, audiovisuals, computers, and multimedia effectively to vary the stimuli.*

Key Terms and Concepts

Purpose of Stimuli
Selection of Stimuli
Content Match
Learner Match
Preview
Novelty
Variation
Interaction
Multimedia Boxes
Community Resources
Guest Speakers
Field Trips
Audiovisual Stimuli
Overhead Projector
Slide Projector
Television
Records and Audiotapes
Videotapes and Films
Bulletin Boards
Demonstrations
Computers
Multimedia

INTRODUCTION

Until now, we have shown you Snapshots of classrooms today, but for this chapter, we are looking at a black and white photo in an old album. It captures an entire school. For those of you in our generation, the picture may bring nostalgia and chuckles. For those of who are too young (we envy you), the picture may bring disbelief.

SNAPSHOT: The Way We Were

It is a Friday afternoon in March at a small private elementary school in western New York. It has been snowing for weeks. At 2:00 P.M., students from grades 1 through 8 file into the auditorium and seat themselves on metal folding chairs. The youngest take the seats in the front rows, and the oldest sit in the back rows.

When everyone is seated, the lights are turned off. There is an immediate ripple of talk and laughter, but some firm "Shs" bring quiet. On the large screen at the front, an image appears and "A Visit to the Andes" begins with music and titles. It is now 2:08 P.M.

At 2:13, we see some of the first-grade students fidgeting and squirming in their chairs and some falling asleep. At 2:19, several third-grade students are scolded for talking. At the same time, we see two sixth-graders talking and pointing to the screen. They are heard discussing the condor, which they read about in their textbooks when they studied South America last fall.

At 2:26, there is a definite hum in the air—some muffled talk, shifting in chairs, and coughing. When the film ends at 2:34, there is quiet applause. The lights come on and the students leave, waving to friends and talking to each other. Back in the classroom, we observe quiet reading of library books, a health lesson, desk cleaning, and, in one classroom, a conversation about the Andes Mountains.

Lest you think that this is a unique Snapshot, let's go to another photo, another state, and look at a public school:

SNAPSHOT: The Way We Were

It is Friday afternoon again, and we're looking at a gymnasium in a rural elementary school in the Midwest. The scenario is similar until the lights go off and the film begins. We see "Division of Fractions" and it lasts 18 minutes. This time, we see heads nodding and students shifting in chairs within the first 3 minutes of the film. The hum in the air is louder and lasts through most of the film.

What's wrong with this picture? It is an understatement to say that there has been no consideration of content, context, or learner in either Snapshot. You may also be wondering why the films were shown or maybe you know the reason. Let's look at the first Snapshot and analyze it together.

Content

Since we have no way of knowing the intent of the teachers for showing the film, or the curriculum being taught in the classrooms, we will look at the content of the film itself. "A Visit to the Andes" contained vocabulary such as *South America, Andeans, agriculture, subsistence farming, condor,* and *Aconcagua* (the highest peak in the mountains). The concepts of weather, geography, culture, economics, and politics were described. Two maps of the mountains were shown. The narration drew several comparisons between life in the United States and life in the Andes Mountains. The content consisted of vocabulary, some concepts, facts, map skills, and comparisons.

If you were to ask some of the students, "What was the film about?" you would probably hear:

"The women carried baskets on their heads."
"The people were very poor."
"The weather in the Andes is hot and dry."
"They don't have cars or trucks."

You may hear a few facts, recognition of differences between life in the Andes and the students' lives, and some misinterpretations. The content in this situation will vary from student to student, and from context to context.

Context

When we look at the immediate context, we see a large room with uncomfortable folding chairs and the lights out. It is Friday, after lunch, and students are sitting for 26 minutes. Put yourself in the context. How do you feel after lunch, in a darkened room? How are you on Friday afternoon?

Consider the community context: a small farming community of families who has lived there for generations and who has seen little outside of the community. This context influenced the film's effect, but even with this commonality of backgrounds, there are learner differences.

Learner

In the Snapshot you could see differences throughout the auditorium. The learners differed first in age and development, then in interest and understanding. If you could converse with the learners, you would find stark differences in their experience with and knowledge of South America, mountains, other cultures, and even with films.

As you watched the learners in the auditorium, you saw their differences exhibited in their responses to the film, a range from boredom and discomfort to interest and recognition. It would have been interesting to question them about why they were seeing the film, to explore the learner sense of purpose.

Purpose

Can you predict what teachers had in mind that Friday afternoon? We will venture a guess. With the time of year, with Friday afternoons, and with the effect of long-term winter weather, the film offered a break from routine. Beyond that purpose, it offered a look at another culture, a life that the students might never experience. It offered some entertainment, because students of all ages will be enthused about a movie, at least, for a while. There was probably an economic purpose for this small school with limited funding to show a film to all 130 students rather than a class of 25.

The film in the Snapshot is one kind of stimuli to use in your teaching. This chapter will describe a wide assortment of stimuli, including community resources, audiovisuals, computers, and multimedia. In addition to the purposes suggested for "A Visit to the Andes," varying the stimuli can help you achieve these additional purposes:

1. *Developing concepts.* For a group of students studying Chile or Argentina, the film could help the students understand concepts of poverty, subsistence farming, and survival, and the differences between urban and rural life in those countries. After the film, discussion and reading would further their understanding.
2. *Enriching experiences.* Enrichment is achieved through appeal to the senses. The film included animal and people sounds, and vivid pictures of mountains and people's faces.
3. *Extending experiences.* The film took students from a small farming community in New York to South America, and from a textbook to audiovisual representations.
4. *Stimulating interest.* The film offered variation from the usual classroom materials and teaching strategies, so there was initial curiosity, even for the youngest students.

Our old Snapshots demonstrated once again that planning to use stimuli begins with consideration of (1) *content,* in terms of vocabulary, concepts, maps or diagrams, skills, and information; (2) *context,* in terms of school, community, time needed for use, location of use, room arrangement, and climate inside and out; and (3) *learner,* in terms of development, interest, experiences, and previous knowledge and understanding.

We have a caution before we proceed with this chapter, and that is for you to plan to teach *with* stimuli. Stimuli will not teach for you. The idea of this chapter is to *vary the stimuli* for teaching and learning.

USING COMMUNITY RESOURCES, AUDIOVISUALS, COMPUTERS, AND MULTIMEDIA

To use stimuli effectively, there is some necessary preparation. We recommend a selection process and a preview process, so that your teaching will be varied with stimuli rather than distracted by stimuli.

TEACHER TALK

I heard that the videotape on space was great and that students really liked it. I ran out of time so I got the VCR and tape just before science. Well, I was having a bad day anyway, but when I turned on the television, the volume was all the way up. The class shrieked and laughed as I turned it on. There was a "soap" showing because I didn't have the right channel pressed. By the time I found the right one and the play button, I was frantic. We finally saw the tape and the class calmed down. I guess it was good, I don't really know. I couldn't concentrate after that.

Eighth-Grade Teacher

Selection of Stimuli

Both the videotape on space and the film on the Andes were selected with minimal criteria. We suggest that you match the stimuli with content and learner. To achieve a *content match,* the stimuli must

1. Be directed to planned objectives or outcomes.
2. Fit the organization and sequence of your plans.
3. Be authentic and accurate.

Mr. Davenport looks for a content match in his choice of guest speakers. His students have been studying and practicing how to get a job by responding to classified ads and applying to desired employers, as part of a study of "Finding a Job." Mr. Davenport has taught resumé development and interview skills, and now plans a simulation session in which all of the job-hunting efforts have been unsuccessful. His content now concerns using an employment agency, so he plans to bring in a guest speaker from an agency in the community.

Mr. Davenport checks with major employers in the area to assess agency reputations. He selects a recommended agency that is quite large and is located close to school. He sets up an appointment with the agency's representative and takes with him an outline of information. During the meeting with his intended speaker, he describes what students have been studying and what information they will be seeking.

Do you see the *content match* in this selection? The speaker will help Mr. Davenport's students meet objectives, so preparation matched stimuli with curriculum.

Next, work for a *learner match.* Begin by considering learner age, development, interest, experience, attention span, and needs:

Will this choice appeal to students of varied ability?
Will it bias student thinking?
Will it motivate learners to think, to want to learn more?

When Flora Weinland selected a visual for her seventh-grade biology class, she decided that her students needed to see pictures of the cell differentiation that they were studying. She found slides, a filmstrip, and large photos in the media center. Which will be best for her class? Flora thought of her students and said to herself: There's a lot of them—31 in the class. Management is always a challenge, but lately, I have been successful grouping them in learning teams to study.

She selected the large photographs, copied them to produce sets for each group, and prepared information cards for matching facts with photographs. She thought to herself: These cards will give the students some control over the activity, and they can use them in different ways. Some students will focus on the information cards and some will focus on the pictures. She felt confident about the match of appropriateness for her learners.

As you watched Mr. Davenport and Ms. Weinland selecting stimuli by matching choices with content and learner, did you notice that they previewed their choices as they planned? *Preview* is the other step in preparation.

Preview of Stimuli

As presented in Teacher Talk, you can find yourself in embarrassing predicaments, losing students' attention and wasting frustrating amounts of time when you vary the stimuli. Previewing stimuli helps you avoid those situations. When you preview, check the content, quality, and potential for problems. For content, listen to the language, to the authenticity of information, to see if the information is up to date, and for evidence of bias. Will Mr. Davenport's speaker dress the part of an agency representative, speak in a pleasant voice, and present in a professional manner? When Flora copied her photographs, did the images remain clear and vivid?

In addition to checking content, quality, and potential for problems, we recommend a *rehearsal* or practice:

1. Check the seating arrangement of students in relation to the screen or board.
2. Locate the source of electricity.
3. Check the timing of the presentation.
4. Check the lighting.
5. Focus the projector.
6. Check the volume.

It can be exciting and satisfying when you use stimuli in your teaching if you are prepared. When you dramatically encourage your students to picture the enormity of Alaska, and smoothly pull down the U.S. map on which you have positioned a mileage indicator, it is effective. What is not effective is struggling to pull the map down or to find Alaska, or pulling down the wrong map. You will get student attention, but it will not be on the enormity of Alaska.

Even after selecting and previewing, varying the stimuli will require more decisions. We describe those decisions in the following sections.

Decisions for Varying the Stimuli

You make two important decisions when you plan to vary the stimuli: when to vary the stimuli and how to vary the stimuli. Additional decisions concern student involvement and evaluation for future planning.

When to Vary the Stimuli

Our worst fear is that you will slip into a routine for scheduling films or field trips, such as before a holiday, a Friday, or the first or last week of school. Instead, your decision should depend on your instructional intent. Look at what stimuli can do for your students:

1. *Stimuli can be used to introduce a topic.* At the beginning of a study of Monet, students view a display of the artist's work and a photo of Monet. Questions and discussions begin.
2. *Stimuli can be used to create interest in a topic.* Before beginning a study of Mexico, a display of photos and tapes of music or a multimedia display on the computer are used to build enthusiasm in the coming unit.
3. *Stimuli can be used to restate or reinforce a process or skill.* During a lesson on using the encyclopedia, the librarian visits and demonstrates how to use it, followed by a filmstrip that restates the process.
4. *Stimuli can be used to summarize or review information or concepts.* After studying about the early pioneers, students use a computer program with a simulated pioneer journey to review.

You see that your scheduling decision depends on what you want the stimuli to do, so your teaching plan is a guide.

How to Vary the Stimuli

The decision of how to vary the stimuli is one of coordination with other teaching and learning strategies. Any of the other strategies in this book are appropriate to use with community resources and audiovisuals. In their study of how teachers used television programming, Yeager and Pandiscio (1993) found a great variety of use. We think that this is true for all the audiovisuals and community resources in this chapter. How to use these stimuli is limited only by your imagination once you consider content, context, and learner. We do suggest, however, two qualities to consider as you combine stimuli with other teaching strategies: novelty and interaction.

Novelty is the quality of variation or change; it is newness. Look at the following examples and determine which provide novelty and which do not:

> **EXAMPLE:** In a high-school political science course, students watch a videotape of a politician giving a speech immediately after a 20-minute teacher lecture. Is there variation?

> **EXAMPLE:** In a high-school biology course, students watch a display of the heart with moving parts immediately after a 20-minute teacher lecture. Is there variation?

Interaction is mutual influencing or action. You will need a variety of other strategies to promote interaction between students and the stimuli. Listen as teachers encourage student interaction:

> **EXAMPLE:** "As we study this unit on drugs and alcohol, one of our objectives is to identify appropriate community agencies and resources. We will visit a display to gather information about community agencies."

When students are aware of the purpose or objectives, they are more likely to interact.

> **EXAMPLE:** "As you listen to the tape of ocean life, keep a list of the different sounds you encounter."

When students have an agenda or an advance organizer for the stimuli, they are more likely to interact.

> **EXAMPLE:** "We are going to take a break halfway through our field trip to see if everyone understands how the production line works before continuing our tour. You will be able to ask questions and check on the terms used by our guide."

When students can check understanding or clarify information at intervals during stimuli use, they are more likely to interact.

Decisions about Student Involvement in Varying the Stimuli

As you continue planning for using stimuli in your teaching, you may question to what extent students can be involved. As far as students selecting stimuli, we know from research (Clark, 1994) that student criteria for making media choices are faulty and based on enjoyment alone. Haugland and Shade (1994) have pointed out that students are not discriminating in their choices of computer games, so it is up to teachers to select appropriate software.

Our caution, then, is to involve students in selection only when they have criteria to follow. Begin by modeling your thinking and decision making for students: "I chose this film because it had such up-to-date photos of mass transportation and because it organized information so clearly." Have class discussions about choosing a resource. Linda Wilson (1998), a teacher educator, frequently discusses educational software with children. She considers their descriptions and evaluations of software an "important way of learning about how computers can be used in the learning process" (p. 250). She encourages discussions as well as uses formal structured ways of eliciting learners' critiques. Wilson recommends the use of student feedback forms, such as the one in Figure 13.1, to help students understand criteria for selection of stimuli. With your guidance, students can develop thinking appropriate for selection of stimuli.

For reasons that include efficiency, self-concept, and smoothness in management, it is to your advantage and to the advantage of your students to involve them in using stimuli. You will have assistance in your teaching and save time for other responsibilities. Even the youngest students (4-year-olds in our experience) are able to operate some audiovisual equipment and computers. Students need training in following directions, maintaining safety, and returning materials and equipment, but the learning will promote the kind of active learning and confident learners we described in Chapter Five.

Organizing for Teaching with Stimuli

Varying the stimuli will require complex decision making on your part: when, how, and why. In addition, you will be faced with many stimuli alternatives from which to choose. Think of it as a shopping trip. Your shopping can begin at most district media centers, university and public libraries, and school supply facilities.

FIGURE 13.1 *Student Feedback Form*

Date ____________________ Time ____________________ Subject ____________________

Describe the stimulus (title, type, length, subject).

____

____

What were the positive qualities of this stimulus?

____

____

What were the negative qualities of this stimulus?

____

____

What did you learn from this stimulus?

____

____

What questions do you have?

____

____

Rate your interest:	1	2	3	4	5
	High				Low
Rate your learning:	1	2	3	4	5
	High				Low

While you are making selections of stimuli, it is a good time to pay attention to organization. One organizing strategy comes from Brown (1993), who suggests that teachers develop Multimedia Boxes, containers of "every form of legitimate material imaginable that is associated with a particular theme." Brown encourages us to go beyond libraries and media centers and collect memorabilia from students' parents and relatives. Your community advancework will also have payoffs in terms of material for your collections. In addition to Multimedia Boxes and various filing routines, we also suggest a system for recording your critique of stimuli for future use. (See the Samples and Examples section at the end of this chapter.)

As you begin, consider the Pyramid of Learning Experiences that we described in Chapter Eleven. Use the pyramid to determine what kind of experience your choice will provide, to further assure your match with content and learner.

Community Resources

We begin with community resources—a broad category that could include objects, clothing, printed materials, models, displays, places, and people. We urge you to return to your Community Context Checklist (Chapter Five) to begin, and then move to the Yellow Pages of your telephone directory.

Many teachers and schools have established partnerships with businesses or organizations as an ongoing and supportive relationship directed to student learning (Hammonds, 1994). Not only do linkages between schools and communities promote your curricular objectives but they also promote additional outcomes, such as communication, workplace skills, career exploration, and so on. Be certain to consider your learner outcomes and have your instructional plans in mind as you initiate partnerships or seek community resources.

For this chapter, we will discuss the community resources of guest speakers and field trips. For many curriculum topics, these resources are likely to have a greater impact on the learners than most classroom activities would.

Guest Speakers

Remember how Mr. Davenport checked with businesses to find out which employment agencies had good reputations? He also went to visit the person who would be meeting with his class. We suggest that you check on your potential speaker to be certain the person can present well, is personable, and is reputable.

Preparing the Guest Speaker

It is important to prepare your guest in order to achieve your teaching purposes. When you meet with your guest, provide some of the following information:

1. The objectives and expectations of his or her visit
2. Information that the students already know and about which they are curious
3. Classroom management routines (e.g., students will or will not raise hands to ask questions)
4. Plans for related teaching and learning experiences

Think about how comfortable your guest will be with this information, and how much better he or she will be able to relate information to the other experiences you have planned.

Preparing Students for the Guest Speaker

Preparing students for the guest can begin with the same information found in the previous items 1, 2, and 3. Encourage them to develop questions beforehand, to discuss expectations, and to connect the speaker's visit with other learning experiences. With most students, you can share the responsibility of greeting the guest, introducing the guest, and expressing appreciation to the guest (verbally or in written form). Be sure to take care of school and district communications regarding your guest (e.g., forms and policies).

After a visit, guide students in processing the information. A discussion time or a writing experience will provide an opportunity for you and your students to hear each other's perceptions and information. You may structure it with directions such as, "List three things you learned from our guest, and three questions that weren't answered." You may simply ask students to write their thoughts about the presentation. Even the task of writing thank you letters will be a processing experience, especially if you ask students to describe specifics of the visit in their letters.

One of the benefits of using a speaker is the connection you make between your curriculum and the community. Field trips accomplish the same link.

Field Trips

A *field trip* is "a visit to a place outside the regular classroom designed to achieve certain objectives that cannot be achieved as well using other means" (Mason, 1977). Although this definition has been with us for some time, its specification, "that cannot be achieved as well using other means" is especially timely with today's limited budgets.

Selecting a Field Trip

School districts have limited resources for field trips, so make careful decisions about using trips to vary the stimuli. They have potential for unique firsthand experiences, but they must be carefully selected.

When selecting a field trip, stop and consider whether the field trip will distract, disturb, or bore students. When you identify a trip that will stimulate, focus, and involve your students, then continue your preparation.

Many teachers have begun their selection process in the immediate environment of their school, eliminating transportation concerns and expense. Johns and Liske (1992) have described opportunities right within the school yard that include observation, classification, hypothesizing, inferencing, predictions, and measurement aspects of learning. Activities on the school grounds can also enhance such skills as comparing, describing, drawing conclusions, investigating, mapping, sequencing, interpreting, and writing for all grades (Finlay, 1991). We suggest that you begin by taking a walk around the immediate area of your school and make a list of possibilities.

Preparing for a Field Trip

To prepare for a field trip, we suggest the following steps:

1. Schedule the location with your school or district, students, and parents.
2. Visit the location to preview what students will see, hear, and learn; to identify potential problems or dangers; and to assess for instructional planning.
3. Arrange for permission forms, transportation, and chaperones or assistance.

In addition to the basic steps, experienced teachers use creative preparations to make field trips even more successful.

TEACHER TALK

During my preparation visit to our field trip site, I took slides of the exhibits and the facilities that we would be seeing. I showed the slides to my class prior to the trip. Then, when we arrived at the site, there was a real excitement over finding the items we saw and talked about in class.

Second-Grade Teacher

When we plan a field trip, I try to assign some of the preparation tasks to the students. One group writes a letter to be sent home that explains the trip. Another group works on logistics—schedule, maps, fees, parent assistance, and so on. Another group works on recording procedures for the trip, and I always have a group write the thank you letters.

Middle-School Civics Teacher

In addition to these logistical steps, we encourage you to make the most of your field trips by previewing with students and coordinating the trips with other learning activities. With the cost and effort that go into a field trip, you want to be assured of maximum learning outcomes.

Processing Field Trips

Student journals are an excellent way of processing the trip's outcomes. We recommend the same attention to processing of field trips that we described for guest speakers—discussions, critiques, and writings. We have also seen students take photographs, make tape recordings, and draw impressions of a field trip during and after the experience.

These two community resources, guest speakers and field trips, provide exciting ways to vary the stimuli in your teaching. Our next type of variation, audiovisual stimuli, requires the same careful preparation and processing.

AUDIOVISUAL STIMULI

Audiovisuals offer you both sound and pictures. We will look at your options, provide brief descriptions and guidelines for use, and suggest some unusual ways to vary your teaching.

Overhead Projector

Notice that on the Pyramid of Learning Experiences (Figure 11.3), this stimulus generally provides high levels of abstraction to your teaching, so use it thoughtfully with younger students. The overhead projector projects a written or graphic image on a screen or wall. You can use it to display a study outline for your class or to list student ideas. Its uses are not limited to any curricular area, and it is easily transportable.

An overhead projector uses a sheet or a roll of transparent film, clear acetate. You can prepare a sheet ahead of time by using a printer or a copy machine or writing with a transparency pen, or use commercially prepared materials. You may also write on the transparency while teaching, but it takes time and skill. An advantage of using the overhead projector is that it allows you to face students; however, if you write on it much during your teaching, you lose the advantage of seeing faces, questions, and behavior.

Using the Overhead Projector Effectively

Some guidelines for using an overhead projector are:

1. Keep your image simple and readable (too much information is distracting).
2. Turn the projector off when not in use (the noise and light are distracting).
3. Use a good quality pen for making sheets (black for most writing; color for interest only).
4. Check the seating of students for clear vision of the image (sit in a few desks to test out the image).

5. Use a piece of white cardboard to cover all the points or items except the one you are discussing.
6. Allow students to write their answers on the overhead.

Unusual Uses for the Overhead Projector

We have seen teachers use this stimulus for numerous activities:

1. *Play a recess game on rainy days.* Children take turns making shadow figures on the screen and the rest of the class guess the figure.
2. *Create suspense or a surprise.* To begin a unit on profit in an economics class, a large $ is drawn to fill the transparency and flashed on the screen.
3. *Provide memory practice.* A list of words is projected for a short time, and then students write all the words they can remember.
4. *Share a small number of materials or materials too small to be seen by many students.* With only one set of counting bears, a first-grade teacher places different quantities of them on the overhead for students to count, add, or subtract.

The overhead projector with transparencies offers stimuli to use with lecturing, discussion, questioning, and with other stimuli, useful for previewing, recording, posing questions, demonstrating, and organizing.

Slide Projector

This machine projects pictures with intense images and you can keep the room lights on. An additional advantage comes with your use of pictures of real people, places, and happenings. Slides can be taken by you, your students, parents, or purchased from commercial producers.

Using the Slide Projector Effectively

When you show slides, remember to do the following:

1. Check the placement ahead of time (images are more effective when they are right side up).
2. Accompany the images with description and questions.
3. Check the vision of students seated in different locations around the classroom.

Slide projectors are lightweight, accessible, and fairly simple to use. You can have students handle the projection task and free yourself to lead a discussion to accompany the visual.

Using the Slide Projector in Unusual Ways

We have seen teachers use this stimulus for various activities:

1. *Develop sequence skills.* Show a small number of slides (3 to 6) in order and out of order.
2. *Develop student ability to predict.* Show a slide and ask, "What is happening here?" or "What may happen next?"

3. *Prompt creative writing.* Show a beautiful or provocative or inspiring picture as a stimulus for writing or drawing.
4. *Review a class project or trip.* Show slides of students to review information and perceptions.

Another advantage of using this stimulus comes with taking the slides. You and your students will gain insights and appreciations while you photograph your subjects.

Television

When you look at the number of hours our students already spend watching television outside of school, you probably question adding more viewing hours in school. We have some compelling reasons for urging your consideration of this stimulus. The first is that television is available in most classrooms, and with a wide selection of quality educational programming. The second is that your classroom use of television can model some good viewing habits for students.

Using Television Effectively

Those good viewing habits we mentioned are incorporated in the guidelines we suggest for use of television:

1. Discuss with students before and after viewing a television program (information, impressions, bias, hidden messages, and so on).
2. Check volume and image for students in different locations.
3. Eliminate distractions.
4. Watch the program with students (rather than work at your desk on some task).
5. Coordinate other learning activities with the program.

Using television to vary your instruction requires that you have a schedule and become familiar with various networks. Many programs are simply another form of lecture, so look for a demonstration or a drama, keeping in mind the qualities of novelty and interaction described earlier.

Research (Tiene, 1994) supports the suggestions we made earlier for effective use of television in classrooms. Payne (1993) has encouraged teachers to focus on the development of critical viewing and thinking skills specifically in regard to visual images. His questions appear in the Samples and Examples section. They will help your students analyze documentaries, television news, and feature-length films.

Using Television in Unusual Ways

We have seen teachers use this stimulus for many activities:

1. Use regular network ads to teach advertising, listening, decision making, and so on.
2. Use only parts of a program (the beginning or ending of a story) and have students write or develop the missing section.

3. Have students plan and produce their own television program.
4. Assign a television program as homework (with parents' approval) and include processing tasks such as questions to raise or answer, or note taking.

Since it looks like television is here to stay, we can best use our energy to make it work for our teaching.

Records, Audiotapes, and Compact Discs

Many of us limit our thinking for these stimuli to music, but there are excellent tapes, compact discs (CDs), and records for every curriculum area. Record players, CD players, and tape recorders are inexpensive and simple to operate.

Using Records, Audiotapes, and Compact Discs Effectively

With the addition of headphones, tapes, records, and CDs can be used by one student or a group of students. Because of the simplicity of operation, there are few guidelines:

1. Check volume for different locations of the room.
2. Keep electrical cords flush with floor or wall so that you and your students don't trip.
3. Have the intended starting point positioned on the tape or record ahead of time.

Cordi (1997) assigned his students the task of assembling 30- to 60-minute thematic audiocassettes of poetry to present to the class. He has shared some good insights for using audiotapes as context for learner assignments: "I spend time discussing how to make tapes. I instruct students to use TDK or Maxwell so as to ensure the durability of the tape. Then I discuss microphone management, care of equipment, and filling blank time" (p. 100). The importance of preparing learners to use equipment appropriately is a reminder that is relevant for many forms of stimuli in this chapter.

Using Records, Audiotapes, and Compact Discs in Unusual Ways

To expand your thinking on potential uses, we urge you to consider different ways to vary these stimuli:

1. Coordinate musical or sound backgrounds with book reports, historical narratives, plays, or science demonstrations.
2. Provide background music for a particular learning center.
3. Have students record their own tapes as journals, correspondence with you or other students, self-evaluation, or progress reports.
4. Have student groups record problem-solving or decision-making sessions, and play back for analysis.

One of our favorite teachers writes the name of a musical composition on the chalkboard each morning and plays it as his students arrive. We have also observed teachers using recordings for management routines, clean-up, or transition.

Films, Videotapes, and Videodiscs

All of these stimuli have appeal for students and can support learner motivation. Technology has even simplified the use of equipment and advanced the quality of programs. The most current of this group of stimuli—videodiscs—has been around for over 15 years but has only recently been used in classrooms. In 1993, 21 percent of school districts in the country had videodisc players available to teachers. Research has already demonstrated that videodisc technology can have positive effects on student outcomes—enthusiasm, motivation, achievement, and confidence (Rock & Cummings, 1994). Videodiscs have currently been matched to textbook and other curriculum materials with the use of a bar code in the texts. "They are much more efficient for teacher use because you can locate an appropriate segment for your lesson much faster than on a video" (Robertson, 1999). Once again, the key to successful use of these stimuli is the teacher role. According to Dowaliby (1993), "Teacher familiarity, if not fluency, with the technology and content would seem to be a necessary condition for the effective use" of videodiscs.

Using Films, Videotapes, and Videodiscs Effectively

The same guidelines regarding vision and volume for students apply here. In addition, we want to focus on one major guideline for using films and videotapes, and that is to use them interactively. Remember that *interactive* means that your students must do more than listen and watch. They must respond to the tape or film or disc, and you can make that happen with questions, advance organizers, and discussions.

Using Films, Videotapes, and Videodiscs in Unusual Ways

The following are some unusual ways to use movies, videotapes, and videodiscs and to make them interactive:

1. Use the film or tape without sound and ask students to supply the dialogue, predict what is happening, or act as an observer on the scene.
2. Stop the film or tape midway and have students dramatize or roleplay the ending, then compare it with the film or tape ending.
3. Have students watch different tapes or discs on the same topic and compare information.
4. Have students make films or tapes to teach other students, present research, describe a group project, record class history, or advertise a class program.

Notice that with these unusual uses, you *cannot* sit at your desk and catch up on your work. Your involvement with questions and suggestions will be needed.

Chalkboards

Chalkboards are everywhere and they come in all sizes, shapes, and several colors. They do not need a bulb or an electrical outlet, and they say what *you* want them to say. You can prepare them ahead of time or use them as you teach.

Using Chalkboards Effectively

Chalkboards get daily use in most classrooms, but they also get misuse. Look at the guidelines for effectiveness:

1. Keep your words large enough, dark or white enough, and clear enough to be seen in locations around the classroom.
2. Avoid filling the board with so much writing that students get confused.
3. Protect the writing surface with proper cleaning and the appropriate writing materials (do your school advancework with the custodian).

Chalkboards offer generous amounts of space on which to write, and are often located in several sides of the classroom. You can move around as you teach, as we suggested in Chapter Six.

Using Chalkboards in Unusual Ways

You can also use the chalkboard creatively:

1. Use colored chalk occasionally to highlight or underline main ideas, or to border information.
2. With tape or other devices, attach pictures and diagrams to the chalkboard with written descriptions, labels, or questions.
3. Reserve space for student messages.
4. On an infrequent basis, write your messages backwards, in a circle, or vertically (see Figure 13.2).

We have also seen teachers use a block of chalkboard space for a Thought for the Day, a riddle, a coded message, or a new vocabulary word. A daily or class schedule on the chalkboard is useful to you and your students. Reminders, directions, assignments and due dates, and announcements are all appropriate for chalkboard display.

FIGURE 13.2 *Sample of Unusual Chalkboard Message*

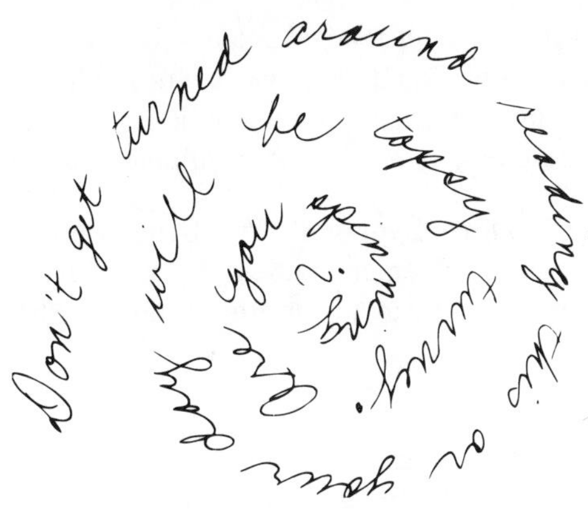

When you combine chalkboards with the other stimuli of this chapter, your teaching will be varied and will capture student attention.

Bulletin Boards

Bulletin boards come in different sizes and shapes. You hear teachers complain if they don't have one, and you hear teachers complain if they do. Like chalkboards, bulletin boards offer ease of use and accessibility.

Using Bulletin Boards Effectively

We have three simple guidelines for the use of bulletin boards:

1. Concern yourself with what your bulletin board says and does, rather than just how it looks.
2. Keep the display up to date, that is, connected to the theme of study, time of year, and so on.
3. Involve students in planning and producing displays.

We want to emphasize the first guideline with a reminder that we are talking about varying the stimuli in teaching. We have seen aesthetically arranged displays that are just part of the wall, never referred to in teaching, never discussed by students, and not connected to curriculum. The intent of these stimuli is to contribute to teaching.

The second guideline won't be a worry if your bulletin board is connected to your curriculum, and following the third guideline will help you keep your bulletin boards up to date.

Using Bulletin Boards in Unusual Ways

As we look at unusual ways to use bulletin boards, you will see the third guideline—students' involvement:

1. Students construct a bulletin board display of what they learned from a unit or course.
2. Each student is assigned a portion of a bulletin board to display what is happening in his or her life.
3. You construct a bulletin board related to future curriculum of unknown objects, places, and people for student guesses or predictions.
4. You and your students construct a bulletin board to communicate appreciation or honor to a student, parent, teacher, volunteer, or administrator.

In Chapter Fourteen, you will see a bulletin board being used as part of assessment. With student involvement, bulletin boards can change from being a responsibility for you to an exciting way to vary the stimuli.

Demonstration

The word *demonstration* means to point out or show by display, so a demonstration helps you vary the stimuli by showing instead of telling. Demonstrations make information more concrete and are often interesting to students.

Using Demonstration Effectively

Figure 13.3 is an example of a rating form to use to evaluate a demonstration, specifically for science instruction (Gillen, Brown, & Williams, 1989). The categories to be rated are our guidelines for using demonstrations effectively with any kind of curriculum:

1. Gain student attention immediately with an interesting title, some humor, an unexpected event, and your own interest and enthusiasm.
2. Check visibility so that all students can clearly see what is being shown.
3. Get students involved (interaction again!) by having them take notes, assist, predict, or ask questions.
4. Check that students understand what you demonstrated by asking questions, reviewing, or repeating parts of the demonstration.
5. Before you begin, familiarize students with the materials and equipment so that they can focus on the process or concept, follow safety procedures, and participate with competence.

Ellis (1998) has added a sixth guideline for effective use of demonstrations: the use of application following demonstration. He cautions,"The danger of the demonstration strategy lies with the passive role of students who may or may not understand the concept of skill (even with guidelines #3 and #4). The solution is to accompany demonstration with application" (p. 141).

When you teach with a demonstration, you can use the evaluation scheme as a checklist to get ready.

Using Demonstration in Unusual Ways

Take a look at how to demonstrate in unusual ways:

1. Demonstrate a cooking procedure or science process the first time with no explanations in a pantomime, then repeat it with directions either from you or your students.
2. Demonstrate a familiar process or concept with some noticeable error, urging students to make corrections when needed.
3. Present a demonstration in a make-believe screen of a television, on a theater stage, or in costume.

If there is a bit of "ham" in you, you will enjoy using demonstrations with your teaching. Demonstrations are also an effective way to involve those community resources like postal service employees, cashiers, and news forecasters, all of whom can demonstrate for students and enhance learning.

COMPUTERS AND MULTIMEDIA

Writing a section, not a chapter or a book, about computers and multimedia seems like an impossible task. We will limit our descriptions to what you can expect from computers and some guidelines for their use. We will skim through an album of classroom snapshots for you to see how teachers vary the stimuli with computers and multimedia.

FIGURE 13.3 *Rating Form for Evaluation of a Science Demonstration*

	Excellent					Poor
	5	4	3	2	1	0
I. Captures Student Attention	___	___	___	___	___	___

1. The demonstration "hooks" student attention with a discrepant event, bright color or catchy title.
2. The volume of the teacher's voice is projected throughout the room.
3. The teacher is enthusiastic.
4. The teacher speaks with confidence.

Communication and audibility: total points earned _____

II. Emphasizes Visibility ___ ___ ___ ___ ___ ___

1. The apparatus and materials being used are of adequate size for class size.
2. The room/demonstration is adequately lighted.
3. The demonstration can be easily seen throughout the room.
4. Materials are supported at an appropriate height from all areas of the room.
5. The teacher does not obstruct students' view.

Visibility: total points earned _____

III. Obtains Student Participation ___ ___ ___ ___ ___ ___

1. The teacher solicits student participation during the manipulations.
2. The teacher gets students to write their ideas down on paper.
3. Students respond to teacher questions and discuss concepts illustrated.
4. The teacher asks questions of both volunteers and nonvolunteers.
5. The teacher questions students throughout the room.
6. The teacher allows time for students to answer.

Student participation: total points earned _____

IV. Checks Concept Understanding ___ ___ ___ ___ ___ ___

1. Asks questions at the appropriate cognitive levels to develop ideas, concepts and principles.
2. Questions are probing in nature and stimulate students to think.
3. Questions direct students through a logical thought pattern.

	Excellent					Poor
	5	4	3	2	1	0
4. Questions permit students to draw their own conclusions.	___	___	___	___	___	___
5. Questions stimulate students to initiate further investigations.						
Checks concept understanding: total points earned ____						
V. Establishes Familiarity with Materials	___	___	___	___	___	___
1. The teacher checks students for familiarity with materials and apparatus.						
2. Students show proficiency in being familiar with apparatus used through oral or written means.						
3. All materials and apparatus are readily available.						
4. Proper safety precautions have been followed.						

Total points earned ____

Preparation: total points earned ____

(Total points possible: 25)

Source: From "How-to-Do-It: Developing Dynamic Demonstration," by A. L. Gillen, W. E. Brown, and R. P. Williams, 1989, *American Biology Teacher, 51*(5), pages 306–311. Copyright 1989 National Association of Biology Teachers. Reprinted by permission.

An important beginning here is a definition of terms. *Computers,* of course, have become well known in homes, schools, and businesses, but current technology has transformed them into fax machines, telephones and cell phones, televisions, and hotlines.

Today's learners and teachers use computers to access the Internet and World Wide Web and to build their own websites. The term *multimedia* describes "virtually any conjunction of media on the computer screen" (Lynch, 1993). It includes various combinations of text, graphics, sound, video, and animation that are controlled, coordinated, and delivered on the computer screen. Multimedia also implies interactivity, so that learners using multimedia are actively involved in the presentation of information.

Expectations from Computers and Multimedia as Stimuli

There is a widespread agreement that our students must be prepared to meet the challenges of technology in tomorrow's workplace and society, and that schools have become a "wired" community for teaching and learning. Other educational priorities—creating integrated and student-centered curriculum, helping learners become critical thinkers and good problem solvers, providing collaborative contexts, and developing authentic assessments—can be served well by thoughtful use of technology in schools.

One of the primary advantages of stimuli such as the World Wide Web is that it is very compatible with the way students now prefer to learn (Owston, 1997): "Most students in public schools, K–12, do not know a world without the computer—it is an integral part of their world" (p. 29). In addition to capitalizing on how students learn and on their preferences, using computers and multimedia can provide the following opportunities:

1. Opportunity for practice—students can use games or programs for review and seatwork (review Chapter 9)
2. Opportunity for development and completion of projects, research, and demonstrations
3. Opportunity for collaboration on problems, practice, and challenges
4. Simulated experiences for application of knowledge and skill, and exploration of attitudes
5. Individual and group assessment of student knowledge, skill, attitude, progress, and achievement
6. Record keeping, management, and storage of student work, assessments, and reflections
7. Collaboration between educators in the development of curriculum, sharing of information, and planning for individual students

You will see examples of how you can use computers and multimedia to meet these expectations as we describe the guidelines for use and as you scan the Snapshots.

Guidelines for Using Computers and Multimedia as Stimuli

Many of us began using computers with little direction or training. Some of the first classroom uses included extra practice for students having difficulty, remediation programs, and games for those students who finished their regular work quickly. These practices limited the effect of computers as stimuli, and few students actually benefited. As we describe guidelines for using computers, our goal is variation for all students. We encourage you to do the following:

1. Assure that each student has equitable access to equipment through alternative and flexible scheduling.
2. Plan for social interaction in computer use with pair and group assignments, tutor teams, and cross-school networks.
3. Connect computer use to whole-class or small group instruction, to home and community.
4. Preview and critique software yourself, and encourage student evaluation.

Following these guidelines will take planning and management because curriculum and schedules affect computer use. Several examples will serve as illustrations for you. The first involves having four practice alternatives following a series of math demonstrations: practice with manipulatives (in pairs), practice with games and card sets (groups of four), and practice with computers (two to three learners). Some of the demonstrations may involve the use of multimedia, and others by teacher or students. Demonstrations and practice sessions can be scheduled for several consecutive days to allow students to practice with each alternative. Related homework assignments can be planned for additional computer use at home or before and after school.

Another example is the use of ongoing assignments such as a research report for history or geography, a writing assignment, or data collection for science. Such assignments can be for individual students, pairs of students, or small groups. Over the week of work on the assignment, each student or group has a time slot and is expected to complete part of the assignment on the computer.

Another example is conducting several evaluation sessions with students after they have used some common forms of multimedia. You may also schedule preview times for small groups to critique and make recommendations for use of a CD-ROM, hypermedia, software programs, or networking technology.

As you look at the Snapshots, you will get more ideas about how to follow the guidelines for using computers and multimedia as stimuli.

Using Computers and Multimedia with Variation

We have photographed elementary, middle-school, and secondary classrooms to help you use computers and multimedia with as much variation as possible. We provide reminders of the guidelines and appropriate expectations of what computers can do as we scan the Snapshots with you.

SNAPSHOT: Secondary Classroom

In a geometry class, small groups of students are asked to create a family album for a specific geometric shape such as a polygon or quadrilateral. First, they use a computer to generate random samples of their group's shape and to obtain measures of specific attributes for each figure. Then they use a ruler and a protractor to reproduce the examples for their albums. Finally, they develop a list of properties for the shape they are investigating. As students construct their own descriptions for a particular geometric shape, there's enthusiasm and creative work. They are engaged in the "doing of mathematics" (Jenson, 1988).

This classroom computer use follows several guidelines with its collaborative use and connection with whole-class instruction. It meets the expectations of computers to provide practice and application.

This classroom use is definitely a social activity, as well as an opportunity for practice, review, and individual assessment. Notice how classroom volunteers could be

SNAPSHOT: *Elementary Classroom*

In a first-grade classroom, children participate in a class discussion about information such as names, birthdays, pets, favorite games, and holidays. After the discussion, each child completes an Information about Me worksheet. A template that duplicates the worksheet is created for the database program. During the day, pairs of students come up to the computer and have their information typed in or type it themselves.

When all the data are entered, children gather around the computer in small groups. They watch as each child's information is found. Children can compare their own information sheet with the information on the monitor. They also quickly learn how to find their own information. Later, questions such as, How many of our classmates have birthdays in March? can be posed and a computer list may be generated for monthly birthdays (Collis, 1988).

used effectively to assist the activity and how a variety of groups is possible for the viewing of data. Review those grouping possibilities in Chapter Ten.

SNAPSHOT: *Middle-School Classroom*

In this English class, the teacher has prepared a format of a book summary using a database program. Each time a student reads a book, he or she enters information about it in the database. As the book report database gets larger, students begin to access it for ideas of books to read. The teacher also uses it to get summaries of the types of books most popular with students to use in planning. Periodically, the teacher searches the entries of each student and conferences with those who are not well represented in the data. Those students sometimes need suggestions for reading material.

Notice how the book report database provides you and your students with assessment information. The format can be tailored to meet the criteria being emphasized in your class.

SNAPSHOT: *Secondary Classroom*

Throughout secondary classrooms, portfolios are being used for assessing (observing, describing, documenting, reflecting, diagnosing, and prescribing) and reporting (progress and achievement). Electronic portfolio systems, such as hypercard sets, have cards for collecting, organizing, and presenting portfolio information. Cards allow students to show actual work samples by copying videotaped performances, scanning works on paper, and recording reflections and feedback. Teachers, students, and families may keep copies of the portfolio on disk for record-keeping purposes (Hunter, Bagley, & Bagley, 1993).

The advantages of using electronic portfolio assessment include an integration of technology with other teaching strategies and with the content learning being evaluated. In the process, learners become competent and confident with technology use.

Such technology use expands the learning community beyond the classroom door and creates new opportunities for teachers to collaborate with other professionals.

When computers are used extensively in classrooms (as described in the next Research Vignette), "teachers inevitably report that they change their teaching style to allow students greater autonomy in their learning—a shift from a didactic to more project-based approach" (Owston, 1997, p. 30).

As we work together to provide students with the kinds of learning we value—critical thinking, problem solving, communication, and collaboration (Uchida, 1996)—we must note technology's potential to foster development of such outcomes when used effectively (Owston, 1997).

Your options with computers and multimedia are many. The bonus you will receive as you use them is that you will probably learn right along with your students, as you use computers and multimedia to vary the stimuli.

VARYING THE STIMULI FOR INCLUSIVE CLASSROOMS

When we look at the enormity of responsibilities that are part of teaching any class effectively, we cannot help but admire good teachers immensely. Fortunately, as we approach more and more inclusive classrooms, teachers and other educators are sharing their insights and experiences to help us be successful in making our classroom places where all learners can be successful. Two very significant guidelines for inclusion are relevant to the topic of varying the stimuli: "(1) inclusion means implementing a multilevel, multimodality curriculum; and (2) inclusion means preparing and supporting teachers to teach interactively" (Sapon-Shevin, 1995, p. 65).

We think that the broad array of stimuli for instruction, which is increasing rapidly, will support you to provide such curriculum and teaching. Some examples and teacher advice will illustrate that support.

Starting with curriculum, teachers are moving away from textbook-based frontal teaching to more student-directed approaches. A look at a group of fourth-grade teachers who planned and implemented a unit on Texas illustrates the kind of curriculum and

Research Vignette: K–12 Teachers

INTRODUCTION

Most educators today feel overwhelmed by the challenge of preparing learners for our increasingly complex technological society. Science teachers feel especially challenged because "computers and other advanced technologies are a vital component of our expanding concept of scientific literacy" (Shroyer & Borchers, 1996). We realize that our efforts to promote scientific literacy have to go beyond purchase of computers and adoption of new curriculum. History has taught us that real change in student outcomes depends on teachers—their beliefs and attitudes and their behaviors in the classroom.

Researchers at Kansas State University engaged in a two-year program to study the factors that influence teachers usage of technology and to help teachers integrate technology into their science teaching.

RESEARCH DESIGN

This two-year study of 14 teachers in rural schools used case study methodology. Both quantitative data (surveys of microcomputer utilization and teacher efficacy beliefs) and qualitative data (observations, interviews, journals, lesson plans, and demographics) were collected before, during, and after the professional development program in which the teachers were engaged.

An overarching research question guided the data collection and analysis: "What organizational, procedural, community, and personal factors enhance implementation of action plans to enhance microcomputer usage in rural science teaching?" (Shroyer & Borchers, 1996, p. 421).

STUDY RESULTS

The Shroyer and Borchers (1996) study yielded extensive findings—too many for this vignette. However, we have highlighted some of the relevant results for your preparation to teach.

First, the study demonstrated that the two-year program of continuous information and experiences increased teachers' use of microcomputers in science teaching. Their students "began using word processing, databases, telecommunications, and microcomputer laboratories to learn and do science" (p. 423). The results also showed an increase in teachers' efficacy, attitude, and enthusiasm toward technology for their everyday teaching. Listen to the teachers:

> "I'm using it everyday. I don't know how we ever did without it. I use it more and more for classroom management" (p. 425).
>
> "I have used the computer for direct instruction, which I never did before.... I had never used the computer for whole class instruction. I had always used it as a supplemental or enrichment or remediation approach but did not see it as a tool for instruction" (p. 425).

The organizational factors of pressure, support, and encouragement from school administration all appeared to be positive influences on teachers' attitudes and use of microcomputers. Ongoing assistance and seminars were found to be more effective in changing teacher beliefs and behaviors (Borchers, Shroyer, & Enochs, 1992) than the intensive two-day workshops.

Community pressure for technology also prompted teacher usage, especially when the teachers received more resources, release time, and technical assistance. Although there were no definite patterns in the data relating personal factors to implementation, novice users of technology tended to embrace the project more enthusiastically than others.

CONCLUSIONS AND IMPLICATIONS FOR PRACTICE

As a preservice or new teacher, you may be feeling unprepared to integrate technology into your teaching. When you are ready to address the challenge, pursue a set of ongoing workshops or a course that extends over several months. Avoid the one- or two-day courses; rather, look for ways to solicit ongoing support and assistance. Check on what kind of administrative and collegial support you can expect. Use the findings from Borchers and Shroyer to maximize the potential for success as you seek to *vary the stimuli* with computers.

teaching that will accommodate a class of diverse learners. As you observe them and their classrooms, look for all the uses of stimuli.

Using a map of Texas as a starting point, the teachers brainstormed interdisciplinary objectives and learning activities, such as roleplaying, cooperative group investigations, the creation of dioramas or murals, song writing and dancing, field trips, letters to state officials, and even planning a state trip. Their planned activities are learner centered, interactive, participatory, multimodal, and fun. "Within a broadly designed curriculum such as this, including students with varying educational needs becomes easier" (Sapon-Shevin, 1995, p. 66).

In the classrooms, Nicole, who has cerebral palsy, is cutting and pasting state landmarks on a wall chart of Texas. She is working with Jose, a student who has just arrived from Mexico and who is teaching the class Spanish words for *town, river,* and *street,* which he has projected on a wall using the overhead projector. After watching a film, a small group of students is preparing a roleplay on the establishment of the state of Texas. Tammy, who is identified as gifted, is preparing a class newsletter on their study. She has used a tape recorder to interview her classmates and will then transcribe and summarize their conversations for her articles (Sapon-Shevin, 1995, p. 67).

Did you notice all the uses of stimuli? Even in the teachers' planning process? More importantly, did you notice how students were learning with and from each other? The interaction with peers and with materials and other forms of stimuli in the class represent changes in both curriculum and teaching. Those changes are recommended for accommodating the diversity of learners you will find in most classrooms and especially an inclusive classroom.

SUMMARY

Did you feel a bit smug when you looked at the old school Snapshots? We have come a long way in our use of stimuli. But return in time with us once more. This time, we are skimming through an old teaching methods handbook. We find a page and a half under a heading, Handling Materials:

> *The problem of management in connection with the physical materials of instruction is growing more pressing, because the materials are growing more numerous. In the classroom today, to the regular texts have been added many supplementary texts: plasticine and clay and sand have their recognized place; paper and cardboard of various sizes and colors for cutting, folding, pasting, and drawing have come to stay. Photographs, stereoscopes, maps, charts, minerals and other specimens for geography, and nature study are all making new demands on skills of the teacher. (Breed, 1922, p. 7)*

The picture sounded overwhelming and exciting in 1922 just as it does today. Substitute videocassettes, computers, overhead projectors, the World Wide Web, and CD-ROMs, and the rest of the narrative fits. There is a need for skills in using resources, audiovisuals, and computers to vary the stimuli.

We remind you to begin with your consideration of the *content, context,* and *learner* when you use stimuli. Your purpose(s) may be *to develop concepts, to enrich experiences, to extend experiences, to stimulate interest, to provide meaningful information,* or *to provide opportunities for practice.* Your selection of effective stimuli is based on a match with content and learner.

Once your selection is made, remember the importance of *preparation.* Include previewing a resource or audiovisual, arranging your classroom for its use, and practice using equipment. Your preparation continues with *scheduling decisions, decisions of how to use, decisions about involving students,* and *decisions about future use.*

From there, you have guidelines for the range of choices available to you. Whether you are using a field trip or a software program, the first guideline is that the stimuli are only part of your teaching. You will need to use other teaching strategies and to connect the stimuli to other learning experiences. A processing step for reviewing impressions, perceptions, understandings, and information is important after any stimuli use. During this step, consider procedures for organizing the stimuli for both present and future use.

With most audiovisual materials and equipment, *visibility and clarity, volume,* and *student interaction* are essential. We have urged you to be creative and to discover unusual ways to vary the stimuli for your teaching. Resources, audiovisuals, and computers are constantly being developed and improved. With their use is support for learning and creative potential for your teaching. *Vary the stimuli!*

REFERENCES

Borchers, C. A., Shroyer, M. G., & Enochs, L. G. (1992). A staff developmental model to encourage the use of microcomputers in science teaching. *School Science and Mathematics, 92*(7), 384–391.

Breed, F. S. (1922). *Public school methods.* Chicago, IL: School Methods Publishing.

Brown, R. G. (1993). Multimedia boxes are more than just fun. *Clearinghouse, 66*(5), 315–317.

Clark, R. E. (1994). Media will never influence learning. *Educational Technology Research and Development, 42*(2), 21–29.

Collis, B. (1988). *Computers, curriculum, and whole-class instruction.* Belmont, CA: Wadsworth.

Cordi, K. (1997, January). Poetry aloud. *English Journal,* 99–101.

Dowaliby, F. J. (1993). *Project 2000: Utilizing interactive multimedia technology.* The Living Textbook—To Improve Science Outcomes (Project Report).

Ellis, A. (1998). *Teaching and learning elementary social studies* (6th ed.). Boston: Allyn and Bacon.

Finlay, J. (1991). Creative minutes in the school yard. *Nature Study, 44*(4), 33.

Gillen, A. L., Brown, W. E., & Williams, R. P. (1989). How-to-do-it: Developing dynamic demonstration. *The American Biology Teacher, 51*(5), 306–311.

Hammonds, K. (1994). Dig into community resources. *Instructor, 104*(1), 72–74.

Haugland, S., & Shade, D. (1994). Software evalution for young children. In J. Wright & D. Shade (Eds.), *Young children: Active learners in a technological age.* Washington, DC: National Assocation for the Education of Young Children.

Hunter, B., Bagley, C., & Bagley, R. (1993). Technology in the classroom: Preparing students for the Information Age. *Schools in the Middle, 2*(4), 3–6.

Jenson, R. J. (1988). Teaching mathematics with technology. *Arithmetic Teacher, 35*(6), 4–46.

Johns, F., & Liske, K. (1992). Schoolyard adventuring. *Science and Children, 30*(3), 19–21.

Lynch, P. J. (1993). Interactive media enlivens learning. *Computing Technology for Higher Education, 2*(3), 8–11.

Mason, J. L. (1977). *Professional teacher education module series: Directing field trips.* Columbus, OH: National Center for Research in Vocational Education. (ERIC Document Reproduction Service NO. ED 149 065).

Owston, R. D. (1997). The World Wide Web: A technology to enhance teaching and learning. *Educational Researcher, 26*(2), 27–33.

Pandiscio, E., & Yeager, E. (1993). Newscasts in the classroom. *Educational Leadership, 50*(8), 52–53.

Payne, B. (1993). A word is worth a thousand pictures: Teaching students to think critically in a culture of images. *Social Studies Review, 32*(3), 38–43.

Robertson, S. (1999). Personal communication. Santa Barbara, CA.

Rock, H., & Cummings, A. (1994). Can videodiscs improve student outcomes? *Educational Leadership, 51*(6), 46–50.

Sapon-Shevin, M. (1995). Why gifted students belong in inclusive schools. *Educational Leadership, 52*(4), 64–70.

Shroyer, M. N., & Borchers, C. A. (1996). Factors that support school change to enhance the use of microcomputers in rural schools. *School Science and Mathematics, 96*(8), 419–431.

Tiene, D. (1994). Teens react to Channel One: A survey of junior high school students. *Tech Trends, 39*(3), 17–20.

Uchida, C. (1996) *Preparing students for the 21st century.* Arlington, VA: American Association of School Administrators.

Wilson, L. J. (1998). Children as software reviewers. *Childhood Education, 74*(4), 250–252.

Yeager, E. A., & Pandiscio, E. A. (1993). Newscasts in the classroom. *Educational Leadership, 50*(8), 52–53.

SAMPLES AND EXAMPLES

The following Samples and Examples are included to assist you when you vary the stimuli:

- Penny Arcade is a writing activity for viewing films that involves the students.
- The Audiovisual Assessment Form is a quick five-item assessment form to judge the effectiveness of a specific audiovisual stimuli (e.g., film, videotape, etc.)
- The Questions to Promote Critical Thinking about Documentaries, TV News, Docudramas, and Movies Based on Historical Events will prompt discussion and insights for your students.

PENNY ARCADE

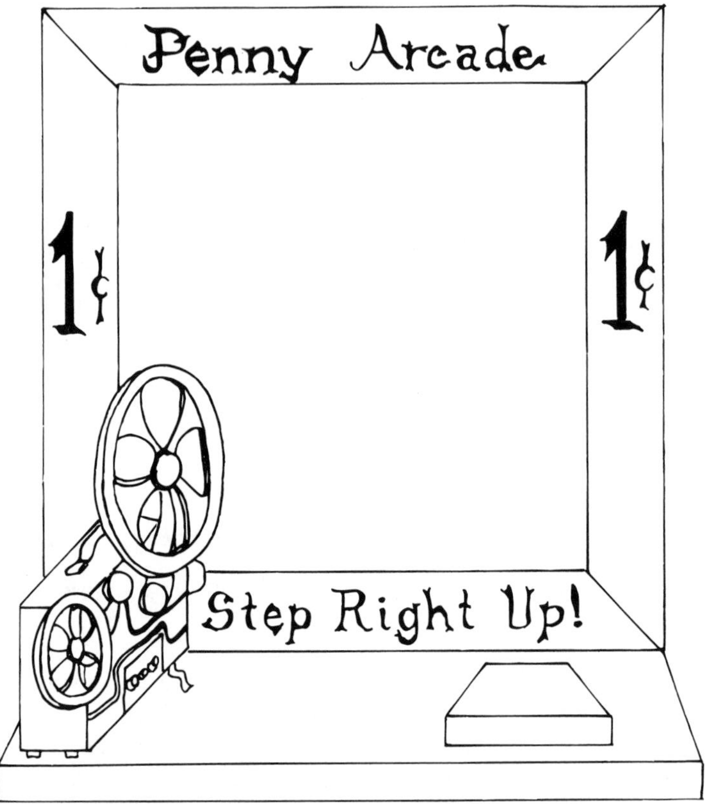

Objective:
After viewing a portion of a film at the center, the student will write a conclusion to the film in a two-page paper, using dialogue and narration with descriptive words and variety in sentence structure.

Directions:
1. Turn on the projector and view the film for 10 minutes.
2. Stop the projector and rewind the film.
3. Now, write an ending to the film you have just seen by taking on the role of one of the characters. Your conclusion should be at least two pages in length. Be sure to use descriptive words and variety in sentence structure.
4. Place your paper in the box when you have completed the center.

Materials Teacher Provides:
The teacher should provide a story film and a projector for the student to view. The story should be at least 20 minutes long, so that after viewing the film for 10 minutes the student will be able to write an original ending to the film.

Source: From Don M. Beach, *Reaching Teenagers: Learning Centers for Secondary Classrooms* (Santa Monica, CA: Goodyear Publishing Co., 1977), pp. 48–49. Reprinted by permission.

AUDIOVISUAL ASSESSMENT FORM

Type	Title	Source	Quality	Student Response
Film	Your Health	Library	Poor	Bored, laughter
Photoset	Geometry	AV Center	Excellent	Entertained - interactive
Filmstrip	Dairy Farms	AVC	Very Good	Best used in small groups—with discussion
Large posters	Environment	Lib.	Very Good	Activity ideas on back - successful; high involvement

QUESTIONS TO PROMOTE CRITICAL THINKING ABOUT DOCUMENTARIES, TV NEWS, DOCUDRAMAS, AND MOVIES BASED ON HISTORICAL EVENTS

Documentaries/TV News

1. Use of Time
   - Does the camera focus on individual scenes long enough for you to understand what is happening?
   - Does one group of people get more time on camera than another?
   - Are events separated by a long period of time shown to happen at or near the same time?
2. Camera Angles
   - Does the camera pan to show you as much of the scene as possible or does it focus on only one part of the action?
   - Are camera angles more flattering to one group than another? (e.g., shadows on faces, squinting in the sun)
3. Editing
   - During the interviews, does the camera switch back to the interviewer or another scene while the person being interviewed is still talking?
   - Compare printed versions of speeches with the segments shown on the news. Were important sections edited out or taken out of context?
4. Music
   - Does the background music change when different people or groups come on the screen?
   - How does the background music affect your attitude toward the topic?

Movies/Docudramas

1. Use of Time
   - Same concerns apply to this category.
   - Does the condensing of time in the movie affect your understanding of the events?
2. Dialogue
   - How much of the dialogue do you believe comes from documents (diaries, etc.) or interviews?
   - Does the dialogue involve the viewer in the personal lives of one group more than another?
3. Camera Angles
   - Same as for documentaries but even more techniques will be used.
   - Is lighting or camera focus used to enhance certain characters more than others?
4. Music
   - Same as for documentaries, though more important.
5. Staging and Cast
   - Are makeup and costumes used to flatter one group more than another?
   - Does the choice of actors affect how you view their role in the movie? Are any of the actors well known for other roles that would lead you to have positive or negative feelings about them?
   - Are there any characters added that were obviously not part of the events dramatized?

6. Historical Accuracy
   - Do any of the events in the movie not follow the order of events as they took place in history?
   - Do any of the events added for entertainment purposes overly distort the movie?
   - Are any individuals or events obviously misrepresented?

Source: From "A Word Is Worth a Thousand Pictures: Teaching Students to Think Critically in a Culture of Images" by B. Payne, 1993, *Social Studies Review, 32*(3), pages 38–43.

CHAPTER

14

ASSESSMENT OF LEARNING

Let Me Count the Ways

Chapter Outcomes

At the conclusion of this chapter you will be able to:

1. *Use and understand the language of assessment.*
2. *Describe and use assessment for multiple purposes.*
3. *Develop and use different assessment strategies.*
4. *Consider the content, context, and learner in assessment decisions.*

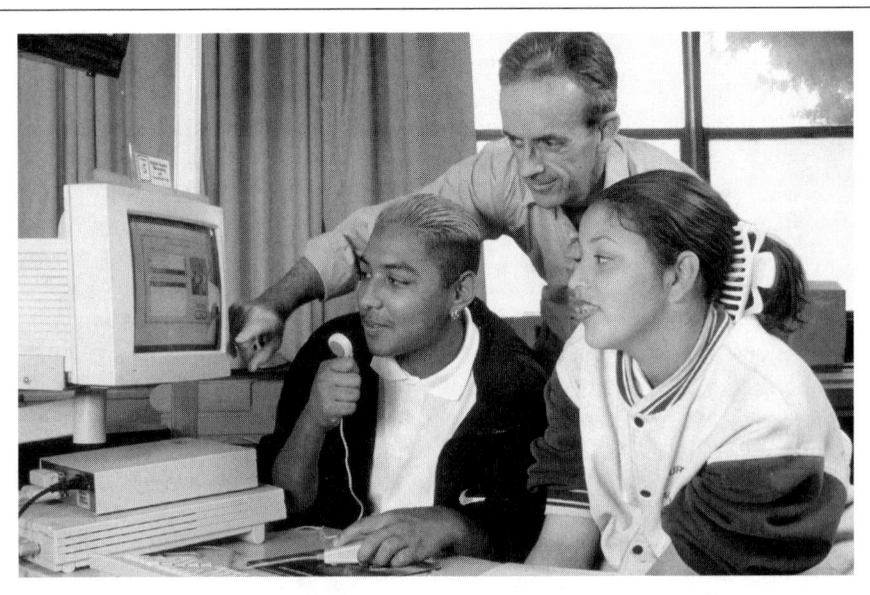

Key Terms and Concepts

Evaluation
Assessment
Diagnostic Assessment
Formative Assessment
Summative Assessment
Informal Assessment
Formal Assessment
Criterion-Referenced Tests
Standardized Tests
Norm-Referenced Tests
Inquiry
Reliability/Validity
Teacher-Made Tests
Anecdotal Records
Checklists
Rating Scales
Fill in the Blank or Short Answer
True-False Tests
Multiple-Choice Tests
Matching Tests
Essay Tests
Questionnaire
Interview
Portfolio
Performance Tasks
Assessment and Inclusion
Student-Led Parent Conferences
Narrative Report Cards

INTRODUCTION

We begin this chapter with a Snapshot that portrays the assessment choices and decisions that teachers face today.

SNAPSHOT: Elementary Classroom

For the past week, Pam Rossio's students have been curious and responsive to a partial bulletin board entitled "Our Environment." On Monday, she urged them to take time during the week to write questions related to the photographs and newspaper clippings, to add items of their own to the board, and to think and talk about the display. During the week, she gave journal writing assignments related to the environmental ecology unit that she was about to plan.

After reading the journal entries, Pam decides to emphasize conservation measures and the immediate environment of her students in her content plans. She reads the students' questions and thinks to herself, "There's some curiosity about forestry and mining—I expected that." She frowns and thinks, "Some of these are very simple ideas, but a few questions get into complex ideas." She checks the content of her unit to see if it will match the range of student understanding.

She thinks about a conversation she heard between Mona and Ardyth. Mona described a TV program about ecology and expressed a mature sensitivity and understanding. Pam noted the conversation because she was stunned by Mona's interest and knowledge, even some unusual vocabulary. As she reflects on the options her students will have to demonstrate their knowledge and understanding of ecology, Pam thinks of Mona: She does so poorly on written tests. Pam wants to be sure that Mona and others will have alternative ways to communicate their learning—ways such as projects and conferencing.

In addition to alternative assessments, however, Pam intends to use three tests from the textbook that her students use. They are criterion-referenced tests, and she plans to use one each week as a review and a check on content understandings. She is also developing a checklist for students to use in recording their own progress and to include in their portfolios.

A major goal of Pam's unit is to develop and improve attitudes toward ecology; she has an intense commitment to this intent. She struggles with how to measure those attitudes and considers doing a student interview, "I don't know how I will find time. Maybe I can use a questionnaire, or perhaps I can get parent volunteers to help."

Pam is especially reflective about her assessment decisions because she is part of a teacher committee on assessment for her school district. Her committee has been surveying the advantages and disadvantages of the district's use of standardized tests. The committee has also been studying portfolios and narrative reporting procedures.

While you were reading this Snapshot, did you feel familiar with the terminology? Did you encounter labels that need definition? Not surprising! Assessment seems to have the most extensive set of language of any teaching and learning strategy and it's expanding even as we write this chapter.

It is important to be able to talk about assessment using terms correctly and knowledgeably with other teachers, with administrators, with parents, and with your learners. Once familiar with the language, it will be even more important for you to develop assessment expertise during this time of school reform. The movement toward national standards of what students should know and be able to do has created a demand for new, improved assessments (Alexander, 1993).

On a national level, there is strong support for "world-class" standards and "tough tests" to show which children meet them and which do not (Allen, 1998). The call for standards and assessment has emerged on many state agendas and it has become common to equate "holding students and teachers accountable with student performance on standardized tests" (Allen, 1998, p. 12).

At the same time, there is increased awareness of and commitment to the role of assessment in the improvement of teaching (Popham, 1998). Assessment is no longer something teachers can "tack on" at the end of teaching and learning. "It is an essential ongoing component of instruction that guides the process of learning" (Simmons, 1994). There are exciting assessment projects being conducted in countless schools, districts, and states, and we will describe many of these examples as we guide you in your development of ways to assess learning.

Language of Assessment

We begin this chapter with assessment language. Many of the terms are interrelated, so we will define them in a framework with examples. As you can see in Table 14.1, the starting point is *evaluation*—that is, the process of making a decision about student learn-

TABLE 14.1 *Framework of Evaluation*

Diagnostic		Formative		Summative	
Formal	*Informal*	*Formal*	*Informal*	*Formal*	*Informal*
Standardized tests	Observations	Checklists	Journals	Inquiry	Discussion
Pretests	Discussions	Quizzes	Observations	Work projects	Observations
Placement tests	Journals	Questions-answers	Questions-answers	Standardized tests	Work Projects
Inquiry		Assignments	Student comments	Classroom tests	Student feedback
Questionnaires		Standardized tests	Assignments	Interviews	
		Classroom tests		Portfolios	
		Portfolios		Performance tasks	
		Performance tasks			
		Interviews			

ing. Evaluation requires us to make a judgment about student knowledge, student behavior or performance, or student attitude. *Assessment* is a strategy for measuring that knowledge, behavior or performance, or attitude. It is a data-gathering strategy. The measurement or data you gain from assessment helps you make the decision of evaluation.

As you can see in the framework, teachers use three major kinds of assessment: *diagnostic, formative,* and *summative.* A simple way of thinking about and remembering these is that you must make decisions *before, during,* and *after* your instruction. Keep the framework in front of you as we describe each of the three kinds of assessment.

Diagnostic Assessment

Pam Rossio used her bulletin board to begin diagnostic assessment. She learned what students already knew and what they were curious about. She learned more as she listened to their conversations and read their journal entries. When diagnostic assessment is used prior to teaching, as in Pam's classroom, it provides planning information. Pam's strategies for diagnostic assessment were *informal*—that is, unstructured. Her alternative would have been a *formal* diagnostic assessment—meaning a scheduled and structured assessment. A commonly used formal diagnostic assessment is a *pretest,* which is a measure of student knowledge about information that is going to be taught before it is taught.

Using both formal and informal diagnostic assessments in your planning process will give you a complete picture of student readiness and interest for your teaching. Diagnosis doesn't have to stop once plans are complete. Effective teachers continue to diagnose student understanding and interest throughout each lesson or unit of teaching. This ongoing assessment during teaching is called *formative assessment.*

Formative Assessment

Formative assessment is conducted during instruction, again either formally or informally. Both teachers and students receive information from this kind of assessment: information about problems, errors, misunderstandings, understandings, and progress. The textbook tests that Pam plans to use and the checklist she developed for student use will formally assess progress. Informally, Pam will listen to student comments and conversations during the activities for formative assessment.

Student portfolios will also provide important formative assessment data. Portfolios are collections of student work that are longitudinal, diverse in content, and collaborative in their selection. Portfolios are intended to emphasize strengths, development of skills, improvement, and personal reflections, thus providing a broad picture of student learning. Informally, Pam will listen to student comments and conversations during activities for more formative assessment.

The information you gather with formative assessment will help you revise your teaching plans to better match the learner, and will tell you whether your teaching has been effective. One possible outcome of Pam Rossio's use of textbook tests is that she will have to reteach a concept. One possible outcome of her use of student checklists is that she may have to change the pace of her unit. If students indicate problems or confusion, she may need to slow the pace; if students indicate boredom, she may have to speed it up. One possible outcome of listening to and observing students and reviewing their portfolios is that she may have to change or clarify content. You can see that it is important for Pam to use both formal and informal strategies because the data from her observations will support and explain the data from her tests and checklist, and vice versa.

Summative Assessment

Summative assessment is conducted at the end of a lesson, a unit, or a course. It is a final measure of what was learned. Most of us have taken numerous summative assessments in the form of final exams. They offer an opportunity for some learners to demonstrate what they have learned. For others, alternative summative assessments, such as projects and performance tasks, are necessary if we are to obtain a true picture of individual learning. When summative assessment is well developed and matched to individual learners, it will tell you about your teaching as well as about your students' learning. Student portfolios can provide such comprehensive information.

Pam is also concerned about measuring student attitudes and is interested in using an inquiry assessment. *Inquiry* is the process of specifically asking students how they feel, what they think, what their likes and dislikes are, and probing their understanding. One possible inquiry strategy is an *interview,* a face-to-face meeting in which one person obtains information from another. Pam thought about asking everyone to respond to an environmental situation or picture. Because of time constraints, she also thought about using a *questionnaire,* which is another inquiry assessment. The efficiency of a questionnaire comes from its written form so that all students answer the questions at the same time, or at least independent of their teacher.

As we described earlier, Pam Rossio is working with other teachers on an assessment committee. One of their tasks is to make recommendations about the use of standardized tests. Standardized tests are commercially designed and administered in the same way to each student or group of students. They are usually nationally norm referenced; that is, they have been administered and scored for groups of students who represent the general population.

By now, the language may be sounding more familiar to you. As we describe the purposes and uses of assessment, you will have a chance to check your understanding of terms. Our goal is to have the vocabulary used with ease and accuracy.

PURPOSES OF ASSESSMENT

Most teachers consider assessment an important part of teaching. The ultimate purpose is to measure student learning. The additional purposes are improvement of teaching, curriculum, and conditions for student learning. In fact, this chapter's subtitle, "Let Me Count the Ways" refers to a broad vision of assessment that addresses multipurposes with multiforms. As you begin to develop your assessment expertise, we suggest purposes that go beyond the measurement of student learning.

Using Assessment Data for Planning

Before you plan a lesson, there is a variety of information that you must know about your students. To plan objectives, you must assess current levels of knowledge and skill. To plan activities, you must assess work habits, independence, interests, previous experiences, social relationships, and learning styles. To plan materials and resources, you must assess previous experiences, competence with materials, comprehension level, and interests.

On the first day of school, Ms. Lewelyn asked her students to complete a questionnaire about their literature preferences and reading preferences and reading experiences. She also facilitated small group discussions focusing on the question: What class activities help you understand and appreciate literature? Her year-long planning then reflected students' tastes in reading, and she used their previous experiences as starting points or comparisons for new literature. Student preferences were reflected in her teaching and learning activities. As a result, students showed high levels of interest in the class and participated enthusiastically in activities. This teacher used assessment data for planning, and the result was appropriate curriculum and activities.

Using Assessment Data for Decision Making

Assessment for decision making calls for the kind of reflection and responsible behaviors we observed in Pam Rossio. Many of the decisions made with assessment data have serious consequences for the lives of students and their families. Look at some of the most commonly made decisions using assessment data:

- Grouping and placement decisions (assignment of students to ability groups or classes for instruction)
- Identification of need for special services (referral of students to remedial or special classes)
- Grades (assignment of letter or number quantification on records and report cards)
- Promotion or retention, graduation, certification

- Educational and vocational counseling (advising for future study and work)
- Curricular decisions (to continue or discontinue a program of studies)
- Personnel decisions (to maintain or dismiss a teacher or other professional)

All seven of these decisions are influenced by data from both standardized tests and those tests that you develop. Although you do not determine the content of standardized assessments, you can influence how they are used if you have basic knowledge about the instruments. The power you hear in the Teacher Talk comes from that knowledge.

TEACHER TALK

We're frustrated with the standardized tests our district selected for language arts. The tests have little to do with how or what our students are learning. They don't describe understanding, and they don't consider attitudes.

The new assessment mandated for our state in writing is ridiculous. They found less than 1 percent correlation between the test items and the curricular approach being used to teach. We're going to write a statewide position paper.

Fourth-Grade Teachers

Here are some basic characteristics of standardized tests that you will need to understand:

1. *Reliability* is the consistency with which a test or item measures whatever it measures.
2. *Validity* defines whether an item or a test measures what it is intended to measure.
3. *Practicality* shows considerations of time, cost, difficulty of administration, and scoring to determine usability.
4. *Norm sample* or *standardized population* is the group whose scores are used as a comparison.
5. *Bias* shows items of test content that could discriminate against specific groups of students in terms of language, experiences, and tests.

These characteristics give you basic criteria with which to examine and discuss standardized assessments. We encourage you to study and develop understanding for using the tests. In this chapter we are also working on competence in developing assessments. That competence will determine the quality of the data you will use to make those critical evaluation decisions. The long-term effects of your assessment processes as well as your immediate needs for information are important considerations in the process.

Using Assessment Data to Promote Learning

Assessment is used in classrooms to promote learning in several ways. Your assessment strategy can get students thinking about a topic or reviewing previous knowledge. As we described in Chapter Three, using an assessment to prompt thinking or review is an effective beginning for a lesson. Look at this teacher who is using assessment that motivates: Mrs. Holgate conducts a lively brainstorming session with her middle-school students on the topic of the Civil War. She begins with, "Think of all the information you know about the war." The lists of information give her data about what her students know, don't know, and have confusions about. The process also gets her students excited as they learn about the Civil War.

Remember Pam Rossio's bulletin board? While she was gathering information about what her students knew about ecology, they were thinking about ecology, developing curiosity and interest in it.

The second way in which assessment is used to motivate students is through the feedback they receive. Some of that feedback is in the form of grades, stickers, or comments. Our own philosophy makes us caution you in your use of assessment for motivation. We are not comfortable with students working only for stars, or happy faces, or 100s. We have seen students working in fierce competition with each other for grades or points. That competition may be contrary to the classroom climate we described in Chapters Five and Six. In the Research Vignette shown later in this chapter, you will learn that students want feedback from their teachers more than they want grades (Weiner, 1998).

Students do need the feedback that is possible from assessment—information about their learning, information about their understanding, and information about their accomplishments. That information is necessary for learning and serves to motivate. We describe how to provide such feedback in Chapter Fifteen and in the next section as we suggest how to communicate assessment data.

Using Assessment Data for Communication

There are four major audiences for your communication of assessment data: *students, parents, school personnel,* and *the public.* For each of these audiences, your assessment data must be clearly communicated.

Student Audience

We begin with students. They have a right and a need to learn about their progress and achievement. Both written and verbal communication can provide such information. Students of all ages desire descriptive information along with grades.

STUDENT TALK

I hate it when I get a paper back and all it has on it is the grade. Even if it's an A, it doesn't matter. I want some feedback, some response to all the work I have done. I sometimes wonder if the teacher really read it completely.

High-School Senior

High-school students are not unique in this desire—all students want such communication. Be sure, however, that your communication is informative, helpful, specific, and unique to the student's work. Look at the contrasting examples for effective communication and ineffective communication to students:

> GOOD WORK—NEAT PAPER
>
> All of your multiplication problems have been done accurately. Your computation is easy to follow because numbers are clearly written.
>
> Interesting paper!
>
> You did extensive background reading before doing this paper. The details you provided on this topic made it both informative and entertaining to read.

Parent Audience

Parents are your next audience, and, as we described in Chapter Six, your relationship with parents influences the teaching and learning in your classroom. It does take time to communicate well, but the payoffs are there for you and your students.

Whether writing or speaking to parents, we encourage you to follow the same advice we gave for communicating to students. Be informative, helpful, and specific, especially when communicating assessment data.

We also encourage you to follow some guidelines for your written communication, whether you are writing informal notes or elaborate reports.

1. Make your notes neat and legible (no cross-outs or misspellings).
2. Be clear and concise (avoid long complicated sentences and jargon).
3. Present facts, not impressions (avoid words such as *seemed, felt, appeared*).

These are basic, commonsense suggestions, but parents have complained and critiqued teachers when such guidelines are not followed. Later in this chapter, you will learn of ways to involve parents in the assessment process rather than just reporting assessment data to them.

School Personnel Audience

When communicating with the third audience, school personnel, we suggest the same guidelines we just listed for parents, with an emphasis on clarity. There is a tendency to use jargon because we think that other professionals will understand; this is not necessarily true, however. We know that educational jargon changes rapidly, so a current phrase may mean something different or nothing at all in a few years or in another part of the country.

When you communicate with other school personnel, it is also important to provide complete descriptions and not leave the reader with questions. Be cautious about your use of abbreviations, again, for clarity.

Finally, remember to include multiforms of assessment. Your professional audience will benefit when your data come from varied sources. Another teacher or administrator will understand the student better if the standardized test scores are accompanied by some observational data, a classroom checklist of work habits, and work samples. Again, as throughout this book, we encourage you to go beyond reporting and to collaborate with other teachers on assessment.

Public Audience

Teachers do not usually communicate assessment data to the general public, partly because school districts and state departments of education generally take this responsibility. Standardized test scores are a regular media item, especially if there are gains or national prominence. What does not appear in the media very often are descriptive data from individual teachers.

For most teachers, this sounds like an overwhelming task, but listen to this teacher's experience. She decided that students' work needs to be communicated to her community.

TEACHER TALK

It's difficult for me to show off and I hate to use the phone, but I felt that my students were doing something worth mention. I checked with my district and was encouraged so I contacted the *Chronicle.* I explained what my fifth-graders were doing and checked possible dates with the paper. They said that someone would be there at a certain time and thought it was great news. The reporter talked with the students and took pictures. I was amazed at how easy it was. I will probably do it again.

Fifth-Grade Teacher

This teacher's experience is not unique. Most teachers are pleasantly surprised at how easy it is to communicate student assessment data to the public.

In sum, using assessment for communication has multiple audiences and therefore a need for multiple forms of assessment. When you look at all the purposes of assessment, you see the reasoning behind our theme, "let me count the ways."

HOW TO ASSESS LEARNING—LET ME COUNT THE WAYS

If you begin by thinking of assessment as an "ongoing part of instruction" and as a component that "guides the process of learning" (Simmons, 1994), you will begin your curricular planning with assessment in mind. Once again, consider the content as you make assessment decisions.

Consider the Content

When you consider all the kinds of objectives you have for your teaching, you quickly see that one kind of assessment will not work for all the learning you intend. Think about the learning domains we described in Chapter Three. Your first assessment decision is to select the appropriate domain. Next, determine the appropriate level of the domain so that you can match it with an appropriate way to assess. We will look at each domain briefly to assist you with the matching process.

Assessing the Cognitive Domain

The *cognitive domain* is most often assessed with tests, especially for measuring knowledge, comprehension, analysis, and evaluation. Tests are systematic forms of measurement, either oral or written. At some levels, such as synthesis and application, specific kinds of tests, such as essay tests, are appropriate. For application, it is also appropriate to listen to or to observe students actually using knowledge. Table 14.2 gives you a list of appropriate options for the cognitive domain.

Assessing the Affective Domain

The *affective domain* is more difficult to assess because of the personal and internal qualities of affect. Again, the domain has levels of difficulty so that you can match your assessment to the level of learning. The inquiry strategy is most commonly used for the affective domain, as shown in Table 14.3.

Assessing the Psychomotor Domain

In the *psychomotor domain,* you also have a hierarchy of difficulty levels, ranging from reflex movements to skilled movements. The levels in this domain are generally assessed by observation of either a behavior or performance. Observational data can be recorded

TABLE 14.2 *Assessment Options for the Cognitive Domain*

Domain	Assessment Options
Knowledge	Written tests (fill in the blanks, matching, simple multiple choice) Observation of student recitations
Comprehension	Written tests (true-false, multiple choice, short answer) Student assignments (summaries, explanations) Observations of student discussions Interviews
Application	Written or oral problem solving Multiple-choice tests (with answers based on solving problems) Observation of simulations, roleplay Performance tasks Projects
Analysis	Essay tests Multiple-choice tests that require classifying, coding, inferring, or using criteria Student assignments (comparisons) Portfolios
Synthesis	Essay tests Student projects with a plan, product Written or oral problem solving Portfolios

TABLE 14.3 *Assessment Options for the Affective Domain*

Domain	Assessment Options
Receiving	Observations of student discussions
	Questionnaires
Responding	Observation of student participation
	Interviews
Valuing	Interviews
	Questionnaires
	Essay tests
Organization	Observation of student choices
Characterization	Student responsibilities
	Student projects (taking a position)
	Student debates

as an anecdotal record, or with checklists or rating scales. In the following Snapshot, you see Mr. Whitfield making decisions as he considers the content for assessment.

SNAPSHOT: Secondary Classroom

It's time for first quarter grades and Mr. Whitfield looks at his data in anticipation of the decisions he must make. Most of the quarter has been spent in review of ideas and skills from previous basic art courses, so students have submitted only two products. Last year he developed a rating scale for use with student work. Other art teachers have critiqued the scale and students have provided comments about its helpfulness, so he feels confident using it. (See his rating scale in the Samples and Examples section at the end of this chapter.)

"The ratings don't seem enough," he thinks. He decides to observe his students for at least half of their work period each day for the next week. "I'm usually so busy talking to them about their work that I don't think I have really watched them." He jots a reminder to himself in his lesson plans.

On Monday, students begin working independently after a demonstration of a shading technique. Mr. Whitfield moves around the room in his usual way, comments to several students, and answers questions for about 10 minutes. Then he picks up a class list and begins recording what he sees...

Advanced Art 3—Mon., Nov. 12
11:10 A.M., Rm. 29, Vista H.S.
Subject: shading, still life

Nathan: Seems unaware of other students; that is, works on his drawing for 12 minutes without looking around at other students. Pauses to look at arrangement; has a serious expression on his face.

Rochelle: Looks at the arrangement for a minute and a half, then holds up her pencil at several angles, looks at the arrangement again, then makes reference points on her paper, looking at the arrangement frequently. Asks Donna, "Do these look right to you?"

Donna: Responds, "Think about your proportions. The bowl is fat, the bottle is skinny..." Turns back to her own work, sighs, looks up at the arrangement for a few seconds, then back to her lines. She uses repetitious lines, 5 or 6, for each surface. She moves her entire arm when making the lines.

After several days of writing the anecdotal records, Mr. Whitfield spends time reading his notes. Feeling anxious about his time, he decides to develop a checklist from the behavior he has already observed. "Next week I will use a checklist and see if each student is using the basic techniques." (The checklist is in the Samples and Examples section at the end of this chapter.)

Back to the psychomotor domain levels: reflex movements, basic fundamental movement, perceptual abilities, physical abilities, skilled movements, and nondiscursive communication—all can be assessed with Mr. Whitfield's observation strategy. You may not have noticed, but he followed some important guidelines, which will be helpful for your own classroom observation:

1. Observe students in natural environments or conditions.
2. Observe students in an unobtrusive manner.
3. Record exactly what students do and say.
4. Avoid using terms of judgment, nonspecific descriptions.
5. Provide contextual data (i.e., time, location).

Notice that Mr. Whitfield began observing students after they had been working for 10 minutes. He also moved about the room as he usually did during the work time. Notice, too, that he described Nathan as "Works on his drawing for 12 minutes without looking around at other students," which is more objective than his first comment, "Seems unaware of other students." When he recorded Donna's techniques, he didn't use "Good," or "Well," or even "Smooth." Instead, he described her technique with, "She used repetitious lines, 5 or 6, for each surface."

In addition to observational strategies for assessing the psychomotor domain, performance tasks are being developed to provide the same kind of information. We will describe those tasks later in the chapter.

We began this section with the importance of matching the *content* of assessment with the *how* of assessment. Mr. Whitfield would have difficulty giving an essay exam on most of the content he teaches. In contrast, another teacher might faithfully observe her students each day and not have enough data to determine if each of her students can spell a specific list of words. After teachers consider the content and determine what kind of assessment is appropriate, they have another decision to make: selecting an assessment, or constructing an assessment.

Selecting an Assessment

Your first step in selection is to find out what is available. Remember Pam Rossio's dilemma? She was uncertain about where to find a test on student attitudes.

Locating Assessments

We suggest to Pam and to you to begin with immediate resources: district media center, school resource personnel, textbook series, and/or curriculum guides. Talk with other teachers. Assessment has become an important topic in teacher conversations, and you will find that your colleagues may be the best source of help. If you do locate an assessment, your next step will be to appraise what you find to be sure that it is a quality instrument or strategy.

Appraising Assessments

Ebel (1965) provided teachers with 10 qualities of a good test. The qualities are universal enough to apply to most assessments. Use them to pose the kind of questions we suggest for appraising an assessment:

1. *Relevance.* Do the items of this test match the objectives and content information of my teaching? Does this test measure the learning that I intended for my students?
2. *Balance.* Does this test represent all of the important content that I taught? Is important information given importance in the test items? Is any information given too much representation in the test items?
3. *Efficiency.* How much time will this test take? Is that amount of time appropriate or in proportion to the amount of time I spent teaching the content?
4. *Objectivity.* When I look at answers to the test items, are they fair?
5. *Specificity.* Is there a match between the curriculum information and the test items? Could a student who missed class do well on this test?
6. *Difficulty.* Can at least half of my students do very well on this test? Could each item be answered correctly by at least half of my students?
7. *Discrimination.* Will my students who worked hard, studied well, and are knowledgeable answer most of these items correctly? Will my students who put little effort, did minimal studying, and aren't knowledgeable answer most of these items incorrectly?
8. *Reliability.* Would my students score similarly if they took this test two days in a row? Does it matter who gives this test?
9. *Fairness.* Will all students have an equal chance on this test? Does it favor a particular group?
10. *Speed.* Will my slow-working students be penalized on this test? Will there be any problem with some students finishing this test?

The most common source of ready-made assessments is a textbook, so it will be important to keep in mind that match between the content of the assessment and the content of teaching and learning (Airasian, 1996). Most teaching deviates from or extends beyond what is in the textbook, so you may find that ready-made tests that accompany the textbook are not appropriate. In this case, your choice is to construct an assessment (teacher-made test) or to design an alternative assessment approach (portfolios, performance tasks, etc.). We will describe both of those options in the sections that follow.

Constructing an Assessment (Teacher-Made Tests)

As a starting point, think about your students and your intent for their learning. Consider the content with knowledge, skills, and attitudes. See if you can describe what you would like your assessment to measure. This is a good place to remind you to consider the content. Now you are ready to develop your instrument, probably in rough form. Review it, revise it, and use the 10 qualities we just discussed. If time permits, we suggest that you pilot the instrument with a group of students, and probably revise it again.

The process we just described is in contrast to a "throw it together the night before" test. We know that you are thinking about how long it will take to develop each assessment you may need. We offer some helpful advice: Give short tests and give them frequently. Be sure to review the time-saving ideas in Chapter Four.

You will also need some suggestions for the various specific kinds of assessments. We begin with the most commonly used paper-and-pencil tests and suggest some cautions:

1. Check your language, grammar, punctuation, and spelling. Avoid obscure or ambiguous vocabulary that could cause confusion.
2. Avoid "irrelevant cues" (Remmers, Gage, & Rummel, 1965) that trigger the correct response without any knowledge or skill on the part of the student.
3. Avoid interrelated items—that is, when the answer to one question furnishes the answer to another item.

As you read the three cautions, can you remember taking tests with such problems? Be sure that you don't repeat them with your own students. Now, we move to strategies for constructing specific paper-and-pencil tests.

Fill in the Blank or Short Answer

Provide enough information in a simple direct question or in a stem (part of a statement), as you see in the samples:

- Tests that ____________ student scores are called *norm-referenced tests.*
- How do norm-referenced tests use student scores?

The first example has more than one possible answer (*compare* or *rank*). Be sure that if more than one answer is possible, you will accept more than one answer.

If you want a definition from students, ask for it directly. The item "Define *evaluation*" is better than "The process of making a decision about student learning is called ____________." For this reason, a question form is preferable for this kind of test.

True-False Tests

This kind of test is efficient to score, but remember to avoid irrelevant cues. Look at the following samples:

- A pretest is always given before teaching occurs.
- A pretest can be given before teaching occurs.

Words such as *always, none, all, never, might,* and *generally* give cues or imply answers. Also, be sure that your "true" statements are absolutely true, and that your "false" statements are absolutely false. When they are not, they cause confusion and errors. Finally, we suggest that you work for a fairly equal number of true and false items. Due to the high levels of guessing, true-false tests should be used sparingly.

Multiple-Choice Tests

These tests ask students to select the answer from a set of alternatives. You provide a stem in the form of an incomplete statement or question. Your stem should be clear, direct, and singular in focus. A direct question is best. Consider our example:

- What is the most appropriate use for criterion-referenced tests?
  a. For a diagnosis of student interest in a topic
  b. For a pass-fail assessment of student learning
  c. For student information about progress
  d. For planning information for teachers

Notice that all of the alternatives are similar and parallel. Again, avoid irrelevant cues and use correct alternatives that are absolutely correct. Contrary to common use, the choice "None of the above" as an alternative answer is not useful. It does not provide enough information about student learning.

Matching Tests

Once again, be clear in your criteria for matching and avoid irrelevant cues and absolute matches. This kind of test should not be too long (5 to 6 items for elementary students, 10 to 12 items for secondary students). It should be placed on a single page.

The left side of your matching items contains the *stimuli,* the information items that should prompt thinking and response. The right side lists *possible responses.* In order to assess learning accurately, more responses than stimuli should be provided. Haven't you been in the situation of matching 8 items, knowing 6 of the items and guessing correctly the last 2? If there were more than 8 responses provided, guessing would not be so effective.

Unlike most of the paper-and-pencil assessments, matching tests can be used with young students and nonreaders. The stimuli and responses can be provided with pictures and symbols instead of words.

Essay Tests

We repeat once more: Clear statements of the response expected and a singular focus are essential. Next, remember what is appropriate content for assessing with essay tests—problem solving, synthesis, commitment, and analysis. Be sure that your item asks students to use those criteria. Some other guidelines for writing essay tests include:

1. Provide several short essay items rather than a few long essay items (this will assess more learning).
2. Give students an indication of amount of time to spend or the value of an item (percentages or points).
3. Require all students to respond to the same question so that you have consistent information for all.
4. Decide beforehand what information and ideas you want to see in students' answers, and rate the worth of each in points or percentages.

Evaluation requires multiforms of assessment. Matching, essay, or fill-in-the-blank tests may not be appropriate for what you want to assess. You may need to construct checklists, rating scales, or questionnaires.

Checklists

Remember the checklist Mr. Whitfield used while observing students in his art class? Checklists are generally used during or after observation. To develop a checklist, begin by breaking down the skill or behavior that you intend to assess. The skill may have steps or it may have components. Ask yourself: When I watch a student performing this skill, what are all the behaviors I should see? If we were to observe you using the skills of this chapter, here is the beginning of a checklist we would use:

Construction of Assessment

Name ______________________________

	Observed	*Not Observed*	*Date*
1. Reviews student characteristics	______	__________	___
2. Considers curriculum	______	__________	___
3. Describes purpose	______	__________	___

To complete the checklist, we would continue listing the steps suggested for constructing an assessment. Remember: The purpose of a checklist is to indicate the presence or absence of a behavior or skill. You have choices in how you indicate—dating the observation of a skill, or checking that it was observed, or not checking when it was not observed.

Rating Scales

These are useful for assessing skills, student products, and behaviors. Again, you must break down the skill or behavior into steps, subskills, or components. From there, use either a qualitative scale or a frequency scale for each step or subskill. A *qualitative scale* uses terms such as "excellent to poor"; a frequency scale uses terms such as "always to never." You can also develop specific descriptions for a scale that is tailored to the particular skill you are assessing. We demonstrate your three options in the samples that follow:

Rating Scale—Writing Fill-in-the-Blank Items

Name ______________________________ Date ____________

1. Writes definite and clear stems.

1	2	3	4	5	
Excellent				Poor	(Qualitative)

2. Uses questions instead of incomplete sentences.

1	2	3	4	5	
Always				Never	(Frequency)

3. Gives credit to alternative answers.

_____ only when absolutely correct
_____ only when student demonstrates serious thinking
_____ only when many students give alternative answers
_____ only when it is acknowledged before the test is given

(Specific to the subskill)

Qualitative and frequency ratings work well for most of your student needs. When you use rating scales for your student products, you often use a "poor to excellent" rating scale or, as Mr. Whitfield did, a scale that reflects the criteria of assigned work.

Questionnaires

When you want to assess attitudes, opinions, and feelings, questionnaires are more efficient than interviews and observational recordings. To design a questionnaire, first decide what kind of information you want. Then develop statements or questions to elicit the information.

In developing questionnaires, you have options for formatting questions and responses. Your choice will be related to the kind of information you are seeking. You may use a *simple checklist* or *open-ended questions.*

For the first option, begin constructing a checklist for your questionnaire by writing a stem and providing choices to complete the stem into a sentence, much like a multiple-choice item. This time, there is no right or wrong answer. Instead, you are looking for a preference, a feeling, or an opinion. Look at the sample:

- This chapter on assessment has made me feel:
  _______ anxious
  _______ confident
  _______ committed
  _______ ready
  _______ bored

Your second option is a sentence completion format, or an open-ended form. You provide students with partial sentences and ask them to complete the sentences with words that best express their feelings, opinions, or thoughts. Look at the last sample:

- After reading this chapter on assessment, I feel ______________________________

  ____

This concludes our suggestions for the most commonly used teacher-made assessment strategies. We want to go beyond these assessments to alternative approaches being designed by individual teachers and by schools and districts. Like Pam Rossio, many teachers are striving to expand and improve their assessment repertoires. We will describe some of the best developed of the alternative approaches—interviews, portfolios, and performance tasks.

Designing Alternative Assessment Approaches

Alternative assessment approaches are being called many different names (authentic assessment, performance assessment, and so on), but *alternative* fits well because these approaches do offer *alternatives* to traditional methods (multiple-choice tests, standardized tests, and so on). Alternative approaches—such as interviews, portfolios, and performance tasks—reflect our expanded notion of pedagogy with innovative practices (Roe & Vukelich, 1998). Much of the interest and popularity of alternative assessment can be traced to the inadequacies of standardized tests.

Interviews

This strategy involves students in conversations to explore their thinking. Rather than seek right or wrong answers, interviews probe for understandings, feelings, opinions, and perceptions. You will generally begin with a developed question or set of questions, and proceed to spontaneously invented questions based on student response.

Interviewing requires sensitivity and will take practice before you are able to probe and develop spontaneous questions. As you begin, review your advancework information and establish rapport with your student. Prepare the student for the interview process by describing your procedures and introducing any materials being used, including recording equipment. Listen as the teacher in Teacher Talk begins an interview with a second-grader.

TEACHER TALK

I'm interested in talking to you to find out how you think about numbers. I've been talking to all the children and do you know what I've been finding out? Everybody doesn't think about numbers in the same way, so every boy and girl that talks to me teaches me something new. The things we'll be talking about may be things you have studied in school and others will be things you haven't studied. I'm not really interested in whether you know the right answer. I'm more interested in how you figure out your answer.

Second-Grade Teacher (Labinowicz, 1985, p. 28)

It is essential that you provide an appropriate amount of time for students to think, so your "wait time" will affect the responses you hear. It is also recommended that you pause after a student's response to encourage more response or elaboration (Labinowicz, 1985). An additional consideration is your response to student answers. You will want to be aware of your body language, facial expressions, and verbal responses. It is recommended that you use a neutral acknowledgment, such as a repetition of the student's answer or a nod of the head. Finally, you will need to decide how to record student answers; you have several options: written notes, audiotapes, and videotapes.

Interviews have numerous benefits in addition to the opportunity to explore student thinking. They include relationships with students, one-to-one interactions with individuals, a chance to check misunderstandings, and an alternative form of assessment that meets learner differences. Interview data can become part of the content of the next assessment approach—portfolios.

Portfolios

Portfolios have the potential to enhance both teaching and learning because they engage you and your students in self-reflection and self-evaluation. Portfolios also accomplish an alignment of curriculum, instruction, and assessment that is seldom achieved with other assessment strategies. An action research project from Bellevue, Washington (Valencia & Place, 1994b), describes how to use and how to evaluate portfolios. The results and conclusions of the Bellevue Portfolio Project will help you understand how to implement portfolio assessment in ways that will actually improve teaching and learning in your classroom. The portfolio model developed by the Bellevue teachers consisted of several categories of evidence to be used in student portfolios:

1. Work selected by the students with periodic self-reflection/evaluation of their progress
2. Several "common tools" included in all portfolios and based on district learning outcomes

3. Other work and notes included by the teacher or student that are important to understanding individual students and documenting their learning processes (Valencia & Place, 1994b)

Other than those three categories, teachers made individual decisions, such as how to organize portfolios or how to coordinate them with other classroom procedures. The most powerful results of the project came from the teachers looking collaboratively at samples of students' portfolios to determine how well they represented individual learners. Some of the questions addressed by the group:

1. What did you learn about this learner?
2. What goals would be approprtiate for this learner?
3. What instructional strategies would be useful for helping this learner achieve those goals?
4. What other items would help this portfolio best represent this learner's abilities.

The teachers also discovered that portfolio information needed to be summarized to report to others. To do so, the teacher had to agree on common expectations for learners and to develop common rubrics (or scoring schemes) to be used to evaluate portfolio work. This process enabled the teachers to use portfolio information to support report cards and to communicate with parents.

In addition to numerous portfolio projects in the area of literacy, similar projects are being conducted in other curriculum areas. Many of the projects have included the use of traditional assessment data (test scores) as part of portfolios. The high school teacher in the Research Vignette uses a variety of assessment examples in his portfolio example.

To further assist you in your understanding of portfolios, we look at developments in mathematics. Some suggestions and examples from math portfolio development will help you be ready to use portfolios. Kuhs (1994) suggested that teachers develop a content guide for learners to help them select appropriate content for their portfolios. She said that students have a tendency to want to include everything possible to demonstrate their work. Figure 14.1 provides a sample content guide for problem-solving

FIGURE 14.1 *Portfolio Content Guide with a Problem-Solving Focus*

Select a sample to show something you did that:
1. You found to be especially difficult,
2. You enjoyed doing,
3. Gave you a chance to use technology,
4. Shows you can apply mathematics to an out-of-school situation,
5. Required knowledge about geometry,
6. Shows your ability in problem solving.

Source: Reprinted with permission from *The Mathematics Teacher, 87*(5), pages 332–335. Therese M. Kuhs, "Portfolio Assessment: Making It Work for the First Time." Copyright 1994 by the National Council of Teachers of Mathematics. Reprinted by permission.

Secondary Research Vignette

INTRODUCTION

Joshua Weiner is a high school teacher who decided to investigate student attitudes toward assessment and invite their input to his development of a grading system. It began at the end of his first teaching assignment (a three-month temporary position) when he gave students his own self-evaluation:

> I *hate* putting points on your papers. Points are an insult to your best work and they put an artificial value on your learning. Nor do I like the idea that I am the only *"judge."* I sense that this system creates an attitude in which you, as students, do not feel connected to (or responsible for) your grades—since all points come from me. This is crazy since you know best what you have or have not learned. (Weiner, 1998)

It is important to note that Josh continued the previous teacher's point system so as not to disrupt too much of the class organization during the last three months of the school year. His self-evaluation did prompt much student response, and for the next two years, he conducted surveys of students and interviews of colleagues for ongoing development of his assessment system. His action research project (Weiner, 1998) is a good example of the kind of inquiry that many teachers are conducting to improve their teaching.

STUDY PROCEDURES

For two consecutive years, at the end of the school year, Josh Weiner asked his students to participate in a survey. The following questions were asked:

1. Do you feel that *you earned* your grades or that *I gave* them to you? Explain.
2. Do you like getting points on your assignments, or would you prefer to just get comments? Explain. (If you say points sometimes and comments sometimes, be specific about when—for example, on in-class work, tests, etc.)
3. Who knows best what grade you deserve—you or the teacher? Explain.
4. Do you feel comfortable evaluating yourself and giving yourself a grade? If you were in that position, would you be honest in grading yourself? Explain.

Student participation in the survey was not required, just requested. Students were directed to respond anonymously and were assured that Josh would not look at responses until all final grades had been submitted.

As part of this action research project, Josh also conducted interviews of teachers (at both secondary and postsecondary levels) about issues of assessment and evaluation and for feedback on his developing assessment system.

STUDY RESULTS

Most of the results were incorporated into Josh Weiner's assessment system (see Samples and Examples at the end of the chapter). It is interesting to look at some of the data to get a sense of how secondary students think about assessment:

- When asked whether grades were earned or given:
  - 87 percent responded that they *earned* their grades.
  - 1.3 percent responded that their grades had been *given* to them.
- When asked about preferences in the current grading system:
  - 79.2 percent responded that they liked the current system.
  - 11.5 percent described changes to make in the current system (with no agreement on the kind of changes).
  - 1.3 percent preferred getting *letter grades only.*
  - 2.6 percent preferred getting *comments only.*
- When asked about who knows best in terms of grades:
  - 42.9 percent responded that they (students) know best.

7.8 percent responded that the teacher knows best.
46.8 percent responded that the teacher and students know best.

- When asked about comfort in evaluating and giving self a grade:
  76.3 percent responded that they would feel comfortable and be honest.
  2.6 percent responded they would be comfortable but dishonest.
  7.9 percent responded that they would be comfortable but would attempt minor grade inflation.
  10.5 percent responded that they would be honest but uncomfortable.

These responses were from the second year's survey and after a year with Josh's revised assessment system. He was especially pleased to note a "dramatic change in the percentage of students who felt that they had earned their grades" (Weiner, p. 2), from 60.2 percent in the first-year survey to 87 percent in the second year. Other changes were a decline (14 percent) in the number of students who felt that the teacher was the best judge of their grade and an increase (13.5 percent) in the number of students who felt that they were the best judge.

CONCLUSIONS AND IMPLICATIONS FOR PRACTICE

Josh Weiner's conclusions took the form of revisions of his assessment system, which is exactly what action research conclusions are intended to do—make changes and improvements for practices. His system (in Samples and Examples) will give you insights and strategies for your own practice. From his perspective, the most important implication is the value of "student voice" in instructional decisions. He would urge you to ask learners for their opinions, feelings, perspectives, and feedback about teaching and learning.

---

curriculum. Notice that it not only guides the student selection of work but it also influences your selection of teaching and learning strategies.

Kuhs (1994) also suggested that students work in cooperative groups to select work to include in their portfolios. In those settings they will hear the strategies used by their peers, will learn how their peers approach problems, and will see how their peers organize their work.

Several approaches have been used by teachers to evaluate or grade portfolios. The first approach is to assign a grade to each work item in the portfolio and average the grades. The second approach is to grade samples of each intended learning outcome and give separate grades for each ability area. The third approach is to develop a scoring rubric or scheme and use it to grade the entire sample of work. Kuhs's work also provided an example of a scoring rubric, again for a portfolio focused on problem-solving content (see Figure 14.2).

The final assessment approach, performance tasks, are in the development phase, much like portfolios. Both approaches offer alternatives to traditional assessment (strategies) in measuring more thinking content.

Performance Tasks

With a performance assessment, learners demonstrate understanding or skill by performing a task. Performance tests or tasks are called *authentic assessment* because they use lifelike situations in which students can demonstrate skills and other forms of

FIGURE 14.2 *Scoring Rubric for Problem-Solving Portfolios*

Level 4

The portfolio contains pieces that show:

- accurate interpretation of problem situations or statements most of the time,
- appropriate use of given information,
- use of appropriate strategies or approaches that logically relate to the problems,
- only rare or insignificant errors in mathematical procedures,
- evidence that answers were reviewed and evaluated in the context of what they would mean in the given problem situations.

Note: One of the following characteristics distinguishes the level-4 portfolio:

a) evidence of creative or insightful, but atypical, approaches to problems;
b) use of technology in either the presentation or solution of a problem;
c) perseverance and tenacity in dealing with complexity, obscurity, or ambiguity.

Level 3

The portfolio contains pieces that show:

- accurate interpretation of problem situations or statements most of the time,
- appropriate use of given information,
- use of strategies or approaches that logically relate to the problems most of the time,
- few mathematical or procedural errors,
- evidence that answers were usually evaluated in the context of given problems.

Level 2

The portfolio contains pieces that show:

- accurate interpretation of problem situations or statements most of the time,
- occasional incorrect use of the given information,
- inconsistent use of strategies or approaches that logically relate to the problems,
- common occurrence of errors in computation or basic procedures,
- answers that seem not to have been evaluated in the context of the given problem situations.

Level 1

The portfolio contains several pieces that show:

- inaccurate interpretation of problem situations or statements or incorrect use of given information,
- rare use of strategies or approaches that logically relate to the problems,
- common occurrence of errors in computation or basic procedures,
- answers that seem not to have been evaluated in the context of the given problem situations.

Level 0

The portfolio is incomplete or contains no work meeting the foregoing criteria mentioned.

Source: Reprinted with permission from *The Mathematics Teacher, 87*(5), pages 332–335. Therese M. Kuhs, "Portfolio Assessment: Making It Work for the First Time." Copyright 1994 by the National Council of Teachers of Mathematics. Reprinted by permission.

learning (Tolman & Hardy, 1999). The following are some reasons why teachers have begun to use performance tasks:

> 1. *They provide clear guidelines for students about teacher expectations.*
> 2. *They reflect real-life situations—problems, issues, and challenges.*
> 3. *They allow for student differences in style and interests. (Marzano, 1994, p. 44)*

Some examples of performance tasks include demonstrations, computer simulations, performance events, debates, development of oral/visual presentations, projects, exhibits, problems, and portfolios. The possibilities for performance tasks are almost unlimited. To begin planning and designing such tasks, ask yourself the following questions:

> *What do I want students to know and be able to do?*
>
> *How will I know they can do it?*
>
> *What resources must be available to ensure that all students can succeed?*
>
> *How can I structure and pace my teaching so that all students are prepared to perform well? (Jamentz, 1994, p. 57)*

Notice that these questions provide a starting point as well as criteria for determining appropriateness of performance tasks. Those teachers and districts that have adopted performance assessment have also confirmed the need for a scoring scheme. For performance tasks, the scoring scheme is shared with the students *prior* to the tasks.

Diez and Moon (1992) described three performance tasks appropriate for Civil War curriculum:

> *Write a diary of the mother of two sons fighting in the war (one fighting for the South and one fighting for the North), and include a statement about what you think was the hardest for the mother.*
>
> *Create a play about a family in the Civil War in which the action revolves around the decision of a family member to join the army. Add commentary about how this family is like or unlike families you know.*
>
> *Create a chart of aspects of the Civil War that affected families, and compare the experiences with those of the Gulf War. (p. 38)*

Diez and Moon (1992) also provided some examples of criteria to be used with the performance tasks:

> 1. *Accurately uses information from the historical period;*
> 2. *Uses sufficient detail to create a sense of what it was like for people who lived at the time;*
> 3. *Draws out relationships or comparisons between that period of history and the present;*
> 4. *Uses affective language in dealing with the experiences of people—in history and today. (pp. 39–40)*

As in the case with portfolios, performance tasks will serve you well in clarifying outcomes for your students. They will also prompt you to examine your teaching to ensure that your students are prepared to perform on the tasks.

As teachers work to improve their assessment practices, more assessment approaches will probably emerge. For now, interviews, portfolios, and performance tasks offer alternative ways to gather assessment information and are appropriate for many content areas. You will find alternative assessment especially useful for your inclusive classroom.

ASSESSMENT AND INCLUSION

The rich array of differences that inclusion brings to our teaching experiences carries with it an important directive for assessment. McLeod (1994) described our responsibility as "best accomplished through a diversity of assessment, involving multiple definitions of competence and evaluation methods" (p. 26). "As important as multiple methods are multiple perspectives" (Allen, 1998, p. 11). Throughout this chapter, our message has been to think of assessment in as many "ways" as possible, but we know that for one teacher working alone, the span of "ways" may be confined by limits of time, expertise and experience, and your own perspective. Throughout this book, we have urged you to collaborate with other teachers, and for purposes of assessment, collaboration is probably the best way to expand the "ways."

We would like to share some of the thinking of teacher collaborations and some examples of how they work as part of your preparation for you to assess with multiple methods and from multiple perspectives. "It is the view of those teachers that, to better understand student learning and improve teachers' capacity to support it, it is important to examine and reflect on the ideas and patterns in the actual work" that learners create rather than the "approximations of learning that grades and test scores offer" (Allen, 1998, p. 1). By collaborating with other teachers, parents and other family members, and "critical friends" (community members, teacher educators, and others), examinations of student work can directly improve conditions for student learning. Several examples will illustrate the potential of such work.

At University Heights High School, students, members of their families, teachers, and invited guests gather regularly for Portfolio Roundtables. Many of the students have had unsatisfactory experiences at other schools but find academic success at this school and go to college after graduation. The school has a well-developed set of standards and criteria for students' work. In the place of state competency tests, content area requirements, grades, and rankings, the school has a well-developed process of assessment and accountability through the Portfolio Roundtables.

As the Roundtable begins, participants are asked to read the portfolio materials and take notes. In addition, the student presents major work samples and learning experiences with evidence. Later in the process, participants are asked to give "warm feedback," from a believing, supportive, and appreciative perspective, and "cool feedback," from a doubting, constructively critical, discerning perspective. The learners are assessed in three ways at a Roundtable: (1) through a review of their cover letter; (2) through the portfolio contents (descriptions and evidence of their work); and

(3) through presentation and discussion during Roundtable. There is a focus on reflection, evidence, and dialogue throughout the Roundtable session (Allison, 1998).

A second example comes from Carrie E. Tompkins Elementary School in Croton, New York. The teachers there have gone "beyond grading papers to examining student work" (King & Campbell-Allan, 1998, p. 147). The faculty adopted portfolios as "vehicles for a different kind of assessment—student self-reflection, teacher reflection on student work, and teacher self-refection" (p. 154). Monthly staff meetings became important occasions to share samples of student work across grades. Teachers kept journals throughout the process and many journal entries revealed teachers' awe at student accomplishments and increased expectations for their own students' achievement. For many teachers, sharing student work caused them to focus and reflect on their own instruction. Soon, teachers were sharing teaching techniques with their colleagues.

Rich debates of assessment issues emerged from the examinations of students' work. Teachers discussed some of the following:

- *What does it mean if student's ideas of best work and teachers' ideas of best work are different?*
- *Whose portfolios are these? Teachers or students?*
- *How do we define best work? (King & Campbell-Alan, 1998, p. 159)*

The debates and the ongoing sharing of student work had significant impact on the teachers' professional development, and ultimately on student learning.

We realize that both of our examples are schoolwide and supported by collaboration. You are probably thinking that as a beginning teacher, you won't be able to be involved in such collaborations, and maybe you're right. Our hope is that you will commit to the importance of multiple methods and multiple perspectives and engage another new teacher, a mentor teacher, or some parents in the examination of student work. In so doing, you will learn more about your students, be better able to assess their learning, and improve the instruction you provide in any classroom.

FINAL CONSIDERATIONS FOR ASSESSMENT

We have already described how the content of your teaching influences your decisions about assessment. Now, as we have recommended with all of the instructional strategies, we will describe some sensitivities regarding the context and some strategies for involving the learner.

Consider the Context

Many environmental aspects will influence students' abilities to respond in interviews, write answers to essay questions, and complete performance tasks. Those factors that require sensitivity include noise, interruptions, crowded conditions, temperature, and lighting. Even the time of day or day of the week can have an impact.

Factors such as these affect students' physical, mental, and emotional states. Fatigue, hunger, and visual strain influence thinking processes. It is difficult to solve problems or analyze information when you are drowsy. There is also the effect of distraction—classrooms that are too stimulating. A new environment or constant interruptions can cause students to lose ideas or give up. There is growing evidence (Tanner, 1996) that anxiety and fear accompany test taking for many learners, so it is critical that we be certain to provide a supportive environment for assessment.

Remember to conduct some advancework before planning your assessment strategies. Consider discussing the context with your students: Is there anything about our classroom that disturbs or distracts you when you are working on a project or taking a test? You will probably gain helpful information, and in the process, you will communicate concern to learners. Those learners are taking new roles in the assessment process and in reporting assessment information. They will need to be well informed and skilled for their participation.

Consider the Learner

Many schools are experimenting with student-led parent conferences in place of the traditional teacher/parent conferences. Teachers Linda Picciotto (1992) and Margaret Reinhard decided that having students explain their progress and plans to their parents would be a good way of directly involving them in their own learning. They thought that the preparation and management of the conferences would be valuable learning experiences for the learners. The teachers created a checklist for the students to follow as they led the conferences (see Samples and Examples) and scheduled the parent conferences. Picciotto and Reinhard described with great enthusiasm the success of their student-led conferences. They are not unique. Many teachers and school districts are experimenting with this approach to reporting assessment information and are describing similar success.

Teacher Madeline Brick (1993) decided to involve her learners in a different way. Instead of her usual midterm progress report, she asked her seventh-graders to write letters to their parents about their progress in English class. She also wanted to encourage her students to assume more responsibility for their learning. Again, this experiment was highly successful. Brick stated, "The letters prompted my students to think about themselves as learners and to involve their parents in that thinking" (p. 63).

In sum, the role of the learner is changing as we teachers encourage much more involvement and responsibility in the actual assessment process and in the reporting of assessment data. With that change in role comes the potential for empowered learners.

SUMMARY

We began by looking into Pam Rossio's classroom and observing her need for "ways" of assessment and the importance of resources. As you read her story, you encountered the language of assessment, an extensive set of terminology. You learned about three major kinds of assessment: diagnostic, formative, and summative, and saw that you could choose formal or informal strategies for each.

From there, we urged you to consider multiple purposes of assessment and to use your assessment data wisely. As you make decisions about how to assess, begin by considering the content, starting with the learning domains in Chapter Three. As you proceed with either selection or development of assessment strategies and approaches, think about your learners, your content, and your context. Be open to multiforms of assessment. Our final reminder is to collaborate with your school colleagues on assessment issues, and to give assessment the time and reflection necessary to do it well.

REFERENCES

Airasian, P. (1996). *Classroom assessment.* New York: McGraw-Hill.

Alexander, F. (1993). National standards: A new conventional wisdom. *Educational Leadership, 50*(5), 9–10.

Allen, D. (1998). *Assessing student learning: From grading to understanding.* New York: Teachers College Press.

Allison, P. (1998). Taking responsibilities for our work: Roundtables at University Heights High School. In D. Allen (Ed.), *Assessing student learning: From grading to understanding.* New York: Teachers College Press.

Brick, M. (1993). When students write home. *Educational Leadership, 50*(7), 62–63.

Dalheim, M. (1993). *Student portfolios.* West Haven, CT: National Educational Association Professional Library.

Diez, M., & Moon, C. J. (1992). What do we want students to know?...and other important questions. *Educational Leadership, 49*(8), 38–41.

Ebel, R. L. (1965). *Measuring educational achievement.* Englewood Cliffs, NJ: Prentice Hall.

Jamentz, K. (1994). Making sure that assessment improves performance. *Educational Leadership, 51*(6), 55–57.

King, S., & Campbell-Allan, L. (1998). Portfolios, students work, and teachers' practice: An elementary school redefines assessment. In D. Allen (Ed.), *Assessing student learning: From grading to understanding.* New York: Teachers College Press.

Kuhs, T. M. (1994). Portfolio assessment: Making it work for the first time. *The Mathematics Teacher, 87*(5), 332–335.

Labinowicz, E. (1985). *Learning from children: New beginnings for teaching numerical thinking.* New York: Addison-Wesley.

Marzano, R. J. (1994). Lessons from the field about outcome-based performance assessments. *Educational Leadership, 51*(6), 44–50.

McLeod, B. (1994). *Language and learning: Educating linguistically diverse students.* Albany: State University of New York Press.

Picciotto, L. P. (1992). *Evaluation: A team effort.* Ontario, Canada: Scholastic Canada Ltd.

Popham, W. J. (1998). Farewell curriculum: Confessions of an assessment convert. *Phi Delta Kappan, 79*(5), 380–384.

Remmers, H. H., Gage, N. L., & Rummel, J. F. (1965). *A practical introduction to measurement and evaluation.* New York: Harper & Row.

Roe, M. F., & Vukelich, C. (1998). Literacy portfolios: Challenges that affect change. *Childhood Education, 74*(3), 148–153.

Simmons, R. (1994). The horse before the cart: Assessing for understanding. *Educational Leadership, 51*(5), 22–23.

Tanner, D. (1996). A lesson from Ms. McGreevey's third grade class. *Education Week, 16,* 36.

Tolman, M. N., & Hardy, G. R. (1999). *Discovering elementary science.* Boston: Allyn and Bacon.

Valencia, S., & Place, N. (1994a). Literacy portfolios for teaching, learning, and accountability: The Bellevue Literacy Assessment Project. In S. Valencia, E. Hiebert, & P. Afflerbach (Eds.), *Authentic reading assessment: Practices and possibilities.* Newark, DE: International Reading Association.

Valencia, S., & Place, N. (1994b). Portfolios: A process for enhancing teaching and learning. *The Reading Teacher, 47*(8), 666–671.

Weiner, J. (1998). *Student perspectives on assessment: Toward authentic assessment.* Unpublished Action Research Project, Graduate School of Education, Portland State University, Portland, OR.

SAMPLES AND EXAMPLES

The following examples and samples provide classroom forms for collecting and reporting assessment information:

- The Assessments for Drawings contains a scale and a checklist for giving feedback on learning in an art class.
- The Checklist for Student-Led Parent Conferences will assist students as they lead these conferences.
- The Primary Progress Report is a narrative report card developed by two elementary teachers who team teach a kindergarten/first-grade classroom.
- Grading Standards, End of Quarter Evaluation, and Third Quarter Portfolio Assignment for a high-school class (see Research Vignette on pages 417–418).

ASSESSMENTS FOR DRAWINGS

Rating Scale

Whitfield—Advanced Art 3

Proportion	Appropriate				Inappropriate
	1	2	3	4	5
	Consistent				Inconsistent
	1	2	3	4	5
Composition	Symmetrical				Asymmetrical
	1	2	3	4	5
Chiaroscuro*	Accurate				Inaccurate
	1	2	3	4	5

Style

____

____

____

*Chiaroscuro is the treatment of the light and shade on an object.

Checklist for Observation of Drawing Techniques

Technique	Observation Date	Description
Looks at subject matter regularly	_______	
Uses pencil to measure proportions	_______	
Maps out proportions with reference points	_______	
Uses hard lines	_______	
Uses soft lines	_______	
Uses repeated lines	_______	

Source: K. Driscoll, unpublished materials, 1990. Reprinted by permission.

CHECKLIST FOR STUDENT-LED PARENT CONFERENCES

STUDENT-LED PARENT CONFERENCE
Linda Picciotto's and Marg Reinhard's Classes
November 28—4:00–5:30 or 6:30–8:00
November 30—1:00–2:30
South Park School

Student's name Frank Parent(s) Diane

Please go to each of the following centers during your visit to discuss each area of your schooling with your parent or parents. You may visit the centers in any order.

Centers	Parent Comments
✓ Reading Share books together Show what you are learning	Surprised to hear how much he could Read without much help!
✓ Writing Share writing folders What have you learned? What skills are you working on? What do you like to write about?	Just overnight his writing and spelling have improved so much that now I can read his work without much correction from him. WHAT a treat!!
✓ Math All-day students— Make a "Raisin Bran graph" Half-day students— Make an "animal cracker graph" All students—Show your parent(s) what math materials you work with during math activity time	The "hands-on" method in teaching math is a GREAT way to "get the picture"
✓ Science Demonstrate and discuss the Magic Milk experiment.	The experiment was not only interesting to observe but very beautiful too.
✓ Portfolio Go through your portfolio together. Tell how each entry shows that you are learning.	I love the way Frank is begining to "take charge" of his own learning.
✓ Art Show and discuss the art work that you have displayed in the room.	Enjoyed the bright colors and variety of pictures.
✓ Gym In the gym tell your parent(s) how to play your favorite game, or demonstrate your favorite activity.	Interesting to hear of some new ways to play tag.
✓ Have a talk with the teacher at the conference table.	Informative as usual.
✓ When you are finished, serve your parent(s) juice and cookies, and enjoy some yourself!	Hats off to the baker!!

Source: From *Evaluation: A Team Effort* by L. P. Picciotto, 1992, Ontario, Canada: Scholastic Canada Ltd.

PRIMARY PROGRESS REPORT

Ministry of Education
Rogers School

Name: ______________________________ Birth date: ____________

Greater Victoria School District #61

Second Report March

OBSERVATIONS AND GROWTH:

Marshall

- Continues to be an enthusiastic member of our class and is becoming a self-directed learner.
- Is becoming a fluent and confident reader and is enthusiastic about many new books. He especially enjoys books by Shirley Hughes, *The Big Cement Mixer* being his favorite! He often reads books to his friends at buddy reading time.
- Is becoming more interested in writing, especially if it's connected to a project he's working on. He often makes lists or writes directions, and has started to notice standard spelling. Occasionally he uses punctuation and demonstrates a beginning understanding of its use. He likes to copy pages of books on the computer.
- Is especially challenged by opportunities for problem solving. In our recent science and math construction unit, he identified problems that most of us didn't anticipate, and delighted in solving them. His plan for displaying our work showed evidence of complex thinking and sensitivity to his classmates.
- Has a good understanding of numeration to 100. He uses manipulatives to perform addition and subtraction and can generalize these concepts to situations that occur in our classroom life. He's very interested in measurement and used good skills in our bridge construction project. His bridge building was impressive.
- Has an amazing memory. This is particularly noticeable when he needs directions for the computer. He only needs to be shown a procedure once. He actually helps other children a great deal with the computers. He takes great pride in his computer skills.
- Has made real efforts to improve his classroom and outdoor behavior especially during the past month. He appears to be more patient with other children, and is realizing that he can't always be in charge. He is better able to describe what he feels during times when he's frustrated.
- Is a good athlete and an eager participant in our floor hockey games.

FOCUS FOR NEXT TERM:

- To continue to support his developing understanding of addition and subtraction.
- To encourage him to find more uses for writing and punctuation.
- To support his efforts to get along with his classmates and express his feelings.

______________________________ ______________________________

Teacher's signature Principal's signature

This report demonstrates impressive growth in reading, writing, math, thinking, and social skills. Wow! TLC

Source: T. Calkins, M. Noll, & W. Payne, unpublished material, 1993. Reprinted by permission.

GRADING STANDARDS

Mr. Weiner — **Benson High School, 1998–99**

	Daily Work	Journal	Exams/Projects	Participation
A	■ At least 90% of assignments completed *and* ■ 1 or no late assignments *General:* ✓ = full credit; – = ½ credit; + = 1½ credit ■ Value of extra-credit work determined on case-by-case basis	■ At least 90% of assignments completed *and* ■ Journal always turned in on time *General:* ■ Value of extra-credit work determined on case-by-case basis	■ Follows directions or negotiates alternatives w/teacher *in advance* ■ Thoroughly discusses all aspects of questions and possible answers ■ Information/ideas clearly expressed ■ Well organized ■ Turned in on time or by alternate date negotiated with teacher *in advance*	■ Often participates "actively" (involved in discussions and activities, sharing ideas in a positive manner) ■ Consistently on task ■ Consistently supportive of others and the general learning environment ■ Consistently in class and on time
B	■ At least 80% of assignments completed *and* ■ 3 or less late assignments	■ At least 80% of assignments completed *and* ■ Journal not late more than once	■ Mostly follows directions ■ Discusses almost all questions and/or possible answers ■ Most information/ideas clearly expressed ■ Mostly well organized ■ *Less* than 3 days late	■ Some "active" participation ■ Usually on task ■ Usually supportive of others and the general learning environment ■ Usually in class and on time
C	■ At least 70% of assignments completed *and* ■ 5 or less late assignments	■ At least 70% of assignments completed *and* ■ Journal not late more than twice	■ Loosely follows directions ■ Discusses most questions and/or possible answers ■ Information/ideas difficult to understand ■ Somewhat organized ■ One week late or less	■ "Active" participation is rare ■ Mostly on task ■ Mostly supportive of others and the general learning environment ■ Often absent or tardy

	Daily Work	Journal	Exams/Projects	Participation
D	■ At least 60% of assignments completed *and* ■ 7 or less late assignments per quarter	■ At least 60% of assignments completed *and* ■ Journal not late more than three times	■ Does not follow directions ■ Does not discuss most questions and/or possible answers ■ Information/ideas not explained ■ Organization is difficult to understand ■ More than one week late	■ Mostly off task ■ Mostly not supportive of others and the general learning environment ■ Regularly absent or tardy
F	■ Less than 60% assignments completed *or* ■ More than 7 assignments late	■ Less than 60% assignments completed *or* ■ Journal late more than three times	■ Off the subject ■ Questions and/or possible answers not discussed ■ Information/ideas not relevant to topic ■ Very disorganized	■ Consistently off task ■ Consistently not supportive of others and the general learning environment ■ Rarely in class or on time

Source: From *Student Perspectives on Assessment: Toward Authentic Assessment* by J. Weiner, 1998, unpublished Action Research Project, Graduate School of Education, Portland State University, Portland, OR. Reprinted by permission.

END OF QUARTER EVALUATION

Mr. Weiner/Government/Economics Benson High School, 1997–98

Name: ______________________________ 3rd Quarter

<table>
<tr>
<td>
Daily Work

______ Completed

(+) ____ (–) ____

Late ____

(XC):
</td>
<td>
Journal

______ Completed

On time

Late ____

Not Turned In __________
</td>
</tr>
<tr>
<td>
Exams & Projects

Adam Smith & The Real World ______
</td>
<td>
Participation

Unexcused Absences ______

Unexcused Tardies ______

Active Participation:

Disruptions:

On Task:
</td>
</tr>
</table>

Source: From *Student Perspectives on Assessment: Toward Authentic Assessment* by J. Weiner, 1998, unpublished Action Research Project, Graduate School of Education, Portland State University, Portland, OR. Reprinted by permission.

THIRD QUARTER PORTFOLIO ASSIGNMENT

Due: *Thursday, April 2* Mr. Weiner/Economics

You cannot pass the class if you do not complete this assignment!!!

Your final project for the quarter is a portfolio of your work and our evaluations.
Your portfolio *must* include:

1. Any six items (daily work, journal entries, handouts, projects, etc.) that were most significant for your learning experience this quarter.
2. The "End of Quarter Evaluation" you got from me.
3. Your Self-Evaluation (see explanation below).

Your self-evaluation can be in any format that you like (essay, story, poem, visual art, etc.), but it *must* communicate all of the following:

1. An explanation of *what you learned* from *each* of the items you chose for your portfolio.
2. An explanation of other significant things, in general, that you learned this quarter (could be related to the material we studied, your behavior, your goals, whatever).
3. Your thoughts on the quality of your class participation this quarter.
4. The final grade you recommend for yourself, with an explanation based on our class standards.

Thursday in class, you will present your portfolio to a small group. Be prepared to discuss what you learned from each of the items in it, as well as the significant things in general that you learned this quarter (basically, parts 1 and 2 of your self-evaluation). You are **not required** to discuss parts 3 and 4 of your self-evaluation, though you can if you want to.

Source: From *Student Perspectives on Assessment: Toward Authentic Assessment* by J. Weiner, 1998, unpublished Action Research Project, Graduate School of Education, Portland State University, Portland, OR. Reprinted by permission.

CHAPTER

15

SELF-IMPROVEMENT THROUGH SELF-ASSESSMENT

Chapter Outcomes

At the conclusion of this chapter you will be able to:

1. *Identify several sources of data to improve your teaching.*
2. *Use the Low Inference Self-Assessment Measure to analyze your teaching.*
3. *Use student feedback as a data source for your teaching.*
4. *Use peer observations with a student off-task seating chart to improve instruction.*
5. *Use the chapter checklists and self-assessment measures to reinforce the use of the teaching strategies presented in the text.*

Key Terms and Concepts

Multiple Sources of Data
Creating Change from Within
Low Inference Self-Assessment Measure (LISAM)
Audiotape Analysis
70 Ways to Vary Your Praise
Guidelines for Effective Praise
Student Feedback
Student Messages
Student Feedback Instruments:
  Teacher Effectiveness Questionnaire (TEQ)
  Off-Task Seating Chart
Student Teaching Research Vignette

A teacher affects eternity: you can never tell where your influence stops.
—Henry Adams

INTRODUCTION

Knowledge Is Power

We began *Universal Teaching Strategies* with a conviction that the teaching profession is facing its greatest challenge in modern history. The economic, social, and political fate of our country rests with the ability of our teachers, administrators, and other educators, to enable all students to learn. The statement *knowledge is power* is a truism that could be applied to both teachers and students.

The changing demographics of students in our classrooms requires both a broader range of teaching strategies and teachers who maintain their viability through the constant seeking of new knowledge. Although *knowledge is power,* knowledge about yourself is perhaps the greatest power. The power of discovering what you are doing and how you can change gives you control of your teaching life. In this concluding chapter of the text, we will provide instruments and measures designed to give you tools to assess your own teaching independent of others' evaluations. You will have the opportunity to reflect on information about your teaching that will ultimately improve your instruction.

How Am I Doing?

Teaching is at once a highly public profession and a uniquely isolated profession. We speak daily before 25 to 150 students but rarely meet peers or other adults during the workday. From the student teacher to the 40-year veteran, the most common questions are: *How am I doing?* and *Where do I need improvement?* These important questions are only rarely answered to the satisfaction of most teachers. Accurate feedback is at the heart of change in teaching, but the process is always dependent on others.

The usual model of observation and feedback for secondary teachers consists of an administrator (principal, assistant principal, or department head) who visits one of six classroom periods from one to four times a year. Elementary teachers receive a similar visiting pattern, except the observations usually occur during reading or mathematics instruction. The administrator may use a checksheet, take notes, or simply observe what is occurring and share those perceptions with the teacher at a later date (Freiberg, 1987).

Providing information about teaching effectiveness may be called *supervision, feedback, assessment,* or *evaluation.* The end goal, however, should be to provide you with usable information about your teaching.

You need accurate information about what is going on in the classroom before you can begin to identify strengths and weaknesses and formulate a plan to institute change. It may not be an understatement to say that the entire school reform movement hinges on the ability of the profession to provide you meaningful data about what is occurring in the classroom and to create opportunities for all teachers to reflect on their teaching.

Sources of Data

Several sources of information are available to you about your teaching, including the following:

- Student gains on teacher-made tests
- Student gains on standardized tests
- Student feedback (verbal, nonverbal, and written)
- Systematic observation by supervisors or principals
- Administrative feedback
- Peer observation
- Self-assessment

In this chapter, self-assessment using audiotape analysis, student feedback from written questionnaires, and classroom observation using an off-task seating chart will be presented as three viable ways of answering the questions: How am I doing? and Where do I need improvement? Self-assessment, student feedback, and systematic observations represent three sources of data that are not used frequently in combination with each other but reflect an emerging trend toward teacher self-assessment (Freiberg & Waxman, 1988).

The seven potential sources of data are rarely collectively provided by schools. Generally, observations by an administrator are the most common source of data and feedback for teachers. Both administrators and teachers have questioned how accurately these brief observations represent the total teaching picture. The number of teachers in a school places limits on the quantity as well as the quality of feedback the principal can provide any one teacher. The average school year requires 1,080 hours of instruction (180 days × 6 hours a day). Most teachers are observed three times a year for 45 minutes each visit, totaling 2¼ hours a year, which represents a 0.2 percent sampling of instruction. Beyond the question of time, judging what is going on in the classroom is a difficult task. Simple checklists rarely provide an accurate picture of the fast-paced interaction of the classroom, and even the most detailed observation systems have their limitations.

…ESSMENT:
…NG CHANGE FROM WITHIN

Imagine an instructional conference between you and your principal. You confidently explain the areas of strength and weakness of a particular lesson, and focus on the types and quality of questions during instruction: "I used 30 percent higher-order questions in my fifth-period tenth-grade literature class. This is a major improvement over the previous lesson when I only used 7 percent higher-level questions. My motivating set was effective in gaining their attention, but my closure was nonexistent—the bell rang before we had the chance to summarize the lesson. I need to pay more attention to my use of time."

The meeting continues for another 20 minutes as you and the principal review information of an audiotape analysis of a lesson you compiled and analyzed. The process described in this scenario is called *self-assessment.* In this example, the teacher met with the principal to discuss his or her analysis of a lesson, but this type of dialogue has also occurred between teachers meeting in small groups of 8 to 10 teachers as part of professional development activities.

Accuracy of Self-Assessment

Self-assessment without an objective data source is usually inaccurate. Being in the middle of a swirl of classroom interactions (up to 1,000 per hour) makes it difficult to reflect back and determine, for example, the level of questions being asked or the degree of teacher or student talk in the classroom. After a six-hour day of teaching, trying to make any accurate assessment of what happened in the morning during a reading activity or in first-period mathematics is rather futile. The research is consistent about our inability, as teachers, to assess accurately teaching effectiveness through self-perceptive data when compared with direct observations of the same lesson (see *Journal of Classroom Interaction,* Vol. 33, No. 1, 1998).

Audiotape versus Videotape

During the past two decades, teachers across the United States have had the opportunity to analyze their teaching by tape recording or videotaping their classes and coding the frequency of different teaching actions (e.g., number of times teacher praises a student) onto a data sheet. The information collected on a data sheet can then be analyzed by the teacher, and areas of strength and weakness may be identified with the intent of enhancing areas of strength and improving areas of weakness.

The question of whether to use audiotape or videotape to collect the data may be determined by the classroom context. The comparisons made between video- and audiotaping in Figure 15.1 reflect the advantages and disadvantages of both systems. Review the advantages and limitations for your own setting and decide which technology would be most effective. Our experience has been that audiotaping a lesson seems to be less obtrusive and more convenient than videotaping. But each classroom setting is unique. If your goal is to focus on verbal classroom interaction, then the audiotaping technology may provide greater flexibility in listening and analyzing a lesson. Videotaping will provide more visual and nonverbal clues about your teaching and classroom interaction.

FIGURE 15.1 *Scoring Strengths and Weaknesses of the Videotape and Audiotape Recorder in Teacher Self-Assessment*

Directions: Place a plus (+) for a strength or a minus (–) for a limitation in each area associated with the type of media: audiotape or videotape recorder.

	Videotape Recorder		*Audiotape Recorder*
____	1. Audio and video qualities	____	1. Audio qualities
____	2. Large	____	2. Small
____	3. Setup time: approximately 10–15 minutes	____	3. Setup time: less than 5 minutes
____	4. High visibility to students	____	4. Low visibility to students
____	5. Permanent record	____	5. Permanent record
____	6. Moderately portable	____	6. Highly portable
____	7. Moderately expensive	____	7. Relatively inexpensive
____	8. Mechanical operation, fairly complex	____	8. Mechanical operation, fairly simple
____	9. Accessibility	____	9. Accessibility
____	TOTAL SCORE	____	TOTAL SCORE

Source: From *Teacher Self-Assessment: A Means for Improving Classroom Instruction* by G. D. Bailey. © 1981, National Education Association. Reprinted by permission.

Low Inference Self-Assessment Measure (LISAM)

Audiotaping allows for greater flexibility in listening and analyzing a lesson. The Low Inference Self-Assessment Measure, or LISAM (Freiberg, 1987; Freiberg, Waxman, & Houston, 1987), focuses on verbal interaction in the classroom. You tape record your class and then listen for and code specific categories of teaching. Studies on changes in teaching behaviors (Freiberg, Waxman, & Houston, 1987) and teacher feedback support using the LISAM (pronounced *leesam*) as a highly effective and efficient self-assessment tool for analyzing teacher-student verbal interaction in the classroom. This section, which describes the use of the LISAM instrument, is adapted from an article that appeared in a journal for the National Association of Secondary School Principals entitled "Teacher Self-Evaluation and Principal Supervision" (Freiberg, 1987).

Common Agreement

The "Low Inference" title of the instrument is derived from the fact that two people listening to the same tape could reach common agreement on what was occurring in the classroom. The LISAM has been used with student teachers, veteran teachers, and beginning teachers at the elementary, middle, or high-school levels.

From Questioning to Use of Student Ideas

The six items on the LISAM instrument (see Figure 15.2) were selected to provide a clear indication of teaching behaviors in key instructional areas. The LISAM instrument focuses on instructional areas that have been highlighted throughout the text (e.g., wait time, questioning, set induction, closure and praise). The instrument builds on the early work of Flanders's (1965) 10-item observation instrument.

LISAM is not the whole picture, but rather a slice of classroom interaction. By listening to the tape and then transferring the spoken words into frequency counts (which are recorded on the LISAM coding instrument), a dimension of objective self-assessment that is missing from other feedback procedures is added.

The audiotaping provides you with an opportunity for reflective inquiry into the teaching process based on specific data. Listening to yourself also adds a perspective that goes beyond the six items on the instrument. Teachers commented about their tone of voice or the dominance of some students in the classroom during questioning and discussion.

The following describes how to use the six elements: (1) questioning skills (recall to opinion), (2) teacher and student talk, (3) set induction and closure, (4) wait time, (5) praise, and (6) use of student ideas of the LISAM coding instrument presented in Figure 15.2.

1. *Questioning skills.* Chapter Eight supports both the advantages and limitations of questioning. Being able to determine the level and tone of your questions will provide an important insight into this dominant instructional strategy.

A balance of 60–40 percent, or 50–50 percent between factual questions (e.g., yes-no and short answer) and higher cognitive questions (e.g., comparison and opinion) may

FIGURE 15.2 *Audiotape Analysis Coding Instrument*

1. *Questioning Skills*

Yes-No:	(Recall/Informational)	TOTAL = ___ = ___ %
Short Answer:		TOTAL = ___ = ___ %
Comparison:	(Reflective/Thought Provoking)	TOTAL = ___ = ___ %
Opinions:		TOTAL = ___ = ___ %

2. *Teacher Talk/Student Talk*

Teacher:	Student:	Other (e.g., Independent Activities with no Interaction):
Total (T) = ______	Total (S) = ______	Total ______ %
Teacher = ______	Student = ______	______

3. *Identification of Motivating Set and Closure*
   Describe each from the tape:
   Set-Induction (Focus):
   Closure (Ending):

4. *Wait Time*
   Time between teacher question and next teacher statement:
   Average Time = ___Seconds
   Place an (*) next to all higher-level questions (comparison and opinion).

5. *Identify Number of Positive Statements Made by Teacher*
   Praise or encouragement
   Class __________ Individual __________ Uses student name Total = ________
   ____
   Identify the praise or encouragement statements directed both toward the entire class and individuals. Also tally the number of times students' names are used with praise statements.

6. *Identify the Number of Times the Teacher Uses Student Ideas*
   Including referring by name to other students' idea:
   Total = ________

Source: Adapted from "Teacher Self-Assessment and Principal Supervision" by H. J. Freiberg, 1987, *NASSP Bulletin, 71*(498), pages 85–92. Reprinted by permission.

be appropriate for many discussion and question-and-answer lessons. Although LISAM uses only four levels of questions, other levels of questions may be substituted by using, for example, the six levels in Bloom's Taxonomy (see Chapter Three).

Many teachers, who before listening to themselves were sure they were asking higher-order questions, were truly shocked to find a void of those questions. Recall-type questions are on the lowest levels of Bloom's Taxonomy and require a recall response from the student. Some forms of questioning appear to be verbal forms of worksheets. There is only one answer the teacher is expecting or accepting. Comparison questions require students to synthesize information before a conclusion can be reached. Opinion questions ask students to express their views on a particular issue. Although student opinion should have some foundation or basis for its response, you should not have a predetermined correct answer in mind. Examples of the four types of questions are provided here:

a. Yes-No	Was George Washington the first president of the United States?
b. Short Answer	Who was the first president of the United States?
c. Comparison	What were the similarities and differences between the inaugural addresses of George Washington's and John F. Kennedy's?
d. Opinion	Which president (from Washington to today's) do you think provided the best leadership for the United States?

In the LISAM analysis, Example I of Teacher A's seventh-grade social studies classroom (see Figure 15.3), the teacher uses 94.8 percent lower-level questions and only 5.2 percent higher-level questions. She commented in her self-assessment, "My overuse of lower-level questions was inappropriate, given the goal to stimulate thinking in my students." The need to provide a balance of questions becomes greater as you move from checking for recall of information to critical thinking.

The questioning levels are not absolute. Determining where a question should be placed is relative to the learner, context, and content of the class. A recall question for a fifth-grader may be a higher-level question for a second-grader. In deciding the best placement for the question on the LISAM, determine what information the question seeks to answer and the mental processes the student needs to achieve to answer the question.

PROCEDURE: To complete the questioning section, place a mark (|) next to the appropriate question for each occurrence (see Figure 15.3). Percentages are calculated for each type of question asked, and a total is given for the actual number of questions.

2. *Teacher talk/student talk.* The teacher talk/student talk balance is an important element in understanding the level of classroom interaction. Teacher talk in secondary classrooms in 1965 was between 80 and 85 percent in math classes, and between 70 and 73 percent in social studies classrooms (Brophy & Good, 1986). Those same figures are consistent with Goodlad's (1983) findings in classrooms of the 80s. Depending on the learner, content, and context, the degree of teacher talk should vary from lesson to lesson.

An introductory lesson designed to give an overview of a unit may require more teacher talk than a lesson that seeks to stimulate student thinking and dialogue. Teacher dominance, which becomes evident in high levels of teacher talk (85 to 100 percent), could inhibit student participation and diminish opportunities for students to take greater responsibility for their learning.

Once the data have been coded onto the LISAM instrument, the analysis of the information is the next step. The low levels of questioning, combined with high degrees

FIGURE 15.3 *Audiotape Analysis, Teacher A, Example 1, 45-Minute Seventh-Grade Social Studies Lesson*

1. *Questioning Skills*
   Yes-No: 卌 卌 卌 卌 I — TOTAL = 21 = 55.3%
   Short Answer: 卌 卌 卌 — TOTAL = 15 = 39.5%
   Comparison: I I — TOTAL = 2 = 5.2%
   Opinions: 0 — TOTAL = 0 = 0%

2. *Teacher Talk/Student Talk*

Teacher:	Student:		Other
Total (T) = 470	Total (S) = 70	(T) + (S)	(e.g., Independent Activities with no Interaction):
Teacher = 87%	Student = 13%	470 + 70 = 540	Total 0%

3. *Identification of Motivating Set and Closure*
   Describe each from the tape:
   Set-Induction: I summarized for the students the issues related to the Lincoln-Douglas debates which had been discussed the previous day.
   Closure: The bell rang before I had time to bring closure to the lesson.

4. *Wait Time*
   Time between teacher question and next teacher statement:

1	1	2	2	1	3	.5
.5	2	2	2	1	*2	
1	3	2	2	2	*1	

   Average Time = 1.63 Seconds

5. *Identify Number of Positive Statements Made by Teacher* — Total = 5
   Praise or encouragement
   2 to the class
   3 to individuals (using students' names twice)

6. *Identify the Number of Times the Teacher Uses Student Ideas* — Total = 5

of teacher talk (87 percent), produced the following analysis from Teacher A, which is presented in the Snapshot.

SNAPSHOT

Teacher A, Seventh-Grade Social Studies (Figure 15.3)

My domination of the classroom discussion is evident from the high teacher talk. This class is the second lesson in a unit on the pre–Civil War period and was designed to give a sense of the issues in the presidential election prior to the Civil War.

I need to consider other strategies in addition to lecture. For example, the students rather than I could have summarized the issues we discussed from the previous day. I realize using original documents that actually show the issues of the time from the Lincoln-Douglas debates would also be more effective. The students could read the materials and first discuss the issues in groups of two, then have a total classroom discussion.

My lack of higher-level questions was surprising. It is easier to think you are asking higher-level questions than to implement them. There seems to be little time to think about questions during the lesson; it's simply a good habit I have not developed effectively. When I did ask higher-level questions, I rushed the students' answers, with one or two seconds wait time. I always feel rushed to cover the content in class, but the audiotape analysis was an eye opener. I need to give more time to being sure my students have some involvement in the class.

I could also improve the quality and quantity of praise statements. I was tired of hearing myself say "good" all the time. I am pleased that of the few responses the students made that I was able to integrate their ideas into the class. Greater opportunities for use of ideas will come with more higher-level questions. I was never a high-praise person, but I feel comfortable with using the students' ideas.

The ability to be self-analytical is the first step on the road to being independent and creating change from within. Teacher A began to explore areas in which a supervisor would need to overcome potential resistance to create the same insight for Teacher A.

In another analysis, a high-school Spanish teacher who used the LISAM coding instrument found that he was talking 90 percent of the time. Given the instructional focus for student use of language in the classroom, he decided that the level of teacher talk was too high. He reduced it for many lessons to 70 percent teacher talk and a corresponding 30 percent student talk. This was accomplished by varying his instructional strategies. He reduced the amount of pure lecture and increased small group activities where the students could practice their Spanish in twos and fours.

PROCEDURE: Using a watch with a second hand or a digital watch, place a checkmark (✓) every five seconds either under the teacher or student column, depending on who is talking. If the students are working in groups, consider it student talk. If the students are doing seatwork and are not talking with each other or the teacher, enter a mark under the other column. You should have 12 marks for each minute if there is continuous interaction in the classroom, or approximately 600 marks for a 50-minute period.

3. *Identification of motivating set and closure.* A set induction, sponge, motivating set, or other focusing activity at the beginning of the lesson has been found by researchers (see Chapter Three) to be highly effective in creating student gains when compared with no formalized instructional beginning (Schuck, 1981). Teacher A (see Figure 15.3)

used an uninspiring set for the students. Reading a brief section from the original Lincoln-Douglas debates or incorporating the Go-Around System into the start of the lesson (see Chapter Eight) may have been a better strategy for gaining the students' interest and attention.

Closure is any device used by the teacher to summarize, review, or bring some finality to the content or procedures being studied or presented. This process usually occurs at the end of a lesson but may take place at several points during the lesson or day. For secondary students, the main points of the lesson should be reviewed before the students move on to the next lesson or unit. Teacher A allowed the bell for change of classes to be the closure for the lesson. Asking a student to provide a nonverbal clue to alert the teacher five minutes before the end of class has been an effective strategy for many secondary teachers. A kitchen timer has been a useful strategy for many elementary teachers to indicate change in subject areas.

PROCEDURE: Describe in writing your set induction and closure for the lesson.

4. *Wait time.* As indicated in Chapter Eight on questioning and discussion, wait time needs to be learner, context, and content friendly. Carlsen (1991) found rigidly applying the three- to five-second rule to all levels of questions may not improve the quality of classroom interaction. Other research generally supports waiting three to five seconds for the student to respond after the teacher asks a question (see Chapter Eight). This is of particular importance when the teacher is asking higher-order questions. Veteran teachers have reported counting silently for three or four seconds before making another statement or asking a question.

PROCEDURE: Time the interval between your question and any teacher statement prior to the student's response. Identify the actual wait time provided for students to answer each higher-order question by using an (*) asterisk (see Figure 15.3).

5. *Identify the number of positive statements made by the teacher.* Flanders (1965) determined that only 1.28 percent of the classroom interaction he observed could be characterized as praising or encouraging. Goodlad's (1983) look at secondary schools in the 80s also concluded that little praise was being used by secondary teachers. Although elementary teachers use greater numbers of praise statements, there is a tendency to use the same phrases repeatedly.

In a study of studies, called a *meta-analysis,* Cameron and Pierce (1994) reviewed 96 experimental studies on reinforcement, reward, and intrinsic motivation. Their review supports the importance of teacher verbal praise and positive feedback as an important factor in improving student motivation. Low levels of positive teacher feedback to students particularly at the secondary level represent lost opportunities to encourage student engagement.

Table 15.1 provides guidelines for the use of praise as determined by extensive research conducted by Jere Brophy (1981). Praise reinforces students' responses and, because of the public nature of the classroom, signals to other students the correctness of the response. The quality of praise is as important as the quantity. A series of "oks" or "goods" provides little to the students. The tone of voice and facial expression also

TABLE 15.1 *Guidelines for Effective Praise*

Effective Praise	Ineffective Praise
1. Is delivered contingently.	1. Is delivered randomly or unsystematically.
2. Specifies the particulars of the accomplishment.	2. Is restricted to global positive reactions.
3. Shows spontaneity, variety, and other signs of credibility; suggests clear attention to the student's accomplishments.	3. Shows a bland uniformity that suggests a conditioned response made with minimal attention to the student's accomplishment.
4. Rewards attainment of specified performance criteria (which can include effort criteria, however).	4. Rewards mere participation, without consideration of performance processes or outcomes.
5. Provides information to students about their competence or the value of their accomplishments.	5. Provides no information at all or gives students information about their status.
6. Orients students toward better appreciation of their own task-related behavior and thinking about problem solving.	6. Orients students toward comparing themselves with others and thinking about competing.
7. Uses students' own prior accomplishments as the context for describing present accomplishments.	7. Uses the accomplishments of peers as the context for describing student's present accomplishments.
8. Is given in recognition of noteworthy effort or success at difficult (for *this* student) tasks.	8. Is given without regard to the effort expended or the meaning of the accomplishment.
9. Attributes success to effort and ability, implying that similar successes can be expected in the future.	9. Attributes success to ability alone or to external factors such as luck or (easy) task difficulty.
10. Fosters endogenous attributions (students believe that they expend effort on the task because they enjoy the task and/or want to develop task-relevant skills).	10. Fosters exogenous attributions (students believe that they expend effort on the task for external reasons—to please the teacher, win a competition or reward, etc.).
11. Focuses students' attention on their own task-relevant behavior.	11. Focuses students' attention on the teacher as an external authority figure who is manipulating them.
12. Fosters appreciation of, and desirable attributions about, task-relevant behavior after the process is completed.	12. Intrudes into the ongoing process, distracting attention from task-relevant behavior.

Source: From "Teacher Praise: A Functional Analysis" by J. Brophy, 1981, *Review of Educational Research, 51*, pages 5–32. Copyright 1981 by the American Educational Research Association. Reprinted by permission of the publisher.

communicate much to the student and the class about the value of students' statements. Students will determine a statement to be negative if either the tone or facial expression is negative, regardless of the spoken words. Figure 15.4, entitled "70 Ways to Vary Your Praise" (Freiberg, 2000), presents three levels of praise: Brief Acknowledgments (e.g., "Good," "Fine," "Outstanding," etc.); Acknowledgments of Specific Effort (e.g., "Robert, I like the way you are using your time to study"); and Extended Praise (e.g., "Alicia, nice job of getting your work in on time and putting thought into your work"). The extended praise example is specific and acknowledges a level of achievement, while the acknowledgments of specific effort praise statements recognizes striving along the way to achieving a goal. You may find need of these examples as you examine your own praise and acknowledgments statements to your students.

PROCEDURE: Count the number of total praise or encouraging statements made during the lesson. Also calculate the number of statements directed to the entire class and individuals and the frequency that student names are incorporated into the positive statements.

TEACHER TALK

Praise is very hard for me to give. Although I increased the number of comments to 10, they were poor expressions that I used of the lowest caliber. I also realize that I tried to teach too much too quickly. If I were to reteach the lesson I would divide the content into two lessons.

High-School Math Teacher

My most glaring weakness, in my opinion, is my tendency to *tell* instead of *ask,* and I frequently restated or answered my own questions without having allowed sufficient time for student thought.

Middle-School English Teacher

6. *Identify the number of times the teacher uses student ideas.* The use of student ideas received some early support from a series of studies reviewed by Dunkin and Biddle (1974). Although the early studies were not always conclusive, the direction for use of student ideas was encouraging. Morine-Dershimer (1982) indicated in her research that students' answers that are expanded or extended by the teacher may signal to students that the answer has greater importance.

Building on his earlier research, Brophy (1998, pp. 114–116) has offered the following guidelines for quality praise:

- Praise simply and directly, in a natural voice, without gushing or dramatizing.
- Praise in straightforward, declarative sentences instead of exclamations or rhetorical questions.
- Specify the particular accomplishment being praised and recognize any noteworthy effort, care, or perseverance.

FIGURE 15.4 *70 Ways to Vary Your Praise*

Always use the student's name in providing praise. You may *acknowledge effort, praise a positive result,* or give a *brief acknowledgment.* The following are examples of each area.

Brief Acknowledgments

OK	Sensational	Correct	Outstanding
Fine	Superb	Accurate	Standout
Great	Astonishing	Perfect	Important
Super	Incredible	True	Noteworthy
Yes	Marvelous	Precisely	Remarkable
I see	Beautiful	Truly	Notable
Nice	Grand	Agreed	Key point
Wonderful	Impressive	All Right	Main point
Much better	Magnificent	Positively	Keep it up
Exactly	Very nice	Noted	Keep up the great work
Excellent	Dazzling	Splendid	Keep up the good work
Tremendous	Brilliant	Better	You're on target
Surely	Good	Much improved	Very nice
Right	Very Good	Superior	Congratulations

Acknowledgments of Specific Effort

- Bill, I like the way you are using your time to study.
- Jose, you have really focused on the lesson.
- Sarah, I see you have tried very hard to complete this English assignment.
- Don, the extra time you are spending on your homework will make a difference in your class work.
- Jasmine, I like seeing you come to class on time.
- Jamie, you almost have it completed.
- Manuel, you are this close (teacher gestures) to finishing your assignment.

Extended Praise

- Juan, excellent, this is the best paper you have written this year in my class.
- Bill, nice job of getting your assignments in on time and putting thought into your work.
- Rose, congratulations, you really discovered another answer to the problem.
- Sarah, great job of completing your Civil War assignment; your writing is very clear and the historical information is accurate and supports the perspective you take in the paper.
- Sam, you really mastered the beginning structure of a topic sentence for your news article.
- David, much better use of first person in your writing.
- Linda, exactly, your answers show you understand and can give examples that explain the concept of gravity.

Source: From "Consistency Management: What to Do the First Days and Weeks of School" by H. J. Freiberg, 1991, *Training Booklet.* Copyright 2000 by Consistency Management Associates, Houston, Texas. Reprinted by permission.

- Call attention to new skills or evidence of progress.
- Use a variety of phrases for praising students.
- Combine verbal praise with nonverbal communication or approval.
- Avoid ambiguous statements that students may take as praise for compliance rather than learning (e.g., "You were really good today").

Education Week (Viadero, 1999) reported on a study of 1,060 students ages 8 to 17 about what kind of rewards they preferred when completing school work: 59 percent preferred praise from their parents and their teachers, 8 percent free time, and another 8 percent food or money. Very few students identified stickers, certificates, or other commonly used reinforcers.

Brophy and Good (1986) stated:

> *Teachers should answer relevant student questions or redirect them to the class, and incorporate relevant student comments into the lesson. Such use of student ideas appears to become more important with each succeeding grade level, as students become both more able to contribute useful ideas and more sensitive to whether teachers treat their ideas with interest and respect. (p. 364)*

The study of mathematics instruction of a third-grade teacher by Peterson (1992), described in the Research Vignette in Chapter Eleven found that "Keisha seems to have discovered the power of what Flanders (1970) referred to as 'use of student ideas'" (p. 172). The use of student ideas acted as a tribute to the students, honoring their views and understandings.

PROCEDURE: Calculate the total number of times student ideas were incorporated into the lesson. For example, a tenth-grade mathematics teacher said, "Sarah's idea of constructing a city of geometric shapes is an excellent way to show how geometry is part of our everyday lives." The teacher was able to make the connection between Sarah's comment and the content being discussed. It is important that the student's name (or the names of several students) be used to indicate where the idea originated.

LISAM Summary

Once the criteria for coding the frequencies of each of the six elements of the LISAM are understood, the following steps should be followed:

1. Determine which class will be taped.
2. Prepare a detailed lesson plan to be used for comparison or as a frame of reference while listening to the tape. (See Chapter Three for possible lesson plan formats.)
3. Tape the class for the entire period or for a complete lesson of 30 to 50 minutes.
4. Using the LISAM sheet, listen for each item. (For example, listen to the types of questions asked and complete the frequencies for item 1, then return to the tape and listen for the frequency of teacher talk to student talk.)
5. Complete the frequency counts for items 1, 2, 4, 5, and 6. Describe the set induction and closure for number 3.

6. Complete all percentages, as described in Figure 15.3.
7. Analyze each of the six elements in the LISAM based on the frequencies collected from the audiotaping.
8. Provide a summary of strengths and weaknesses for the lesson.
9. Describe the changes you would make if you were to reteach the lesson.
10. Provide some conclusions (or lessons learned) about your teaching analysis.

Theory into Practice

You are encouraged to use the LISAM several times during the school year. The LISAM has been implemented in real as well as simulated teaching situations. It has been used in peer teaching situations where teachers in training teach a group of five or six other peers a 10- or 20-minute lesson. The "teacher" records the simulated teaching event and analyzes the lesson. Peers may give feedback using the Peer Feedback Sheet provided in the Samples and Examples section of this chapter.

A second use of the LISAM is during student teaching. The LISAM has proven to be highly effective in enabling student teachers to reflect and change their instruction during student teaching (Freiberg, Waxman, & Houston, 1987). The student teacher tapes and then analyzes the lesson. The analysis could be shared with the cooperating teacher and/or supervisor. The *student teachers are not graded* on the effectiveness of the lesson but on the ability to analyze and reflect on their teaching. The emphasis is placed on learning how to be self-analytical rather than being judged on a single teaching episode.

The LISAM has been used extensively with experienced teachers in Texas, California, West Virginia, and Missouri with gratifying results. Veteran teachers who have used the LISAM described the experience as "enlightening," "challenging," "sobering," "exciting," "beneficial," and "encouraging." We have included two additional examples of self-assessments from a high-school geometry teacher and a fifth-grade teacher. The LISAM data sheets and their analyses of their teaching are included. Examine the data sheets (see Figures 15.5 and 15.6) and compare your analysis with that of the two teachers presented in the Teacher Talk that follows.

TWO TEACHERS ANALYZE THEIR CLASSROOMS

The LISAM analyses of an eleventh-grade geometry class and a fifth-grade class are presented to provide additional perspectives on the process of self-improvement through self-assessment for different grade levels.

Teacher B's Eleventh-Grade Class

Teacher B teaches geometry to eleventh-grade inner-city students. She has analyzed her geometry classroom twice using the LISAM audiotape analysis. Teacher B's second critique of her class is presented in the Teacher Talk* section after her LISAM audiotape analysis (see Figure 15.5).

*Kathleen Gandin-Russell. Used by permission.

FIGURE 15.5 *Audiotape Analysis, Teacher B, Example 2, Eleventh-Grade Geometry Lesson*

1. *Questioning Skills*
   Yes-No: TOTAL = 16 = 31%
   Short Answer: TOTAL = 20 = 38%
   Comparison: TOTAL = 16 = 31%
   Opinions: TOTAL = 0 = 0%

2. *Teacher Talk/Student Talk*

Teacher:	Student:	Other (e.g., Independent Activities with no Interaction):
Total (T) = 147	Total (S) = 42	Total = 0%
Teacher = 78%	Student = 22%	

3. *Identification of Motivating Set and Closure*
   Describe each from the tape:
   Set-Induction: As the students walked into the classroom they were each handed an orange card with a geometrical figure on each.
   Closure: They raised their cards in order to identify polygons—convex or concave.

4. *Wait Time*
   Time between teacher question and next teacher statement:
   Average Time = 1.69 seconds

5. *Identify Number of Positive Statements Made by Teacher* Total = 38
   Praise, encouragement, suggestions, etc.

6. *Identify the Number of Times the Teacher Uses Student Ideas*
   Including referring by name to other students' idea:
   Total = 1

Note: Teacher B completed an earlier LISAM version that did not include the identifying of higher-level questions or whether the individual or group was receiving praise.

Source: Kathleen Gandin-Russell. Used by permission.

TEACHER TALK

Teacher B, Eleventh-Grade Geometry Lesson (Figure 15.5)

I asked a majority of lower-level questions; however, I did ask more higher-level questions than last time. I asked yes/no questions 31 percent of the time, and short-answer questions 38 percent of the time. In this lesson I asked 31 percent of comparison questions, which was better than last time's 3 percent. I still feel that I could have asked more had I consciously prepared the questions. Again, I asked no opinion questions. I now see the importance of preparing questions ahead of time at all levels. When you are actively teaching you do not always have time to ponder or remember to ask higher-order questions. I am sure, in retrospect, that I could have come up with at least one opinion question; for example, "Why do you suppose it is important to classify polygons?"

My *teacher talk/student talk* ratio leaned a bit more to the students' side the second time around, but not much. This time I had 78 percent of teacher talk to 22 percent of student talk, as opposed to last time I had 80 percent teacher talk and 20 percent student talk. My students talked a whole 2 percent more than before. Even though the data do not support it, the students were more involved in this lesson. Many of my questions had silent responses and therefore the students were participating, even though they were not verbalizing it in order to verify it on tape. Many questions they answered by showing me cards that matched the descriptions I was looking for. So, even though student talk appears low on the data sheet, the students were actively involved.

Since the *set induction* that I had originally planned on was not very motivating, I changed it. Originally I was going to have the geometrical figures drawn on the chalkboard. Instead, I drew them on orange cards and handed each student one as they walked in the door. This little change in the set induction had a tremendous effect on the rest of the lesson. Active planning went into effect and the lesson took a 180 degree turn for the better.

Actually having the figures in their hands caused them to actively discuss their figures before class even started. Since they had the figures, when it was time to discuss the difference between a polygon and a nonpolygon, I had them raise their cards to participate in the answers. Thus, the new *set induction* helped increase class participation. After we discussed the definition of a polygon, we talked about how to classify the polygon as convex or concave and by the number of its sides. Again, they raised their cards in response to the questions. Then an in-flight idea came to me—to group them to practice the new concepts. This worked very well.

The *closure* was also altered because of the set induction. Since they had the cards in their hands, they again raised them at the appropriate times to prove that they had or had not mastered what a polygon was and that they could classify the polygons as convex or concave and by the number of its sides. The evaluation was also different in that they classified figures in their textbook.

I am not sure how I feel about the *wait time* data. My wait time on questions went from 2.14 seconds to 1.69 seconds. I realize the ideal is 3.0 seconds and that I went further away from that, but they quickly answered many of the questions and more wait time was not always appropriate. Longer wait time is appropriate for higher-level questions. Fast-paced drill will give you shorter times. I felt that I waited sufficient time when necessary. However, I notice that now I am constantly aware of my wait time in class and frequently try to glance at my watch without the students knowing about it.

The number of *positive statements* that I made increased greatly from last time. I made 38 positive statements; last time I made 9. Unfortunately, I decreased in the number of times that I used student ideas. Only once did I refer to a *student's idea,* as compared to last time with 16. I feel that this new lesson did not lend itself well to my being able to use student ideas. However, if I had really put my mind to it, I'm sure that I could have done better.

If I were to reteach the lesson, I would make sure that I prepared higher order questions ahead of time. I would use the same set induction (motivating), stimulus variation, and closure as before. But I would see to it that I improved on the items mentioned as my weaknesses.

I see how important it is to have a motivating set induction; it could be the difference between a good and bad lesson. I also see how important it is to be flexible. I feel that analyzing my teaching has helped me to improve greatly.

Kathleen Gandin-Russell

FIGURE 15.6 *Audiotape Analysis, Teacher C, Example 3, Fifth-Grade Mathematics Lesson*

1. *Questioning Skills*
   - Yes-No: TOTAL = 7 = 12.1%
   - Short Answer: TOTAL = 38 = 65.5%
   - Comparison: TOTAL = 5 = 8.6%
   - Opinions: TOTAL = 8 = 13.8%

2. *Teacher Talk/Student Talk*

Teacher:	Student:	Other
Total (T) = 83	Total (S) = 71	(e.g. Independent Activities with no Interaction):
Teacher = 53.9%	Student = 46.1%	Total = 0%

3. *Identification of Motivating Set and Closure*
   Describe each from the tape:
   Set-Induction: The class purchased some land. Fences had to be built as well as other improvements.
   Closure: A short quiz spanning the material covered

4. *Wait Time*
   Time between teacher question and next teacher statement:
   Average Time = 4 seconds

5. *Identify Number of Positive Statements Made by Teacher*
   Praise, encouragement, suggestions, etc.
   Total = 6

6. *Identify the Number of Times the Teacher Uses Student Ideas*
   Including referring by name to other student's idea:
   Total = 3

Note: Teacher C completed an earlier LISAM version that did not include the identifying of higher-level questions or whether the individual or group was receiving praise.

Small Changes

Small changes can produce great results. The movement of the geometric figures from the chalkboard to cards in the students' hands created greater stimulus variation (see Chapter Thirteen) and higher levels of student involvement. The point of nonverbal student response is a limitation of the audiotape, but the teacher is aware of the discrepancy. It is evident from Teacher B's description of the lesson that student learning and involvement also produced high levels of involvement and satisfaction for the teacher. She also used a student feedback instrument at the conclusion of the lesson, which is included in this chapter (see Figure 15.8). The student assessment of the class was very positive and validates the data from the audiotape analysis.

Teacher C's Fifth-Grade Class

Teacher C, who is teaching a fifth-grade mathematics lesson on perimeters for advanced students, was less satisfied with his lesson. The audiotape analysis (see Figure 15.6) highlighted areas he wanted to change in future lessons.

TEACHER TALK

Teacher C, Fifth-Grade Math Lesson (Figure 15.6)

The objective for this lesson was to have the students calculate the perimeter of any rectangle or square. I decided to ask the students to build a fence around a small plot of land the class would buy. This plot of land would be used later to build a house and determine the land area needed for the house and other possible improvements.

- *Questioning skills.* I was pleased with the overall coverage of the four different types of questions, but higher-level questions only accounted for 22 percent of the total.
- *Teacher/student talk.* My balance of teacher to student talk was much better than in previous lessons. However, in listening to the tape, I felt the lack of patience on my part inhibited some student discussion.
- *Identification of motivating set and closure.* The set induction was mediocre at best. The idea was good, but the delivery was poor. After listening to the tape, I realized the set was rushed and poorly organized. I realize the importance of more planning time in developing a motivating or facilitating set. The closure was sidetracked. One of the students did not understand the entire lesson. I spent the time allocated for closure using the example of a football field to explain the idea of perimeter to David, who wants to be a football player. He finally understood the example, but we had to move on to PE (physical education).
- *Number of teacher positive statements.* I was surprised by the lack of positive statements (only 6). Also, listening to the tape, the statements I did use came across as very impersonal (e.g., yes, good, ok). I definitely need to take care to personally give more positive recognition to the students.

- *Teacher use of student ideas.* I need to be more responsive to students' ideas. I was set to plow through the lesson as I had imagined it should go and gave little thought to increasing student contributions to the lesson.
- *Student feedback on the TEQ.* I had the students complete the Teaching Effectiveness Questionnaire (see Figure 15.7). Of the 16 items, the students gave high marks on 13 items. The three lowest items, although above the mean, included "preparation" "attitude" and "what is expected of student." The fact some students saw me as somewhat biased was an eye-opener. I need to use a place on the board for assignments and help the students, perhaps through a syllabus or outline on the board, understand what is expected of them.

There are several changes I would make in a future lesson. First, I would give more thought and planning to the set induction. For example, after listening to the tape I realized that we could have used our classroom to measure the perimeter. I need to help the students learn how to learn and be successful in my classroom. When I was a student I disliked trying to guess what the teacher wanted, and here I am doing the same thing. I like the idea of using an outline on the board and providing opportunities for greater student involvement in the lessons.

Teacher C is perhaps harder on himself than necessary, but self-assessment has the potential to create greater change because the change comes from within. When this realization that change is needed is combined with effective inservice programs or college classes, continued professional growth can be achieved.

Conditions for Success

There are several ways the LISAM can be used. You may use the LISAM as an ongoing professional development activity, where a group of teachers meets once a month to share their audiotape analyses and propose solutions for each other. However, certain conditions are necessary if the use of LISAM is to be successful:

- A climate to learn and an opportunity to share both successes and failures should be supported by your principal, other teachers, and the district administration.
- You should be willing to make changes in your instructional approaches based on actual classroom data analyzed from the LISAM.
- Discussions between you and other teachers relating to the LISAM analysis should be held in confidence.
- Staff development activities should support teachers who use the self-assessment instrument.

Critical Insight

Self-assessment can be done independently or with the support of your principal or other teachers. The audiotape analysis enables you to examine one aspect of classroom life.

Self-assessment, using objective sources of information, empowers teachers to be more reflective and self-analytical. The comments in the Teacher Talks highlight this willingness to explore teaching from a more introspective and reflective basis. The insights and critical analyses provided by the teachers are far beyond what any administrator would give in the normal course of providing feedback.

STUDENT FEEDBACK

The greatest source for feedback on the effects of teaching sits directly in front of you each day—your students. However, they are rarely tapped as a data source. Within the classroom setting, you measure the reactions of the students to lessons, content, and strategies, and other elements of teaching on an instantaneous basis but little time is available for reflective and measured responses. Students are constantly giving nonverbal and, in some instances, verbal clues and messages about their level of comfort (or discomfort) to instructional activities in the classroom. Reading these messages can provide a valuable source of information to both neophyte and veteran teachers.

Student Messages

Once routines and teaching patterns are established during the first few weeks of school (see Chapters Five and Six), changes in the content, context, or instructional strategies could result in mixed reactions by the students. "The stronger the student response, either positive or negative, the stronger the message to the teacher about his or her performance" (Smylie, 1985, p. 10). An example of this interaction between teacher and student is evident when teachers begin to move away from worksheets to more interactive, reflective instructional activities.

Teachers report that students, particularly lower-achieving students, are resistant to changes that require more thinking and are at greater risk of failure in the highly public classroom environment. Worksheets require less risk (students are rarely asked to read from the sheet) and minimize interactions with both peers and teachers (students work independently at their seats). The tradeoff of using *worksheets* for both teacher and students is a lack of opportunity to think and interact with others. Introducing activities that require greater "academic exposure" and new skills (e.g.,working in groups, thinking aloud for answers, problem solving, and brainstorming) require the teacher to be a careful observer of student responses to change. The following list should be considered in identifying students' messages as you introduce instructional changes into the classroom:

Student Concern Messages

___ Students are excessively fidgety prior to and during highly interactive activities, including grouping, discussion, and reports to the class.

___ Students are very quiet when asked to think aloud or explain an answer to the class.

___ Students are less willing to participate when called on or volunteer to answer.

___ Students begin acting out, including calling out, tapping pencils, rocking chairs, tapping fingers.

___ Students look down when class discussion is about to occur.
___ Students stare blankly at objects around the room.
___ Students allow themselves to be distracted more easily.

Student messages are signals that teachers may use to make in-flight corrections during instruction. However, some teachers are overwhelmed by students' responses or miss the meaning of some messages.

Student Change

There is an assumption that the young respond to change more readily and with greater comfort than adults. There is no evidence to support this assumption. Presenting an unknown situation for some students is seen as a challenge to be tackled, while others see potential failure. Link these negative experiences together and *some students will seek monotony over challenge and worksheets over dialogue.*

Student negative messages may indicate a degree of anxiety or discomfort with a new procedure or instructional strategy that is requiring rapid change and adjustments. Preparing students for changes will diminish or alleviate the sources of many messages on the list. For example, preparing students for working in groups (see Chapter Ten) through practice, assigning specific roles, reporting and grading procedures, and gradually increasing the difficulty of the task to be solved will make the unknown known and lessen the impact of change on students. The transition is gradual and ordered, allowing students to progress at a reasonable rate.

Formal and Informal Messages

There is a need for some disequilibrium in which students' notions are challenged and ideas are tested, but there is no requirement that students become frustrated, inhibited, and alienated from learning. Being aware of student messages is an important source of information about your effectiveness and the comfort level of your students. Other forms of student feedback, including surveys and questionnaires, are also available to you. Although observing student messages is informal and ongoing, survey feedback is more formalized and would occur less frequently (a few times a year). The advantages of using student surveys of classroom environment or specific teaching areas is realized by the opportunity to reflect on the information and prepare some specific planned changes. If student messages influence in-flight corrections, then student surveys influence both post- and preplanning. Examples of student questionnaires are discussed next.

STUDENT FEEDBACK INSTRUMENTS

Two student feedback instruments are presented here. The first questionnaire, entitled Teaching Effectiveness Questionnaire (TEQ) (Freiberg, 1972), is a 16-item bipolar (e.g., from good to bad) adjective (e.g., preparation, organization, and subject matter knowledge) questionnaire. The TEQ has been used in research and practice with students in elementary, middle, and high-school classrooms. The second instrument is a 21-item teacher-developed questionnaire designed from the TEQ by the geometry teacher (B) highlighted in her Teacher Talk. She used the questionnaire with her eleventh-grade students.

Teaching Effectiveness Questionnaire (TEQ)

The Teaching Effectiveness Questionnaire (see Figure 15.7) uses a seven-point scale and has 16 verses and 40 questions. It has been determined to be valid and reliable for use with students in grades 6 through 12 as a feedback measure of teaching effectiveness (Freiberg, 1972).

Scoring Procedures

The Samples and Examples section of this chapter has a template that can be used for scoring this instrument. To eliminate the possibility of a student checking down one side or the other, the poles (e.g., thorough–unprepared) have been reversed for items #2, 5, 7, 8, 10, 12, and 15. The template should be made into an overhead transparency and placed on top of each completed questionnaire. The scores for each line would be written on the right side. The highest score possible will be 112. A score above 80 should be considered good, although you may want to examine any trends for a particular item. You may also want to add one open-ended question (e.g., What do you like best or least about this class?) in the space provided at the bottom of the page. The students should not place their names on the questionnaires.

Modified TEQ

A second questionnaire was designed by Teacher B for her eleventh-grade geometry class (see Figure 15.8). She modified the TEQ to a five-point scale and added smiley faces to indicate the range of responses. It has "face validity" (no pun intended) for the teacher who designed it. The questions have meaning for the teacher and provide a measure of feedback to the question: How am I doing? Teacher B received feedback from 25 eleventh-grade geometry students. One of the students wrote in the open comment section: "I wish she would teach me all the subjects. This is a great teacher. I really never liked math, but the way she teaches it makes it interesting. I really enjoy coming to this class. I look forward to it throughout the whole day." It is clear from the student's comments that his or her teacher has made a difference in geometry. Teachers who seek to meet the needs of their students and are willing to learn from mistakes and capitalize on success can increase their effectiveness and improve their own satisfaction with teaching and student motivation for learning.

Summary

Each instrument provides an element of feedback to judge the effectiveness of your teaching. You may wish to adapt an instrument for your particular class. Students are a valuable source for data about your teaching and their learning, and they should become part of your repertoire for teaching.

The LISAM and the student questionnaires are sources of data that you may implement without assistance from other teachers or administrators. You may wish to

FIGURE 15.7 *Teaching Effectiveness Questionnaire*

Teacher: ______________ Expected Final Grade: ________________ Grade Level: _______

Instructions: The following lines represent traits commonly noted by students when describing their teachers. Please place a checkmark (✓) on that part of the line which would indicate how you would rate your teacher. Please read each question carefully as the words on each end of the line have been reversed for specific questions (e.g., thorough–unprepared). Each line should be checked.

Poor	Organization	Good
Thorough	Preparation	Unprepared
Limited	Subject matter knowledge	Current
Dull	Presentation	Interesting
Open minded	Attitude	Biased
No	Sense of Humor	Yes
Interesting	Personality	Poor
Encourages	Discussion	Prohibits
Boring	Speaker	Effective
Respects	Student	Belittles
Ignores	Student's needs	Recognizes
Clear	What is expected of student	Unclear
Unfair	Fairness	Fair
Not	Warmth	Very
Very	Flexible	Not
Not	Enthusiastic	Very

Comments:

What did you like most about this class?

Source: From *An Investigation of Similar and Different Ability Groups in Secondary Classrooms* by H. J. Freiberg, 1972, Amherst, MA: University of Massachusetts. Reprinted by permission.

FIGURE 15.8 *Teacher B Feedback Sheet*

Teacher Name: ______________________ Expected grade: ________ Grade level: _________

Instructions: Please place a check mark (√) on the face that best tells how you feel about each statement.

1. My teacher is well organized. ☺☺😐😑☹
2. My teacher is well prepared. ☺☺😐😑☹
3. My teacher is knowledgeable about the subject he or she is teaching. ☺☺😐😑☹
4. My teacher presented the lesson in an interesting way. ☺☺😐😑☹
5. My teacher has an open-minded attitude. ☺☺😐😑☹
6. My teacher has a sense of humor. ☺☺😐😑☹
7. My teacher has an interesting personality. ☺☺😐😑☹
8. My teacher is happy when we ask questions. ☺☺😐😑☹
9. My teacher is an effective speaker. ☺☺😐😑☹
10. My teacher respects students. ☺☺😐😑☹
11. My teacher recognizes students' needs. ☺☺😐😑☹
12. My teacher is very clear about telling us exactly what he or she expects of us. ☺☺😐😑☹
13. My teacher is fair. ☺☺😐😑☹
14. My teacher is a warm individual. ☺☺😐😑☹
15. My teacher is flexible. ☺☺😐😑☹
16. My teacher is enthusiastic about teaching. ☺☺😐😑☹
17. I understand what my teacher just taught us. ☺☺😐😑☹
18. If I had to grade my teacher, I would give him or her a(n) ________ . ☺☺😐😑☹
19. I would like to take another class from this teacher. ☺☺😐😑☹
20. I enjoy coming to class. ☺☺😐😑☹
21. I have always liked math. ☺☺😐😑☹

Additional Comments:

Source: Kathleen Gandin-Russell. Used by permission.

share this information with others in your school who also receive feedback from their students and talk about strategies for improving instruction. A third source of data about your teaching may be derived from an off-task seating chart, which requires the assistance of a colleague to collect the information. However, only you should analyze it and make any final assessments about your ability to focus student attention.

DATA FROM PEER OBSERVATIONS

Colleagues can provide an important source of data for you. School systems throughout the United States have moved to peer coaching and collegial teams. However, many teachers feel uncomfortable giving feedback to a colleague or receiving it. The difficulty rests with the perception that feedback is an evaluation about one's teaching from one's peer. If, however, the colleague is a data gatherer, not an evaluator, then the peer can be an invaluable source of information in answering the questions: *How am I doing?* and *Where do I need improvement?* The off-task seating chart developed by Jane Stallings (1986) is effective in identifying off-task student behavior. The feedback and analysis of the seating chart has shown to be effective for increasing teaching academic time and reducing organizing time (Stallings & Freiberg, 1991). (See the Research Vignette in this chapter.)

Off-Task Seating Chart

The use of the off-task seating chart requires another person (teacher, administrator, parent, or high-school student) to code what the students are doing when the teacher is involved in various instructional activities. The teacher, for example, is instructing and 25 students are listening, but 2 students are chatting and 2 are uninvolved during the presentation.

Sweeps

The observer begins with a seating chart of the class and "sweeps" (or looks) from left to right in the classroom and notes what the teacher is doing (e.g., instruction [I]) and where the teacher is located on the seating chart (e.g., T1). There are 10 sweeps per observation. If the class is 50 minutes in length, each sweep is 5 minutes (50 minutes ÷ 10 sweeps = 5 minutes per sweep). If the class is 60 minutes or 55 minutes, then the sweeps would be 6 minutes and 5.5 minutes respectively. For an elementary-school lesson, the time period can be decided prior to the observation. The observer codes only those students on the seating chart who are off-task during instruction. In the case of the example (see Figure 15.9), Joshua, Matthew, and Ann during instruction (I) are uninvolved in sweep #1, the first 5 minutes of class. In the case of Joshua, a *1 U/I* is placed in his seating chart box. The number *1* indicates the first sweep, the *U* shows uninvolvement, and the *I* identifies the type of instructional activity, which in this case is instruction.

Instructional Activity Codes

The instructional activity codes reflect seven common instructional practices:

C	Cooperative group	Q	Question/Answer
G	Games	R	Oral reading
I	Instruction	S	Seatwork
O	Organizing		

Each of the criteria for coding the activity codes follows.

The teacher may be *instructing (I),* which includes lecture, explaining, or presenting; *organizing (O),* including passing out papers, taking attendance, or grading papers in class; *question/answer (Q),* including teacher's questions, fast-paced oral drill, and student responses; *oral reading (R),* including reading aloud; *seatwork (S),* including students working independently at their seats, reading or writing; *games (G)* for the entire class, including board games, teacher-made games, and computer games; and

FIGURE 15.9 *Off-Task Seating Chart #1*

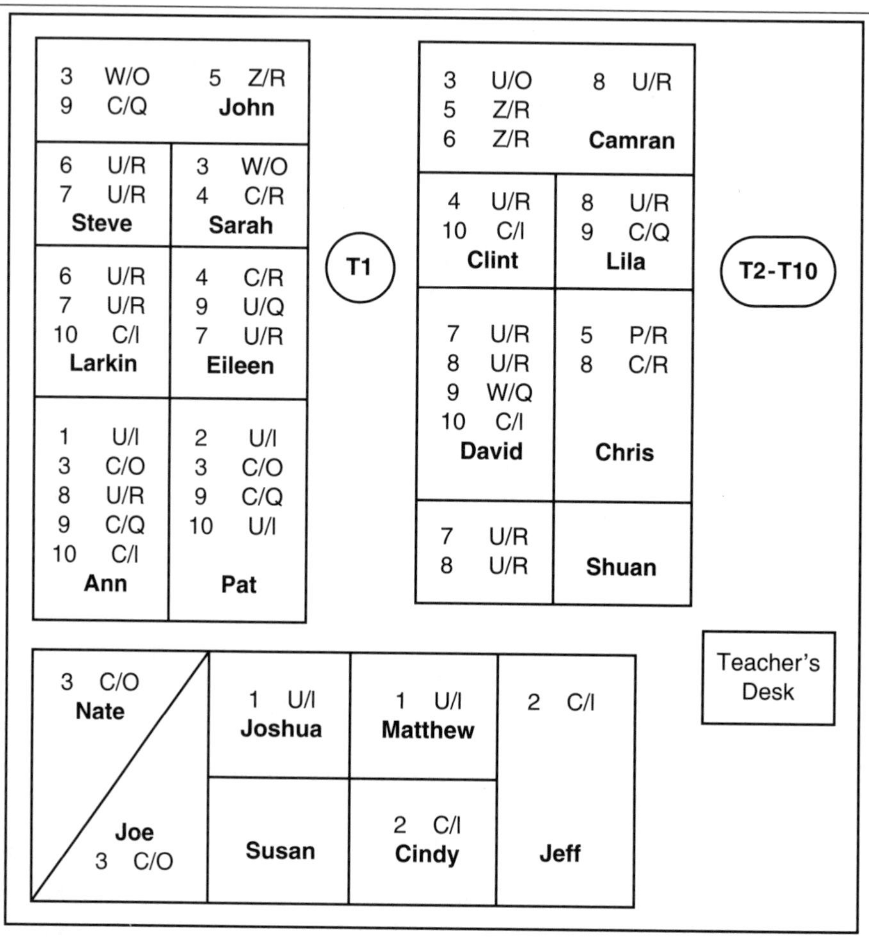

3 W/O
9 C/Q

5 Z/R
John

6 U/R
7 U/R
Steve

3 W/O
4 C/R
Sarah

6 U/R
7 U/R
10 C/I
Larkin

4 C/R
9 U/Q
7 U/R
Eileen

1 U/I
3 C/O
8 U/R
9 C/Q
10 C/I
Ann

2 U/I
3 C/O
9 C/Q
10 U/I
Pat

T1

3 U/O
5 Z/R
6 Z/R

8 U/R
Camran

4 U/R
10 C/I
Clint

8 U/R
9 C/Q
Lila

7 U/R
8 U/R
9 W/Q
10 C/I
David

5 P/R
8 C/R
Chris

7 U/R
8 U/R

Shuan

T2-T10

3 C/O
Nate

Joe
3 C/O

1 U/I
Joshua

1 U/I
Matthew

2 C/I

Susan

2 C/I
Cindy

Jeff

Teacher's Desk

Teacher Activity During Sweep

Organizing = 3
Instruction = 1, 2, 10
Question/Answer = 9
Oral Reading = 4, 5, 6, 7, 8
Seatwork
Games
Cooperative Groups

Codes

Off Task:
C = Chatting
D = Disruptive
P = Personal Needs
U = Uninvolved
W = Waiting
Z = Sleeping

Activity:
S = Seatwork
O = Organizing
I = Instruction
R = Reading Aloud
Q = Question/Answer
C = Cooperative Group
G = Game

(T1) = Teacher location during the first 5 minutes.
(T2–T10) = Teacher location during the remainder of the observations (45 minutes).

Source: Jane Stallings. Used by permission.

cooperative group (C), including students working in groups of two, four, or six on academic tasks.

Off-Task Codes

There are six off-task codes:

C	Chatting	U	Uninvolved
D	Disruptive	W	Waiting
P	Personal needs	Z	Sleeping

Chatting (C) is any conversation between students during instructional time that is not sanctioned by the teacher and is unrelated to the task. *Disruptive (D)* behavior is coded when the teacher needs to stop instructional activities and respond to a student or when the disruptive student is drawing attention from other students in the classroom. *Personal needs (P)* represent students going to the bathroom, combing hair, applying make-up, or other personal activities during instructional time. *Uninvolved (U)* students are identified by their lack of focus on the teacher or instructional activities. Students reading a book during a teacher's or other student's presentation, doing homework for another class, looking out the window, and involved in activities indicate they are not focusing on the lesson. A student who is looking down or glances away from the teacher may actually be involved. Some judgment may be required. If the observer is unsure, then the student should not be coded as uninvolved. *Waiting (W)* connotes the student waiting in line to see the teacher, raising a hand during seatwork until the teacher is able to respond, or other behaviors that indicate the student is waiting to proceed. *Sleeping (Z),* which is perhaps more common at the secondary level (student working the late shift), is a particularly troublesome off-task behavior and is provided a separate code.

Off-Task Behavior Summary

Figure 15.10 provides a summary of off-task behaviors. We can see from Figure 15.10 that there are 44 off-task behaviors in a 50-minute time period. The most common off-task behaviors are chatting (17) and uninvolved (20) in this classroom. Students were off task most often during oral reading (20) and instruction (11), with teacher organizing attributing to some (7) students also being off task. Determining the percentage of time the students were off task requires inserting the numbers from the summary of off-task behavior into the formula below.

$$\frac{\text{number of off-task behaviors}}{\text{number of students} \times \text{number of sweeps}} = \%\text{ off task}$$

Going back to Figure 15.10, we see the following:

$$\frac{\text{number of off-task behaviors (44)}}{\text{number of students} \times \text{number of sweeps}} = 22\%\text{ off task}$$

(20) × (10) = (200)

FIGURE 15.10 *Seating Chart #1: Summary of Off-Task Behaviors*

Sweeps	1	2	3	4	5	6	7	8	9	10	
Observation #1	3	3	7	3	3	3	5	6	6	5	= 44

Behaviors	Chatting	Disruptive	Personal Needs	Uninvolved	Waiting	Sleeping	
Observation #1	17	0	1	20	3	3	= 44

Activities	Organizing	Instruction	Question/ Answer Discussion	Oral Reading	Seatwork	Games	Cooperative Groups	
Observation #1	7	11	6	20	0	0	0	= 44

GRADE 3 READING CLASS, Stallings Observation System

Source: Jane Stallings. Used by permission.

Possible Solutions

Off-task behavior is both a teacher and student concern. Mrs. Smith spent 25 minutes in oral reading (5 minutes × 5 sweeps). This may be too long for the 20 third-graders. The teacher could have shorter oral reading sessions or ask the students to read to each other in pairs for part of the oral reading time while the teacher works with small groups. The teacher used three instructional strategies: instructing, question and answer, and oral reading. A better balance of the two and the addition of other strategies like cooperative groups, discussion, and five minutes of guided or independent practice could add greatly to the interaction in the classroom. Cipani (1995) suggested asking if the frequency of the student's off-task behavior escalates during specific types of instruction or activity. The seating chart will enable you to determine the possible reason for off-task behavior.

Procedures for Observers

- Remind the observer of strict confidentiality prior to the seating chart activity. If students will be moving to a laboratory setting, learning centers, or cooperative groups, then name tags are placed on the back of the students with high-mobility activities.
- Provide a seating chart of the students in the classroom to your colleague.

Student Teaching Research Vignette

INTRODUCTION

> *I think the time I invested in the LISAM is going to pay for itself in the long run. I think it's priceless really. I mean every student teacher should have the opportunity to look at themselves through the LISAM. Some of them I've talked to have only been observed by their college supervisor one or two times. I don't see how you could get better without the type of in-depth feedback you get from the LISAM analysis. I don't think you could get it anywhere else. (Student teacher comments in Anderson & Freiberg, 1995, p. 9)*

This study explores the use of the LISAM instrument by 10 teacher education students during their student teaching placements in suburban secondary schools in the state of Colorado.

STUDY DESIGN

The 10 secondary student teachers (4 teaching mathematics, 3 social studies, 2 science, and 1 in English) participated in four stages of involvement in the study. The first-stage students audiotaped themselves for one class period (60 minutes). In stage two, participants received instructions in analyzing their tapes. Stage three involved a seminar where research findings and suggestions for using the LISAM data by each student teacher were discussed. The students developed individual goals for the next lesson they would tape and analyze. The fourth stage of the study involved in-depth semi-structured interviews of the 10 student teachers' perceptions of their use of the LISAM after the completion of the second audiotape analysis. Twenty audiotapes were analyzed using the LISAM procedures to determine changes in pre- and post-teaching of the student teachers. Qualitative data from the interviews were analyzed to determine themes or patterns across the 10 students' experiences with the LISAM.

STUDY RESULTS

Three teaching areas showed statistically significant improvement from the first to second teaching analysis: closure of the lesson increased in its duration, wait time increased for higher-level questions, and the frequency of all positive teacher statements increased. Listening to their tapes resulted in 19 additional insights about their teaching not included in the LISAM instrument, including interrupting their students, talking too quickly, and using "OK" to excess. Based on the interviews, the following comments were representative of the group:

> It was helpful to me to see my numbers down in black and white.
>
> Where you gain insights is when you do the analysis yourself. It's hard to argue with your own data.
>
> I never realized how many yes-no questions I did ask. It was actually going through it and putting down all those marks that made me realize what I was doing.
>
> Before I analyzed my tape it always seemed to me that the kids were doing most of the talking. (*Note:* This student teacher talked 79.6 percent of the time in the lesson recorded on the first audiotape.)
>
> I really thought I was being more divergent in my questioning, and then I listened to my tape. It's like hard facts evidence that's right there in front of you. It really opened my eyes.
>
> I had no idea I was rushing so much until I listened to my first tape. When I timed myself it became obvious that I wasn't giving them enough time to answer.
>
> I heard myself interrupt a thought process that was happening. A child was thinking through a problem and I took the ball away from him. I thought, "My God, how can I be doing this?" (p. 9)

DISCUSSION AND IMPLICATIONS FOR PRACTICE

Although much of this chapter has discussed the use of LISAM with veteran teachers, this study shows the potential for LISAM procedures to be a catalyst to accelerate the pedagogical growth of student teachers. Using concrete data from one's teaching has the power to give new members of the profession an insider's view of teaching. It also moves the locus of control about "How am I doing?" from others to yourself.

- Remind the observer that he or she is only a collector of data and should not make value judgments about what is being observed.
- Analyze your own data and complete the formula to determine the percentage of off-task behavior.
- Share your chart and discuss possible solutions with another teacher whom you are observing.

Our experiences with the seating charts and the teachers who have worked with them have proved to be very positive. As with the other feedback tools for answering the questions, *How am I doing?* and *How may I do better?* the off-task seating chart is but another sliver of life in the classroom.

LISAM and Caring

Many of the instructional areas measured by the LISAM can also be found in the need for students for a caring learning environment. A study of by Wentzel (1997) of 375 eighth-graders asked them to respond to two key questions: (1) "How do you know when a teacher cares about you? List three things that teachers do to show that they care about you" and (2) "How do you know when a teacher does not care about you? List three things that teachers do to show they don't care about you." Table 15.2 describes the student responses listed under the caring category in the first column and the percentage of students who identified this as an important area in the second column. We have matched those LISAM categories that are congruent with the four caring categories (modeling, democratic interactions, expectations based on individuality of student as learner, and the need for nurturance).

SUMMARY

This chapter is designed to give you independent measures of your own effectiveness. You, your students, and your colleagues are valuable sources of data that may be tapped to gain an insight into your teaching. The instruments included in this chapter are selected to foster independence and reflection, and are based on a belief that learning to be an effective teacher is a lifelong pursuit, requiring a variety of sources of information.

The LISAM should give you a measure of how the students hear you and an indication of how you are doing in six areas of instruction. The Snapshot and Teacher Talks of the chapter were devoted to elementary, middle, and high-school teachers analyzing and critiquing their own instruction.

The student feedback instruments—the TEQ and Teacher B's Questionnaire—are designed to provide different measures for both classroom instruction and climate.

The off-task seating chart (Stallings, 1986) is included to give you an opportunity to see your classroom from the eyes of an observer using a systematic observation instrument.

Lya Kremer-Hayon, in her book *Teacher Self-Evaluation* (1993), talks about self-assessment allowing teachers to be their own mirrors. We hope the resources in this chapter and the entire text will guide you in your own personal development as a professional. Teaching provides challenges and opportunities for you to reflect on your practice and build a profession. We wish you all the best.

TABLE 15.2 *Student Responses about Caring Shown by Teachers*

Caring Category	Student Responses	LISAM Category
Modeling *Caring examples:* makes a special effort, teaches in a special way, makes class interesting. *Uncaring examples:* teaches a boring class, gets off task, teaches while students aren't paying attention	30%	**Motivating Set and Closure** **Teacher Talk/Student Talk** Students are involved in learning at the start of class and they are asked to summarize their learning at the conclusion of the lesson.
Democratic Interactions *Caring examples:* asks questions, pays attention, listens *Uncaring examples:* ignores, interrupts	47%	**Questioning Skills** Using the "Go-Around" to provide fairness and allowing students to "Pass" with accountability involves everyone. Using a range of lower- to higher-order questions allows for creativity and higher levels of thinking.
Expectations Based on Individual Student as Learner *Caring examples:* asks if I need help, takes time to make sure I understand, calls on me *Uncaring examples:* doesn't explain things or answer questions, doesn't try to help you	54%	**Wait Time** **Using Student Ideas** Allowing students "think time" and urging students' ideas builds meaningful student involvement.
Nurturance *Caring examples:* tells you when you do a good job, praises me *Uncaring examples:* gives bad grades, doesn't correct work	22%	**Praise Statements** Provides students with feedback by using a variety of praise statements

Sources: "Student Motivation in Middle School: The Role of Perceived Pedagogical Caring" by K. R. Wentzel, 1997, *Journal of Educational Psychology, 89,* pp. 411–419 and "Teacher Self-Assessment and Principal Supervision" by H. J. Freiberg, 1987, *NASSP Bulletin, 71*(498), pp. 85–92.

Key Points

The instruments individually and collectively will enable you to test the influence of using different strategies with your students. The following list of concepts and terms highlight the key points of the chapter.

- Knowledge is power, but knowledge about yourself is the greatest power of all.
- There are at least seven sources of data about your teaching.

- Self-assessment is not accurate without an objective source of data.
- Audiotaping and videotaping are effective tools for collecting information about your teaching. Generally, audiotaping is less obtrusive in the classroom.
- The LISAM focuses on six areas of instruction, including questioning, teacher/student talk, set and closure, wait time, praise and encouragement, and use of student ideas.
- The research supports 12 guidelines for effective praise.
- Student messages about your teaching are constantly being provided during instruction.
- Students need to be prepared for change in the classroom.
- Student feedback is an important but neglected source of information about your teaching.
- Formal student feedback can be acquired by presenting student questionnaires.
- Off-task seating charts will enable you to measure the amount of time and during what instructional activities students are most frequently engaged in learning.
- Learning to be an effective teacher is a lifelong pursuit and requires a variety of information sources.

REFERENCES

Anderson, J. B., & Freiberg, H. J. (1995). Using self-assessment as a reflective tool to enhance the student teaching experience. *Teaching Education Quarterly, 22,* 77–91.

Brophy, J. (1981). Teacher praise statements: A functional analysis. *Review of Educational Research, 51,* 5–32.

Brophy, J. (1998). *Motivating students to learn.* Boston: McGraw-Hill.

Brophy, J. E., & Good, T. L. (1986). Teacher behavior and student achievement. In M. C. Wittrock (Ed.), *Handbook on research and teaching.* New York: Macmillan.

Cameron, J., & Pierce, W. D. (1994). Reinforcement, reward, and intrinsic motivation: A meta-analysis. *Review of Educational Research, 64,* 363–423.

Carlsen, W. S. (1991). Questioning in classrooms: A sociolinguistic perspective. *Review of Educational Research, 61,* 157–178.

Cipani, E. C. (1995). Be aware of negative reinforcement. *Teaching Exceptional Children, 27*(4), 36–39.

Coker, H., & Coker, J. G. (1982). *Classroom observations keyed for effective research.* Atlanta, GA: Georgia State University.

Dunkin, M., & Biddle, B. (1974). *The study of teaching.* New York: Holt, Rinehart and Winston.

Flanders, N. (1965). *Teacher influence, pupil attitudes and achievement.* Cooperative Research Monograph No. 12. Washington, DC: U.S. Office of Education.

Flanders, N. (1970). *Analyzing classroom behavior.* New York: Addison Wesley.

Freiberg, H. J. (1972). *An investigation of similar and different ability groups in secondary classrooms.* Amherst: University of Massachusetts.

Freiberg, H. J. (1987). Teacher self-evaluation and principal supervision. *NASSP Bulletin, 71* (498), 85–92.

Freiberg, H. J. (Ed.). (1998). *Journal of Classroom Interaction, 33*(1), 1–35.

Freiberg, H. J. (2000). *Consistency management and cooperative discipline: Strategies for the classroom.* Houston, TX: Consistency Management Associates.

Freiberg, H. J., & Waxman, H. C. (1988). Alternative feedback approaches for improving student teachers' classroom instruction. *Journal of Teacher Education, 39*(4), 8–14.

Freiberg, H. J., Waxman, H., & Houston, W. R. (1987). Enriching feedback to student teachers through small group discussion. *Teacher Education Quarterly, 14*(3), 71–81.

Goldhammer, R. (1969). *Clinical supervision.* New York: Holt, Rinehart and Winston.

Goodlad, J. (1983). *A place called school. Prospects for the future.* New York: McGraw-Hill.

Joyce, B., & Showers, B. (1988). *Student achievement through staff development.* White Plains, NY: Longman.

Kremer-Hayon, L. (1993). *Teacher self-evaluation: Teachers in their own mirrors.* Boston: Kluwer Academic Press.

Morine-Dirshimer, G. (1982). Pupil perceptions of teacher praise. *Elementary School Journal, 82,* 421–434.

Peterson, P. L. (1992). Revising their thinking: Keisha Coleman and her third-grade mathematics class. In H. H. Marshall (Ed.), *Redefining student learning.* Norwood, NJ: Ablex.

Redfield, D., & Rousseau, E. (1981). A meta-analysis of experimental research on teacher questioning behavior. *Review of Educational Research, 51,* 273–245.

Rosenshine, B., & Furst, N. (1973). The use of direct observation to study teaching. In R. Travers (Ed.), *Second handbook for research on teaching.* Chicago: Rand McNally.

Schuck, R. (1981). The impact of set induction on student achievement and retention. *Journal of Educational Research, 74,* 227–232.

Smylie, M. (1985, April). *Improving the accuracy of teacher self-evaluation through staff development.* Paper presented at the annual meeting of the American Educational Research Association, Chicago.

Stallings, J. (1985). *Effective use of time program: Notes for trainers.* Nashville: Peabody Center for Effective Teaching, Vanderbilt University.

Stallings, J. (1986). Using time effectively: A self-analytical approach. In K. Zumwalt (Ed.), *Improving teaching. ASCD yearbook.* Alexandria, VA: Association for Supervision and Curriculum Development.

Stallings, J., & Freiberg, H. J. (1991). Observation for the improvement of teaching. In H. Waxman & H. Walberg (Eds.), *Effective teaching: Current research* (pp. 107–133). Berkley, CA: McCutchan.

Stallings, J., Needles, M., & Stayrook, N. (1978). *How to change the process of teaching basic reading skills in secondary schools.* Final Report to the National Institute of Education. Menlo Park, CA: SRI International.

Viadero, D. (1999). The value of praise. *Education Week, 44.*

Wentzel, K. R. (1997). Student motivation in middle school: The role of perceived pedagogical caring. *Journal of Educational Psychology, 89,* 411–419.

SAMPLES AND EXAMPLES

There are two samples and examples in this section:

- A template is given for scoring the Teaching Effectiveness Questionnaire (see Figure 15.7).
- The Peer Feedback Sheet will assist the teacher.

SCORING TEMPLATE FOR FIGURE 15.7: TEACHING EFFECTIVENESS QUESTIONNAIRE

Teacher: ______________ Expected Final Grade: _________________ Grade Level: ________

Instructions: The following lines represent traits commonly noted by students when describing their teachers. Please place a checkmark (✓) on that part of the line which would indicate how you would rate your teacher. Please read each question carefully as the words on each end of the line have been reversed for specific questions (e.g., thorough–unprepared). Each line should be checked.

1	2	3	4	5	6	7
Poor			Organization			Good
7	6	5	4	3	2	1
Thorough			Preparation			Unprepared
1	2	3	4	5	6	7
Limited			Subject matter knowledge			Current
1	2	3	4	5	6	7
Dull			Presentation			Interesting
7	6	5	4	3	2	1
Open minded			Attitude			Biased
1	2	3	4	5	6	7
No			Sense of Humor			Yes
7	6	5	4	3	2	1
Interesting			Personality			Poor
7	6	5	4	3	2	1
Encourages			Discussion			Prohibits
1	2	3	4	5	6	7
Boring			Speaker			Effective
7	6	5	4	3	2	1
Respects			Student			Belittles
1	2	3	4	5	6	7
Ignores			Student's needs			Recognizes
7	6	5	4	3	2	1
Clear			What is expected of student			Unclear
1	2	3	4	5	6	7
Unfair			Fairness			Fair
1	2	3	4	5	6	7
Not			Warmth			Very
7	6	5	4	3	2	1
Very			Flexible			Not
1	2	3	4	5	6	7
Not			Enthusiastic			Very

PEER FEEDBACK SHEET

After participating in a simulated teaching situation, please provide the following information to the "teacher."

Identify (by placing a check mark) up to three strategies used by the teacher in this simulated lesson:

____ Lecture
____ Questioning
____ Discussion
____ Drill/Recitation
____ Cooperative Grouping
____ Reflective Teaching (Discovery, Inquiry, and Problem Solving)
____ Roleplay
____ Simulation
____ Drama
____ Media
____ Computers
____ Assessment

Please be specific (e.g., using the diagram helped me visualize the concept) in giving feedback:

1. Describe the set induction (beginning) and the closure (ending) of the lesson.

2. Describe a strength of the lesson.

3. If the lesson is to be retaught, what changes would you recommend?

Use the other side for additional comments.

Author Index

Subject Index